*Tenant Right and Agrarian Society
in Ulster
1600–1870*

To Joe and Betty

Tenant Right and Agrarian Society in Ulster

1600–1870

MARTIN W. DOWLING

IRISH ACADEMIC PRESS

DUBLIN • PORTLAND, OR

First published in 1999 by
IRISH ACADEMIC PRESS
44, Northumberland Road, Dublin 4, Ireland,
and in the United States of America by
IRISH ACADEMIC PRESS
c/o ISBS, 5804 NE Hassalo Street,
Portland, OR 97213 3644

Website: http://www.iap.ie

British Library Cataloguing in Publication Data

Dowling, Martin W.
    Tenant right and agrarian society in Ulster, 1600–1870
    1. Landlord and tenant – Northern Ireland – History 2. Ulster (Northern Ireland
    and Ireland) – History 3. Ulster (Northern Ireland and Ireland) – Social conditions
    I. Title
    941.6'06

    ISBN 0–7165–2592–5 hardback
    ISBN 0–7165–2656–5 paperback

Library of Congress Cataloguing-in-Publication Data

Dowling, Martin W., 1960–
    Tenant right and agrarian society in Ulster, 1600–1870 / Martin W. Dowling.
      p.   cm.
    Based on the author's thesis (Ph. D.—University of Wisconsin—Madison).
    Includes bibliographical references and index.
    ISBN 0–7165–2592–5 (hb). — ISBN 0–7165–2656–5 (pb)
      1. Landlord and tenant—Ulster (Northern Ireland and Ireland)—History.
    2. Peasantry—Ulster (Northern Ireland and Ireland)—History. 3. Ulster
    (Northern Ireland and Ireland)—Rural conditions. I. Title.
    HD1331.I73D68   1999
    333.5'4'09416—dc21   98–43172
                                                          CIP

Typeset in 11.5 pt on 13.5 pt Dante by
Carrigboy Typesetting Services, Durrus
Printed by Creative Print and Design (Wales), Ebbw Vale

Contents

Abbreviations	vi
Acknowledgements	vii
Map of Ulster and Environs	x

PART I. CONTEXT

1. Tenant Right and Agrarian Capitalism	3

PART II. THE SOCIAL BASES OF TENANT RIGHT

2. Historicity	47
3. Production	117
4. Visuality	176
5. The Advance of Estate Management	241

PART III. THE END OF TENANT RIGHT

6. Tenant Right and the Land Question	269
Bibliography	355
Index	378

Abbreviations

Bessborough commission evidence	*Minutes of evidence*, pt. i [c 2779–i], HC 1881, xviii, 73; pt. ii [c 2779–ii], HC 1881, xix, 1; *index to minutes of evidence and appendices* [C 2779–iii], HC 1881, xix, 825.
Bessborough commission report	*Report of her majesty's commission of inquiry into the working of the landlord and tenant (Ireland) act, 1870, and the acts amending the same* [c 2779], HC 1881, xviii, 1.
Devon commission evidence	*Minutes of evidence from her majesty's commissioners of inquiry into the state of the law and practice in respect to the occupation of land in Ireland*, pt. i [606], pt. ii [616], pt. iii [616], HC 1845, xxi, 1.
Devon commission report	*Report from her majesty's commissioners of inquiry into the state of the law and practice in respect to the occupation of land in Ireland* [605], HC 1845, xix, 1.
I.E.S.H.	*Irish economic and social history*
Maguire commission evidence	*Report from the select committee on the tenure and improvement of land (Ireland) act; together with the proceedings of the committee, minutes of evidence, appendix, and index.* HC 1865 (402), xi, 341.
N.L.I.	National Library of Ireland
P.R.O.N.I.	Public Record Office of Northern Ireland
T.C.D.	Trinity College Dublin

Acknowledgements

After nearly a decade of sporadic research and writing, it is a great pleasure to attempt to acknowledge here all those who have helped in some way in the creation of this book.

I must begin by thanking my first teachers in Irish Studies, Emmet Larkin and the late Frank Kinahan of the University of Chicago and James S. Donnelly, Jr., of the University of Wisconsin-Madison. Professor Donnelly has had a huge influence on this work, both directly and indirectly. First he has influenced it by example, with his work. *The land and the people of nineteenth-century Cork: the rural economy and the land question* continues to set a well-nigh unattainable standard of scholarship for the historian of Irish rural society. More directly, he made an enormous editorial contribution to the Ph.D. dissertation on which this book is based. His heroic reading of an over-lengthy, ungainly, and immature manuscript in 1993 contributed greatly to the present form of the central chapters of this work. If some of those earlier weaknesses remain, it is more the result of my stubbornness than his sage advice.

The Ph.D. research conducted in 1987 and 1988 would not have been possible without the support of a Dissertation Fellowship from the North American Conference of British Studies and travel awards from the Department of History and the Graduate School of the University of Wisconsin-Madison. In Ireland, the staff of the National Library, the library of Trinity College, and the Royal Irish Academy were most cooperative and helpful. I thank the National Library and The Board of Trinity College Dublin for allowing me to cite the manuscripts listed in the bibliography. The greatest debt I incurred during that year was at the Public Records Office of Northern Ireland in Belfast. The very scope of this book was made possible by the work of the director and staff of that institution in identifying, collecting, and cataloguing an enormous archive and in providing an unparalleled environment in which to conduct research. Thanks are due to P.R.O.N.I. for allowing me to quote extensively from manuscripts owned or held there. Thanks are also due to the following individuals and institutions for allowing me to cite materials deposited at P.R.O.N.I.: the marquess of Anglesey (Anglesey papers), Viscount Dunluce (Antrim papers), Sir Charles Brett (Ardglass papers), the Essex Record Office

(Barrett-Lennard papers, D/DL C28–42), the earl of Belmore (Belmore papers), the Berkshire Record Office (Blundell papers), Viscount Brooke-borough (Brookeborough papers), the earl of Caledon (Caledon papers), Earl Castle Stewart (Castle Stewart papers), Lord Dunleath (Clifford papers), the marchioness of Dufferin and Ava (Dufferin papers), the Nottinghamshire Record Office (Foljambe papers), the Scottish Record Office (Guthrie Castle papers), the National Trust (Castleward and Lennox-Cunningham papers), Lady Mairi Bury (Londonderry papers), Lord O'Neill (O'Neill papers), Mrs N. Hughes (Perceval Maxwell papers), Lord Rossmore (Rossmore papers), Dr. J. Whyte (Whyte papers), the Honourable Irish Society, the Drapers' Company, the Haberdashers' Company, and the Archbishop of Armagh. Thanks are also due to the following owners of materials deposited in the National Library: Hon. Desmond Guinness (Conolly papers), The Honourable Irish Society, Leeds City Libraries (Lane Fox papers), West Devon Record Office (Playdell papers), Major J.E. Shirley (Shirley papers), the British Museum (Southwell papers), and the Drapers', Fishmongers', Merchant Tailors', and Skinners' companies.

The Institute of Irish Studies at Queen's University of Belfast provided me with a fellowship to write this book in 1996 and 1997. I am grateful to all my colleagues in that noble institution for their spirited support. During that year my manuscript benefitted from a number of careful readings. Bill Maguire read the entire manuscript and made a number of enlightening suggestions. Paul Bew read and commented on the last chapter. Bill Crawford gave chapters 3, 4, and 5 a very engaged reading, allowing me to make numerous dramatic improvements. None of these individuals, of course, can be blamed for the many errors that remain.

Since the majority of the work for this book was done without the financial support of any institution, pride of place in these acknowledgements must go to my family and friends. My wife Christine has lived for over a decade with the uncertainties surrounding both this project and the more general tribulations of beginning a career as a historian in the 1990s. I would not have had the financial wherewithal, the stamina, or the spirit to complete this book without her constant support. The communities of traditional musicians in Madison, Minneapolis, Chicago, Milwaukee, Belfast, and Dublin also deserve to be mentioned for the safekeeping of my sanity and artistry during the many stretches of research and writing. Finally I thank the rest of my family, the Dowlings and the Plochmans, but especially my parents, to whom this is dedicated.

Key to estates listed on map

1. Abercorn
2. Anglesey
3. Annesley
4. Antrim
5. Barrett-Lennard
6. Belmore
7. Brookborough
8. Brownlow
9. Caledon
10. Castleward, Dufferin, Londonderry, Perceval-Maxwell, Sharman Crawford
11. Conolly
12. Clothworkers'
13. Donegall
14. Downshire
15. Drapers'
16. Dufferin
17. Fishmongers'
18. Irish Society
19. Kerr (McGildowney)
20. Merchant-Tailors'
21. Montgomery
22. Murray of Broughton
23. O'Hara
24. Ogilvie
25. Skinners'
26. Trinity College
27. Vernor
28. Vintners'
29. Waring
30. Whyte

Principal Estates (see list)

• Towns mentioned in the text

Ballycastle 19

18

Coleraine 12

11 20

Limavady

NDONDERRY

• Dungiven

4 Glenarm

ANTRIM

MOUNTAINS

• Ballymoney

• Ballymena

25 Bellaghy

raperstown• 15 28

Ahoghill

Desertmartin•

Magherafelt Castledawson

Moneymore• 15

Carrickfergus

Bangor

O N E

LOUGH

NEAGH

10

13 Newtownards

Belfast

Dungannon

27

Lisburn

8

cloy• Lurgan

9 6 29 Waringstown

Benburb

16

D O W N

Caledon

• Armagh

Loughbrickland•

Banbridge

Downpatrick•

26 ARMAGH

30

Dundrum 14

24

Castlewellan 3

Ardglass

ONAGHAN

• Newry

MOURNE

MOUNTAINS

N

Carlingford 2

LOUTH

Part I

Context

A sign that has been withdrawn from the pressures of the social struggle – which, so to speak, crosses beyond the pale of the class struggle – inevitably loses force, degenerating into allegory and becoming the object not of live social intelligibility but of philological comprehension. The historical memory of mankind is full of such worn-out ideological signs incapable of serving as arenas for the clash of live social accents. However, inasmuch as they are remembered by the philologist and the historian, they may be said to retain the last glimmers of life.

V.N. Volosinov

CHAPTER ONE

Tenant Right and Agrarian Capitalism

THE HISTORIOGRAPHY OF TENANT RIGHT

This book investigates the origin, meaning, and regulation of the Ulster custom of tenant right, a practice by which rural tenants claimed property rights above and beyond their contracts with landlords, allowing departing tenants to exact a payment well in excess of the yearly rent from those who wished to replace them. Tenant-right payments not only compensated departing tenants for the improved value of their farms, they also served to transfer their 'goodwill' to the new occupier, thereby allowing the latter to enjoy the 'peaceable possession' of the farm. James Hamilton, the land agent responsible for the estate of the Abercorn family surrounding Strabane, Co. Tyrone, told the eighth earl of Abercorn in 1785 that tenant right was 'a thing well understood on your lordship's estate.'[1] Hamilton's statement refers not only to the nature of the thing itself, but also to the nature of that understanding, its historicality and its social context. Neither of these is self-evident. The thing itself, in its actuality, was embodied in a particular act of exchange of a sum of money for the right to occupy a parcel of land. Events such as this were permeated by abstractions. They abstracted from the real difference between the things exchanged, a sum of money and a plot of land. The exchanged things were also abstractions. The sum of money was a quantitative abstraction from the accumulated labour that created it. The parcel of land, on the other hand, was an abstraction from the harnessed and cultivated prodigality of the ecosphere. The property right to that land was an historical abstraction from the material relationships between people and their collective mode of production. As for each individual exchange, so for the social and historical abstraction that gathers the entire collection of exchanges into a 'custom': it was based on a narrative that selected and distilled an abstract story from the heterogenous actuality of unfolding events. Societies can only function by abstractions such as these. Without them the chaos, heterogeneity, and unpredictability of human history reign. They are none the less historical, collectively produced, and occasionally fragile compromises between a society and its unfolding reality. The custom of tenant right was one such compromise.

By examining how it developed and then died out over the course of two centuries and more, this book purports to explain how the inhabitants of rural Ulster understood their social reality and made their history.

This is no straightforward task, for it is not clear how such a complex and ambiguous thing as tenant right came to be 'well understood.' The archive of estate papers and other printed material reveals that contemporaries, even those with the benefit of direct experience, still relied on the impressions of others allegedly closer to the facts, on the traces of textual and numerical evidence, and above all on their own widely varying interpretive capacities and biases, to explain the custom. Like the many interested parties whose arguments and opinions are rehearsed in the following chapters, the historian must approach this thing and this understanding not directly, but through a textual thicket. After scrutinizing the private correspondence and public writing of contemporaries, the historian begins to feel a kind of partnership with individuals like James Hamilton who came to the question in the wake of its development, after it was already 'well understood' by an often inscrutable tenantry. It is as if the passage of time has neither increased distance from nor opened new avenues toward the subject.

The Ulster custom has been relatively neglected by recent historiography. In the concluding pages of his pathbreaking work on an Irish landed estate over twenty years ago, W.A. Maguire suggested that

> a more generally rewarding line of investigation [than the study of an individual estate] may be the study of particular topics and problems. An obvious example is the study of the custom of tenant right in its origin and early development. When it became a legislative issue, in the third quarter of the nineteenth century, the Ulster Custom attracted the attention of numerous writers, and there is a great deal of evidence as to its nature and distribution at that stage. The circumstances of its origin, and how it came to be established in a variety of forms in different parts of the country, are still obscure, and can only be illuminated by the patient study of a large number of estates.[2]

Maguire's suggestion is still pertinent. The question of the origin and development of the custom remains largely unexplored, even in detailed accounts of Ulster estate society.[3] The most significant discussions of the custom are still to be found in studies of single estates, many of which have not been published.[4] Historians have been somewhat more assiduous in mining the vast quarry of Victorian evidence, much of it in printed sources, concerning the nature, usage, distribution and legislation of tenant right,[5] all of which has culminated in W.E. Vaughan's penetrating analysis of the mid-Victorian period.[6] However, none of this important literature takes the custom of tenant right as a central theme, and none, including the present work, have fully exploited the wealth of relevant evidence available from the records of Ulster landed estates.

The pertinence of Maguire's suggestion is not merely that the painstaking exploration of seventeenth, eighteenth, and early nineteenth-century sources will fill a historiographical gap and supplement our understanding of Victorian tenant right. This research agenda has the further ramification of expanding the historical context of the discussion to unsettle those narrowly economic interpretations of tenant right which trace their intellectual roots to Victorian political economy. One circumstantial result of the fixation of historical interest on mid-Victorian questions has been the tendency to treat tenant right primarily as an economic rather than a historical subject.[7] The meaning of tenant right has traditionally been unequally divided into two aspects: the question of tenure and occupancy, and the question of financial function.[8] For various reasons, the latter has been given more attention and higher importance than the former. This strategy dates from a mid-nineteenth-century treatise on the subject by William Dyer Ferguson and Andrew Vance, who identified tenant right as 'the right of a tenant to continue in possession as long as he paid his rent and until the landlord required possession; the right of the outgoing tenant to sell "all the interest in the farm recognized by custom to belong to him".'[9] Ferguson and Vance quietly subordinated the right of continuous possession to the discretion of the landlord. Barbara Solow gave this approach a forceful and rigorous restatement by separating the simple mathematics of 'compensation for improvements' from what she called 'pure tenant right,' which was 'something beyond' compensation for improvements. Intolerant of the ambiguity of this 'something beyond,' from where more thorny social or ontological aspects of the question might return, Solow reduced it to the lease contract, with all its neoclassical presumptions about the equality between renters and takers in a free market for land.[10] Vaughan provides more empirical detail but draws essentially the same conclusion as Solow. He praises Ferguson and Vance's characterization as 'cautious, but capacious,' even though it excludes the right of renewal from the definition of tenant right. Definitions of the custom that went beyond the right to sell when leaving a farm, according to Vaughan, 'could be seen as mere aspirations that formed an insubstantial halo around a substantial core.' There is 'nothing remarkable' about the right of occupancy, if the most remarkable aspect of the right of occupancy – the right of renewal – is categorically excluded. All that remains for this explication of the meaning of tenant right is a logical breakdown of the various financial components of the exchange: compensation for unexhausted improvements, the blackmail required to secure peaceable possession, the opportunity cost of landlessness, and the 'capitalization of uncollected rent.'[11]

Economists find nothing surprising in the Ulster custom because as an economic entity it is similar to the traditional English tenure system where tenants pay high entry fines for 'beneficial leases' whose rents are set below a rack-rent, competitive, or Ricardan level. The only difference is that in the case of tenant right the outgoing tenant, not the landlord, receives the entry fine. The related issues of the circulation of capital, incentives for investment of capital in land, and choice of farming technique can be analyzed similarly in both cases.[12] These financial and economic implications of tenant right warrant further research. After all, by the middle of the eighteenth century the payment of tenant right for rented property had become, after rent itself, the most significant form of exchange occurring on Ulster estates. Amounting as it did to five, ten, or more times the yearly rent of a farm, it was one of the largest expenditures that tenants faced in their lifetimes. Only the cost of a major improvement or the financial burden of dowries could rival this investment in size, and even these outlays came to be intimately related to the nexus of tenant right. A common complaint on the part of landlords and managers was of course that high tenant-right prices proved that rents were well below their 'lettable value.' One traveller through the north of Ireland in 1773 noticed that the highest-rented farms were attracting very elevated prices for the sale of their leases, proving the absence of rack-renting.[13] As another Abercorn estate agent noted in a letter of 1755, a lease could be a valuable hedge against inflation: 'Your lordship's tenants never had so light a burden of rent upon them in my remembrance or in the remembrance of any other person, and if there is no reason for it but one, it is proper it should be so when leases draw near their conclusion.' This windfall must have been quite high, for on many plots rents were doubled three years later in 1758.[14] Abercorn was certainly aware of the loss in income. In 1767 he made a complaint that must have been repeated frequently by landlords over the next century:

> I must think it hard on me that when leases are selling at ten and eleven years' purchase and people are struggling for the preference of buying them, the tenants should be as backward in the payment of their rents as they were. . . . You must bring the rents six months forwarder at least. This can be no real inconvenience even for those who are behind from misfortune, as they may dispose of their leases to great advantage. . . .[15]

To consider only these undeniably critical financial and distributive aspects of the custom is to miss the more extensive historical meanings of the term that project themselves through individual transactions. There is a difference between definition, function, and quantification, and only the first incorporates the social and historical relations between landlord and tenant. The implication of the accounting analysis is that if an aspect of tenant right only figures into a payment insignificantly, then that aspect cannot be significant to the meaning of tenant right. If the total price paid for tenant right was small, the custom itself could not have much meaning. While some historians have been sensitive to the early importance of the hereditary aspect of tenant right,[16] most have adopted the view that tenant right was not historically significant unless and until it became financially significant.[17] Even then, historians are more concerned with speculating how much rents might have been increased (at a time when it was widely recognized that sharp increases were socially impossible) than with investigating its broader meanings.[18] This approach to the meaning of tenant right is not wrong, only limited. It is relevant to the subject at a certain minimal level of abstraction, namely the level of the exchange itself. But at a higher level of abstraction, tenant-right payments were entangled in a historical web of significations in which economic analysis is itself caught. This book argues that on the historical plane, tenant right signified the process of establishing an economic structure within which classical-economic analyses can operate. The focus, therefore, is at the level of the social process of forming a private property system and transforming the landscape and the economy, beyond the level of particular capitalizations of uncollected potential rent. The strategy of shifting the focus from the narrowly economic to the social, historical, and political plane will not be without its critics. Solow, for example, castigated Gladstone and other half-hearted advocates of the traditional meanings of tenant right for confusing morality with economics and clinging to what she calls 'romantic historical arguments about tenant's rights.'[19] For Vaughan and Solow reality is transparent, non-contradictory, and immediately empirical. Their definition must also be clear, simple – and unreal. Attention to more capacious definitions brings the question of the meaning of tenant right into forbidden ideological waters: the recognition of the artificiality of private property rights, the recognition of the plantation as a human project, not a natural order, and the nature of the historical weakness of Irish landlordism. Tenant right caused such controversy in the nineteenth century not merely because of its status as 'a capitalization of the uncollected rental.' It clearly disturbed prevailing, and for some historians, presupposed, conceptions of property rights.

CUSTOMARY TENURE AND AGRARIAN CAPITALISM

The inadequacy of recent writing to this 'something beyond' of tenant right points to the much larger issue of its adequacy to the analysis of the phenomenon of capitalism itself. In order to grasp this 'something beyond' capitalist relations of production in the countryside it is necessary to take account of the historical and conceptual formation of capitalism, and the nature of the 'ensemble of social relations' which characterize the individual in societies transisting between feudalism and capitalism.[20] If these can be clarified, then the meaning of customary tenures in the historical transition to capitalism may come more clearly into view. Capitalist property relations, embedded as they are in a complex social network, are not simply a choice of technique. What distinguishes modern economic growth is not the adoption of certain technologies, practices, and organizations; rather, it is in Brenner's terms 'the presence in the economy of a systematic, continuous, and quite generalized drive on the part of the direct producers to transform production in the direction of greater efficiency by whatever means possible.'[21] This drive on the part of direct producers has had two essential and interrelated historical prerequisites: the orientation of all production toward exchange value and away from use value, and the separation of the producers of value from the means of production. Adam Smith's invisible hand of the market works only when producers, according to Brenner, 'must buy on the market the tools and means of subsistence needed to reproduce themselves. It is only [then] . . . that they must also be able to sell competitively on the market . . . and produce at the socially necessary rate.'[22] The crucial event in terms of the transformation of peasant economies into a capitalist system is the separation of the peasantry from the immediate sources of sustenance: the land or livestock from which they derive their subsistence.

The timing of, and therefore the explanation of, this transformation is a vast and much controverted question. Some medieval historians have emphasized the very early development of commerce and individualism in English society. It is clear from this literature that the economic differentiation of the peasantry, and the importance of the market for land in that differentiation, were already highly developed phenomena in medieval England.[23] On the other hand, modern social historians have traced the resilience of pre-capitalist forms of production well into the eighteenth century.[24] This book argues that customary tenures were among those remnants of precapitalism which survived into the modern period. In order to understand these transitional tenures, it is necessary to draw a clear distinction between the late feudal situation and the conditions of full-blown agrarian capitalism. In the former a market for land may operate within peasant society to differentiate between larger and smaller producers, arbitrate the distribution of landed resources within communities and across generations, and allow peasants to alter their portfolios to changing economic conditions. The operation of such a land market might allow for greater commercialization and productivity, but it operated in a context of a tight bond between land and family and strong productive, social, legal, and political connections both between families in a village and between each of those families and the lord. Historically, feudalism developed above already established, locally oriented, authochthanous peasant communities that were inseparable from the land they used to directly satisfy their subsistence needs. E.P. Thompson notes that 'both agrarian and legal historians appear to agree that the notion of the origin of common rights in royal or feudal grants is a fiction.' These were often said to have been 'enjoyed from time immemorial.' 'Anglo-Saxon and Norman monarchs and lords did not graciously institute but, rather, regulated and curtailed' such property rights.[25] This aboriginal collective attachment to their primary means of production survived into the post-feudal age in widely varying common-use and tenurial rights. In the vast period that lay between medieval vassals and serfs, whose right of inheritance arose from an arrangement based on violence as well as monetary and nonmonetary obligation, and early modern tenants, who competed one against the other as individuals in a market for rented land, customary tenures appeared. Customary tenures attest to the reality that agrarian capitalism was historically imposed on an authochthonous society whose conceptions of property were fundamentally incompatible. This incompatibility was *economic* in that it included certain communal productive practices and orientations, and *visual* in that it required communities to alter and inhabit the landscape in certain ways. But most importantly, it was *social* in that it carried forward what E.P. Thompson called a certain 'social or communal psychology of ownership' along a 'grid of inheritance:'

> This customary grid was as intrinsic to inheritance as the grid of banking and of the stock exchange is to the inheritance of money. Indeed, one could say that the beneficiary inherited both his right and the grid within which it was effectual: hence he must inherit a certain kind of social or communal psychology of ownership: the property not of his family but of his-family-within-the-commune.[26]

While the development of capitalism has a number of characteristics (commercialization, the expansion of wage labour, increased productivity, etc.), each with distinct though interconnected historical trajectories, the transformation in property relations is highlighted here. Full-blown agrarian capitalism incapacitates or completely destroys traditional bonds and connections so that all potential agrarian producers, including the landlords themselves, appear in the land market as free and individual competitors. Land becomes a commodity in the specific sense that Marx gave to the term, whereby the relations between people assume 'the fantastic form of relations between things.'[27] The relationships among persons in feudalism, which are made possible by legal or customary ties of persons to the land, are transformed and reinterpreted as relationships among things in capitalism. Property was once distinct from capital in that it was meaningless without reference to its own particular content – in the possession of a particular family, subservient to a particular lord, bound by the custom of a particular manor, etc. Capitalism renders these particularities into a homogeneous mass of mathematically and visually defined individual units, reducing each individual tradeable parcel to a general form of value.[28] Land becomes 'fictitious' capital, held *as if* it were capital.[29] This is for Marx 'the culminating point of the development of private property,'[30] the transition of property into capital. Its value becomes an abstraction, measured only in relation to other commodities and finally only as a pure quantity.[31]

The transition from feudalism to capitalism is therefore characterized by the emptying-out of private properties of their disparate contents and the universalization of their meaning and value in terms of money. This characteristic of the transition to agrarian capitalism is both economic and discursive. It applies not just to the organization of production and exchange but also to the language used to describe it, so that the emptying-out occurs not only to what is intuitively perceived as the content of private property (land, factories, machines, etc.), but also to discourse and texts.[32] A new unitary language, the language of capitalism, is imposed. In early modern England, for example, landholders became generically named as 'tenants' rather than disparately as copyholders, freeholders, or other various customary titles. The generic term is a unifying signification of a social relationship formerly defined by various 'heteroglossic forces, local traditions.'[33] The object of negotiation between landlord and tenant is therefore more than just the physical land and the rent, it is also a discursive negotiation of the meaning of the objectification of past human efforts in the landscape.[34] Discursive battles such as these are a peculiar feature of social and political life in capitalism. The relatively transparent and particular nature of pre-capitalist economic relations and the relative stability of ideology in premodern society create the context in which, in Giddens's words, 'private property has *content*, it *is* something.'[35] But the abstract and inscrutable nature of capitalist economic relations corresponds to an instability and contestability of the discourse or ideology applied to it.[36] One form this contest takes is a conflict between the language of capital and the customary language of agrarian communities.

The existence of custom is finally incompatible with agrarian capitalism. The capitalist threat to customary tenure takes a double form: it severs the agrarian community from its direct relationship to the means of production, and it drains the descriptions and legal definitions of customary tenure of their alleged content. The economic and the discursive aspects of this process are homologous, so that the sentences written about the one are always penetrated by the problem of the other. In order to properly render the meaning of tenant right, one must hold at arm's length the commonsensical view that a definition represents a transcendental, univocal rendering of a word in terms of a stable and universal language. A sign, a word, or a concept, is a refraction of social contradictions; it develops out of a contested social field of force where hegemony and resitance are entangled. This quality is often suppressed, however, because, in the words of the Russian linguist Volosinov, 'the ruling class strives to impart a supra-class, eternal character to the ideological sign, to extinguish or drive inward the struggle between social value judgements which occurs in it, to make the sign uni-accentual.'[37] The effort 'to make the sign uni-accentual' is the work of hegemony, defined by E.P. Thompson as

> the dominant discourse, which imposes a structure of ideas and beliefs – deep assumptions as to social proprieties and economic process and as to the legitimacy of relations of property and power, a general 'common sense' as to what is possible and what is not, a limited horizon of moral norms and practicable probabilities beyond which all must be blasphemous, seditious, insane, or apocolyptic fantasy – a structure which serves to consolidate the existent social order, enforce its priorities, and which is itself reinforced by rewards and penalties.[38]

The language used to describe relationships between landlords and tenants is intrinsic to the nature of those relationships. The survival of a customary tenure like tenant right in the commercializing, expanding, capitalist Ulster economy of the eighteenth and nineteenth centuries is not a nominal accident of history. In the face of the unitary language of private property, an alternative terminology survived. This terminology articulated a more fluid relationship between the three components of the relationship of rural communities to the land (past labour, living labour, and the farms in which they are conserved) and between the three components of the social whole (the individual-within-commune, the lord and his property, and the state and its constituents). Customary tenures created an open and flexible mapping between these various components, a mapping that conserved and propelled the social ensemble forward in time while adapting to changing demographic and economic circumstances. The struggle to establish a purely capitalist land market in Ireland has lasted for centuries and, as has recently been argued, has still not been entirely successful.[39] The thesis of this book is that terant right signified this continuous struggle, and this signification evolved to reflect the changing contexts of that struggle.

AGRARIAN CAPITALISM AND PRECOLONIAL ULSTER

To understand how a customary tenure developed across the entire province of Ulster, it is necessary to view the development of a capitalist private property system from the broader perspective of the relationship between the capitalist core and its various peripheries in the British and Irish Isles. This process had a vast chronology and a distinct geographical differential. The transition was marked in lowland England and Scotland by the War of the Roses and the wars of independence, in the Borders by the Union of the Crowns in 1603, in the Scottish Highlands by the defeat of the Pretender in 1745, and in Ireland by repeated plantation and conquest of property in the sixteenth and seventeenth centuries.[40] The explanation of the advance of agrarian capitalism in England comes down to crucial differences in the con- stellation of élite and peasant relationships concentrated in class conflict.[41] In comparative perspective, the English aristocracy was neither strong enough to keep peasants enserfed (as in eastern Europe), nor so weak that peasants maintained their relatively autonomous status (as in France).[42] This situation allowed English landlords to create a competitive market for land, so that 'holders of plots (leasehold farmers) had little choice but to treat their holdings as commercial investments, as a source of profit (if they wished to keep them), and could no longer view them as a *directly* self-sufficient basis for a family.'[43] Gordon Batho indicates the competitive atmosphere in the early seventeenth century by quoting Robert Churton's declaration that tenants 'by reason of this greediness and spleen one against the other [are] more their own enemies than is either the surveyor or the landlord.'[44] Amalgamation of holdings, investment in improvements, enforced adoption of new agricultural techniques, conversion of tenures to leaseholds, increasingly accurate surveying and calculation of fines, and other 'positive action to support the rental' were the hallmarks of progressive landlordism during the flowering of English agrarian capitalism.[45] The result was a transformation in landholding on a vast scale. By gradually annexing non-freehold land through the aggressive use of fines on the exchange and subdivision of farms, English landlords had gained control of perhaps 75% of all cultivable land by the end of the sixteenth century, and they used that control 'to engross, consolidate, and enclose, to create large farms and lease them to tenants who could afford to make capitalist investments.'[46] In Cambridgeshire, for example, the average size of landholding doubled from fifteen to thirty acres; in the Wiltshire chalk lands, most of the land was in the hands of capitalist farmers by the sixteenth century; in the west midlands the 30- to 100-acre farm became common by the late sixteenth century; and in Leicestershire 'the average and typical unit was already 45 acres in the second half of the sixteenth century.'[47] The importance of this uniquely English development can hardly be overestimated. According to Robert Brenner,

> Over the course of the early modern period, customary peasants were reduced to market-dependent, commercial tenants, losing the full possession

of the land that formerly, to a significant degree, had shielded them from the necessity to compete productively on the market in order to hold on to their land. The emergent class of commercial tenant farmers, subjected to competition both in the market for leases and in the market for their output, had little choice but to maximize their profits by specializing to the greatest extent possible, reinvesting their surpluses, and applying improved agricultural methods.[48]

In spite of the 'futile legal wrangling' instigated by tenants in the manor courts, progressive landlordism gradually ground down customary tenures.[49] The hallmark of the transformation was the replacement of the beneficial with the commercial lease, allowing landlords to gain more control over the process of production. According to Clay:

> Copyholders who did not fulfil their obligations in respect of repairs, or who exceeded their customary rights in such matters as subletting or ploughing up meadow and pasture, had either to be dealt with through the unreliable mechanism of the manor court, or by means of a full-dress legal action to terminate the tenancy altogether. In the case of leaseholders, however, the conditions could be spelt out more explicitly in a series of covenants, breach of which could bear a monetary penalty to which a tenant would automatically become liable if he overstepped the mark.[50]

This revolution in property relations is crucial to the relationship between the early modern English state and its more recalcitrant and problematic peripheries, and in particular to the antagonistic relationship which developed between the English crown and Ulster's Gaelic aristocracy. Here the relevant aspect of this relationship was the tension between two utterly different social formations and forms of political accumulation.[51] Like so many other non-capitalist forms of tenure, the tenure of the Irish middling sects was impenetrable and undefinable to English legal experts. In Ulster the communal nature of the traditional pre-capitalist agrarian community permeated the entire legal superstructure. Ownership of land was communal and individual units of land were periodically redistributed among kin. Under the custom of 'tanistry,' inheritance normally fell to the most worthy male member of a group with a common great-grandfather, which led to 'a constant transfer of property in land from the weaker and declining groups to the stronger and expanding ones, either through formal legal transfer or through annexation of unoccupied or under-utilized lands.' Such redivisions normally occurred at the death of co-heirs, but in some areas redistribution was annual at Mayday. The fluid and negotiable nature of Irish property rights had as its basis the pastoral orientation of the productive forces. More than any other factor, control over cattle and labour determined possession of property rights; hence the crucial role of the cattle raid in Gaelic power relations, which could 'reduce even a relatively prosperous group to beggary and to the need to part with part or even the whole of their lands.'[52] Control of land followed on the ability to control *creaghts*, large herds of cattle and the communities that tended them, not upon any other legal right. Without this following, the acquisition of land was pointless.[53] Pastoralism and fluid tenurial relations created a context in which occupiers of land exerted their power within the Gaelic hierarchy by frequent and sudden moves between competing sects. The result, according to Sir William Weston, was that 'the tenants do oftentimes change their dwellings, sometimes being tenant to one and within a half a year after tenant to another of those chief men, and many times wandering into other counties, often changing and not long continuing in one place, whereby great loosening and idleness is maintained and the ground slenderly or not at all manured.'[54]

It would be difficult to imagine a greater contrast in social formations than that which existed in the sixteenth century between Gaelic Ulster and the nascent agrarian capitalism of the south of England. In Ireland the direct production of use values by communities was for the most part restricted to the care of herds of cattle. The development of a market was inhibited by frequent cattle raiding and violent conflict between kin-based communities, and capital accumulation limited by the relatively weak control of chieftains over their highly mobile creaghts. 'The sixteenth century system of landholding,' according to Gillespie, 'did not centre on profit or on the concept of an economic rent for land but on a token render or 'ceart' to a lord who did not own any land. The land was held by family groups who paid this token sum, fixed by custom, and therefore theoretically immutable, to a lord in return for services such as protection.'[55] Gaelic customary rents were therefore far too low to allow sufficient income for chieftains to develop estates along commercial lines. Objectified labour was embodied in the cattle herd and only indirectly in the land that supported it, whereas in England the labour of a community was embodied in and identified with the visibly demarcated landscape as well as in the cattle, corn, etc., that were produced out of the landscape. In Ireland property rights were never more than a temporary and renegotiable contract between groups of people, but in England they were cemented into commercial contracts governing visible and discrete parcels of land. The Irish formation tended toward an economic steady-state, whereas the English combination of keen competition between tenants and 'positive action to support the rental' by the landowning class unleashed a revolutionary potential for the accumulation of capital and political power.

The geographical proximity of these starkly contrasting social formations, combined with their entanglement in a volatile international imbroglio, could not but produce political antagonism. In an unstable international context, the accumulation of political power by various Gaelic earls was perceived to be a dangerous threat to the Tudor state. In this context, the fate of a distinctly Gaelic tenurial system in Ulster was governed by both internal and external pressures. Its demise began in the sixteenth century, when the relations of power between competing Gaelic sects were first mediated by Tudor governments. Nicholas Canny demonstrates how the conflict between the brothers Shane and Matthew O'Neill over the right of inheritance to their father's lands in central Ulster led to an attempt to overthrow the whole traditional system of inheritance and succession and to replace it with a system of primogeniture and hereditary kingship. The strife between these brothers was typical of Gaelic power struggles, but the recourse that Matthew and his allies took with the English government in 1542 was novel and portentous. For the first time Ulster chieftains set out 'to fend for themselves totally outside the Gaelic institutional system.'[56] Matthew was murdered by his brother, but during the troubled decades of the 1560s and 1570s his descendants sought the support of the English government for their claim to inheritance by right of primogeniture. After the violent confrontation between Ulster Gaeldom and the Elizabethan state at the end of the century, the transformation of the remaining Ulster élite into an English-style aristocracy subservient to the crown was nearly complete. After the Treaty of Mellifont in 1603 Hugh O'Neill, the earl of Tyrone, held nothing short of 'palatinate jurisdiction' over his family kingdom. But for the casual oversight of the lord deputy and the easily dodged visits of relatively powerless assize justices, Tyrone held the rule of law completely in his own hands. After 1603 Tyrone used his powerful legal rights to the land to tyrannize those families in the area that had taken an independent stance in the Nine Years' War.[57] Once Tyrone's property rights were set on an English footing, the next strategy was to universalize the freehold system and distribute their possession more widely among Tyrone's competitiors.[58] The famous flight of the earls in 1607 simplified the task of Sir John Davies, who oversaw the legal transformation of Gaelic Ulster into a system of private property, by allowing him to use legal disputes between a much weakened Gaelic aristocracy to abolish tanistry and gavelkind and install freeholds and a system of common law.[59] South Ulster was particularly susceptible to this infiltration, where, according to Moody, 'the Irish system of landholding was rapidly being superseded in Ulster by English feudal tenure.'[60] While these legal tactics began the dissolution of Gaelic landed power, the central thrust of the colonial endeavour in Ulster was to escheat all the land held by Gaelic chiefs in six counties in western Ulster, thereby severing their inheritance and replacing the former proprietors with an entirely new class of immigrant undertakers, servitors, and acceptable natives.[61]

The decapitation of the Gaelic polity and the plantation of Ulster that followed were not inevitable, and the history of agrarian capitalism in Ulster might have taken a much different path. Canny, for example, makes the conjecture that had Tyrone not fled in 1607,

> there can be little doubt that he would have revolutionized the landholding and succession systems within the lordship, and in bringing them to conform with English practice would have promoted the interests of his immediate relatives at the expense of the collaterals. Tyrone in striving to accomplish this was both ruthless and avaricious, but such traits were absolutely essential to survival in the age of Machiavelli, and in any event Hugh was attempting nothing that would not have been attempted by his adversaries had they found themselves in a similar position.[62]

In the event, some Gaelic freeholders were given opportunities to accumulate property in the parlous decades before 1641. In general, however, they were characterized 'by an apparent inability to cope with the new demands of landownership. The crown rents and their poorer farming techniques meant that they were in constant difficulties.'[63] For those below the status of freeholder, the customary tenures were illegitimate under the new system based on the English lease contract. This meant that Gaelic customers had no defence against the new class of landlords who could easily evict them and renew the tenures on a new contractual and more exploitive footing.[64] If they were to survive, it would only be under a new contractual régime.

THE COLONIZATION OF ULSTER AND THE ORIGIN OF TENANT RIGHT

The meaning of customary tenure in Ulster must be set against the relationship between the Gaelic polity of sixteenth-century Ulster and the colonizing grasp of Europe's most precocious capitalist state. Here lay the origin of a vital distinction between English and Irish agrarian capitalism. The former developed organically – though not without considerable violence – behind the backs of historical actors, a fortuitous result of the peculiarly English constellation of peasants, lords, church, and state. In the escheated territory of Ulster, by stark contrast, agrarian capitalism was instituted as a model imbedded in the 'orders and conditions' of the plantation. E.P. Thompson distinguished between the organic development of English agrarian capitalism and the visual and legal model which served as the superstructural mechanism for the colonization of more communally oriented societies:

> Capitalist notations of property rights arose out of the long material process of agrarian change, as land use loosened itself from subsistence

imperatives and the land was laid open to the market. But now those concepts and this law (or lex loci of that part called England of a European island) were transported and imposed upon distant economies in various phases of evolution. Now it was law (or 'superstructure') which became the instrument of reorganizing (or disorganizing) alien agricultural modes of production, and on occasion, for revolutionizing the material base.[65]

The goal of the plantation was to place the tenure of land in Ulster on a fundamentally new foundation, to reorganize the landscape accordingly, and to populate that landscape with British landlords and tenants who would embody the new legal and productive régime. The keystone of the plantation scheme, as W.H. Crawford rightly emphasizes, was the requirement that all undertakers 'shall not demise any part of their lands only, but shall make certain estates for years, for life, in tail, or fee simple'[66] to the colonists. Without this requirement, Crawford judges, 'it is probable that many of the landlords would have farmed their estates in the traditional Irish way, employing Irish tenants.'[67] This requirement amounted to the adoption of any tenurial contract that was then current in England. The lease officially became the exclusive repository of authority over property rights, excluding any other forms of tenure or claims to the soil, and allowing the property owner to enjoy and allocate, in Marx's words, 'a monopoly over definite portions of the globe as exclusive spheres of their private will to the exclusion of all others.'[68] All customary or communal claims to land were made null and void, to be replaced by the terms of leases. So, for example, where common land and common rights survived in England and the English Pale in Ireland well into the eighteenth century, they were eliminated at a stroke in escheated Ulster.[69]

In the face of some recent revisionist historical writing, it needs to be emphasized that it is entirely appropriate to apply the term 'colonization' to the project of the plantation of Ulster. In the seventeenth and eighteenth centuries agrarian capitalism in Ulster would not result from a fortuitous combination of class forces but rather from the implementation of a colonial model by an immigrant population over the course of two centuries. The African critic V. Y. Mudimbe provides the following definition of colonialism:

Colonialism and colonization basically mean organization, arrangement. The two words derive from the Latin word colere, meaning to cultivate or design. . . . Colonists, those settling a region as well as colonialists, those exploiting a territory by dominating a local majority, have all tended to organize and transform non-European areas into fundamentally European constructs.

This reorganization, according to Mudimbe, takes place on three levels:

> the procedures of acquiring, distributing, and exploiting lands in colonies; the policies of domesticating natives; and the manner of managing ancient organizations and implementing new modes of production. Thus, three complementary hypotheses and actions emerge: the domination of physical space, the reformation of the natives' minds, and the integration of local economic histories into the Western perspective.[70]

The colonization of Ulster has often been rewritten in terms of neutral economic, demographic, and even environmental forces. Robinson, for example, defends a structural and social-scientific 'environmental' approach to the plantation over 'historical' accounts of the seventeenth century. His environmental approach emphasizes population distributions, building types, agricultural capital, and markets. This approach has a certain value, but when 'history' is replaced by 'environment' and terms like 'plantation' are replaced by the more value-free 'colonial spread,' the danger is that the human historical aspect of the plantation of Ulster is mystified.[71] Moody set out to disprove the conception that the 'plantation set on foot in the six escheated counties of Ulster in 1610 involved an immediate and extensive displacement of the native population,'[72] pointing out that only one demarcated category of land, that which was granted to British undertakers, was to be completely rid of the Irish. He preferred to characterize the period in terms of separate but equal competition between native and newcomer: 'The process by which they were driven out of the more fertile land and their places taken by British colonists was a gradual one and was the product of economic forces rather than of any deliberate act on the part of the state.'[73] This distinction is founded upon the premise that economic contact between distinct groups in an historical situation can be separated from its military and political context. By preparing the rhetorical stage for the telling of a story whose narrative force is economic competition, Moody and others efface the crucial military and political context of the story, namely, the pulverization of the native Ulster polity and economy from within and from without over the previous decades. The empty countryside can then be portrayed not as an economic disaster, but rather as an economic incentive, a place in whose 'turmoil lay glittering opportunity.'[74] Under this procedure Elizabeth's Irish wars signify a fortuitous clearing of the ground, enabling the immigrants to develop the only type of economy worthy of the name, not the destruction of a dynamic economy that was well adapted to the social and geographical environment. This artificial separation of the political from the economic sphere isolates the strictly 'political' activity of the crown (warfare, legal revolution, colonization) from the 'economic' activities of both the crown and the colonial planters (the raising of fines and rents, the segregation of settlement, discrimination in leasing policy). The state, being political, only acts politically. The economic activities of the crown may be suppressed or placed under the category of 'economic forces,' relieving the state of its responsibility and agency in the economy, despite the obvious economic effects of political actions.[75] It is important to register the economic effects of the activity of the state, and in particular, the relationship between the destruction of an old society and the potential for subsequent economic development. This relationship is implied in Perceval-Maxwell's account of the period:

> To add to Ulster's attractiveness, war had decimated her population. The whole of Ireland had suffered during Elizabeth's Irish wars. . . . But though all of Ireland suffered, of all her provinces Ulster had received the severest blows: 'Despoiled,' wrote an English settler in 1610, 'she presents herself (as it were) in a ragged sad sabled robe, ragged (indeed), there remaineth nothing but ruins and desolation, with very little show of humanity.'[76]

The rubric of neutral economic forces fails to explain the history of seventeenth-century Ulster because it neglects the political transition from *one* form of economy to *another*, a transition instituted and sponsored by the geographically expanding apparatus of the British state. Focussing on the *economy* in the most abstract sense of the term blurs this distinction. Without a positive conception of the mode of production or social formation constituting the earlier society, its characteristics can only be expressed negatively, as the absence of the characteristics of the capitalist economy. The result is that a narrative of Irish economic development suffers from the same explanatory weaknesses that Brenner identified in conventional histories of the transition to capitalism: an excessive reliance on the naturalized and self-perpetuating forces of commercialization and demographic expansion. Ireland's underpopulation, its undeveloped commercial and mercantile infrastructure, its shortage of capital, all serve as naturalized backdrops to the predictable and passively narrated story of their eventual development. For example, Gillespie's succinct and definitive account of this transitional period leaves the impression that the Irish economy was merely lacking components of a healthy capitalist economy (a robust merchant class, a workable monetary system, etc.), not that a fundamentally different type of economy was in the process of destruction.[77] He does emphasize the importance of changing property relationships, echoing Canny by saying that native Irish lords were already making the transition from warlords to commercial landlords by accepting surrender and regrant arrangements from the crown and extinguishing the rights of their own freeholders. But he fails to make Canny's point that it was antagonistic pressure from the English crown which forced these adaptive measures on to the native aristocracy. The monopolization of authority for 'trading arrangements and land allocation' under the English crown created 'the structures necessary for a market economy.' The predominant social force in this process was the English state. Gillespie, however, would rather have it that 'Ireland was moving in this direction even before the arrival of large numbers of settlers in the seventeenth century.'[78] The abstract phrasing used to describe the transition to capitalism ('Ireland was moving') casts it as a natural process with a self-generating momentum independent of the social forces propelling the changes.

For those historians for whom concepts like commercialization, demographic expansion, and 'colonial spread' take a sovereign position within their narratives, it is a short step to the abandonment of the term 'colonization' altogether. For Connolly, truly colonial enterprises are defined by geographical distance, immigrant settlement, and racist distinctions, and Ireland fulfils only the second of these. He claims that natives, colonists and metropolitans in Ireland shared a common European character. Since colonialism necessarily subjugates people and territories defined as other than European, no European people can therefore be colonised, especially by a state so close to and a culture so intermingled with its own.[79] The economic role of colonialism, to erase the crucial differences in the relations of production between the dominating and the colonial society, irrespective of racial or religious differences, remains unspecified and unexamined in Connolly's argument.[80] The thrust of the comparative work of Brenner and others is surely that the colonial erasure of older social formations within Europe, far from being excluded from European history, actually preceded and continued along with the European colonization of the rest of the world. As Karl Polanyi put it in 1944, 'what the white man may still occasionally practise in remote regions today, namely, the smashing up of social structures in order to extract the element of labour from them, was done in the eighteenth century to white populations by white men for similar purposes.'[81] It is not surprising then that the strand within eighteenth-century Irish Protestant society which identified itself as colonial was made up predominantly of landlords and Anglican churchmen, for they occupied crucial strategic positions in terms of the colonization of Ireland – the land settlement and the state religion.[82]

This plea for the applicability of the term 'colonization' is motivated by a view of history which gives privilege to the force of social and political agents over socioscientific forces. The danger is that the source of agency (class consciousness, class conflict, *mentalités*, etc.) may take an equally passive and abstract place in the historical narrative.[83] But one can go too far in the devaluation of the social force of class consciousness or the *mentalité* of groups. In their survey of the colonial period Gillespie and Brady downplay any continuity, evolution, or systematic repetition in favour of the contingency of changing circumstances: 'Anglo-Irish relations between 1534 and 1641 can no longer be seen as a progressive and irresistible process of conquest but rather as a result of a series of changing attitudes and opportunities.'[84] This seems to imply a rather Sartrean view of the human subject, a one-sided emphasis on the ability of historical subjects to remake themselves irrespective of social determinants or processes. Gillespie's concluding assessment is that 'the relationship between native and newcomer cannot be seen simply in terms of the confrontation of mutually exclusive interests and ideologies. The contours of the relationship can only be traced by the analysis of individual instances, at specific times, and in particular places.'[85] The first statement is reasonable enough, since the 'mutually exclusive categories' are themselves only ideological 'actants' created by historical narratives, not historical realities *per se*.[86] But this move from larger to smaller stories, without a proper dialectical understanding of their context, risks failing to grasp that 'specific times and particular places' have no meaning outside their relationship to those contexts. The demonstration that 'mutually exclusive interests and ideologies' do not fully capture the nature of particular relationships between natives and newcomers does not lessen their social force. The battle between mutually exclusive conceptions of property, for example, proceeds apace in this period even though there are pronounced ambiguities in particular cases, such as those of the O'Neills of central Ulster discussed above. Native but modernizing landowners like Sir Phelim O'Neill, who ousted natives and replaced them with British tenants, were no less significant to the transformation than the stereotypical planter of English stock.[87] And at the level of the actual occupiers of land in colonial Ulster, it cannot be said, to paraphrase Gillespie, that the newcomers confronted the natives with a new régime of private property so that the two groups had 'mutually exclusive interests and ideologies.' The mass migration of Scots and northern English to Ulster was a result of displacements caused by capitalist transformation in the British countryside. These newcomers were in many cases victims of the same economic régime in Scotland and England that they were helping to establish in Ulster. There is a fine but important distinction between the active ideological agency of individuals or groups and their passive participation in social forces not of their own making. Whether the historian has the intellectual and linguistic tools to properly make these distinctions is an open question.[88]

THE ORIGIN OF TENANT RIGHT

Seventeenth-century Ulster immigrants arrived from areas in Britain where customary tenures embodying the remnants of pre-capitalist landlord-tenant relations such as border tenant right in northern England and kindly tenure in Scotland had relatively recently been extinguished. In the search for the origin of Ulster tenant right, it seems safe to connect the following phenomena in one context: first, the political stabilization and agrarian modernization of the north of England and the attendant emigration to Ulster from areas where border tenant right had only recently been extinguished; second, the dramatic influx of English settlers into the fragile network of landed estates in Ulster in the third quarter of the century; and third, the reuse of the term 'tenant right' to assert a claim to the soil.

Although it is often maintained that tenant-right payments first occurred during the plantation of Ulster by James I and had their origin in the relationship that developed between capital-starved landlords and their immigrant tenants, no convincing evidence has yet been given for this hypothesis. The idea may have originated in the early nineteenth century, for it surfaced for the first time in the inquiries of the Devon commission of inquiry into the occupation of land in Ireland of 1843–5. For example, it was the opinion of John Sinclair, a Tyrone landowner, that tenant right originated with this new population. He told the Devon commission:

> As far back as the plantation of Ulster the tenant right has been respected and has been valuable only to the tenant. The notion is that it originated in the manner in which the settlement was made. The settlement here was quite a feudal settlement. The tenants in capite got a certain proportion of land on condition that they were to sublet a portion and be ready to defend the place; and it appears to me that we can trace the present indefeasible tenant right up to that; for those who were settled by the original patentees were in some sort fosterers or kindred and were engaged in the defence of the country and became a friendly tenant rather than a tenant for money. And I think that from that time to this the tenant right has been continued.[89]

It is interesting that this witness made a connection between Ulster tenant right and both pre-capitalist feudal relations and kindly tenure by identifying the first settlers as kindred in defence of the country. This was precisely the situation of the first customary tenants in England and Scotland in earlier centuries.[90] Mildred Campbell described English border tenant right as 'a kind of cross between customary tenure and knight service in its ancient form, with features drawn from both,' using a feudal terminology to articulate these features.[91] As for Scottish kindly tenure, Margaret Sanderson argues that 'the word kindly derives from the word kin and came to express belief in the rightness of possession by inheritance, a claim to hold the land because one was kin, usually nearest of kin, to the previous holder.'[92]

These connections are suggestive, but there is little evidence to support Sinclair's hypothesis. Chapter 2 explores in greater detail how the new owners of land west of the River Bann were generally dependent on the Irish occupants and their landholding and productive practices. To take the example of the London companies' proportions, in 1614 there were no colonists, only workmen and a few voluntary immigrants. Robert McClellan, the head tenant of the Clothworkers' proportion, who held land in perhaps the most challenging territory of the Londoners' plantation, found himself paying for the transport of tenants, only to have them run away to other landlords because of their dissatisfaction with the poor surveying and the wild condition of the estate. According to Macafee's study of a locality in nearby Maghera, Co. Londonderry, 'the planters were mainly concentrated on the church lands while the Irish occupied the lands of the London companies, a situation directly opposite to that envisaged by the plantation scheme.'[93] This evidence suggests that the origin of tenant right must have been established later than the reign of James I when a much greater number of poor and disaffected tenants emigrated to colonial Ulster and established geographically distinct communities of settlement.[94] While it is conceivable that the original plantation leases that were renewed in the 1630s might have provided the context for the articulation of an extra-economic form of customary tenure, little evidence for this has appeared.[95] Nor does the term tenant right seem to have been in use in the reconstructive 1650s. In a detailed written agreement over the exchange of three townlands in County Antrim in 1653 which refers to the sale of 'all the interest, title, and right' held by one of the parties, the term tenant right is conspicuous by its absence.[96]

The context proposed here for the origin of tenant right was not set in place until much later in the century, when the total numbers of immigrant settlers began to increase, and the proportion of English-born among them began to rise.[97] The archive surviving from seventeenth-century Ulster is too sparse to allow for broad generalization, but the circumstantial evidence suggests that tenants who fled the north of England for colonial Ulster in the late seventeenth century took with them the memory of tenant right and found in tenant right an allegory for the new colonial situation. In the north of England up until at least the 1620s, tenures of service to protect against raiding supplemented otherwise strictly commercial contracts. Hereditary tenures which secured the very ground on which exclusively economic contractual relationships might be agreed had only recently become extinct. The willingness of emigrants from these areas to occupy land under the unfavourable and sometimes impossible conditions in Ulster, and later to farm, occupy, and produce in a certain way, may have appeared as an iteration of the difficult conditions which had originally produced the border tenant right of their ancestors. There are some indications that the term 'tenant right' was in common usage by the end of the century. Gillespie unearthed the following early evidence of tenant right:

In 1680, for example, Hugh Rowley, a tenant to the bishop of Derry, complained that he should not have been removed from his holding: 'my present tenant right should oblige you to use me better than any other.' The tenant right, or right of renewal, could be dissociated from the lease itself. Thus, on the Molyneux estate at Castledillon [County Armagh], one Mr. Sargeant sold his lease to Thomas Calvert but reserved the tenant right for himself, and on Calvert's death he exercised the 'right' to renewal in a petition to the agent on the estate. In contrast to this, one tenant on the Conway estate, Major Stroud, was keen 'to sell his lease and tenant right.[98]

Another piece of evidence comes from a 1693 lease assignment to a grave-yard. The lease assignees were 'to have and to hold the said graveyard as it is now set out to them and their heirs, exes, admes, and assignees, during all the said Robert Richardson's and John Marshal's lease, and the tenant right thereof after the expiration of said lease.'[99] The sellers of the tenant right were also to be allowed access to bury their dead. Two entries in a county Down rent book from before 1720 used tenant right in the specific context of the right of sons to inherit the tenant right from their mothers: 'Jane McMechan [is] to have her present holding at the present rent, and surrenders her waste tene-ment to us in consideration of which she and her family renounce and quit their tenant right after the said Jane's death to the said holding.'[100] Another entry in the rental a couple of years later reads: 'John Brown remitted his tenant right to his mother's holding, she paying him what he lay out. She quits a year of her freedom of her tenement on having liberty to build her new house of clay on the back part, and stones on the front.'[101] Evidence of the use of the term tenant right is more common after the first decades of the eighteenth century. The first recorded sale of tenant right on the Abercorn estate around Strabane, Co. Tyrone, occurred in 1715.[102] Another early example of the sale of tenant right comes from Derry city in 1717, where £422 was paid for three tenements, the seller sacrificing in exchange 'his right, tithe, interest, tenant right, term of years and lives, property, claims, and demand' of the land.[103] A County Down rental of 1722 includes the following entry:

> Hugh and Murtagh Diamond of Dromnavaddy [near Banbridge, Co. Down] hereby surrender and deliver up unto Joseph Savage all our tenant right in and to the farms we hold under Thomas Fitz – esq. in Dromnavaddy and hereby give and grant leave to said Savage and assigns to build houses, ditches, etc., on the premises, carry turf, corn, and any other effects they have occasion for to said lands at any time till November next. Witness our hands this 9th of August, 1722.[104]

In 1745 a County Down agent reported that 'James Blackwood has purchased Thomas Cowden's tenant right of the house adjoining his and I would wish that what he proposes would be agreeable to my lord and you as it is exchanging a very good for a very bad tenant.'[105] A will of 1747 mentions the 'residue including tenant right of farm to wife not named.'[106]

THE MEANING OF TENANT RIGHT

Why did a customary tenure called tenant right arise in late seventeenth-century Ulster? Historians have traditionally attached no significance to the fact that the practice of selling leases and later any other form of tenancy came to be named 'tenant right.' This book argues that the custom itself was important both economically and discursively, and that the particular way in which it came to be named may also have historical significance. This is not to say that mere existence is deeply meaningful in itself, only that the language used in reference to social relationships during a period of rapid and sometimes violent transformation is significant. Still, the usage of the term 'tenant right' can only be significant if its referent actually existed.[107] The lease contract, the keystone of the new property relations of the plantation settlement, was intended to be exhaustive and comprehensive. In a régime governed by lease contracts, tenant-right tenures had no legal legitimacy. A publication of 1731 entitled *An inquiry into the tenant right of those who hold lands of church or other foundations* claimed that the Irish Society, the development corporation for the Londonderry plantation which held land in Derry and Coleraine, 'did not consider themselves bound to respect any tenant right to renewal and in many cases accepted the proposals of strangers.'[108] Some surviving leases specifically abrogated any such rights. Robert Maxwell, the bishop of Kilmore and a prominent head tenant on the Trinity College lands in the manor of Toaghy, Co. Armagh, wrote to the provost and fellows in 1671 to gain acceptance of his son as tenant of three townlands, asking their 'consent and approbation [to] pass over my whole title, interest, and term of years to me yet remaining to said James [his son], according to a clause in my lease whereby I am bound not to alienate any part of my lease except by my last will and testament, provided it be to some of my children.'[109] For later commentators, the orders and conditions of the plantation provided a *prima facie* case for the non-existence of tenant right. The marquis of Dufferin, a leading Victorian opponent of tenant right, argued that James I stipulated that the new landowners 'should grant leases of smaller portions of lands to other settlers for a definite duration, at a moderate rate, it being expressly laid down that these tenants should, on security of their leases, build houses and cultivate land. Now the fact of a definite and terminable contract having been entered into at once excludes the idea of an indefinite understanding, such as that which is claimed for Tenant Right.'[110] It is understandable that modern historians, disciplined to assess the empirical evidence at face value, tend to restrict the existence of tenant right *within* the bounds of the legal framework of the plantation. Cullen reckons that 'what is sometimes described as a tenant right by later writers referring to this period in the eighteenth century was simply the right of the tenant to sell his interest in a lease.'[111] Crawford, whose mastery of the sources remains unsurpassed, concludes that surviving seventeenth-century leases generally gave 'clear indication that at the termination of a lease the tenant had no legal claim to renewal; nor could he claim for compensation for improvements unless the terms of the lease specifically allowed him to do so.' He quotes from wills left by Ulster tenants in 1740, 1769, and 1792 in which they assign their right of renewal to their heirs '. . . if this can be obtained' or with the proviso 'in case same is not renewed. . . .' The tenant right of renewal, according to Crawford, was merely a claim of 'priority among the tenants themselves' determining who, if anyone, held such a right, and it fell far short of a right to perpetuity. 'To demand rather than request tenant right,' he insists, 'would have meant depriving a landlord of a say in the disposal of his own property.'[112] The reticence of tenants to make such demands can be seen in the following petition from a County Louth tenant to his landlady, which clearly distinguishes 'right' from 'discretion':

> I applied to Sir Nicholas to add about eleven years that is elapsed of a term of thirty-one years in some concerns . . . , or that he would be pleased to change the term of years into three lives . . . , but he seems to think it would be doing an injustice and disservice to his eldest son. . . . What I requested was a matter of common right, though discretionary in Sir Nicholas to grant to every good tenant.[113]

The new private property system, in this bluntly empirical view of the period in question, contains within it all of social reality, leaving nothing outside itself. Evidence showing deference to the rules of private property is held to be definitive. This book argues otherwise. The private property system is not ontologically exhaustive of historical reality. Tenant right existed anterior to and on a more fundamental plane than either the lease or the legal title to the land. In many of the first usages of the term tenant right, it was clear that the term referred to something other than the property right delimited by the lease and existed after its expiration. In this respect, the crucial aspect of the 1693 lease assignment cited above is the clear distinction between the lease contract itself and the custom which supplemented it. In the entries in the County Down rent book of 1720 cited above, tenant right was presumed to apply *after* the expiration of the landlord-tenant contract at the death of the tenant. From the very earliest point in its history, tenant right referred to 'something beyond' contracts with landlords. Tenant right and the sale of interest in a lease have from the very beginning two separate meanings, the former referring to the right of inheritance and renewal, the latter the market value of a tenancy.

Tenant right has a certain 'in-betweenness' or 'limnality.'[114] Discourse about it is marked by a conflict between the language of an older customary society and the new society governed by contracts. Mudimbe complains that most theories of colonialism misapprehend that third space between the typical dichotomies traditional/modern, oral/written, agrarian/urban, customary/rationalized, subsistence/market. 'This marginal space,' he claims, 'has been a great problem since the beginning of the colonizing experience.' Rather than being a step in an imaginary evolutionary process, 'it has been the locus of paradoxes that called into question the modalities and implications of modernization. . . .'[115] The custom of tenant right took root in this 'third space' between the economic and the transgressive foundation of plantation Ulster society, between the operation of a capitalist economy and the colonial structure of that economy, between the laborious production of surplus value and the establishment and maintenance of the conditions of such production. Customary tenures traditionally served to signify the customers's places both *within* an ancient community and *between* that community and the estate or manor, relationships that were maintained through labour and service from a distant date in the feudal past. Tenant-right in colonial Ulster was an iteration of the old function of customary tenure, a repetition with a crucial difference. Here the labour and service of the tenant was oriented toward the establishment of commercial relationships in a colonial market, not toward the preservation of feudal relationships. Landed estates were established in Ireland only by way of landlord-tenant relationships in which the need to recognize ties to the land always haunted the new landlord class. Strictly capitalist property relations founded on the commercial lease required the alliance of a tenantry recruited from both the native Irish and the immigrant British populations. This class alliance, which gave substance to the model, was 'something beyond' capitalism and was signified in the discursive relationships between landlords and tenants by 'something beyond' plantation contracts, tenant right. There was a gap between the political requirement to transform the Irish countryside and the economic potential of doing so. One result of this, as Gillespie recognizes, was a system of landlord-tenant relations 'which were conditioned by non-economic considerations.'[116]

If it can be said that tenant right had an existence, however marginal and tenuous, what is its meaning? What did the users of the term intend to signify and make significant? Tenant right was an allegory in the sense that Spenser gave to that term: a 'dark conceit' of discourse by which a text works with words that have complex historicities and multiple usages to preserve meaning beneath the surface of a narrative.[117] Allegory works out the relationship between a text and that which is 'interior and absent' to it, that is, its social context. It is the key of a text in a musical sense, the thematic harmony or constellation of key words within the text that resonate with reality.[118] Capitalism, which empties the individual tenant, landlord, and farm of their particular meanings and relationships, abhors allegory.[119] Preferring the thing itself, redefined by surveying, parcelling, and leasing, as a unit of production without history, the capitalist landlord conceives of the farms at his disposal in terms of the annuity they will return and the contracts which govern their disposition. The lease delimits the relationship between landlord and tenant to the text of the contract, and in particular, closes off any other possible figuration of the history of the property or the tenant's relationship to it. The customary tenant, therefore, adhered to allegory. The *literal* history of the relationship with the landlord could never be entirely adequate because its temporal boundaries excluded historical relationships that continued to haunt the contract and supplement its meaning. The customary tenure, as allegory, was a *figurative* history signifying the temporal structure of those larger relationships within which contracts were made literal. The landlord-tenant relationship had an inescapable *historicity* which the lease contract struggled to efface.[120] To reiterate: the object of negotiation between landlord and tenant was not merely the mute materiality of the farm of land, but also the status of that farm as a repository of past and continuing labour, a component in a larger project of transformation. The farm itself had a history imbedded in its presence, and this historicity was conserved discursively by a narrative which attached the past labour of a tenant to a right to a property. The Irish land question revolves around the disruption of the literal by the figural history of the relationships between owners and occupiers.

The following chapters examine how Ulster landlords, faced with the struggle to establish and maintain a colonial system, were dragged from their sovereign throne of private property and forced to come to terms with the historicality of that system. They were displaced from this throne by the repeated reminders, petitions, and claims of their tenants concerning the foundations of the system. These tenants undermined the ahistorical and universal pretensions of the land law with a rhetoric grounding property rights on labour and, therefore, history. These tensions surrounding the conceptual and historical foundations of property had to be worked out both theoretically and practically. For John Locke 'property originated in the mixing of labour (man's original God-given "property") with the common: "Whatsoever, then, he removes out of the state that nature hath provided and left it in, he hath mixed his labour with . . . and thereby makes it his property".'[121] Thompson notes that this origin of property in labour was not a particularly popular position among eighteenth-century judges, unless of course they could identify it with the labour of an improving capitalist:

Legal decisions in the eighteenth century introduced arguments from 'labour' in terms of the general reasons of 'improvements.' More often they fell back in the question of custom of lex loci upon the legal fiction that customary usages must have been founded on some original grant, from persons unknown, lost in the mists of antiquity. The law pretended that, somewhere in the year dot, the commons were granted by benevolent Saxon or Norman landowners, so that uses were less of right than by grace. The fiction was purely ideological: it guarded against the danger that use rights might be seen as inherent in the users, in which case the successors of the Levellers or Diggers might arise and plead their original title.[122]

Locke's definition rested on the undefinable and contestable term 'labour,'[123] a term to which he could only attribute meaning negatively by inventing the 'other' of labour. Locke found Native Americans to be a suitable signifier for this 'other' of labour. The absence of labour is present in 'the Wild Indian . . . who knows no enclosure and is still a tenant in common.' The Indians, like the Irish, were poor 'for want of improving' the land by labour, and 'since labour (and improvement) constituted the right to property, this made it all the more easy for Europeans to dispossess the Indians.'[124] For the capitalist-minded adjudicator, the definition of labour and the definition of 'reasonable act' both collapsed into one concept: 'improvement.' The definition of custom as originating in a reasonable act had its use once the law had detached customary right from the person of the user. Thompson suspects that 'the common law allowed 'reasons' to be considered which had more to do with the political economy of 'improvement' than with strict attention to the terms of the law. . . .'[125] So the dominant discourse, when it was unable to contain the meaning of relationships within leases, entered the fray of figural history to articulate a language of 'improvement' which conforms to the requirements of capital accumulation. This, as the following chapters will show, became a central element of the history of Ulster tenant right.

The allegorical nature of tenant right, the tension between figural and literal readings of the relationship between Ulster landlords and their tenants, is revealed in the evidence of tenant petitions to their landlords justifying their continued tenure. Tenants were often moved to tell elaborate stories in their defence rather than leave the question of their renewed tenures to competition or the caprice of the land agent. These stories are the clearest evidence that the lease alone could not contain the totality of the tenurial relationship. Consider for example the petition of Solomon Martin of Culmore, Co. Londonderry. He claimed in 1782 that his father purchased a farm in 1720 that was held by 'one widow Moore mother to the said Samuel Moore now in possession of said lands. . . .' The widow was at one point in heavy arrears and the agent McCausland approved Captain John Martin's purchase of 'her right title and interest of said lands, and the crop that was on said lands, and got possession of the whole, and paid all rents and arrears due on said lands, and held said lands for several years without lease . . .' until he was given a lease at £6 13s. 4d. for a £30 fine. In the meantime Solomon inherited the lease, it expired, and 'Lord Cunningham came into said estate at Limavady.' The latter threatened a lawsuit to dispossess him and since he had no lease he could not defend and so gave up the lands. He and the immediate tenant expressed their willingness to pay 14s. per acre for all that was out of lease in the townland.[126] In a dispute on the Barrett-Lennard estate around Clones, Co. Monaghan, between John Armstrong and Hugh Willoughby, the decision as to who should get a new lease for the townland was stated to be a question of which of the two had the better 'tenant right.' The claim for tenant right was not based on their past economic behaviour, since 'neither of them has made any improvements, for they only graze cattle on them.' Nevertheless, the agents attempted to judge who would be more likely to improve in the future. Willoughby was apparently wealthier and more powerful than Armstrong and received Barrett's support for his bid for a parliamentary seat, but the renewal went to Armstrong. Armstrong had held the lease to the land in question that had expired in 1714. The motivation for renewing to Armstrong was, 'first, to get the best improved rents, and second, to get good improvements made where never any was before.' Armstrong promised this and therefore got the lease. Willoughby even offered to pay more rent than Armstrong

> out of spite to John Armstrong because he knows he has taken it, but John Armstrong's rent improvements is much better for your honour than what Mr. Willoughby offers, for he told me it was for his servants and cotters or he would not take it, which will destroy the land, and besides old Willoughby is angry that his son should offer to take it from Armstrong, being, he says, that Armstrong, as soon as he came to live at Carrow after the late wars, offered to give him [your?] father's lease, and he would not take it. [Since] that makes Armstrong's tenant right good, so I humbly presume that John Armstrong ought to have it.[127]

This evidence appears to suggest that tenant right was associated as closely with Armstrong's occupation 'after the late wars' as with his potential as an improver. Finally, consider this elabourate plea from a County Louth tenant:

> That petitioner's grandfather had the honour of serving under your lordship's noble ancestor the great Bagnel of worthy memory in the wars as a trooper and whitesmith and after the settlement that nobleman settled him in the farm of Mullattee at a very low rent for the convenience of having him to do his work. . . . That since that time he and his successor up

to petitioner have been tenants and lived on the estate of that nobleman. But one Mr. Brabazon took Mullatee over petitioner's father's head and raised the rent considerably. That when the honorable Sir Nicholas Bayly was here in Ireland he found that petitioner was firmly attached to the interest of him and family, as he made manifest on being the chief means of gaining the lawsuit with Miss Morrow. That as petitioner was in suspense, not having a lease worthy of improvement, the honorable Sir Nicholas gave him his word and honor that he nor his heirs forever should be disturbed out of Mullatee while he the honorable Sir Nicholas or any of his heirs successfully should inherit the same, and desired petitioner to go on and improve the premises without any fear of being turned out. That petitioner then having surety, from that time forward, has spared neither labour nor cost to improve both the said land and strand so that he has now in full perfection 130 perches of ditches well quicked, 160 fruit trees and 180 forest trees on the said farm and that he has laid out upwards of sixty guineas from time to time since on improving the strand by levelling the same by drawing stones and laying them for the wreck, or seaweed, to grow on. That as petitioner's family relied on that nobleman's promise, he used the best means to improve the said farm and premises and make the same commodious and comfortable, divided the land into five parks or fields, having four children . . . , and built houses for that purpose. So he now depends as firmly on the noble earl of Uxbridge that his lordship will not turn him, his wife, four children, and nine grandchildren to desolation and beggary. And if it must be that petitioner and his family must turn out, he is well pleased it should and will be done by the right honorable successor of the noble worthy family, that he nor any of his forefathers disobliged. But as there are few men who have not enemies, petitioner would not wish his place should fall into such hands as covet it on account of the improvements he has made, it being the only place on your lordship's estate here that is in the least improved. So as petitioner has no expectations but from your lordship, he therefore humbly leaves himself entirely under your mercy. . . .[128]

These humble narratives, and many others like them, condense a wide variety of circumstances into justifications for customary tenure. The next three chapters separate the evidence of the history of Ulster agrarian society according to three themes, each of which addresses the question: What is the social basis of a claim of tenant right to a farm on an Ulster estate? These themes are: (1) the establishment and maintenance of a commercial tenurial relationship with a planter family (historicity); (2) the adoption of a productive practice that oriented the farmer toward a colonial market economy (production); and (3) the creation and maintenance of a visually and socially distinct unit of production (visuality). Each of these served to develop the plantation economy in a crucial way. Continuity of tenure and occupation by Protestant tenants constituted the primary bulwark against the deterioration of estates caused by middleman structures, emigration, and waste. Commercially-oriented economic practices and strategic occupation promoted the maximization of output and the marketing of produce in urban centres, integrating young estates into a colonial market economy. Enclosed settlement formed visually distinct units conducive to the storage of power relations by rationalized estate management. Each mark of a stable and developed economy, by distinguishing itself from the Gaelic economy that preceded it, surrounded it, and continued to influence it, opened a gap between the one and the other. The making of these marks was an effort to transform the ensemble of social relations that made up traditional agriculture, a labouring on the part of the entire Ulster population – settler, native, and owner – whose meaning was contestable. The unfolding of that contest in the eighteenth and nineteenth centuries is the subject of the following chapters.

The specification of three *separate* discourses – historicity, production, and visuality – is necessarily artificial and abstract. The tripartite construction of the subject is in one sense nothing more than an organizing principle and a vehicle for propelling the narrative forward. As the foregoing examples show, the evidence surveyed rarely isolates one of these themes from the others. In the particular instances of tenant-right claims or sales, these categories tend to overlap or replace each other, so that each case appears as a bundle or constellation of themes. The problem, to extrapolate from a penetrating critique of Edward Said's influential discourse analysis, is that 'if particular representations and discursive statements – if in fact they *are* discursive statements – can float so easily in and out of various discourses, then in what sense *can* we designate any one of them a discourse . . . ?'[129] This tripartition of the subject has been adopted because it corresponds to the earlier characterization of the productive life of agrarian communities in terms of social, economic, and visual elements.[130] It corresponds to three ways in which capitalism is organized and sustained: socially through class alliances, economically through the forced marketing of labour and the products of labour, and visually and organizationally through the creation of discrete and measurable units of production.

NOTES

1 James Hamilton to eighth earl of Abercorn, 18 September 1785, P.R.O.N.I., Abercorn papers, T2541/IA1/15/24.

2 W.A. Maguire, *The Downshire estates in Ireland, 1801–1845: the management of Irish landed estates in the early nineteenth century* (Oxford, 1972), p. 354.

3 For example, W.H. Crawford grants the custom only a brief mention in his two excellent characterizations of Ulster estate society. See his 'Landlord–tenant relations in Ulster, 1609–1820' in *I.E.S.H.*, ii (1975), pp. 5–21, and 'The significance of landed estates in Ulster,' in *I.E.S.H.*, xvii (1990), pp. 44–61.

4 See Olive Robinson, 'The London companies and tenant right in nineteenth-century Ireland' in *Agricultural history review*, xviii (1970), pp. 54–65; Robert Gourley, 'The social and economic history of the Gosford estates, 1610–1876' (M.S.Sc. thesis, Queen's University of Belfast, 1974); Martin W. Dowling, 'The Abercorn estate: economy and society in northwest Ulster, 1745–1800' (M.A. thesis, University of Wisconsin – Madison, 1986), pp. 165–210.

5 For the political question, see B.A. Kennedy, 'The struggle for tenant right in Ulster, 1829–1850' (M.A. thesis, Queen's University of Belfast, 1943); idem, 'Tenant right before 1870' in T.W. Moody and J.C. Beckett (eds.), *Ulster since 1800: a political and economic survey* (London, 1955), pp. 39–50; Robert Kirkpatrick, 'Landed estates in mid-Ulster and the Irish land war, 1879–1885' (Ph.D. dissertation, Trinity College Dublin, 1977); Francis Thompson, 'Land and politics in Ulster, 1868–1886' (Ph.D. dissertation, Queen's University of Belfast, 1982).

6 W. E. Vaughan, *Landlords & tenants in mid-Victorian Ireland* (Oxford, 1994), pp. 67–102.

7 The economic approach to tenant right began with William Neilson Hancock, *The tenant right of Ulster, considered economically . . .* (Dublin, 1845); see also, more recently, Barbara L. Solow, *The land question and the Irish economy, 1870–1903* (Cambridge, 1971), pp. 24–45; Joel Mokyr, 'Uncertainty in prefamine agriculture' in T.M. Devine and David Dickson (eds.), *Ireland and Scotland, 1600–1850: parallels and contrasts in economic and social development* (Edinburgh, 1983), pp. 89–100; Joel Mokyr, *Why Ireland starved: a quantitative and analytical history of the Irish economy*, 1800–1850 (London, 1983), pp. 81–101, 133–4; Timothy Guinnane and Ronald I. Miller, 'Bonds without bondsmen: tenant right in nineteenth-century Ireland' in *Journal of economic history*, lxi, no. 1 (March, 1996), pp. 113–142.

8 Maguire, *Downshire estates*, p. 140.

9 Vaughan, *Landlords & tenants*, p. 67, quoting William Dwyer Ferguson and Andrew Vance, *The tenure and improvement of land in Ireland, considered with reference to the relation of landlord and tenant and tenant right* (Dublin, 1851), p. 302.

10 Solow, *Land question*, pp. 26–7. In Liam Kennedy's equally careful exposition, 'pure tenant right' is nothing more than 'the extent to which the holding was being let at below the competitive level.' Liam Kennedy, 'The rural economy, 1820–1914' in Liam Kennedy and Philip Ollernshaw (eds.), *An economic history of Ulster 1820–1939* (Manchester, 1985), p. 39.

11 Vaughan, *Landlords & tenants*, pp. 67–76.

12 Lawrence Stone, *The crisis of the aristocracy, 1558–1641* (Oxford, 1965), p. 315, n. 2. Tenant right has been analyzed in terms of economic analyses of risk expectations and transaction and enforcement costs. See Mokyr, 'Uncertainty in prefamine agriculture' and Guinnane and Miller, 'Bonds without bondsmen.'

13 'Journal of a tour of parts of England, Wales, and Ireland, 3 June to 12 Aug. 1773' by Reverend J. Burrows, N.L.I., MS 23,561.
14 Nathanial Nesbitt to eighth earl of Abercorn, 12 Sept. 1755, P.R.O.N.I., Abercorn papers, T2541/IA1/3/106; idem, 22 Jan. 1758, ibid., T2541/IA1/5/3.
15 Abercorn to Hamilton, 14 Feb. 1767 ibid., D623/A/18/83. In a letter to James Hamilton in 1769 he calculated a loss of £2,349 on one eleven-acre holding alone because of long leases since 1704. Hamilton responded that this sum was gained by the sellers of tenant right. Hamilton to Abercorn, 11 and 17 May 1778, ibid., T2541/IA1/8/120 and T2541/IA1/9/19.
16 Gillespie emphasizes the hereditary nature of tenant right by comparing it in function to the three-life renewable lease. Raymond G. Gillespie (ed.), *Settlement and survival on an Ulster estate: the Brownlow leasebook 1667–1711* (Belfast, 1988), pp. liv–lvi. Maguire also carefully distinguishes between the hereditary right of occupancy from the financial function of tenant right in his study of the Downshire estates. Maguire, *Downshire estates*, p. 140.
17 Crawford implies that tenant right was not an important part of the rural scene until the nineteenth century. Crawford, 'Landlord-tenant relations,' p. 20. See also Cormac Ó Gráda, *Ireland: a new economic history 1780–1939* (Oxford, 1994), pp. 31–32.
18 Vaughan makes much of the fact that 'actual' rents were much lower than 'potential' rents on mid-Victorian estates. But the limitations on extracting these economically potential rents from tenants is demonstrated in Vaughan's quotation from the infamous Nassau William Senior's journals: 'Such a tenant right', I said, 'implies that the rent is too low. Why do you not raise it?' 'I cannot', he answered, 'ask a larger rent than that which is usually paid in this neighbourhood for land of this quality. I should not, certainly, incur personal danger by doing so, but I should become unpopular, which might affect my position.' Nassau William Senior, *Journals, conversations, and essays relating to Ireland* (London, 1868), ii, p. 171 quoted in Vaughan, *Landlord & tenants*, p. 72. The social and political context of setting rents is examined further in chapter 6.
19 Solow, *Land question*, p. 26.
20 The term 'ensemble of social relations' is taken from Karl Marx, 'Theses on Feuerbach' in Marx and Frederick Engels, *The German ideology: part one with selections from parts two and three and supplementary texts*, edited with an introduction by C.J. Arthur (New York, 1970), p. 122. The literature on the transition to capitalism is of course too massive to cite fully here. The position taken in this book is guided by the work of Robert Brenner. See his 'Agrarian class structure and economic development in pre-industrial Europe' in T.S. Aston and C.H.E. Philpin (eds.), *The Brenner debate: agrarian class structure and economic development in preindustrial England* (New York, 1985), as well as his response to his critics, 'The agrarian roots of European capitalism,' ibid., pp. 213–327; also Brenner, 'The origins of capitalist development: a critique of neoSmithian Marxism' in *new left review*, no. 109 (1977), pp. 25–92; idem, 'Economic backwardness in eastern Europe in light of developments in the west' in Daniel Chirot (ed.), *The origins of economic backwardness in eastern Europe: economics and politics from the middle ages to the twentieth century* (Berkeley, 1989), pp. 15–52; idem, 'Bourgeois revolution and transition to capitalism' in A.L. Beier, David Cannadine, and James M. Rosenheim (eds.), *The first modern society: essays in English history in honour of Lawrence Stone* (Cambridge, 1989), pp. 271–304. For productive critiques of Brenner, see Paul Glennie, 'In search of agrarian capitalism: manorial land markets and the acquisition of land in the Lea valley c. 1450–1560' in *Continuity and change*, no. 1 (1988), pp. 11–40,

and Surendra Munshi, 'Social formation and the problem of change' in *Science and society*, lv, no. 2 (Summer, 1991), pp. 175–96.

21 Brenner, 'Economic backwardness,' p. 17.

22 Ibid., p. 19.

23 See, for example, Alan MacFarlane, *The origins of individualism: the family, property, and social transition* (Oxford, 1978); Richard Britnell, *The commercialization of English society, 1000–1500* (Cambridege, 1993); Richard Britnell and Bruce M.S. Campbell, *A commercializing economy: England 1086 to c. 1300* (Manchester, 1995); Richard Smith (ed.), *Land, kinship, and lifecycle*, (Oxford, 1984); P.D.A. Harvey (ed.), *The peasant land market in medieval England* (Oxford, 1984).

24 See E. P. Thompson, *Whigs and hunters: the origins of the Black Act* (New York, 1975); idem, *Customs in common: studies in traditional popular culture* (New York, 1991); J.M. Neeson, *Commoners: common right, enclosure, and social change in England 1700–1820* (Cambridge, 1993).

25 E. P. Thompson, 'Custom, law, and common right' in *Customs in common*, p. 133. The immediate attachment between communities and their means of production should not be romanticized as a kind of primitive communism in the autochthonous peasant communities. The exploitation of women's labour, the exploitation of the younger generation by the older, and the exploitation of the foreigner by the autochthon are among the more common characteristics of traditional agrarian communities. See Maurice Godelier, *The mental and the material: thought, economy, and society* (London, 1986), pp. 71ff.

26 E.P. Thompson, 'The grid of inheritance: a comment,' in J. Goody, J. Thirsk, and E.P. Thompson (eds.), *Family and inheritance* (Cambridge, 1976), p. 337. The historical debate over the 'land-family bond' in early modern England is relevant to Thompson's argument. For a persuasive revision of the Alan MacFarlane's thesis that landholding and the market for tenancies were dominated by tenant individualism, see Govind Sreenivasan, 'The land-family bond at Earls Colne, Essex, 1550–1650' in *Past and present*, no. 131 (May, 1991), p. 19. The original argument was made in MacFarlane, *Origins of individualism*, pp. 68–9. See also Alan MacFarlane, *The culture of capitalism* (Oxford, 1987); R.W. Hoyle, 'The land-family bond in England: comment' in *Past and present*, no. 156 (Feb., 1995), pp. 151–74; Sreenivasan, 'The land-family bond in England: reply' in ibid., pp. 174–188.

27 Karl Marx, *Capital: a critique of political economy*, vol. 1, trans. Ben Fowlkes with an introduction by Ernst Mandel (New York, 1976), p. 165.

28 See Crystal Lynn Bartolovich, 'Boundary disputes: surveying, agrarian capital and English renaissance texts' (Ph.D. dissertation, Emory University, 1993), pp. 89, 98–99, 216.

29 '*Landed property*, as distinct from capital, is private property, capital, which is still afflicted with *local* and political prejudices, which has not yet entirely emerged ,rom its involvement with the world and come into its own; it is capital which is *not yet fully developed*. In the course of its *formation on a world scale* it must attain its abstract, i.e. pure, expression.' Karl Marx, 'Economic and philosophical manuscripts' in *Early writings*, trans. Rodney Livingstone (New York, 1975), pp. 340–41, cited in Bartolovich, 'Boundary disputes,' p. 210.

30 C.J. Arthur, *Dialectics of labour: Marx and his relation to Hegel* (Oxford, 1986), p. 25.

31 Land 'only acquires a general expression of its value if, at the same time, all other commodities express their value in the same equivalent.' Marx, *Capital*, i, p. 159.

32 This book adopts neither the traditonal Marxist position that economic transfor-
    mations determine changes in discourse and ideology, nor the lately fashionable
    position know as the 'linguistic turn.' Social historians who cast out as reductionist
    the work of economic historians often do so without realizing that the linguistic model
    they adopt is in many ways the same as the science they left behind. Even a cursory
    reading of the literature on deconstruction reveals that deconstructive readings do not
    deny or efface the economic basis of social reality; rather, they insist on the textu-
    alization of the economic. Derrida's point of contact to this question is to the linguist
    F. Saussure's investigation of the synchronic and diachronic character of language.
    Saussure relates this fundamental duality of the science of linguistics – its separation
    of itself from itself in terms of synchronicity and diachrony – to the same duality in
    economic science, divided as it is between political economy and economic history.
    Since these two sciences concern themselves with value, their subjects are split
    between the determination of value and the way value changes over time. 'In both
    cases, we have a system of equivalence between things belonging to different orders.
    In one case work and wages, in another case signified and signifier.' Jacques Derrida,
    'White mythology' in Jacques Derrida *Margins of Philosophy*, trans. with additional
    notes by Alan Bass (Chicago, 1982), pp. 217–18. The promising feature of the 'linguistic
    turn' is therefore not the replacement of economics or social history by linguistic
    analysis, but the interpenetration of these two fields: the social and economic field is
    textualized while texts are subjected to the determininations of the economy and to
    conflicting social forces.
33 Bartolovich, 'Boundary disputes,' p. 57. She quotes the Russian linguist Mikhail
    Bakhtin's description of a 'unitary language [that] gives expression to forces working
    toward concrete verbal and ideological unification and centralization, which develop
    in vital connection with the processes of sociopolitical and cultural centralization.'
    Mikhail Bakhtin, 'Discourse in the novel,' in *The dialogic imagination*, trans. Caryl
    Emerson and Michael Holquist (Austin, Texas, 1981), p. 271.
34 'Objectification' is used here in the Hegelian sense of the transformation and mediation
    of the natural world through labour. A farm, for example, via the labour of the farmer,
    becomes a human, not a natural, object. See Arthur, *Dialectics of labour*, pp. 5–19.
35 Anthony Giddens, *A contemporary critique of historical materialism, volume 1: power,
    property, and the state* (Berkeley and Los Angeles, 1981), p. 113.
36 This distinction between the transparency of pre-capitalist economic relations and
    the opacity of capitalist economic relations was developed by Samir Amin in his *Class
    and nation, historically and in the present crisis* (New York, 1980). For a concise sum-
    mary, see his 'Modes of production, history, and unequal development' in *Science and
    society*, xlix, no. 2 (summer, 1985), pp. 196–7.
37 V.N. Volosinov, *Marxism and the philosophy of language*, trans. Ladislave Matejka and
    I.R. Titunik (London, 1986), p. 23.
38 E.P. Thompson, *Witness against the beast: William Blake and the moral law* (Cambridge,
    1993), pp. 108–9, quoted in Marc W. Steinberg, 'Culturally speaking: finding a commons
    between post-structuralism and the Thompsonian perspective' in *Social history* vol.
    21, no. 2 (May 1996), p. 205.
39 Irish agriculture continues to resist 'market pressures and the ultimate triumph of
    agro-capitalism.' Liam Kennedy, 'Farm succession in modern Ireland: elements of a
    theory of inheritance' in *Econ. history review*, xliv, no. 3 (1991), p. 498.
40 The literature on the history of other customary tenures in the northern British Isles
    in the early modern period must fall outside the scope of the present work. For develop-

ments in Scotland and the history of 'kindly tenure' there, see W. Croft Dickenson, *Scotland from the earliest times to 1603*, third ed., ed. Archibald A.M. Duncan (Oxford, 1977); T.M. Devine, 'Social responses to agrarian 'improvement': the highland and lowland clearances in Scotland' in R.A. Houston and I.D. Whyte (eds.), *Scottish society 1500–1800* (London, 1989). For discussions of 'border tenant right' in the north of England, see R.H. Tawney, *The agrarian problem in the sixteenth century* (London, 1912); E. Kerridge, *Agrarian problems in the sixteenth century and after* (London, 1968); S.J. Watts, 'Tenant right in early seventeenth-century Northumberland' in *Northern history*, vi (1971), pp. 64–87; R.W. Hoyle, 'Lords, tenants, and tenant right,' *Northern history*, xx (1984), pp. 38–63; and idem, 'An ancient and laudable custom: the definition and development of tenant right in northwestern England in the sixteenth century' in *Past and present*, no. 116 (1986), pp. 24–55 .

41 Brenner, 'Agrarian roots,' pp. 258, 313–15; Bartolovich, 'Boundary disputes', p. 13, n. 12 and p. 84, n. 52; Glennie, 'In search of agrarian capitalism'; Richard Lachman, *From manor to market: structural change in England, 1536–1640* (Madison, Wisconsin, 1987); Gordon Batho, 'Nobleman, gentlemen, and yeomen' in Joan Thirsk (ed.), *Agrarian history of England and Wales, iv: 1500–1680* (Cambridge, 1967), pp. 276–305; Christopher, Clay, 'Landlords and estate management in England' in Joan Thirsk (ed.), *The agrarian history of England and Wales, v: 1640–1750, pt. ii, agrarian change* (Cambridge, 1985), pp. 119–251; and Jerome Blum, 'English parliamentary enclosure' in *Journal of modern history*, liii (1981), pp. 477–504.

42 'It was the English lords' inability either to re-enserf the peasants or to move in the direction of absolutism (as had their French counterparts) which forced them in the long run to seek novel ways out of their [feudal] revenue crisis.' Brenner, 'Agrarian roots,' p. 293.

43 Idem, 'Agrarian roots,' p. 303.

44 Batho, 'Noblemen, gentlemen, and yeomen,' p. 304.

45 Clay, 'Landlords and estate management,' pp. 214–24, 230–51; Stone, *Crisis of the aristocracy*, p. 323.

46 Brenner,, 'Agrarian class structure,' pp. 48–9.

47 Idem, 'Agrarian roots,' pp. 305–6. See also Richard Lachmann, *From manor to market: structural change in England, 1536–1640* (Madison, Wisconsin, 1987), p. 98.

48 Idem, 'Bourgeois revolution and transition to capitalism,' p. 299.

49 Clay, 'Landlords and estate management,' pp. 198–99. At-will tenancies were replaced in the sixteenth century either by more secure forms of tenure or by elimination of the tenancies altogether. Tawney, *Agrarian problem*, p. 283. Peter Bowden, 'Agricultural prices, farm profits, and rents' in Thirsk (ed.), *Agrarian history*, iv, p. 686.

50 Clay, 'Landlords and estate management,' p. 204. This management revolution was also made possible by actuarial and geometrical advances which allowed more accurate surveying and calculation of value. 'The curtailment and abandonment of the beneficial lease thus depended firstly on the production of more sophisticated mathematical data which showed up the folly of the system, and secondly the growth of credit facilities to provide an alternative source of ready cash in time of need.' Stone, *Crisis*, pp. 319–20.

51 For a comparative discussion of Europe-wide dimensions which links different social formations to different forms of political accumulation, see Brenner, 'Economic backwardness,' especially pp. 28–30. See also Perry Anderson, *Lineages of the absolutist state* (London, 1974).

52 K.W. Nicholls, *Land, law and society in sixteenth-century Ireland* (Dublin, 1976), pp. 7, 13, n. 39, p. 20; Mary O'Dowd, 'Gaelic economy and society' in Ciaran Brady and Raymond Gillespie (eds.), *Natives and newcomers: The making of Irish colonial society 1534–1641* (Dublin, 1986), pp. 120–147. Pawlisch explains that by 'avoiding the uncertainties associated with minority or regency government,' tanistry's lateral system of succession was particularly suited to societies where agriculture is extensive rather than intensive. Hans Pawlisch, *Sir John Davies and the conquest of Ireland: a study in legal imperialism* (Cambridge, 1985), pp. 60–1.

53 A.T. Lucas, *Cattle in ancient Ireland* (Kilkenny, 1989), pp. 68–124; Katherine Simms, 'Warfare in the medieval Gaelic lordships' *Irish Sword*, xii, no. 47 (1976), pp. 99–100.

54 Nicholls, *Land, law, and society*, p. 10, quoting Sir William Weston in *Cal. S.P.I.*, 1692–9. Another Elizabethan, Sir Richard Bingham, described Connacht in similar terms in 1592. In 1596 the Bishop of Cork wrote 'the tenants continue not past three years in a place, but run roving about the country like wild men fleeing from one place to another.' *Cal. S.P.I.*, 1592–6, pp. 481–2.

55 Raymond G. Gillespie, *Colonial Ulster: the settlement of east Ulster 1600–1641* (Cork, 1985), p. 141. A Victorian researcher uncovered a contemporary description of tenure under the O'Neill earldom by Tobias Caulfield which held that the tenants held 'no certain portion of land,' that rents were paid partly in kind and were chargeable on the number of cows in milch or in calf, not the extent of their land, and that such rents were uncertain because counting the livestock was 'a procedure marked by corruption and deceit' and because 'by the custom of the country the tenants may remove from one Lord to another every half year as they usually do.' H.F. Hore, 'The archaeology of tenant right' in *Ulster journal of archaeology*, vi (1858), pp. 119–120.

56 Nicholas Canny, 'Hugh O'Neill, Earl of Tyrone, and the changing face of Gaelic Ulster' in *Studia Hibernica*, x (1970), p. 20.

57 Ibid., pp. 10–11, 15, 19.

58 Pawlisch, *Sir John Davies*, p. 67; P.J. Duffy, 'The evolution of estate properties in south Ulster 1600–1900' in William J. Smyth and Kevin Whelan (eds.), *Common ground: essays on the historical geography of Ireland presented to T. Jones Hughes* (Cork, 1988), p. 91.

59 'In the wake of the mysterious flight of the earls in September, 1607, the abolition of 'tanistry' and 'gavelkind' by judicial fiat served as a device to circumvent native rights in land whenever the more usual methods of attainder and revived medieval titles proved unsatisfactory.' Pawlisch, *Sir John Davies*, pp. 78, 80.

60 T.W. Moody, *The Londonderry Plantation 1609–41: the city of London and the plantation of Ulster*, Belfast, 1939, pp. 25–6; Pawlisch, *Sir John Davies*, pp. 78–80; William J. Smyth, 'Society and settlement in seventeenth-century Ireland: the evidence of the "1659 census",' in William J. Smyth and Kevin Whelan, *Common ground: essays on the historical geography of Ireland* (Cork, 1988), p. 68; P.J. Duffy, 'The territorial organization of Gaelic landownership and its transformation in County Monaghan 1591–1640' in *Irish geography*, xiv (1980), pp. 1–26; T. McErlean, 'The Irish townland system of landscape organization' in T. Reeves-Smyth and F. Hammond (eds.), *Landscape archaeology in Ireland* (Oxford, 1983), p. 68.

61 Philip Robinson, *The plantation of Ulster: British settlement in an Irish landscape, 1600–1670* (Dublin, 1984), pp. 60–65.

62 Canny, 'Hugh O'Neill,' p. 24. According to Canny, these characteristics are not unique to Tyrone. This sort of aggressive behaviour was common among the major figures of Ulster Gaelic society: extremely autocratic rule in defence of the immediate family with little respect for Gaelic tradition.

63 Duffy, 'Evolution of estate properties,' p. 91.
64 Gillespie, *Colonial Ulster*, pp. 141–142.
65 Thompson, 'Custom, law, and common right,' p. 164.
66 George Hill, *An historical account of the plantation of Ulster at the commencement of the seventeenth century, 1608–1620* (Belfast, 1877), p. 84, quoted in Crawford, 'Landlord-tenant relations,' p. 6, n. 9.
67 Crawford, 'Significance of landed estates,' p. 51.
68 Marx, *Capital: a critique of political economy, volume 3: the process of production as a whole*, ed. Frederick Engels (New York, 1967), p. 615. Anthony Giddens developed the idea that power is exercised in modern societies via instruments that store authorative and allocative resources. Such instruments are crucial to the administration of capitalism in general. The importance of the lease as a capacitor of authoritative and allocative resources – i.e. management, surveillance, and promotion of economic rationality – has already been noted and will be examined in later chapters. See Anthony Giddens, *Central problems in social theory: action, structure, and contradiction in social analysis* (Berkeley and Los Angeles, 1979), pp. 100, 162–3. See also Giddens, *Contemporary critique*, p. 41.
69 Thompson, 'Custom, law, and common right,' pp. 97–186; Neeson, *Commoners*, pp. 55–80; J.H. Andrews, *Plantation acres: an historical study of the Irish land surveyor and his maps* (Omagh, 1985), p. 123.
70 V.Y. Mudimbe, *The invention of Africa: gnosis, philosophy, and the order of knowledge* (Indiana, 1988), pp. 1, 2.
71 Robinson, *Plantation*, pp. xvii–xx.
72 T.W. Moody, 'The treatment of the native population under the scheme for the plantation of Ulster' in *Irish historical studies*, i, no. 1 (1939), p. 59.
73 Ibid., p. 63. Johnston's opinion concerning the plantation is similar: 'What James I could not do, economic circumstances compelled, and the Irish were removed to the uplands.' J.D. Johnston, 'The plantation of County Fermanagh 1610–41: an archaeological and historical survey' (M.A. thesis, Queen's University of Belfast, 1976), p. 86.
74 Karl Bottigheimer, 'Kingdom and colony: Ireland in the westward enterprise in Nicholas Canny, et. al (eds.), *The westward enterprise: English activities in Ireland, the Atlantic, and America 1480–1650* (Liverpool, 1978), p. 48.
75 For example, the penal restrictions on Irish land ownership, according to one petitioner, 'in all much abate the industry of the said natives to gain any greater or further estates.' The enforcement of the law against ploughing by the tail was also a major grievance, which in addition to the exacting fines prevented them ploughing their land and led to starvation of their cattle in the winter. Perceval-Maxwell, *Scottish migration*, p. 48; Lucas, *Cattle in ancient Ireland*, pp. 110–11.
76 M. Perceval-Maxwell, *The Scottish migration to Ulster in the reign of James I* (London and New York, 1973), p. 17. R.A. Butlin estimates that rural population density in 1600 was one-fifth its present-day value, pointing to famines resulting from the combination of war and bad weather. R.A. Butlin, 'Land and people, c. 1600' in T.W. Moody, F.X. Martin, and F.J. Byrne (eds.), *New history of Ireland, vol iii: early modern Ireland* (Oxford, 1976), pp. 146–147.
77 Gillespie, *Transformation*, pp. 54–56; Gillespie, *Settlement and survival*, pp. xxv–xxxii. Gillespie recognizes the importance of conflict in a more recent piece that argues that the switch from live cattle to provision exports even before the Cattle Acts of 1665 'was only possible because older patterns of economic activity had been broken

down by war.' Gillespie, 'The Irish economy at war, 1641–1652' in Janet Ohlmeyer (ed.), *Ireland from independence to occupation, 1641–1660* (London, 1995), p. 180.

78 Ibid., pp. 58–9.

79 Sean Connolly, *Religion, law, and power: the making of Protestant Ireland* (Oxford, 1992), pp. 111–13.

80 L.M. Cullen shows a greater appreciation of this role in *The emergence of modern Ireland* (London, 1981), p. 35.

81 Karl Polanyi, *The great transformation: the political and economic origins of our time* (Boston, 1944), p. 164.

82 Thomas Bartlett, *The fall and rise of the Irish nation: the Catholic question, 1690–1830* (Dublin, 1992), pp. 37ff.

83 Brenner has been criticized on these grounds. See Munshi, 'Social formation and the problem of change.'

84 Ciaran Brady and Raymond G. Gillespie, 'Introduction' in Brady and Gillespie, *Natives and newcomers*, p. 12.

85 Ibid., p. 17. They attack the concept of cohesive group ideologies, finding a wide range of opinion within native Irish, Old English, Palesmen, and Planter groups. The argument against the categories of process adopted by Canny and Bradshaw – renaissance and reformation respectively – is similar: 'this discovery of the gradual inadequacy of interpretive categories is, of course, a natural result of the progress of research.' Ibid., p. 16.

86 For a provocative, though jargon-filled, analyis of the way historical narratives transform abstractions into active historical agents, see Sande Cohen, *Historical culture: on the recoding of an academic discipline* (Berkeley, Los Angeles, and London, 1986).

87 Michael Perceval-Maxwell, *The outbreak of the Irish rebellion of 1641* (Dublin, 1994), pp. 45, 47.

88 The social theorists, having taken a few steps back from empirical reality, have had better luck. See for example, Giddens, *Central problems*, and Pierre Bourdieu, *Outline of a theory of practice*, trans. Richard Nice (Cambridge, 1977).

89 Sinclair also felt that this close personal relationship was as important in the origin of tenant right as was compensation paid for improvements. *Devon comm. evidence*, pt. i, xix, 743–6.

90 Kerridge, *Agrarian problems*, pp. 43–4.

91 Mildred Campbell, *The English yeomen under Elizabeth and the early Stuarts* (New York, 1968), p. 148.

92 Margaret Sanderson, *Scottish rural society in the sixteenth century* (Edinburgh, 1982), p. 58.

93 William Macafee, 'The colonization of the Maghera region of south Derry' in *Ulster Folklife*, xxiii (1977), p. 76; Perceval-Maxwell, *Scottish migration*, pp. 126, 134, 136, 151, 161, 171, 173, 178–82. Freeholders made up only ten to fifteen per cent of the tenantry in 1614. Ibid., pp. 244, 247; R.H. Rutherford, 'The plantation of the Lagan and its economy 1600–1900' in *Donegal annual* (1959), pp. 122–140; Moody, *Londonderry plantation*, pp. 184, 188.

94 R.J. Hunter, 'The Ulster plantation in the counties Armagh and Cavan 1608–41' (M. Litt. thesis, Trinity College Dublin, 1969), p. 425. Gillespie, *Colonial Ulster*, pp. 57–60. Perceval-Maxwell finds a marked continuity of names between the 1622 and 1630 surveys, arguing that new immigrants followed their neighbours and kin in Ulster, and that many landlords populated their estates with cadet members of their own families. Perceval-Maxwell, *Scottish migration*, pp. 286–8.

95 J.D. Johnston, 'Settlement on a plantation estate: the Balfour rentals of 1632 and 1636' in *Clogher record*, xii, no. 1 (1985), p. 101; Hunter, 'Ulster plantation,' p. 524.

96 Agreement of Patrick McClennon, Ballydonnelly, Co. Antrim, with William Conyngham, Oldstoun, 24 October 1653, P.R.O.N.I., Castle Stewart papers, D1618/15/2/5.

97 Irish historical geographers distinguish two major components of 'British' settlement in Ulster: 'an outer area to the north-east, north, and north-west where the non-Irish population is primarily of Scottish origin, and an area in mid and south Ulster where it is predominantly of English origin.' Robinson, *Plantation of Ulster*, pp. 110–12. In addition to the mid-Ulster belt of English settlement, 'County Londonderry appears in the seventeenth century to have been predominantly English rather than Scottish . . ., while south Tyrone apparently contained a relatively higher proportion of Scots.' Ibid., p. 113. Quakers in Lurgan were 'drawn from the north of England: about a third from Yorkshire, a fifth from Cumberland, and the remainder from Lancashire, Northumberland, and Westmoreland. . . . Lisburn was 'one of the most English places in the kingdom,' and the inhabitants of Blaris parish near Lisburn were almost entirely English, to judge by their surnames.' Gillespie, *Settlement and survival*, p. xviii.

98 Ibid., p. lv.

99 Lease assignment to graveyard, 1693, P.R.O.N.I., T1062/45/124.

100 Rental of Clanbrassil estate, n.d. [c. 1714], P.R.O.N.I., T776, p. 93.

101 Ibid., [c. 1718], p. 95.

102 Joseph Calhoun to eighth earl of Abercorn, 19 October 1753, P.R.O.N.I., Abercorn papers, T2541/IA1/7/5.

103 Alderman James Lennox to Frederick Gordon, 22 March 1717, P.R.O.N.I., Lennox-Conyngham papers, D1449/1/30.

104 Rental of Portaferry, 1722, P.R.O.N.I., Nugent Estate papers, D552/A/B/3/2/93.

105 Charles Brett, Bangor, to Judge Ward, 27 Feb. 1745, P.R.O.N.I., Castleward papers, D2092/1/7, p. 88. See also a letter to Michael Ward where the right of a man to renew the lives of a lease was discussed in terms of his alleged 'tenant right'. [?] to Michael Ward, n.d. [c. 1740], ibid., p. 1.

106 Will of Archibald Douglas of Ballynahinch made 2 November 1747, P.R.O.N.I., T808/4249.

107 Historians of English customary tenures have also grappled with this problem. The strength of customary tenures against the new contractual regime of leases in early modern England is the subject of an old and unresolved controversy. The debate revolves around the ability of tenants to protect their customary tenures from landlord attempts to exact arbitrary fines for the renewal of those tenures. Compare Tawney, *Agrarian problem*, pp. 296–310, especially p. 296, note 2, with Kerridge, *Agrarian problems*, pp. 38–40. Tawney used the term 'security' to question the ability of customary holders to prevent themselves from being 'subjected, sooner or later, to economic, uncertain, market-determined rents, or whether they held with fixed payments, and by inheritance, whether customary land was ultimately theirs or their landlords.' Brenner, 'Bourgeois revolution,' p. 299, n. 36. For Kerridge, on the other hand, 'security of tenure can only mean the legal security of the tenant against the wrongful eviction or ouster, not against all the hazards of this fleshy world. One thing security of tenure cannot mean by any stretch of the imagination is a perpetual an inalienable right to possess a certain property.' Kerridge, *Agrarian*

problems, p. 54. The tendency in more recent historiography has been to give credence to Kerridge's position.

108 Quoted in J. Bigger, *The Ulster land war of 1770*, p. 19, and Kennedy, 'Tenant right,' p. 5.

109 Robert Maxwell to provost, 15 May 1671, T.C.D., MUN/P/24/144(11).

110 Marquis of Dufferin to Charles William Hamilton, 14 Feb. [1866], Hamwood papers, Hamwood House, Co. Meath, A/26/3.

111 L.M. Cullen, 'Problems in the interpretation and revision of eighteenth-century Irish economic history' in *Transactions of the Royal Historical Society*, 5th ser., xvii (1967), p. 9. See also Maguire, *Downshire estates*, pp. 144–5.

112 Crawford, 'Landlord-tenant relations,' pp. 7, 11, 12.

113 He also told her that he had invested £300 of borrowed money in the improvement of the land. James Rooney to 'her ladyship,' 4 July 1752, P.R.O.N.I., Anglesey papers, D619/21/B/107.

114 Victor Turner uses the term 'liminality' to describe the characteristics of a 'transitional period or space in which ordinary rules do not apply so that reorganisation and change can take place.' Bartolovich, 'Boundary disputes,' p. 207; Victor Turner, 'Betwixt and between: the liminal period in rites of passage' in *The forest of symbols* (London, 1962), pp. 93–111.

115 Mudimbe, *Invention of Africa*, pp. 4–5.

116 Gillespie, *Transformation*, p. 54.

117 In an allegorical narrative like Spenser's *Fairie Queene*, the plot unfolds as an investigation 'into the literal truth inherent in individual words, considered in the context of their whole history as words.' Maureen Quilligan, *The language of allegory: defining the genre* (Ithaca, 1979), pp. 33, 53.

118 Bartolovich, 'Boundary disputes,' p. 5.

119 Quilligan, *Language of allegory*, pp. 156–7.

120 Paul Ricoeur makes the distinction between the literal and the figurative referents of historical narrative in his *Time and narrative*, vol. 1, trans. Kathleen Blamey and David Pellauer (Chicago, 1984), pp. 57–82. See also Hayden White, 'The metaphysics of narrativity: time and symbol in Ricoeur's philosophy of history' in his *The content of the form: narrative discourse and historical representation* (Baltimore, 1987), pp. 172 and 233, n. 4. Ricoeur associates figurative history with the German term *Geschichtlichkeit*, translated both as 'historicity' and 'historicality' in the works of Hegel, Heidegger, and Marcuse. The important aspect of the term in the present context is the difference between literal, causal, or scientific history and figural, phenomenological 'historicity.' In Heidegger's reading of the term, 'the historical past has a continuing effect on the present, is, as Heidegger claims, 'stretched along into' the present and that effect cannot be treated as a causal effect. That is, historicity cannot be understood as a 'scientific' theory about the relation between events, and certainly not a causal theory, because the historicity thesis is that there *are* not 'separate' events 'in' history affecting each other. One of the events *is* what it is only in relation to its past.' Robert Pippin, 'Marcuse on Hegel and historicity' in *Philosophical forum*, xxv, no. 3 (Spring, 1985), pp. 183–4. See also Selya Benhabib, 'Introduction' to Herbert Marcuse, *Hegel's ontology and the theory of historicity*, trans. Seyla Benhabib (London, 1987); Michael Roth, *Knowing and history: appropriations of Hegel in twentieth-century France* (Ithaca, 1988), pp. 28–40; and David Carr, *Time, narrative, and history* (Bloomington, Indiana, 1986), pp. 102–116.

121 Thompson, 'Custom, law, and common right,' p. 160. The quotation within the quotation is from Locke.

122 Ibid., pp. 160–1.
123 On the subject of the inscrutability of labour in modern political economy, see Michel Foucault, *The order of things: an archaeology of the human sciences*, trans. anonymous (New York, 1970), pp. 189–95, 221–6, 235–6.
124 Thompson, 'Custom, Law, and common right,' p. 160.
125 Ibid., p. 137. In the nineteenth century, J.S. Mill and his followers argued for the reasonable basis of property rights in the concept of economic improvement against the absolute rights of Irish property owners. See E.D. Steele, 'J.S. Mill and the Irish question: the *Principles of political economy*, 1848–1865' in *The historical journal*, xiii, no. 2 (1970), pp. 220–25. See also *The constitutional rights of the landlords; the evils springing from the abuse of them in Ireland . . .* (Dublin, 1844) and Denis Caufield Heron, *Should the tenant of land possess the property in the improvements made by him?* (Dublin, 1852).
126 Petition of Solomon Martin of Culmore, County Londonderry, to Thomas Conolly, 23 March 1782, T.C.D., Conolly papers, MS 3974–84/750.
127 Edmund Kaine to Dacre Barrett, 10 Oct. 1712, P.R.O.N.I., Barrett-Lennard papers, film 170/2; idem, 8 Dec. and 2 Feb. 1713/14, ibid. A month later, he wrote as follows: 'I have now concluded with John Armstrong, and Mr. Willoughby says he is very well satisfied and that he bid the £17 out of spite to Armstrong.' Idem, 14 Mar. 1714, ibid. Hugh Willoughby offered to pay £12 a year for the land held from Barrett, which was formerly set at £8. Idem, 10 Oct. 1714, ibid.
128 The humble petition of Ross Farley, one of your lordship's tenants in Mullattee in the parish of Carlingford and County of Louth, 6 August 1785, P.R.O.N.I., Anglesey papers, D619/11/73.
129 Aijaz Ahmad, *In theory: classes, nations, literatures* (London, 1992), pp. 230–31.
130 See above, p. 9.

Part II

The Social Bases of Tenant Right

CHAPTER TWO

Historicity

THE UNCERTAIN TENURES OF THE EARLY PLANTATION

This chapter investigates the establishment and maintenance of commercial tenurial relationships in colonial Ulster, the infrastructure of the estate system, the relations which developed between the different strata of estate society, and the ramifications of the tenurial dynamics of this multi-layered society for the meaning and operation of the custom of tenant right. The evidence presented highlights various obstacles in the way of the visual and economic model of the plantation: tenurial uncertainty, rapid tenant mobility, bickering between rival head tenants, and confusing multilevel tenurial relationships. To the extent that these difficulties were overcome, the goals of the plantation were manifested in visible and narratable characteristics.

The first decades of the seventeenth century were characterized by massive uncertainty over the tenure of land in Ulster. The first difficulty faced by the plantation project was the lack of knowledge of the newly colonized territory and the vagaries of the early surveys. Planter use of the Irish 'ballyboe,' a unit of land whose size and boundary was determined by the number of cattle which it could support, caused much uncertainty.[1] Planters crudely translated the ballyboe into sixty Irish plantation acres of profitable land, but poorer ballyboes (in mountain areas, for example) could be many times the size of more fertile ones. These unexpectedly huge ballyboes presented undertakers with their greatest difficulties, and the natives with their greatest opportunities.[2] In the turbulent decades which followed, the vagaries of an unfamiliar landscape could undermine tenurial claims. For example, Robert Maxwell, the bishop of Kilmore, who held and became the rector of two glebes in a parish on the Trinity College lands in Armagh, was ousted in 1641. The legal basis for the establishment of these glebes appears to have been ruined at some point because of a dispute revolving around a plantation clause dealing with subsequently discovered inaccuracies in the survey and with whether certain townlands could be annexed as glebes.[3]

A more serious cause of uncertainty was the activity of the crown. The plantation land grants had forfeiture clauses for noncompliance with the orders and conditions of the plantation. In the five years after 1617 James repeatedly used these clauses to threaten the tenures of the undertakers because of their failure to adequately plant the lands with new British tenants. But by the end of the 1620s the crown had completely revised its policy, officially allowing the native Irish to have legal tenures and removing forfeiture clauses from new patents.[4] This was an admission of political and economic failure, a tacit recognition that the economically most beneficial arrangement was to allow the native Irish to produce a surplus and to exploit that arrangement to the fullest by raising fines. Compromise notwithstanding, the threat of forfeiture of titles and the accompanying noise-making by the crown after each successive survey was nevertheless a real danger, with the result that British tenants were increasingly reluctant to lease land in the 1620s.[5] Furthermore, the uncertainty over newly created estates was not exclusively a problem of the lesser and impoverished undertakers, nor for grantees of the wilder interior of Ulster. In Antrim and Down, areas outside plantation territory, even landowners with powerful political connections were affected. Chichester, Hamilton, and Montgomery, the three predominant new landowners in east Ulster, all endured serious legal claims against their property in Ulster.[6] According to Roebuck, in addition to Chichester's difficulties with rival claims to his property,

> there was also the threat, which periodically intensified, that political developments would result in the investigation of the manner in which Chichester had benefitted from Hamilton's grants, and be followed by reconfiscation of the property. The family was obliged to part with some of its interests, but in this case also longstanding uncertainty was ultimately more detrimental than actual loss of property.[7]

One ramification of this uncertainty was the rapid mobility of tenants and the development of a market for abandoned leases. There is abundant evidence of a vigorous market for leases and properties early in the century. Hunter found considerable evidence from the Fishe estate in County Armagh of the sale of leaseholds and tenant mobility. For example, it was noted in 1622 that 'many of the first leases had been passed over from one party to another, with covenants of planting not performed.'[8] Although some landlords were able to use the active market to attract promising tenants to their estates, especially in the 1630s,[9] generally landlords tried to restrict the market by banning the alienation of leases without consent, hoping thereby to pin their tenants to their leased lands.[10] Many new landlords soon recognized that their attempts to enforce covenants could not prevent the tenants leaving the land waste, and might even encourage them to do so.[11] Crawford correctly observes that many a seventeenth-century tenant was 'liable to leave an estate in search of a better bargain, and landlords were ready to permit him to sell to a newcomer rather than deny him, only to find that he had slipped away, leaving the land waste.'[12] Arthur Brownlow's tenants around Lurgan had established the right to alienate leases by 1660, so that he had to penalize or ban alienation in his first leases. After 1671 Brownlow and many others adopted the widespread tactic of securing 'the preemption or first right of refusal to purchase the lease himself.'[13]

Another ramification of the general uncertainty was a state of confusion over the respective rights of undertenants and head tenants. The uncertain legal footing of crown titles, coupled with the granting of subleases of questionable validity, and compounded over the years by dubious exchanges and inheritances, caused vexing uncertainty and complexity for all involved. One example of this may be found in the records of the Trinity College property in Donegal.[14] Hunter recounts another complicated dispute on the college's Armagh lands in the 1630s between two tenants, one a former fellow of the college and another the second husband of a widow who held one of the first leases granted on the property. Even though the dispute concerned events going back at most two decades, the argument was infused with rhetoric about the 'right and equity of the ancient tenant' over the pretensions of 'mere strangers.'[15] The complications of multi-layered tenancies were even worse if, as was often the case on the frontier of the plantation, the undertenants were native Irish still holding land in an older evolved settlement pattern. In 1624, for example, the governor of Monaghan, noting 'the waste which characterized the whole country,' complained that the McMahons, the predominant Irish clan in the area, were unwilling or unable to pay rent.[16] One troublemaker named John Price cast doubt on the validity of a sixty-year lease of lands made to one Petrie in 1623. Price had convinced twenty-five occupying tenants, most of them with the surname McMahon, to refuse to attorn, leaving Petrie helpless to recover arrears of rent from them. The result was that 'divers of the English tenants by reason of some threats and speeches of the said Mr. Price . . . were put in fear to be distrained for the said arrears [and] were departed from part of their lands and had left the same waste. . . . '[17]

The uncertainties of the early plantation notwithstanding, many historians emphasize the definite progress of colonial settlement up to 1640, particularly in east Ulster. The high mobility of tenants operated as a kind of centripetal force, strengthening core areas of settlement, and weakening more peripheral areas. The flow of immigrants slowed dramatically in the 1620s, but the internal mobility of the recent immigrants continued, resulting in further concentration and segregation of settlement. A few successful areas saw an internally generated demographic increase, as the younger sons of immigrant tenants moved away to find land.[18] But it was still just as likely that the sons of immigrants would return to Scotland and England.[19] The 1630s, however, were marked by an economic buoyancy and further rationalization of the

British settlement pattern. Some landlords were apparently able to renew leases at an increased rent.[20] At Trinity College, for example, there was a notable improvement in expectations concerning the fate of their Armagh lands. In 1622 the provost felt that 'the rent hereafter may be improved; this is uncertain, it being as like that it will be disimproved.'[21] But in 1629 an undertenant named Robert Maxwell offered to pay an increased rent for a direct lease from the college. In 1636 advances of rent of between 5s. and £5 per quarterland were paid by seven college tenants.[22] After the general renewal of leases in 1638 the rent received by the college had doubled over the 1614 total. The rent appears to have been well-paid in the late 1630s and the college was for the first time bold enough to enter specific building covenants into the new leases, and tried to displace Irish tenants with more newly arrived British. Balfour in Fermanagh was also able to take advantage of the opportunity to relet lands in the buoyant 1630s to displace natives to uplands and set lowlands to planters.[23]

Bolstered by good harvests, by the centripetal force of tenant resettlement into core areas, and by the demographic regeneration of the colonists themselves, the theory and the reality of the plantation scheme began to converge in some areas during the 1630s. But much of the territory still resembled the pattern established in the southern provinces, where the general result was that feudal and Irish forms of landholding were intermixed. According to Clarke, 'it was neither unusual for land to be held in common 'without partition' in the Irish manner, nor uncommon for it to be held according to the most elabourate stipulations of feudal overlordship.' Clarke identifies 'a kind of pastiche feudalism through surrender and regrant arrangements designed to replace irregular Irish exactions by fixed charges and to introduce formal manorial structures, though the effect was perhaps more often to put an English veneer on Irish arrangements than to replace them.'[24] This general pattern was particularly true of the crucial territories granted to the London companies, the former heart of the O'Neill earldom. Colonial settlement in south Ulster was also seriously compromised by asset-stripping, subletting, and mortgaging by financially strapped undertakers and overburdened servitors.[25] In Armagh and Cavan the holders of twenty-one-year or three-life leases were mostly natives or relatives of the grantees. It was most common among absentees there to arrange with one of their more substantial tenants for the supervision of their estates. Many freeholds on these estates which were granted to relatives of the grantee were sublet to the Irish and managed by Irish agents.[26]

If the economic buoyancy of the 1630s brought a measure of stability, the uncertainties that marked the plantation from its beginning resurfaced during the economic and political collapse of the 1640s and the 1650s. Collapsing

prices, shrinking estate incomes, and frequent farmer bankruptcies were widespread throughout the British Isles in these years. In Ulster these troubles
were compounded by political strife and nine years of war.[27] The problem of
landlord insecurity of tenure and tenant skittishness which plagued the early
plantation turned from bad to worse.[28] Over the next decade the land system
established by the plantation ceased to exist as a practical reality. When the
blood dried and the dust settled in the 1650s, a crippled land system had to be
rehabilitated. The awards of lands to Cromwellian soldiers who were unwilling
to settle on their properties produced a vigorous trade in land debentures in
the 1650s. George Blacker lamented in 1656: 'If I had not adventured my
money, for that I could have gained much more and bought soldiers' lands,
but the time is past.'[29] One result of this debenture trading was concentration
in land ownership.[30] The new purchasers, and those who managed to hold
on to or renew their titles, had a difficult time in the 1650s and 1660s. The
evidence available is sketchy, but there are some examples of the types of
problems faced by Ulster grantees.

A royal letter of 1661 to the provost and fellows of Trinity College inter-
cedes for two tenants, Sir John and Thomas Temple, who 'being [enforced]
to renew the said lands during the late troubles from persons taking advantage
thereof, do endeavour to make void their interest and take new leases from
you, the provost and fellows of said college, notwithstanding they and their
father William Temple have been tenants of them for almost these fifty years
last past.'[31] William Waring, who purchased lands in north-west County
Down from a Cromwellian soldier in 1656, appears to have had problems
securing his right of ownership almost immediately. Confronted by the renewal
claims of the Catholic Magennis family, who held the land in question under
a grant from James I but forfeited it due to their implication in the 1641
rebellion, Waring petitioned a brigadier to put him in possession in 1659. The
questions seem to have been whether Waring returned to the land soon
enough after hostilities to satisfy the requirements of a royal proclamation to
return and occupy land, and whether he took up arms against the king.[32] He
succeeded in 1668 in securing the land which would eventually become the
village of Waringstown and there is some evidence of his efforts to rent lands
in the 1670s.[33] But during the upheaval of 1688 to 1690 Waring, like many
others, left his estate and went to the Isle of Man as a refugee. Arthur
Brownlow commiserated with him on 12 April 1689: 'I am sorry you left this
kingdom. Yourself, your tenants, and some of your neighbours have suffered
by it. I believe you might have stayed as well as any man, for I know none of
your station in Ulster that behaved themselves more innocently and inoffen-
sively to all.'[34] The Magennises were briefly reinstated into their lands by
James II, but Waring was able to return after the victory of William's forces.[35]

Another dispute, involving lands near Raphoe, Co. Donegal, reveals itself in correspondence among two men named Leslie, one of whom was the bishop of Raphoe, a Scottish absentee owner named Francis Guthrie, and one Lennox, a prominent tenant who was also of Scottish origin. Guthrie had abandoned his Irish property after the disastrous 1640s, and Lennox also threatened to return to Scotland leaving behind heavy arrears of rent. But he did not attempt to – or was unable to – sell his leases until the 1660s. Guthrie appears to have held leases from the bishop. A letter of 1652 explains that

> landlords have a third part allowed unto them out of their estate; the lessees have a third part of whatsoever the land can be valued at more than the rent payable to the chief landlord. Francis Guthrie would have got his third had he appeared on the estate to show that he had not acted anything contrary to the state or commonwealth of England.[36]

In 1656 the bishop urged Guthrie to visit the estate and stop tenants from abandoning their land without paying. He drew special attention to one major tenant, 'Mr. Lennox, who I hear is now to go to Scotland to live there. His arrears of rent I believe is very much, and which I believe will not be got until you come.'[37] Other correspondents implored Guthrie over the next six years to take a hand in the management of his deteriorating house and estate, one of them warning that the storehouse and land were in a ruinous condition. Another correspondent declared that his land was 'decaying yearly and wasting,'[38] and a third claimed that 'some tenants have a greater arrear on them than they are able to pay.'[39] Finally, Pat Leslie informed 'Laird Guthrie' in 1663 that he had heard that Guthrie was selling his leases and, referring to the neglected estate and his own devotion to the property, he offered to pay whatever anyone else would give for it.[40]

The issue of improvements, a perennial bone of contention surrounding tenant right, first appeared in the context of this recovery from the mid-seventeenth-century crisis. What little building and investment occurred in the early decades, by its very scarcity, brought forth much discussion of its meaning in terms of tenure. Robert Maxwell, who held Trinity College lands in County Armagh leased to Francis Ruish in the 1620s, pointed out to Ruish's widow in 1629 that he was the only one of her chief tenants who had erected buildings. This fact he linked directly to his right to renew his present lease:

> Before the renewing of the lease or leases be made of the aforesaid lordship, [the supplicant requests that] there may be a caveat entered that the said two town[lands] and a half upon which your petitioner hath built and planted may not be passed to any other than your supplicant, he giving such reasonable augmentations of rent . . . as you shall think fit, . . . desiring only that he may be immediate tenant himself . . . and that in

respect of the great cost and changes that he hath bestowed, his rent for the next settings may not be raised or enhanced, but made proportionable to what you think fit.[41]

The destruction and depreciation of the 1640s heightened concern over the question of who deserved credit for buildings still standing in later decades. Martha O'Neille, who let half a townland to Colonel Robert Stewart for five years, observed in 1653 that the rent 'clears all, in consideration and relation of what building he made upon the said half town [land] . . . , which buildings the said Col. Robert Stewart is to leave stiff stance [sic] and tenantable at the expiration of the said five years.'[42] An anonymous writer who offered to rent a townland on the Castle Stewart estate in 1655 endeavoured, before he took the land, to clarify his rights to the buildings that might still have been standing on it, 'lest those who may hereafter claim interest in it, if it should be let without their knowledge, have buildings erected on that town[land].'[43] In 1661 petitioners in Derry claimed that their heavy pre-1641 investments had been destroyed by the rebellious Irish and all their effects taken. They claimed that they could not continue to hold their leases if the country was to be settled, and they asked for new leases at lower rents. They were allegedly the first to have been harmed by the rebellion and had suffered most.[44]

While the rebellion, the civil war, and the ensuing economic, political, and tenurial turmoil brought the plantation to a crashing halt, the decades between 1650 and 1690 amounted to a new colonial departure, with a dramatic influx of Scottish Presbyterians in the 1650s, followed and superseded by an influx of English colonists.[45] The signs of improvement were clearly visible. William King's report on the state of the Protestants in 1691 trumpeted that 'lands were everywhere improved, and rents advanced to near double what they had been a few years before. The kingdom abounded with money, trade flourished, even to the envy of our neighbours. . . .'[46] For the social historian, the now classic citation is Crawford's table compiling the data contained in the leasebook of the Brownlow estate.[47] The evidence from this prosperous estate shows decreasing farm size, increasing rent per acre, and increasing entry fines in the period 1650–1709, with the exception of the years of the Williamite war.[48] A rent-roll of Fermanagh lands held by Trinity College shows how one estate attempted to phase out beneficial rents.[49] Three men reporting to the provost and fellows of Trinity College in 1707

examined upon oath some of the old Protestant inhabitants, men of good repute, and it appeared to us that the highest value that ever was paid for said lands before the late troubles by the [ground] tenants was £171 per annum and £11 15s. 6d. receiver's salary and duties, and that from the year 1693 to the year 1699 the said lands paid but £81 together with receiver's fees and duties, and that at present and since the lands pay £151 and £10.17 receiver's salary and duties.[50]

The three men then certified that the lands were worth £200. The evidence of hearth-money returns for Ulster counties in the period 1672–85, displayed in Table 1 in order of the scale of change, also show substantial if uneven improvement. The poor ranking of Antrim and Down is readily explained by their already advanced position in 1672. The escheated counties of Tyrone, Cavan, and Donegal stand out as areas where the aims of the plantation may have finally begun to manifest themselves, whereas Londonderry (in the hands of the twelve London companies), Monaghan (much of which was still in the hands of native middlemen), and Fermanagh lagged behind.

Table 1
Hearth money returns (£), 1672–85

County	1672	1682	1683	1684	1685	% increase
Tyrone	563	868	879	879	907	61
Cavan	460	609	643	654	634	38
Donegal	605	880	913	914	941	36
Armagh	517	567	574	621	671	30
Londonderry	705	880	887	897	900	28
Fermanagh	350	494	478	489	445	27
Monaghan	355	379	402	424	474	25
Down	1105	1365	1408	1458	1481	25
Antrim	1353	1620	1662	1712	1737	22
Ulster	6013	7612	7846	8058	8190	36

Source: 'A view of the hearth money in the several provinces and counties of Ireland as let to farm in the following years' in *A natural history of Ireland*, T.C.D., MS 883/1.

These developments continued into the next century. Although the agricultural economy remained unstable, with frequent harvest crises and heavy out-migration plaguing the young Ulster estates, a sufficiently continuous and peaceful period of occupation, combined with some price inflation, allowed many Ulster landlords to increase their rentals and for the first time to establish management structures and to formulate consistent tenure policies.[51] The early decades of the eighteenth century were marked by further efforts to increase rent, especially at the expiration of leases and after the inheritance of estates. Fines and increases of rent were imposed on those who renewed leases that commenced after 1689 and expired in the 1720s on many estates throughout Ulster. On the Castletown estate in County Fermanagh in the

1720s the landlord renewed expired leases to the highest bidders and took fines for the renewal of leases to the sitting tenant.[52] In 1718 Thomas Conolly renewed six- and seven-year leases commencing in 1712. Fines ranging from double to five times the yearly rent were taken.[53] On his Ballyshannon estate in 1726, William Conolly raised rents from the levels set in 1718.[54] Many letters of the early eighteenth century in the Downshire papers refer to the old rent and an 'improved' rent which was double or triple the old rent.[55] The owner of the Castleward estate criticized his agent in the 1720s for not pushing for an inflated rent and for fining down rents.[56]

The success of these decades should remain open to qualification. Scottish Presbyterian immigration tapered off significantly, with only one new congregation founded in the last quarter of the century, though existing congregations must have continued to grow. New immigrant settlement was concentrated largely in Belfast and the Lagan valley.[57] The financial buoyancy of some estates notwithstanding, Ulster rural society continued to experience distress and hardship. Some tenants were hurting on the Waring estate in County Down in the late 1660s,[58] but by the early 1670s the difficulties had become more widespread. William Gore, a head tenant of Trinity College, in an apology for remitting the rent so late, wrote in 1672 that 'the poverty of the tenants in these hard times, being seconded by the necessities of their landlord, who is paying his grandfather's and father's debts, is the cause of it. . . . I abated every tenant I had in Donegal a fifth part of their rent for three years during the last Dutch war.'[59] The harvest of 1674 appears to have been a disaster. 'The poor tenants of this country have not bread to eat,' observed William Waring. 'There is such a great scarcity of victuals that many give up their farms, and those that hold them are not able to pay the rent and of yours there is a part of two townlands now waste and a great part of the tenants expect abatement.'[60] The same situation, according to William Rawdon, obtained around Lisburn: 'Really, except in 1641, there has not been so sudden and general a destruction heard of in this country: whole stocks of cattle dead, very little ploughing for want of horses and seed, and families starving for want of bread.'[61] Again in the following decade many landlords were facing an impoverished and resistant tenantry, with the years 1684 and 1689 being particularly bad.[62] Planters were also faced with continued political uncertainty and the religious disaffection of both Presbyterian immigrants and the native Irish. The earl of Rossmore, the bishop of Derry, and Trinity College each made provisions in the leases of their respective lands for the eventuality of rebellion.[63] A correspondent to the Irish Society felt that the most successfully planted estates were the most vulnerable: 'Improvements would [be] more especially exposed to the covetous eye of officers. There often happens rebellions in this country, by which means, though the rent may be abated if the company pleases, yet the term of years, for which a great fine was paid, is thereby lessened, to the considerable loss of the lessees.'[64] In 1687 Rossmore ordered the distraint of all unpaid rent on his Monaghan estate in order to raise money for the purchase of land in Essex.[65] He abandoned his Rathmore estate in 1687, left the big house in the hands of a head tenant/agent, and bid him farewell with these words: 'God preserve you and keep you from going to law.'[66]

These concerns turned out to be well-founded. The Williamite wars destroyed much of Cavan, Monaghan, Fermanagh, and Derry, although east Ulster was not severely damaged.[67] A report on the state of the diocese of Derry mentions that in the parish of Maghera 'the parishioners are very disaffected, there not being above forty or fifty comfortable persons in the union.'[68] The agent to Captain William Jackson, a lessee of the Clothworkers' lands, pleaded for an extension of his lease in 1691, which had twenty-nine years left to run, because of 'sufferings during the late wars in which . . . most of the tenants lost their lives.'[69] The Goldsmiths' estate had also been completely ravaged by the war.[70] Gabriel Whistler, head tenant of the Salters' proportion, claimed that the Irish 'burnt much of the countryside during the wars.'[71] The destruction also extended into south Ulster. In 1688 Dacre Barrett's agent was advised to 'take what the tenants will give if they but stay on the land till times mend . . ., for all the north is [perfectly?] in arms.'[72] Clones was garrisoned under the command of a Colonel Singons in 1690. The tenants in the surrounding countryside had for the most part abandoned the estate, and 'what poor people live in town are ready to run away, for they can keep neither horse nor cow but what is stolen from them.' He went on to warn that the loss of horses and hay would prevent next year's ploughing.[73] The disruptive effects of the war and the disturbing presence of militia did not subside in many areas until after the turn of the century,[74] with a number of estates producing evidence of tenant difficulties keeping up with increased rents.[75]

It is difficult to condense the experience of seventeenth-century colonial Ulster into a summary assessment. Historians striving for a balanced and objective account grapple with the tension between socio-scientific tropes of demographic and economic expansion and intensification and the more linguistic tropes emphasizing consciousness and *mentalités*.[76] Neither of these strategies are satisfactory in themselves, nor does the tension between them resolve itself in even the most skilfully wrought narratives.[77] The difficulty is heightened by the awareness of political readings of the narrative. As Foster recognizes, the emphasis on inexorable social forces feeds into unionist arguments about Ulster's inherently different nature while the emphasis on conflict, policy, and *mentalité* jibes with nationalist grievances.[78] If the bias of the present narrative is toward the latter, it is because these seem to best explain the context in which the custom of tenant right developed. The emphasis on progress, continuity, and inexorability does not do justice to the struggle faced by so many, natives and planters, to take their place in the plantation estate sytem. Consider, for example, the 1691 testimony of Gabriel Whistler, whose family had been head tenants of the Salters' proportion for most of the century. Defending his unsuccessful efforts as a planter and pleading for a rent reduction, he complained about the failed early plantation and the effects of war and English politics,[79] and recollected mournfully that in 1656 'there was not so much as a single [Protestant] on your lands, nor upon any other of the companies' lands that I ever heard of,'[80] and claimed that he went to England to find tenants and that 'he had laid out considerable sums of money to rebuild tenants' houses.' The arrival of James II on the English throne 'put the Protestants in fear, so that trade and rents began to cease, and the people that had anything considerable began to remove out of that kingdom, and so it continued to the happy revolution.'[81] For Gabriel Whistler, William Waring, and many others, the artifice of the plantation was never naturalized; it never became 'second nature' to the members of Ulster society and remained vulnerable and unfinished.

THE WEAKNESS OF ESTATE INFRASTRUCTURE

The new property system required that a legal and managerial structure be set in place, manned by a colonial personnel. The struggle to meet these requirements revealed the regional weaknesses of the plantation. The primary vulnerability was the weakness of the Irish lease, the cornerstone of the plantation system. Evidence from all over the island shows that it was almost impossible to enforce husbandry or alienation covenants in leases in Ireland. Even though alienation was usually prohibited without consent, sales routinely occurred. In Cork *post hoc* validation of the sale of leases that contained clauses specifically prohibiting any such alienation was routine. Indeed, attempts in the 1740s to put penalties into leases for the first time failed since no tenants could be found to take them. The best that could be accomplished was to adjudicate between competing buyers of a lease.[82] In Tipperary the degree of enforcement of covenants banning alienation varied greatly, and in one case that ability appears to have weakened as the century drew to a close, only to be rehabilitated after 1815. 'Most landlords,' Power reports, 'did not intervene in the subletting activities of their head tenants. This partly reflected the entrenched position established by the latter over a wide area of the county after 1690, and it partly demonstrates the lack of resolution by landowners to confront a major social group.'[83] Ferguson and Vance, in a well-informed survey published in 1851, considered that 'covenants in leases are for the most part a dead letter, that a most shameless disregard of covenants prevails throughout the lower class of tenantry. . . .' Juries would not find against tenants, they argued, and the legal difficulties of breaking a lease in Ireland were well nigh insurmountable.[84] Landlords were powerless to enforce covenants in the lease specifying improvements. Enforcement of improvement through bonds of performance with fines for noncompliance 'was a cumbersome method, and the legal problems involved in suing a tenant were a deterrent, of which tenants themselves were well aware.' The problem was that juries were made up of tenants.[85]

Likewise, contractual prohibition of subletting, particularly to Catholics, was also a dead letter. In Cork, 'the only effective sanction against the subletting was non-renewal of the lease.'[86] Stephen Silthorp of Drogheda objected strenuously in 1756 to such clauses in his lease, complaining that

> no reputable tenant fit to be entrusted with the payment of £320 a year . . . can by any means comply with [them], particularly the clause for the augmentation of any rent to be paid by the lessee if he should sell, alien, assign, or demise to any person or persons so granted and for the reasons following. First, that such a penal clause, if in equity binding, would take away the benefit of the tenant's lease by depriving him from letting his land to any person, except first approved by the lessor, for as our farms in this country are generally parcelled out in small holdings and for a short term of years, . . . no tenant qualified to pay such a rent could submit to such a clause, for how can a landlord who lives in England judge whether the tenant I would chose to let ten or twenty acres be a proper tenant or not.[87]

One portentous strategy was to punish sublettors by defending their undertenants. Thomas Noble of the Barrett-Lennard estate wrote of one tenant: 'I shall attack Cotman, [who is] holding for the advanced rent, for the nonperformance of covenants in regard to improvements, and defend the undertenants as far as I well can against him according to your directions . . . , but if he has bound the undertenants by their leases in the same manner as he is bound himself in that case, I fear the additional rent will fall upon them. . . .' Noble hoped to force them to make the improvements and also to avoid entering into any lawsuits with the attendant expense and trouble, but he was resigned to the fact that it might be necessary to make an example of someone.[88] The legal attack on Cotman had to be directed at his failure to abide by covenants for improvement and against alienation, but this plan bore a great deal of risk, for Noble felt that 'if we proceed at law for the breach of covenant, it must be tried by a jury, who perhaps may be for the most part tenants themselves, and if so, will most probably favour the tenant.'[89] The only option available to the estate managers in Clones appeared to be to wait for all leases to expire before dismantling the lease structure erected by the middlemen.[90] The failure of the enforcement of lease covenants was eventually mitigated by the rapid proliferation of non-agricultural linen production on farms. During the heyday of the weaving and spinning farmhouse, estate managers stopped concerning themselves with the typical covenants.[91]

The weakness of the lease was related to the problem of inadequate personnel. Landlords were dependent on agents who were untrustworthy, incompetent, self-aggrandizing, or just uncontrollable. They were also often saddled with an agent who was weak and vulnerable to the disputatiousness of outsiders, or, equally undesirably, one who held too much local power.[92] The effects of this dependence were especially strong in times of crisis. Although historians generally emphasize how quickly Ulster estates recovered after 1689, it is nevertheless remarkable how fragile the structures of some estates revealed themselves to be. Dacre Barrett seems to have completely lost control of his estate in the 1690s to an agent who 'pretends to have a power from Mr. Barrett for the management of this concern and persuades the people to observe no other agent but him, so that if you do not come hither yourself, there is no likelihood of any of the old tenants returning to their former habitations [for the] reason [that] there is no one here that has power to give them encouragement.'[93] In Sligo the O'Haras could not trust a member of their own family to act in their interest. Keane O'Hara was allegedly attracting tenants to another landlord's property and leaving the O'Hara property untenanted in 1692.[94] A head tenant of Trinity College property in Donegal was apparently in league with the appointed seneschal and abused the undertenants, rack-renting at a great profit.[95] The seneschal was also accused of concealing land on the estate in order to grant it to a neighbouring undertaker. A lawsuit between two rivals for the office of seneschal over who possessed the right to hold court followed. This situation could not have done much to bolster the plantation or the rule of colonial law in the area.[96] On the Castleward estate near Bangor, Co. Down, the agent was fining down rents instead of pushing the tenants to pay more as instructed, and was eventually served with an ejectment from his own holding in 1734.[97] Tenants on the Anglesey estate were refusing to pay rent to a new agent, preferring to pay to another man more to their liking.[98] 'Lord Boyn' was robbed of the profits of his estate by an overmighty agent in the 1720s. Charles Ward explained:

> My Lord Boyn was disobliged by his agents in the County of Donegal and [was] very resolved to remove them, for they had planted his estate for the most part with their own friends and dependants, who had very beneficial bargains under his lordship. When their leases were expired, their credit in

conjunction with the said agents was so great that no one durst [sic] or at least would bid for the lands, so that my lord could not raise his rents in any way proportional to the value.[99]

The same problem occurred on the Downshire estate, where there were no knowledgeable or capable candidates for the job of estate agent who were not already tenants. Henry Hatch, the head agent resident in Dublin, complained to the landlord: 'No agent ought to be tenant to any of his employer's lands, for who is to set it to them but themselves? And who will venture to take lands over the agent's head? So, of course, he will have it at what rate he pleases.'[100] On both the Downshire estate and the Anglesey estate members of the Savage family disrupted the management of the estate by usurping agent power and threatening undertenants.[101]

In the context of weak legal power and ineffective management, many landlords could only minimally adhere to the orders and conditions of the plantation. The problem was of course that the native Irish, though largely excluded from this undermanned infrastructure, might still dominate the landscape. Because of the religious discrimination embodied in leasing policies, areas with a large Catholic population necessarily had more middlemen, often absentees, who then sublet to Catholics. Presbyterian areas had less lopsided landholding patterns.[102] The result was that a stable lease structure on the English model was established only in areas in Antrim, Down, and parts of Armagh where the Irish were from the beginning of the plantation a less dominant presence on the land. Where an Irish settlement pattern, if not also Irish occupants, remained entrenched, the lease structure was much more lopsided and practically impossible to control. In general, the larger the native population, the more likely was the establishment of the pattern of large middlemen subletting to Catholic farmers. Over much of Munster and south Leinster, 'large head tenants became entrenched and established a vested interest as well as social prominence in rural society. . . . Attempts by the landlord or the agent to remove such interests were rare, difficult, and where eventually successful, costly.'[103] Acts of 1696 and 1701 to promote English Protestant settlement combined with the penal statutes against Catholics holding long leases conspired to create a situation in which a small number of Protestant head tenants bought up large tracts of land on long leases, subletting them to Catholics.[104]

Evidence from Trinity College clearly shows the problem of overpowering middlemen. James Hamilton, a major County Down proprietor, was present in London in 1610 and helped the college secure its grant of lands in Fermanagh, Armagh, and Donegal. Having no background in English or Scottish landed society, the college was ill-equipped to attract tenants to fulfil the duties of the plantation, so that it was forced to take on major head tenants, servitors, and undertakers from elsewhere in the province. But according to Hunter, 'apart from an offer from James Hamilton proposals to it were not numerous.'[105] Hamilton described his strategy to the provost in a letter of 1610. This is an excellent characterization of the difficulties which would face plantation landlords well into the next century:

> Every undertaker is seeking tenants all that he can because they would have help to perform their conditions and agreements, every of them, even he that is best moneyed. . . . But now we are wooing of people to come thither [to remote lands] who, if they have any competent being here, are loath to remove from hence, and if they be beggars and lean people without money, they are not fit for us. . . . I could let some of your lands to some great men here and to some captains there, but I had rather let it to such honest men of meaner rank, who if they do not pay me their rent shall, whether they will or not, permit me to fetch away their distress, than to deal with such Monsieurs who, being our tenants, we must petition on to and entreat for our rent.[106]

There was disagreement within Trinity College over how to deal with Hamilton. Temple defended a fee-farm grant to Hamilton over the objections of others who feared that it would sacrifice the possible increase in value of the property in the future. He was opposed to giving out the land on short leases, asserting that 'these Ulster lands [having] now a long time rested barbarous, rude, unhusbanded, undistinguished by enclosures, fences, and bounds, unfurnished of houses for habitation or defence, naked of all sorts of buildings for necessary use, no man of wisdom will for a short time take a lease of any proportion thereof.' A lessee holding for a short period would 'wear out the whole virtue and heart thereof, spoil the woods, and build no more than of necessity he must.'[107] In the end Hamilton did not get a fee farm but received a twenty-one-year lease in 1614.[108] The argument over the terms which he received, and the handwringing over what type of British tenant he was best advised to woo, appear to have been a wasted effort, for he sold part of the Slutmulrony lease almost immediately, and the following year he sold the rest to James Carroll of Finglas.[109] Hunter speculates that he let large tracts to Irish and to other servitors. Eight years after the grant to Hamilton, 'the essential lines of a fairly permanent leasing arrangement had been drawn – a system involving a small number of middlemen.'[110] The lands were later said to be in the hands of the 'O'Quines' and 'Connylies' of Mulroney, the 'principle woodkerne of Ulster.'[111]

At the other end of the century, Joseph Hamilton, lessee of the Trinity College lands in Donegal, had similar problems finding suitable tenants. In a detailed letter of 1697, he described his reasons for entrusting the lands to one John Payne, and explained how he was abused by Payne:

> When I let the place, I preferred John Payne, being of English descent, to
> my countrymen, believing he would improve better, and settled him in
> that house and got him as many fruit trees, gratis, as planted the orchard,
> and gave him a lease of the half-quarter for fifteen years, engaging him by
> words to bring in Protestant tenants. But to the contrary, he settled papists
> and in a few years gave up his lease, all to a sixth part, which I was forced
> to accept. . . . And within a very little time after, the house which I built and
> put him in was burnt to ashes by flax, as he said, but whether designedly or
> otherwise I cannot be positive. All this I freely forgave, and on this new
> settlement, I give him the fourth part of the land again, the first year for
> half-rent, three years more for less than two parts the old rent, and for the
> remainder of the seven years a little more than two-thirds. The old rent
> was £26 p.a. Neither he nor any other of the tenants would enter into
> writing with me, but still as opportunity offered, threw the land in my
> hands. At All Saints last was a year, Joseph Payne, unknown to me, made
> over his whole right in Glassbole to Irish fellows and took a farm elsewhere,
> designing to make what advantage he could for the seven years and then
> throw it up to Irish.[112]

Hamilton finally persuaded Payne to give it up to him and set it to Protestants.
They paid the same amount as Payne, but they would do no more than 'try
the place one year and give me their answer' as to whether they would hold
it at the increased rent for seven years. He was not optimistic about them:
'There is not one tenant I have as yet taken [with] a lease from me, but are on
the watch.'[113]

Evidence from the estates of the London companies suggests that the 'chief
tenants' and middlemen were also granted lands at huge fines and steep rents.
In order to pay these rents, many resorted in turn to exacting rack-rents from
others. Far from granting security of tenure and peaceful possession to
undertenants, English or native, those middlemen increased rents, evicted,
and confiscated capital on very short notice. Less demanding middlemen
were soon replaced by the companies because of their lack of zeal in rent
collection.[114] The London companies had the most difficulty attracting men
of prominence to their estates. They were granted the 'wildest' part of central
Ulster and correctly perceived the plantation to be a poor investment. The
shortage of men to occupy key positions in the new society was acute. One
observer complained that on the London companies' estates 'poor, mean, and
unfit persons are summoned to attend at every assize and sessions. Where
such of them do appear, [they] are incapable of doing service as aforesaid.'[115]
According to this observer, the lessees of the London companies who offered
fines for conversion to freeholds also wanted to fine down their rents because,
aside from four or five gentlemen, there were no lessees of any of the twelve
companies to occupy the various offices of justice of the peace, commissioner

of array, captains of militia troops and companies, commissions of assessments, knights of the shire 'and other offices and employments of his Majesty's service and the good of the country.' Lower rents at more secure tenures were necessary to attract suitable personnel. Otherwise the estate would continue to stagnate: 'The said lands never since the City's plantation here, being above seventy years, have been well-inhabited nor improved . . . [the] English, who are the best improvers, will not come into a another kingdom for a lease. Nor have said lands been improved . . . , and at last it is left untenanted. That the undertenants will not be bound to any of those improvements on any lease whereupon, on a more certain holding they would be willing to do so. . . .' This observer described the intractable problems facing the planters from the very beginning. But the gist of this commentary is that even when landlords had the opportunity to rectify these problems upon the expiration of leases, they failed to alter the circumstances:

> It happens in a few years' time that one of the twelve companies' proportions is to be set to farm, and one striving to undermine and outbid another, is sometimes an occasion of the old lessee's having it taken from him, and always [this] is the continued occasion of animosity and differences amongst the gentlemen of the country. . . . Nor can making, in each proportion a few more freeholds answer all, perhaps any of the aforesaid particulars: for that those new freeholds may in short time come into the hands of a few persons, as all the former freeholds already are, for, as the counsel says the law cannot restrain any person from selling his freehold.[116]

The shortage of freeholders induced an almost frantic effort on the part of early eighteenth-century estate managers to attract solid men of capital to their estates, in spite of the obvious risk of dealing with overmighty tenants. An abusive and troublesome middleman could easily be mistaken for a promising gentleman of capital. In a letter to a prominent head tenant, the agent of the Blundell estate wrote of the advantage of renting to middlemen on his estate in County Down in 1720:

> I must observe to you that I can let this estate to a single tenant of undoubted credit and substance at a greater rent than I am likely to make by letting it to several persons, and if I find there is any confederacy to my prejudice, I may chance to make a bargain for myself. But this method I shall not so willingly come into unless by a combination I have reason to suspect and which if any such tie impossible to be unknown to you I am driven to it. I confess I had rather have it rented by Protestant tenants under me.[117]

The estate agent reported later in that year that Blundell had nearly missed his opportunity to keep Hugh Gwynn.[118] The agent of the Downshire estate, of which the Blundell property had then become part, was still recommending that the landlord search for substantial men of capital in 1790:

> With regard to Dundrum I would recommend the encouragement of men of property to settle there and to lay out their money. Then it will be their interest to promote the prosperity of the place. If you lay out your own money, needy persons, men of broken fortune, idlers, etc. will get in upon you, and the improvements go to ruin. If any bar [sic] lies in the way of granting proper leases, the omnipotence of parliament can soon remove them, which is better to do than to suffer the place to continue a waste till a future day.[119]

Despite the apparent longevity of this attitude, the managers of the estate were eventually to suffer for their penchant for wealthy tenants. In the 1740s and 1750s they were plagued by a tenant named John Trimble who, along with his undertenants, resisted paying rent to Downshire and prevented all distraint and efforts toward his arrest from 1747 until his death ten years later. Trimble died in 1757, but he continued to have an impact on the behaviour of many other tenants on the property, especially his son Joshua, and his tactics spread throughout the estate.[120]

HISTORIES OF A MULTI-LAYERED TENANTRY

The development of a multi-layered tenantry was one of the most serious ramifications of the incomplete plantation of Ulster and a great challenge to the managers of Ulster estates, who in the eighteenth century began to take an interest in developing the financial potential of their estates and sought to clarify the property rights of the occupants of those properties. The nature of the surviving evidence prevents a systematic geographic analysis of the layered relationships between head tenants, undertenants, and estate managers. The following paragraphs focus on four properties: the properties of the London companies in County Londonderry, the Abercorn estate in the Foyle valley on the Tyrone-Donegal border, the Barrett-Lennard estate in Clones, Co. Monaghan, and the Anglesey estate in County Louth. This sample is geographically skewed towards the west and the south, areas where the influx of immigrants was thinner and the native settlement more persistent. Of the four areas examined here, only the London companies' proportions and the Abercorn estate were part of the plantation scheme. The problem of multi-layered tenancies certainly existed in east Ulster as well, but the nature of that problem was different where colonists were more densely settled.[121]

* * *

The study of eighteenth-century estates in County Londonderry is greatly inhibited by the fact that the crucial territories held by the various London companies completely disappear from our view. Following the restoration of their titles in 1663, the companies set their estates, called 'proportions,' on perpetuity leases.[122] From the colonial standpoint this was crucial territory because it was the core of the Gaelic stronghold dominated by the O'Neills. This area west of the Bann river, 'hither Ulster,' was a well-defined geographical and cultural territory, bounded on the west by the Irish-dominated Sperrin hinterlands of Loughlinsholin, and on the south by 'a broad strip of wild country, including the Carlingford mountains, Slieve Gullion, and the "Fews" in south Armagh, where the dominance of the Irish population, their language, and culture was not seriously challenged.'[123] In the reign of James I the various London companies had become important sources for the financing of colonial endeavours. Moody observed that 'under the Tudors the City became more and more the financial agent of the crown. With increasing frequency in the sixteenth century the crown applied to the City for loans, and in its main undertakings it habitually sought the help of the City in men and money.'[124] The City of London's undertaking in Ulster was, however, a departure from the typical pattern of colonial undertakings by joint-stock companies:

> The latter, while encouraged by the crown, were promoted by private individuals for motives of profit, and the capital was voluntarily subscribed. The former was initiated by the crown as a means of carrying out part of its programme for the anglicanization of Ulster, and was foisted upon the City as the most capable body for that purpose. The prospect of reaping large profits was used by the crown to induce the City to enter into the desired contract, but once this was concluded, the crown concentrated on enforcing the City's public obligations and discouraged profit-making tendencies. . . . The companies were compelled to pay their quotas, and within the companies individual members were compelled to pay the amount levied on them by their courts of assistants.[125]

Unlike the other Ulster undertakers, the London companies were placed under the supervision of a special body, the Irish Society, which closely monitored the management of their lands. The companies showed 'no enthusiasm for, and some positive hostility to, investing money in Ireland,' and so they had to be strong-armed into complying with the articles of plantation.[126] The result, notwithstanding massive investments in Derry and Coleraine, was the nearly complete failure of the plantation in the countryside. Macafee observes that 'by the middle of the seventeenth century there was a wedge of planter settlement lying between the bog-lands of the Moyola to the south and the Irish [and the Loughlinsholin woods] to the north. Judging from the limited evidence available for the latter part of the seventeenth century there was not a great deal of change in this pattern before the late 1690s.'[127]

Currie's painstaking reconstruction of the landholding patterns in two Londonderry manors from the 1659 census, hearth counts, and eighteenth-century maps and surveys is all the more valuable because of the paucity of other estate evidence for this period. The picture that he draws is the familiar one: perpetuities on large plots located along waterways and near established towns were initially offered in the seventeenth century to attract tenants, while in the remote hinterlands shorter terminable leases were offered. The rents of terminable leases climbed much faster in the eighteenth century than the more rigid perpetuities. Improvement spread slowly from towns and villages under perpetuity leases and along waterways, the traditional areas of Protestant dominance.[128] But on terminably leased lands some distance from the towns the situation deteriorated. John Spotswood, who was familiar with the Bellaghy estate, told Thomas Conolly in 1800:

> I never experienced such distress as the people are in general in, and assure you that there are very few on your estate [that] have their bread unbought, and you will not be surprised at it when I can with truth inform you that there are but four who live on your estate that have above fifty acres of land in their own occupation, and not twenty who occupy twenty acres, and the general average of this estate do not occupy more than seven acres, so you may judge our situation.[129]

Some of the companies were lucky enough to have tenants who behaved like model improvers. The Vintners' proportion had been leased in its entirety to Lord Massereene in 1673. Amos Strettle observed in 1718 that the rents which Massereene extracted from his undertenants in the 1670s 'were very inconsiderable, if any at all, for the tenants in those days were very poor and they are still not able to pay fines, and the landlords were then glad to get tenants at any rate.'[130] Lord Massereene claimed that he had since then been unable to lay fines on the tenants. Strettle believed this to be true because 'several of the leases were made by the late Lord Massereene, who set them at the highest rents he could get, and for as long a term as he had himself and in some instances longer, from whence I imagine that he could at any time easily renew and was glad to get tenants for longer terms.'[131] Apparently, Massereene wanted to get as many tenants under him for as long a term as possible in order to secure his own right of renewal to the property. This may have been an attempt to establish his own right of renewal through a claim that he had secured tenants with long leases and therefore effectively planted the land. The Earl of Tyrone, head tenant of the Fishmongers' proportion, also gave beneficial leases to Protestants in the 1750s which were for the same duration as he held from the company.

If a significant number of the ascendancy élite like Masserene took effective control of a company property, an element of stability in the tenurial history of an estate might result. But uncertainty was just as common. The greatest factor inhibiting the improvement of the Clothworkers' proportion, and this must have been true of most of the other proportions,[132] was uncertainty among tenants as to who would be the next in a never-ending series of petty landlords. The Clothworkers' proportion was let to one Richard Jackson, who paid £20,000 for the lease and who apparently raised the purchase money 'by taking fines and granting leases at reduced rents' to the occupiers. According to the Irish Society deputy, 'Sir George Jackson, the son of the purchaser, after granting renewals on similar terms, disposed of the estate to a Mr. Harrington, a banker, upon whose failure and bankruptcy a series of litigations followed, and the estate was in the Court of Chancery for many years. . . .' Leslie Alexander, the most recent purchaser, held for the lives of three old people. In 1836, when this account was given, there was very little improvement evident on the estate.[133]

Church lands in County Londonderry were in no better condition than the surrounding company estates. One eighteenth-century source claimed that they were unimproved partly because of 'the confined power of such churchmen and partly by their immediate tenants exacting large fines from the undertenants or occupiers of the land, a practice highly injurious, as it takes that fund that would enable them to cultivate the land. . . .'[134] The undertenants of Hercules Rowley, the head tenant of Bishop Hervey-Bruce's land in Londonderry, complained in 1769 of Rowley's offer to give them twenty-year leases only if they paid heavy fines both at the beginning of the tenure and at six-year intervals.[135] It is not clear whether Rowley would have succeeded in extracting these rents and fines, because four years later, he abandoned the enterprise and allowed the occupiers to hold directly from the bishop.[136] Rowley and the bishop were responding to pressure from the undertenants themselves. Around this time Hervey-Bruce also received 'the humble address of John Kennedy and co-partners, tenants of Leitrim in Donaghkeady, to the lord bishop of Derry to set their land to no petty landlord, but as he has renewed life, hope, and vigour once more in all the drooping, sinking hearts of Ulster, those poor, honest people hope to be redeemed from bondage, misery, and oppression.'[137] In 1780 a head tenant on the Hervey-Bruce property was informed that 'your lordship requires that all your tenants immediately deriving under you should give leases of twenty years duration to any undertenants' to whom they sublet lands.[138] Another undertenant who attempted to renew or to buy the interest in his land from a head tenant of the See of Derry commented dejectedly in 1785: '. . . after many attempts to prevail upon him to renew or to sell to me his interest, or to permit me to renew with your lordship, I was advised to sue him at law. . . .'[139] He had gone to court, but as his lease had expired, he found that he was not protected by law and had 'lately been served with an ejectment.' He sought the benefit of the bishop's power to renew directly to him since all the leases concerned had expired.[140]

While the foregoing retrospective commentaries are revealing, more concrete evidence of the tenurial developments on the London companies' lands would be desirable. Unfortunately, such evidence with respect to central Ulster is especially rare. One interesting morsel is an account given by tenants of a townland three miles from Derry on the road to Strabane, adjoining the Goldsmiths' proportion and separated from the rest of the Irish Society's proportion in the Derry suburbs.[141] This account contains many of the themes associated with customary tenure: the efforts of the head of a family to secure his or her children on the land, the contestation over tenure between head tenants and undertenants, the relationship between capitalist improvement and holding land in common with others, and the relationship between improvement and the length of tenure. Half the townland of Rosnagallagh, fifty-six acres, was leased to Roger Brown, a linen merchant, in 1754. The other half of the townland was held by one John Ewing. Brown's son William inherited the half-townland and during his lifetime divided half of it between his two sons, reserving the other half to himself. Thomas, one of the two sons, occupied his part, but William, another son, emigrated and sold his quarter to one John McKinley. William the elder left a quarter of his half to his daughter Frances, who married a Matthew Mahary. Upon Brown's death two other daughters got the remainder of his half, and upon their marriage their husbands divided the land so that each would enjoy his own share. Mahary and Kinley were co-authors of a memorial to the Irish Society in which both asserted their right to hold on to the land in their possession, Mahary claiming that he held 'in right of his wife.'

In the space of one generation the tenurial situation on Rosnagalegh became even more confused and uncertain. These various occupiers, who held land either by right of purchase or by marriage, were nevertheless insecure about their tenures because the term of years in the lease expired in 1815 and the existence of the lives was uncertain. More importantly, they wished to be completely separated from each other by new agreements with the Irish Society. The emphasis on 'improvement' and the trend towards parcellized landholding tend to blend together in petitions such as this one from Thomas Brown:

> That memorialists, owing to the uncertainty of their tenure, the lives being old, and the years nearly expired, feel themselves incapable of giving the land that degree of improvement which would make them productive,

fencing them in a permanent manner, and being desirous of having the rent of each man attached to his own proportion, so that he may be responsible for no more than his own, are willing to surrender the advantage they have in their present unexpired tenure and to take out leases separately from such tenure. . . .[142]

The complaints about the lack of incentive to improve the land most likely derived from the fact that the townland was poor and ill-cultivated. Thomas Brown was reported to be a bad character lately out of gaol, but his son Major Brown was known to be honest and reputable, and it was urged that he should be given a lease instead of the father. The other tenants, according to the account, were, 'like most of the occupying tenants in the north of Ireland, bad farmers and not willing to work on what they deem short tenures, which has occasioned their having neglected their land very much, seeing that the lease thereof was so near expiring.'[143] The deputies of the Irish Society recommended that nine leases for twenty-one years and the life of one public figure be given to the various occupiers shown in Table 2. This was a change from the sixty-one years and three private lives granted in the existing lease.[144] Another report two years later mentions that the townland was let for sixty-one years and three lives in two halves: one to Roger Brown and the other jointly to William Magee and Alexander Major. None of these lessees ever occupied the townland or paid much attention to the condition of the undertenants, nor did they fulfil any of their covenants, 'so that at this

Table 2
Landholding on the townland of Rosnagallagh, Co. Londonderry

Tenant	Acres	Rent
Thomas Major, Jr.	31	£51
Robert McReevy, Jr.	10	£19
Robert McReevy, Sr. and Patrick Brown	10	£18
John Grumbley	10	£18
John McKinley	16	£32
Matthew Mahary	6	£13
Robert Watson and Daniel McCadanes	6	£10
	13	£28
Major Brown	13	£21
Total	119	£211

Source: See note 145

moment the lands are probably in a worse state than they were in the year 1754, and appear to be occupied by a variety of undertenants, several of whom are at variance with each other, and some appearing to be characters which by no means recommend them as worthy to be trusted with the management of those improvements contemplated by the deputation.' This report recommended accepting the offer of Mr. Babington, the legal agent for the Irish Society, for a sixty-one-year lease.[145] Babington underlet it at a profit rent of about £30 to the above-mentioned individuals, who were apparently receiving a further considerable profit from the occupying tenants. The reporters concluded that in order to avoid the further delapidation of townlands such as this one, 'we think it right to recommend to the Society on all further occasions of granting determinable leases, to cause a clause to be inserted restraining the tenants from underletting their lands under the penalty of double rent or forfeiture of the lease.'[146] In the following year Babington was ordered to give up his lease or be ejected from Rosnagallagh because he had not complied with the terms of his lease.[147] Whether they succeeded in ousting him is uncertain, but the problems other landlords were having enforcing lease covenants makes their success doubtful.

The case of Rosnagallagh demonstrates the confusion inherently produced by the demographic development of localities held under multilayered tenancies. The ideal three-way mapping between tenant, land, and contract proved nearly impossible to maintain, so that responsibility for improvement of the land was not clearly established. The Irish Society was caught in a typical bind: the only prospective tenants whose representations to the company appeared attractive were uninterested in farming the land themselves, and the only tenants offering to occupy and produce were not 'worthy to be trusted.' Inevitably, it was these latter who remained in occupation, while the former were more likely to acquire direct leases, a situation whose instability revealed itself when the lease came up for renewal. This was also the occasion on which various antagonists might attempt to offer a coherent but subjective narrative, in the form of a petition to the landlord, which might make some sense of the objective mess created by the growth of families, inheritance, marriage, and exchange.

Undertenants on the proportions of the various London companies were anxious to assert their right of renewal over head tenants in the early nineteenth century, as in the case of Rosnagallagh. In one case the issue revolved around both 'peaceable possession' of the land and the right to negotiate directly with the landowner. Upon the expiration of leases in the early nineteenth century George Hill received a forty-one-year lease of Garvagh, Co. Londonderry, from the Irish Society in 1805, on the condition that the undertenants were granted twenty-one-year leases. But the latter refused to acknowledge Hill as their rightful landlord or to pay him any rent. Hill was therefore unable to pay for the improvements for which the Irish Society had stipulated in his lease. Hill solicited the Irish Society 'to take such steps . . . for putting him into quiet and peaceable possession for the lands for which he has long since paid his rent, although he has not received it from the tenants.'[148] Two years later, in another memorial to the Irish Society, Hill expressed concern about losing the heavy investment which he had already laid out, and urged the Society to either force the undertenants to pay him or to eject them. He warned the Society not to 'throw a doubt upon their own act by entering into any communication with the undertenants, upon the propriety of having granted their lease to him.' He claimed that he had already agreed to give many of the undertenants twenty-one-year leases 'at the former rent, or [their] option of value in money, computing [their] interest at the rate of the adjoining lands by the acre,' and he urged the Society to eject those who refused this agreement.[149]

* * *

Between the heartland of Gaelic power in what is now called Londonderry and the remote Gaelic periphery of western Donegal lay another region whose peculiar character was significant for the plantation. A tenuous strip of Scottish settlement extending down the Foyle valley from the city of Derry separated the Tyrone earls from the more remote Gaeldom of highland and coastal Donegal. There were two different Donegals. The mountainous coastal baronies of Boylagh and Banagh in the south-west were granted to Scots undertakers, while Kilmacrennan in the north-west was granted to servitors and natives, and Innishowen was given to Chichester. These three areas were clearly distinct from 'the more flat and fertile country that lies between the mountains and the river Foyle – the eastern boundary of the county. It is largely Protestant and from a very early period in history has been known as the Lagan, i.e. the low and level country.'[150]

In the Foyle valley, where Protestant settlement before and during the plantation had been heavy, estate managers may have had an easier time curbing the middleman system, had they been so inclined. An investigation of the leases issued in 1835 on the closely managed Abercorn estate showed that the land jobber was apparently all but nonexistent.[151] Three observers testified a decade later at the Strabane and Omagh sessions of the Devon commission about the scarcity of middlemen in their neighbourhood. One man, himself a farmer of 170 acres, declared that 'there is no such thing as a middleman in the Strabane area.'[152] This pattern of landholding was the direct result of aggressive policies by the Abercorn management. Unlike other eighteenth-century landlords, the eighth earl of Abercorn had, effectively eliminated the opportunities of prospective middlemen by requiring lessees to occupy the land they held under lease and by prohibiting single tenants from renting more than one farm.[153] But after 1765 the pace of rising population and the pressure on the landholding structure increased faster than the estate managers were able to respond. Agents were forced to deal with dozens of tenants who had divided their farms and sublet the 'skirts' to cottiers. Abercorn directed James Hamilton to devise a procedure for governing the division of farms in 1767. Hamilton informed him: 'I do direct that any tenants desirous of a division may put their leases in your hands under assurance of having them restored when the divisions shall be made, by my order, as equally and conveniently as may be. And I will support no division made hereafter by themselves.'[154] But even as diligent an agent as Hamilton was not up to this impossible task. 'It is scarcely possible to prevent the tenants from dividing their land,' he wrote in 1773, noting that on one farm 'there are three [tenants where there once was one], and each must have a horse and some little business to do in the land, and I am convinced that had one kept it, he would have been better able to pay than if he had one of these little parts for nothing.'[155] By 1778 Abercorn was obviously tired of this bothersome but unavoidable problem. He sternly admonished his agent: 'Samuel Smith of Ballymagorry can upon no account split his farm. This is, I hope, the last time you will give me occasion to write on this sort of subject.'[156] But Hamilton was uncomfortable with the responsibility of controlling the occupation of land when tenants believed that they were within their own rights. He had already timidly explained to Abercorn three years earlier:

> I am afraid to let Pollock or Timoney know that your lordship has been pleased to refer this matter to me. The time draws near when your lordship, I fear, will have many troubles of this sort. No one endeavour of mine should be wanted to lessen them, but I find a diffidence in myself for fear of being wrong. I never pretend to do more than advise among the tenants, when in many cases it requires something more peremptory to be said to them.[157]

Unhappy with efforts to stop tenants from breaking covenants in their leases by alienating land, Abercorn responded harshly and perhaps irrationally by announcing that he would shorten the length of tenure of the new leases:

> I wish you to make it generally understood that when the present leases are out, new ones will not be made for more than seven years. . . . I think it an act of lunacy to enter into covenants for a long term with people who profess not to think themselves bound on their parts. The only justification for letting leases even for seven years is that the shortness of the term may make the tenants reflect – they cannot break covenants with impunity.[158]

The existence of a new population of undertenants, holding their land under widely varying contractual arrangements, posed a great challenge to Hamilton and Abercorn. A number of large farmers who paid low rents granted short leases to undertenants in the 1760s at a sizeable profit. Upon the expiration of these leases, which may not have coincided with that of the head lease of the property, the undertenants' claims for renewal caused a conflict between two leaseholders of the same property. Abercorn described in detail one grievous case of 1766, showing as he did so his sensitivity to the rhetoric typically used to justify claims for tenant right:

> In 1761 I let a farm to Rogers at £12 rent for twenty-one years. This, I have the right to say, was less than three-fourths the value because Rogers immediately let the half of it for £8 10s. for a shorter term. And in this very advantageous bargain I surely compensated all the merit Rogers could be imagined to desire from his forefathers having lived there under very easy rents for several generations. And this advantageous bargain he made under a well-known obligation not to alienate the land, and especially not to split it. . . . [He] has alienated for a term not coextensive with his own, endeavouring thereby to establish and keep up the troublesome and pernicious tenure of a rack-rent tenant right distinct from the possession. Thus the foundation is laid for a litigation that may last as long as I live.[159]

The confiscation of tenant right paid to a smallholder, or of his lease or property through legal proceedings, was rarely carried out by the agents of the Abercorn estate, although it was standard practice among its wealthy tenants.[160] Abercorn did threaten the tenure of much wealthier and more powerful tenants who abused the rights of their undertenants. Tristram Carey, a wealthy tenant of the townland of Tonagh, complained confidently to Abercorn in 1769 that certain of his subtenants would not leave farms on which he had planned to put three of his sons. Carey suggested that to 'prevent their being put to any inconvenience, I would like to take their farm and give them one [of] what size they chose and twenty-one-years' lease,' but Abercorn upheld the undertenants' petition to remain.[161] Another large renter, Robert Harper from Listimore, had the same difficulty and with the same result. Abercorn ruled that Harper could not remove subtenants from good farms in order to replace them with his offspring.[162] In a case that resembles that of George Hill of Garvagh, Co. Londonderry, another Listimore middleman named George Leitch linked the issue of peaceable possession with the right to negotiate directly with the landlord. He tried to prevent Abercorn's intervention into the tenure of his undertenants by forcing them to agree not to treat with Abercorn before they got possession of their farms. He attempted to frighten one tenant who petitioned Abercorn by 'threatening to throw him into gaol for a £50 penalty he had undergone at the time of taking the land,

to give it up peaceably and never petition your lordship for it.' Although
Leitch was allowed to evict one undertenant 'who beat and abused him,' he
was informed that Abercorn 'considered him as forfeiting' the part held by the
tenant whom he had threatened.[163] Abercorn's defence of subtenants' claims
was also motivated by his desire to develop the land. In reference to George
Leitch, one of the prominent farmers on his estate, James Hamilton revealed his
opinion on the whole matter and suggested a policy that might reconcile both
sides:

> Was I to lean to either side, it would be to that of the undertenants, who
> generally labour with great industry and pay exorbitantly dear for their
> earning and improve much more land, I am sure, than the immediate
> tenant, and if he was found on the land at the end of the lease, I would
> wish him to be continued, but if he bargains and obliges himself to give it
> up, I think his pretension is the less, and the case of such is certainly hard.
> . . . Many of your lordship's farms as well as Listimore have rough tracts
> that want active hands. . . . I apprehend that the improvement will be more
> where the tenant may avowedly set off parts for some years than when it
> is otherwise, for he may think it best to hold all, though he cannot manage
> it, than to run the risk of losing part of it. . . . Perhaps one year of a lease
> would be reserved, and if by that time they had not fixed a child in it, the
> undertenant would no doubt lay in his pretensions, and it might be
> thought best by your lordship to let him have it.[164]

This type of evidence will be considered again in Chapters 3 and 4 in the
contexts of the changing economic determinants of viable farm sizes and
demographic growth of the rundale system. The focus here is on the contest
between landlord, head tenant, and undertenant over property rights. By
granting to the undertenants head leases at the expiration of their subleases,
Abercorn sought to maintain his control over the length of tenure and the
level of rent charged on his property. In cases such as those of Smiley and
Tagert, where the subdivision had been too minute and the tenants were
insolvent, the subleases were not to be renewed, 'and this with a view to maintaining my own right not to have lands occupied by poor tenants instead of
substantial ones, and for a shorter time than I give in it.'[165] Policy on this estate
varied with perceptions of the productive relationships between the various
residents of a particular leasehold or townland. In one scenario, the head
tenant and undertenants were part of a single loosely knit enterprise, where
the undertenant may have been partially employed in spinning, weaving, or
labouring on the farm of the head tenant. But another scenario existed whereby
the subtenant operated autonomously on remote virgin land or as an independent weaver. Hamilton drew the following distinction:

The cottier in [the former case] would be helped by his landlord. He would give him assistance in many ways. He would give him weaving and labour to help him pay his rent. They would live as friends. Whereas [with respect to] the tenant who would get a mountainy bit, your lordship's tenant who considers the farm all his right is seldom friendly to the little tenant who lives on a part he intended for a son on a future day.[166]

In the former case tenant right would rarely be sought or granted. In the more common latter case the claims of the undertenants depended on Abercorn's defence, and it was in this circumstance that smallholders conceived of an attachment between occupier and owner against the middleman that would be voiced as a tenant-right claim.

More often than not as the decades passed, landlords began to turn their backs on these cottiers. Though Abercorn and others like him were adjusting their policies to the shrinking size of economically viable farm units, they maintained a crucial distinction between a tenant 'splitting' a farm and one who disposed its underused margins in order to exploit the labour of a cottier: 'It would be to the advantage of the estate that tenants were allowed to let skirts of their farms, without fearing to lose the tenant right of it, and to avoid splitting as much as possible.'[167] Abercorn and Hamilton were doing their best to distinguish between undertenants who had become successful farmers and cottiers who remained in a dependent status.[168] As the decades passed, landlords successfully detached themselves from any responsibility for the tenure of cottiers. By the middle of the next century, they were in a position to blame the by then much deteriorated condition of the cottiers on the behaviour of the more aggrandizing and troublesome strong farmers on their estates. J.R. Rowley, agent to the Drapers' company, remarked on the treatment of cottiers by their head tenants in 1857:

The nine-tenths of the farmers do not look after their cottiers, and many, very many of them and their families have to go into the workhouses. . . . The generality of tenants who are allowed to have cottiers treat them very unfeelingly; they oppress them with a heavy rent and get as much work out of them as they are able to bear. The very men who call the loudest for tenant right and who abuse landlords right and left have no idea of cottier right. It is very difficult to regulate cottier rents, as the poor labourer is anxious to get a house for his family at almost any cost.[169]

Rowley wrote during a time when farmer-landlords had galvanized a politically potent tenant-right movement, but the abusive relationship which he described had been in existence for over a century.

★ ★ ★

The deeper one travelled down the Foyle valley, the weaker was the Scottish presence. In 1708 one traveller left this account of his passage down the Foyle river and into County Tyrone and south Ulster: 'After dinner we went along the fine river Foyle through an open sort of country for about four hours and arrived at Lifford, which is a very nasty, ugly sort of town, the county town of Donegal; across the river lies Strabane, which is a somewhat better town in Tyrone belonging to Lord Abercorn, who has here something of the linen manufacture.' From Newtownstewart to Omagh was 'a very woody country, Omagh from hence through a wild country enough to Clogher.' He then 'left Clogher and came in about four or five hours through the miserablist, wild, uncultivated mountains that can be seen to Monaghan, which is a very thriving village.'[170] As this account suggests, the strength of the colonial presence diminished as one moved into the more differentiated territories of south Ulster. Evidence from south Ulster, where a Gaelic landholding system remained on the ground, indicates how lightly the plantation touched the area.[171] Cavan had closer historic links with the Old English of the Pale, some of whom were confirmed in their Cavan estates during the plantation of Cavan. But according to Duffy, the result in terms of the pattern of landholding was no different from that in escheated Monaghan: 'the ultimate territorial pattern of estates was not radically different from the ballybetagh/ tate structure of Monaghan, which did not experience such a proprietal [*sic*] upheaval.'[172] According to Johnston, the Mount Sedborough and Balfour estates in Fermanagh were almost unaltered by the plantation. Most of their freeholds were sublet to the Irish. Johnson suspects that these tenants may have been leading members of clans, thus providing continuity with pre-plantation settlement.[173] Hunter found that dispersed settlement was nearly universal in Armagh, and that only the most active planters were able to establish centralized, enclosed settlement on their estates.[174]

There were difficulties with overpowering middlemen on various estates in south Ulster. Edmund Kaine, the agent of the Barrett-Lennard estate around Clones, abandoned the strategy of attracting substantial head tenants and took steps to prevent them from entrenching themselves in the lease structure. A gentleman named Bellingham asked in 1711 to rent the whole of the Moore estate, part of which was held by Dacre Barrett, but Kaine advised Barrett that 'your honour will find that setting your part of that estate to Mr. Bellingham will not be to your daughter's advantage for three reasons, as I find it: first, that country gentlemen [are] generally the worst paymasters when they get lands in their hands; secondly, the rent is hardly ever to be advanced; and thirdly, the lands [are] never to be got [away] from them . . .'[175] because middlemen were often in the habit of giving their undertenants leases longer than their own.[176] In 1773 Noble argued against renewing the lease of one

Hamilton, as it would contradict his scheme to renew only farms of no more than fifty acres, and took the opportunity to reiterate his beliefs concerning the treatment of undertenants by their middlemen:

> I must say that what has and is hurting this kingdom is your petty landlords, who take lands and then rack them out to a parcel of poor creatures in small parcels at an exorbitant rent. Now the poor creatures are broke and so [low?] that the high-set lands are now left waste by them, and they going to America and other places out of the kingdom. I have and always will give your tenants to understand that they that live and reside in the lands may always expect to get their holdings at the value when they fall in, and that such of them as set to poor people at a rack-rent, that I shall recommend it to you not to set to them again, but to set to such of them as will live thereon.[177]

So, for example, when James Fisher's lease expired, the agent punished him for abusing his undertenants by denying him a renewal. Fisher was attacked in a petition by his undertenants as an 'insinuating land jobber' who would never have been able to give 'five shillings for a tenant right' except for the 'buying and selling of cattle for gentlemen agents.'[178] Discussing the opportunity to increase the rent on a holding whose lease had expired in 1777, Charles Mayne felt that a new tenant would be required because 'the present tenant will never be able to hold it without setting to undertenants, and your leases does and has been to the contrary.'[179] By the early nineteenth century the agents had set in place a renewal policy favouring the undertenants. The general policy on the Barrett-Lennard estate in 1812, according to William Mayne, was to 'let to the resident tenant and to keep the middleman out of your estate as much as possible.' As the old leases expired, Mayne would show preference to 'the occupying man . . . if of good character.'[180] Four years later, another agent concurred: 'As leases determine, I let to the occupying tenants as much of the premises as I consider they deserve or can occupy without subletting.'[181] After over a century of effort the Barrett-Lennard estate seems to have finally been rid of its middlemen.

Head tenants on the Anglesey estate in County Louth also endeavoured to prevent their undertenants from usurping their tenures and spoiling their plans to pass their holdings on to their children. In 1757 a tenant who offered to pay 'the outside value' for his farm warned that he and his three sons would leave if the entire townland was given to another over his head. 'There are rookers and oppressors who have given in proposals for whole towns,' he complained. 'To live under such men would be nothing else but a wretched state of slavery and bondage.'[182] In a case where the head tenant was a widow, she might be particularly vulnerable to such usurpation. One widow of a head tenant attempted to secure her own tenure by introducing a clause in the leases of her undertenants guaranteeing her the right of renewal of her own lease. Her nephew explained that he 'was left in care of an aunt now resident upon the farm, but being then too young to take on the management of an extensive farm, she was induced to let it to neighbouring farmers with a special clause against their building upon it, reserving only fifty acres in her own hands. This clause, my lord, she had inserted in their lease to preclude them from any pretensions of stepping in between her and the landlord at the expiration of her lease.'[183]

When arguing for renewal, head tenants who based their claims on the improvements they had made would emphasize the poverty and inefficiency of the undertenants. John Clarke, another head tenant on the Anglesey estate seeking renewal, claimed in 1778 that he had improved his farm as much as possible barring a vast further expense, and he offered what 'any man who means to pay the rent honestly' would. He too was afraid that Anglesey would not renew to him land occupied by undertenants:

> Your directions are that Mr. Hutchinson should agree with me . . . for what I have in my own hands or occupy myself, exclusive of what they pay. But I humbly beg leave to observe to you that those tenants on my part are so exceedingly poor, they could not nor did they ever pay me but by labouring work, and notwithstanding I was well pleased to take it in that way, there are, some of them, greatly in arrears; their small little tenements happen to be so interspersed through what I have in my own possession that my holding one part without the other would be very inconvenient.[184]

But in this case the undertenants made rival claims, and their investment, labour, and long occupation stood them in good stead with the landlord. Two of the undertenants, Peter and James McGuire, claimed that they held land 'that they and their forefathers held since the wars of Ireland.'[185] Patrick Matthews of Irish Grange, another undertenant of Clarke's, asserted in 1785 that though he had held his ten acres for only the past four years, he did so at such an exorbitant rent that he had to invest greatly in marl and to lay out other money while 'striving to bring it into heart.' He asked for 'the favour, blessing, and comfort of becoming tenant of his present holding' under Lord Uxbridge.[186] Apparently, this behaviour alarmed Clarke's widow, who was alerted by the activity of this industrious undertenant and decided to oust him if she could. But the agent took a different view of these undertenants' 'striving to bring the land into heart:'

> At the decease of Mr. Parks, [the] lands were in great heart and condition. Soon after, they were set to the Whitestown people, who made the most of them by keeping them under tillage and expending the manure on Whitestown, by which the greatest part of them are impoverished greatly. I was glad to get them to sign the attornment anyway; by this you have them in your power and may do with them as you please.[187]

The Anglesey estate records provide another more complete example of tenurial controversy consequent upon the death of a head tenant. The poor and mountainous strip of land called Benagh, which had been out of lease for most of the eighteenth century, was let to James Hanlon in 1780 over the heads of the undertenants who had been occupying at the will of the landlord.[188] The tenants of Benagh submitted a petition

> setting forth their situation under their petty landlord Mr. James Hanlon, having laboured under his oppression for five years past, taking all methods to distress them, wanting to banish them out of the town wherein they and their forefathers have been residing tenants before and since the wars of Ireland; as he was in doubt that if the right honourable earl should come to know that he let land to undertenants, that he would not grant him lease of the same, but would, as was in his noble father's rule, give the land to the residing tenants.[189]

Unfortunately for the undertenants, after Hanlon's death a pretender to the head lease appeared on the estate. John Hanlon, a son-in-law from Dundalk who claimed the inheritance of Hanlon's lease, arrived on the scene, manured a field, set about abusing two widows, and harrassed other tenants in a variety of ways. In a letter to Uxbridge he complained cleverly that 'all my manure is on said field, and beg of you that I may not be so hardly dealt with as to lose the benefit of it. . . . If you are so good as to let me have it, you will find me a good and peaceable tenant.' But when he moved from Dundalk to claim possession, the agent warned him that 'it was more than probable he would not get leave to continue here, as there were too many tenants at present on the estate, and that Lord Uxbridge rather wished to diminish rather than add to the number.' This was belittling language to a man who aspired to a status above that of the other residents of the townland. Aside from the fact that he was encroaching on an already crowded townland, there were other good reasons to keep Hanlon off the estate, since he seems to have abused his new neighbours at every opportunity. The elder Hanlon had let the land to the undertenants in order to cultivate potatoes, which were sold to the neighbouring tenants. The son-in-law was evidently demanding the rent from them too early in the year. Traditionally, they harvested them in the fall and paid at Christmas. A row ensued and some neighbouring tenants occupied the potato ground. Robert Hutchinson, the agent, thought that one of the undertenants should get the potato ground. A witness to the affair claimed that Hanlon, a man who regularly beat his wife, came to the potato fields shirtless in order to box with anyone. Others complained that Hanlon had doubled the rent in the past four years and charged them church and county cess for the part that he kept. Furthermore, Hanlon denied them access to sea wrack, to which they were accustomed under his father. Armstrong argued that 'this indulgence, which may possibly rather be called a right,' should be continued, and that the sea wrack remained the property of the landlord, not the tenant. But as there was nothing about it in the lease, Armstrong was uncertain how to proceed.[190]

The occupants made every effort to escape the heavy abuse poured on them by Hanlon. Hutchinson reported that the 'Benagh tenants have been all with me and declare they will never pay Mr. Hanlon another shilling.' They wished to 'come immediately under his lordship's protection and pay the value of their respective holdings to me.' One tenant offered 'undeniable security' to be continued directly, claiming that Hanlon had distrained his cattle and sold them outside the estate. Another petitioner insisted that after having 'laboured sore this many years past,' he was 'still hoping that he might become the tenant of the right honourable earl of Uxbridge' rather than suffer 'under the tyranaciousness [sic] of a petty landlord.' In the end, Hanlon agreed to give up all but his own portion. He was lucky to have even this, for Hutchinson had warned Harrison: 'I fear they are so small that unless they get what Hanlon at the present holds, which is about one-third of the town-land, they will make but indifferent tenants.'[191]

TENANT RIGHT AND MULTI-LAYERED TENURE

Who had the better claim to the soil and to the renewal of their tenure? For what reasons? What influence did the overlap of rights between tenant and undertenant have on the meaning of the term tenant right? Powerful middle-men sometimes prevented renewals going to occupiers if they could put pressure on the occupiers or on the agent. Arthur Young, who popularized the term 'middleman' and demonized them in his influential *Tour of Ireland*, lost his job as agent for Lord Kingsborough's estate in Cork because of the intrigues of powerful middlemen families on the estate.[192] In Cork and Tipperary the tenurial strength of middlemen had not diminished by the end of the eighteenth century. The first Earl of Bantry wrote of one such family in 1806: 'All the Warner family are honest men and have been under my grandfather, father, and myself, they are improving tenants, have always got their several farms reasonable and have got considerable incomes under our family, they should certainly get a preference whenever their lives expire.'[193] To be sure, Ulster middlemen were often in a position to look back on their eighteenth-century tenures and make the same claims concerning improvements and management as their counterparts further south. William Armstrong, the tenant of 3,158 statute acres on Trinity College lands in County Armagh, prefaced his request for a rent reduction with the following preamble:

that the lands I now hold as tenant of the college have been held by members of my family since the time when they were granted by the crown as part of the college endowment, that by my ancestors those lands, then a wilderness, were brought into a state of cultivation and the property of the college in them protected, secured, and improved by every means which industry, perseverance, and intelligence could do during the centuries that have elapsed since the college obtained their grant. . . .[194]

He warned that the decline of the small landlord class, of which he was a member, would leave no one to 'guide the improvement of the land and impart knowledge and civilization upon the tenantry.'[195] A similar claim on the part of substantial middlemen stood behind their offer to purchase the Clothworkers' proportion in 1871. They asked the managers to reconsider their decision to sell the proportion to Sir Hervey-Bruce, politely admonishing them not to

overlook the claims of the tenants whose forefathers emigrated from England and Scotland and settled the estate with a loyal and peaceable people, in times of great trouble and danger, and by whose toil and industry the Clothworkers' Company's estate has been so much increased in value since your company sold their estate in 1727 to the Richardson family at £70,000.[196]

Of course, any such property claims made by middlemen had to be balanced against both the huge profits which they were often able to extract from the actual occupiers of their landlord's property and the pattern of occupation they allowed to flourish on their estates.[197] An agent for Charles O'Hara's County Sligo estate complained in the 1820s that

those tenants who are most anxious for abatements at this moment receive profit rent from their undertenants, and if willing to dispose of their farms, require a sum of money for their interest therein; you will find upon inquiry this to be the fact. Would it not be incorrect to give an abatement when the very poor people on your estate will not derive the smallest benefit, as their landlords, who should be punished for having introduced such a number of people on the estate, will not give the most trifling abatement to them?[198]

The agent of the Barrett-Linnard estate held a similar opinion:

Although I am very unwilling to involve you in suits with your tenants, there are some of them who deserve to be punished. I mean those who live off the lands and let them at a rack-rent to a parcel of poor tenants, which is the reason your rents are so badly paid, for those who don't live on the lands leave the poor creatures to pay your last November with their present May rents. And in that case I think it hard to distress the poor wretches.[199]

The general trend was therefore against the middleman.[200] On the Shirley estate in Monaghan the landlord turned away from the middlemen in the 1760s, writing that he would 'never again let an inch of land to any gentleman to let again for a profit rent, as it is only the means of making slaves and beggars and impoverishing the lands. . . .' Twenty-one year leases were given to the occupiers in 1777.[201] In 1808 Edward McGildowney, agent to Lord Mark Kerr's property in County Antrim, set about reorganizing the tenure of that estate after the expiration of a life named in the leases of eight head tenants holding over 400 acres each. He told Kerr not to 'give the landlords of the lands out of lease any more of them than what they hold in their own hands unlet to undertenants.'[202] Over the next few years McGildowney established a consistent policy, informing one correspondent in 1814 that 'the practice for some years past in the Antrim estate has been, on the expiration of the lease, to give right of renewal to the occupying tenants.'[203] A report to the Irish Society, the umbrella body for the twelve London companies, recommended that renewals should go to occupying tenants and that the former middlemen should be compensated for any improvements. 'We consider it advisable to recommend the adoption of this as the best means of bringing the tenants under the immediate protection of the society and preventing oppression by the middleman.'[204] Henry Smith of the Drapers' company estate directed in 1821 that only occupiers were to get a lease.[205] Edward Driver, agent to the Clothworkers' company, noted in 1840 that he had been assigned to relet the estate and, whenever possible, to dismantle the middleman system.[206] By the early nineteenth century polices prejudicial to middlemen seem to have become routine on Ulster estates.[207]

HISTORICAL CLAIMS FOR CONTINUOUS TENURE

The thesis of this chapter is that the establishment and maintenance of a commercial tenurial relationship between a farming family and a landowning family was an important source of a claim for continuous tenure. The evidence presented in the previous sections provides a backdrop for the formation and maintenance of these relationships. The following two chapters will deepen this context by introducing economic and visual developments. This chapter looks at the relationships which form the very structure of the estates. The emphasis on the difficulties of maintaining these structures is intended to highlight the obstacles that had to be overcome, not to assert that all or the majority of Ulster estates were dysfunctional. For landlords and tenants who overcame political upheaval, economic uncertainty, and legal handicaps, and who recognized the threats of these difficulties on other estates or in other parts of the province, these relationships had a special meaning. Tenants articulated this in terms of their right to continued tenure.

Over the course of the eighteenth century the rhetoric justifying this extra-economic relationship changed its emphasis. Claims for continued attachment between families occurred in five different contexts: first, where the tenant and the landlord were about to re-establish what was for one or both of them an original or foundational relationship, either in the first generations of the plantation or later at the inauguration of the tenure of a new landlord; second, where the tenant and the landlord came to share a continuous historical relationship of 'peaceable possession' that originated soon after the violent episodes of the seventeenth century; third, where, with the passage of time and labour, the person-to-person historical relationships attenuated to the point where all that remained was a more vague relationship between families that may not have been directly founded on the primordial tenancies of the seventeenth century; fourth, where, upon further attenuation of these historical relationships, other climactic violent events such as the 1798 rising or more localized threats to landlord hegemony came to serve as the anchor of a personal relationship between tenant and landlord; and finally, fifth, where the context permitted no appeal to personal or family history nor to any climactic historical events. In this last situation, the tenant had only the present potential of his labour and capital to justify his continued tenure, although this was supplemented by the collective potential of the tenantry as an enfranchised and politically powerful class which put pressure on landlords and legislators to recognize the legitimacy of their customary claims to the soil. Usages of the term tenant right found in estate records do not fall discretely within any one of these categories. Neither do these five categories fit snugly into specific historical periods, following one upon the other in a linear succession. There is, however, a general movement from the first to the last which corresponds to the movement from the immediate extra-economic relationships of the early plantation, to the mediated relationships that developed as the plantation estate structure, the market economy, and agrarian capitalism slowly congealed, to the wholly different form of immediacy resulting from the purely commercial relationship between landlord and tenant, and finally out into the realm of parliamentary politics.

During the early years of the plantation and throughout the latter half of the seventeenth century, the sitting tenant who sought renewal or whose tenure otherwise became the subject of estate correspondence more often than not was the first occupant ever to have farmed the land under the new conditions and requirements of the plantation. By his very occupation until the expiration of his lease the tenant defined and embodied the plantation estate structure, and the naturalization of a new order of property relations stood squarely on his shoulders. The status and attachment of the occupier to the land became a central element of the sitting tenant's social standing because it brought into relief the high mobility of most tenants. Where there was a stable tenantry, where family-landlord relations as a rule spanned generations, the force of this circumstance was diluted. But when both tenants and landlords were relatively new to the land, and when they could both easily imagine the precariousness of their tenure, made painfully obvious to them in 1641, 1689, and even in the 1740s, there was an added urgency to their property claims that supplemented straightforward leasehold agreements. This is the context of the first use of the term tenant right in the late seventeenth century.

The situation in which a tenant faced his landlord in a foundational relationship was not restricted to the first century of the plantation but occurred repeatedly throughout the next two centuries at the change of the landlord. The arrival of a new landlord after the purchase or inheritance of an estate provided the opportunity for the reciprocal recognition of the landlord-tenant relationship. These were tense periods in the social life of an estate, with new landlords investigating the extant leases and rent-rolls and tenants anxiously awaiting new policies. If an heir showed signs of adopting a threatening posture with regard to tenure, tenants defended themselves by referring him back to their past behavior in support of the threatened legal rights of his family. The testimony of tenants in support of landlord claims, or their supportive behaviour as jurors, stood them in good stead when the issue of their right of renewal arose at a later date. A number of examples of this survive in the Anglesey estate papers. An encroachment on to the estate by the undertenants of a tenant on a neighbouring estate was successfully thwarted in court with the help of a crafty young Newry lawyer. Some of the undertenants then attorned to the landlord, Lord Uxbridge.[208] Another, earlier lawsuit requiring the testimony of certain tenants formed the basis for the following petition: 'Old inhabitants and tenants for several years . . . lately incurred the displeasure of several neighbours and gentlemen [by testifying] in your honour's favour with regard to your suit at law at Dundalk and humbly hope your honour will consider the same and not leave us in the powers of any other landlord.'[209] In the 1780s tenants on the border between the estates owned by one Brabazon and Uxbridge were again caught in the middle of a boundary dispute. One such tenant was ejected by Brabazon because of his testimony in a suit between Brabazon and Uxbridge.[210] One tenant complained 'that the petitioner's late father was the only man who stood up for supporting the property of Sir Nicholas [Bayly] in this place, when several attempts were made to deprive him of it, and even a lawsuit commenced to take away his right. The said father was for time out of mind esteemed by Sir Nicholas as an honest man, and one who had his landlord's interest truly at heart. . . .' He called attention to 'his distressed situation having a large family of children grown to maturity and little or no land to support himself and them.' He asked for an adjacent field presently held by a man from another estate.[211] Similar evidence survives from County Antrim. A tenant of Lord Mark Kerr found himself on the wrong side of a litigation in 1819. Kerr's agent, Edmund McGildowney, dismissed his claim to a lease:

> I find that Mr. Hutchinson on behalf of himself and John McElhargy has served you with a notice. McElhargy came here last Monday and offered to pay me down whatever I would charge for getting him a lease of his part of Ballymacrea. I told him that I had heard he allowed his name to be used to go to law with Lord Mark Kerr for what I considered his just right and that he was now in possession of it, and that he or any other who would act so should never get lease or accommodation from his lordship that I could keep from them. Indeed, it was hardly worth Mr. Hutchinson's while to set such an example for two or three acres of bog if he was even sure to succeed, but perhaps it is what he hopes to make by the suit that induces him.[212]

The personal and legal alliance between landlord and tenant was sometimes sealed by attornment. When Lord Anglesey forced his tenants to sign attornments, committing them to the landlord apparently without the legal protection of a lease, the petitions for renewal that were showered upon the agent all cited ancient residence and improvement as justifications for renewal.[213] A change in policy with regard to the attornments in 1778 for the first time included a new clause with a promise to give up 'quiet actual possession' at the end of the term of attornment.[214]

It is clear from estate records that the most forbidding threat to customary relationships on an estate was the arrival of a modernizing and presumptuous heir or purchaser. When William Conyngham inherited his estate in 1765, a member of his family told him that he had 'been with all the tenants, who gave up their possessions very quietly and also gave security that they will not pay any rent to any but you, except John O'Haggan and James O'Haggan, who will not give possession, and when Matthew asked them the reason of taking a defence, they told him they intended holding over until you came into the country.'[215] Examples abound of new heirs objecting to, in their eyes, the overly generous leasing policies of their forbears and attacking the legitimacy of the agreements.[216] One Antrim heir complained that he could not 'be blamed for his father's error in the leases being for a term of forty-one years, twenty years longer than normal term in that part of the country, and though the tenants have come to the end of their term, no improvements, repairs, etc., have been made.'[217] New members of the landowning family were often bad enough, but an unknown purchaser was more dangerous still. Tenants of Bishop Frederick Hervey-Bruce in County Londonderry, who had recently surrendered their old leases for new ones based upon a revised valuation, expressed fear that the heir to the estate might sell, and that they would 'come under some low landlord who might distress us in our old age or oblige us to send our young families to America.'[218] In the last anarchic years of the century wild rumors spread about the behaviour of Abercorn with regard to his tenants and country:

> When I was seen in town by some of the men, it was generally regarded that your lordship was in town; then it was said that you were never to see Ireland, that you had sold the estate and were so determined that Baronscourt should not exist that you had commanded the stones of the house to be picked asunder, [or alternatively] that you had abandoned England and [were] determined, as soon as peace would admit, to sell all your property there and in Scotland and remain in Ireland until you had brought Ireland to a sense of her duty.[219]

It took the unsettling crises of the 1790s to create this attitude on the part of Abercorn's tenants, who lived on a very well managed estate. But a similar attitude on the part of the tenants on the very poorly managed London companies' properties, where the landlords had essentially abandoned their estates to the type of people found so onerous by the Abercorn tenants, was more or less a chronic condition. A deputation called the Goldsmiths' proportion

> good, low land, but nevertheless, as to improvement, it is stationary, and in this respect it is very unlike its neighbours the Grocers' and Fishmongers'. This is no doubt to be attributed to the uncertainty felt by the tenants as to who are to be their landlords; one half the estate, which was sold a few years since under a chancery decree, was purchased by Mr. Leslie Alexander, and the other half, it is expected, will soon be disposed of, so that the occupying tenants, seeing that no one is interested in their prosperity, are careless and indolent.[220]

Such dangers dramatically increased in the nineteenth century, especially after the passage of legislation facilitating the sale of encumbered estates.

The second form of the claim for continued tenure appeared as plantation estate structures began to stabilize in the second quarter of the eighteenth century. Around this time the violence and artifice of the plantation began to fade into memory and history. This was the context in which tenants cited the heroic occupation of a father, grandfather, or great-grandfather who had saved the estate from collapse by occupying it in the 1690s. For example, Charles Doherty proposed for a three-life lease of lands near Virginia, Co. Cavan, in 1726, noting that 'my father and grandfather have been tenants to said lands time out of mind, my said grandfather being the person who had given the first possession thereof to the right honorable Lord Fingal in a time when the inhabitants thereof with strong hand withheld possession from his then lordship.'[221] Cornelius Dormollen, another tenant on this estate, observed in 1726 that he was

> tenant to the said lands these thirty-four years past and came to inhabit Virginia when the whole lordships were waste and untenanted, and paid rent all along and encouraged several persons to come and inhabit, and after the first fourteen years the late Lord Fingal . . . encouraged and desired said Mr. Dormollen to build and improve, which he did, and that for the future he should be preferred to said lands before any other person.[222]

The tenant James Plunkett requested an abatement from his Londonderry landlord Thomas Conolly in 1783 owing to 'the very bad markets we had these two years past. My family have been tenants to your family for more than a hundred years past, and it would make me very unhappy to surrender my land.'[223] A tenant named O'Dolan on the Playdell estate in Leitrim sought a renewal of his lease based on his 'having, as I flatter myself, a priority of claim from the fact that my forefathers occupied said lands for 300 years and faithfully performed the conditions imposed on them for that length of time.'[224]

The point of statements such as these was to establish extra-economic claims for tenure which might be deemed superior to economic ties between landlord and tenant. The following petition from a tenant on the Anglesey estate in 1785 shows the clear link which this tenant felt between the relationship of his family to the landlord and the right of his family to continue on the estate despite changing economic circumstances. Patrick McFarland claimed that his

> forefathers have been tenants in Belleghan since before the wars of Ireland, that petitioner has lived in one house in same town these forty years past; but in the course of that time he was dispossessed of all the land he held, only what he holds from the man who took it over his head. . . . That since petitioner has been greatly wronged and distressed, it is very hard to think of newcomers being supplied with land they do not want in the place where petitioner cannot get a foot, though being born and bred in it, and though his children are able to pay for and cultivate land if they could get it, and since he is an infirm, sickly, disordered man not able to provide for himself, and without his children's help must beg during the rest of his life, and that they will not stick to him unless they get some spot of land to live on.[225]

Another Anglesey tenant, Brian Murnaghan, emphasized those things which he had done to prove his strong attachment to the lord: 'When Sir Nicholas was here and understood how firmly this petitioner was attached to him and his interest and gave proof of it on various occasions, he then promised that petitioner and his offspring should never be molested in his little holding or be deprived of it.' He claimed that he had been deprived of a lime kiln even though he offered to pay the same rent as any other person, and requested that he be allowed to pass it on to his now full-grown daughter.[226] Alexander Hogg Lecky argued that his 'predecessors have been tenants of the society ever since the memorable siege of Derry in the year 1688, [and] that renewals have been made to his family ever since. . . .' He then appealed for new terms 'in consideration for his having built a capital dwelling house and offices, and erected walls to protect the same, together with his garden, farm, and plantations, by granting him a term of sixty-one years for such his demesne lands, consisting of forty acres, in like manner as has been granted to Mr. Scott, his next adjoining neighbour. . . .'[227] The point is thrown into relief by the undated petition of a stranger to the Anglesey estate seeking a tenancy. Since he did not have a long tenure on the estate to boast of and had no hereditary ties to the estate, he noted his former residence and emphasized his ability to labour hard.[228] Without a recognizable historical attachment to the estate, he could offer nothing else.

These memories of behaviour above and beyond the requirements of economic performance were particularly strong on the properties of the Irish Society and the London companies near Derry and Coleraine. Robert Hazlett, who in 1860 held one of the largest farms on the Merchant Tailors' estate, benefitted from the now legendary behaviour of his ancestors. A deputy of the company admitted to the managers: 'This tenant and his ancestors have held the farm for nearly 200 years. The Hazletts took an active part in the defence of Derry and underwent great vicissitudes of fortune in those eventful times. The present tenant is a kind, benignant old man of nearly eighty years of age' who wanted a lease so that one of his eight sons might inherit the farm.[229]

Of course, it was quite rare for a tenant like Hazlett to be able to claim direct and continuous lineage extending back to the first post-1689 occupants. As the century aged, the historicity of particular tenures became severed from their moorings to the cataclysmic foundation of 1689. Tenants began to make claims based on a continuous past relationship between the families of the landlord and the tenant even though no evidence of a direct link to the seventeenth-century plantation may have existed. Tenants might claim to have an 'ancient' tenure, one that had lasted time-out-of-mind, or might refer to their forefathers and the landlord's forefathers, or merely draw attention to their names on the gravestones dating from the plantation period. Omeath tenants of four years' standing on the Anglesey estate claimed in 1770 a right to bog taken by another tenant because their parents and grandparents had also been tenants.[230] Another tenant claimed to be the third generation of his family on the same farm and therefore deserving of a lease.[231] A tenant on the Drapers' company estate hoped to be allowed to stay on his farm because his family had resided on the estate for over a century – ever since an ancestor

had purchased a farm on the estate. An eighty-year-old tenant facing an ejectment served by Lord Dufferin's agent in County Down begged for another
year to pay the arrears he had accumulated because of a recent failure of his
flax crop, adding that he 'and his ancestors have been tenants of your lordship
for upwards of 100 years,' and that he was the sixth generation of his family
on the estate.[232]

The volatile political history of the eighteenth and nineteenth centuries
occasionally gave tenants the opportunity to replace their attenuated attachment to the foundations of the estate system with arguments about their
participation in more recent events. Loyalty and patriotism were crucial
concepts in the politics of the eighteenth century. War with continental
enemies, normally an 'occasion of danger for Irish Catholics,' after the Seven
Years' War became an 'opportunity to draw up addresses, to stress their loyalty
and, especially, to beat the recruiting drum. It would be no coincidence that
the major Catholic Relief Acts of the late eighteenth century were put through
in a time of war.'[233] Loyalty and patriotism were also important at the level
of the estate. Two of the most important bases for the renewal of tenure
were the creation of political leases in the period 1770–1815, and the disposition and behaviour of tenants during the 1798 rebellion.

In the first two-thirds of the eighteenth century there appear to have been
no pronounced changes in the relationship between land tenure and electoral
politics. The electorate was small, though in Ulster counties it must have
been relatively larger than the rest of the island due to the concentration of
Protestant leaseholders who, because of the opportunities presented to them
by the linen trade, were able to show forty shillings net profits over their rents
and other charges and thus qualify for the franchise. By contrast to Irish
electoral politics in the nineteenth century, this period appears rather torpid.
There was only one general election between 1728 and 1768. By-elections,
bundled together as they were at the opening of parliamentary sessions,
could amount to mini general elections, but the issues at stake were restricted
to the familiar nexus of paternalism and deference, and rarely extended to
'opinion' concerning the business of parliament. Tenant voters might on
occasion be able to extract from their landlords abatements of rent, cancel-
lation of arrears, or the promise of lease renewal on favourable terms in
exchange for their votes.[234] The infrequency of elections and the small minority
of enfranchised tenants together lessened the significance of electoral politics
in estate management. This scenario began to change rapidly in the last third
of the century. The Octennial Act of 1768 mandated that general elections be
held at no greater than seven-year intervals. After 1771 by-elections were
contested immediately upon the vacation of a seat, not at the beginning of
the next parliamentary session. Parliamentary elections therefore became

more frequent and less predictable so that landlords concerned with the management of their electoral patronage 'knew not the time nor the hour when a maximum exertion would be required.'[235] At the same time, the role of 'opinion' in parliamentary politics was expanding rapidly. Thomas Conolly, MP for Londonderry, the head tenant of the Grocers' company proportion, was forced to appease his Presbyterian constituents after they threatened to field an independent candidate in the 1776 election. In a letter concerning the search for a new provost for Strabane, James Hamilton abandoned his characteristically impartial demeanor: 'Nor do I know where to turn myself in Strabane, the next class of people being Presbyterians, and at this instant we apprehend, [rather than being] much averse to Steelboys, they [are] made up, I may say, to a man, of them. Besides, I must own that in general I think [them] a plodding [i.e. plotting] discontented people, valuing themselves much on their consequences, which is no doubt greatly increased by the Octennial bill. . . .'[236] The following decade saw the growth of Catholic influence on parliament and the passage of a series of relief acts which culminated in the Catholic Relief Act of 1793, giving forty-shilling freeholders the vote and the right to bear arms.[237] Patrons were forced to come to terms with a new electoral constituency on their estates. James Hamilton, Jr., reported in 1793 that 'the Roman Catholics in [the] Donegal [portion of the estate] are very few, not exceeding sixteen, I think, but such as there are shall be put on a footing with the others, as your lordship desires. Their holdings are comparatively small, few exceeding £5 yearly.'[238]

Thomas Bartlett has identified the year 1793 as the definitive end of the sleepy and oligopolistic equipoise of eighteenth-century rural electoral politics.[239] In terms of political life on landed estates, this date also marks the beginning of a practice Edward Wakefield called 'political agronomy,' a rough science practised by landlords to weigh the political benefits of giving freehold tenancies and votes to smallholders on their estates against the economic cost of doing so. If their political ambitions were high, and the political competition in the constituency evenly balanced, patrons might be quite reckless in their creation of political tenancies. This tendency was particularly strong in County Londonderry, where, according to an anonymous report of 1869,

> many of the middlemen had close parliamentary connections: Henry Carey of the Skinner's proportion was a member for Coleraine and his son a member for the county, Richard Jackson of the Clothworkers' proportion was a member for Coleraine, Thomas Conolly of the Grocers' proportion was a member for the county, the earl of Tyrone, a member of the House of Lords, held the Fishmongers' proportion, Sir William Rowley of the Drapers' proportion was the son of a member for the county, and William Conolly, Speaker of the Irish parliament, held the Vintners' proportion.[240]

One observer reported to the Fishmongers' court in 1808 that the Beresford family had acquired leases of large tracts from various London companies for the sole purpose of adding to their 'enormous political influence.'[241] The Mercers' proportion had been in the hands of that company since the expiration of the lease of the marquis of Londonderry, who 'had cut up the estate into forty-shilling freeholds for electioneering purposes.' Rents on the estate were £12,000 in arrears.[242] Edward Oseland found the forty-shilling-freeholder system to be rampant on several London company estates, though not on the Merchant Tailors' proportion.[243] It is difficult to gauge how widespread was the practice of political agronomy without a more comprehensive survey of leasing practices and local politics. William Blacker claimed that landlord-sponsored subdivision to create forty-shilling freehold voters was rare, and that subdivision was more often the result of land-jobbing, especially on Church lands.[244] Much depended on the concentration of land ownership and the political ambitions and skills of landowners in a constituency, and on varying judgements about the economic costs of political leases.[245] It is hazardous to generalize even about a single estate. The third marquess of Downshire, for example, was a far more reckless practitioner of political agronomy than her heir.[246] The ninth earl of Abercorn was much more politically active than his father, and much more concerned to maximize political patronage on his estate. It was observed that in the parish of Ardstraw, Co. Tyrone, 'the same mistake is made here as elsewhere: short leases with old lives to enable the tenants to vote and the landlords to keep them in subjugation.'[247] This would not have been said of the eighth earl. James Hamilton recognized the loyalty of tenants who paid rent as fully as possible, given economic circumstances, and who, if voters, obeyed their landlord's wishes at the polls.[248] Whatever the extent of political agronomy may have been, it is important to recognize the historic link that Victorians made between the forty-shilling franchise, the expansion of political tenures, and the per-petuation of tenant right. For mid-nineteenth century tenants, there was a political basis to the tenures held by their fathers and forefathers. The tenant-right advocate Robert Donnell was wildly exaggerating when he wrote of the eighteenth century that 'the ordinary lease in Ulster was political. It was granted as a qualification for the franchise, at the desire of the landlord more than that of the tenant. . . . The truth is, the tenant was not half as desirous of dividing his farm as the landlord was of doubling his votes.'[249] But Donnell did have a point. Even the agent of the earl of Belmore's County Tyrone estate linked the forty-shilling freehold boom with the perpetuation of the custom of tenant right in 1873: 'Tenant right has greatly increased and has been very materially changed by custom since 1785. I think the tenancies increased to a very injurious extent in those years when voters were in great demand, and the difficulty since is to reduce them.'[250]

The forty-shilling freehold was not the only political basis for tenant right. The behaviour of tenants during the United Irish disturbances and uprising of the 1790s, or in relation to less political and more localized outrages against landlords, agents, or tenants, served as even stronger pretexts for 'updating' tenant-right claims. When paternal alignment of the tenantry underneath its gentry leadership became frayed at the end of the century, great confidence was placed in the ability of landed and wealthy men to maintain a threatened hegemony. Thomas Pemberton, the ninth earl of Abercorn's trusted political advisor, insisted in 1793 that 'nothing will more effectually tend to produce quiet than the public declarations of persons of respectability expressive of their loyalty.'[251] James Hamilton, Jr., in his typically optimistic manner, expressed the same confidence six years later: 'The people of the north and the rich merchants especially are every day more and more reconciled to a union, and their opinions are always retailed among the lower class, who never fail to be governed by them.'[252] Lapses in loyalty were accordingly blamed on the social weakness of the gentry, as Hamilton implied in this oddly phrased remark: 'The self-dread so very early discovered by the middling sort of gentry in the north give[s] greater confidence to the lower class than any other circumstance.'[253] As the end of the century neared, religious groups became more self-consciously vocal, and none more so than Presbyterians. Their close affiliation with the radical and revolutionary politics of Belfast was alarming to the estate agents, who felt that even the Catholics on the estate were more loyal than Presbyterians.[254] A large region south of Derry, which included the estate, was the only area outside the linen triangle to be defined as a proclaimed district by the government in 1798.[255] In this atmosphere tenants might take the opportunity to rest their claims to renewal on their loyal behaviour. F. E. Foljambe wished to restrict his Fermanagh tenantry to twenty-one-year leases 'except for those yeomenry who stood forward with so much honor to themselves and advantage to the country in the late unnatural rebellion who I wish to reward for their loyalty and patriotism by such additional terms according to their merits as you who are the best able to judge of them may think proper not exceeding the term of 28 years.'[256] General Knox, a commander of yeomen wrote in 1797 that in order to secure the Union of Great Britain and Ireland all landlords should give a preference of 10% to the old tenants.[257] The agent on the Barrett-Lennard estate, having considered the claim of a tenant with one life left in his lease, remarked to Barrett in 1812: 'At present I shall only say that his family during the last unfortunate rebellion were deeply implicated and his brother lost his life in consequence.'[258] An Antrim tenant, David Kennedy, explained in 1816 his behaviour during the uprising in the following terms. He claimed that he occupied a small part of the farm held in his family for at least a century past. Your petitioner inherited with this small patrimony the affection of his ancestors for the British constitution, and zealously active in its defence, he exerted his utmost ability to them though [sic] spreading torrent of disaffection; when marked out by reason for its victim, he with the greatest difficulty saved his life by flying to Scotland, and when the fury of the rebellion burst forth, his house, furniture, and every movable effect became prey to the flames. With other suffering loyalists, your petitioner received . . . encouragement to build on his farm and in consequence laid out in building dwelling house and offices about the sum of £400.[259]

Finally, it should be remembered that it was not necessary to refer specifically to the universal crisis of the late 1790s if one's behaviour in a more localized dispute could be articulated. One example of a more local nature concerns a Leitrim man whose father's life-lease from Lady Playdell had expired. He pointed out that he was the eldest son of Philip O'Dolan, 'a tenant that was of infinite use to your father when a Mr. Carleton, who held seven farms on his estate, proposed to pay no rent. . . .' His defence of the landlord against Carleton 'made a number of enemies of our family since.'[260] The agent referred to Andrew O'Dolan a month later as 'the last of that old stock that has a claim on you; his father certainly was the most respectable resident tenant on the upper Doobally estate.'[261] Later in the nineteenth century, tenants again found useful expressions of support for landlord hegemony. A memorial of 1869 from the Orange Order on the Drapers' company estate claimed for its members ancestral ties to the planters and declared that they 'have no desire to see any change in our landlords, as advocated by a small section of the community led by a few designing men.'[262] The appeal to a moral economy between landlord and tenant, whose rules superseded the market economy and the legal contract, was sustained by a wide variety of responsible behaviour, and did not depend only on the heroic feats marked in the collective consciousness by the dates 1641, 1690, and 1798.

PRIVILEGE, COMPETITION, AND DISPLACEMENT

The essential policy of the plantation élite and its predominant legacy was to segregate the natives and the newcomers geographically and in terms of their tenure. This strategy was especially aggressive in the early decades of the plantation. In 1616, one Robert McClellan was to pay 8d. an acre and 'erect and build a road and village of twenty houses at the least within the tenure of one year next, beginning from May next and to settle inhabitants therein of British. He is likewise to plant and people the country with British tenants within the time aforesaid and to muster and keep horses and footmen.'[263] As a result of the compromises of the 1620s, the native Irish, originally excluded from the plantation scheme, were allowed to hold legal tenures. A 1630 lease of Castle Stewart, County Tyrone, specified that the lessee be allowed to make leases to mere Irish no more than forty-one years or three lives, and that they were required to build houses together and not dispersedly.[264] But under the penal laws of the eighteenth century, only Protestants were allowed to hold leases for lives, and between 1704 and 1778 Catholics could hold leases for no longer than 31 years.[265] Throughout this period, leases typically included a clause stating that the tenant 'shall not set same nor any part thereof to any but a British tradesman nor alien any part to any person whosoever without consent.'[266] Those natives who were given determinable leases early in the century out of economic necessity were replaced as soon as sufficient numbers of newcomers were available, or give shorter or at-will terms.[267] Oliver Plunkett, the Catholic archbishop of Armagh, linked the mobility of Catholics to the discriminatory leasing policy of local landlords in a letter of 1675:

> Sometimes it happens that a parish which one year has 200 Catholic families will not have thirty the following year, as happened in various parishes of the diocese of Armagh this year, because the Catholics, being as a rule lease-holders, often lose their leases, which are given to Protestants or Presbyterians or Anabaptists or Quakers. These are the dominant sects here and every time a new colony of them arrive, the poor Catholics are put aside.[268]

A detailed leasebook *c.* 1700 from the manor of Castledillon in Armagh reveals a similar policy.[269] On the Bath estate around Farney in County Monaghan a pattern emerged in which the initial terminable leases given to Catholics were replaced with shorter leases or at-will tenancies to those Catholics seeking to renew their tenure.[270] As the eighteenth century advanced, these strategies continued to operate in piecemeal and opportunistic fashion. 'I would prefer Protestant tenants whenever it can be done without oppression to the poor people, the ancient inhabitants of the land,' wrote the agent on Lord Uxbridge's land south of Newry in 1768.[271] Two years later, Uxbridge directed his agents to replace troublesome tenants with good Protestants from the nearby town of Omeath. These were to be given a minimum of twelve acres each, and some worthy souls were to have their holdings expanded. Uxbridge concluded: 'It is wholesome to seek opportunities of turning out tenants and never omit using them when they happen.'[272] Court minutes of the Drapers' company in 1821 record that despite attempts to be non-sectarian, the court had concluded that Protestants were the only tenants with the necessary civility to warrant leases.[273] The Fishmongers' company awarded renewals with leases only to Protestant occupiers in the more fertile lowlands of the estate.[274]

The success of these policies varied widely in Ulster, with the result that there were marked geographic differences in the balance of sectarian occupation in the province. Smyth explored evidence listing immigrants as 'English' and 'English and Scots' and found that the areas of Ulster most successfully colonized were Antrim, most of Down and Londonderry, north Armagh, east Donegal, and a core surrounding the lakes of Fermanagh. Smyth envisioned a 'segregation-dislocation index' by which the intensity of colonial settlement might be measured. The index would produce the following picture:

> This core of planter settlement pivots around three interlocked areas – east Londonderry, coastal and mid-Antrim, . . . and north and central Armagh where eighteen to twenty-eight percent of all townlands enumerated appear to be the sole preserve of the settlers. A domain area with eight to twelve percent of townlands segregated can be identified for the remainder of northeast Ulster, with secondary cores of equal strength emerging in east Donegal and Fermanagh.[275]

Smyth also noticed that the cementing of economic and cultural links through an urban network was a defining characteristic of the settlement cores.[276]

The nineteenth-century inheritance of these sectarian policies was widespread ethnic segregation.[277] On the Abercorn estate in the 1830s, 'the valleys are filled with Protestants chiefly of the Scotch churches, the mountains are tenanted by Catholics.'[278] The Catholics on the Gosford estate were heavily concentrated in the poorer rented lands.[279] On the Drapers' company estate the Protestant population was concentrated in the prosperous division of Moneymore surrounding that town, while the Catholics resided for the most part in the mountainous and infertile areas. On the southern Brackaslieve-gallon division, according to one report of 1817, 'the larger part of the inhabitants of this division are descended from the aboriginal Irish.' This was in contrast to the Ballynascreen division, described by the Drapers' company agent in 1821 as follows:

> It appears probable that the inhabitants of it were descended from Scotch ancestors who settled there anterior to the Reformation; the reason for this supposition as to the period of settlement being formed arises from the circumstance of the great proportion of Catholics above that of Protestants. The difference in appearance of the inhabitants of the Ballynascreen division and the Brackaslievegallon division is very striking and illustrates the well-known distinction between the leading features in the Scotch and Irish characters.[280]

On the Fishmongers' estate, according to one observer, 'the Protestant tenantry are principally settled in the vicinity of Lough Foyle and towards the southern extremity of the estate, and we were informed that the proportion of Protestants to Catholics is greater on this estate than most of the others in the county.'[281] A Fishmongers' deputation recorded in 1820 that the several mountainous districts of the estate were inhabited chiefly by Catholics.[282]

The geographic differential of the ethnic makeup of estates is an important context for the nature of the Protestant colonial *mentalité* in general and the nature of historical claims to tenure in particular.[283] The seventeenth-century plantation became concentrated in collective memory in the dramatic events of 1640s and 1689. While much of the eighteenth century might be considered a period of stability with regard to the land question, the resilience, relevance, and power of these memories can easily be understated. Bartlett describes the *mentalité* of eighteenth-century Protestant society as follows:

> During this period the dizzy fluctuation of fortunes, the constant revolutions actual or feared, had shaped a distinctive Protestant mindset. Brought to the very edge of destruction; then redeemed by the actions of Cromwell and the Cromwellians; then threatened by Charles II's complaisant attitude towards Irish Catholics, he had dammed himself forever in Protestant eyes by inventing the category 'innocent papist' to whom some land could be restored; then once more plunged into mortal peril through the action of the Catholic King, James II, and his Catholic Lord Deputy, Richard Talbot, earl of Tyrconnell; and then deliverance at the hands of William. These experiences and the interpretation put on them by Protestants were of vital importance in determining both the character of the Protestant state and the attitude of the Protestants towards the vanquished Catholics.[284]

This attitude towards vanquished Catholics was bound together with attitudes toward property. 'The image of the dispossessed Catholic masses patiently waiting and indeed scheming to recover their ancestral lands,' writes Bartlett, 'was largely a Protestant invention, through one that proved remarkably resilient, surviving well into the nineteenth century and beyond.'[285] In terms of their security of tenure, the privileged position of Protestants was threatened not so much by the apocalyptic return of an avenging material and political force (although the importance of this has already been recognized), but by the more mundane threat of economic and tenurial competition from Catholics. This threat was particularly serious in the first century of colonization. The evidence suggests that the native Irish as a group were able to pay higher rents than the newcomers during the first phases of the plantation,[286] though 'British and Irish tenants paid the same rents for the same sort of land' on the Balfour estate in Fermanagh.[287] A report of 1627 found that the natives

> are content to take the land for less a time and to give a greater rent than the English are willing or able to do, not only because they may better do

it, who spend not the tenth part which the English spendeth in buildiing and fencing, in diet and apparel, but also because out of an inveterate malice towards the English they will rather impoverish themselves than not outbid the English, that so they might get the lands into their own hands and in the end overthrow the English plantation in that important part of the country, which, excepting the mountainous part, were most fit to be all planted with English.[288]

The ability of newcomers to outbid natives for land indicated the economic and political success of the plantation, and this came to prevail only gradually.

Given the ambiguities associated with the productive abilities of natives and newcomers, some landlords whose properties were peripheral to the areas of intensive colonization preferred Irish tenants to Scots or Englishmen in the eighteenth century. The Williamite military chaplain William Storey wrote in 1692 that landlords 'who still smart of their former calamities will rather set their land to an Irishman or a Scot that shall give them sixpence an acre more and never improve it further, than to an English farmer that, if he had encouragement, would in a few years make good improvements.'[289] Some landlords preferred that the native tenants stay as they were, dominated by priests and with no threatening social aspirations. Henry Moore, the fourth earl of Drogheda, preferred them to Protestant tenants because 'there is not one of them but wears a sword and thinks himself as good a gentleman as I am; and possibly would offer to fight me should I find fault with him.' Archbishop William King said that the 'covetousness' of Protestant landlords led them to prefer papist tenants 'who live in a miserable and sordid manner and will always outbid a Protestant.' And again: 'The gentle[men], I mean Protestants, govern their popish tenants by their priests and the more obnoxious these are to the laws the more the people will be under the landlords' power.' This opinion was held mostly by Church of Ireland officials and landlords, not so much by merchant or placeholding Protestants.[290] Lord Rossmore of County Monaghan regarded Irish tenants as better than English, and instructed that their tenures be set for seven years.[291] Robert Molesworth reported in 1710 that tenants in Fingal, Co. Dublin, had exhausted the land during the last thirty years without a rent increase and complained that 'unimproving, idle people would not live on an estate though it were their [sic] own property, much less than when tenants, and all those bastard, degenerate English tenants, to whom John gave leases for lives soon after the reducing of Ireland, are ten times worse than the mere Fingalians, though those be bad enough.'[292] Irish tenants on the Barrett-Lennard estate around Clones, Co. Monaghan, were thought to be better at paying rent than the Protestants. The agent remarked in 1764 of three Protestant tenants offering to renew: 'The people I know not, but if they are industrious and the times be good, I fancy they may, from what I hear of them, be able to pay the rent. The rest of the land west of the river is held by Papists in small parcels, and [they] will agree to pay 14s. or 14s. 6d. per acre rather than quit, for they say they know not where to go. These poor people oftentimes pay their rents better than abler tenants.'[293]

The geographical context and the particular characteristics of an estate are crucial determinants of the severity of this competition for land between ethnic groups. In areas of weak Protestant presence, as in Cork, there was a softening of sectarian tenure policy by mid-century. The estate agents of one landowner were told in 1716 that 'you may turn out as many Papists as you think fit, provided you can get good Protestant tenants and that you are sure will pay their rents as well.' But by 1750, he felt that a tenant's 'religion is nothing to him if he pays his rent well . . . ' and he refused to allow a Catholic to be turned out.[294] In areas with a more substantial but not dominant Protestant presence, the situation differed. The Abercorns were said to be relatively tolerant of Catholics, compared to other landowners in the area. A Protestant minister testifying before the Devon commission praised the managers of the Abercorn estate for their tradition of religious tolerance, which he contrasted to the behaviour of George Knox, a neighbouring landowner, who habitually replaced Catholic tenants with Protestants.[295]

As Chapter 3 articulates in greater detail, Protestant tenants were in the paradoxical position of claiming rights as tenants and as citizens for helping to establish a system of competition for land and employment that was blind to the particular ethnic characteristics of the competitors. Because they survived by competiton with the natives, 'they had roots in the land virtually as strong as those natives.' This generated 'a popular kind of settlement colonial legend. The settlement had survived because of its masses.'[296] Chapter 1 explained how under full-blown agrarian capitalism the actual landlords, and the actual tenants, are irrelevant so long as property relations function properly. In the colonial situation, however, the particular relationship between the landlord and the tenant was subsumed under the universal rules of private property only with great difficulty. Planters established landed estates in Ireland only by way of landlord-tenant relationships in which the need to recognize ties to the land always haunted the progressive landlord. Although economic solvency was universally required of tenants, the right of renewal was still considered by many landlords to be more important than the landlord's desire to maximize the rent.[297] The plantation project offered clear and important privileges to immigrant Protestants, but it never fully protected them from native economic competition. The protection they did receive dwindled as landlords lost control of the distribution of economic opportunities with the rise of the rural textile trades and as penal restrictions on tenure were relaxed with the reforms of the later eighteenth century. 'The onset of capitalist economic relationships, the extension of centralized state power in opposition to landlords who had previously been the only power in their domains, and eventually democratization,' according to Wright, 'opened up spaces for the native society,' which in turn 'ensured that *de facto* dominance of the citizen element could no longer be preserved without more visible and conscious effort.'[298] Wright named the effects of the dissolution of this privilege the 'settler displacement effect.'

One of the ways the displacement effect manifested itself politically was in the Catholic presence in the agitation for tenant right in the 1840s. A priest speaking at the Loughbrickland Tenant Right meeting in 1848 emphasized to his largely Protestant audience that Catholics were no different in terms of property rights than Protestants because plantation landlords had broken the rules and let to Catholics as well.[299] Another manifestation was Orangeism. William Mayne felt the displeasure of local Protestants when he was seen to be encouraging industrious Catholics on the Barrett-Lennard estate around Clones. He wrote in 1810 about a 'respectable Catholic who is very wealthy' who he thought should be encouraged to establish a tanning business. But he added: 'there are a description of creatures in Ireland denominated Orangemen that can't bear to see a Catholic encouraged. As I have uniformly dealt perfectly equal to all description of religions, I am considered by the Orange party as only a so-so kind of man, and have received many anonymous letters thereon, which I take no notice of.'[300] The question of the land was never far beneath the surface of Orange-Catholic conflicts. The crucial function of the Orange-men, according to Wright, was to give threatened Protestants west of the Bann 'courage to stay rather than emigrate.'[301]

The final threat to customary tenures, blind to ethnic character, dismissive of both geography and history, destructive of ties between and among tenants and landlords, was the market itself. Tenants who might have only voiced a hereditary claim to their farms were forced to proclaim their competitiveness and to recognize the market value of their farm if they were to continue in possession. When Augustine Brogan proposed to rent land near Virginia, Co. Cavan, in 1726, he noted that it had been enjoyed by his father and grand-father, but he also added an offer to pay 'as much as any responsible tenant will bid for said lands.'[302] The most limited expression of the right of renewal, the greatest contraction of ancestral claims, the near abandonment of extra-economic justifications for continuous tenancy, was based on the mere existence of the tenant as an economic competitor. For the marginal and impoverished smallholder it may have reflected the claim for renewal at its weakest point; for a capitalist strong farmer it may have indicated the ascendant strength of his purely economic claim for tenure. In this way it may be seen as an empty claim – totally dependent upon its context – a short step from the total disappearance of the custom under the rule of private property. The anxiety produced by the uncertainties surrounding one's ability to compete in the market for land, combined with political uncertainties over the relationship between landlords and the state, brought the issue of tenant right into the public sphere of the nineteenth century. The final chapter examines this subject in greater detail.

NOTES

1 The pre-existing Gaelic pattern had a great influence on the plantation settlement pattern in Tyrone, as Robinson has pointed out: 'At every level the native social hierarchy was replaced by a new order which had remarkably similar spheres of influence to the old: the ballyboe was perpetuated as the territorial unit in leases granted to plantation tenant farmers just as the ballybetagh became the new estate, while the larger 'countries' of the local Irish chiefs were invariably the preplantation equivalents of the baronies or plantation precincts; each of the latter was to have its principal undertaker in the plantation scheme.' Robinson, 'British settlement in county Tyrone, 1610–1660' in *I.E.S.H.*, v, 1978, p. 11.

2 Perceval-Maxwell, *Scottish migration*, pp. 148–9. This was also a problem for McClelland, the head tenant on the Haberdashers' and Clothworkers' proportions. Ibid., pp. 173–9. See also Gillespie, *Colonial Ulster*, pp. 7–28; David Dickson, 'An economic history of the Cork region in the eighteenth century' (Ph.D. dissertation, Trinity College Dublin, 1977), p. 58; Roy Foster, *Modern Ireland 1600–1972* (London, 1988), p. 61.

3 Robert Maxwell to Provost [?] Seele, T.C.D., MUN/P/24/144. Ambrose Bedell to provost, n.d. [c. 1661], ibid., MUN/P/24/152.

4 T.W. Moody, 'The treatment of the native population under the scheme for the plantation in Ulster' in *I.H.S.*, i, no. 1 (1939), pp. 62–3. Perceval-Maxwell, *Scottish migration*, pp. 211–14.

5 Ibid., p. 212.

6 Ibid., pp. 235–42. For the details of the grants to these three men and their activities during the early plantation, see ibid., *passim*.

7 Peter Roebuck, 'Making of an Ulster great estate: the Chichesters, 1599–1648' in *Proceedings of the Royal Irish Academy*, lxxix, sect. C, no. 1 (1979), p. 15.

8 Hunter, 'Ulster plantation', p. 424. The mortgaging of leaseholds is also documented in Gillespie, *Colonial Ulster*, pp. 79–80. The details of one sale on Chichester's County Antrim property reveal the operation of this market. Article between Patrick McClennon and William Conyngham, 24 Oct. 1653, P.R.O.N.I., Castle Stewart papers, D1618/15/2/5.

9 The Fermanagh agent Eleazar Middleton was able to threaten one tenant in 1632: 'I have not as yet set anew, but unless he take it of me shortly, I will set it to another.' Johnston, 'Balfour rentals,' p. 101, 158.

10 Lease from Trinity College to James Hamilton, 1622, T.C.D., MUN/P/24/16; lease from Earl of Donegal to Timothy Taylor, 1 Nov. 1656, P.R.O.N.I., Castle Stewart papers, D1618/15/2/11; lease by James Wills to James Boyd, Drumellton, Co. Cavan, 1728, N.L.I. *Reports on private collections*, x, no. 273, Fegan papers (second report) in the custody of A. G. Fegan, Market Square, Cavan.

11 Concerning one of her leases of land in County Down, Lady Ardglass was informed in 1688: 'there is a clause that he shall not sell his interest but no penalty if he does. The clause runs in these words, viz, "shall not sell his interest in said premises to any person whatsoever without consent".' Anthony Lock to Lady Ardglass, n.d [c. 1688], P.R.O.N.I., Ardglass papers, D970/1/19. In 1636 tenants of the earl of Antrim were pardoned for alienating land without a crown licence. Randolph Buthill to earl of Antrim, 14 July 1636, P.R.O.N.I., Lenox-Conyngham papers, D1449/1/3.

12 Crawford, 'Landlord-tenant relations,' p. 10.

13 Gillespie, *Settlement and survival*, p. lii; mortgage of Bryan oge McMahon to Sir Robert Forth, 9 Nov. 1631, N.L.I., *Reports on private collections*, i, no. 9, p. 190, Madden Papers in possession of J. W. R. Madden, Hilton Park, Clones, Co. Monaghan; William Layfield to William Waring, 24 July 1674, P.R.O.N.I., Waring papers, D695/98; entry book of tenancies on Clanbrassil estate, Ards, Co. Down, 1615–1678, p. 1, P.R.O.N.I., Clanbrassil papers, T761/3; Mary, Dowager Lady Shelbourne to Alexander Murray, 22 Nov. 1705, P.R.O.N.I., Murray of Broughton papers, D2860/9/7; Edmund Kaine to John Armstrong, 13 Mar. 1713, P.R.O.N.I., Barrett-Lennard papers, film 170/2.

14 'A true relation concerning the tenure of the quarter of Mullynesoll, being a parcel of land within the Baroney of Tirhugh in County Donegal, by John Knox' n.d. [c. 1641], T.C.D., MUN/P/24/134.

15 Hunter, 'Ulster plantation,' p. 517–24.

16 Duffy, 'Evolution of estate properties,' p. 96.

17 Petrie also claimed that he built a slated house of lime and stone besides four more houses for English and British tenants at a cost of £300, and that his own and his tenant's cattle had been driven and impounded on Price's orders, 'the place being frequented much with thieves and rebels.' Chancery bill of Thomas Petrie and William Sandes, attorney of the Exchequer court, 1625, N.L.I., *Reports on private collections*, v, no. 142, p. 1326: Shirley Papers, in the possession of Col. E.C. Shirley, Lough Fea, Carrickmacross, Co. Monaghan.

18 Perceval-Maxwell, *Scottish migration*, pp. 140–1. Bodley found that one estate in south Tyrone had been abandoned almost as soon as the immigrants set their eyes on it. Gillespie, *Settlement and survival*, pp. xvi–xxv; J.D. Johnston, 'Plantation of county Fermanagh,' pp. 195–8; Hunter, 'Ulster plantation,' pp. 424–5. Philip Robinson, 'British settlement of county Tyrone, 1610–66' in *I.E.S.H.*, v (1978), p. 25. Gillespie provides a number of examples of tenants in east Ulster abandoning one landlord for another to get better leases and therefore higher social standing. Gillespie, *Colonial Ulster*, p. 118.

19 Johnston, 'Balfour rentals,' p. 95.

20 Moody, *Londonderry plantation*, p. 336; Hunter, 'Ulster plantation,' pp. 400–406; Johnston, 'Balfour rentals', pp. 96–7. Gillespie highlights the practice of vetting prospective tenants who petitioned for land. Gillespie, *Colonial Ulster*, pp. 132–33, 136.

21 Comment on lease, c. 1622, T.C.D., MUN/P/24/16.

22 Petition of Robert Maxwell, 16 Mar. 1629, T.C.D., MUN/P/24/76. Consent of various tenants to increased rent, 11 Apr. 1636, T.C.D., MUN/P/24/105. Years were added to the leases of these tenants. Notice from William Newman to various tenants, 16 Apr. 1636, T.C.D., MUN/P/24/106.

23 R.A. Gore to Provost and Senior Fellows, 21 April 1636, T.C.D., MUN/P/24/109; Hunter, 'Ulster plantation', pp. 520–25; Johnston, 'Plantation of county Fermanagh,' pp. 196–8.

24 Aidan Clarke, 'The Irish economy 1600–60' in Moody, Martin, and Byrne, (eds.), *New history of Ireland*, iii, pp. 170–1.

25 Duffy writes that 'the emergence of about twenty large estates in both counties is testimony to the ultimate failure of the plantation' in Cavan and Monaghan. Duffy, 'Evolution of estate properties,' pp. 98–100.

26 Hunter, 'Ulster plantation,' pp. 407, 417.

27 Clay, *Economic expansion*, i, p. 91; Gillespie, *Colonial Ulster*, p. 191; Rosalind Mitcheson and Peter Roebuck, 'Introduction' in Mitcheson and Roebuck (eds.), *Economy and society in Scotland and Ireland, 1500–1939* (Edinburgh, 1988), p. 2. James Stevens Curl, *The Londonderry plantation* (Chichester, 1986), p. 97. John Temple, lessee of Slutmulrony, claimed that all his English tenants were murdered in the first days of the rebellion, 'some of them as they were ploughing on ye said lands.' Memo on Sir John Temple's leases, n.d. [c. 1661], T.C.D., MUN/P/24/153. The estate of Hugh Crofton in Sligo was untenanted and lying waste in 1640 because of 'the trouble of the times.' Lord Crofton to Henry Crofton, 10 Nov. 1640, P.R.O.N.I., O'Hara papers, T2812/1/3.

28 Perceval-Maxwell, *Scottish migration*, p. xxiii. See Gillespie, *Colonial Ulster*, pp. 81–83 and Gillespie, 'The Irish economy at war, 1641–1652' in Janet Ohlmeyer (ed.), *Ireland from independence to occupation, 1641–1660* (London, 1995), p. 178.

29 George Blacker to James Judgan, 6 Oct. 1657, P.R.O.N.I., Castle Stewart papers, D1618/15/2/14.

30 Brendan McKinney, 'The seventeenth-century land settlement in Ireland: towards a statistical interpretation' in Ohlmeyer, *Ireland from independence to occupation*, p. 198. Clarke concludes that 'by 1641 the depression of the small freeholders was almost complete.' Clarke, 'The Irish economy 1600–60,' p. 170.

31 'Copy of king's letter to provost, etc., in favour of Sir John Temple, master of the rolls, and his brother Thomas Temple,' 13 Mar. 1661, T.C.D., MUN/P/24/149.

32 Captain Throgmorton [?] to Rev. Magennis, 31 May 1659, P.R.O.N.I., Waring papers, D695/141.

33 William Waring to William Layfield, 17 Mar. and 26 June 1674, ibid., D695/9, 13B.

34 Gillespie, *Settlement and survival*, pp. xii.

35 Edward Dupre Atkinson, *An Ulster parish, being a history of Donaghcloney (Waringstown)* (Dublin, 1898), pp. 18–47, 34–48. Thanks are due to Dr. Bill Crawford for alerting me to this source.

36 James Leslie to Francis Guthrie, 4 Apr. 1652, P.R.O.N.I., Guthrie Castle papers, T1547/27.

37 Idem, 11 Jan. 1656, ibid., T1547/308.

38 Robert Buchanan to Guthrie, 13 Jan. 1656, and William Lennox to Patrick Leslie, 23 Jan. 1660, ibid., T1547/31, 46.

39 Bishop of Raphoe to Laird of Guthrie, 18 Apr. 1662, ibid., T1547/49.

40 Pat Leslie to Laird of Guthrie, 13 Apr. 1663, ibid., T1547/51.

41 'Petition of Robert Maxwell, subtenant to Lady Ruish, widow of Sir Frances Ruish, of two and a half townlands in the parish of Toaghy, Co. Armagh,' 16 Mar. 1629, T.C.D., MUN/P/24/76.

42 Martha O'Neille to Colonel Robert Steward, 29 Mar. 1653, P.R.O.N.I., Castle Stewart papers, D1618/15/2/4.

43 Unsigned letter, c. 1655, ibid., D1618/15/2/9.

44 'Report of the bishop of Derry and the archbishop of Armagh on the petitions of the tenants of London companies' land in Co. Derry,' 18 Oct. 1661, P.R.O.N.I., Ellis papers, D683/133.

45 Macafee, 'Maghera region,' pp. 72–75. According to Alan Gailey, much of the dissemination of Presbyterianism in the period 1641–60 was limited to areas easily accessible from the coast: north Down and south Antrim, north Antrim and Derry, the Lough Swilly region and the Lough Foyle area. Gailey found only one more new Presbyterian settlement in the period 1661–90. See Alan Gailey, 'The Scots element in north Irish popular culture' in *Ethnologia Europaea*, viii, no. 1 (1975), pp. 2–22. See also E.A. Currie, 'The evolution of cultural landscapes in the northwest and southeast regions of County Derry in the eighteenth and nineteenth centuries with particular reference to the Rae and Moyola valleys' (Ph.D. dissertation, Queen's University of Belfast, 1981), pp. 59–60, and Robinson, *Plantation of Ulster*, p. 97.

46 William King, *The state of the protestants* (London, 1691) cited in Curl, *Londonderry plantation*, p. 98.

47 Crawford, 'Landlord-tenant relations,' p. 13; Gillespie, *Settlement and survival*, p. xi.

48 The rental of nine townlands of the Trinity College estate also dropped from £201 to £137 as a result of the wars. 'An account of how the college lands held by Captain Hamilton are now set and how before the wars,' [n.d.], T.C.D., MUN/P/24/273.

49 Thirty-two tates of land were rented to thirteen tenants for eighteen years from 1693, and the rent-roll divided the rent into six-year intervals, with an increase of twenty to thirty percent added to each successive interval. 'A rent-roll for what the lands are set for eighteen years remaining from May next [16]93 in the county of Fermanagh,' May 1693, T.C.D., MUN/P/24/244.

50 Certificate of the investigation of Adam Nixon, Thomas Richardson, and Alexander Montgomery into the value of Slutmulrony, 27 Mar. 1707, T.C.D., MUN/P/24/343.

51 L.M. Cullen, *An economic history of Ireland since 1660* (London, 1972) pp. 7–25.

52 Jonathan Cooper to Thady Coane, 28 Oct. 1714, P.R.O.N.I., Castletown papers, T2825/C/25/22; Lucy Folliott to William Conolly, 28 [June] 1724, ibid., T2825/C/29/3.

53 Memo by Robert McCausland, 2 Jan. 1721, 'An account of leases soon out in Limavady, 1728,' 'An account of leases and terms of years to come from November 1725,' N.L.I., Conolly papers, film 6950. See also E.A. Currie, 'Fining down the rents: the management of the Conolly estates in Ireland, 1734–1800' in *Derriana* (1979), pp. 25–38.

54 John B. Cunningham, 'William Conolly's Ballyshannon estate, 1718–26' in *Donegal Annual*, no. 33 (1981), pp. 27–44.

55 These refer to the Edenderry estate in Leinster. Letters of Meredyth to Blundell, 1707–19, P.R.O.N.I., Downshire papers D607/A/11.

56 Letters to Michael Ward, 1725–1728, P.R.O.N.I., Castleward papers, D2092/1/3, 4.

57 L.M. Cullen, 'Population trends in seventeenth-century Ireland' in *Economic and social review*, vi (1974–5), p. 149; Currie, 'Evolution,' pp. 53–6.

58 George Rawdon to William Waring, 11 Oct. 1667, P.R.O.N.I., Waring MSS, D695/146.

59 William Gore to Provost [?] Seele, 28 Nov. 1672, T.C.D., MUN/P/24/180. Strettler remarked that in 1672 when the estate had been leased to Lord Massereene, 'the landlord was anxious to get tenants at any rate,' indicating that there were few to choose from. Rental of the Bellaghy estate by Amos Strettle, P.R.O.N.I., D2094/21.

60 Gillespie, *Settlement and survival*, p. xxxii; see also William Waring to William Layfield, 16 March 1674, P.R.O.N.I., Waring papers, D695/10.

61 Gillespie, *Settlement and survival*, p. xxxii.

62 Edward Fletcher to Dacre Barrett, 22 Jan. 1684 and 21 May 1684, P.R.O.N.I., Barrett-Lennard papers, film 170/2; Anthony Lock to Lady Ardglass, various letters 1688–89,

P.R.O.N.I., Ardglass papers, D970/1; [?] Conolly to the Corporation of Derry, 25 July 1691, P.R.O.N.I., Lenox-Conyngham papers, D1449/12/5; Mary Aldworth to Keane O'Hara, 14 Jan. 1697, P.R.O.N.I., O'Hara Papers, T2812/4/198.

63 Memorandum of proposals for a lease with Symon Richardson, excusing him from certain obligations in the event of a rebellion, n.d., [c. 1676], T.C.D., MUN/P/24/199.

64 'An appeal to the Honourable Society of the Governor and Assistants of London for the new plantation of Ulster to let their lands to their respected lessees in fee farm,' n.d. [c. 1680], P.R.O.N.I., Lenox-Conyngham papers, D1449/1/6.

65 Thomas Bligh to Peter Westenra, 11 Jan. 1687, P.R.O.N.I., Rossmore papers, T2929/1/6; idem, 4 Oct. 1688, ibid., T2929/1/21.

66 Idem, 26 Nov. 1687, ibid., T2929/1/16. In 1688 he decided to wait for the next parliament before making any decisions about his estate. Idem, 7 Feb. 1688, ibid., T2929/1/18.

67 Gillespie, *Settlement and survival*, p. lxiii; Walter Dawson to Dacre Barrett, 12 Mar. 1689, P.R.O.N.I., Barrett-Lennard papers, film 170/1; Curl, *Londonderry plantation*, pp. 102, 105. Most of the houses of Derry and Coleraine were demolished. Much timber was lost from the Vintners' proportion in 1688 and in the rebuilding of Derry and Coleraine. 'Rent-roll of Vintners' proportion of lands,' 10 Oct. 1718, P.R.O.N.I., D2094/21.

68 In the parish of Killelagh the old church had been demolished and in the words of the report, 'neither does there seem any necessity to rebuild it.' 'State of the diocese of Derry, 1693,' P.R.O.N.I., T505; Macafee, 'Maghera region,' p. 76.

69 Letter from Captain William Jackson's agent, 22 June 1691, P.R.O.N.I., film 146/9; Curl, *Londonderry plantation*, p. 97.

70 Currie, 'Evolution,' p. 55.

71 Gabriel Whistler to the Salters' company, 1691, reproduced in W.H. Maitland, *History of Magherafelt* (Cookstown, 1916), pp. 5–7, cited in Macafee, 'Maghera region,' p. 75.

72 Edward Fletcher to Lord Barrett, 29 Jan. 1684, P.R.O.N.I., Barrett-Lennard papers, film 170/2.

73 He gave a list of a dozen old tenants now residing in the town and 'out in the country.' George Hammersly to William Westgarth, 6 Nov. 1690, ibid., film 170/3; William Westgarth to Dacre Barrett, 31 July 1690, ibid., film 170/1; Thomas Wilson to Barrett, 8 July 1693, ibid., film 170/3.

74 Letters of Robert McCausland to William Conolly 1718–29, P.R.O.N.I., Castletown papers, T2825/C/27: Thomas Bligh to Peter Westenra, 28 May 1691, P.R.O.N.I., Rossmore papers, T2929/1/30; Edmund Kaine to Dacre Barrett, 1 Dec. 1716, P.R.O.N.I., Barrett-Lennard papers, film 170/2.

75 Hugh McNeely to Dacre Barrett, 22 May 1704, P.R.O.N.I., Barrett-Lennard papers, film 170/2; Edmund Kaine to Barrett, 14 Feb. 1710, ibid.; John Bayly to Edward Bayly, 1 May 1731, P.R.O.N.I., Anglesey papers, D619/21/A/6; George Knipe and Brian [?] Nevill to Barrett, 5 Feb. 1723, ibid., film 170/3. See also the O'Hara's efforts to keep tenants from leaving the estate. John Fleming to Keane O'Hara, 7 June 1692, P.R.O.N.I., O'Hara papers, T2812/4/45

76 See chapter 1, pp. 20–1.

77 See, for example, Roy Foster, *Modern Ireland, 1600–1972* (New York, 1988), pp. 1–78. He makes use of demographic generalities ('the great expansion of settler stock,' p. 14; ' . . . the continuity rather than displacement of population is what strikes us now', p. 72), but he concludes with an impressive cascade of adjectives embellishing 'the plantation idea, with its emphasis on segregation and native unreliability' p. 78.

78 Ibid., p. 78.

79 'The Whistler family had leased the entire estate from the company in 1627 and Gabriel had come into the lease in 1657 on the death of his uncle. The letter in 1691 was in reply to a demand for rent by the company and Gabriel was trying to argue that payment was not possible because of the serious losses incurred during the Williamite wars.' Macafee, 'Maghera region,' p. 75.

80 Macafee claims that the 1659 census proves otherwise but the statement that they were all on church lands seems to support Whistler; ibid.

81 Gabriel Whistler to the Salters' company, c. 1691, cited in Macafee, 'Maghera region,' p. 75.

82 Dickson, 'Cork region,' p. 186–189.

83 Thomas Power, *Land, politics, and society in eighteenth-century Tipperary* (Oxford, 1993), pp. 157–8. After 1815, 'a slump in cereal prices undermined the solvency of middlemen, allowing landlords the collective incentive to proceed against them more resolutely.' Ibid., p. 158.

84 Ferguson and Vance, *The tenure and improvement of land in Ireland*, p. 210.

85 Dickson, 'Cork region,' pp. 84, 183.

86 Ibid., p. 216. Earl McCartney expressed confidence in the strength of a covenant in a lease against alienation in 1802. The covenant was 'sufficiently strong. The lease will to a certainty be forfeited if alienated without consent.' [Earl McCartney] to [?], 12 Jan. 1802, P.R.O.N.I., McCartney papers, D572/18/51. The Cork landlord Viscount Perceval entered restrictive covenents into leases in order to 'have a just excuse for dividing their farms and setting the land to the utmost penny on turning them out as [his family will] judge most advisable'. Dickson, 'Cork region,' p. 185.

87 Stephen Silthorp to Arthur Maguire, 10 May 1756, P.R.O.N.I., Derby papers, film 368/1. He also complained that he might have to mortgage the lease or turn it into money.

88 Noble to Barrett-Lennard, 18 Feb. 1760, P.R.O.N.I., Barrett-Lennard papers, film 170/2.

89 Idem, 24 Apr. 1760, ibid. Still they never wavered from the policy of restricted leases. Thomas Noble explained in 1760: 'On any new leases to be made on your estate there will be proper care taken to throw in covenants against alienation or setting in small parcels without your consent, or in case of such alienation, to pay an additional acreable rent, which I think will prevent the same.' Barrett-Lennard was apparently applying this rule inconsistently, leaving many tenants with a grievance. Idem, 20 Apr. 1760, ibid.

90 The death of head tenants was often as useful as a lease expiration for those who sought to give the undertenants a direct lease. Henry Hatch to Blundell, 6 Dec. 1746, P.R.O.N.I., Downshire papers, D607/A23.

91 'Ever-rising rent-rolls made landlords less eager to enforce restrictive clauses in leases.' W.H. Crawford, 'The rise of the linen industry' in L.M. Cullen (ed.), *The formation of the Irish economy* (Cork, 1969), p. 33.

92 For the problems of Cork landowners with their autonomous and uncontrollable agents, see Dickson, 'Cork region,' pp. 218–19, 226, 233–4.

93 George Hammersly to William Westgarth, 6 Nov. 1690, P.R.O.N.I., Barrett-Lennard papers, film 170/3. The 1694 letters of Thomas Smith to Dacre Barrett record theft of cattle., ibid., film 170/2. 'Most of your tenants are very unwilling to own you as landlord until the kingdom be quite settled.' Walter Dawson to Dacre Barrett, 13 June 1692, ibid.

94 Rose Peyton to Keane O'Hara, 12 Mar. 1692, P.R.O.N.I., O'Hara papers, T2812/4/42.
95 Basil Brooke to provost, 27 June 1631, T.C.D., MUN/P/24/87. In 1682 a crooked seneschal in Donegal held court on a fair day in another town to frustrate the tenants. Ambrose Bedell to Provost Marsh, 14 May 1682, and Robert Spence to Marsh, 22 June 1682, T.C.D., MUN/P/24/222, 226. Hans Stevenson noted in reference to the troubles of the dissenting owners of the Clanbrassil estate in litigating to secure titles: 'the corruption of judges and juries is such that no man can be secure, let his title be [ever] so good.' Hans Stevenson to William Hamilton, 19 Jan. 1697, P.R.O.N.I., Clanbrassil papers, T761/7.
96 Hunter, 'Ulster plantation,' pp. 533–4.
97 Robert Ward to George Hamilton, 9 Nov. 1726, P.R.O.N.I., Castleward papers, D2092/1/4. Francis Lascells to Justice Ward, 6 Mar. 1734, ibid., D2092/1/4.
98 John Bayly to Edward Bayly, 29 Aug. 1734, P.R.O.N.I., Anglesey papers, D619/21/A/18.
99 Charles Ward to Michael Ward, 9 Nov. 1723, P.R.O.N.I., Castleward papers, D2092/1/2.
100 Henry Hatch to Henry Blundell, 7 Feb. 1746, P.R.O.N.I., Downshire papers, D607/A/23.
101 See the letters referring to Rowland Savage in P.R.O.N.I., Anglesey papers, D619/11, D619/21, D619/22/H, and the letters referring to James Savage in P.R.O.N.I., Downshire papers, D607/A.
102 E.A. Currie, 'The evolution of cultural landscapes in the north-west and south-east regions of county Derry in the eighteenth and nineteenth centuries' (Ph.D. Dissertation, Queen's University of Belfast, 1981), p. 195.
103 Power, *Tipperary*, pp. 132–33.
104 Ibid., pp. 122–24; Dickson, 'Cork region,' pp. 19–20, 94–5, 186–7.
105 Hunter, 'Ulster plantation,' pp. 501–3.
106 Sir James Hamilton to provost, 28 May 1610, T.C.D., MUN/P/24/4.
107 Ibid.
108 Hunter, 'Ulster plantation,' p. 503.
109 'Perspective on the Hamilton disinvolvement can be got from the fact that at this time the family acquired estates in Armagh and Cavan.' ibid., p. 508.
110 Ibid., pp. 506, 509.
111 Ibid., p. 533.
112 Joseph Hamilton to Provost George Brown, 6 Apr. 1697, T.C.D., MUN/P/24/245.
113 Ibid.
114 Moody, *Londonderry plantation*, pp. 311–35.
115 An appeal to the Honorable Society of the Governor and Assistants of London for the new plantation of Ulster to let their lands to their respected lessees in fee farm, n.d. [c. 1680], P.R.O.N.I., Lenox-Conyngham papers. D1449/1/6.
116 Ibid.
117 Blundell to Henry Gwyn, 3 Jan. 1720, P.R.O.N.I., Downshire papers, D607/12/A.
118 Meredyth to Blundell, 1 July 1720, ibid.
119 John Macoughtny to Lord Hillsborough, Nov. 1790, ibid., D607/A/406.
120 See P.R.O.N.I., Downshire papers, D607/A.
121 For Antrim middlemen, see Peter Roebuck, 'The making of an Ulster great estate.'
122 Currie, 'Evolution,' pp. 53–4; Curl, *Londonderry plantation*, p. 97. County Londonderry surpassed all other counties in Ireland in absenteeism. Ó Gráda, *New economic history,*

pp. 124–5. A history of the tenures of the various London companies is summarized in *The Irish land question and the twelve London companies in the county of Londonderry* (Belfast, 1869).

123 F.H.A. Aalen, *Man and the landscape of Ireland* (London, 1978), p. 144. Moody remarked that 'geographical circumstances have tended to isolate the whole Sperrin region and to make communications difficult between the Foyle and the Bann.' Moody, *The Londonderry plantation*, p. 52.

124 'During Tyrone's rebellion, when Elizabeth called on the City for men and money, loans of £20,000 and £60,000 were raised in successive years, 1598–9.' Moody, *The Londonderry plantation*, p. 62.

125 Ibid., p. 97.

126 Ibid., pp. 72, 158. A nineteenth-century surveyor of the Drapers' company estate felt compelled to make the same point as Moody: 'A very strong impression prevails in Ireland that the Company's Irish estates were free grants by James I and therefore that as no money was paid for them, the tenantry and others conceive that the companies are bound and can well afford to be liberal. It is not generally known that a very large sum was paid by the companies for their estates in Ireland, and that they were not by any means willing purchasers.' Report of a surveyor, minutes of the court of assistants, extracts relating to Irish estates, 20 Nov. 1856, Drapers' Hall, London, N.L.I., film 1530.

127 Macafee, 'Maghera region,' p. 75.

128 Currie, 'Evolution', pp. 50, 219.

129 Spotswood considered fining down the rents but realized that these Catholics could not afford the fines. John Spotswood to Thomas Conolly, 9 June 1800, T.C.D., Conolly papers, MS 3974–84/1350.

130 'Rent-roll of Vintners' proportion of lands, 10 Oct. 1718, by Amos Strettle,' P.R.O.N.I., D2094/21.

131 Ibid.

132 Commentary from the early nineteenth century is often contradictory. For example, one deputy to the Fishmongers' company claimed that a policy of giving long leases at stable rents induced the Protestant tenants to cultivate rather than sublet to others, which 'had prevented the injurious system of middlemen, or persons procuring leases for the purpose of underletting at increased rents. . .' though the 'lands in many cases passed into new hands and had been much subdivided: large sums of money had been given, even at late periods, for the interest in the term that remained, although its duration was so very uncertain.' Letter entered into the minutes, 27 July 1820, Fishmongers' Hall court minutes, N.L.I., film 1514. Not all reports from the Fishmongers' estate were so favourable. A letter entered into the Fishmongers' minutes in 1809 listed 'the chief causes which have operated against the improvement of the estate: first, the proprietors of the soil having no connection with the occupying tenant; second, the number of middlemen between the proprietors of the soil and the actual cultivators of it; third, the uncertainty of tenure; fourth, the want of education among the lower orders.' Minutes concerning the state of the Irish estate, 16 Mar. 1809, Fishmongers' Hall records, N.L.I., film 1514.

133 Report of a deputation, 3 Dec. 1836, Irish Society court minute books, N.L.I., film 1523.

134 He proposed the adoption of legislation to allow them to give leases for lives to occupiers now holding for years and to outlaw fines for renewal. [?] to [?] [n.d.], P.R.O.N.I., Hervey-Bruce papers, D1514/1/4/11.

135 Petition of tenants of 'Raistown' to Bishop Frederick Hervey-Bruce, 17 Apr. 1769, P.R.O.N.I., Hervey-Bruce papers, D2798/3/2.
136 Hercules Rowley to Hervey-Bruce, 16 June 1773, ibid., D2798/3/12.
137 Ibid., D2798/3/79.
138 Rowley to Hervey-Bruce, 5 Aug. 1780, ibid., D2798/3/29.
139 John Galbraith to Hervey-Bruce, 31 May 1785, ibid., D2798/3/44.
140 Ibid.
141 Report of memorial of Thomas Brown and others, tenants on lands of Rosnagalegh,' 3 Feb. 1814, Irish Society court minute books, N.L.I., film 1512.
142 Ibid. They explained further that the neighbouring landlords prohibited the sale of turf, thereby blocking their access to fuel.
143 Ibid.
144 Major, the McReevys, Brown and Grumbley were the former undertenants of John Ewing on the other half of the townland. McKinley purchased his portion from William Brown, the younger grandson of Roger Brown. Mahary married Frances, the eldest daughter of William Brown the elder. Watson and McCadanes were the husbands of William Brown's two younger daughters Margaret and Anne. Major Brown was the son of Thomas Brown and the great-grandson of Roger Brown.
145 Ibid.
146 Report of deputation to Irish Society lands, 9 June 1832, N.L.I., film 1523.
147 Letter to Andrew Babington, Irish Society court minutes, 2 Feb. 1833, N.L.I., film 1523.
148 Letter entered into Irish Society court minutes, 31 May 1805, Irish Society court minute books, N.L.I., film 1521.
149 Report on the memorial of George Hill, 17 June 1807, Ibid.
150 Rutherford, 'Plantation of the Lagan,' p. 129.
151 There were relatively few very large farms. Of the 324 farms whose tenants were given leases in 1835, only twenty-one were above 80 acres and only six above 100 acres. Dowling, 'Abercorn estate,' pp. 67–116.
152 *Devon comm. evidence*, pt. i, HC 1845, xix, p. 824. Young found such scarcity throughout the north of Ireland. Young, *Tour*, i, p. 174.
153 John McClintock to eighth earl of Abercorn, 13 June 1745, P.R.O.N.I., Abercorn papers, T2541/IA1/1B/52; Abercorn to James Hamilton, 1753, 5 January 1773, ibid., D623/A/14/83, 92; D623/A/21/15.
154 Abercorn to Hamilton, 12 Apr. 1767, ibid., D623/A/18/90.
155 Hamilton to Abercorn, 28 December 1773, ibid., T2541/IA1/10/119.
156 Abercorn to Hamilton, 10 Jan. 1778, ibid., D623/A/23/7.
157 Hamilton to Abercorn, 7 Sept. 1775, ibid., T2541/IA2/1/43; the same sentiment is expressed in Hamilton to Abercorn, 5 Feb. 1788, ibid., T2541/IA1/16/8.
158 Abercorn to Hamilton, 25 July and 2 Aug. 1773, ibid., D623/A/21/44, 51.
159 Idem, 26 Apr. 1766, ibid., D623/A/18/60.
160 Hamilton to Abercorn, 26 Feb. 1779, ibid., T2541/IA2/2/71; idem, 24 Jan. 1801, ibid., T2541/IA2/10/2.
161 Tristram Carey to Abercorn, 28 July 1769, ibid., T2541/IA1/8/143.
162 Hamilton to Abercorn, 1770–71, ibid., T2541/IA1/9/87, 96, 99, 102.
163 Idem, 4 Aug. 1771, ibid., T2541/IA1/9/134; idem, 2 Aug. 1771, ibid., T2541/IA1/9/133; idem, 6 Sept. 1771, ibid., T2541/IA1/9/139.
164 Hamilton to Abercorn, 2 Aug. 1771, ibid., T2541/IA1/9/133. See also idem, 6 March 1774, ibid., D623/A/42/11, idem, 10 Jan. 1785, ibid., T2541/IA1/15/2. Crawford

points out that Hamilton admitted two years later during a depression that the head tenants were better able to pay the rent and that anyway head tenants had stopped giving leases to their undertenants and were treating them as cottiers. W.H. Crawford, 'The political economy of linen' in Ciaran Brady, Mary O'Dowd, and Brian Walker (eds.), *Ulster: an illustrated history* (London, 1989), pp. 139–140.

165 Abercorn to Hamilton, 9 May 1773, ibid., D623/A/A/21/35.

166 Hamilton to Abercorn, 29 Feb. 1788, ibid., T2541/IA1/16/9.

167 Ibid.

168 Abercorn to Hamilton, 7 Mar. 1773, ibid., T2541/IA1/9/2/23.

169 J. R. Rowley to W.H. Sawyer, 1 July 1857, P.R.O.N.I., Drapers' company papers, D3632/1/2.

170 'A journey to the north, 7 Aug., 1708' in *A Natural History of Ireland, memories and notes relating thereto, made from communications to the Dublin society*, 2 vols (1683), ii, p. 148, T.C.D., MS 883/1.

171 Duffy, 'Evolution of estate properties,' p. 91.

172 Ibid., p. 94.

173 Johnston, 'Plantation of County Fermanagh,' p. 204; Johnson, 'Balfour rentals,' pp. 97–9.

174 Hunter, 'Ulster plantation,' pp. 420–22.

175 Edmund Kaine to Dacre Barrett, 27 Mar. 1711, P.R.O.N.I., Barrett-Lennard papers, film 170/2. In another letter Kaine reported on a neighbouring landowner who rented part of Barrett's land 'joining to his own.' He wanted to advance the rent, 'but as I told your honour, when gentlemen get land, they are not to be got from them, nor the rents to be advanced.' Kaine to Barrett, 26 Mar. 1712, ibid.

176 The problem of the overlapping tenures of middlemen and undertenants was addressed two generations later by another agent. Edward Mayne to Barrett-Lennard, 20 Mar. 1779, ibid.

177 Thomas Noble to Thomas Barrett-Lennard, 20 Mar. 1773, P.R.O.N.I., Barrett-Lennard papers, film 170/2.

178 Petition of William Hendry and Robert Hendry, sons of Widow Hendry, n.d. [c. 1785], ibid., film 170/2.

179 Charles Mayne to [Thomas Barrett-Lennard], 21 June 1777, ibid.

180 William Mayne to Thomas Barrett, 5 Dec. 1812, ibid., D1232/1/172.

181 William Mayne to Lord Barrett, 20 Feb. 1816, ibid., film 170/2. On the Foljambe estate a similar policy was adopted. A note in the margins of a rental of Cecil manor in Newtown Saville, Co. Tyrone, indicates that all holdings were to be held 'by the occupying tenants.' Rental of Cecil Manor, 1800–01, P.R.O.N.I., Foljambe papers, T3381/5/48. Barrett-Lennard inserted a penalty for subletting in the new leases of 1829. Ellis to Barrett-Lennard, 27 Mar. 1829, P.R.O.N.I., Barrett-Lennard papers, film 170/3.

182 George Lister to N. Bayly, 7 July 1757, P.R.O.N.I., Anglesey papers, D619/22/A/46

183 [?] MacNeill to earl of Uxbridge, 27 Oct. 1790, ibid., D619/22/C/54.

184 John Clarke to Henry Bayly, 24 Mar. 1778, ibid., D619/22/B/50. Hutchinson gave leases directly to undertenants in 1778. Robert Hutchinson to Bayly, 6 June 1778, ibid., D619/21/C/174.

185 Mary Bellamy to earl of Uxbridge, 26 July 1785, ibid., D619/11/55. At the expiration of the Belleghan lease, three petitioners of 1778 began their justification of their right to a renewal with these words: 'As my grandfather and father were your tenants for so many years. . . .' Tenant petitions, Feb. 1778, ibid., D619/22/B/46/47/48.

186 Petition of Patrick Mathews of Irish Grange, 27 July 1785, ibid., D619/11/56.

187 Robert Hutchinson to Henry Bayly, 17 Feb. 1778, ibid., D619/21/C/167.

188 Benagh was 'only a long strip of mountain land, for the most part fit for grazing cattle in the summer season.' Surveys were done in order to prevent a dispute resulting from the expiration of a lease. In 1750 Benagh had for nearly twenty years 'been inhabited by beggars at the rent of £12 12s.' James Rooney to Bayly, 15 Mar. 1750, ibid., D619/21/B/89.

189 Petition of tenants of Benagh, July 1785, ibid., D619/11/58.

190 Petition of widows Hanlon and McManus, 26 July 1785, ibid., D619/11/53; John Hanlon to earl of Uxbridge, July 1786, Jan. 1787, ibid., D619/22/C/25, 31; Robert Hutchinson to Thomas Harrison, 24 Dec. 1786, ibid., D619/21/D/17; Daniel McNeal to Harrison, 3 Jan. 1787, ibid., D619/22/C/30; Hutchinson to Harrison, 24 Dec. 1786, ibid., D619/21/D/17; petition of Hanlon's undertenants, 12 Mar. 1788, ibid., D619/11/6; [?] Armstrong to earl of Uxbridge, 19 July 1810, ibid., D619/23 /A/55.

191 Robert Hutchinson to Thomas Harrison, 23 Aug. 1787, ibid., D619/21/D/20; Samuel Corbett to John Bayly, n.d., ibid., D619/11/29; tenant petition, n.d., ibid., D619/11/95.

192 Dickson, 'Cork region,' pp. 246–7, 253, 298. In one nineteenth-century tract, however, middlemen were blamed for insecurity of tenure, impoverishment of both the soil and the people cultivating it. W.W. Simpson, *A defence of the landlords of Ireland, with remarks on the relation between landlord and tenant* (Dublin, 1844).

193 Dickson, 'Cork region,' p. 254.

194 William J. Armstrong to provost and fellows, 10 May 1850, T.C.D., MUN/P/24/421.

195 Ibid.

196 Stuart Hunter, John Matthews, et al. to Samuel Fischer, 24 Apr. 1871, Merchant Tailors' Hall minutes, N.L.I., film 1519.

197 For various complaints about excessive profit rents, see 'Note on the ejectment of Ballyhendry,' n.d. [c. 1780], P.R.O.N.I., T2825 and, N.L.I., Conolly papers, film 6950; Irish Society court minutes, 31 Jan. 1812, N.L.I., film 1521; Tenant petitions, n.d., P.R.O.N.I., Anglesey papers, D619/11/18, 25; Hamilton to Abercorn, 16 July 1787, ibid., T2541/IA2/4/p. 45.

198 [?] Beer to Charles O'Hara, n.d. [c. 1823], N.L.I., O'Hara papers, MS 20,321(1).

199 Brabazon Noble to Barrett-Lennard, 17 May 1773, P.R.O.N.I., Barrett-Lennard papers, film 170/2.

200 Dickson, 'Cork region,' p. 307.

201 *On 'Tenant-Right' or 'goodwill' within the barony of Farney, County of Monaghan, Ireland* (London, 1874), pp. 12–14. This text goes on to claim that by 1798 it was apparent that middlemen were not the cause of poverty and subdivision, which had proceeded unabated despite restrictive covenants in the leases.

202 He suggested later that some undertenants might have their rents reduced on renewal. Edmund McGildowney to Lord Mark Kerr, 14 Feb. 1808, P.R.O.N.I., McGildowney papers, D1375/4/7/1. See also McGildowney to Mrs. Jane Moore, 24 Sept. 1809, ibid., D1375/1/1.

203 McGildowney to James Gaston, 3 Mar. 1814, ibid., D1375/1/6. One tenant in Antrim was denied renewal because he was cutting down trees and he refused to provide a list of his undertenants. Robert McNaghton to McGildowney, [Dec.] 1816, ibid., D1375/2/4/55 and 4 Feb. 1817, ibid., D1375/2/5/4.

204 Survey of report of deputation, 21 Aug. 1827, Irish Society court minute books, N.L.I., film 1522.

205 Henry Smith to Messrs Grassen and Sons, 5 Mar. 1821, P.R.O.N.I., Drapers' company papers, D3632/3/1.

206 Survey of the Clothworkers' estate by Edwin Driver, 1840, Merchant Tailors' Hall,, N.L.I., film 1517.

207 [?] Rutherford to Thomas Beer, 3 June 1842, P.R.O.N.I., Anglesey papers, D619/23/B/67; diary of Matthew Saukey, agent, 9 Feb. and 4 Apr. 1859, P.R.O.N.I., Brookeborough papers, D998/8/5; agent memorandum, 1875, ibid., D998/8/21; Frederick Wrench to [?], 22 Jan. 1877, ibid., D998/6/1, p. 112; Frederick Wrench to Mrs. Duffy, 15 Oct. 1878, ibid., p. 403. Edward Lawford to Rowley Miller, 3 Mar. 1836, P.R.O.N.I., Drapers' company papers, D3632/3/4; Lawford to Rowley and J.R. Miller, 21 Nov. 1842, ibid.; Lawford to Millers, 23 May 1848, ibid., D3632/1/1; Millers to W.H. Sawyer, Oct. 1858, ibid., D3632/1/2; Rowley Miller to Sawyer, 9 Jan. 1864, ibid., D3632/1/3; Lawford to Miller, 25 Feb. 1830, ibid., D3632/3/3; D Tierney, 'The tabular reports,' in William Greig, *General report on the Gosford estates in County Armagh 1821*, intro. F. M. L. Thompson and D Tierney (Belfast, 1976), p. 61–62. The general rule from the Devon evidence was that 'the occupying tenant–middleman or sub-tenant–was entitled to the tenant right of the portion he actually occupied.' Robert Donnell, *Reports of one hundred and ninety cases in the Irish land courts; with preliminary tenant right chapters* (Dublin, 1876), p. 74.

208 P.R.O.N.I., Anglesey papers, D619/21/C/136.

209 Petition of Taaffe, Taaffe, Toole, Toole, and Kelly, 26 Aug. 1760, ibid., D619/11/2.

210 [?] Nugent to earl of Uxbridge, 4 July 1785, ibid., D619/22/C/5.

211 Petition of John Macken and son James Macken, 29 Feb. 1788, ibid., D619/11/82.

212 Edmund McGildowney to Robert McNaghton, 13 Nov. 1819, P.R.O.N.I., McGildowney papers, D1375/1/14.

213 The word attornment is derived from the French word *tourner*, to turn or change. It is an acknowledgment of the turning of a tenant to a new landlord. A landlord may grant the services of his tenant to another for a term of years, a term of life, or in tail, or in fee; the tenant must attorn to the grantee for the life of the grantor by force and virtue of the grant. See the alphabetical listing in Matthew Dutton, *The law of landlord and tenants in Ireland* . . . (Dublin, 1726). Attornments were taken from the tenants on the Anglesey estate in 1712, (P.R.O.N.I., Anglesey papers, D619/5/1–2) and again in 1765. There were over sixty signatures on an attornment dated 1765. All of the tenants paid a 6d. fine and attorned themselves to Bayly with these words: 'being the tenants, undertenants, or occupiers of certain cottages.' Attornment, 9 Oct. 1765, ibid., D619/5/4. Another twenty attorned as 'tenants to Sir Nicholas Bayly whose estate of inheritance we do acknowledge said lands of Muckgrange to be,' and paid a 1d. fine. Attornment, 3 Apr. 1766, ibid., D619/5/5. Attornments normally specified both 'tenants and occupiers.' Attornment, 5 Dec. 1768, ibid., D619/5/6. All tenants were forced to sign the 1765 attornments. Attornment, 11 Aug. 1770, ibid., D619/21/C/23. One tenant was to be ejected for refusal to sign an attornment in 1770. Lord Uxbridge's directions to agents, n.d. [c. 1770], ibid., D619/ 14/C/3.

214 Petitions (two identical), 14 Feb. 1778, P.R.O.N.I., Anglesey papers, D619/5/13, 14.

215 John Conyngham to William Conyngham, 14 May 1765, P.R.O.N.I., Lenox-Conyngham papers, D1449/12/100.

216 A. Edmonstone to [?], 15 Dec. 1769, P.R.O.N.I., Edmonstone papers, D233/2; Richard Fletcher to Samuel Heron, n.d., ibid., D233/3; James Rooney to Nicholas Bayly, 28 Sept. 1742, P.R.O.N.I., Anglesey papers, D619/21/B/42.

217 Edmonstone to [?], 31 Mar. 1770, ibid., D233/4.

218 Tenant letter to Bishop Frederick Hervey-Bruce, 9 Mar. 1802, P.R.O.N.I., Hervey-Bruce papers, D2798/4/24.

219 James Hamilton, Jr., to ninth earl of Abercorn, 11 Feb. 1796, P.R.O.N.I., Abercorn papers, T2541/IA2/6/2.

220 Ibid.

221 Charles Doherty to earl of Fingal, 31 Jan. 1726, N.L.I., Earl of Fingal papers, MS 8025(2).

222 Cornelius and Andrew Dormullen to earl of Fingal, 17 Jan. 1725, ibid.

223 James Plunket to Thomas Conolly, 25 Oct. 1783, T.C.D., Conolly papers, MS 3974–84/811.

224 Petition of John O'Dolan to John Dickson, n.d. [c. 1848], N.L.I., Playdell papers, film 7648. He took £500 to leave. William Johnston to John Dickson, 6 July 1848, ibid.

225 McFarland requested five or six more acres so that his family would not be split up and impoverished. Petition of Patrick McFarland, 25 July 1785, P.R.O.N.I., Anglesey papers, D619/11/49.

226 Petition of Brian Murnaghan, 25 July 1785, ibid., D619/11/42.

227 Report on memorial of Alexander Hogg Lecky, 5 Feb. 1806, Irish Society court minute books, N.L.I., film 1521.

228 Tenant petition, n.d. [c. July 1785], P.R.O.N.I., Anglesey papers, D619/11/67.

229 Report of deputation, 5 Sept. 1860, Merchant Tailors' Hall, Irish estate committee of management minutes, N.L.I., film 1517.

230 Petition of Stephen Rice and Hugh McManus, 16 Jan. 1770, P.R.O.N.I., Anglesey papers, D619/22/B/8.

231 Tenant petition, n.d. [c. 1795], ibid., D619/11/88.

232 James Gough to Lord Dufferin, 23, 24, 25 Feb. 1865, P.R.O.N.I., Dufferin papers, D1071A/K, Box 1. Another tenant complained of his ejectment after nearly sixty years as tenant. James Maxwell to Dufferin, 23 Jan. 1866, ibid.

233 Bartlett, Catholic question, p. 59.

234 J.H. Whyte, 'Landlord influence at elections in Ireland, 1760–1885,' in English historical review, lxvvv (Oct., 1965), p. 741.

235 Anthony Malcomson, John Foster: the politics of the Anglo-Irish ascendancy (Oxford, 1978), p. 317.

236 James Hamilton to Abercorn, 17 April 1772, P.R.O.N.I., Abercorn papers, T2541/IA1/10/23. Disloyalty was in evidence in 1768 when, contrary to Abercorn's wishes, James Hamilton's brother, William, was soundly defeated in a County Donegal election. Idem., 5 Aug. 1768, ibid., T2541/IA1/8/80.

237 See Bartlett, Catholic question, pp. 82–172.

238 James Hamilton, Jr., to ninth earl of Abercorn, 19 Apr. 1793, P.R.O.N.I., Abercorn papers, T2541/IA1/19/35.

239 Thomas Bartlett, 'An end to moral economy: the Irish militia disturbances of 1793' in Past & present, no. 99 (1983), pp. 41–64.

240 The Irish land question and the twelve London Companies in the county of Londonderry (Belfast, 1869), pp. 22–23.

241 Anonymous letter entered into the court minutes of the Fishmongers' Company, Fishmongers' Hall records, 26 Sept. 1808, N.L.I., film 1514. Another letter entered into the minutes and describing the poverty and subdivision of those estates recommended not renewing to Beresford.

242 Report of a deputation to the Irish Society, 3 Dec. 1836, Irish Society court minute books, N.L.I., film 1522.

243 Third report of Edward Oseland, 8 Nov. 1838, Merchant Tailors' Hall, Manor of Clothworkers' extracts from accounts, box 131, N.L.I., film 1518.

244 William Blacker, *Prize essay on the management of landed property* (Dublin, 1834); [William Hickey], *An address to the landlords of Ireland, on subjects connected with the melioration of the lower classes, by Martin Doyle* (Dublin, 1831).

245 Malcomson, *John Foster*, p. 305.

246 Maguire, *Downshire estates*, pp. 121–9; Malcomson, *John Foster*, p. 299.

247 *Ordnance Survey Memoirs of Ireland, volume 5: parishes of Co. Tyrone I*, eds. Angélique Day and Patrick McWilliams (Belfast, 1990), p. 12; Malcomson, *John Foster*, pp. 305, 310.

248 James Hamilton, Jr., to ninth earl of Abercorn, 9 May 1798, ibid., T2541/IA2/7/20.

249 He felt that after 1829 and the disenfranchisement of the forty-shilling freeholder, consolidation of tenancies was also politically motivated. Donnell, *Reports*, pp. 26, 30–33.

250 R.C. Brush to earl of Belmore, 1 Feb. 1873, P.R.O.N.I., Belmore papers, D3007/V/56.

251 Thomas Pemberton to ninth earl of Abercorn, 5 Feb. 1793, P.R.O.N.I., Abercorn papers, T2541/IA1/19/9.

252 James Hamilton, Jr., to Abercorn, 17 Jan. 1799, ibid., T2541/IA2/8/3.

253 Idem, 24 June 1797, ibid., T2541/IA2/6/30.

254 Idem, 17 June 1797, ibid., T2541/IA2/6/29.

255 Nancy Curtain, '"Traitors, miscreants, and wicked men:" mobilization, social composition, and aims of the United Irishmen in Ulster, 1791–8' (Ph.D. dissertation, University of Wisconsin-Madison), 1980, pp. 222–4.

256 'Instructions for Mr. Speer' by F.E. Foljambe, n.d. [c.1800], P.R.O.N.I., Foljambe papers, T3381/10/4.

257 Brigadier-General Knox to Thomas Pelham, 19 April 1797, P.R.O.N.I., Pelham papers, T755/4/2.

258 William Mayne to Thomas Barrett-Lennard, 20 May 1812, P.R.O.N.I., Barrett-Lennard papers, D1232/1/158.

259 His last life had expired and he entreated 'your lordship to confirm to him the possession of his holding,' which was large enough to support two cows and a horse. Petition of David Kennedy to Edmund McGildowney, n.d. [c. 1816], P.R.O.N.I., McGildowney papers, D1375/4/12/35B.

260 [Andrew] O'Dolan to Lady Playdell, 15 Aug. 1828, N.L.I., Playdell papers, film 7648.

261 James Fawcett to Lady Playdell, 19 Sept. 1828, ibid.

262 Memorial of Orange Order, 1869, Drapers Hall, London, Minutes of the court of assistants, extracts relating to Irish estates, N.L.I., film 1529.

263 Articles of agreement between Sir Robert McLellan and Adrian Moore, 8 Apr. 1616, P.R.O.N.I., T2208/1.

264 Lease of Castlestewart, County Tyrone, 1 Nov. 1630, P.R.O.N.I., Lenox-Conyngham papers, D1449/1/1.

265 Currie, 'Evolution,' p. 74.

266 'Survey of several leases and other holdings within the manor of Brownlow's Derry, County Armagh,' 1667–1708, P.R.O.N.I., T970, p. 3. The managers of the Downshire property in King's County also struggled with the alienation of farms leased to

Protestants to Catholics. [?] Meredyth to [?] Hunt, 9 Oct. 1719, P.R.O.N.I., Downshire papers, D607/A/12; Henry Blundell to [?] Meredyth, [?] Dec. 1720, ibid., D607/A/12; Meredyth to Blundell, 1 July 1720, ibid.; A. M. Blundell, M. Raymond, and J. Trumbell to Henry Hatch, 11 Mar. 1758; Henry Hatch to Henry Blundell, 11 Apr. 1758, ibid.

267 Perceval-Maxwell, *Scottish migration*, p. 247; Currie, 'Evolution,' p. 98.

268 Gillespie, *Settlement and survival*, p. xxiii.

269 Leasebook of the Manor of Castledillon Co. Armagh, with observations by William Molyneux, P.R.O.N.I., Film 80/3.

270 Lorcan O'Meirain, 'The Bath estate 1700–77' in *Clogher record*, vi, no. 2, 1967, pp. 333–60.

271 Nicholas Bayly to Robert Hutchinson, 26 Dec. 1768, P.R.O.N.I., Anglesey papers, D619/21/C/3.

272 Lord Uxbridge's directions to agents, n.d. [c. 1770], ibid., D619/14/C/3.

273 The head agent recommended that Catholics should be harassed for rent and put out if possible. Henry Smith to Rev. Murphy, P.P., 11 Dec. 1821; Henry Smith to Rowley Miller, 12 Dec. 1821, P.R.O.N.I., Drapers' company papers, D3632/3/2.

274 Letter concerning Beresford's lease, 27 July 1820, Fishmongers' Hall court minutes, N.L.I., film 1514.

275 Smyth, 'Society and settlement,' p. 75.

276 Ibid., p. 59.

277 This is not to say that leasing policies were the sole cause of segregation. Chapter 4 explores in more detail how geographically distinct ethnic communities developed during the demographic expansion of the eighteenth century.

278 *Ordnance Survey Memoirs*, vol. 5, p. 12. Two adjacent townlands on the Abercorn estate named 'Scotch Letterbin' and 'Irish Letterbin' that have retained the ethnic character reflected in their names to this day. Personal communication with Dr. Brian Trainor of P.R.O.N.I.

279 William Greig, *General report on the Gosford estates in Armagh, 1821*, ed. with intro. by F.M.L. Thompson and David Tierney (Belfast, 1976), p. 11; Tierney, 'Tabular reports' in ibid., p. 57.

280 Report by Nathanial Stonard and W. Hamond, 27 Feb. 1817, Minutes of the court of assistants, extracts relating to Irish estates, Drapers' Hall, London, N.L.I., film 1529. 'The farmers on the Moneymore division or south side of the estate having the advantage of a better climate, and much better land, and larger farms generally as well as the great majority of the tenants being Presbyterians, whilst the great majority of the Brackaslievegallon tenants are Roman Catholics, will easily account for improvement making more rapid strides than in the mountain districts of Brackaslievegallon and Ballynascreen divisions. It is notorious that Protestants of all denominations are more tidy than Roman Catholics and more anxious to improve their condition in life.' Rowley and J.R Miller to Edward Lawford, 1 October 1845, P.R.O.N.I., Drapers' company papers, D3632/1/1.

281 Letter entered into the minutes describing the revaluation and reletting of the Fishmongers' proportion south of Lough Foyle at the expiration of the lease of Beresford, 27 July 1820, Fishmongers' Hall records, court minutes, N.L.I., film 1514.

282 Report of a deputation, 30 Nov. 1820, Fishmongers' Hall court minutes, N.L.I., film 1515.

283 For a masterful analysis of how local sectarian imbalances and economic changes combined to structure local politics and community relations in the nineteenth

century, see Frank Wright, *Two lands on one soil: Ulster politics before home rule* (Dublin, 1996). A general picture of the religious demographic balance in Ulster has been gleaned from the religious census of 1766. See the map in Crawford, 'The political economy of linen,' p. 153.

284 Bartlett, *Catholic question*, p. 10.

285 Ibid., p. 5. Bartlett quotes one moderate Presbyterian's response to Tone's plan for Catholic Emancipation and parliamentary reform in the early 1790s. Such a plan posed a direct 'danger to property by renewing the court of claims and admitting any evidence to substantiate Catholic titles.' Ibid., p. 11.

286 Moody, 'Treatment of the native population,' p. 62. Moody quotes a '"Discourse" on the settlement of natives in Ulster, c. 1613' to the effect that 'the Irish were willing to pay higher rents than the men from either England or Scotland.' See also Robinson, *Plantation of Ulster*, p. 183; Hunter, 'Ulster plantation,' p. 26.

287 Johnston, 'Balfour rentals,' p. 99.

288 *Phillips MSS* (H.M.S.O, 1928), p. 103 cited in D. L. Armstrong, *An economic history of agriculture in Northern Ireland, 1850–1900* (Oxford, 1989), p. 4.

289 Gillespie, *Settlement and survival*, p. 1.

290 Bartlett, *Catholic question*, p. 28.

291 Thomas Bligh to Peter Westernra, 15 Dec. 1678, P.R.O.N.I., Rossmore papers, T2929/1/17.

292 Robert Molesworth to Mrs. [?] Molesworth, 13 Nov. 1710, Historical Manuscripts Commission, *Reports on various collections*, viii (1913), p. 241.

293 Brabazon Nobel to Richard Barrett-Lennard, 27 Oct. 1764, P.R.O.N.I., Barrett-Lennard papers, film 170/2.

294 Dickson, 'Cork region,' p. 149.

295 *Devon comm. evidence*, pt. i, xix, 824.

296 Idem, *Northern Ireland: a comparative analysis* (Dublin, 1987), p. 10.

297 Brabazon Noble to Thomas Barrett-Lennard, 17 May 1773, P.R.O.N.I., Barrett-Lennard papers, film 170/2; Mayne to Barrett-Lennard, 12 June 1809, ibid., D1232/1/98; Lord Mark Kerr to Edmund McGildowney, 11 Mar. 1814, P.R.O.N.I., McGildowney papers, D1375/4; McGildowney to Dr. M. Leslie, 2 Oct. 1815, ibid., D1375/1/7; McGildowney to [?] Dobbs, 11 Nov. 1817, ibid., D1375/1/11.

298 Ibid., p. 2 and chapter 3; Wright, *Two lands on one soil*, pp. 8–9, 35, 71, 84–86, 98–9. 'It was upon this section of the population that the displacement effect might work in its most volatile and subjective ways: they were the people who were least susceptible to control by landowners on account of the very looseness of their connections with the land.' Ibid., p. 29. Greig argued that Linen had dismantled differences between natives and newcomers. Greig, *General report*, p. 76 Another contribution to the displacement effect was the movement for Catholic emancipation, which gave an enormous boost to northern Catholicism, especially outside of Presbyterian inner Ulster. The effect was reduced in the north east by high eighteenth-century emigration combined with the strategic location of the linen industry, and outlets for agricultural products in Belfast. Wright, *Two lands on one soil*, p. 140.

299 *Northern Whig*, 28 March 1848; Wright, *Two lands on one soil*, p. 173.

300 William Mayne to Thomas Barrett-Lennard, n.d. [c. May 1810], P.R.O.N.I., Barrett-Lennard papers, D1232/1/113.

301 Wright, *Two lands one soil*, pp. 97–8.

302 Augustine Brogan to Earl of Fingal, 29 Jan. 1726, N.L.I., Earl of Fingal papers, MS
    8025(1). Anglesey estate tenants commonly voiced this attitude in their petitions for
    renewal. Tenant proposal to Nicholas Bayly, 28 July 1734, P.R.O.N.I., Anglesey
    papers, D619/6/4; three petitions from tenants, 11 Dec. 1840, ibid., D619/6/105,
    106, 109. One tenant whose lease had expired in 1751 proposed to pay what he
    claimed was more than his farm was worth, 'which I hope will be agreeable to you,
    and as I am a present tenant, I would expect the preference before a stranger.'
    Nicholas Dromgool to Nicholas Bayly, 3 Nov. 1751, ibid., D619/22/A/40. The agent
    felt, however, that a better rent might be had for the farm if he allowed other
    bidders. Robert Hutchinson to Bayly, 14 Sept. 1790, ibid., D619/21/D/24. The head
    tenant of the townland of Irish Grange on the Anglesey estate asked for a renewal
    in 1778 and claimed that his farm had been improved as much as possible, barring a
    vast further expense. He concluded by offering whatever sum 'any man who means
    to pay the rent honestly' would think reasonable. John Clarke to Henry Bayly, 24
    Mar. 1778, ibid., D619/22/B/50.

CHAPTER THREE

Production

A COMMERCIAL AND COLONIAL ECONOMY

The previous chapter examined the complications of establishing plantation estates and stable tenurial relationships between owners and occupiers of Ulster soil. This chapter shifts the focus from the relationships themselves to the purpose of those relationships. The new landed estates provided the framework for the development of a commercialized economic culture in rural Ulster. But just as the structures and relationships were fragile, so too were the productive forces of the economy. Two phenomena greatly protracted the nature of this transformation: the slow evolution of the productive practices of native and immigrant farmers, and the propensity of those farmers to abandon rented property for more promising prospects elsewhere. The vicissitudes of the plantation itself prevented the quick adoption of the new productive model and perpetuated the defensive and mobile behaviours of the Gaelic mode of production. Those familiar with the experience of the Munster plantation of the sixteenth century were already aware of the problem. Colonists perceived the resilience and mobility which characterized Irish pastoralists as an intractable problem. The historian of the sixteenth-century plantation of Munster explains contemporary perceptions of its economic goals:

> Plantation theorists would not have been happy about Munster's concentration on wool and cattle exports. The equation hammered home by every English commentator was that pastoralism encouraged sloth, instability, and the Irish way of life. The settler's job was to transplant the new England to Munster, and in agricultural terms this meant the promotion of arable farming. Yet the incontestable increase in agricultural produce in our period came from wool and stock, both found mainly in south Munster and among large numbers of enthusiastic new English landlords.[1]

One tacit admission of the inevitable dominance of livestock production occurred when officials of the Munster plantation reluctantly accepted the fact that the number of cattle on the land was more important than the number of tenants.[2] The problem is not one of production *per se*, but of the form of production.

This and the following chapters focus on the social meaning of eighteenth-century economic development. Chapter 4 attends to the actual farms themselves, the buildings and fences constructed and maintained by those who remained and settled as visual and organizational components of the estate sytem. In this chapter a different type of remnant, one that was both more and less tangible than mere improvements, is analyzed: the commercial economy itself. The establishment of a market economy with factors of production that imparted to plantation estates a basis for tenurial stability was crucial to the settlement of the plantation and the transformation of the inherited pastoral/subsistence economy. This chapter argues that it was also a central social basis of the meaning of tenant right. Chapter 2 explored how the gaps and fissures created by the political conflicts of the seventeenth century, or more locally by the inheritance or sale of an estate, opened a space for a tenant to articulate an extra-economic narrative about his tenure. Likewise, economic crises and their disruptive effects interrupted the natural state of property relations and allowed for the articulation of a narrative about tenure in which individual agency superseded larger and more impersonal economic forces. The custom of tenant right related to these developments in a number of ways. By providing an exchange system for commodified tenancies, it abetted the mobility of the tenants. By representing the historicity of tenant production, it provided a vehicle for the resolution of the issue of 'compensation for improvements.' Most important, the pursuit of an economic practice that oriented the farmer toward the colonial market economy became a crucial ideological basis for the claim of tenant right. Just as the establishment and maintenance of a commercial landlord-tenant relationship was articulated as an artifice created by the tenant, so too was the growth of the economy attributable to the efforts of tenants.

To revisit a theme from Chapter 1, the central question of the economic element in tenant right was one of 'agency:'[3] who could claim credit for economic practices oriented toward the colonial market economy? On the one hand, successful agrarian capitalism was not the result of the agency of tenants, but rather the result of a structure, a context or web of social relations, a social formation. The success of the plantation did not depend on what type of tenant was attracted to Ulster but instead on the development of property relations and colonial markets along capitalist lines. The position of farms and estates in relation to colonial markets and tenant-right prices was spelled out by a tenant in Donegal in 1702. He claimed that 'if the world does not mend, you may have cattle enough out of your estate but little money. I protest if Ireland is much worse for another year as it has [been] these six months past, I would not give five years' purchase for any estate that does not lie within reach of the markets of [Dublin].'[4] On the other hand, the prosperity of the plantation was the result of the labour of many agents. A particular social organization (a market, for example) is held together not only by those individual labours, but also by the consent and legitimacy each participant gives to that structure. Such consent and legitimacy depends on the acceptance of certain descriptions of that labouring, ways of attributing the products of labour to the labourers, ways of mapping the connections between members of a community and the objects it produces, preserves, and exchanges. Who would take credit for establishing and maintaining the plantation economy? The landlords, the middlemen, the tenants, the undertenants, the cottier-weavers, the native Irish – all these overlapping groups had different, and potentially legitimate, answers to this question. Tenant right was implicated in this conversation.

The issue of economic performance was related to another term closely associated in use with tenant right: improvement. Throughout the seventeenth century the economic basis of tenant right amounted to no more than the ability to remain in continuous possession of a farm under very adverse circumstances. 'Improvement' was nothing more than keeping a farm or an estate from a wasted condition. Landlords were not unaware of this idea that the labour of the tenant was integral to the very existence of an estate in a colonial setting. Edward Coke wrote in Tipperary in 1737: 'I and every other gentleman would have good substantial Protestant tenants if we could get them, but as they are not to be had we must take the best we can get, or have our land waste which is next to having no estate.'[5] Wasteland is not an estate. Private property is meaningless unless inhabited by occupants of a certain kind. It was only after the plantation of Ulster had been naturalized that this minimum definition of improvement disappeared from view and different methods of economic production became comparable in the context of claims for tenure. At a certain point in its history an estate became integrated into an urban mercantile nexus, and the tenantry became more distinguishable in terms of their own productive integration into that nexus. The range of occupations varied from enclosed stock farming to improved arable production and engagement with the linen industry, but all of these distinguished themselves from the surviving pastoralism of the native Irish. The visual and economic marker of this difference was the reinvestment of the surpluses back into the farm, thereby improving its housing and fences.

The denigration of Irish productive capacities and the overestimation of the abilities and endowments of the newcomers to seventeenth-century Ulster is an interpretive bias with a very old pedigree. Early seventeenth-century writers such as Spenser, Moryson, and Davies held that the economic inferiority of the Irish, which justified their subjugation, stemmed from primitive tenurial relationships. Plantation theorists and legal experts interpreted tanistry as a form of property right that extended no further than the life of the tanist, and therefore as antithetical to their perception of a settled polity and an economy firmly based on private property. 'Since a tanist came to office by way of election,' Pawlisch points out, 'freehold was held in suspense.'[6] The inherent fluidity of all tenurial relationships was and still is associated with a shiftless, uneconomic, even barbaric productive practice. Nicholls states this position plainly in his influential monograph on early modern Irish society, arguing that the fluid mechanisms of inheritance characteristic of Gaelic society were responsible for 'the instability of Irish settlement patterns and the under-utilization of Irish land in the sixteenth century.' He argues that 'it is difficult to see how such frequent, even annual, redistributions could have been possible if either the normal dwelling houses of the Irish were permanent ones or the occupation of the agricultural land [was] at all complete.'[7] In Perceval-Maxwell's recently reprinted The *Scottish migration to Ulster in the reign of James I*, the role of the native Irish in the economy is all but ignored while the impoverished and landless Scottish emigrants receive a much more careful and nuanced treatment.[8] To bolster their image, he cites evidence that some Scots introduced superior breeds of livestock into Ulster, and that exports of livestock from Ulster increased after the Scots arrived.[9] Evidence showing that responsibility for this trade gradually changed hands from landlords to merchants is then adduced to suggest that the Scots were responsible for a qualitative change in the economy. But the real significance of this remains 'a matter of opinion.'[10]

The immigrant population that was so instrumental to the success of this colonial endeavour, may have been culturally more familiar to the planters, but it still could not easily be formed into their image of the ideal capitalist tenant. This difficulty was owing not just to the hostile and alien cultural landscape in which the immigrants planted themselves but also to the heritage of practices and relations which they carried with them.[11] Scottish and English emigrants to plantation Ulster for the most part came from areas that were peripheral to the developed agrarian capitalism of the south of England, areas in which customary tenure restricted the commodification of land. The confrontation between Gaelic agriculture and the forms of production characteristic of lowland Scotland was not so much one between core and periphery as one between two different peripheries. Perceval-Maxwell establishes that the Scots migrants came mostly from 'some eight counties adjacent to the English border and up the west coast to Argyllshire, in neither of which areas can agriculture conditions have been significantly more advanced than those which had obtained in Ulster prior to the plantation.'[12] The 8,000 Scots and nearly as many English males who had emigrated to Ulster by 1622 were probably 'neither equipped nor disposed to introduce any drastic economic or social change in Ulster.'[13] Those who followed in the next century were most likely refugees from an increasingly competitive and commercialized Scottish rural economy.[14]

Rather than distinguishing between primitive pertinacity and progressive economic interest, the evidence indicates that in the unstable atmosphere of plantation Ulster both the natives and the newcomers appeared equally indifferent to ploughing and settling.[15] Whatever may have been their abilities, endowments, or inclinations, it is clear from the surveying and commentary conducted early in the plantation that the unwillingness to adopt an enclosed, visible, arable-based form of production was widely shared. The Irish were needed as tenants not so much to pay rent and provide labour as to produce enough food to feed the emigrants in their first winters in Ireland.[16] According to the 1622 commissioners, it was the 'English' who neglected ploughing and devoted too much of their land to grazing. Clarke surmises that

> the plantation does not seem to have altered the pattern of land use in Ulster dramatically. This arose partly from the fact that arable production had in any case been a component part of the Irish system, as a proclamation of 1610 acknowledged when it postponed the removal of natives until the following year so that the land might be prepared and sown with seed as usual; but it arose also from the fact that many settlers were slow to plough the land, the English, it was alleged, being particularly reluctant to do so.[17]

Those historians who believe that the plantation immigrants brought a dramatic change in the economic structure of the Ulster countryside, a position Nicholas Canny called 'one of the "myths" of "Ulster history",'[18] have yet to make a convincing case. Even in work that is as dismissive of the Irish as Perceval-Maxwell's we may read here and there between the lines: the Irish remained demographically dominant, they paid the highest rents, and they were especially successful in maintaining themselves in tenancies in Fermanagh and Cavan lands held by absentees.[19] The discrepancy is then bridged by undocumented appeals to the 'pertinacity'[20] and land hunger of the native Irish, with no serious analysis of how they managed to pay such high rents. Both Canny and Perceval-Maxwell have explored the depositions of the 1640s for further evidence of agricultural practice during the early decades of the plantation. Canny's conclusion that Ulster agriculture was not fundamentally altered by the plantation is based on the striking absence of husbandmen, the rarity of claims of losses of ploughs or crops, and the predominance of claims of losses of livestock among Ulster deponents as compared with Munster deponents.[21] The continued resilience of a pastoral economy in Ulster was rightly regarded as a fundamental obstacle to the goals of the plantation in the first half of the seventeenth century, causing the Irish House of Commons to appoint a committee in 1634 'to draw up a bill to prohibit the conversion of arable land to pasture.'[22]

Why was the pastoral economy, which was regarded as backward and ill-fitted to the colonial settlement, so resilient? The ability of the native Irish to compete for land in the early stages of the plantation suggests that the plantation had not fundamentally changed the situation of uncertainty and instability to which native producers had been forced to adapt themselves for two or three generations. The instabilities created by the confrontation between the O'Neills and the English government in the mid-sixteenth century forced native occupants of Ulster to adapt their agricultural practices so as to coexist with uncertain tenures, discretionary extraction of surpluses, and intermittent warfare. Ulster farmers in these circumstances ranged between a pastoral orientation with more fluid and tributary relations of power, and a more settled orientation of arable production with more stable, reified, and individualistic relations of production. The Gaelic style of agricultural production was therefore not a monolithic pastoralism but a flexible system that, because of the instability of much of its recent history, tended towards pastoralism and demographic stagnation. As Clarke argues, arable agriculture was pursued in a context of a transhumance economy: 'It was customary to move the site of cultivation periodically, so that the process of intensive cultivation was actually short term and took place within a context of an extensive system of land use.'[23]

A crucial component of production and settlement in Ulster was the paradoxical interconnection between tillage and warfare. On the one hand, militarization of the countryside promoted an evasive pastoralism. On the other hand, it increased the demand for grain and the requirement that tenants be tied down to their farms. Thus, 'there clearly was some tillage practised in the Irish areas of Ulster and Connacht, though little evidence can be gleaned about it save that it was customary for English soldiers to devastate it along with the farm settlements so as to weaken Irish resistance.'[24] A ban on exports from the Pale and government orders to imitate English farming practices were all relevant to the level of arable agriculture in sixteenth-century Ulster, but, according to Canny, 'the chief motivation for tillage was probably the increased militarization of the province: food was needed to feed extra troops.'[25] Extensive tillage cultivation was consistent with the very temporary tenurial and productive structures by which it was practised. At the same time, corn grown for troops was an obvious target, and the more settled the agriculture, the more attractive was that target.

Tillage was an important part of the essentially pastoral economy of colonial Ulster, but it was dispensable, especially in times of crisis and uncertainty. This high mobility and flexibility in terms of occupation, tenurial relations, and productive mix allowed tenants to be more resilient in the face of political and economic uncertainty. In England also, according to Clay, the pastoral small farmer was much more economically resilient than was a small farmer in a mixed farming district. The latter would not have had access to common fields and would have been dependent on the produce of a smaller holding, while the pastoralist, having had a clearer opportunity to accumulate a surplus, in the form of livestock feeding on the commons, would have been better prepared to survive a crisis. The pastoralist's labour was also less extensive, allowing him the opportunity to pursue nonagricultural marginal activities. In short, he was more diversified and more resilient.[26] This was the case in Ireland as well. Both native and colonist had a tradition of oat consumption in an economy dominated by dairy, cattle, and sheep production.[27] Cullen argues that while the tillage sector of the economy was always important for domestic food supply, i.e. subsistence, price trends before the 1760s dictated that Irish farmers with a commercial orientation steered way from specialized grain production.[28] Ulster farmers who might still consider marketing grains were further discouraged from doing so by the poorer soil and harsher climate of the north. This bias against tillage should not be overstated. A pattern of marketing barley for sale in the Dublin market had developed in the Lecale district of County Down.[29] There is also some evidence of grain marketing in the rapidly developing Lagan valley in the late seventeenth century. A traveller to Armagh commented in 1682 on 'the vast majority of wheat that is yearly carried hence into the county of Antrim, besides the maintenance of about two thousand families with bread, which number I find to inhabit this small barony, most whereof being English. [These facts] do plainly demonstrate it to be the granary of Ulster.'[30] But in the west of the province, tillage agriculture in eighteenth-century Ulster appears to have been geared toward subsistence, and the staple of that subsistence was oatmeal. Serious depressions in the 1740s and again in the 1770s were caused primarily by poor grain harvests.[31] Abercorn estate agents occasionally purchased oats shipped into Derry from Scotland and sold them well below the market value in the years 1745, 1770, 1784, and 1793.[32] The planting and harvesting of oats, the local price of oatmeal, and the flow of that commodity through the nearby port of Londonderry were of constant concern to Lord Abercorn's agents. Oat prices are the most frequently reported in the correspondence. In his account of the area surrounding the Abercorn estate Wakefield criticized the practice of 'raising successive crops of oats.' 'But,' he continued, 'are not oats as much the grain of a northern climate as wheat is of a southern?'[33] Grain production was crucial to the livelihood of Ulster tenants, but it would not be the basis of a commercial economy centred on compact and enclosed farms in the eighteenth century.

SETTLEMENT AND MOBILITY

During the turbulent century after 1570, when the top of the entire social structure of Ulster was decapitated and the body reformed, the native Irish were to depend completely on the mobility that pastoralism allowed them.[34] Landlords and other commentators in the seventeenth century complained frequently of the propensity of the Irish to scatter suddenly and leave estates wasted. The bishop of Derry explained the situation to the Irish deputy in some detail in a letter of 1640:

> The Irish are loathe to pay money where they can get grass by stealth, or to pay a valuable rent where they can compound for wasteland. . . . This they that have farms see, and no sooner envy than imitate, knowing that what land they leave now shall be set as wasteland shortly thereafter. And to help this they have a custom of fealty or welcomes. That is, when any man leaves his farm, they that have one entertain him and his family and his cattle for a fortnight gratis upon trial, so as the natives in these parts all most generally are turning, flitting tartarians responsible to no law of God or man.[35]

The intermittent harvest crises of the late seventeenth century exacerbated this problem. The impoverished state of commerce in the 1670s caused many to leave their lands waste, which, according to one observer, 'threatens an undoing to the country.'[36] Nothing could be worse for a landlord than to have farms lying unoccupied through an entire agricultural season. With each passing year the farm would decrease in value either from lack of cultivation or from plunder and trespass, and it was not uncommon for tenants to capitalize on this fact.[37] Many concerned estate managers recognized that the inattentive absenteeism of the owners only exacerbated this problem. Murray of Broughton's agent implored him in 1728 to come from Scotland to his Donegal estate to urge the tenants to plough their farms, for he feared that the estate might degenerate to waste:

> I had no small difficulty this season to persuade many of your tenants to plough their farms, always encouraging them and telling them that you would surely be here in February, and if they hear now you won't come, I fear it will not be in my power to keep them any longer. But this I can assure you: if you are not here before May, much of your estate will be turned [to] waste. Land is likely to fall to a greater degree, and bread is so exceeding

[scarce] here that a famine is feared among the poorer sort. Captain Conyngham's tenants, though bound in firm leases for four years ending next May, are throwing them up daily. I have writ pressingly to him to Brussels, where he now is, to come over this spring and give his tenants abatements, otherwise he will have a waste estate. Col. Montgomery's tenants have many of them run away [because his estate] was so highly set, yet I could not get the rents collected.[38]

These circumstances significantly reduced the value of estates. One potential purchaser of an estate in Monaghan was warned in 1728 that 'in case of bad times waste rents would soon ruin your freehold.'[39] But it was not clear even to careful managers what could be done about waste rents. In Cork landlords entered covenants into leases prohibiting the surrender of the lease before the expiry of the term. 'The argument,' according to Dickson, 'was that the sight of tenants surrendering their farms would damage the reputation of an estate, while finding substitute tenants prepared to take the land at rates approaching the existing levels might be impossible.'[40] The weakness of the legal infrastructure notwithstanding, some chose to chase down tenants and attempt to hold them to their contracts in court. One head tenant, who apparently expected the worst upon the reletting of a townland occupied by five undertenants, warned them that 'if any man offered to move and leave his house or ditches out of repair, he would sue them for committing waste, and if they stayed within the three kingdoms, he would be at them. . . .'[41] The agent of the Barrett-Lennard estate was forced to buy up leases to prevent farms from going to waste. One tenant, according to Edmund Kaine, 'came and said he would give your honour up his lease, for he was not able to pay it or build anything. So I thought it best to take up his lease, which I did, for they would have been waste. And if your honour pleases, I have set these three waste gardens to Michael Clarke of Clones . . . , the best improver in the town.'[42] The Monaghan landowner Thomas Bligh refused to take leases back from those who wished to depart from his estate. 'After they have ploughed the heart out of the land,' he wrote in 1687, 'to throw it up is neither honest, nor, I hope, will [it] be approved of by the courts now, I having contracts under their hands.' Similar problems faced nineteenth-century agents.[43] In 1818 the agent of the Nugent estate 'proceeded at law' against a tenant to compel him to occupy a farm which he had abandoned. But in the following year he was warned against such high-handed behaviour: 'Should I act as you wished me to with your tenants, the consequences would be [that] you would not have either rent or tenants; after these two years nothing but a nursing indulgence will keep them up.' Two years later the agent claimed that 'tenants will not be bound any longer than two years, given the present circumstances.'[44]

Some landlords went so far as to abandon giving leases altogether to combat the wasting of their estates by mobile tenants. 'I am quite against making any leases in parchment,' maintained the earl of Fingal, [and prefer] 'only letting all our tenants be tenants at will. They are so already at their own will, and it is but just [that] they should be so at ours. It is not the intention by this to turn out or raise the rents upon good tenants, but to keep them in awe and hinder them from destroying our estate. . . .'[45] The earl of Rossmore expressed a similar opinion regarding the wisdom of giving leases.[46] The trouble with this hasty solution to the problem of waste rents was of course that these landlords lost all hope of attracting the more stable tenants. The weakness of the at-will tenancy suited the uncertain situation, but it violated the ideals of the plantation, as Lady Shelbourne recognized in the case of the tenants on the Murray of Broughton estate in 1705: 'You will be persuaded to consider your poor tenant in abatement for some time, at least till times mend, and add to our term, for no good, improving, substantial tenants will take land for so short a time, which obliges us to send for the poorer sort and makes the rent very ill-paid, nay sometimes they run away with all.'[47]

The failure of landowners to secure leaseholders on their lands was a significant threat to the integrity of the plantation model. Landlords were clearly attempting to tie down their tenants with leases, committing the relationship between landlord and tenant to a legal script so that their estates might take on the appearance of prosperity and stability. Leases were essential: 'You are to observe that tenants will not hold land in Ireland from year to year, as in England, but expect leases of twenty-one years, sometimes forty years or three lives. For in Ireland the tenants make all repairs and improvements at their own charges; consequently, the lands there must be leased out or lie waste.'[48] The growing prevalence of at-will tenancy signified the weakness of landlords and the incompleteness of the plantation. It was only much later, when landlords attempted to rationalize the occupational organization of their messy and crowded estates by ousting leaseless smallholders, that the insecurity of at-will tenure became an issue. Here, it represented the freedom, mobility, and power of the tenant to threaten the integrity of the estate.

This pattern of high mobility can be considered a structural obstacle to plantation goals, the overcoming of which was accomplished by maintaining the type of landlord-tenant relationships discussed in Chapter 2. Neither the native Irish nor the immigrant Scots and English possessed some fundamental cultural attribute by which they were naturally more prone to skittish occupation and the wasting of farms, nor should either group be distinguished by their 'pertinacity' or economic rationality. The circumstances of the early plantation dominated over the different cultural attributes of Ulster farmers. Indeed, in much of the evidence concerning tenants abandoning their leases, it is impossible to determine whether the tenants were of native or newcomer stock. None the less, there may be reasons to distinguish between native and colonial attitudes towards their mobility. Miller speculates on the reason why Protestant emigration far exceeded Catholic emigration before the American revolution in the following terms:

> Although most Protestant emigrants sought an 'independence' still defined in pre-capitalist terms – as the security and self-sufficiency enjoyed by yeoman farmers and self-employed artisans – most Catholics retained an outlook best characterized as 'dependent,' formalized in life-styles associated with clachan settlements and rundale cultivation, and expressed in Irish-speakers' traditional strictures against innovation and self-aggrandizement.[49]

While the cultural underpinnings of the tendency toward mobility may have been different – an 'independent' vs. a 'dependent' form of mobility, perhaps – from the perspective of plantation theorists and colonizing landlords those differences were not apparent, and both were threatening to the plantation. The form of dependence which Miller attributes to Irish speakers – their strong attachment to Ireland, homeland, etc. – is not inconsistent with their clear lack of attachment to particular farms, estates, or even entire regions of Ireland. In the demographic and political context of the century before the American revolution, they could remain mobile and pastorally-oriented without any threat to their cultural dependencies, just as the newcomers could practise their 'independence' by resettling on estates in developing core areas or by setting off across the Atlantic.

Certainly the newcomers, having uprooted themselves once, continued their mobile tendencies. The evidence from the Brownlow estate in County Armagh clearly shows that this sort of mobility persisted right through the middle of the century.[50] Many Ulster estate managers observed with great alarm that ships were leaving for America full of passengers of British origin. James Hamilton, the agent who had expressed his exasperation at his employer's disinterest in his Donegal estate, told John Murray in 1728 that 'several in the barony of Raphoe are selling their freeholds and going to America.'[51] In 1729 he warned that ships in Killybegs harbour were full of gentlemen tenants, many of whom were in arrears. Good tenants were obliged to indenture their families for three years to gain passage. He was plainly struggling in this letter to communicate to Murray the gravity of the situation:

> I declare before God it is not in my power to get it managed. . . . Let me entreat you now once again more fully to resolve to come here before All Saint's rent, otherwise I doubt much if even the tenth man will plough their farms. There are two ships in Killybegs ready to sail with passengers, wherein are some of your tenants and several other gentlemen tenants in

arrear. [There is no] help for it, for there is no more to be got of the cat than the skin. . . . I can assure you there is a great deal more rent due you in your estate than will ever be paid you.[52]

An agent for the Vintners' company explained in 1718 that

> most thinking, intelligent people are of opinion that lands here must fall soon chiefly by reason that a great many of the inhabitants and tenants of that part of the country are going off to America and leaving their inhabitations and lands, which must of necessity reduce the rents very low in all the Northern counties.[53]

The popularity of emigration extended far inland.[54] A resident of Clones, Co. Monaghan, complained in 1684 about a tenant on the Barrett-Lennard estate who 'by the maggot of his wife is persuaded to sell all his stock and go for Carolina, [for] which I am sorry, for he was an excellent tenant – an honest man and paid his rent well.'[55] This was not the only such instance on the Barrett-Lennard estate. Edmund Kaine informed Barrett in 1718 of the widespread movement of the colonists in Monaghan:

> I have no news, but there is a hundred families gone through this town this week past for New England. . . . Mr. Bellffore . . . has set fifty tates of land . . . this day that is all waste, the tenants being all gone to New England, I believe, nor shall [he] have anything left but Irish at last. But I hope your honour's estate will be safe enough, for they complain most [that] the hardship of the tythes makes them all go, which is true, for the clergy is unreasonable.[56]

The problem was certainly not unique to the western and southern periphery of the province. In 1724 Carrickfergus was reported to be 'so miserably poor and gone to ruin and so many houses gone to waste that you must just take what we can get from the present tenants.' Only the presence of army officers kept the houses of the town occupied.[57] In a letter of 1729 in response to a request by the Lords Justices to 'their circuits to enquire into the reasons of the Protestants of the north of Ireland transporting themselves to New England and other foreign plantations,' Ezekiel Stewart of County Antrim tried to give a comprehensive answer. Wealthier tenants, he believed, feared that 'if they stay in Ireland, their children will be slaves, and that it is better for them to make money of their leases while they are worth something, to enable them to transport themselves and families to America. . . .' The poorer sort, on the other hand, were deluded by the talk of great wages for working men, and by Presbyterian ministers, some of whom left along with members of their congregations, 'bellowing from their pulpits' about 'rackers of rent and servers of tythes, with other reflections of this nature, which they know is pleasing to their people. . . .' But in general, Stewart believed that their reasons for leaving were as various as their circumstances: 'That many have cause to murmur and complain cannot be denied, some by the oppression of their landlords, these gentlemen, I will venture to say, are for the most part strangers to our country, others by tythe managers, some by the country courts, and a good number by the justices of the peace . . . ,' but not so many he thought, as were emigrating.[58]

Emigration reached its most alarming scale yet in the 1770s.[59] Paradoxically, as its scale increased the prevailing view of emigration among estate managers began to change. During the first half of the eighteenth century the increasing popularity of emigration to the American colonies allowed this tendency towards mobility to continue, and concern for its effects persisted. Wright suggested that the 'settler displacement effect' – the effect of the threat to immigrants from economic and political competion of the natives – operated forcefully in the early eighteenth century. With stable state power and plentiful and docile Catholic labour, 'Protestant tenants who spoke of their rights became more dispensable than hitherto.' When they left for America in huge numbers, landlords were nonchalant. Examples of such nonchalance do appear in estate records. Rose Peyton declared to her agent in 1694: 'As to those tenants you say will go away if they have not my land this year as they had it last year I am satisfied to let them go, none shall set my land till I go myself . . . I will endure no longer to be so abused.'[60] But the evidence presented here suggests that Peyton's intemperence was out of step with the general attitude of landlords towards emigrating Protestant tenants.[61] The foregoing evidence of concern about emigration before 1760 suggests that while Wright's concept is correct, the timing of its effects is wrong. The threat which Protestant emigration raised to the integrity of estates and to the supply of capital available to improve those estates was an overriding concern before 1760. Later, however, agents began to show some appreciation for the benefit which emigration had on now populous and complicated estates. 'It is wonderful to see the emigration to America,' declared James Hamilton, Jr., in 1792, and in the following year he took approving note of 'a vast many carloads of people from the upper part of Tyrone [passing] by this and every day these ten days on their way to Derry for America.'[62] Hamilton might have been less sanguine had the majority of this emigrant population not been Catholics. A large exodus of Catholics from Armagh and southwest Down to Westport, Co. Mayo, following the battle of the Diamond in 1795, may also have been welcomed by local landowners.[63] The sight of Protestants abandoning south Ulster, on the other hand, remained worrisome. A member of the Beresford family lamented to Lord Farnham in 1829: 'I am sorry to hear of many Protestants preparing to emigrate. I wish there was an enactment to prevent them, but I am quite sure that the union . . . [which] there has lately been cemented between all classes will be a great means of preventing them.'[64]

EMIGRATION AND TENANT RIGHT

The tenant-right market and the market for leases helped organize this exodus. While this was cause for much resentment among weak landlords in the early eighteenth century, by the end of the century it was widely recognized that tenant-right exchanges were fuelling the much-desired emigration of smallholders.[65] It was also clear to estate managers that if they were to retrieve the debts of their impoverished emigrants, they must come to grips with the tenant-right system. Estate managers were generally aware that many emigrants were leaving behind large debts not only to their landlords but to other tenants.[66] Managers were also generally aware that many of these indebted emigrants were selling the tenant right of their farms to facilitate their departure. Abercorn noticed that tenants 'with the best bargains' were more prone to emigrate than others because they drew higher tenant-right prices.[67] Lord Donegall's agent, who was sensitive to the economic ramifications of the heavy emigration of the 1770s, reported that 'some of the people might be spared, but the money taken with them is what makes this country wretched. The sums gone and going out is inconceivable.' The same, he declared, was true of the neighbouring Hillsborough and Hertford estates.[68] Two other agents in the north of Ireland noticed the link between the enormous migration of Presbyterians to America in the early 1770s and their ability to sell their leases at exorbitant prices: 'Many of them who rented farms upon lease in places which were let at the highest increased rents, raised a great deal of money from the sale of their leases, which proves that the misery of Ireland does not proceed from the landlords' racking their tenants.'[69] Tenant-right sales also facilitated some of the migration of Armagh weavers to Mayo in 1795.[70]

Agents soon realized the connections between indebted tenants, emigration, and the sale of tenant right. In 1719 Kaine attempted to gain some control over this situation: 'I have been with all that has got your honour's life [in their leases] and showed them your honour's directions about their selling and buying without your honour's consent. Your honour may be sure [that] none will do it again. [We would] rather renew them that has a mind to live in the country but them that sold is gone to New England.'[71] Robert McCausland expressed similar concerns about the district around Limavady to Thomas Conolly in 1728:

> As to the generality of your lordship's tenants in the manor of Limavady, I
> see no danger of the least loss to your lordship if some of them should go
> to the West Indies, for they will sell their leases. But all the danger I foresee

is they may sell to bad tenants that may be troublesome hereafter in paying their rents. But all care should be taken to prevent such evils if it be possible.[72]

Later in the century James Speer, an agent in Aughnacloy, Co. Tyrone, had mastered the system. He explained that some of the tenants on the Foljambe estate

> are selling in order to go to America, which is in some measure the cause of the rents being gotten in better last year and the arrears somewhat lessened. When a tenant sells, I insist upon almost all of the arrear being paid, and as the spirit of emigration is increasing every day, I suppose the arrear will be considerably lessened in a few years. Indeed, I enforce the payment of the rents over the estate more punctually than formerly, by which I find the tenants are becoming more industrious. Some few of the leases, I believe, would not sell for the amount of the arrear due on them, so that in such instances a part will be lost, and if proper steps be not taken soon, the loss will be greater. . . .[73]

The nineteenth-century management of tenant-right sales, which is explored in greater detail in Chapter 5, was directed toward the promotion of emigration. This strategy was most prominently used during the crisis decades of the 1830s and 1840s. On the Drapers' estate in the nineteenth century tenant-right sales were often not of sufficient magnitude to allow the seller enough money to emigrate, so the company supplemented the proceeds of the sale with further subsidies to guarantee that the seller was safely removed from the country with no outstanding debts.[74] The correspondence of the Drapers' company managers is peppered with examples of this subsidization.[75] These ad hoc policies were transformed into a large scale program during and after the famine. Of eighteen tenants who applied for assistance to emigrate in 1847,

> nine have [disposed] or are about to dispose of their farms, which nine farms have or are to be amalgamated and the houses either at present down or are to come down. Four others lost their farms at the squaring of the townlands in 1842, and other farms were enlarged by these four being amalgamated with them, and these four families have squatted down upon the estate. We took [the] liberty of recommending some assistance be given to them, as they were unable to pay their passage to America. Of the remaining five of the eighteen, four of the farms were disposed of to sons of tenants where we could not get them amalgamated. The fifth was a son of a tenant who with his wife and family settled with his father, and we recommend that the land should be sold and all should go to America.[76]

In a decade when astute managers wished to avoid the opprobrium associated with mass clearances, the Millers of Draperstown were careful not to appear to be encroaching too much on the 'tenant right' of the emigrants. The Millers explained their strategy in a letter of April, 1847: 'We do not mean to purchase the interests of the tenants out, who were anxious to emigrate, but only to assist them to procure their passages when the purchase money of their farms would not enable them to get away. We stated that after the arrear of rent was paid and more or less of small debts, that too often the sum left was not sufficient to pay passage money.'[77] The Drapers' company officially ended the policy of subsidizing emigration in 1854, since the 'times have considerably changed.'[78] The policy was not only tactful, it made financial sense as well. Each ejectment would cost the company £2 5s. If their poor rates were added to this, the Millers figured that it was worth getting rid of them through assistance. They urged the reluctant management committee in London that if they 'had money to spare, it would be worth their while, if there were no tenant right, to purchase at their sole expense many of the small farms and add them to others, charging a moderate interest for the capital so expended, but so long as the tenant right exists there is no occasion for such a proceeding.'[79] Later in the year they gave an example of a woman and her family who had sold their farm but were denied assistance to emigrate and were now a charge on the poor rates: 'Looking at matters in a business-like way, it would have been cheaper for the court to have assisted her and her children to get to America than to pay for perhaps the duration of their lives the greater portion of their support.'[80] Landlords and agents who looked at the matters of emigration and tenant-right sales in a businesslike way discovered a marvellously efficient and relatively peaceful mechanism for accomplishing the often ugly task of clearing their estates of unwanted tenants. The evidence suggests that in the eighteenth century managers began to use the tenant-right market to their advantage. It was not until the nineteenth century that managers like the Millers of Draperstown were in a position to actually subsidize emigration. By then, requests for assistance to emigrate submitted by the tenants themselves begin to appear more often in estate correspondence.[81]

TENANT RIGHT AND IMPROVEMENT

The preceding evidence shows how important tenant-right sales were to those who left Ireland. But this outward mobility was also critical in shaping perspectives on the society that was left behind. Tenant mobility, supported by pastorally-oriented productive practices and propelled by an active market for leases and other tenancies, disturbed the settlement of plantation estates, interrupting improvement and settlement. Improvement, the settlement and alteration of the landscape, complemented this tradition of mobility. The constructive remnants left behind by emigrants practising settled arable farming – more solid houses and fences, enclosures – signified the colonial transformation of the estate system. In the context of the tendency toward emigration by the newcomers and the resilient mobility of the natives, the colonists could view the decay, deterioration, and depletion of landed estates as a natural force against which human labour operated.

The first and foremost issue with regard to responsibility for improvements was financial compensation. The issue was anticipated in an agreement between the provost of Trinity College and Thomas Vincent in 1658. Trinity College, according to the agreement,

> in setting their lands in the county of Donegal, did covenant with diverse tenants to whom the said lands were set, for their encouragement in building and planting, that if after the term granted to them by said agent they should not be continued any longer tenants on their said demise, that they should be contented for what they should build or plant upon the premises according as it should be valued by four men, whereof two for the college and two for the tenants, as will further appear by said contracts. . . .[82]

Evidence of significant compensation for improvements is hard to find before the eighteenth century.[83] It is well to remember the considerable risks involved with major improvements, as the experience of a tenant on the Anglesey estate who was financially ruined by 'an indiscreet expense which he brought upon himself and led me into in the reclaiming of the strand of Greenore . . .'[84] The greater frequency of claims and the higher level of compensation by that time may have been the result of the construction of more substantial houses.[85] Thomas Dawson revealed his conception of improvement when he informed Thomas Barrett-Lennard that his estate was 'very much improved and several new houses built and buildings, I mean good farm houses, not little smoky cottages.'[86]

The past efforts of tenants to improve their farms or houses, or the promise to do so in the future, became the basis for a successful claim for renewed tenure. In an uncertain economic and political climate a claim could be made by tenants for merely reproducing their status as tenants, for preserving the minimum base upon which future improvements might be erected, and this meant simply reproducing farms and families physically. Those who abided by the letter of their contracts were then in a position to undercut the most crucial aspect of the lease contract – that it ended when it ended – by articulating the more fundamental historicity that joined their farms and their labour together in a narrative. One Cork landlord was of the opinion that 'improvers were by definition those who had kept their contract; it was "a sort of justice" to prefer them or their heirs; all other things being equal – it was 'reasonable, though not strictly a duty' – and those who improved beyond what they undertook should not suffer.'[87] In Castledillon, Co. Armagh, in 1700, the landlord paid very close attention to the history of improvement on specific farms when deciding on what type of lease to give, treating improvers or their close relatives most beneficially.[88] On the Barrett-Lennard estate the sitting tenant was allowed the first right to renew if he offered to improve, but quite often he or she was not acceptable owing to past misbehaviour.[89] A tenant on the Anglesey estate petitioned for the right of renewal, resting his claim entirely on his long history of investment in the property. He testified

> that your petitioner in the year 1730 took the old Abbey Garden, which was then waste and uninhabited, from your honourable father Sir Edward Bayly at the yearly rent of £1.10s. p.a., and with labour and industry built and planted until 1740, and then it came into the hands of Mr. Robert Draper and Mr. James Rooney, who raised your petitioner's rent to £3 p.a. [Your petitioner] then was obliged to improve yet more to enable him to pay the raised rent. Therefore your honourable petitioner leaves it to your honour's consideration and most humbly begs that [as] he has but about two years of his lease to come, he may not be turned out or left desolate of a place to dwell in his old days.[90]

In the nineteenth century petitions similar in tone and content to this became more common.[91]

Improvement meant more than residence and the building of houses and fences; it also referred to a new form of production which not only produced the wealth necessary for physical improvements but was organizationally distinct from Gaelic pastoralism. The artefacts of improvement were not so remarkable on their own, but when contrasted with the less substantial infrastructure of the traditional Gaelic pastoral communities, they stored a social charge that they would not have otherwise possessed. This is very clear in the commentary of some Munster landlords. 'Improvements' on the Perceval/ Egmont estate were associated with arable production, i.e. 'farm building and planting,' distinct from the more flimsy fixed assets of the pastoral economy.[92] One steward observed in 1747 that 'most people here think that every shilling which is laid out in trade viz in buying cattle in cheap seasons and selling in dear answers infinitely better than burying it as they call it in improvements.'[93] The agent of a Kerry property in 1690 observing the small rental, wondered 'what the same would yield had their natures allowed them Irish gentlemen to build good houses, plant orchards, set on fields with double ditch and quicks and other improvements as by their leases were bound to do.' A Protestant prospective tenant to a farm described in 1710 'how he had found it like a Papist's farm without either bounds made on a bush on the same, [no] cabin but three such as our cowherds generally live in. . . .'[94] Speaking of three estates of the Earl of Cork, one commentator wrote that 'he would not set a lease to a native, because they are quite the reverse to improvements.'[95] The problem in Ulster as well as Munster was that the envisioned tidy geometry of compact and enclosed farms would never prosper on the basis of arable production alone. The danger was therefore that a largely subsistence-based yet commercialized form of production might degenerate in a downward spiral of poverty as communal natives and individualist newcomers alike subdivided the holding of ethnically cohesive townlands amongst close and distant kin. The remainder of this chapter investigates how the combination of the spinning wheel, the loom, and the potato helped landlords and tenants to forestall this danger.

THE WEAKNESS OF PLANTATION TOWNS

For the structure of plantation estates to survive, a market network that tied together the dispersed settlers in an economic fabric was essential. The military conquest of Ulster had established an archipelago of fortified posts.[96] The goal of the plantation was to develop these into urban centres with commercial links to the outside world. Robinson shows that by the 1660s 'most British-owned farms were within three miles of a market, and ninety per cent were within a five-mile radius. Irish-owned hearths, on the other hand, were not so closely distributed in relation to the market centres. Occupying marginal lands, substantial numbers of Irish farms were outside the effective ranges of the markets.'[97] As in the previous chapter, this distinction should not be overstated. Robinson finds that 'although the articles of plantation required settlers to live in towns or villages, more than two-thirds of the plantation estates contained neither. . . . In fact, the great majority of plantation colonists did not live in nucleated settlements of any sort, but were scattered among the townlands they leased and farmed.'[98] The weakness of towns, according to Robinson, was directly related to two fundamental characteristics of Ulster society: the productive bias toward pastoralism and the fragmentation of tenancies.[99] In east Ulster, for reasons which are made apparent below, these characteristics were less in evidence and urban centres developed with greater success. West of the River Bann, the complete dependence of the towns on the success of the surrounding agricultural and industrial forces of production is clear from estate records.[100]

The essentially rural character of the towns is one reason why town parks were so important to the management of estates. To develop towns, landlords had to offer suburban agricultural parks at beneficial leases to attract capitalists and rural cultivators.[101] The managers of the Barrett-Lennard estate, for example, struggled to maintain the integrity of Clones, the urban seat of their estate, throughout the eighteenth century.[102] Thomas Noble suggested that offering leases with lives renewable forever in the town with parks attached 'would encourage numbers of the Protestant tenants to come to the town. . . . I have no doubt but in a short time Clones would be a flourishing little town and not a tenant in it that would not slate their houses they having that tenure of them.'[103] Even as late as 1808 William Mayne was concerned to talk up what had in fact been only modest development: 'The town of Clones is increasing in buildings, population, and wealth. Indeed, all matters appear [to be] doing well through the estate, and after you look over the new rental, [I] shall prepare leases for the deserving.'[104] But Clones more closely resembled the towns of the south of Ireland, overrun as it was with poor Catholics, than the prosperous markets of the northeast. The owners of the town of Edenderry in King's County, who also held a County Down property, sought to get rid of all Catholics from the town except those involved in the linen trade. Henry Blundell's agent responded helplessly in 1721:

> You are pleased to order that I should think of a method to get rid of the popish inhabitants of this town. I heartily wish I could, that it were in my power to remove them speedily, for then there should be none left but a very few that are useful to carry on the manufacture and are earnest and inoffensive in their dealings. All I can do in that affair is to threaten those that take them as tenants with double rents and your displeasure, in answer to which most of them tell me that their own holdings being too large for themselves, they do the better to enable them to pay their rents to set some parts to papists.[105]

In a town like Clones, it was a struggle to preserve the distinction between town parks and farms, as Nicholas Ellis did in 1843:

> Town parks and farms come under very different rates. A farm is set to a man for the purpose of being used as ground out of which he is to make his rent and support his family. Not so town parks: they are for the conveniences of the undertenants of the town, for their cows and horses and hay and potatoes. It never was intended that town parks should be let at such prices as to enable them – with the superior advantages of manure, of market, [and] of setting conacre – to compete with the farms at a distance and to injure them.[106]

Even though it was ideally located in the Foyle valley, managers of the Abercorn estate also had some difficulty developing the town of Strabane. Although in 1750 it was one of the few Ulster towns boasting a twice-weekly provision and linen market, a new town hall, constructed by Abercorn, and boat traffic from the port of Derry at the rate of over 100 vessels per year, the Abercorn estate records provide little evidence for the growth of Strabane later in the century.[107] The town hall constructed in 1750 was overcrowded immediately and was still the only building in town in which to do business thirty years later.[108] There is little evidence of other construction. In 1770 it was found that most of the tenements on the east side of Patrick street, which had been available for over three years, were lying waste, with the former tenants heavily in arrears, and that 'no building goes on this season.' Some of the departing tenants left Strabane to colonize bog-land in the nearby townland of Backfence. Much of the unleased acreage, whether urban or freehold, was of high value in Strabane.[109] But the parks to the south of the town were held by wealthy urbanites who were not necessarily farmers. Those parks that were 'too distant to the town to be used by the town are held by poor people' underwent very little improvement.[110]

CAPITAL SHORTAGE AND THE LINEN INDUSTRY

Why was this urban infrastructure so weak? The master notion of seventeenth and eighteenth-century Irish history, the Aristotlean cause without a cause, is capital shortage. In the effort to understand the 'underdevelopment' of the Irish economy, the backwardness of agrarian productivity, the tardiness of non-agricultural expansion, the dysfunctionality of the relations of production in the countryside, all roads lead to the scarcity of capital. For most historians, this *prima facie* explanation is satisfactory, adequate for the classroom and for terse contextualization of other historical issues, and in need of little elaboration.[111] Gillespie, for example, explains that capital shortage constrained non-agricultural economic growth. He emphasizes higher interest rates and undeveloped capital markets in Dublin, but he believes that the real reason for the capital shortage was that 'the great magnates of Tudor and Stuart England and Scotland had not, in the main, shown great interest in acquiring land. Those who were attracted by the prospect of cheap land and quick profit were men with few assets to support them.'[112] He goes on to complain of the lack of a workable credit system, but surely if the investment was forthcoming, the credit system would have followed. Apparently, the smart and concentrated money was to be expended elsewhere.

Why? The question leads directly to serious theoretical and empirical difficulties. Before one can explain why capital is scarce one must explain how it is produced. This in turn depends on an understanding of the conditions of its existence, and the processes of its production and reproduction. In short, without an understanding of the genesis of capitalism, its development in long waves of accumulation punctuated by periods of crises and reorientation, and the geographically uneven and differential character of these developments, there can be no understanding of capital shortage. But should the following paragraphs succeed in succinctly clarifying these conceptual matters, they will only serve to introduce the unwieldy historical problem of grasping the movement of the capitalist system in the seventeenth and eighteenth centuries, the erosion of pre-capitalist systems coming under its domestic, colonial, and imperial influence, and the place of Ireland in these developments. The problem is especially difficult because much of the best writing on the empirical aspects of the question is sorely inadequate on the conceptual side, while conceptually elegant writing rarely adequately fleshes out the empirical details.

The first step toward an answer to the question is to place the period of the plantation of Ulster within the orbit of a capitalist world-system suffering a profound crisis and reorientation. The explanation of Irish capital shortage must therefore take account of both the primitive accumulation of capital in Ireland and its place within an international economy also accommodating itself to the capitalist transformation. The seventeenth century was a period of stabilization and retrenchment of a capitalist world system, now firmly established by the long sixteenth-century expansion, and of a reordering of the dominant nation-states within that system by the thirty years' war.[113] Explanations of the crisis of the seventeenth century in general, and the capital shortage facing rural Europe in particular, are very hard to come by.[114] Jan de Vries rehearses the explanations on offer, rejecting in turn Malthusian arguments (the century is often one of labour shortage, not oversupply), the bellicosity of the thirty years' war (warfare was an important economic stimulus rather than an alternative to productive investment), and contraction in the money supply (the empirical link between contractions in the money supply and periods of stagnation is quite weak). The only explanation left is Hobsbawm's argument that the century is best characterized as a crisis of 'capitalism within a feudal framework.' Hobsbawm offers a 'portrait of an economy in which capital is misinvested out of frustration,'[115] but one in which the relative success of Britain and the Netherlands pointed the way to the rapid economic expansion of the the next century.

Any analysis of the capital shortage facing Ireland in this period must be placed in the context of the reaction of the British state to the general crisis, and the direction toward which capital flowed as a result of that response. England, unique in Europe, experienced an enormous transformation and significant capital accumulation. Why didn't Ireland benefit from English investment? Ulster faced a capital shortage because in the seventeenth century it was not a capitalist economy, even though some halting steps were taken in that direction. Without capitalism, no capital. To go briefly back to the basics, social production is an interrelation of (1) labourers, (2) the means of production, that is, that part of nature taken as the object of labour and the means by which that object is transformed, and (3) non-labourers. Capitalism is a mode of production where these three are connected by the constitution of the object of labour as private property. This creates a framework in which 'the labour process is an operation between things which the capitalist has purchased.'[116] One of these things is the power of the labourer, now separated from the direct relation which he or she might have had with the realization of value.[117] This framework frees the capitalist to explore the endless possible combinations of labour, objects of labour, and means of labouring in the effort to realize value. Capital is mediated labour. A capital shortage is, in this sense, the shortage of a particular kind of labour. Successful colonization always involves more than the exploitation of resources, it must establish this kind of labour, and, necessarily, a new kind of property, on a frontier.[118] How was this accomplished in Ulster?

This chapter has already argued that tillage production on enclosed farms would not alone fulfil the requirements of capital accumulation. In the absence of a vigorous accumulation based on traditional agricultural products, the linen industry became a crucial link between the successful development of Ulster towns and the stabilization of the unsteady rural economy and the accumulation of capital. How does one accumulate capital with nothing but an estate with a dysfunctional settlement pattern? The answer was to extract it from the available labour by promoting a trade with both low capital investment requirements and available market outlets. The putting-out system of the linen trade fit these requirements perfectly. To understand the origins of the linen trade in Ireland, the scope must be widened to an Atlantic proto-imperial economy. In this context, the promotion of textile production can be seen to have a strong political content. The elimination of duties from all Irish flax products in 1698 was done expressly to 'encourage "foreign Protestants" to settle in Ireland.'[119] The English linen act of 1705, extended in 1717, allowed Irish linen to travel directly to the West Indies for sale. The debate surrounding the passage and extension of this act pitted the representatives of English linen interests in the English parliament against both the Irish linen interests in the Dublin parliament and the English executives who were concerned to solidify the colonial administration in Ireland.[120] Manchester linen merchants complained to parliament that direct Irish access to American markets would be 'extremely detrimental to them and many counties in England, it tending greatly to the discouragement, not only of the English linen manufactory, which cannot be made at so low a price as in Ireland, but also the woollen manufacture . . .' because they were trading wool for German flax and yarn to make linen for American markets.[121] A report of a House of Lords committee appointed to consider the Irish House of Commons request for direct access to American markets reiterated that it was the intention of earlier legislation to protect English woollen production from any Irish competition, but if the Irish 'turn their industry to the settling and improving [of] the linen manufacture, they should receive all countenance, favour, and protection for the encouragement and promotion of the same.'[122] In 1715 the earl of Sunderland felt that 'the linen trade is in a manner all that is left to Ireland and ought therefore to be encouraged as much as possible.'[123]

The system of bounties for Irish linen passing through English ports also had the effect of 'strengthening English commercial institutions' while continuing to 'frustrate the development of a domestic market-oriented linen manufacture in the American colonies.' The linen bounty was in effect 'a tax on the subjects of Great Britain' for the benefit of Dublin merchants, Ulster producers, and English shippers.[124] Developing the Ulster production occurred at the expense of both Lancashire and the colonies. France, Holland, and Belgium were locked out of this market by prohibitive duties, though German duties were low enough to allow Hamburg merchants to operate in London. Under the Navigation Acts any Irish linen destined for America had to travel through English ports. London merchants who dealt in German cloth in America petitioned the House of Commons on 5 April 1717 against extension of the 1705 Act claimed that the act 'was enacted for the support of the Protestant interest in Ireland and for the encouragement of the linen manufacture of that kingdom.' Another petition from City of London linen drapers urged that 'the trade of the plantations may be carried on as much for the advantage of Great Britain as Ireland.'[125]

What was the impact of these concerted efforts to promote Irish linen in the world market? Protected markets and bounties gave Irish exporters a narrow price advantage over even domestic production in the colonies, but this protection should be viewed within a scenario of comparative advantage to American agricultural production. Americans were better off specializing in agriculture and trading for linen. 'It was because the real price of imported linen continued to decline, as the real cost of domestic manufacture increased, that Irish linen imports roughly doubled between 1750 and 1760, and doubled again between 1760 and 1770.'[126] Still, the political efforts may have been decisive in encouraging landlords to invest in the industry. As Cullen has concluded, 'grudging and incomplete though it was, the encouragement of the Irish linen industry in the form of the removal of import duties was one of the decisive factors in its evolution.'[127] The Linen Bounty Act of 1745, according to Truxes, 'was the single most important encouragement to Ireland's transatlantic linen trade. After its passage, Irish linens competed in America on better terms than the German fabrics that had been long established there.'[128]

After the abolition by the British government in 1696 of import duties on Irish plain linens entering England, the landlord-sponsored linen industry in Ulster responded, so that Irish exports of linen climbed from less than 1.5

million yards in 1712 to 5.5 million in 1734, 11 million in 1750, and 46 million in 1796.[129] Crawford writes: 'It is difficult to conceive what eighteenth-century Ulster would have been like without the linen industry.'[130] Contemporaries would have certainly agreed with this statement. A number of Munster landlords attempted to attract Ulster Protestant linen artisans into the towns of their estates.[131] One articulate Cork landowner drew a clear link between the lack of promising opportunities for the development of estates, the serious dangers facing landlords whose improvements were rapidly deteriorating, and the necessity of establishing the linen industry. Northern landlords anxious to develop the incomes of their estates aggressively promoted this growth.[132] Lord Hillsborough, Arthur Brownlow, Sir Richard Cox, William Waring, and other proprietors invested heavily in urban construction, roads, canals, and linen equipment in centres of trade such as Lurgan, Hillsborough, and Cookstown. The first 'manufacturers' of linen were immigrant Quakers and Huguenots who settled in what became the 'linen triangle' region bounded by Lisburn, Dungannon, and Newry in east Ulster.[133] For example, Waring gave one lease in 1699 on his estate in County Down in exchange for an advanced rent and the promise to build a bleach yard.[134] Arthur Brownlow's efforts in the town of Lurgan were described by a traveller in 1708:

> This town is at present the greatest mart of linen manufacturers in the north, being almost entirely peopled with linen weavers, and all by the care and cost of Mr. Brownlow. On first establishing this trade here, [Brownlow] bought up everything that was brought to the market. [He] lost at first considerably, but at length the thing fixed itself, and he is now by the same methods a considerable gainer.[135]

Lisburn was the major linen centre before it was destroyed by a devastating fire. The developments in the linen triangle were already pleasing to this traveller's eye in 1708. From Lisburn, he remarked, 'we went on . . . to Belfast through a country all the way from Armagh extremely pleasant, well improved, and inhabited by English.'

Leasing policies and landlord sponsorship were crucial to the promotion of the linen industry. Wright suggested that 'the Ulster bleaching trade – which required heavy investment in fixed immovable assets – was virtually the exclusive preserve of Protestants who could legally acquire long leases.'[136] The agent of the Anglesey estate showed some excitement in 1783 over some Newry merchants who wanted to rent land in Omeath for summer residences,[137] and advised Uxbridge that if he was to develop Omeath into a centre of trade, he must give leases in perpetuity to encourage building, as 'it is the custom everywhere in the kingdom.' There were other plans to build a harbour to compete with Warrenpoint and Newry.[138] Dacre Barrett also invested the surplus income of his estate in linen and butter production, and agents on the Barrett-Lennard estate paid close attention to the development of linen production there, remarking on the completion of a bleach yard in the spring of 1741.[139] John Todd submitted this report to Barrett-Lennard in 1744: 'As to the linen trade on your estate, I think it goes on very well; several of the tenants have weavers in their houses and pretty bleach yards on their farms, and Mr. Ramadge bleaches vast quantities of linen every season.' Todd added that despite being recently cheated by a linen factor in Clones, 'he pays his rent very well and so do the Quakers,' although the latter had not yet built bleach yards or improved according to the covenants in their leases.[140] He compared the market for yarn and butter in Clones favourably with any found in the 'north of Ireland' in 1748, observing that the men in the town purchased green cloth, whitened it, and sold it. He also commented on the many weavers in the neighbouring countryside, though there were none in the town. The Clones dealers eased the difficulty of rent collection by bringing money to the area. Todd hoped that Clones would develop into a market for cloth and corn in addition to yarn and butter.[141] Although this never happened, Thomas Noble boasted about the 'great number of buyers from County Down and Newry' appearing in Clones in 1771.[142] The eighth and ninth earls of Abercorn supported the linen industry in the Foyle valley by obtaining weaving equipment from the Linen Board, by completely funding the construction of a canal on the river Foyle between Strabane and Londonderry, and by encouraging the practice of spinning and weaving among tenants whose rents were overdue.[143] He stopped short of building a linen hall in the town, leaving it to 'the provost and the burgesses and commonalty, to whom the market belongs.'[144] He was, however, willing to supply the estate with the machinery necessary for linen production.[145] Most of these donations were acquired from the Linen Board in Dublin and reflected Abercorn's place in the parliamentary pecking order as much as his generosity.[146] The estate also acquired grants from the Linen Board to subsidize the planting of flax.[147]

Linen production in south Ulster was underdeveloped by comparison to the northeast, for according to Edmund Kaine of Clones, the better linen was unavailable in south Ulster in 1721 because weavers were forced to sell their yarn: 'My wife is using all means to get your honour's good lady four pieces of linen that is good. She designs to go to Lurgan to get it right, for it is not to be got in this country, for they have sold all their yarn to keep their necessity this bad winter.'[148] But the dependence on the trade had increased dramatically outside the linen triangle by the last quarter of the century. In Monaghan, recovery from the depressed 1740s depended on a mixture of a good corn crop, healthy cattle, and a strong linen market.[149] The Barrett-Lennard agent was hopeful in 1747 that 'with this good weather a fine prospect of corn and grain of all kinds amongst us, and with the yarn and linen cloth, which now give a good price as well as the young cattle and dry cows, will enable them to pay their rents more regularly than they have been able to do for some time past.'[150]

The specialization of small farmers in spinning and weaving first became apparent in the years preceding the American revolution. After 1770 rents due on the Abercorn estate in the autumn generally could not be collected until after the harvest was completed and tenants had time to spin, weave, and sell yarn and cloth. This dependence became distressingly obvious in both 1773 and 1778, when estate income was crippled by a slumping linen market even though the oat harvest had been abundant. Even in good years for oats and linen, such as 1775, tenants would delay paying rent until after market conditions were suitable for the sale of their yarn and linen. In April 1776 Hamilton offered his employer this apology for tardy payments: 'some know times will mend, and others will not forego the profit they can make by keeping a web or two of yarn in their hands until they are forced' to pay rent.[151] Hamilton believed in 1777 that 'the most substantial of the tenants have their money in cloth and yarn'[152] in order to speculate in a rising market, but that small farmers had an even greater stake in the industry. In 1776 he observed:

> The times of late have been as favourable as ever I remember them to tenants who hold small farms. I have spurred them more than I usually did, especially since the harvest, and many of them have paid pretty well, yet I find if I was to press some hard, that they could not do, as it would be taking from them the money [with which] they buy the yarn that keeps them weaving. They promise that in the course of this winter they will do a great deal.[153]

By 1784 James Hamilton had cause to complain that the number of local bleach greens was insufficient. The steady decline of yarn exports and the rapid rise in cloth exports after 1780 are evidence of a significant development in the regional economy. The rapid decline of linen imports also supports the thesis that more cloth was being produced in the hinterlands of Londonderry. The Abercorn estate correspondence reveals more concern for spinners and weavers toward the end of the century. By the 1790s spinners on the estate had become dependent on local rather than foreign demand for yarn. That dependence was in evidence in the middle of the decade when many weavers either emigrated or joined the militia in greater numbers.[154] The fall of the linen market in the years before 1816 was considered to be the dominant cause of the large arrears accumulating on the Barrett-Lennard estate. In 1815 the agent declared: 'At present, honourably moderate as your estate is let in Ireland, your rents can't be paid by agriculture; the linen trade is all we can look to for existence in this country.'[155]

Perhaps the most revealing evidence of the importance of linen production in the eighteenth century was the continual shortage of flax and flaxseed. The seasons immediately following a poor flax harvest, such as those of 1758, 1778, 1783, and 1794, were disastrous for the Abercorn estate.[156] Tenants were forced to buy their supplies of flaxseed on credit at exorbitant prices, on 'nearly a third more than their value.'[157] Those who could not afford the peak seasonal prices might be forced to delay their purchases until too late in the planting season. The poorest tenants were often dependent on aid from the landlord. Landlord and agent were agreed that the success of the industry depended on self-supplied flax, but the cottiers' plots were too small, and the supply from large farms became increasingly deficient. Estate agents were forced to depend on Derry merchants who imported American seed. But the foreign supply of flax and flaxseed was highly volatile and could not be relied upon.[158] James Hamilton described this chronic problem in 1783:

> We must grow greater quantities or import much more flax than we do at present, [or] else our spinners would want flax half of their time at least. [Even] with all [that is grown here], flax is scarce almost every year. The cottier, if he can, must grow flax, [but since] he gets the refuse of the tenant's land, he is generally disappointed. Since our American war we seldom get good seed or enough of it. I wonder why much more flax is not imported.[159]

The small farmer had always been the most aggressive cultivator of flax. It was reported of Carrickfergus in 1722 that flax-seed 'is the chief thing they have hereabouts to live by.'[160] In spite of the generally poor quality of their land James Hamilton felt that an abundant flax harvest had the effect of 'enabling those of smallholdings to get forward.'[161] The concentration of flax production among small farmers was revealed by the subsidization of the planting of flax by the Linen Board in 1781.[162] No less than 729 tenants on the Abercorn estate received a total of £233 at the rate of £1 10s. per acre of flaxseed sown. But these tenants held only 716 acres between them, 350 of which must have been under flax. The recipients of the subsidies held on average less than an acre and cultivated flax on roughly half that land. Abercorn clearly felt that the success of the linen industry depended on the ability of these cottier-weavers to supply themselves with flax. Flax culture may even have supplanted the growth of oatmeal for subsistence, for Hamilton found that 'many who have ten and some who have farms as high as twenty [acres] have been buying their bread for a long time.'[163] This dependence on flax presaged an important development. With the mechanization of textile production and the collapse of the cottier-weaving economy in the nineteenth century, flax production was to become the only remaining profitable rural employment in the linen industry.

The linen manufacturers of Strabane, as in most localities where linen production had become entrenched, were the main bearers of commerce and the source of currency. Local economies became almost entirely dependent on linen commerce to keep money in circulation so that, among other things, the rents could be paid. Those who provided working capital to linen producers maintained a critical link to creditors in the Dublin market as well controlling the importation of flaxseed. The agent Nathanial Nesbitt observed in 1760: 'Ever since I knew business, bank notes have been of little use in this part of the kingdom where the linen trade is carried on, as nothing will carry that branch but ready money. There is no such thing as a bank note in the hands of a dealer in this country.' When the linen trade slumped temporarily in 1764 and again in the early 1770s, the money supply dried up and incomes suffered. In 1764 there was 'the greatest scarcity of bills, owing chiefly to the linen drapers not having money in Dublin.'[164] Money scarcity inhibited rent collection in 1736, 1758, 1764, 1767, 1776, 1778, and 1788.[165] The eighth earl's decision to transmit rent payments through Dublin merchants because no qualified candidate could be found in Strabane revealed the financial weakness of the urban seat of his estate.[166] The Abercorns used Dublin bankers throughout the century. The Nugent estate on the Ards peninsula of County Down also depended financially on Dublin.[167] Clones had no monetary connections directly with England or with Belfast.[168] According to William Mayne, sometimes acute shortages of cash had a dramatic effect on the local economy around Clones:

> Where money can be had by your tenants until after next harvest I cannot say. Your drawing is dangerous at present. I shall do my utmost to uphold our credit. . . . Though moderately let, yet in so numerous a tenantry some either from extravagance, indolence, or misfortune had not paid me . . . , so that I received no [?] except advancing their rent for sometime. Indeed, some of your good tenants often have given me cash for my bills on Dublin, which served me and answered their demands.[169]

On the Downshire estate in 1746, getting a bill to Dublin depended on 'linen dealers going up or corn exported from this season. The last £200 paid and the cash in my hands was all by the produce of linen.'[170] This was especially true during harvest crises. The Downshire agent noted in 1746 that 'the bulk of the rent here was always paid by manufacturing of sundry kinds, especially linen cloth, and not by the produce of the lands, and that has been so low of late, occasioned by the rebellion.'[171] On the Anglesey estate in 1778, rents were forthcoming only after the cloth sales.[172] Thomas Noble reported from the Barrett-Lennard estate in 1773 that distraining for rent was of no use: there was no money because of the linen-market slump.[173]

LINEN COMMERCE AND LANDHOLDING

The development of linen commerce was crucial to the accumulation of capital, the expansion of economic opportunity, and the general stability of the plantation estate system in eighteenth-century Ulster. The nature of this development was complicated both in terms of its geographic spread and its social effects. Linen production developed most intensively in an area of south-east Ulster, known as the 'linen triangle,' between Lisburn, Dungannon, and Newry. In this district a growing population of weavers settled on small plots, paid their rents and secured their livelihoods exclusively by their work at their looms, supplied with yarn by merchants connected to a far-flung population of hand spinners. A pattern of subdivision in which leaseholders sublet to weavers and spinners rather than farming the land themselves began in many areas of eastern Ulster as early as 1740.[174] The growth of this system had a dramatic effect on landholding and the value of rented land. The geographic dispersal of linen production corresponds with geographic differences in rent levels and occupational density. Higher rents per acre and lower farm size were found in the eastern linen country, whereas the opposite characteristics prevailed in the more agriculturally-oriented southern and western counties.[175] As the century progressed, the specialization of smallholders began to spread westward on to estates whose tenants had previously only been engaged in the linen trade on a part-time basis. This expansion brought with it increased opportunities for many, but also a new set of problems for tenants, landlords, and agents. How much expansion would linen markets bear? What would happen to agricultural production in this proto-industrial scenario? Most critically, how was the great intensification in landholding, with its attendant tenurial complications, to be managed? In the relatively buoyant middle decades of the century these questions did not press themselves too urgently on estate managers. But by the 1790s they were unavoidable.

Specialized production was not traditionally the norm in the eighteenth-century Ulster countryside. Tenants were willingly eclectic in their productive pursuits and survived by combining together any number of activities, depending on local circumstances. To find money for their rents Omeath tenants were travelling in their fishing boats as far as Belfast to bring fish to Newry to sell there. In 1773 the agent could conduct no estate business with 'scarce one head of a family in all Omeath being at home.'[176] On the Downshire estate in 1748 'the Murlough tenants, as soon as they sell the remainder of their rabbit skins, promise to do their best to get their rent cleared.'[177] This is the context in which households, wives and daughters particularly, alighted on the relatively lucrative practice of hand-spinning prepared flax into yarn. The Revd. William Henry wrote in 1739 that the typical Donegal farmer 'generally contents himself with no more land than is necessary to feed his family, which he diligently tills, and depends on the industry of his wife and daughters to pay by their spinning the rent, and lay up riches.'[178] The growing dependence on yarn and cloth was at first incorporated into the traditional farming household, with little visible change, as Arthur Young observed on his way from Antrim to Derry: 'The farmers themselves have yarn spun for them in their houses, which they give to weavers to have it spun into cloth – the farmer himself tending to nothing but the management of his land. This appears to me a sign that I have quit the linen country, for there are more farmers than any set I have met with for some time.'[179] But appearances were deceptive, because such households rapidly came to depend on the linen income, even if they remained active in farming. Agondish Vesey was warned by James Hutchinson in a letter of 16 March 1708 that 'the poor people's rent' on his estate in Ballyclare, Co. Antrim 'depends on their cloth.' It was reported in Derry in 1720 that trade had been brought to a standstill by the recession in Manchester, 'where we used to have an annual demand for all the yarn we could spin.'[180] McEvoy's 1802 survey of County Tyrone shows that few smallholders could survive by farming alone. Because of the size of their holdings agricultural earnings had to be supplemented 'by the industry of the loom.'[181] Many tenants on the Abercorn estate were equally dependent on the sale of cattle and linen to pay their rents. James Hamilton of the Abercorn estate thought specialization in the cattle industry to be particularly risky:

> The prices of lean and fat cattle are very precarious, nor have I found for more than these seven years past that a man can compute with any certainty their profits in that branch of business. Cattle that we think will weigh when fat and fit for sale in October 400 lbs. will cost from £3 5s. to £3 10s, but when we come to sell, the merchant tells us there is no foreign demand.[182]

A failing linen market and the vulnerability of cattle stock in bad weather were the two crucial components of the failure to collect rent on the Conolly estate in County Londonderry in the 1770s. The agent Andrew Spotswood gloomily reported in June 1778: 'I have been using my utmost endeavours to bring in the November rents and assure you, sir, when I have impounded the tenants' cattle, [I] have been obliged to return them again for want of purchasers. And little or no money [is] given for cloth or yarn, so great is the distress of this part of the country.'[183] Henry Major in Ballyshannon corroborated Spotswood's report from Derry. The people around Ballyshannon were getting little or nothing for their poor black cattle and yarn, and this coupled with the harvest failure left many destitute and dependent on meal imported from Derry, Sligo, and Scotland.[184] He too had to release impounded cattle for lack of purchasers. In the following year Major continued to complain of 'an extraordinary scarcity of money' and 'bad markets for black cattle, which is at present almost the only article the tenants have for the payment of their rents, the failure of their crops of flax last season having in great measure deprived them of the usual assistance which the purchase of that article afforded them.'[185]

The problems created by expanding linen production concerned relationships, and therefore tenure, as well as livelihoods. With the expansion of the boundaries of the linen country came a mutation in the relationship between tenants and cottier/weavers. Traditionally, head tenants regarded the cottier's membership in the extended family as an apprenticeship, somewhat analogous to and interchangeable with that of the farmer's sons. After noting that the local production of yarn had become dependent by 1775 on both foreign and domestic demand, Abercorn remarked: 'I always think it right that the tenants should not be discouraged from keeping labouring servants in distinct tenements, provided the greater part of their labour be employed in the service of the tenants.'[186] In certain circumstances James Hamilton approved of farmers who let to cottiers:

> I really think I can observe the tenant's farm who has a working cottier in better order than one who has not one; his employing his cottier costs him, as he conceives, no money, and [he] wishes to get in his rent that way. . . . It would be good for the estate and for the cottier that he hold under the tenant [since the tenant] would give him weaving and labour to help him pay his rent. . . . They would live as friends.[187]

In Armagh cottiers were most commonly associated with tenant households where the 'holder is unmarried, or without children, or where the family is very young; where the tenant is very old, or . . . follows a full-time occupation other than farming.'[188] But weavers, although they may have remained dependent on the head tenant's bleach green or flax mill, also depended on the market for income to pay the rent and to purchase their sustenance. Their status was not that of an apprentice but rather of a mature and often independent producer of a final good. In the linen triangle smallholders who were directly employed by merchants or who worked independently 'secured small plots of land in the vicinity of a good market town and were able to pay a higher rent than any farmer who was prepared to earn his living by farming alone.'[189] Moreover, as the following chapters demonstrate, the land occupied by the cottier was often formerly an underdeveloped plot that he had transformed and improved into a viable unit of agricultural subsistence.

This new-found independence was translated into a claim on the soil. In the fifteen years after 1770 agents on the Abercorn estate were inundated with complaints concerning tension between tenants who sought to replace cottiers with their mature sons and cottiers seeking extension of their tenure or direct leases from Abercorn. The first such cases concerned George Leitch and Robert Harper, both of Listimore in the manor of Strabane, who attempted to oust undertenants immediately after they had enclosed and ditched a great deal of land.[190] Tristram Carey had the same problem with the relatively prosperous cottiers employed at his bleach green whom he sought to replace with his three sons.[191] John Smyly and James Kerr, two large farmers and operators of bleach greens and flax mills, had similar problems with undertenants demanding extended tenure in spite of the restrictive covenants to which they had earlier agreed.[192] In all these cases the root of the tension was a conflict between the new-found permanence claimed by colonizers and linen producers and the traditional transitory role of the cottier in the family tenancy.

In townlands with a multi-layered tenantry, where the head tenant might control considerably more capital than the undertenants, the latter might be dependent on the credit of the head tenant to pay rent. A 1753 petition of the twenty undertenants of the deceased Robert Ross on the Anglesey estate claimed that Ross, 'to enable your petitioners to pay the £49 rent, frequently lent them money to traffic with, not being able to pay said rent by the produce of the land.' This practice ended with his death, whereupon the agent Rooney began serving notices to quit.[193] James Hamilton, Jr., was aware in 1780 of 'many rich farmers who in common years would have been ready and willing to help their poorer neighbours with the loan of the rent.'[194] Local lenders around Strabane, however, were often far more rapacious than the landlord. In fact, loans or gifts given to tottering tenants by estate administrators often went straight into the hands of a lurking creditor.[195] Tenants who controlled crucial factors of production such as cows or flaxseed were often the most notorious creditors in a locality. Writing from the Dartrey estate in Dawson's Grove, Co. Monaghan, in 1773, J. Burrows criticized 'the oppression frequently exercised in this country, for the extreme poverty of the people makes them liable to extortion a thousand ways.' Burrows explained how those who needed a cow to subsist on buttermilk were exploited by cattle dealers:

> One of these undertakers sells a cow to two or three of these poor people, who give their own and their friend's security for it, for six or seven guineas, which is worth only three or four, and agrees to take the money by the week, the bond for this purpose an expense of three or four shillings. On the first failure of payment he seizes for seven guineas and recovers what he can get and his cow, and by a quick law process peculiar to this country, which they call a civil bill, puts the suffering party to the expense of twelve shillings and either ruins him beyond recovery, or keeps him in eternal slavery.

The benevolent landlord, he argued, could counteract this usury by hiring these people to work on his demesne and by providing them with the means to hold a cow, 'the reasonable price of it taken out in labour.'[196] The supply of linseed on the Abercorn estate was quite volatile, and many tenants had to borrow in order to purchase it. Some of Abercorn's tenants were lucky enough to receive a loan from the estate, but most had to rely on their more rapacious neighbours.[197] Another crucial point of contact revolved around the supply of oatmeal, which greatly affected the behaviour of tenants. The output of agricultural labourers, spinners, and weavers was highly elastic with respect to the food supply. James Hamilton noticed in the bountiful 1750s that provisions were so cheap that few labourers were willing to work or join the army, and farmers were obliged to keep their sons at home longer:

> Upon your lordship's orders to enlist men, I applied particularly to the tenants of Derrygoon . . . , but the fathers called out that if their sons, who are mostly weavers, or their journeymen or apprentices should leave them, they would not be able to pay their rents. Nothing will be done in these cheap times but by those who make use of the recruiting methods sergeants do, which is to entice people to drink, and when drunk, to enlist them.[198]

During the recovery of 1794 the willingness to take a vacation from the loom in a good harvest year, in spite of buoyant prices in the linen market, was evident: 'Potatoes and meal are at present much too low for the price of land, which I can't consider good for the country, as the means of support being too easily obtained encourages idleness and drunkenness among the lower orders and discourages the farmer from pursuing his crops.'[199]

But it was in times of dearth rather than plenty that the differences between social groups were most starkly revealed. In the summer and fall after a bad harvest the combined pressures of high food prices and rent payments forced smallholders into debt to local creditors. The grain seller, petty landlord, and linen dealer to whom debts were owed might even be the same person. In order to discharge their rent and buy food, backward tenants on the Abercorn estate in 1759 'got money advanced, mostly [from] yarn buyers to whom they were obliged to give their yarn as they spun it, at much under value, nor durst [sic] they dispute any price offered by the lenders, as that could destroy their credit with them.'[200] As the century progressed, high grain prices bene-fitted fewer and fewer tenants. Economic circumstances could force those who held reasonably large farms to reduce the size of their holdings to the subsistence minimum. In 1781 Hamilton found that

> many of the tenants went greatly into debt in order to keep themselves in their holdings, and many of them . . . gave [up] acres of their best land [to creditors] for years without rent to raise this money and pay it. . . . Nothing could be more ruinous than their giving [up] their land. The fodder was

carried away, which impoverished their land, and when they got their land back, it was worn out. Besides, they were obliged to buy their bread at a high price on credit.[201]

During the dearth of 1783 Hamilton judged that 'the high price of corn greatly benefitted those of the tenants who had to sell, but they are very few compared to those who were obliged to buy, and who could not get what could barely sustain them but for ready money.'[202] The active market and high demand for meal presented an opportunity for speculation that many agricultural capitalists could not miss. In 1792 speculators were observed laying up stores of meal in anticipation of the high prices that followed.[203] By lending provisions at an exorbitant rate of interest, the speculator was able to retain his market position even in the subsequent years of recovery: 'The farmer that has provisions to spare will not, if he can help it, dispose of them now that they are cheap, but depends on what the poorer sort owe them for provisions that they bought at exorbitant prices. By this means those of that class are almost forever in distress.'[204]

Reaction to this type of behaviour became more and more angry and violent as the century wore on. In 1798 one large farmer on the Abercorn estate lost property worth £1,700 to an arsonist. 'Very few pity him,' recorded James Hamilton, Jr., for 'he has an overgrown fortune, and he never took pains to be popular among his parishioners or neighbours.' Another tenant named Bob Cochran was equally callous. He 'speculated very deeply in the meal and corn trade, by which it is supposed he will clear £1,500. It has got him double that number of curses from the poor, but he would just as soon have them as so many blessings.' A violent mob, most of whom were women, rioted outside Cochran's warehouse in 1801 and had to be dispersed by the militia. Other rich farmers who sold potatoes at the extraordinarily high market price in 1798 'had their barns and houses set fire to.'[205] These patterns of behaviour were completely absent from the Abercorn estate during the devastating famine of the mid-1740s. What had changed in the meantime was the degree of social differentiation. The evidence suggests that as the eighteenth century progressed tenants were identifying themselves as members of specific groups and responding collectively to these tensions between groups for the first time. 'The servants and cottiers,' Hamilton noticed, 'have taken advantage of the defenceless state of the rich farmers' because of the preoccupations of the militia in those years. They 'have gone about for some nights robbing and plundering. Although disguised, their persons have generally been discovered, which . . . has effectually destroyed that confidence they once had in each other.'[206] The level of organization was considerable, as the following passage suggests: 'There has been for the past ten days a universal nightly plunder for cash, clothes, even provisions. The perpetrators are all cottiers and servants who exchange their districts to avoid detection and mutually furnish each other with information. This has brought about a meeting of the wealthy tenants [who established mutual protection and night surveillance].'[207] These social tensions – concerning land tenure, indebtedness, the control of capital and critical commodities – are the stuff of which class struggle is made.[208] Out of these tensions came the realization of like circumstances, the awareness of conflicting positions, and finally the desire to act collectively. It is important in this respect to recognize the smallness of estate society. The sublandlord who attempted to control the tenure of his cottiers, the rapacious creditor, and the grain speculator may have been, for any number of peasants, the same man. In this face-to-face world, 'that confidence they had in each other' was easily jeopardized.

This rending of the moral economy had as its basis the growing uncertainty about the direction of the development of the real economy. Maguire has argued that 'there is little or no evidence in estate records to suggest that landowners initiated, or even actively encouraged, the trend towards subdivision.'[209] This may apply to the nineteenth century with some accuracy, but just the opposite was true in the eighteenth century when subdivision was accepted and in many cases actively promoted by landlords. Rev. William Henry remarked in 1739 on 'the happy success which this method of dividing the land into smaller partitions and encouraging the cottager and the manufacturer has had in enriching both landlord and tenant.'[210] Tenants were unreservedly encouraged to supplement agricultural incomes with the wheel and loom in the subsequent decades, but after 1780 new concerns began to surface. Now agents were apprehensive that many smallholders had become completely dependent on rather uncertain occupations and that the occupants of larger tracts were so preoccupied with weaving that they neglected their farms. James Hamilton lamented this situation in 1786, a poor year for the linen market, wishing 'that the people of northern Ireland branch out into other trades and not be solely dependent on the linen-cloth business.'[211] Coincident with and related to the sea change in attitudes towards emigration, discussed above, was a similar about-face concerning the value of small farms. Like McEvoy, Young found the agricultural specialist to be all too rare in the north of Ireland. After a lengthy attack on middlemen he remarked:

> Let me next mention the circumstances of the occupiers. The variety of these is very great in Ireland. In the north, where the linen manufacture has spread, the farms are so small that ten acres in the occupation of one person is a large one, five or six will be found a good farm – and all so subservient to the manufacturer that they no more deserve the name of farmers than the mere occupier of a cabbage garden.[212]

In short, the experts viewed small farms not so much as the appropriate and desirable response to economic conditions but as an unfortunate aberration from a new ideal. As James Hamilton wrote in 1785: 'There can hardly be any instances where it is not hurtful to split farms. The larger the farms, the surer the rent.'[213] Small farms were seen to be intimately linked to an outmoded productive practice. Where even as late as 1800 polemicists could argue that farmers were secure with a mixed output of corn and linen, as the nineteenth century progressed this delicate balance lost its efficacy. John Spotswood, agent to Thomas Conolly, considered fining down the rents in 1800 but judged that the Catholics could not afford the fines: 'Few of the Roman Catholic tenants, if any, are able to fine down to the rent of the lands granted in 1734. The farms each man occupies are so small [that] it is impossible for them to be rich, and it is by the linen manufacture all live.'[214] The Drapers' company, for example, adopted a policy not to allow tradesmen to inherit farms in 1824.[215] Two surveyors of the Drapers' company also lamented

> the deficiency of capital and the habits of the people. The habits which are alluded to are the application of the industry of the same persons to agriculture and manufacture. This tends, by division of a very diminutive capital to two objects, to lessen its insufficient ability to answer either, to which may be added the almost total insensibility of the people to the comforts and luxuries of good lodging, furniture, and clothing.[216]

A similar observation was made of the Gosford estate in Armagh: 'Among the small farmers of this district there does appear to be the least idea of bringing up any of their sons to any other mode of life than agriculture; for, though some are taught weaving, yet that trade is never looked on as an exclusive mode of support. The weaver is also a farmer, and still retains the same anxiety for a small portion of land.'[217] The agriculturist P. O'Connor toured the Whyte estate in Loughbrickland, Co. Down, in 1849 and strongly urged the adoption of different crops and a different system of cultivation. He anticipated that some tenants would adapt to the changes, but he warned that

> there are others who, though well inclined to follow a good system of farming, are incapacitated from want of means to do even anything on their holdings. They have to work at their trades to keep body and soul together in their families, hence the land must be in a great measure or altogether neglected. To be candid, things are very near as bad as in the west of Ireland some twelve months ago, and were it not for the manufactories along the Bann, they would now be on the same level as the people of that district.[218]

According to J. R. Moore, the townland of Clerkhill on the Annesley estate near Newcastle, Co. Down, contained many Protestants, 'but the townland has been so cut up and subdivided by cottiers, etc., [that] it will require much attention to put the tenants in a thriving state.'[219] A deputation to the Clothworkers' company in County Londonderry reported in 1849 that small farms of ten to twenty acres were observed to be poorly cultivated and poorly capitalized, and the soil exhausted.[220]

The main concern was therefore the lack of specialization, not the inadequacy of either agricultural or industrial production. Still attached to the subsistence and security their small farms provided them, weavers were willing neither to abandon them for a completely proletarian status nor to give up the cash income they drew from the linen trade to put their farming on a competitive commercial footing. Land hunger was not an ahistorical characteristic of the smallholding farmer. Rather, it was a result of the rapid expansion and sudden collapse of economic opportunities which allowed families to survive on smaller plots. The predominant bearers of this new attitude toward the land were the rapidly proliferating class of weavers. Their preoccupation with the loom and spinning wheel prevented their participation in land-extensive agriculture and thus made impossible their holding more than the minimum acreage necessary for subsistence. A large group of tenants in these circumstances competing in the small-farm land market inflated prices. Holders of smaller farms on the Abercorn estate, for example, paid a much higher price for their acres or portions of acres. James Hamilton found many cottiers paying from 10s. to 15s. per acre, about average for the estate, but just as many 'who pay much more than double' that sum to their tenant-landlords.[221] Three holders of between three and five acres were paying £3. 3s., £2. 5s., and £2. 4s. per acre in 1787 – or roughly triple the 1835 average.[222] On leased farms in 1835 the inverse relationship between farm size and rent per acre was much weaker.[223] None the less, the fewer acres a tenant occupied, the more highly each acre was valued. As one neared the subsistence level, each unit of land and labour was of critical value, and the prospect of renting less land became more hazardous, because it lowered the probability of producing a subsistence income,[224] and less possible, because the landlord might hesitate to let smaller units. Herein lay the economic basis of the peasant's 'tenacious' and 'irrational' desire to hold land at any cost. James Hamilton, Jr., observed this trait after a proposed rise in rents in 1799:

> Hood [the surveyor] and I agree that the terms are so extravagant that there will not be ten in one hundred who will continue to hold, and those only will be of the sixth class, who will be ready to promise any rent, rather than at this season of the year [October] be forced from their miserable cabins with wretched family. Several of this description have for the last fifty years existed on their little spots, [to] which they feel the strongest attachment.[225]

The agent on the Barrett-Lennard estate had a similar experience:

> My father in 1767 set an estate in County Longford by [soliciting] proposals. Different people having proposed a high rent, indeed a rent then going for lands, the poor tenants on the lands, rather than turn out, agreed to give what was proposed by other persons and accordingly took leases thereof and paid their rents for a year or two. They then began to complain [that] they were not able to hold the lands, nor could they make the rent, which they had engaged to pay, out of the lands.[226]

After some years of growing arrears Noble had the property revalued, 'and it really surprised us to think that the tenants ever agreed to give such prices, but they said they must either give the rent proposed by others or turn out.' He lowered rents by 4s. to 6s. an acre and gave 'abatements to the tenants in possession [rather] than have the lands lying waste for a year or two.'[227]

Under these circumstances, some landlords continued to promote the linen trade on farms that were apparently not otherwise commercially viable in the nineteenth century. Robert Galt complained to the earl of Caledon in 1790 of beggarly tenants on his estate near Ballycastle, Co. Antrim: 'There are many of your tenants who have sold their leases to people who do not live on the land and have it set to cotters.' He suggested supplying spinning wheels from the Linen Board to these cotters.[228] James Hamilton, Jr. reflected the prevailing attitude in a letter of 1806: 'In the future the rise of land will depend much on the success of the linen trade. Without looms and weavers the land would be as cheap in the north as it is in Connaught.'[229] The Anglesey estate agent concurred: 'if manufactures to any considerable extent could be introduced amongst them, in that case numbers would not be a grievance but a benefit.'[230] William Ogilvie, a landowner in Lecale, Co. Down, enquired of his agent in 1807 whether the linen manufacture had been introduced among his tenants, and if not, what would be the best method of doing so. He believed that the problem of smallholders could be solved in only two ways: either promote the linen industry among them or get rid of them.[231] His agent argued that because the soil on his estate was much better suited to wheat and oats than flax cultivation, spinners and weavers were at a disadvantage. But Ogilvie insisted that flax could be grown on the bogs and that merchants could be found to come and buy flax in its less prepared form, and he hoped to introduce hackling and spinning later. In the following year Wilson reported that he was trying to tempt a few good weavers to Ardglass, as 'that would set the whole machine of the linen manufacture agoing.'[232]

This optimism was disastrously misplaced. The larger technological developments in linen production after 1815 doomed these efforts to promote handloom weaving, even though a rump of more highly skilled cambric weavers survived. Poor livestock prices compounded the crisis. Unfortunately, the mechanization of linen production began to affect many areas of Ulster after the waves of subdivision of holdings had created a mass of 'independent' smallholders whose economic dependence on hand spinning and handloom weaving was almost complete.[233] Nicholas Ellis described the harsh realities of this dependence in 1829: 'The linen trade is hopeless yet still is not quite extinct. A man by hard [work] may earn a shilling a day by weaving, and a woman may earn two pence by hand spinning. This is bad encouragement. Our women [have] taken to field labour and lose all their beauty.'[234] A deputation from the Drapers' company reported in 1832 that the most common reasons for petitions from tenants were the diminution of cattle prices and the decline of spinning.[235] A report of a deputation to the Merchant Tailors' estate in 1844 registered the profound change that had recently occurred:

> If we look to the north, we find villages without a loom where formerly the shuttle almost unceasingly plied at every window. The poor son of the once flourishing weaver poorly tills his thirty acres, passing for a farmer of respectable extent, and even the growth and cultivation of the flax crop leaves him [with] but the shadow of those comforts of which the march of machinery has deprived the farming tenants of this part of Ireland.[236]

A 'memorial from the ladies of Moneymore' in 1846 complaining of the lack of sufficient employment and high prices provoked the following observations from the Drapers' company agent: 'In former days they were able to support themselves comfortably by the spinning wheel, but machinery for spinning linen yarn has knocked [out] almost entirely the hand spinning, and although the mill work gives employment to many hands, still it cannot employ the multitude. . . .' Formerly, he claimed, all the members of every household joined in spinning, 'from the child of six years of age to the man or woman of seventy.'[237] Wright summarizes the post-famine situation as follows:

> Until the mid-1860s, the old weaver belt population, held up in rather marked contrast to other regions. And although this was partly a consequence of urban growth, it also reflected the continued presence of rural weaving and textile activity. Between 1862 and 1872, however, the cotton famine, 1861-66, destroyed what remained of the cotton weaving industry. Then the break in the flax boom in the late 1860s undermined the demand for agricultural labour and the viability of smallholder farming. In Maghera for example, emigration in 1872 was at its worst level since 1847.[238]

By the mid-nineteenth century the only significant factor of production in the linen industry, with the exception of the Cambric weavers who continued to operate within the putting-out system, was the small-to-middling flax producer.[239] In 1847 Miller noticed that tenants were planting flaxseed where they had once set potatoes.[240] In 1852 he reported that 'to make a year's rent in time, all hands are employed about preparing the flax, in pulling, steeping, drying, and scutching it. Consequently, the making of drains cannot be brought forward until the flax is brought to market, hence the difficulty of making the drains and having the rent paid before the 30th of September.'[241] An agent on the Dufferin estate insisted in 1853: 'If the flax fails this year, we will be all undone. It is nothing more or less than a gambling transaction with our farmers.'[242] Bad weather threatened the harvest of 1862 on the Drapers' company estate, and the Millers worried in October that 'the only prospect we have for the payment of rent is from the flax crop, which is turning out well, but when the tenant has no flax, the rent, we fear, must fall behind.'[243] In 1864 Rowley Miller observed a fine-looking harvest. 'Potatoes look magnificent, nothing like them since 1844. Unless we soon shall have rain, very many of the scutch mills will remain idle for want of water. Many farmers are in great straights for want of water to steep their flax.'[244] On the other hand, heavy rains in 1875 flooded some areas of the estate which prevented scutching and delayed rent payments.[245] H. R. Miller remarked in 1877 that 'it has been a very wet, bad season, the price of flax and pork, on which the tenants chiefly rely, being considerably lower than former years.'[246]

ECONOMIC OPPORTUNITY, LAND HUNGER, AND TENANT RIGHT

This long, halting and painful transition of rural Ulster society from the heterogenous mixture of cottiers, smallholding weavers, and middling to large capitalist farmers to the more stratified, homogenous, and less densely settled society of the post-famine period had enormous ramifications for tenure and estate management. The ramifications for Irish landholders of important transformations in the United Kingdom economy of the period 1780-1850 began to take hold in the 1830s. These can be characterized briefly as the now chronic deflationary trend in the prices of cereals, punctuated only by the equally disastrous spikes in the trend due to harvest failures, and the irreversible transformation of textile production which rapidly destroyed all the hand-spinning and many sectors of the handloom weaving trades.[247] It is best to bear in mind that the experience of poverty was as singular as were its immediate causes, even if structural shifts in the entire economy lay at their base. We may get an inkling of the range of factors causing tenants to go into debt from a report by the agent of a Cavan estate about nine tenants who were in arrears in 1844:

(1) a widow suffering from the death of a son, her only means of support; she also spent money on improvements; (2) man erected a comfortable dwelling house in 1842, the same year he was forced to buy provisions; (3) the death of two cows in 1842 put this tenant in trouble; (4) death of pigs, 1842; (5) tenant's parents died of cholera and unable to acquire grazing cattle, thus his farm lies waste; (6) widow suffers the death of her stock and unable to acquire more, her farm also lying waste; (7) tenant with partial blindness but will recover; (8) death of pigs; (9) chronically in arrears.[248]

The dilatory effects of this crisis should not be overstated. After all, slumping prices have a positive aspect for the consumer which must balance the negative effects on the producer. Even in terms of production, farmers, weavers, and spinners responded to lower prices of their products by increasing the volume of output, by producing more efficiently and exploiting themselves, their families, and their labourers more intensively. By no means was this an economy grinding itself down into a Malthusian or Ricardan crisis of production. But the transformation that did occur had a dramatic effect on the nature of the land question.[249]

Agents were forced to reassess productive relationships on their estates, and alter their tenurial policies according to their perceptions of what would be the most viable mix of farm sizes. This task was fraught with uncertainties about the relationship of those at the bottom of the economic pyramid to the productivity of the larger farmers. One spokesman for tenants on the Merchant Tailor's proportion argued that the ban on cottiers disallowed tenants from taking 'a tradesmen as cottier,' and that furthermore the wording of the ban 'leaves uncertain what is meant by an 'agricultural labourer,' the great body of cottiers upon the estate being employed in agriculture during perhaps one third or one half of the year, and in weaving linen cloth the remainder.'[250] As part of a longstanding policy of 'extending the farms to respectability and of limiting the holdings of artisans and mere labourers to mere potato gardens,'[251] the Drapers' company allowed any tenant paying at least £20 rent to have one cottier 'to assist him in labouring his farm provided that he the cottier was made comfortable by having a stone and lime house, etc.,' recognizing the need for cottiers on large farms with no mature sons.[252] They had explained the reasoning behind this policy in a letter the previous year:

It must *never be forgotten*, that even in farms of 30 statute or 18 Irish acres the occupier would require generally to have the undertenant, or cottier, which cottier, if not looked after – and sharply too by the Landlord or his Agent – will *be ground to the dust by heavy rent* and hard work with a *comfortless cottage* to reside in. Now much as we approve of large farms, we are concerned that, if every farm on this estate contained 40 or 50 statute acres, and that each tenant was permitted to have as many undertenants or cottiers under the pretence of labourers as he might deem necessary, which is too much the practice in many Estates in this part of the country, there would be more poverty by one hundred percent upon the proportion, than there is under the present system. The court no doubt is aware that the large number of tenants was caused by their orders through the Deputation of 1820, when the cottiers were *emancipated*, and received as tenants. Suppose then, that the court came to the resolution of enlarging the farms to 40 or 50 statute acres each. By either removing half the present occupiers or by purchasing them out they would then have 800 in place of 1,385 tenants. Then supposing that each of those tenants would have two cottiers – and we are confident, that they would tell the Company, if they here asked, that less would not do them – it would introduce upon the estate exclusive of the 800 tenants *1,600 cottiers otherwise paupers*. Then the question arises which is the best plan for the landlords to adopt, for not only the *improvement of their estates*, but for the *general improvement of the country*. This point or subject has occupied our minds for a length of time and although we have been always favourable to the enlarging system, and have acted upon it for years, still there's a question, whether the larger farms, combined as they necessarily must be with the cottier system, be better for the Country than the *maximum* of land, which a farmer may be able to manage without the assistance of cottiers – which maximum would be about 15 Irish or 24 English or statute acres. The Grocers' company, and we believe the Mercers' also, fell as we consider into a great error, when they took possession of their estates in this Country, by allowing the cottier system to a very great extent indeed upon each of them. The Drapers' plan of emancipating the cottiers, and making them free men by making them their tenants was preferable, inasmuch as free men are always better that slaves. And it is unhappily too true that the cottier system in this Country, if not closely looked after, and kept in check, is analogous to slavery, and you will almost invariably find that those tenants, who complain most of their own rents, being too high, are the greatest grinders of their under-tenants or cottiers. When cottiers are permitted on this estate, and we are happy in having it in our power to state, that there are fewer upon it, than on any large property in this country, we insist upon the tenants making their cottier houses comfortable, and to the uttermost of our power prevent them oppressing the poor creatures with heavy rent.[253]

The tenant right of smallholders in the nineteenth century is best understood in the context of these economic changes and managerial decisions. During most of the eighteenth century these smallholders might have enjoyed a purely economic legitimation of their tenure by working toward an independent tenurial position on the formerly under-utilized fringes of much larger holdings. But when the economic basis for this collapsed, smallholders were left with nothing but the now hollow-sounding claims based on their ancestry and their continuous histories of occupation, translated by hostile managers and polemicists as irrational pertinacity or backward ideology. Their only remaining economic justification for continued occupation was their willingness to allow larger farmers to profit from their labour. This ascendant population of middle-to-large-holding flax and livestock producers could look back on their tenurial history from this side of the famine decade and make confident arguments about their role in the development of the Ulster rural economy. The ambiguous difference between these two classes lies at the heart of the contested multiple meanings and uses of the custom of tenant right. Each had its own rhetoric. The argument from economic strength was occasionally invested with a rhetoric of ethnic superiority. It was often remarked in the early nineteenth century, for example, that Protestant participation in the linen industry was responsible for the qualities of industriousness, frugality, tidiness and dependability for which Ulster was so renowned.[254] The sectarian overtones were often overwhelming, as in this classic statement of anti-Catholic sentiment in an editorial commenting on the clerical *Catholic Examiner's* motto 'Pro Aris et Tous' ('for our altars and firesides') in the *Portadown and Lurgan News* of 26 July 1873: 'In other words for superstition and mud cabins, and bogs, when all the civilized world was for true religion, and good drainage and ventilation.'[255] Chapter 6 examines the potential convergence between landlords and capitalist strong-farmers on the issue of a strictly economic definition of tenant right which allowed landlords to exploit the operation of the custom to manage the debts of smallholders and rationalize landholding on their estates. But it must not be forgotten that the smallholders also had their historical justification for tenant right. The Millers of Draperstown described it in a letter of 1848. The importance of this description is the way it combines the central basis of tenant right identified in this chapter (participation in the linen industry) with an important theme of chapter 2 (the political nature of tenancies):

> We are of opinion that the great curse of tenant right, crept in from this province being for very many years the seat of the linen manufacture. Every farmhouse, nay every cottage be it ever so small, was a manufactory in itself – it had its wheel and its reel and its loom and employment to every being in the house from six years of age and upward. This coupled with the anxiety of the Romish Priesthood to increase their flocks by every possible means, not only on account of increasing their wealth – for the Priests are paid so much on baptisms, churchings, marriages etc. etc. and so much for every head in each family every year – but also in a political point of view to increase their numerical strengths, so that they might be able to carry their point by brute force if necessary. These two things

caused a vast increase of population and hence the anxiety to procure the *'bit of land'* for which they were willing to pay almost any sum demanded. They would not only consent to give a smart rent for a few acres, but they would give also an 'input' as it is called for the tenant right of the ground, and immediately erect a cottage thereon. The linen trade was doing so well that perhaps a month's work of man and his family would pay his years rent and considerably more. The Landlords too for two reasons encouraged the cutting up of farms, because in the first place they obtained a great increase of rent and also when the Roman Catholics got the elective franchise from the Irish Parliament in 1792 in order to increase their political influence they, the landlords, granted leases and made forty-shilling freeholders of the lowest and most ignorant of the peasantry. These all combined caused the tenant-right system to be firmly fixed in this province, and which no enactments we are persuaded can ever do away with. . . .[256]

If tenant right could not be abolished by legislation, then landlords and their agents had to face the distasteful task of ridding these tenants from their estates by some other means.

NOTES

1 Morrogh, *Munster plantation*, p. 226.
2 Ibid., pp. 128–9.
3 Giddens, *Central problems*, pp. 49–95; see Chapter 1, pp. 35–7.
4 Henry Conyngham to John Murray, 10 Nov. 1702, P.R.O.N.I., Murray of Broughton papers, D2860/5/12.
5 Power, *Tipperary*, p. 148.
6 Pawlisch, *Sir John Davies*, p. 77. According to Pawlisch, 'the instability of succession by tanistry and the frequency of land distribution associated with the Irish variant of gavelkind allowed critics like Davies to argue that the limited tenancy associated with these Irish customs prohibited the intensive exploitation of land and deterred formation of a stable body politic.' Ibid., p. 61.
7 Nicholls, *Land, law, and society in sixteenth-century Ireland* (Dublin, 1976), p. 18. For a synopsis of Nicholls's and Hayes-McCoy's view of Gaelic landholding, see Pawlisch, *Sir John Davies*, pp. 57–61.
8 Perceval-Maxwell orders paragraphs describing the problems of the plantation with themes of violence, more violence, terror, the 1615 conspiracy, 'seething undercurrents of Irish discontent,' and the devious 'Irish idea of turning Scot against Englishman.' Perceval-Maxwell, *Scottish migration*, pp. 152–5, 274–89. As opposed to the monolithic characterization of the Irish as rebels and robbers, he carefully breaks down the emigrant population so that 'fugitives and criminals' are but one isolated and de-emphasized part. Ibid., p. 277. He uses a typical fragment from the promotional literature, a source he attacks two paragraphs later as 'a ringing tribute to the toughness and resilience of the Scots which made them ideal material for the population of a frontier.' Ibid., pp. 278–9.

9 His authority on the introduction of superior livestock into Ulster is Philip Robinson, but Robinson provides no proof of the claim. But this only shows that pastoralism may already have been more developed in Ulster. Perceval-Maxwell makes the most dubious claim that 'we may also assume that the quality of the livestock matched or surpassed that in the market to which it was sent.' Ibid.

10 Ibid., p. xxx.

11 J. Michael Hill argues that the Celtic Scottish migrants to Ulster had far more in common in terms of productive practices with the natives than historians have recognized. J. Michael Hill, 'The origins of the Scottish plantations in Ulster to 1625: a reinterpretation' in *Journal of British studies*, xxxii (Jan., 1993) pp. 24–43.

12 Perceval-Maxwell, *Scottish migration*, p. 22.

13 Ibid., p. 22. Roebuck quotes Chichester's opinion that neither the English nor the Scots emigrants were endowed with much capital. Roebuck, 'The making of an Ulster great estate,' p. 16. Roebuck follows this quote from Chichester with the notorious quote from Andrew Stewart stating that Ulster was then populated by 'the scum of both nations.'

14 For the Scottish background, see T.M. Devine, *The transformation of rural Scotland, 1660–1815* (Edinburgh, 1994).

15 Moody, 'Treatment of the native population,' p. 61. Moody further states: 'In May 1611 we find Davies assuring Salisbury that the natives were more willing to leave the undertakers' lands than the undertakers were to part with them.' Ibid., pp. 61–2.

16 Ibid.

17 Clarke, 'The Irish economy 1600–60,' p. 176. According to Pynnar in 1619, 'were it not for the Scottish, who plough in many places, the rest of the country might starve.' quoted in Robinson, *Plantation of Ulster*, pp. 178–9; Hunter, 'Ulster plantation,' p. 408.

18 Nicholas Canny, 'A reply,' in *I.E.S.H.*, xiii (1986), p. 98, n. 3.

19 Perceval-Maxwell, *Scottish migration*, pp. 200–02.

20 Moody, 'Treatment of the native population,' p. 61.

21 Nicholas Canny, 'Migration and opportunity: Britain, Ireland, and the new world,' *I.E.S.H.*, xii, 1985 pp. 7–32. Hunter also analyzed the planters' claims of losses in the 1641 depositions. He found the proportion of crops to livestock by value to be in the range of 2:3 and 3:7. Hunter cites the example of Sir Thomas Waldron of Loughtee, who was stated to have had in 1622 'very good tillage, enclosures, and store of English cattle.' Hunter, 'Ulster plantation,' p. 432. Perceval-Maxwell points to the deposition of one Thomas Crant, who lost considerable stores of corn, wheat, barley, and hay in Cavan, Fermanagh, Monaghan, and Meath, to support his position that 'farming took place in south Ulster on a fairly large scale and at a level of technology well above anything that has been discovered for the preplantation period.' Perceval-Maxwell, *Scottish migration*, p. xxix. But this man also owned fifty horses and eighty cattle, which suggests diversity and flexibility rather than specialization, and an unusually large scale of farming. Is this one example enough to overturn Canny's interpretation? Canny has not yet presented any quantitative results of his research on the depositions, but his generalizations appear to carry more weight than Perceval-Maxwell's one example.

22 Raymond G. Gillespie, *The transformation of the Irish economy 1550–1700* (Dundalk, 1991), p. 33.

23 Clarke, 'Irish economy, 1600–60,' p. 173; Nicholls, *Land, law, and society*, p. 9; Aalen, *Man and the landscape*, p. 138.

24 Ibid.

25 Canny, 'Hugh O'Neill,' p. 27.

26 Clay, *Economic expansion*, i, pp. 94, 101.

27 Cullen, *Emergence*, p. 144.

28 Idem, *An economic history of Ireland since 1660* (London, 1972), pp. 46–8, 67–71; Kevin Whelan, 'Settlement and society in eighteenth-century Ireland' in Gerald Dawe and John Wilson Foster (eds.), *The poet's place: Ulster literature and society* (Belfast, 1991), pp. 54–56. p. 48.

29 Letter books of Justice Ward, Bangor, Co. Antrim, 1724–32, P.R.O.N.I., Castleward papers, D2092/1/3,4.

30 'A description of Oneilland barony in the county of Armagh by William Brooke, Portadown,' 26 Oct. 1682, in *A Natural History of Ireland, memories and notes relating thereto, made from communications to the Dublin Society* (2 vols), i, p. 222, TC.D., MS 883/1.

31 James Hamilton to eighth earl of Abercorn, 31 July 1778, P.R.O.N.I., Abercorn papers, T2541/IA2/2; 15 Apr. 1770, ibid., T2541/IA1/9/27; 12 Mar. 1745, ibid., T2541/IA1/1B/40; 4 May 1745, ibid., T2541/IA1/1B/48.

32 Joseph Calhoun to Abercorn, 21 July 1745, ibid., T2541/IA1/1B/5; James Hamilton to Abercorn, 5 Mar. 1770, ibid., T2541/IA1/9/53; Hamilton to Abercorn, 5 Dec. 1783, ibid., T2541/IA2/3/58; Charles Youngman to Abercorn, 1 May 1793, ibid., T2541/IA1/19/38.

33 Edward Wakefield, *An account of Ireland, statistical and political*, 2 vols (London, 1812), i, p. 371.

34 Canny has noticed more intense competition between Ulster and Pale landlords for these mobile tenants. Ibid., pp. 27, 30, 31, 33. See also Clarke, 'Irish economy, 1600–60,' p. 173; Aalen suggests that 'the protracted warfare of the seventeenth century, which often forced the Irish to abandon their settlements and find refuge in the hills and bogs, may have encouraged the use of the potato . . . , [which] required less attention and [was] less easily spoiled than cereals.' Aalen, *Man and the landscape*, p. 138. One Fermanagh landlord complained in the 1640s that 'the Irish who practise creaghting and live dispersed everywhere take advantage of their opportunity to help the Irish soldiers although they are peaceable themselves.' Masterson, 'Land use patterns and farming practice in county Fermanagh 1609–1845' in *Clogher record*, vii, no. 1 (1969), p. 65.

35 John Bramhall to Christopher Wandesford, 16 Apr. 1640, Historical Manuscripts Commission report, Hasting MSS, iv, 1947, 86–8.

36 'A representative of the present state of the city and county of Londonderry,' n.d. [c. 1670], P.R.O.N.I., Ellis papers, D683/185; Michael Porkrich to Dacre Barrett, 22 May 1674, P.R.O.N.I., Barrett-Lennard papers, film 170/3; Gillespie, *Settlement and survival*, pp. xxii–xxiii; Andrew Hutchinson to William King, 18 Sept. 1691, T.C.D., MSS 1995–2008; William Waring to William Layfield, n.d. [c.1675], P.R.O.N.I., Waring papers, D695/7. Macafee, 'Maghera region,' p. 76. The agent on the Downshire estate promised in 1747 to watch tenants in the townland of Murlough so that they did not 'run off' with the 'effects' of their farms. Robert Isaac to Henry Blundell, Sept. 1747, P.R.O.N.I., Downshire papers, D607/A/48. See also ibid., D607/A/89.

37 A Carrickfergus agent wrote in 1721 that a waste plot formerly worth 30s. would only earn 20s. from bidders. James Kirk to Agmondisham Vesey, 8 Sept. 1721, P.R.O.N.I., Kirk-Vesey papers, T2524/6; Thomas Edgerton to Justice Ward, 20 Apr. 1744, P.R.O.N.I., Castleward papers, D2092/1/1–6, p. 98.

38 James Hamilton to John Murray of Broughton, 4 Feb. 1728, P.R.O.N.I., Murray of Broughton papers, D2860/12/21.

39 Captain John Henderson to Alex Cairnes, 3 Nov. 1713, P.R.O.N.I., Rossmore papers, T2929/2/16.

40 Dickson, 'Cork region,' p. 155.

41 Hans Stevenson to William Hamilton, 14 May 1696, N.L.I., Hans Stevenson correspondence, MS 1702, p. 65.

42 Edmund Kaine to Dacre Barrett, 3 May 1718, P.R.O.N.I., Barrett-Lennard papers, film 170/2.

43 Thomas Bligh to Peter Westenra, 15 Dec. 1687, P.R.O.N.I., Rossmore papers, T2929/1/17. In this letter Bligh also expressed his preference for Irish tenants. Given the date of the letter, it is likely that this preference was political in nature rather than economic.

44 James Nugent to Andrew Nugent, 23 Mar. 1818, P.R.O.N.I., Nugent papers, D552/A/7/6/25; idem, 27 May 1819 and 2 Apr. 1821, ibid., D552/A/7/6/40 and D552/A/7/6/75.

45 Robert Molesworth to Hon. Mrs. [?] Molesworth, 13 Nov. 1710, N.L.I., Historical Manuscripts Commission, *Reports on various collections*, viii (1913), p. 249.

46 Thomas Bligh to Peter Westenra, 7 Feb. 1688, P.R.O.N.I., Rossmore papers, T2929/1/18.

47 Mary, Dowager Lady Shelbourne, to Alexander Murray, 22 Nov., 1705, P.R.O.N.I., Murray of Broughton papers, D2860/9/7.

48 [?] Meredyth to [Edward Bayly], 16 July 1714, P.R.O.N.I., Downshire papers, D607/A/11.

49 Kerby Miller, *Emigrants and exiles: Ireland and the Irish exodus to North America* (New York, 1985), pp. 167–8.

50 Gillespie, *Settlement and survival*, pp. xxi–xxii.

51 James Hamilton to John Murray of Broughton, 4 Feb. 1728, P.R.O.N.I., Murray of Broughton papers, D2860/12/21.

52 Idem, 11 July 1729, ibid., D2860/12/22. These papers also include letters critical of Hamilton's performance, in particular his inability to collect arrears. Ibid., D2860/13, 14.

53 'Rent-roll of the Vintners' proportion of lands, 10 October 1718, by Ambrose Strettle,' P.R.O.N.I., D2094/21.

54 A 'List of fourteen persons in Limavady gone or going to New England and how they disposed of their lands in 1718' identified 'the tenants in their places,' and noted that 'many more [were] just now upon terms of selling their land.' 'A list of persons in the manor of Limavady that is gone and going to New England and how they disposed of their land,' n.d. [c.1718], N.L.I., film 6950. News of emigration from Sligo was reported by the agent for Charles O'Hara's estate. Patrick Brett to Kean O'Hara, 14 Nov. 1718, P.R.O.N.I., O'Hara papers, T2812/6.

55 Edward Fletcher to Dacre Barrett, 21 Oct. 1684, P.R.O.N.I., Barrett-Lennard papers, film 170/1.

56 Edmund Kaine to Dacre Barrett, 17 Mar. 1718, ibid., film 170/2.

57 Hamilton Maxwell to Agmondisham Vesey, 15 Aug. 1722 and 22 June 1724, P.R.O.N.I., Kirk-Vesey papers, T2524/16,20

58 Ezekiel Stewart to [Michael Ward], 25 Mar. 1729, P.R.O.N.I., Castleward papers, D2092/1/3.

59 R.J. Dickson, *Ulster emigration to colonial America* (London, 1966), pp. 19–81. Reports came from the Anglesey estate that many of the poorer classes were emigrating from Newry, 'which was beginning to affect the value of lands, especially in the North,' and that 'a great part of Mr. Hall's estate is now waste, particularly that opposite to Omeath, and people are going to America.' Robert Hutchinson to Henry Bayly, 16 May 1773, P.R.O.N.I., Anglesey papers, D619/21/C/77; Hutchinson to Bayly, 29 Mar. 1774, ibid., D619/21/C/94; [George Portis] to Lord Donegal, 4 May 1773, P.R.O.N.I., Donegall papers, T1893; Portis to Donegall, 22 Apr. 1773, ibid. Emigration from the Abercorn estate around Strabane, Co. Tyrone, on the other hand, was minimal during the eighteenth century, even during periods of crisis. In 1772 James Hamilton reported: 'Never did I see so many going from all parts, yet fewer from your lordship's estates than from any place else in these parts.' Abercorn's efforts to attract labour away from the estate to work in his Scottish mines in that year totally failed. James Hamilton to eighth earl of Abercorn, 10 July 1772, P.R.O.N.I., Abercorn papers, T2541/IA1/10/44. Those who did leave were not established producers but 'chiefly young men, few landholders to my knowledge, and . . . the poorer sort.' Ibid., 15 Aug. 1784, ibid., T2541/IA1/14/41.

60 Rose Peyton to Kean O'Hara, 8 May 1694, P.R.O.N.I., O'Hara papers, T2812/4/108.

61 Wright, *Two lands on one soil*, p. 13; Wright cites Dickson, *Ulster emigration*, pp. 4, 13, 21, 35, 69, 150, 182–3.

62 James Hamilton, Jr., to ninth earl of Abercorn, 6 June 1792 and 24 May 1793, P.R.O.N.I., Abercorn papers, T2541/IA2/5 and T2541/IA1/19/47.

63 Patrick Hogan, 'The migration of Ulster Catholics to Connaught, 1795–6,' *Seanchas Ardmacha* vol. 9, no. 2 (1979), pp. 286–301. The earl of Moira's estate near Ballynahinch, Co. Down lost ninety-one tenants in 1795, most of whom, according to State Paper Office records and a list drawn up by Moira, ended up in Ballina and Foxford, Co. Mayo. One State Paper Office document lists 1,074 immigrants, 390 from unspecified counties, 305 from Tyrone, 99 from Armagh, 87 from Monaghan, 100 from Derry, 26 from Cavan, and 30 from Antrim, 9 from Down, and 8 from Fermanagh. All were Catholics.

64 Rev. M.G. Beresford to Lord Farnham, 26 Mar. 1829, N.L.I., Farnham papers, MS 18,160(8).

65 The tenant-right system should be added to Ó Gráda's list 'reasons for the preponderant role of the northern counties' in pre-famine emigration. See Ó Gráda, *New economic history*, pp. 74–75.

66 'Rental of Cecil manor, 1801,' Mar. 1802, P.R.O.N.I., Foljambe papers, T3381/5/50; William Mayne to Thomas Barrett-Lennard, 9 June 1816, P.R.O.N.I., Barrett-Lennard papers, film 170/2; James Fawcett to John Dickens, 24 Feb. 1824, N.L.I., Playdell papers, film 7648; James Nugent to Andrew Nugent, 2, 7 June 1826, P.R.O.N.I., Nugent papers, D552/A/7/7/51, 52.

67 Eighth earl of Abercorn to James Hamilton, 29 July 1783, P.R.O.N.I., Abercorn papers, D623/A/25/198.

68 [George Portis] to Lord Donegall, 4 May 1773, P.R.O.N.I., Donegall papers, T1893. Idem, 22 Apr. 1773, ibid.

69 'Journal of a tour of parts of England, Wales, and Ireland compiled by Reverend J. Burrows, 3 June to 12 August 1773,' N.L.I., MS 23,561.

70 Patrick Tohall, 'The Diamond fight of 1795 and the resultant expulsions,' *Seanchas Ardmacha*, iii, no. 1 (1985), pp. 17–50.

71 Edmund Kaine to Dacre Barrett, 5 Nov. 1719, P.R.O.N.I., Barrett-Lennard papers, film 170/2.

72 Robert McCausland to Lord Justice Thomas Conolly, 23 Nov. 1728, T.C.D., Conolly papers, MS 3974–84/9.

73 James Speer to F.E. Foljambe, 15 Mar. 1788, P.R.O.N.I., Foljambe papers, T3381/5/10.

74 The court of assistants wished to avoid any newspaper revelations that they were subsidizing emigration to Liverpool, so they urged that subsidies be large enough to pay for passage all the way to America. Edward Lawford to Rowley and J.R. Miller, 16 Apr. 1847, P.R.O.N.I., Drapers' company papers, D3632/3/5. In order to ensure that subsidies were not misused, assistance for emigration was given directly to the ship agent in 1847. Rowley and J.R. Miller to Lawford, 1 May 1847, ibid., D3632/1/1.

75 Rowley and J.R. Miller to Edward Lawford, 9 Dec. 1843, 25 Mar. and 2 May 1844, 25 Jan. and 6 Feb. 1845, ibid.; minutes of court of assistants, extracts relating to Irish estates, Drapers' Hall, London, 23 Jan. 1851, N.L.I., film 1529.

76 Millers to Lawford, 12 Apr. 1847, P.R.O.N.I., Drapers' company papers, D3632/1/1.

77 Millers to Lawford, 12 Apr. 1847, ibid. Other tenants who were given money to emigrate in the 1830s and 1840s are mentioned in the following letters: Lawford to Rowley Miller, 3 Dec. 1831, 4 July 1832, 23 Feb. 1844; Millers to Lawford, 28 June 1844, 17 Jan. 1848, ibid. But even in 1846 the court of the Drapers' company began to pull back even further from these commitments, perhaps because of the successful departure of some unsubsidized emigrés. In 1846 the tenant-right price of a nine-acre farm was considered to be 'more than enough to clear the arrear owing by him and to pay for his passage to America. The court thought they should not be called upon to assist him in the latter object.' Lawford to Millers, 18 Dec. 1846, ibid., D3632/3/5. The managers of a Trinity College estate also gave cash to insolvents to emigrate. James Johnston to provost and fellows, 16 Nov. 1850, T.C.D., MUN/P/24/429.

78 Lawford to Rowley and J.R. Miller, 19 Jan. 1854, ibid., D3632/3/5. Ten years later, Rowley Miller reported that emigration from the estate had been reduced sharply, and that there were very few applicants for assistance. The great emigration was from the south, west, and centre of Ireland, but not many from Ulster. Rowley Miller to W.P. Sawyer, 30 Jan. 1864, ibid., D3632/1/3.

79 Rowley and J.R. Miller to Lawford, 31 May 1847, ibid., D3632/1/1.

80 Idem, 16 Aug. 1847, ibid.

81 Tenant petitions, n.d. [c.1850], P.R.O.N.I., Anglesey papers, D619/23/B/251,252; Samuel McCullen to Dufferin, 19 Jan. 1866, P.R.O.N.I., Dufferin papers, D1071A/K/Box 2; William Stannus to W.P. Sawyer, 2 Dec. 1879, P.R.O.N.I., Drapers' company papers, D3632/1/4; Elizabeth Rowan to William Sharman Crawford, 29 June 1883, P.R.O.N.I., Sharman Crawford papers, D856/B6/44.

82 Agreement between Nathanial Hoyle, vice-provost and Thomas Vincent, 17 July 1658, T.C.D., MUN/P/24/140. See also letters of Nathanial Cooper to Rev. Benjamin Span, [n.d.] c. 1695–1715, ibid., MUN/P/24/272.

83 Conveyance of premises at Omagh between Charles Young of Omagh and George Steward, 28 Apr. 1715, P.R.O.N.I., Stuart papers, D847/27/1; John Lennox to William Lennox, 27 May 1744, P.R.O.N.I., Lenox-Conyngham papers, D1449/12/51; Edward Ford to Keane O'Hara, 19 Feb. 1715, P.R.O.N.I., O'Hara papers, T2812/8/37.

84 Rooney to Bayly, 6 Aug. 1751, P.R.O.N.I., Anglesey papers, D619/21/B/103. Initiatives to rehabilitate or improve houses or farm offices might easily be cut short by all manner

of misfortunes. See, for example David Wilson, Rahorn, Fivemiletown, to Mrs [Jane] Graham, 15 Feb. 1866, P.R.O.N.I., Stuart papers, D847/27/4; William McCormick to Richard Legard, 7 Feb. 1801, P.R.O.N.I., McGildowney papers, D1375 /3/10/31; Mary Bellamy to Uxbridge, 26 July 1785, PRONI, Anglesey papers, D619/11/51.

85 See Alan Gailey, 'Changes in Irish rural housing, 1600–1900' in Patrick O'Flanagan, Paul Ferguson, and Kevin Whelan (eds.), *Rural Ireland: modernization and change, 1600–1900* (Cork, 1987), pp. 86–103.

86 Thomas Dawson to Thomas Barrett-Lennard, 6 Oct. 1750, P.R.O.N.I., Barrett-Lennard papers, film 170/2.

87 Dickson, 'Cork region,' p. 198.

88 Leasebook of the manor of Castledillon, Co. Armagh, with observations by William Molyneaux, P.R.O.N.I., film 80/3.

89 Brabazon Noble to Richard Barrett-Lennard, 26 July 1757, P.R.O.N.I., Barrett-Lennard papers, film 170/2; Thomas Noble to Richard Barrett-Lennard, 17 Sept. 1769, ibid.

90 Petition, n.d. [c. 1780], P.R.O.N.I., Anglesey papers, D619/11/22.

91 Petition of George Hill to Richard Legard, agent and receiver of Sir Henry Vane Tempest, 14 Aug. 1800, P.R.O.N.I., McGildowney papers, D1375/3/10/23; Frederick Hamilton to earl of Caledon; David McCool to earl of Caledon, n.d. [c. 1790], P.R.O.N.I., Caledon papers, D2433/A/2/5/14,15; Francis Fawcett to Lady Playdell, 21 July 1806, N.L.I., Playdell papers, film 7648; [?] to Thomas Barrett-Lennard, 28 Apr. 1828, P.R.O.N.I., Barrett-Lennard papers, film 170/3; Robert Fitzgerald to Sir Thomas, 25 May 1830, ibid.; William White to Thomas Barrett-Lennard, 7 Oct., 1830, ibid.; unsigned proposal, 27 Sept. 1839, P.R.O.N.I., Anglesey papers, D619/ 6/104; James O'Hanlon to [?] Rutherford, 23 Mar. 1843, ibid., D619/23/B/90.

92 Early seventeenth-century surveys emphasized the lack of permanent buildings: 'the Irish inhabitants always lived in creaghts which they remove from place to place to enrich the small plots of arable for tillage.' William J. Smyth, 'Society and settlement in seventeenth-century Ireland: the evidence of the 1659 census' in W. Smyth and Kevin Whelan (eds.), *Common ground: essays on the historical geography of Ireland,* (Cork, 1988), p. 68

93 Richard Coley to Lord Perceval, 5 Oct. 1747, cited in Dickson, 'Cork region,' p. 192.

94 Dickson, 'Cork region,' p. 146.

95 Ibid.

96 'During the great struggle with Tyrone, a network of fortified posts had been spread out over the province–Ballyshannon, Enniskillen, Omagh, Lifford, Dunalong, Derry, Culmore, Dungiven, Coleraine, Toome, Masserene, Dungannon, Mountjoy, Armagh, Charlemont, Moyry, Monaghan, and Cavan.' Moody, *Plantation,* p. 24.

97 Robinson, *Plantation of Ulster,* p. 166.

98 Ibid., p. 158. Leases on Trinity College lands required the construction of English-style houses and prohibited building 'dispersedly or scatteringly.' Hunter cites the worried commentary of plantation theorists about the dispersed nature of settlement in about 1620. Hunter, 'Ulster plantation,' pp. 418–19.

99 Ibid., pp. 160–1. See also Robinson, 'Urbanization in northwest Ulster' in *Ir. geog.,* xv (1982), pp. 35–50; Hunter, 'Towns in the Ulster plantation' in *Stud. hib.,* xi (1971), pp. 40–97.

100 For Carrickmacross, Co. Monaghan, see Smyth, 'Society and settlement,' p. 68. See also Clarke, 'The Irish economy 1600–60,' p. 175.

101 Coleraine houses were standing without tenants in 1613 because 'the tenants would take no leases without some lands thereto.' Report by Alderman Smith and Mathias

Springham on the Londonderry plantation, 1613, P.R.O.N.I., Ellis papers, D683/27. George Cunningham to John Watt, 7 Feb. 1753, P.R.O.N.I., Lenox-Conyngham papers, D1449/12/55; James Kirk to Agmondisham Vesey, 25 Feb. 1718, P.R.O.N.I., Kirk-Vesey papers, T2524/1.

102 James Knight to Dacre Barrett, 12 Feb. 1718, P.R.O.N.I., Barrett-Lennard papers, film 170/2. Edmund Kaine to Dacre Barrett, 10 July 1718, ibid. The letters of John Todd in the 1740s are concerned primarily with leases and the construction of houses in Clones, including a market house. Another agent was searching for 'persons of substance' to occupy the town in 1750. Richard Dawson to Thomas Barrett-Lennard, 7 June 1750, ibid.

103 Thomas Noble to Barrett-Lennard, 5 January 1771, ibid., film 170/2.

104 William Mayne to Thomas Barrett-Lennard, 17 Jan. 1808, P.R.O.N.I., Barrett-Lennard papers, D1232/1/65.

105 [?] Misset to [?] Blundell, 22 July 1721, P.R.O.N.I., Downshire papers, D607/A/12. 'The few tenements in the town which are mighty bad we had no bidders for, except beggars, wherefore I have directed Gwynn to make the best bargain he can for you from year to year till we can find able persons to take them that will build.' [?] Meredyth to Blundell, 1 July 1720, ibid.

106 Nicholas Ellis to Barrett-Lennard, 27 June 1843, P.R.O.N.I., Barrett-Lennard papers, film 170/3. McGildowney disallowed the sale of town parks because they were meant for the residents of Ballymoney. Edmund McGildowney to Adam Hunter, 20 Feb. 1815, P.R.O.N.I., McGildowney papers, D1375/3/12/20.

107 W.H. Crawford, 'The evolution of Ulster towns' in Peter Roebuck (ed.), *Plantation to partition: essays in Ulster history in honour of J.L. McCracken* (Belfast, 1981), p. 141; Nathanial Nesbitt to eighth earl of Abercorn, 18 May 1750, P.R.O.N.I., Abercorn papers, T2541/IA1/2/1.

108 James Stevenson to Abercorn, 26 Dec. 1769, ibid., T2541/IA1/8/1; James Hamilton to Abercorn, 10 May 1778, ibid., T2541/IA2/2/28.

109 John Hamilton to Abercorn, 18 Feb. 1770 and 12 June 1768, ibid., T2541/IA1/9/14, T2541/IA1/9/41l, T2541/IA1/8/65; John Hamilton to Abercorn, 1 Mar. 1771, ibid., T2541/IA1/9/106; James Hamilton to Abercorn, 23 Apr. 1769, ibid., T2541/IA1/8/1. No fewer than 110 of the 125 freeholds on the estate were located in the manor of Strabane, ibid., D623/C/4/1,3,5,7,8.

110 James Hamilton to Abercorn, 17 May 1785, ibid., T2541/IA1/15/14; Dowling, 'Abercorn estate,' pp. 72–77.

111 See, for example, Gillespie, *Transformation*, pp. 37–8; Foster, *Modern Ireland*, p. 66; L. M. Cullen, *Anglo-Irish trade, 1660–1800* (Manchester, 1968), p. 26; Reter Roebuck and Rosalind Mitcheson, 'Introduction' to idem (eds.), *Economy and society in Scotland and Ireland, 1500–1939* (Edinburgh, 1988), pp. 1–14.

112 Gillespie, *Transformation*, pp. 37–8, 53.

113 Immanuel Wallerstein, *The modern world system ii: mercantilism and the consolidation of the European world-economy, 1600–1750* (London, 1980), pp. 12–35.

114 Wallerstein and Gunder Frank are content merely to describe this long phase of history as a 'secular' event. Wallerstein, *Modern world system, ii*, p. 19; Andre Gunder-Frank, *World accumulation, 1492–1789* (New York, 1978), pp. 65–103.

115 While lamenting the ambiguities surrounding his use of terms 'obstacles,' 'forces,' 'feudalism,' and 'capitalism,' de Vries finds the Marxist interpretation much the best. Jan de Vries, *The economy of Europe in an age of crisis, 1600–1750* (Cambridge, 1976), pp. 21–25.

116 Etienne Balibar, 'The basic concepts of historical materialism' in Louis Althusser and Etienne Balibar, *Reading capital* (London, 1970), pp. 209–16.

117 For Marx, this means that indirect production is the basis for the notion of commodity fetishism, whereby the relations between labouring individuals appear not as direct social relations between producers, but as social relations between things. This appearance hides the fact that labour time is the only commodity capable of producing value.

118 The establishment of a certain form of labour is a necessary, but not sufficient, condition for the accumulation of capital. There is also the problem of realizing accumulated capital, which is dependent on successful marketing. The failure of the Virginia company was paradigmatic of seventeenth century colonialism. At first, stockholders hoped to avoid the question of labour. 'Stockholders relinquished earlier hopes of quick windfalls through discovery of precious metals or trade with Indians. Facing the hard reality that nothing could be gained without the production of staple crops, they initiated a full-scale effort at colonization.' Robert Brenner, *Merchants and revolution: commercial change, political conflict, and London's overseas traders, 1550–1653* (Cambridge, 1993), p. 93.

119 N.B. Harte, 'The rise of protection and the English linen trade 1690–1790' in J.B. Harte and K.G. Ponting (eds.), *Textile history and economic history* (Manchester, 1973), p. 92.

120 'The increasing political initiative of the Anglo-Irish in the early eighteenth century led them to formulate a body of Irish legislation that may, without exaggeration, be said to constitute a form of Irish mercantilism.' Francis Godwin James, *Ireland in the empire 1688–1770: a history of Ireland from the Williamite Wars to the eve of the American revolution* (Harvard, 1973), p. 194.

121 *Journals of the House of Commons*, 27 January, 1704/5.

122 *Journals of the House of Lords*, 17 March 1703/4.

123 Earl of Sunderland to Secretary Stanhope, Bath, 4 June 1715, P.R.O.N.I., T448/45. On the extension of the linen act of 1705 for another 10 years in 1717, see Leo Francis Stock (ed.), *Proceedings and debates of the British parliaments respecting North America*, 5 vols (Washington, 1924–1941), iii, pp. 383–384; Conrad Gill, *The rise of the Irish linen industry* (Oxford, 1925), pp. 66–67.

124 Thomas M. Truxes, *Irish-American trade, 1660–1783* (Cambridge, 1988) p. 180.

125 Stock, *Proceedings and debates of British Parliaments respecting North America*, iii, pp. 383–4.

126 Ibid., p. 192.

127 Cullen, *Anglo-Irish trade*, p. 2

128 Truxes, *Irish-American trade*, p. 177.

129 Crawford, 'Origins of the linen industry,' p. 146; Conrad Gill, *The rise of the Irish linen industry*, London, 1925, pp. 341–2.

130 Crawford cites both Walter Harris, *The antient and present state of County Down* (Dublin, 1744) and L. Slater, *The advantages which may arise to the people of Ireland by raising of flax and flaxseed* (Dublin, 1732) on the crucial role played by the linen trade in raising the poorly endowed province out of the doldrums of poverty. Crawford, 'The political economy of linen,' p. 137.

131 *A letter from Sir Richard Cox, Bart., to Thomas Prior Esq., showing . . . a sure method to establish the linen manufacture* (Dublin, 1749); Richard Cox, *Some observations on the state of Ireland* (London, 1731) cited in Dickson, 'Cork region,' p. 144, 148. See also Power, *Tipperary*, p. 1, 68, 155–6.

132 W.H. Crawford, 'Ulster landowners and the linen industry' in T.J. Ward and R.G. Wilson (eds.), *Land and industry: the landed estate and the industrial revolution* (New York,

1971), p. 135; Gillespie, *Transformation*, p. 44. Sligo landlords also hoped to retain their Protestant tenantry by promoting the linen manufacture. Cullen, *Emergence*, p. 209.

133   W.H. Crawford, 'The origins of the linen industry in north Armagh and the Lagan valley' in *Ulster folklife*, xvii (1971), p. 142. Lurgan was said to contain the largest linen manufacture in Ireland in 1682. 'A description of Oneilland Baroney in the County of Armagh by William Brooke, Portadown,' 26 Oct. 1682 in *A Natural History of Ireland, memories and notes relating thereto, made from communications to the Dublin society*, 2 vols., i, p. 222, TC.D., MSS 883/1.

134   William Waring to Samuel Waring, 9 Aug. 1699, P.R.O.N.I., D695, Waring papers, D695/54.

135   'A journey to the north, 7 August, 1708' in *A Natural History of Ireland, memories and notes relating thereto, made from communications to the Dublin society*, 2 vols. ii, p. 130, T.C.D., MSS 883/1.

136   Wright, *Northern Ireland*, p. 2.

137   Robert Hutchinson to Henry Bayly, 4 June 1783, P.R.O.N.I., Anglesey papers, D619/21/D/3.

138   [?] Benson to earl of Uxbridge, 3 Aug. 1785, ibid., D619/22/C/12. Robert Hutchinson salivated in 1790 about two 'gentlemen of capital,' both of whom were experienced Newry merchants, who proposed to rent and build bleach greens in Omeath. Rental of Mullarton, 14 Sept. 1790, ibid., D619/21/D/24. One man offered one guinea per acre for parts of the townland of Muckgrange. He was reported to have had a house in Dublin, an estate worth £2,000 a year, and a 'very good character. The rent would be well paid.' Hutchinson to Bayly, 10 June 1775, ibid., D619/21/C/118. A Dundalk merchant was interested in renting Muckgrange because he had become fond of rural life and wanted to raise cattle. He noted that the present cottiers paid a guinea an acre for a small part of it, 'and this to be collected with the utmost difficulty, without their making the smallest improvement on your estate, but on the contrary, have almost wore out entirely the substance of the grounds.' He suggested taking it for the same price. [?] to Bayly, 10 June 1775, ibid., D619/22/B/36. A Dundalk merchant was told that Bayly had promised not to dispossess the present tenants of Muckgrange, and therefore the proposal was denied. He tried again after some of their leases expired in 1778. [?] to Bayly, 14 Feb. 1778, ibid., D619/22/B/49.

139   James Knight to Dacre Barrett, 12 Feb. 1718, P.R.O.N.I., Barrett-Lennard papers, film 170/2; John Todd to Barrett, 30 Oct. 1741, ibid.

140   Idem, 5 June 1744, ibid. Master bleachers were also consulted.

141   Todd to Barrett, 17 July 1748, ibid.

142   Thomas Noble to Thomas Barrett-Lennard, 16 Nov. 1771, ibid.

143   Nathanial Nesbitt to eighth earl of Abercorn, 8 Dec. 1753, P.R.O.N.I., Abercorn papers, T2541/IA1/2/17; see also ibid., T2541/IA1/8/182, T2541/IA1/10/76, 84; James Hamilton to Abercorn, 15 Nov. 1778, ibid., T2541/IA2/2/55; Crawford, 'Ulster landowners,' p. 132.

144   Eighth earl of Abercorn to James Hamilton, 15 Apr. 1778, P.R.O.N.I., Abercorn papers, D623/A/23/32; petition of inhabitants of borough of Strabane to Abercorn, n.d. [c. 1765], ibid., T2541/IA1/6C/164; A.P.W. Malcomson, 'The politics of "natural right:" The Abercorn family and Strabane borough, 1692–1800' in G.A. Hayes (ed.), *Historical Studies*, x (1976), pp. 43–87.

145   'Wheels and reels' were given away on numerous occasions. Nathanial Nesbitt to Abercorn, 10 Feb. and 17 May 1753, ibid., T2541/IA1/2/144,152; Hamilton to Abercorn, 24 Apr. 1770, ibid., T2541/IA1/9/30.

146 Charles Coote described the 'scramble for wheels and reels' in Dublin. Charles Coote to Abercorn, n.d. [c. 1748], ibid., T2541/IA1/1D/13.

147 James Hamilton to Abercorn, 19 Aug. 1781, ibid., T2541/IA1/13/125.

148 Edmund Kaine to Thomas Barrett-Lennard, 14 June 1721, P.R.O.N.I., Barrett-Lennard papers, film 170/2.

149 John Todd to [Richard Barrett-Lennard], 10, 16 Sept. 1747, ibid., film 170/2.

150 Idem, 23 May 1747, ibid.

151 James Hamilton to eighth earl of Abercorn, 7 Dec. 1770, 3 Dec. 1771, P.R.O.N.I., Abercorn papers, T2541/IA1/9/86, T2541/IA1/9/147; idem, 25 Apr. 1773, 21 June 1778, ibid., T2541/IA1/10/85, T2541/IA2/2/36; idem, 7 Apr. 1776, ibid., T2541/IA1/12/1.

152 Idem, 28 June 1778, ibid., T2541/IA2/2/37.

153 Idem, 1 Dec. 1776, ibid., T2541/IA1/12/47.

154 Idem, 26 Sept. 1784, ibid., T2541/IA1/14/48; on Londonderry imports and exports, see Dowling, 'Abercorn estate,' pp. 39–46; James Hamilton, Jr., to ninth earl of Abercorn, 5 July 1794, P.R.O.N.I., T2541/ IA1/20/19; idem, 6 Aug. 1794, ibid., T2541/IA1/20/26.

155 William Mayne to Thomas Barrett-Lennard, 22 Jan. 1815, P.R.O.N.I., Barrett-Lennard papers, D1232/1/212. And in the fall of that year he observed: 'It is true a large portion of your rents are not made by tillage. Linen, linen yarn, flax, butter, pigs, and all sorts of cattle are proportionately low in price. Your tenantry don't deserve censure for being tardy in paying.' Mayne to Barrett-Lennard, 4 Sept. 1815, ibid., D1232/1/223.

156 For 1758: P.R.O.N.I., Abercorn papers, T2541/IA1/5/37; for 1778: ibid., T2541/IA1/12/5, 10; for 1783: ibid., T2541/IA2/3/44; for 1794: ibid., T2541/IA1/20/19. Linen was sometimes sold at a loss in order to acquire American flaxseed. Truxes, *Irish-American trade*, p. 182.

157 James Hamilton to eighth earl of Abercorn, 27 Apr. 1759, P.R.O.N.I., Abercorn papers, T2541/IA1/5/84.

158 Idem, 21 May 1780, ibid., T2541/IA1/13/30; idem, 20 Feb., 7 April, and 13 April 1776, ibid., T2541/IA1/12/5, 10, 113. Abercorn to Hamilton, 20 July 1783, ibid., D623/A/25/106. Hamilton to Abercorn, 2 June 1778, ibid., T2541/IA2/2/33; Dowling, 'Abercorn estate,' graphs 6 and 7, pp. 45–6.

159 Idem, 9 July 1783, ibid., T2541/IA2/3/44.

160 Hamilton Maxwell to Agmondisham Vesey, 13 Jan. 1722, P.R.O.N.I., Kirk-Vesey papers, T2524/12. Five barrels of flax-seed were divided among Protestant tenants on a list drawn up by agents on the Castleward estate in 1732. Robert Ward to Michael Ward, 28 Feb. 1732, P.R.O.N.I., Castleward papers, D2092/1/4.

161 James Hamilton to eighth earl of Abercorn, 7 Nov. 1784, P.R.O.N.I., Abercorn papers, T2541/IA1/14/49.

162 Idem, 25 Aug. 1781, ibid., T2541/IA1/13/125.

163 Idem, 22 June 1783, ibid., T2541/IA2/3/36.

164 James Hamilton, Jr. to ninth earl of Abercorn, 25 Sept. and [early Sept.], 1788, ibid., T2541/IA1/16/26, 28; Nathanial Nesbitt to Abercorn, 17 Feb. 1760, ibid., T2541/IA1/6A/1. James Hamilton to Abercorn, 8 June 1764, ibid., T2541/IA1/6C/3; Cullen, *Anglo-Irish trade*, p. 13.

165 1736:, ibid., T2541/IA1/1A/15; 1767: T2541/IA1/7/112; 1758: T2541/IA1/5/31; 1776: T2541/IA1/12/122; 1788: T2541/IA2/2/36; 1788: T2541/IA1/16/28. Money shortages occurred for other reasons in 1745, when fear of a Scottish war caused

hoarding. Nathanial Nesbitt to Abercorn, 22 Sept. 1745, ibid., 6 Oct. 1745, T2541/ IA1/1B/59, 60.

166 Abercorn to John McClintock, 15 Oct. 1745, ibid., D623/A/12/25.

167 James Nugent to Andrew Nugent, 21 Apr. 1822, P.R.O.N.I., Nugent papers, D552/ A/7/6/110. Arthur and Thomas Robinson to Andrew Nugent, 3 Mar. 1815, P.R.O.N.I., Nugent papers, D552/A/75/3. In 1835 the Northern Banking Company demanded a £5,000 minimum deposit to locate at Moneymore. Edward Lawford to J.R. and Rowley Miller, 16 Apr. 1835, P.R.O.N.I., Drapers' company papers, D3632/ 3/4.

168 William Mayne to Thomas Barrett-Lennard, 7 May 1808, P.R.O.N.I., Barrett-Lennard papers, D1232/1/74.

169 Idem, 9 June 1816, ibid.

170 James Gwynn to Henry Hatch, 22 Oct. 1746, P.R.O.N.I., Downshire papers, D607/ A/24. W.H. Crawford discovered a hardware merchant in Ballymena dealing in linen bills of exchange in Ballymena in the 1780s. Crawford, 'A Ballymena businessman in the late eighteenth century' in J. Gray and W. McCann (eds.), An uncommon bookman (Belfast, 1996).

171 Gwynn to Hatch, 28 June 1746, ibid., D607/A/12.

172 Robert Hutchinson to Henry Bayly, 6 June 1778, P.R.O.N.I., Anglesey papers, D619/21/C/174.

173 Thomas Noble to Thomas Barrett-Lennard, [?] 1773, P.R.O.N.I., Barrett-Lennard papers, film 170/2.

174 W.H. Crawford, 'Ulster as a mirror of the two societies' in David Dickson and T.M. Devine (eds.), Ireland and Scotland, 1600–1850: parallels and contrasts in economic and social development (Edinburgh, 1983), pp. 43–62.

175 Peter Roebuck, 'Rent movement and agricultural development, 1730–1830,' in Roebuck, Plantation to partition, pp. 86, 263; Dowling, 'Abercorn estate,' p. 71. The Whyte estate near Banbridge, Co. Down, had an artificial value from its location in near manufactures. John Doran to N.C. Whyte, 7 Feb. 1850, P.R.O.N.I., Whyte papers, D2918/3/8/4.

176 Robert Hutchinson to Henry Bayly, 8 Sept. 1773, P.R.O.N.I., Anglesey papers, D619/ 21/6/86. It was impossible for Hutchinson to collect rents in the fall of 1774. The townlands of Crobane and Mullerton were now as bad as Omeath in this respect. Revenue agents who shut down contraband trade further reduced rent payments. Also, the Carlingford Lough fishery failed. Hutchinson to Bayly, 1774, ibid., D619/ 21/C/101–4, 109.

177 Robert Isaac to Henry Hatch, 2 Apr. 1748, P.R.O.N.I., Downshire papers, D607/ A/76. Savage reported the sale of rabbit skins from the estate in Dublin in 1756. James Savage to Hatch, 3 Apr. 1756, ibid., D607/A/145. William Curlett and his partners in the townland of Murlough on the Anglesey estate informed Henry Hatch that a hard frost in the autumn of 1746 had destroyed their rabbits and oats, forcing them to buy bread. They promised they would pay, anticipating a good crop of fine flax. Petition of William Curlett and Partners, c. 1747, ibid., D607/A/608.

178 'Hints toward a natural and topographical history of the counties of Sligo, Donegal, Fermanagh, and Lough Erne by Rev. William Henry . . . 1739,' P.R.O.N.I., film 198.

179 Young, Tour, i, pp. 137, 165. W.H. Crawford, 'Change in Ulster in the late eighteenth century' in Thomas Bartlett and David Heyton (eds.), Penal era and golden age: essays in Irish history, 1690–1800 (Belfast, 1979), pp. 186–203; Graeme Kirkham, 'Economic diversification in a marginal economy: a case study' in Roebuck, Plantation to partition, pp. 64–81.

180 Nicholson to Wake, 6 Dec 1720, Dublin Municipal Library, Gilbert MSS, Bishop Nicholson to Archbishop Wake of Canterbury. Cited in Connolly, *Religion, law, and power*, p. 52.

181 McEvoy, *Statistical survey of Tyrone*, p. 39.

182 James Hamilton to eighth earl of Abercorn, 1 June 1758, P.R.O.N.I., Abercorn papers, T2541/IA1/5/31. Although this situation may have been somewhat ameliorated by the passage of the Cattle Acts, exports of cattle products did not become significant until after the turn of the century.

183 Andrew Spotswood to Thomas Conolly, 2 June 1778, TC.D., Conolly papers, MS 3974–84/514.

184 Henry Major to Conolly, 23 June 1778, ibid., MS 3974–84/522.

185 Major to Conolly, 6 July 1779, ibid., MS 3974–84/581.

186 Abercorn to Hamilton, 3 Apr. 1776, P.R.O.N.I., Abercorn papers, D623/A/22/59.

187 Hamilton to Abercorn, 26 Feb. 1788, 16 Jan. 1789, ibid., T2541/IA2/4 p. 58, T2541/IA1/16/9.

188 Tierney, 'Tabular reports,' p. 68.

189 Crawford, 'Ulster landowners,' p. 135.

190 Hamilton to Abercorn, 13 Dec. 1770, 2 Aug. 1771, P.R.O.N.I., Abercorn papers, T2541/IA1/9/87, T2541/IA1/9/133.

191 Tristram Carey to Abercorn, 19 Dec. 1766, ibid., T2541/IA1/7/52; Abercorn to Hamilton, 7 Mar. 1773, ibid., D623/A/21/23.

192 Hamilton to Abercorn, 24 May 1772, 25 Apr. 1773, 17 Feb. 1775, ibid., T2541/IA2/1/25, T2541/IA1/10/85, T2541/IA1/10/35.

193 Tenant petition, 23 Dec. 1753, P.R.O.N.I., Anglesey papers, D619/11/9.

194 James Hamilton, Jr., to ninth earl of Abercorn, 9 June 1780, P.R.O.N.I., Abercorn papers, T2541/IA2/9/22.

195 James Hamilton to eighth earl of Abercorn, 18 Dec. 1778, ibid., T2541/IA2/2/59.

196 Journal of a tour of parts of England, Wales, and Ireland compiled by Reverend J. Burrows, 3 June to 12 Aug. 1773, N.L.I., MS 23,561.

197 James Hamilton to eighth earl of Abercorn, 22 Mar. 1776, P.R.O.N.I., Abercorn papers, T2541/IA1/12/8.

198 Idem, 19 Sept. 1759, ibid., T2541/IA1/5/108. See also idem, 18 Nov. 1759, ibid., T2541/IA1/5/127.

199 Robert Jamison to ninth earl of Abercorn, 6 Dec. 1794, ibid., T2541/IA1/20/45.

200 Hamilton to Abercorn, 5 July 1759, ibid., T2541/IA1/5/102.

201 Idem, 1 Apr. 1781, P.R.O.N.I., Abercorn papers, T2541/IA1/13/82.

202 Idem, 21 Sept. 1783, ibid., T2541/IA2/3/50.

203 James Hamilton, Jr., to ninth earl of Abercorn, 4 April 1792, ibid., T2541/IA2/5/17.

204 James Hamilton to eighth earl of Abercorn, 1 Dec. 1775, ibid., T2541/IA2/1/47.

205 James Hamilton, Jr., to ninth earl of Abercorn, 20 Aug. 1798, ibid., T2541/IA2/6/29; idem, 4 May 1800, ibid., T2541/IA2/9/19; idem, 4 Mar. 1801, ibid., T2541/IA2/10/7; idem, 23 April 1798, ibid., T2541/IA2/7/15, 16.

206 Idem, 21 Mar. 1797, ibid., T2541/IA2/6/19.

207 Idem, 25 Mar. 1797, ibid., T2541/IA2/6/20.

208 E.P. Thompson, 'Eighteenth-century English society: class struggle without class?' in *Social history*, x, no. 2 (1978), pp. 133–65.

209 Maguire, *Downshire estates*, p. 248.

210 Henry, 'Hints;' Crawford, 'The political economy of linen;' Crawford, 'Origins of the linen industry in north Armagh and the Lagan valley.'

211 Hamilton to Abercorn, 19 Feb. 1786, ibid., T2541/IA2/4/3.

212 Young, *Tour*, ii, p. 29.

213 Hamilton to Abercorn, 10 Jan. 1785, P.R.O.N.I., Abercorn papers, T2541/IA1/15/2.

214 John Spotswood to Thomas Conolly, 9 June, 5 July 1800, T.C.D., Conolly papers, MS 3974–84/1350, 1361.

215 Henry Smith to Rowley Miller, 15 Dec. 1824, P.R.O.N.I., Drapers' company papers, D3632/3/2.

216 Report by Nathanial Stonard and W. Hamond, 27 Feb. 1817, Minutes of the court of assistants, extracts relating to Irish estates, Drapers' Hall, London, N.L.I., film 1529.

217 Tierney, 'Tabular reports,' p. 44 n. 2.

218 P. O'Connor to J.P. Kelly, [?] Mar. 1849, P.R.O.N.I., Whyte papers, D2918/3/7/165.

219 J.R. Moore to [?] Lees, 2 Sept. 1840, P.R.O.N.I., Annesley papers, D1854/6/2, p. 51.

220 Report of deputation to Irish estate of Clothworkers' company, 1849, N.L.I., film 1517.

221 James Hamilton to eighth earl of Abercorn, 16 Jan. 1789, P.R.O.N.I., Abercorn papers, T2541/IA2/4, p. 58.

222 Idem, 16 July 1787, ibid., T2541/IA2/4/p. 45.

223 Dowling, 'Abercorn estate,' pp. 68–70.

224 For analyses of risk and farm size, see J.C. Scott, *The moral economy of the peasant: rebellion and subsistence in Southeast Asia* (New Haven, 1976) and J. Roumassett, *Rice and risk: decision-making among low income farmers* (Amsterdam, 1976).

225 James Hamilton, Jr., to ninth earl of Abercorn, 7 Oct. 1799, P.R.O.N.I., Abercorn papers, T2541/IA2/8/19.

226 Thomas Noble to Thomas Barrett-Lennard, 12 Feb. 1774, P.R.O.N.I., Barrett-Lennard papers, film 170/2.

227 Ibid.

228 Robert Galt to earl of Caledon, 13 Mar. 1790, P.R.O.N.I., Caledon papers, D2433/A/2/6/4.

229 James Hamilton, Jr., to ninth earl of Abercorn, 25 May 1806, P.R.O.N.I., Abercorn papers, D623/A/94/39.

230 'Observations for Mr. Parks' assistance,' 18 July 1787, P.R.O.N.I., Anglesey papers, D619/14/C/4.

231 William Ogilvie to John Wilson, 18 Sept. 1807, P.R.O.N.I., Ogilvie papers, T1546/1.

232 Wilson to Ogilvie, 20 Oct. 1807, ibid.; Ogilvie to Wilson, 2 Nov. 1807, ibid.; Wilson to Ogilvie, 14 Feb. 1808, ibid.

233 Liam Kennedy, 'The rural economy, 1820–1914,' pp. 1–16.

234 Nicholas Ellis to Thomas Barrett-Lennard, 30 Dec. 1829, P.R.O.N.I., Barrett-Lennard papers, film 170/3.

235 Report of deputation, 3 Dec. 1832, minutes of the court of assistants, extracts relating to Irish estates, 1805–24, Drapers' Hall, London, N.L.I., film 1529.

236 Report to the Irish estate committee on the Merchant Tailors' estate by Samuel Angell, surveyor, 22 July 1844, Merchant Tailors' Hall, Irish estate committee of management minutes, 1840–53, N.L.I., film 1517.

237 J.R. Miller to Edward Lawford, 2 Mar. 1846, P.R.O.N.I., Drapers' company papers, D3632/1/1. William Mayne of the Barrett-Lennard estate encouraged a local manufacturer in 1816 to employ women who had no more spinning work. William Mayne to Thomas Barrett-Lennard, 16 Apr. 1816, P.R.O.N.I., Barrett-Lennard papers, film 170/2. The Drapers' company lent £500 for a spinning manufactory in

1838. Minutes of the court of assistants, 31 July 1838, Drapers' Hall, London, N.L.I., film 1529. The collapse of the linen trade also caused the reduction of the rent for the Draperstown hotel, which was to get a water closet. J.R. Miller to Edward Lawford, 25 Jan. 1847, P.R.O.N.I., Drapers' company papers, D3532/1/1.

238 Wright, *Two lands on one soil*, pp. 383–4.

239 W.J. Smyth, 'Flax cultivation in Ireland: the development and demise of a regional staple,' in Smyth and Whelan (eds.), *Common ground*, pp. 234–252.

240 J.R. Miller to Edward Lawford, 17 Mar. 1847, P.R.O.N.I., Drapers' company papers, D3632/1/1.

241 Rowley and J.R. Miller to Edward Lawford, 17 Dec. 1852, ibid., D3632/1/2.

242 Mortimer Thomson to James Kennedy, 19 May 1853, P.R.O.N.I., Dufferin papers, D1071/A/K/box 1.

243 Rowley and J.R. Miller to W.H. Sawyer, 25 Oct. 1862, ibid., D3632/1/3.

244 Rowley Miller to Sawyer, 16 Aug. 1864, ibid.

245 H.R. Miller to Sawyer, 12 Dec. 1875, ibid., D3632/1/4.

246 Ibid., 10 Mar. 1877, ibid.

247 Wright counts five forms of pressure on pre-famine Ulster smallholders: the decline of weaving and spinning, the shrinking potential for developing marginal land, the decline of cottage whiskey distillation, shrinking supplies of turf, and declining opportunities for harvest labour in Scotland, England, and Leinster. Wright, *Two lands on one soil*, pp. 74–75, 89, 172, 189.

248 Agent report on increasing arrears on the Royal School, Cavan estate, 11 Mar. 1844, N.L.I., Dr. Michael Quain papers, Royal School, Armagh, MS 17,912.

249 Donnelly, *Cork*, pp. 9–72; Ó Gráda, *Ireland*, pp. 153–70.

250 Letter of S.W. Greer, 29 July 1841, Merchant Tailors' hall, Irish estate committee of management minutese, N.L.I., film 1517. For the confusion over the definition of cottiers, see Tierney, 'Tabular reports,' pp. 67–8; The terminology used in eighteenth century Cork is rehearsed by Dickson, 'Cork region,' pp. 205–6.

251 Henry Smith to Rowley Miller, 2 Mar. 1821, P.R.O.N.I., Drapers' company papers, D3632/3/1.

252 Rowley and J.R. Miller to Edward Lawford, 17 Mar. 1846, ibid., D3632/1/1.

253 Idem, 1 Oct. 1845, ibid.

254 Letter on the estate entered into the minutes, January 1809, N.L.I., Fishmongers' records, film 1514; Greig, *General report*, pp. 104–5.

255 Frank Wright, *Two lands on one soil*, p. 401. See also the marquis of Dufferin's testimony to the Bessborough commission on the prosperity of the north of Ireland and the industriousness of its people. *Bessborough comm. evidence*, Q. 1474–8.

256 Rowley and J.R. Miller to Edward Lawford, 25 May 1848. 'The origin of tenant right, it appears to me, may be altogether ascribed to the manner in which the linen manufacture has been carried on in the province of Ulster. . . . The introduction of tenant right was not originally based upon the value of antecedent improvements, but may fairly be ascribed to the factitious value which small holdings had acquired, as useful adjuncts to that which was the main business of the population of Ulster, namely, their trade as weavers.' Conway E. Dobbs, *Some observations on the tenant right of Ulster* (Dublin, 1849), pp. 3–5. See also Wright, *Two lands on one soil*, pp. 92, 96–7.

CHAPTER FOUR

Visuality

RUNDALE, ENCLOSURE, AND THE PLANTATION OF ULSTER

The purpose of this chapter is to examine the dynamics of the rundale system as it came under the demographic and economic pressures of the eighteenth century, the efforts of landlords, estate managers, and individual tenants to reorganize landholding into individualized and parcelled units, and the role which the custom of tenant right played in this reorganization. The antithesis of the plantation model of large, cohesive, Protestant-occupied farms was a variant of the traditional system of land settlement known in Ireland as rundale.[1] In these systems, the landscape was generally divided between the most fertile and intensively cultivated area of the community (the infield), and the less fertile areas used predominantly for summer pasturing (the outfield). The characteristics of these traditional systems can be described in overlapping economic, social, and visual terms. Economically, local eco-systems and the technical and capital requirements of harvesting resulted in the arrangement of infield farms in long, narrow strips. This visual pattern was reinforced by the piecemeal colonisation of land by the demographically expanding community in a spatial context where cultivators 'leapfrog' each other. Socially, common rights to winter grazing on the infield and summer grazing on the outfield or waste were determined collectively. The infield strips were also formed and distributed with a view to equalising land quality among families, so that individual cultivators only temporarily possessed separate and scattered strips. The community relied on some form of disciplinary assembly such as a manor court, and not the market, to adjudicate between the competing claims of individuals. Finally, local systems were reproduced within traditions of joint tenancy and partible inheritance.[2] The Irish rundale system had many of these characteristics. Tillage shares were divided between members of the community and were ploughed collectively. This labour was followed by the gathering of sea wrack for fertilizer, cutting turf, driving stock to summer pasture, mowing hay, harvesting, and the opening up of infield parcels to winter pasturing.[3] This system possessed neither an inherent tendency toward livestock farming nor any aversion to arable production,[4] but as Chapter 3 showed there was a strong correlation in Ulster between the type of landscape, rundale landholding, and the form of transhumance pasturing known as booleying.[5]

The previous chapter emphasized the economic or productive facet of the ensemble of social relations that composed the Ulster farm. Here the focus shifts to the organizational and visual aspects of that ensemble. Plantation theorists promoted settled and enclosed farms over pastoral farms not so much because of their 'economic' superiority, but because they served the crucial function of visually dominating the unwieldy landscape and controlling the native and colonial population. The transformation was one of economic practice *and* visual organization. Enclosed farms held under severalty tenures facilitated what Foucault identified as new disciplinary methods atomizing and depersonalizing power relationships in modern society. Foucault articulated an interrelationship between *visual* control over populations and labour processes with the *economic* processes of capitalism:

> If the economic take-off of the West began with the techniques that made possible the accumulation of capital, it might perhaps be said that the methods of administering the accumulation of men made possible a political take-off in relation to the traditional, ritual, costly, violent forms of power, which soon fell into disuse and were superseded by a subtle, calculated technology of subjection. In fact, the two processes – the accumulation of men and the accumulation of capital – cannot be separated. . . . Each makes the other possible and necessary; each provides the model for the other. The disciplinary pyramid constituted the small cell of power within which the separation, co-ordination, and supervision of tasks was imposed and made efficient; an analytical partitioning of time, gestures, and bodily forces constituted an operational schema that could easily be transferred from the groups to be subjected to the mechanisms of production. . . . But, on the other hand, the technical analysis of the process of production, its 'mechanical' breakdown, were projected onto the labour force whose task it was to implement it: the constitution of those disciplinary machines in which the individual forces that they bring together are composed into a whole and therefore increased is the effect of this projection. . . . The growth of a capitalist economy gave rise to the specific modality of disciplinary power, whose general formulas, techniques of submitting forces and bodies, in short, 'political anatomy,' could be operated in the most diverse political régimes, apparatuses, or institutions.[6]

The particular capitalist institution under examination here, the Irish landed estate, is an excellent example of the development of this disciplinary power over tenants and visual sovereignty over properties. Both of these aspects, disciplinary power and visual sovereignty, were important to efficacious estate management. The enclosed farm was not only an efficient productive unit, it was an objective, readable, discoverable, mapable space. An estate that was organized, viewed, and known as a collection of such space-units was made more amenable to the management of the complexities produced by demographic intensification and grids of familial inheritance. The work of mapping and rationalizing estates was intended to retrain the eyes of the tenantry 'to see estate boundaries as distinct from relations among inhabitants and as emanating from 'within' the land itself as an intrinsic property of mathematically ordered nature (which included the market). Landowners [and tenants], and therefore social positions, alter, but property is absolute.'[7] No longer is a farm conceived of as a site of agricultural labour measured in terms of the number of days ploughing or the number of livestock it could sustain. Now it is geometrically 'divisible into capitalised space-units.'[8] It took some time for this form to become a model, but once it did so, agrarian capitalism became more than just an economic practice; it was now a visuality.[9]

The visual and organizational reform of the rundale system was important to the plantation at a number of levels. At the most general level, enclosed farms were a crucial signifier of the 'civility' that plantation strategists sought to insinuate into the countryside. One example of this was the description of the Savages, a Norman family of the Ards peninsula of County Down. They were said to be

> stout and warlike and loyal to the crown, who, however they might have had some civil broils [sic] amongst themselves and became (as many noble English families in Leinster, Munster, and Connaught) too much addicted to Irish customs and exactions, yet they are now as much civilized as the British and do live decently and conformably to the church and enjoy houses, orchards, and enclosed fields. . . . [10]

William Brooke portrayed a north Armagh barony similarly in 1682: 'Those few Irish we have amongst us are very much reclaimed of their barbarous customs, the most of them speaking English, and for agriculture they are little inferior to the English themselves. In a word, the fertility of the soil, the curious enclosures, the shady groves, and delicate seats that are everywhere dispersed over this barony do concur to make it a paradise of pleasures.'[11] The large, orderly, prosperous farmer modelled on the English yeoman was an enduring ideal for Irish propagandists throughout the eighteenth century. Arthur Young had a sharp eye for and an obvious preoccupation with the strong farmer. The sequence of anecdotes and observations in his *Tour of Ireland* is punctuated with detailed investigations of those large-scale agriculturists with whom he visited.[12]

But the enclosed farm was more than an empty signifier of colonial civilization, a kind of lace curtain on estate windows. The rundale system was a huge obstacle to managers seeking a rational ordering of farms, clear individual relationships between landlord and tenant, perfectly exchangeable units of land, and accurate knowledge and control over tenants and productive processes. For example, rundale greatly inhibited the ability of estate managers to place a value on the land. A townland on the Anglesey estate which had been let to a large group of joint tenants under a lease that expired in 1778 was, according to the agent, 'all divided into smallholdings among a number of poor tenants, the lands not being calculated for farmers and they upon all inquiry I can make pay the full value they would set for. . . . The lands of Irish Grange are so various, some mountains and some course and good land that it is difficult to say what their general value might be by the acre, but much depends on the sort of tenants.'[13] Another indication of the complexities involved was provided by a list of twenty-one tenants who shared a mountain's grazing on Richard Waring's County Antrim estate in 1804. This mountain was divided into 32 'sums,' a unit of measure equivalent to the grazing of one cow, between the tenants. A tenant named McDonnell had bought a total of seven sums from four tenants. The agent noticed that

> they grazed it in common, no division or partition being made amongst them. The list shows what share each of them grazed, ranging from 1/32 to 1/16 of the total: Mr. Randall McDonnell purchased from [four of these tenants] their proportions of the above mountain which would entitle him to graze thereon seven sums in all. But in place of seven he put to graze on said mountain thirty-seven and on 21 July last I impounded twenty-five head of his cattle off said mountain, leaving behind twelve which was five more than the number he was entitled to graze or keep on said mountain; and for the impounding of which I was served with the enclosed replevin. You will be pleased to take defence for me. . . .[14]

Waring responded to this by enquiring into the lease of the mountain: 'I perceive they are all joint tenants at present, but as they might be tenants at will, or have a subsisting interest of lives or years which would in this case make a considerable difference, I shall decline giving any further answer. . . .'[15] A single serpentine farm prevented the resetting of a townland on the Earl of Lanesborough's estate near Belturbet in 1860: 'If the object be to let them in town parks, a glance at the map will show that according to the present arrangement of the fields, this could never be advantageously done. The straggling position of the Leo Storey farm running serpent-like through the entire length, presents an insuperable obstacle in the way of town parks.'[16] The rundale system also stood in the way of a landlord's political control over tenants, because rundale partners were barred from registering for the franchise as freeholders.[17]

The orders and conditions of the plantation of Ulster legally destroyed many aspects of the open-field and rundale systems.[18] Landlords were given an absolute right over all property within the townlands specified in their patents, including bog, mountain, waste, and any other land that might otherwise fall under the category of commons. The requirement that all land be held under lease also technically replaced the lateral tenurial relationships of the rundale system (younger sons sharing rights with older brothers, the passage of leased property from father to son-in-law, or the lending and borrowing of land between neighbours) with the strictly vertical landlord-tenant relationship. Success in implementing the new order depended on aggressive managerial practice. These legal requirements did not automatically change the occupation of land.

The revisualization of the countryside was a slow and piecemeal process. Responsibility for mapping the escheated counties of the plantation was left to soldiers such as Josias Bodley in the early seventeenth century, and to the planters themselves. Quality mapmaking was rare, and the outstanding work of the mapmaker Thomas Raven in the 1620s in Londonderry, north Down, and Monaghan was certainly not the norm.[19] The new landlords were just as likely to rely on the native Irish to identify old and create new boundaries. Hunter cites this advice given to a British tenant of the archbishop of Armagh: 'Learn of the natives the confines of the territories and sessiages [sic, an Irish unit of land] in every ballyboe.'[20] Clearer definition of properties was brought about haphazardly, at the renewal of patents and leases, for example, or on the occasion of a dispute between neighbours. One such dispute from County Armagh in 1617 was resolved with the advice of government officials and a prominent native Irish inhabitant. The rather primitive way in which the boundaries were clarified was revealed in the following passage:

> Beginning at the usual ford where now a bridge is over the river in the tradeway to Newry from Dundalk called the Four Mile Water, about two stones cast from the river, [we] did drive a stake into the ground upon a ridge of a hill, and so driving another stake upon a right line by comerture [sic] from the first stake to a heap of stones called Firrbreage, and so as a man's eye will direct upon a right line through a corner of a wood every eight or ten score or thereabouts, driving stakes till you come to a rocky mountain called the ffadd, to the height of the mountain, which seems like a saddle from the first rock called Firrbreage, to which all parties agreed.[21]

The government showed its preference for this sort of negotiated creation of boundaries in 1637 when Wentworth issued a proclamation 'for the avoiding of lawsuits . . . concerning mears and bounds,' establishing instead commissions of perambulation and requiring that four-by-five-foot ditches and rows of quicksets be made and kept in repair.[22] In the eighteenth century estate managers made more concerted attempts to maintain a rational view of their estates, but the quickening pace of economic and tenurial change frequently made rent-rolls, maps, and other estate documentation obsolete. The agents on the Anglesey and Downshire estates complained of the difficulties of updating the rent-rolls because of the many leases that had been sold and tenancies changed, and the many abandoned cottier houses.[23] By the early nineteenth century, the useful life of an estate map had shortened considerably. Edward Driver, agent to the Clothworkers' company, remarked in 1840 on the dramatic changes that had occurred on the estate since the maps of the estate were drawn in 1825:

> There have been many alterations in some and in others additional fences made, thereby materially altering the enclosures or fields. The homesteads comprising the farm houses, cottages, outbuildings, and small closes in the towns are in most cases very imperfectly and in frequent cases inaccurately thereon; in many other cases considerable proportions of land have been enclosed and brought into cultivation from the mountains since the maps were made, which ought to be accurately measured and delineated thereon.[24]

Because the survey was so out of date, Driver found 'in a great many instances large quantities of land have been heretofore subdivided amongst several persons without any survey being made, but only into proportions [that] persons taking them might be able to agree upon.'[25] In the second third of the nineteenth century great strides were made in reforming Irish land in terms of this new visually based rationality. This work was accomplished not only an an estate-by-estate level but also on the grander scale of the entire island by the topographer Samuel Lewis and the surveyor Richard Griffith.[26]

The new way of seeing property was intended to increase management control over the population on that property. Organizational and the economic control were inextricable; the reform of the first allowed for the control of the second. Giddens identifies the crucial distinction between class-divided societies and class societies as the intrusion of the capitalist into the labour process itself. In class-divided societies generally there is autonomy between the labour process and the expropriation process. Under capitalism they are wedded together.[27] Land held in the open-field or rundale systems was subject to common rights and was cultivated by the community collectively. Landlords could interfere with these rights and practices only with great difficulty. The practice of letting lands in severalty, the identification by the landlord of one parcel to one person, was therefore just as significant for the management of an estate as physically enclosing the farm.[28] The lease was a crucial capacitor of these new arrangements, but only to the extent that its referent (a parcel of land) was accurately defined and made visible. On the Acheson estate in Cavan tenants were bound in a lease of 1635 to make every year

> forty perches of good and sufficient ditches set with the like quicksets . . . upon the firm ground and upon the bog, . . . with sallow and such other quicksets as will thereupon best prosper, . . . according to the manner . . . used in England, until the [lands] be fully enclosed and ditched about and divided into convenient closes and closures.[29]

Early leases on the Brownlow estate directed that tenants perambulate the boundaries of their farms annually. It was only later in the seventeenth century that recognized boundaries could be specified in leases; only after an estate was accurately carved up into parcels could a landlord investigate and monitor the level of production for which a single family was to be held responsible.[30] Managers saw a close link between an accurate map, a well-specified lease, and an optimal extraction of rent from the tenant.[31] This may explain the rarity of evidence concerning agricultural practices before the nineteenth century. Eighteenth-century pamphlets on Irish agricultural practice concerned themselves primarily with the state of tillage in Ireland. They argued for the expansion of tillage and specified methods for improving it.[32] But this propaganda was useless without the ability to implement change. For example, the Dublin Society introduced a system of premiums for farmers who produced high wheat crops, but the system depended entirely on verifiable acreages. Only those farmers whose plots had been verifiably surveyed needed apply.[33] In the early nineteenth century the emphasis changed, one indication of which was the outpouring of published works related to more effective cultivation of the soil.[34] Another sure sign of the growing interest of estate managers in the productive practices of their tenants is the evidence of their sponsorship of farming societies, agricultural schools, competitions, and the like.[35] Perhaps the most influential pamphlet in this line of thinking was William Blacker's *An essay on the improvements to be made in the cultivation of small farm* . . . (Dublin, 1834). Originally an address to Gosford and Close tenants, the tract recommended house feeding of cattle with turnips and rape, cleanliness, temperance, draining, squaring, neat manure heaps, new ploughing and weed techniques, and the consumption of turnips instead of potatoes. He claimed that a system of continuous tillage was possible with the right rotation.

The concern here is not so much with the actual techniques themselves as with the fact that landlords believed that their adoption required rationalizing the layout of farms. Smout argues that rotations using turnips and clover were incompatible with rundale in sixteenth-century Scotland.[36] Even in the nineteenth century arable cultivation on the infield by partnership farmers was limited to rotations of spring-sown oats and barley, potatoes, and flax.[37] The key to the more 'scientific' farming practices promoted by landlords was the adoption of new rotations in which turnip husbandry played a large role and dependence on the potato was reduced,[38] and the use of the 'Scotch' plough, which required that fields be organized into straight furrows.[39] The agent of the Nugent estate in the Ards peninsula of County Down, who explained in 1817 that the typical cropping method of one tenant was to exhaust the land and then let it lie fallow until 'time shall have brought it to some little skin of grass. Then [he would] begin to crop [it] again. In the meantime, how is the rent to be paid?' This tenant was denied a request for abatement of rent as he was a bad example to his neighbours.[40] James Nugent wrote of tenants who practised in the traditional way: 'The habits and management of the people in the North and this part are as different as possible, where your man made his fortune a Dysart man would starve, it is the most difficult thing possible to get them to change their system.'[41]

Ulster landlords generally attempted to force a change in productive practice by entering specific instructions into leases which required that tenants leave fields fallow periodically or specified the use of certain crop rotations and methods of fertilization.[42] Landlords also began to restrict the right of renewal only to those whose productive practice was acceptable.[43] The agent to the McCartney estate warned a tenant in 1792 that he was 'restricted from ploughing any but what he has first laid thirty Carlisle bushels of lime upon each acre,' and that he must follow the specified field rotation.[44] As noted above, the effectiveness of specifying new rotations in leases was limited by the landlord's ability to enforce them in court. Very few husbandry covenants were placed in Irish leases because of the futility of enforcing compliance with them. In 1779 Sir George Savile, a Tyrone proprietor, advised James Murray of Broughton to insert clauses regarding timely payment, over-ploughing, and repairs, but he warned him not to take legal action against the breaking of covenants if the tenant paid his rent on time, since there was little chance of success in court and a good chance of losing control over tenant practices altogether:

> I have heard it doubted whether such a clause which I have above mentioned would not leave a landlord to prove his damage and consequently give him no remedy at all if the tenant paid his rent and gave no other cause of complaint. This doubt has influenced me so much [that I would] rather wink and give leave when they asked it, which they have sometimes done, rather than losing by a trial the little hold it has upon them, for it is not without its effects.

Instead, he recommended rack-renting and granting regular abatements if the tenant obeyed the clauses and did not sublet.[45] Not until the judicial and managerial advances of the nineteenth century did agents become more sucessful in regulating productive practice.[46] Landlords began to prohibit the burning of bogs for fertilizer, practised by those without manure.[47] Detailed warnings such as this complaint about the sale of fifty tons of turnips by a farmer would have been unheard of in the previous century: 'I met a person called Malone yesterday in Armagh who informed me that he had purchased 50 tons of turnips from you. I hope there is some mistake about this, as I conceive such an act at this season of the year of selling turnips off your farm would be a violation of the condition on which you got it and very much opposed to the opinions I have heard you express of good farming.'[48] Four years later this agent harangued the same tenant again: 'I must beg to call attention to the quantity of grass land you are breaking up in your farm for tillage which will render it impossible for you to adopt a fair rotation of crops according to the covenants in your lease. Your having sold your straw of your farm last year will not give you the means of manuring the proper quantity of land next year for a future rotation of crops.'[49] Eighteenth-century efforts to increase productivity were generally limited to promoting linen production. This may have been a result of the high marginal productivity of land in a period lacking the demographic and productive pressures of the nineteenth century. In any case, landlords' growing interest in agricultural techniques collided with the traditional productive practices of the smallholding rundale communities on their estates. The violence of this collision derived from the incompatability of new tillage techniques with old systems of landholding, and from the intransigence of those involved in these old systems.[50]

THE RESILIENCE OF THE RUNDALE SYSTEM

Though nearly half of England's surface area had been enclosed by 1600, in the period 1600-1760 the back of the traditional open-field system in England was irrevocably broken. Nearly half of all enclosure occurring between 1500 and 1914 took place in this period.[51] In contrast to England, the enclosed farm was not yet a dominant component of the seventeenth-century Ulster landscape. It was still a fragile and only partially visible unit of land, created with considerable difficulty and preserved by a continuous labour.[52] *Advertisements for Ireland*, 1623, described the typical agricultural practice of the early plantation: 'their fields lie open and unenclosed, where wood is plentiful, they hedge in all their corn with stakes and bushes and pull them down in the winter and burn them.' At the other end of the century another anonymous tract, *A brief character of Ireland*, 1692, observed: 'enclosures are very rare amongst them, and those no better fenced than a midwife's toothless gums.'[53] It is for this reason that contemporary commentators were so exuberant about the enclosure that had been accomplished. Thomas Ashe's 1703 survey of the lands of the archbishopric of Armagh celebrated the successful plantation of the estate with glowing descriptions of the buildings of some English-style tenants on lands in south Ulster in the 1690s. Ashe frequently referred to destruction during the great rebellion and to the construction of mearings and planting of trees since then. The very enthusiasm expressed over some fine-looking houses suggests how rare they were in the countryside. Another mark of plantation success was the taming of the wild Irish woods by destroying them and replacing them with orderly plantations.[54] Ashe mentioned the 'once great woods' of which there was nothing left.

Historians have recently endeavoured to provide a more systematic account of the extent and distribution of enclosure in plantation Ulster. Robinson has gathered the most definitive evidence and drawn maps, based on evidence from the Ordnance Survey Memoirs, of timber hedges which give an impression of the areas where enclosure occurred earliest. According to this evidence, the Foyle valley extending down through mid-Tyrone, the Erne basin of Fermanagh, and the Lagan valley extending southwestward to north Armagh and north Monaghan were the three areas where enclosures were established earliest and most extensively.[55] Desmond McCourt's research on the extent of surviving rundale in eighteenth-century Ulster complements Robinson's findings. McCourt identifies four areas where rundale may have been absent from at least the early eighteenth century: the lowlands east and west of Lough Neagh, mid-Armagh, the northern sectors of the Ards peninsula, and much of County Fermanagh. He argues that heavy Scottish and English settlement east of Enniskillen was the primary reason for the absence of rundale there. Of course, the linen triangle showed no sign of clachans.[56] Enclosed farming was most intensive in the areas of Ulster having the most ancient Scottish influence, or those areas which were never strongholds of Gaelic society,[57] that is, in areas where the plantation met with the least resistance. Enclosure became particularly well established in areas with longstanding seafaring ties to Scotland, such as the County Down coast.[58] The same was true of the Foyle valley, although the rundale system was not finally eclipsed until well into the nineteenth century.[59] Rundale survived into the nineteenth century in the Glens of Antrim, and also in remote parts of Cavan and Fermanagh, the Omeath peninsula of County Louth, and high in the Sperrin mountains.[60] Rundale dominated the landscape on most London company estates until the nineteenth century. An 1849 deputation to the Clothworkers' proportion gave this report of their visit to a mountainous district on that estate:

There they saw a large population living together in tenements scattered over the mountain without order or regularity, without any proper road, dependent principally upon cultivation of the mountain land. While in some few cottages the loom was seen, this is unquestionably the poorest part of the estate, the great mass of the people living in extreme poverty. Still, they were not importunate for anything for themselves; they had no personal request to make.[61]

Some farms on the Fishmongers' proportion, both pasture and tillage, were found to be held in rundale in 1820.[62]

Why did the rundale system persist when the social relations it embodied were so incompatible with commercial agriculture and the legal script of the plantation? Landlord weakness and disinterest certainly played a part, but the more fundamental reason may have been that natives, newcomers, and estate managers all preferred the social cohesion and productive flexibility given by the system.[63] Common rights and traditions had a long evolutionary history in the English countryside. But in Ireland these were subjected to revolution, not evolution, by the plantation. As Connolly points out, 'the rural lower classes became subject to the same broad body of property law as in England, but with none of the multiple accretions of use rights and customary entitlements that offered the population there and elsewhere a measure of protection from the pressures of a rapidly developing market economy.'[64] Very little evidence of the socio-cultural aspects of the rundale communities is to be found in the business records of landed estates. But it is clear that in the absence of a poor law or the development of a heritage of common use rights as in England, tenants who might otherwise be exposed to the vicissitudes of a 'free' market for labour and land depended on the wide range of support given by the rundale system. The most important characteristic of the rundale system was its capacity to preserve the land/family bond by yearly redistribution of the scattered strips of land among the members of the clachan. This yearly redistribution of land eventually gave way to a system of fixed rundale, whereby specific strips were continually farmed by one family. The fixed rundale situation may be one where land is not redistributed but labour decisions are still made collectively and other mobile capital resources are shared. With greater demographic intensity the scope of collective redistribution and shared labour was reduced from the entire village to smaller kin-based groups within the village. Parts of a townland might be fixed between families but the rundale system continued to operate within and between networks of families linked by marriage and descent.[65]

The rundale system was also economically resilient. In a context of a high land/labour ratio and relatively poor soil, the so-called 'backward techniques' employed on small rundale farms were economically rational. 'Even rundale,' notes Ó Gráda 'the much maligned Irish version of the open-field system, has been reinterpreted in this light, as an adaption to difficult soil and cropping conditions.'[66] Historical geographers emphasize the rationality and modernity of rundale settlement. Jones Hughes emphasized the relatively late settlement of rundale areas in the west and Ulster. For Whelan it was an adaption to peculiar ecological and economic circumstances. High and unproductive land which provided low returns to capital could be cultivated with the intensive supply of labour characteristic of the rundale system.[67] Buchanan organizes evidence from *A view of the great tithes of the deanery of Down for the year 1732* to distinguish partnership farms from individual farms. Buchanan was able to calculate the share of each crop grown under the traditional system as well as on enclosed farms.[68] In the five parishes of the deanery over half the cultivated acreage was devoted to oats, and oats and barley together comprised over ninety percent of the arable acreage. The evidence indicates that partnership farmers were required to produce the same goods as efficiently as those holding in severalty. In the five parishes only thirty percent of the cultivated land was held in severalty in 1732. There was no difference between the two forms of tenancy in the cultivation of subsistence crops, and very little difference in the cultivation of cash crops, wheat and barley. For both, a high proportion of land, 45.1 percent, was devoted to cash crops, and in fact partnership farms devoted proportionally more land to wheat cultivation. Buchanan argues that this wheat cultivation must have put a severe strain on the livestock-producing capabilities of the rundale system, since it must have reduced the availability of winter pasture. This may be one explanation for the severity of harvest crises early in the century, with cattle hard-pressed to survive what was routinely a hungry winter.

Table 3

Output Mix on County Down Farms, 1732

	Barley	Wheat	Oats	Potatoes	Flax
Total acreage	**2574.5**	**190.25**	**3113.0**	**142.25**	**119.25**
% of total	42.0	3.1	50.7	2.3	1.9
% on partnership farms	66.5	73.0	70.0	70.0	70.0
% on severalty farms	33.5	27.0	30.0	28.8	27.0

Source: Buchanan, 'Barony of Lecale,' pp. 156–7, Tables 10, 11, 12.

Finally the rundale system, or at least some diluted variant of it, survived because the system had a positive symbolic relationship with certain aspects of the plantation estate system itself. For example, the rundale system adapted readily to the propensity to maintain ethnically separate and defensible communities. For the planters, social cohesion and strategic location were at a premium. The attractiveness of good land should not be underemphasized, but the location of newcomer settlements in the seventeenth century appears to have been determined by strategic position as well as by the quality of land. By projecting nineteenth-century evidence on the quality of land back onto the seventeenth-century settlement pattern, Robinson found that on land occupied since the seventeenth century, the areas of highest value in the nineteenth century were those with the most dense concentration of English and Scottish surnames. Significantly, though, areas without good land but with good locations with regard to transport and communication were also densely populated with immigrants, and much land called high quality in the nineteenth century had been left unoccupied by both natives and newcomers in the seventeenth century.[69] Macafee's examination of demographic data from a locality in southeastern Derry corroborates Robinson's findings.[70] Macafee speculates that the need to establish a connected colonial community outweighed considerations of profitability:

> Judging by the location of the townlands chosen for settlement by the majority of the early settlers, the fact that they lay along the major natural routeways converging on Maghera from the northeast to the southeast may have been just as important as the quality of the land. There is also a suggestion that some of the townlands lay on the edge of areas dominated by the Irish rather than in the middle of them. By moving into [certain] townlands . . . , planters were occupying an area which marked the edge of a zone dominated by [Irish] families because to the east and southeast was another area dominated by [Irish] names. . . . The occupation of this zone running northeast from Maghera, whether intentional or not, drove a wedge between these two groups of Irish.[71]

The settlement pattern on the Balfour estate in County Fermanagh reveals a similar set of preferences where British settlers congregated near the Dublin-to-Derry road, 'the only thorough-fare into the country.' The lands near this road were more attractive not because of their quality but because of their accessible and defensible location. For this reason the newcomers were willing to pay a higher rent than the natives. On the other hand, the Irish preferences led them to occupy land that was 'out of all good way.'[72]

Once again, leasing policies had a strong effect on the perceptions and practice of both native and immigrant settlers.[73] Macafee speculates that 'perhaps the key factor which led to particular groups of planter families becoming concentrated in and dominating certain townlands was the way in which the land was leased from the landlord.'[74] In a system where the unit of leasing was often the entire townland, which might not even have been accurately measured or fully occupied, the lease symbolized that status associated with ties to the landlord and the estate system. Within that lease, a myriad of permutations could be concocted between the occupiers. It is in this sense that Currie writes that open-field farming was practised in Derry 'within a coarse network of enclosure.'[75] The habit of renting entire townlands jointly to groups of tenants cultivating the land in rundale, thereby securing a contiguous area from the outside, intensified segregation. For example, Macafee reports that on the Vintners' proportion, 'where the leases were taken by groups of families, the character of settlement was likely to be more permanent, and so it became a feature of the planter area that certain townlands were dominated by particular families.'[76]

Once established, some landlords and agents helped to preserve this arrangement by renewing joint leases to co-partners because it facilitated rent collection, improvement, and general management of estates whose growing populations prohibited close attention to individual tenants.[77] The Anglesey estate agent felt that leased lands were better improved. 'This may naturally suggest to your lordship the idea of leasing generally,' he wrote to the landlord, but he went on to note the practical impossibility of this due to the 'immense population' and all the 'partial grievances' that would have to be settled.[78] Middlemen commonly took this view. Currie blames both William Rowley, the late eighteenth-century middleman of the Drapers' company, and Thomas Conolly, who for a time held the Vintners' proportion, for the spread of rundale and infield-outfield husbandry in those areas at the same time that it was being eliminated in other parts of the province.[79] William Mayne in Clones reported of one townland in 1790 that he was 'satisfied the rent promised will be well paid. To ensure that past doubt, I have taken care to have a man of wealth to join in the leases with those I was not acquainted with personally.'[80] This policy was adopted even if the tenants were all poor. The Abercorn estate tenant Samuel McCrea advised Thomas Conolly in 1760 of a survey of two townlands near Castlefin:

> The tenants in both are busy reclaiming the barren improvable grounds and on that account deserve to be encouraged, but the Bealalt tenants, being too numerous and mostly poor on that account, though they are desirous of separate leases, I rather advise to bind them in one, for in that case if any of them run in arrear or break, the rest will on their own account take care to see your rent paid, which in the other case they would not be liable to pay.[81]

Townlands on the Anglesey estate were leased as a whole rather than in parcels in the early eighteenth century, and in one letter there is a hint that the agent felt that the communally-bound partners were best able to regulate and advance the colonization and improvement of wasteland themselves: 'the land is better set, leased as a whole than in parcels, and there is a great deal of wasteland in the country.'[82] In fact, the Anglesey manager was so confident of the ability of a rundale partners to improve the estate that he gave them preference over aggressive individuals willing to pay stiff prices for land,[83] arguing that the present jointly-bound tenants would be able to offer sufficient security by themselves: 'When they are bound one for another in a lease, they will always have the value of two or three years' rent on the premises. . . .'[84] In one case from this estate the landlord protected the integrity of the rundale community even against one of its poorer members. In 1770 an at-will tenant on the estate was given notice to quit and his land was to be 'disposed of in common to the other tenants' at a higher rent.[85] Later, when rundale came under attack, agents still recognized the value of the pressure of the community on the behaviour of a tenant. The Drapers' managers were hesitant to give a smallholder a lease 'if he be a contentious, ill-behaved person, whereas if he be a tenant at will he must conduct himself properly to all around him else he will be directed to sell his holding and reside somewhere else.'[86]

The pattern on Ulster estates, where ethnically cohesive neighbours joined together to secure for themselves entire townlands at the most secure form of tenure available, occurred in the Irish communities as well as the planter communities, but with a crucial difference: the Irish faced the legal handicap that they could not hold lengthy determinable leases. As the concern for community defence receded in the early eighteenth century and estate structures began to assume a more stable, capitalist form, it became apparent that the Irish were forced to compete for leases under management régimes whose main goal was to secure good Protestant tenants on as much of the best land as possible. Macafee concludes that 'land was not scarce until the later part of the eighteenth century, and there seems no reason to suppose that some Irish would not have remained in the planter townlands. However, with the increase of planter population in each townland during the eighteenth century, the Irish, with no security of tenure, would have found it more difficult to retain a firm foothold in the planter zone.'[87] Thus, whereas the Protestant tenants inscribed in rent-rolls as co-partners held long terminable leases or perpetuity leases, and many others had long leases under head tenants, there were only a few Irish conformists who got direct leases, and most held at will from head tenants.[88] These points should not be overstated. The length of lease was not so important as confidence that the lease or the at-will tenancy would be renewed to the sitting tenant. And the scenario that

Table 4

Percentage Change in Land Use on the Abercorn Estate, 1756–1834

Year	Arable	% Increase	Mtn. Grazing	% Decrease	Bog	% Decrease
1756	31.2		42.1		18.2	
1777	36.7	5.5	36.9	5.2	13.7	4.5
1806	43.0	6.3	31.4	5.5	9.0	4.7
1834	59.9	16.9	19.8	2.8	6.2	6.2

Source: Peter Roebuck, 'Rent movement and agricultural development' in Roebuck (ed.), Plantation to partition, p. 124

Macafee describes cannot be generalized until similar studies are performed on other localities. None the less, by the time penal restrictions on Catholic tenures were lifted, a pattern of settlement whereby Protestants held the most productive and commercially central land had already been established.

Patterns established in the early eighteenth century became more deeply entrenched as the century advanced, population increased, and ethnically segregated townlands became more densely settled.[89] The characteristic pattern of growth of a rundale community was to expand on to previously uncultivated land, particularly bogs which, although legally they belonged to the landlord on escheated lands, had been previously regarded and used as commons.[90] The alteration of estates by growing tenant populations is demonstrated in one study based on a succession of surveys of the Abercorn estate (see Table 4) which shows that the use of arable land had been extended at the expense of mountain grazing and bog by an impressive twelve percent between 1756 and 1806.[91] In the late 1750s the colonization of bog-land was sluggish, and some plots set out for rental by estate surveyors remained unoccupied.[92] Changing policy on the Abercorn estate after 1765 reflected the widespread colonization of land. Two surveyors were hired to organize the development of bogs and to oversee drainage, road construction, and the rental of plots. Prospects for renting nineteen new acres of reclaimed bog were assessed optimistically in 1764.[93] By the 1780s, however, the problem for the Abercorn managers was not one of finding tenants, who were plentiful and offering over ten shillings per acre, but of securing adequate supplies of lime to fertilize the land.[94] Currie's analysis of the change in land use over the period 1698–1782 on two Londonderry estates corroborates the evidence of the Abercorn estate. The reclamation of bog was too systematic and widespread to be attributed only to fuel-cutting. Middlemen anxious to make the most of their bargains induced much of the bog reclamation, but most of the bog was improved 'collectively' by rundale farmers. Improved land increased by 2,585 acres, or sixteen percent of the total, on the Bellaghy estate between 1730 and 1830.[95] In other areas colonization was not so rapid in the eighteenth century and did not accelerate until the early nineteenth century. Much land in the Maghera region was still waste in the middle of the eighteenth century. Referring to a 1752 survey of the Salters' estate, Macafee surmises that

> there was still considerable land to be cleared in each townland even by the middle of the eighteenth century. Frequent mention is made of large parts of each townland 'being mostly covered with shrubs of wood, rocks, moss, and bog' or having 'very little arable land.' A survey of the Mercers' estate carried out in 1749 to fix rents on each townland indicated that in the northern part of the . . . region thirty-three per cent of the land was arable, but by 1831 the figure had almost doubled to sixty-four per cent.[96]

One portentous ramification of the colonization of land within the rundale system was the great expansion in potato cultivation. As rundale communities grew in size, their population expanded into previously uninhabited areas. Bog and mountain land provided, with modest investment and considerable labour, a potentially self-sufficient agricultural unit. Digging the bog was the first step, which supplied the farm with fuel. Then, as Salaman was the first academic to point out, the potato served as 'an excellent crop to plant in freshly broken up ground.'[97] Subsequent draining, liming, and planting of the virgin land with potatoes supplied the farm with food and prepared the land for oat and flax cultivation in later seasons. Buchanan concludes that in the highly commercialized district of Lecale, Co. Down,

> only when the potato came into more general use during the eighteenth century could the area of cultivated land be extended onto land which was otherwise useless for arable cropping. Colonization of waste land by means of the potato not only made more land available for tillage, it also allowed the infield to be more exclusively devoted to grain crops.[98]

James Hamilton described the process in reference to the enclosed mountainous part of a farm rented by the tenant James Quinn, 'which was little more than an outlet to his cattle . . . [before] the great labour done in the enclosure, where there is four and a half acres covered with a compost of clay and about 100 barrels of lime to the acre which is now set with potatoes; this will be a great beginning of a farm.'[99] An agent in Ballinamore, Co. Cavan, noticed this same development on his estate in 1830.[100]

The role of the potato in the colonization of land grew slowly in the early eighteenth century. It is clear from the correspondence of the agents on the

Abercorn estate that the potato did not become dominant in the diet of the tenantry until very late in the century. Potatoes had previously been cultivated on a limited scale, grown in rotation with grains as a 'renovating crop'[101] rather than for subsistence. Potatoes were also rarely found in the marketplace. Prices were not regularly reported by agents of the estate until very late in the century, even though the reporting of other commodity prices was routine. Potato prices were mentioned by Abercorn agents on 23 occasions between 1744 and 1800, compared to over 100 times each for oats and linen in the same period.[102] The changing use of potatoes was revealed in reports of poverty in bad harvest years. The potato crop did not warrant a mention in a report on the disastrous harvest of 1744, which emphasized instead the high price of oats and the widespread consumption of 'the flesh of dead carrion cattle.'[103] After the harvest crisis in 1769 the situation had already changed. James Hamilton commented in April of 1770 on exorbitant potato prices. 'Vast numbers that are able,' he reported in one letter, 'continue buying [imported meal], but the poor are forced to use their potatoes.' Under similar circumstances in July 1778 Hamilton observed that 'the decay in people's looks is visible in a few days; they are beginning to fall on their potatoes.' The poor harvest of 1782 again brought exorbitant grain prices in the following summer, and again the crisis was somewhat relieved by the early digging of potatoes in mid-July.[104] But it was not until the last fifteen years of the century that the potato came to dominate diets in all seasons. Aside from fluctuations in bad harvest years, the market price of potatoes appeared to be generally stable until 1800. A stronger dependence on the potato crop was revealed by James Hamilton, Jr.'s closer attention to the size of that crop in 1783, 1794, and 1800. Hamilton was hoping in 1800 for a 'tremendous potato crop if no accident happens, but the poor and rich must fall on them as soon as they are the size of pigeon's eggs.'[105] In 1800 potato prices were double those of any year in the previous century, and the demand remained strong thereafter.[106] The volatility of the market was demonstrated in the observations for 1783 and 1800. Early in the growing season of 1783 potato prices were high, but the harvest in late July of that year cut the price by two-thirds. Conversely, between February and July in 1800 pressure on the poor harvest of 1799 caused prices to soar.[107] The evidence suggests that from about 1785 the potato became an element of daily sustenance for a large section of the tenantry and a regular market commodity, and a crucial component of the success of small farms. As one observer wrote of Hugh Crofton concerning his Co. Cavan tenants: 'I should never have expected you would wish to deprive the poor miserable peasant of the only recourse he has of raising potatoes, his chief support by burning sods to supply the place of animal manure, which your agent Mr. Lowther has forbid [sic]. [This was] their last and only effort to pay rent, as wheat and oats must be all sold to raise money, and nothing [is] left to exist on but potatoes and salt.'[108]

On the various properties of the London companies dependence on the potato was greatest among tenants who had moved up the mountain sides and on to the recently colonized bogs. In these areas the productive situation by the nineteenth century had become very fragile. Even though the absolute dependence on the potato characteristic of districts in the south and west of Ireland did not exist in Ulster, the health of the crop was still crucial to the economic survival of smallholders. The minutes of the Irish Society for 20 November 1845 observed: 'Happily, there are but few of your honour's immediate tenants so poor as to be entirely dependent upon their potato crops for their subsistence, but many will be severe sufferers and will require perhaps some abatement in their rent but certainly time to make up the amount.'[109] The total failure of the potato crop would painfully reveal the social division between those for whom it was only one factor of production and those who depended on it more or less completely. Here are two other descriptions, one from the Fishmonger's proportion and the other from the earl of Antrim's estate, which identify the social differentiation exposed by the potato failure:

> The appearance [of the estate] was a most dreadful one from the total failure of the potato crop, an important one in Ireland with every farmer but the mainstay of your mountain tenants. Growing only potatoes and oats, they depend entirely on the former for the support of their families throughout the year and for the means of fattening their pigs, the sale of which furnished one half a year's rent. For the means of paying the other, they look to the sale of their oats, which are this year their sole resource and a very inadequate one for meeting all their demands. . . .[110]

> No class felt the loss of the potato crop more keenly than the small farmers – the bulk of the tenants on this estate – who, cultivating small patches on the mountainside, depended wholly upon it for their living. For themselves and their families they usually asked no other food or higher reward for their toil than plenty of potatoes, but when these failed, their condition became so deplorable that many of the resident gentry left the country rather than witness the distress.[111]

The famine, according to this agent, had not curtailed potato dependency or encouraged turnip cultivation in the glens of Antrim. 'One fact, however, is worth noticing,' he remarked: 'the potato has suffered little during all that time on lands planted for the first time out of a state of nature, the new soil and free use of lime favouring its healthy cultivation.'[112] The Millers explained the stubborn economic logic of potato dependence facing mountain smallholders, even in the face of declining marginal productivity and the risk of monoculture: 'Three acres of even good oats will not feed so many as one middling acre of potatoes.'[113] By the middle of the nineteenth century it had become widely recognized that the traditional place of potato cultivation in the process of colonization and expansion had met its limit.

COLONIZATION OF LAND, IMPROVEMENT, AND 'PEACEABLE POSSESSION'

Demographic expansion, increasingly intensive cultivation, narrowing economic opportunity and more competitive rents ran the rundale system up against strict social and economic limits.[114] Rural communities had traditionally been able to adapt to these stresses and maintain a balance between individuals, families, and their communities. Methods of establishing individual rights to land and other resources evolved with the demographic context. McCourt identifies both the transformation of nucleated settlements into clachans and the reverse process of the dissolution of clachans into nucleated settlements, concluding that 'we are dealing not with opposing types of settlement but with a single dynamic scheme within which dispersal and nucleation were alternative developments. The predominance of either at a given time depended, probably, on social and economic conditions and their relation to the physical background.'[115] Robinson makes a similar point with respect to seventeenth-century Tyrone:

> The introduction of English and Scottish settlers into the lowland areas and the movement of the Irish to permanent settlement in the marginal ballyboes caused an increase of population pressure in these marginal areas, so that in 1660 the poll tax lists show that some Irish-occupied ballyboes contained as many as ten or eleven families, with an average of about five. Evidently, Proudfoot's assertion that single farmsteads became clachans within a few generations as population increased could apply to the seventeenth century as well as the late eighteenth and nineteenth centuries.[116]

The expansion onto the frontier of a community brought autonomous tenure claims and more isolated and individualized agricultural practice, but this was only a temporary movement. There was no 'unilinear drift' toward individualism and private property embedded in the system. Nor was there an inevitable trajectory towards demographic crisis, as some historical demographers have argued.[117] Still, it is important to avoid this demographic determinism without demoting the demographic context to irrelevance.[118] Demographic forces set in motion a dialectical movement between communalism and individualism. The original colonists of outlying areas held in severalty, but, through the mechanism of inheritance, the colonial areas of a townland fell gradually back within a communal space.[119] In turn, the overcrowding of the communal space required increased specificity of individual rights. Simpson conjectured that common rights

> arose as customary rights associated with the communal system of agriculture practised in the primitive village communities. At a very early period such villages would be surrounded with tracts of wasteland. . . . On such land the villagers as a community would pasture their beasts and from it they would gather wood and turf and so forth. In the course of time, when the increase of population and the reduction in the quantity of uncultivated land started to produce crowding and conflict, their rights would tend to become more clearly defined but would still be communal rights, principally over wastelands regarded as the lands of the community itself.[120]

To complete this sketch, it should be noted that the tension between the individual and the community in the rundale system was filtered through discernible hierarchies based on age, gender, and inherited control over resources. The male holders of the largest herds of livestock, for example, held much greater power than those (predominantly young males and women) dependent on arable or marginal industries. Also, members of rundale communities sublet portions of the outfield to outsiders, cottiers, who may or may not have been able to successfully integrate themselves into the community. These were second-class citizens, and the rents they paid were used to pay the head-rent the entire village owed to the landlord.

The collapse of the rundale system involved the ascendance of the individual farmer as the unit of production and as the social unit, at the expense of communal and hierarchical determinations of distributive and productive activity. These latter were subsumed under the operation of a market for individual property rights and other capital assets. This collapse was therefore not simply a demographic crisis. Indeed, demographic dynamics may be viewed as in some ways endogenous to the system. McCabe makes the point that 'the fluidity of landownership, and the tendency for marriage to occur within a relatively exclusive family circuit, actually lessened the impact of subdivision in the west, at least for families at a certain material level-though this was not always clear to observers dumbfounded by the intricate maze of tiny fields developed in rundale.'[121] The fluidity of landholding before the onset of fixed rundale is an important limit on family formation. Joint tenancies were used, for example, to share a holding between an older and a younger married couple for an indefinite period to maximize the options of both couples.[122] McCabe suggests that external commercial and managerial pressures had a much greater effect on the system than population pressure.

Evidence from Mayo shows that 'until the later eighteenth century, and the increased dependence of the tenantry on their corn and flax crops as a means of paying rent, there may have been no need for individual shares of arable land; if purely a food crop it would have been more practical to grow oats for the entire village in a common field.' But the increasing need to market oats destroyed the collective basis of rundale arable. This pressure prompted larger and more successful farmers to extricate themselves from collective responsibility for the rent payments of their insolvent, ex-linen producing neighbours.[123]

Was rundale in a steady-state equilibrium in the absence of the potato, oat, and linen markets, a demographic equilibrium spoiled by the limited opportunities these markets presented to those on the lowest rungs of the rundale hierarchies? As was argued in Chapter 3, the collapse of both small-scale arable and linen production was the root of the post-Napoleonic disaster. The causes of that disaster cannot therefore be attributed exclusively to the weakness of rundale productive forces. That landlords, polemicists, and later historians routinely made such attributions is testimony to their ideological distaste for the relations of production inherent in the rundale system rather than to their grasp of reality. Rundale landscapes appeared messy and inefficient compared to the more rational, enclosed, severalty farms. Landlords also complained about the fractious nature of its social relations. But this fractiousness and messiness should be viewed contextually, not as a transcendant quality. Most disputes concerned the fencing and ditching of land, issues of shared access and trespass, loans and theft, collective responsibility for rents, taxes, tithes, marriage arrangements, etc. The fluidity of arrangements was especially pronounced with regard to the sale of land, which always took place against the backdrop of the long habit of redistribution of strips of land and the custom allowing those who sold land to retain the right to buy it back. All of these areas of dispute persisted under autonomized managerial capitalism. The crucial difference is that social relations in the rundale system were visible, open, discursively argued, and collectively resolved, with the result that the operation of the system appears fractious. On the other hand, the social contract embodied in the severalty tenures of parcelled farms replaced these mechanisms with the more enigmatic and tyrannical determinations of the market and the estate office. The market introduces a mute fractiousness, replacing the loud-mouthed traditional methods. This change was widely celebrated, especially by agents who could take credit for sponsoring market solutions to disputes. But it should be remembered that the boxing matches and other skirmishes between rundale members at least had the benefit of transparency, in stark contrast to the opacity of market competition.[124]

The crucial point is that by forcing the market determination of disputes over property, estate managers could more easily assert their outside control over matters. The demise of rundale has as much to do with the rise of managerial power as it does with its alleged social and economic weaknesses. Estate managers routinely criticized the disorder of the rundale system and the violence and argumentativeness of joint tenants, and used such occasions to boast of their own management skill and of the calming and beneficial effects of parcellized landholding.[125] A new manager of the Anglesey estate found in 1841 that the rundale tenants were in a constant state of warfare, fighting over who would pay what share of the total: 'The Omeath tenantry are in many instances at open war with each other, the consequences of their own unallowed bargains, and they expect the agent to solve all their difficulties.' After getting accustomed to the routines of management, the Omeath agent wrote again: 'The nearest relatives are the most ready foes, and this arises from Col. Armstrong having allowed them to subdivide their original holdings into the most minute patches . . . ; they receive my suggestions with great civility.'[126] A deputy to the Fishmongers' property was compelled to report in 1827:

> The deputation cannot refrain from observing that the system adopted and pursued by the late valuable and indefatigable agent, the Rev. G.V. Sampson, deceased, for abolishing the practice of rundale, for providing for the gradual removal of the dwellings of the tenants from off the holdings of their neighbours to their own land, thereby taking away a perpetual source of bickering and quarrelling, for the straightening [of] the mearings or divisions of the respective occupancies, so that when two or more are united, they will form large and compact farms, has caused his memory to be greatly esteemed by a numerous tenantry.[127]

The Drapers' company agent also claimed that destroying rundale made the typical tenant happier: 'When he gets over his first difficulties, he gradually improves in his circumstances, because he has his land together and he has no contra [?] with his neighbours: he doesn't trespass on them nor they upon him.'[128] The judgment by estate managers against the rundale system masked the real reasons for the internal strife of rundale communities: the strain of reaching the productive limits of the land and the enormous macroeconomic disaster facing heavily indebted smallholders. If the rundale system could be faulted, it was only on the grounds that it was incapable of adapting to an economic crisis not of its own making.

Estate managers were naturally caught up in this volatile combination of demographic expansion, tension between the individual colonization of land within a communally organized settlement pattern, and the need to identify settlement boundaries and reintegrate them into a new, expanded whole. The options for the colonization of land, which were restricted by the requirements of strategic location, market access, and ethnic cohesiveness had narrowed considerably by the end of the eighteenth century. Once the density and fragmentation of the settlement pattern reached a certain level of complexity, the shrinking supply of open land and fuel overshadowed all other concerns. The mechanisms of the communal organization of production, which were not without their violent and recriminatory episodes, were abhorrent to estate managers who preferred the more peaceful and orderly – though equally if not more ruthless – operations of a market for land. While colonization of land greatly enlarged the profitable acreage of their estates, the dense confusion of demographically developed rundale communities radically complicated the visual and organizational complexity of estate management duties. Efforts to increase the rent or update the rent-roll plunged estate managers directly into the wiry thicket of rundale settlement.

Perhaps the most tedious ramification of the demographic expansion for estate managers was the requirement that they be closely involved with the actual colonization of the bogs, the construction of roads, and the distribution of access rights.[129] Almost all discussion of roads and road construction in the correspondence of Ulster estate managers occurred in the context of colonizing bogs or gaining access to them.[130] In many areas colonization was completely dependent on the construction of roads. An agent on the Lane Fox estate in County Leitrim remarked: 'there are many hundreds of acres of mountain, moor, and bog-land upon this estate, which is now rendered accessible by new roads and extensive drainage which thirteen years ago were quite inaccessible.' These he recommended should be let from year to year to impoverished families, widows, and about 200 young men with no land now resident on the estate.[131] Tenants on a townland on the Hart estate in Inishowen called Backlands claimed in 1876 that 'they or their predecessors would never have gone to live in the Backlands if it had not been understood that a road would be made connecting their holdings with the village.'[132] The Millers of Draperstown emphasized the importance of road access in 1845: 'Almost every tenant on the estate can drive a horse and cart to his house. If this be not an improvement . . . , we are certainly ignorant of what improvement is.'[133]

The shortage, inaccessibility, and maldistribution of turf in the most populous areas of estates introduced perhaps an even greater pressure for new roads than colonization.[134] To the evidence rehearsed in Chapter 2 of the complicated historicities of landholding produced by the effects of colonization, mobility, subdivision, inheritance, marriage, exchange, credit, and debt may now be added disputes over the right to access to fuel, which were sometimes linked with tenant right. The bishop of Derry received the following account of a conflict over turf between two of his tenants, John Rogers and the correspondent William Maxwell, in 1773:

About six and forty years ago, [John Rogers's] father assisted in parcelling out the turbary and fixing every man's share who was to be accommodated. At the same time, those who could not help drawing their turf through John Rogers'[s] arable land agreed to give him the enjoyment of some arable in their own adjoining farms, in consideration of the trespass they might commit, which ground then given off continues yet in the occupation of John Rogers. . . . By multiplying tenants on his farm he has quite wasted his own portion of bog, and therefore he inclines to invade that of my neighbour [George White] and me. However, if he should insist on that point that he pays a fine to the bishop for the bog, both my neighbours and I are quite willing to pay our proportionable part of that fine, or any other that your lordship will impose, provided we may have a power to enclose our shares to enjoy the benefits thereof and preserve our turf from being trodden by his cattle.[135]

Such disputes could easily escalate into serious fights, as in the case of a dispute over a bog called 'the Freedoms' on the Hart estate in the 1870s.[136] Hart's agent impressed upon him in April of 1877 how unfairly those who lived a great distance from the sources of fuel were treated. He reported that 'those who are put out of the Freedoms will destroy the turf of those who are put in their place, and that they will all fight with pitchforks.' The agent personally marked out the new boundaries of these farms, and access to the bog was to be determined by lots. The tenants concerned threatened 'with the most tremendous curses and oaths that they would lose their lives before they would give up their bank, and that they would attempt to take the life of any man who attempted to cut it.'[137]

As with many other aspects of estate management, agents seem to have delayed their involvement in these issues until it was nearly too late and the pitchforks had already been brandished. It seems likely that the great majority of eighteenth-century landlords allowed the free and unregulated use of the bogs on their estates.[138] But as demographic pressure curtailed the supply of land and fuel, rights to communal assets became a nearly universal bone of contention.[139] In 1839 an agent reported that 'people in the interior of the country in the neighbourhood of Carlingford' came down to the sea-shore of the estate 'in immense numbers, with carts, cars, bludgeons, pitchforks, and other weapons, and attempted to carry off by force the sea wrack – both that which had been collected by the tenants throughout the winter and what still remains attached to the nooks on the shore.'[140] The legal agent suggested bringing the case to quarter sessions, and a long series of legal disputes ensued.[141]

Predictably, some agents sought justifications for minimizing their role in this process, especially since long-established rundale communities might resist their interference. An agent on the Inishowen peninsula in 1815 recommended that reclamation be done by the tenants themselves for two reasons: 'First, the part they at present hold will be a support [until] the other is reclaimed. Second, their farms are small and the people numerous and perhaps strangers and they would not mix well.'[142] But the conversion of former bog into valuable farms laid greater pressure on agents to intervene. Landlords and agents involved themselves in the disputed tenure and possession of bog and former bog not simply because they were intolerant of the apparent disorganization resulting from concentrated settlement or because of an altruistic or paternal desire to help members of local communities to resolve their differences. These were manifestations of much more serious problems involving the question of the right of property to the bogs and the extraction of profit from the process of mining them for fuel and transforming them into arable land. For example, the ninth earl of Abercorn did not grant leases to holders of newly colonized farms until after they had become established and viable units.[143] In 1800 the increase in revenue on the Abercorn estate was owing primarily to these potential farms. James Hamilton, Jr., boasted in 1800: 'Your Lordship will be pleased to observe the increase in the bog rent. Wherever bog could be let through the estate, I have done it, especially where there was no apparent scarcity of turf to neighbouring tenants.'[144] Agents for the Irish Society recommended offering leases for the cut-out bogs to adjoining tenants in the Derry suburbs. Apparently, other local landowners had been 'much annoyed by the forcible and unlawful settlement in their neighbourhood of the marauders and freebooters who have taken up residence upon the said bogs without a colour of right thereto and so greatly to the prejudice of the peace and good order of the country.'[145] George Joy believed in 1843 that every inch of his property, even the remotest mountain area, should be subject to rent. When leases fell in, reclaimed bog was added to the farm to increase the acreable rent.[146] A deputation to the Fishmongers' estate reported in 1832 that a considerable acreage of mountain farms had been broken up and brought into cultivation and explained how the new farms would be dealt with:

> Mr. Simpson is of the opinion that the best mode of setting out mountain farms is that which he has hitherto pursued, viz., to ditch deeply and to drain the bog – which is done at an expense of about one shilling per perch – so as to draw off the water as much as possible, and to endeavour to find tenants of respectable character possessing some little property, whether already on the company's estate or not. . . . No new farms should be set out until a further portion of the bog has been cut off to put the land in a state capable of cultivation.[147]

In response to an inquiry in 1844 into the amount of wasteland that could be reclaimed as farms on the Drapers' estate, the Millers claimed that, aside from one farm of only about 60 acres,

> any other part at present uncultivated of the estate lies too high to prevent [i.e., to allow] much improvements ever being made thereon, but at all events it is almost the only place now in the estate where fuel is and where the tenants are obliged to go for their firing, and consequently it is more valuable for fuel than it could possibly be in any other way. The position of turf bogs that were cut out in the lower part of the estate have been [sic] either planted or put into the adjoining farms. We let last year about £50 p. a. of cut-out bog. In a very few years all of the turf bogs in the low lands will be exhausted.[148]

The Drapers' agents felt that the regulation of turf was the bailiff's 'most challenging duty.'[149]

Ambivalence over the tenant right of bogs was not a marginal issue; it bore directly on the sovereignty of private property. The earl of Antrim's tenants were allowed free access across a mountain to a bog, but with the following warning: 'his lordship is always ready and willing to give any accommodation to your tenants as far as he can, provided that such accommodation be not afterwards claimed as a right on their part.'[150] One indication of this was the difficulty which a landlord faced in selling his property with this ambivalence hanging over him. Archdeacon Trail expressed his wariness of purchasing perpetuities on land managed by Edmund McGildowney because the legal rights to bogs were so unsettled: 'My brother writes me that Jack Dunlop conceives himself entitled to his bog and will maintain his claim to it. So say several of the other tenants. Until this point is ascertained, I am not prepared to say how many years' purchase I would give, as it would make a material difference in the value of some of the denominations.'[151] Another corre-spondent referred to this letter from Trail, telling McGildowney: 'I don't . . . altogether agree with him about the bogs, I mean as [to] the tenant right to them, but it certainly appears to me that those acting for Lord Caledon will not hastily close a bargain with a purchaser until all doubt as to his lordship's title to the bog is removed.'[152]

This situation bears directly on two of the most contentious issues asso-ciated with the custom of tenant right: the peaceable possession of farms and compensation for improvements. Both of these issues arose from claims on the part of individual families who pitted rights arising from their own labour of colonization and improvement against the rights of both their landlord and the surrounding community. Once again, the custom of tenant right served to mediate between these conflicting claims and landlords who gained control of the custom were able to conduct such mediation to their own advantage. The focus here is on the place of the term tenant right *within* the rundale system, *between* socially and geographically distinct rundale communities, and *between* rundale partners of a specific community and their landlord. At first sight it appears that neither the term 'peaceable possession' nor 'improvement' was appropriate to the communal aspect of rundale systems. It was unnecessary for kinsmen or rundale partners to seek a tangible assurance of 'peaceable possession' of infield strips in a rundale community if it was guaranteed by their membership in the community. Similarly, there was little need for economic compensations for improvement, since the value of the land accrued to the collectivity. As the necessity for clear boundaries and privatized rights increased, individuals within rundale communities began to assert positions in terms of their own possession, the improvements which they had made, and their tenant right. Conflicts between neighbours were fuelled by the increasing value of formerly unattractive plots of land. At mid-century a piece of undeveloped land still might be considered a burdensome expense to a tenant forced to take it in a lease. But by the 1780s a different view prevailed, and if the tenant's father had alienated the land to a neighbour a conflict might ensue.[153]

The terms 'tenant right' and 'peaceable possession' were often used in these contexts. One of the earliest appearances of the term 'tenant right' in estate papers occurs in the context of a 1679 dispute over the boundaries between land owned by one John Tasburgh near Cong, Co. Mayo, and adjacent land owned by the Protestant archbishop of Tuam. Tasburgh claimed that his family had traditionally leased that portion of the archbishop's land which was intermingled with theirs. It appears that the archbishop threatened Tasburgh's right of renewal. In a letter complaining about the situation in March 1679, he made explicit reference to this assault on his 'tenant right:'

> If the bishop's land in Cong were yet more convenient than profitable to me, I should not desire to meddle with it. My only aim is to prevent grief and troubles which will necessarily arise between my tenants and that stranger that comes to possess the said lands. For you know the bishop's lands and mine are so contiguous, if not intermixed, that I suspect there will be perpetual clashing and quarrelling, and for this reason my ancestors always held the said bishop's land in lease. And truly I must say I have had hard measure if my tenant right be not considered and preferable to all other pretences.[154]

Though the term tenant right was absent from early plantation usage, the related term 'peaceable possession' appears to have been in use since the very beginning. A letter from James I to Chichester refers to Lord Balfour's 'peaceable possession' against abuse by the Maguires, sheriffs, or 'any other officers and persons of the country.' The letter concerned a dispute over the surrender and regrant of lands by Maguire. In the end 'Burley bought out Maguire by purchasing some lands from him.'[155] Landlords in Antrim and Down guaranteed peaceable possession to tenants who would defend those landlords in legal disputes.[156] And Gillespie cites the case of one Savage, who 'mortgaged land from Dowltagh Smith for £90, and the land was to be given to Savage in peaceable and quiet possession.'[157] The agent of the Anglesey estate in County Louth used the term 'peaceable possession' in a letter of 1716 threatening a tenant named Stannus. He was given notice that he had 'no term or time of the house or tenements' in Carlingford and was instructed to 'deliver up the quiet and peaceable possession thereof the first of November next, otherwise I will sue you for double the value of the tenement. . . .'[158] A change in policy with regard to the attornments on the Anglesey estate in 1778 also reflected the importance of the term. For the first time attornments included a clause with the promise to give up 'quiet actual possession' at the end of the term of attornment. This was different from all previous attornments; the specific clause about delivery of rent while in possession and giving up the 'quiet actual possession' was new. Petitions thereafter took the following form:

> We, the inhabitants and occupiers . . . , [attorn as] tenants to Sir Nicholas Bayly . . . baronet for all the lands and tenements . . . now in our occupation or possession, . . . [and we] agree and promise to pay . . . as he or they shall think proper, to continue us tenants for said premises, such sum or sums of money by the year as are respectively set to our names, and we do further promise and agree to deliver up the quiet actual possession of our respective holdings in said lands when thereupon required by the said Sir Nicholas Bayly.[159]

Early uses of the term 'peaceable possession' by the agents of the Anglesey estate referred to disputes over ditches. Peaceable possession of undemarcated land justified the drawing of visual boundaries. Concerning one mearing dispute on the estate border in 1745, the agent decided that it was only a small bit of ground, but since it had been enclosed 'with a ditch where there never was the least mark or sign of one before, which might hereafter cause disputes, I thought proper to interpose and throw it down . . . ,' whereupon the antagonist filed a bill claiming that he had been 'three years in peaceable possession.'[160] On the Abercorn estate disputes over peaceable possession often occurred between relatively wealthy farmers in the lowlands and the colonists of poorer mountain land who were faced with a reduced supply of open grazing and bog, and who were forced by the geography to trespass on lowlander property.[161] The encroachment of new enclosures brought about conflicts over territory that had traditionally been regarded as property with common use rights and thrown open to the herds of the community.[162] A group of petitioners on the Anglesey estate claimed that the 'deceased John Baily took part of their land from them and enclosed it in a field and kept the same for his own use and in lieu thereof gave unto your petitioners liberty in the mountain. Now your petitioners are stopped from the liberty of the mountain,' and they requested that the field be returned to them.[163] Another group of partners objected that they 'formerly held about 120 acres of said lands, but by the applications of some undermining people they have been taken from petitioners in small pieces to about one half.' They asked to be continued as tenants to the whole.[164] Six other petitioners claimed in 1841 that a newcomer named McCann, by virtue of a marriage portion from another estate, had had forty or fifty acres of their mountain surveyed, and reminded their landlord that 'as we have but a few acres of arable each, your lordship knows that unless we have recourse to the mountain . . . , we could not support our cattle. The said McCann did obstruct us and will obstruct us in getting our turf off the mountain.'[165]

By what mechanisms were such disputes resolved? It is important to recognize the uncertainty of landlord legal power. One boundary dispute in 1836 on the Anglesey estate was disrupted by 'a jury who could not or would not divest their minds of a bias which rendered them totally unfit to discharge the duties imposed upon them.'[166] Clarifying the rights to the mountain bogs in the glens of Antrim caused considerable trouble to the managers of estates in that area. In three letters of 1802, Richard Waring discussed the rather poor prospects of breaking one Adam Hunter's lease of a bog.[167] McGildowney's decision to go to court to gain control of the Lord Kerr's bog bore great risks since a victory would produce resentment in the locality and a defeat would set a damaging precedent against landlord property rights.[168] After one case McGildowney warned that 'another defeat, such as at last assizes, would be attended with bad consequences and would prevent those who have agreed and are willing to pay for Ballywillan bog to pay anything for it after a defeat.'[169] Referring to threatening letters he had received over the following four years, McGildowney claimed that 'our asserting and maintaining Lord Mark Kerr's right to the bogs . . . will never be forgiven or forgotten to us.'[170] In 1835 a notice from 'Captain Rock' demanding free distribution of bog to the poor was posted on the O'Hara estate in Sligo. In 1844 the tenants from that estate won lawsuits against landlords protecting their right to bogs, with the courts allowing bogs to be cut freely. The agent fumed that 'such a system of humbugging no one ever witnessed, I am sure, on any estate. People put in as caretakers five years ago are now claiming their compensation money before they give possession.'[171]

If the courts were an ineffective mechanism for resolving disputes over bogs, they were even less capable of settling issues of peaceable possession created by subdivision, inheritance, and undertenancy, which recurred in many contexts throughout the nineteenth century. In the late eighteenth and nineteenth centuries the tenant-right market, and not the courts or the less formal social arena of the rundale community, was the mechanism of choice to resolve such disputes. This solution to the problem obviously gave the advantage to the protagonist with the most capital. In a protracted dispute over the line of a mearing between two townlands in County Derry in the 1770s, the tenants of one townland, according to two third-party adjudicators, had 'an equitable claim to some part of the lands in dispute, but being a poorer sort of people, they were not able to support their pretensions as to possession against their neighbours, the tenants of [the other townland], who were more numerous and more wealthy.'[172] An example from the earl of Belmore's estate in the 1870s clearly demonstrates the difficulties. The agent R.C. Brush explained that James Galbraith held a lease of lands that expired in 1863 under which he had sublet to two tenants named James McKelver and George McFarland. The layout of the farms was such that access to McFarland's farm could be achieved only by passing close to McKelver's door, which was a source of annoyance to McKelver. McFarland stubbornly refused to accommodate his neighbour in any way and exarcerbated matters by attempting to place his niece and her husband John Clements on the farm in 1870. This was a further threat to McKelver, because Clement and the niece already 'occupied a farm not exactly adjoining, but on the other side of McKelver.' Brush prohibited the transaction. McFarland died in 1874 and accomplished his goal in another way by leaving the farm to his niece in his will. Brush then made every effort to accomplish an exchange between Clements and McFarland to rationalize the boundaries, but Clements would not co-operate. Clements was not only an unaccommodating neighbour, but also was apparently something of an ideologue:

> If he had retired, the full value of the tenant's interest would have been paid him by McKelver. McKelver only wants it because of the lane, not for the land. Clements is one of those hot-headed leaders of the Orange body there, and a tenant-right advocate. . . . As in any proceedings, I would not advise [this] to be had at quarter sessions, since he would bring one of those Belfast attorneys who are engaged more to abuse landlords than to fight cases.[173]

With legal proceedings out of the question, in cases like the dispute between McKelver and Clements the parties might resort to a financial solution whereby McKelver would purchase Clements's tenant right. Failing this, the landlord might purchase the tenant right and then sell it again at a loss.[174]

Both of these options depended on the willingness of one party to sell or on the landlord's ability to force such a sale; the latter condition might obtain if the tenant was heavily in arrears. But for a stubborn tenant-righter like Clements, who was probably solvent, though certainly no improver, neither of these options was available. Brush concluded on Christmas Day 1875: 'From the situation of the respective houses there would be no hope of squaring the lands now. McKelver has the farm in such good order while the part claimed by Clements is very bad and in a rough state. I found it impossible to reconcile the interests of both parties by exchange in any way.'[175] Finally, a week later, he persuaded Clements to give the farm up to Lord Belmore on the promise that he would get it back after the road had been adjusted.[176]

Peaceable possession of land was the representation of an individual's property right not only to the landlord but to the surrounding community. A claim of improvement was a similarly-directed representation. Given the high mobility of Ulster tenants in the seventeenth century, it was inevitable that the question of the distribution of the improved value of a townland between its co-residents would surface. Examples of conflict over this question date from the very beginning of the plantation. Hunter gives an account of two original tenants of Trinity College in County Armagh who in 1615, with the consent of the provost and fellows, agreed with a third tenant to whom they were in debt that all three of them would occupy the lands as tenants-in-common without receiving individual leases. But they soon found that as they had transformed the property with their own labour, the communal arrangement no longer sufficed, so that the partnership led to 'barrattings and fallings-out in a very uncivil and unchristian manner.' No one, including the landlord, was happy with the ambiguities of the communal arrangements that blurred the history of an individual's contribution to improvement. Dissatisfaction with the way in which communal tenancies resolved the problem of compensation for improvements might drive many of them away and allow the Irish to secure undertenancies.[177] With the structural solidification and increasing density of plantation settlements in the eighteenth century, this problem gave way to the larger one of the carving up by individuals of communally held bog and waste. The process of the colonization of formerly uncultivated bog and mountain did more than just provide subsistence to the impoverished and land-hungry; it also represented a dramatic 'improvement' of the particular estate in question. The labour involved in that improvement had an indeterminate social meaning and therefore formed the basis for subsequent tenant-right claims.

The agent of the Barrett-Lennard estate was cognizant in 1753 of the long-run benefit of allowing landless members of local communities the opportunity to improve the waste:

> Mr. Nixon has got three cottiers or labourers to settle and build houses or little cabins in the island. I have advised him to get two or three more and to give off to each of them a particular quantity of the bog for a few years rent free, to encourage them to reclaim the same by making little gardens every year and setting potatoes therein and to take payment from them in labour [so that they may] work for the freedom and liberty of grazing their cows on the island and on the bog, by which means a good deal might be got by degrees.[178]

This, he insisted, was a better plan than giving the bog free to neighbouring tenants who, since they already held farms, would do nothing to reclaim it. John Todd did not recommend throwing in bog adjacent to farms 'gratis' on the promise that the tenant would then set about 'retaining some part of it,' as he felt they 'would never trouble themselves to put it in practice.'[179] When a lease expired on Sir Hugh Crofton's lands near Swanlinbar, Co. Cavan, in 1811, the former undertenants had received leases at quadruple rents, which they were now unable to pay. The tenant memorialists asked Crofton to 'send some gentleman experienced in mountainous land to view our separate holdings and see our situations. And we your honour's and forefathers' tenants these hundred years and upwards; although our lands are set very high to us, we are still reclaiming it and bringing the barren bog into arable.'[180]

Tenant farmers also realized how the process worked. Although they might not be interested in expanding the size of their holdings, they might offer to improve their landlord's estate in order to satisfy their demand for more turf. A tenant in Ballyshannon explained the potential for bog improvement to his landlord Thomas Conolly in 1800:

> Would you be pleased to admit me as one of your tenants for some turf bog, my own being nearly cut out? . . . I shall consider it, therefore, as a great favour if I may have two, three, or four acres at any rent you may think proper to name, for such a tenure as may encourage me to build a cabin and enclose a turf yard for a place of safety against depredations, and a sort of repository for my turf, till I find a convenient opportunity of drawing them home. Should you be so fortunate as to succeed in this request, I may have the pleasure of finding that I have led the way to an improvement of your rental from a species of landed property which is now getting into great request, in many places indeed equal to and beyond that of the best arable, and of which you have many valuable acres.[181]

This tenant may have been overstating the case. On another farm on this estate, it was discovered that there were diminishing marginal returns – in terms of rent – to this reclamation and colonization of the bogs. An example of extensive reclamation occurring during the eighteenth century which actually reduced rent per acre comes from the Derry property owned by Thomas Conolly. [182]

The difference between the first case of John Alcock's farm on the Conolly estate, where colonization of the bog was thought to have produced a dramatic improvement, and the second case of the Terrydremont farm on the Castletown estate, where such colonization met with diminishing marginal returns, opens up the contested social terrain upon which the meaning and value of labour is determined. How would John Alcock's contribution to the improvement of the estate be measured? How would the fact that he offered to pay rent for land normally given freely to tenants affect that measurement? Did the diminishing marginal increase in rent on the Terrydremont farm reflect diminishing marginal productivity of the soil under constant inputs of labour, a situation contrary to Alcock's claim? Or did such a diminishing marginal increase of rent represent a reward to the colonizing tenants for their labour of improvement? Such questions could be resolved by reference to the exchange value of the improved land as represented either by the rent or the tenant-right price. But even if the exchange value could be given an unquestionable determination, the difficult questions of measuring the value of the labour that had created the exchange value and of the mapping of property rights onto that labour remained. In conflicts between middlemen and undertenants,[183] between owners and occupiers, among rundale co-partners, and between neighbouring severalty farmers, the issues were manifold: did occupiers have a traditional right to hold the bog and waste adjacent to their holdings rent-free? In terms of the labour of improvement, what was the threshold between wasteland and arable that was subject to rent? How would the relationship between the labour of improvement, the rent paid, and the tenant's property rights be figured? The contentious and individual nature of these issues, and the necessity for agents to find some way to manage them, was widely recognized.

MANAGING THE RUNDALE SYSTEM

The modern system of enclosed farms and severalty tenures was established on Ulster estates in two ways. It was created alongside the rundale system as part of the plantation settlement. Later, however, it was established within rundale communities by a process that was both explosive and implosive. Aggressive managers exploded the rundale system with policies designed to rationalize the layout of farms and break community influence on the occupation of land. At the same time, this communal power was imploding as individuals stepped out from their jointly-bound relationships with their neighbours to receive direct tenures from their landlords. The tenant-right system flourished on this threshold between the implosion of rundale communities and the creation of individual tenancies. It also played a crucial role in managerial attempts to eradicate the system. In order to secure exclusive and individual contracts with each tenant, landlords and agents were forced to come to some understanding of a system to which they had previously paid little attention. Indeed, some displayed a complete ignorance of the workings of the system. Henry Smith, for example, surmised that the request of a tenant to alienate his holding in 1824

> is connected with some circumstances as to a holding by him and his father which I do not understand. He says his motive for selling is to purchase a piece of land 'which is held by 'deal about' with petitioner's father who has promised to give petitioner possession of all.' In your note at the foot of the petition you say, 'he would buy half the farm that is in rundale with his father.' What is meant by 'deal about' and 'rundale?' Were Woods to buy his father's share, what is to become of the father?[184]

Edward Lawford expressed similar bafflement in 1828 when he asked Rowley Miller to 'explain exactly what you mean by a number being held 'in common' or, as you now seem to think it would be better expressed, 'in connection.' Has any one of those tenants an equal right with his neighbour to use and occupy the same identical spot of ground at the same time, just in the same manner as if it were demised them jointly?'[185]

Given the incompatibility of rundale with prevailing notions of private property, and its perceived visual disorganization and fractious social relations, these early nineteenth-century agents had gut-level objections which lay at the root of this rhetorical mixture of confusion and intolerance. One deputation to Londonderry elaborated on the rundale system in these terms:

> Rundale, which is a most mischievous way of occupying land, was until of late years a common practice in the north of Ireland. It is thus: three or four persons become tenants to a farm, holding it jointly, on which there is land of different qualities and values. They divide it into fields and then divide each field into as many shares as there are tenants, which they occupy without division or fence, being marked in parcels by stones or other landmarks. Each [tenant] occupies with such crops as his necessities or means of procuring manure enable him, so that there are at the same time several kinds of crops in one field.[186]

Witnesses before the Devon commission also occasionally attempted to explain this strange system to the uninitiated. Masterson cites this example of the pejorative tone employed by one witness:

> Instead of each subtenant or assignee of a portion of the farm receiving his holding in one compact lot, he obtains a part of each particular quality of

land so that his tenement consists of a number of scattered patches, each too small to be separately fenced and exposed to constant depredations of his neighbour's cattle, thus affording a fruitful source of quarrels and utterly preventing the possibility of the introduction of any improved system of husbandry.[187]

These general reflections on the part of agents and Devon witnesses were the result of hard experience in the 1830s and 1840s dealing with districts within their estates still held in rundale.[188] Landowners who began to manage their estates closely after a century or more of neglect found that nothing but the complete reorganization of the layout of the farms on the estate could rectify these problems. The Millers of Draperstown strongly urged that all mountain farms be squared because improvement was impossible without detached farms,[189] but they also acknowledged that

> in a great change like this some individuals for a time will suffer much inconvenience. For instance, if a tenant holds several fields, some low down and some high up on a mountain, and the lowland is taken from him and he is put on a highland farm without a house, he must for at least a couple of years and perhaps more feel inconvenient because he has not only to build a house but to break in new ground.[190]

Great expense and inconvenience were by no means the greatest obstacles to rationalizing the layout of estates. In his cover letter attached to another report of 1856 the agent Richard Wilson told Lady Londonderry that the consolidation of farms was difficult because of 'there being such an insituate hatred to a tenant who is even suspected of wishing to add to his own holding.' This was for him the most objectionable characteristic of the rundale system:

> That system of 'rundale,' which I am sorry to say exists on the estate, although but to a small extent, . . . should be completely exterminated. But a difficulty exists in the townland in question in consequence of some of the holdings being under old leases granted in the year 1787, some of the lives of which are still in being. . . . To give some idea of this pernicious system and how this townland is divided, there are 42 acres, 2 roods statute measure in cultivation held by seven tenants in 79 divisions![191]

As Henry Smith of the Drapers' company feared, this reordering affected not just the physical layout of the farms but also the social relations which were the basis of that layout:

> We are quite determined not to treat the tenants or any sets of them as having a common interest. We shall offer terms to each of them individually and will endeavour to arrange that such individuals shall except or reject the terms offered without communication with any other tenant.

> We shall resist anything like combination to the utmost, and the sensible part of the tenants will see at once that if the estate was to lay waste for four or five years without yielding any rent, it would only stop improvements and expenditures in Ireland without producing any inconvenience to the company's concerns here.[192]

But the only way to resist their combination was to buy them out at a price at which they would be persuaded to leave peaceably. And even then they had to be persuaded to go as far away as possible.[193] The agents of the Drapers' company felt that nothing short of emigration to America would break up rundale communities, otherwise 'no person could be got to take their farms.'[194]

These late-comers to close estate management were first learning in the 1820s what had been obvious to others for many decades. James Hamilton of the Abercorn estate was conscious of how important property claims were to the tenantry and to the smooth and peaceful operation of the estate. Even in the case of backward tenants Hamilton had great difficulty in overcoming the force of popular belief. He informed Abercorn in 1780:

> If I could once get a farm sold cleverly, I am very confident that some would struggle to pay, who, as your lordship observes, are waiting for the event. But the loss I am at is getting purchasers while the tenant is in possession; if he is himself not earnest in selling, not a man will offer to buy. To bring the tenant to consent, I must either take of all he has or bring a writ for him and send him to gaol.[195]

In fact, some tenants could be quite obstinate about their claims, particularly when agent-regulated purchases conflicted with traditional familial or inherited claims to property. If the offended tenant remained in the neighbourhood, he might also create considerable trouble for all concerned. Thomas Addi observed of a Donegal tenant in 1730 that he could get no rent from him, even though the farm was a good one and undervalued, and that 'while he possesses it, no other will propose any rent.'[196] In 1777 Abraham Boys, a tenant on the Abercorn estate, lost his holding for some unmentioned reason to William Carland, 'who paid on account of Boys two years' rent, and [he] assures me [Hamilton] that he gave him [Boys] over and above that about fifteen in order that he might leave the place without trouble.' This apparently did not satisfy Boys, for soon afterwards the house on the holding was burned to the ground. Ten years later, after Carland had built a new house and was leaving the plot, Boys's son was still asserting his right to the property.[197] Tenants on the Anglesey estate also wielded considerable influence over their landlord's selection of tenants. In 1816 Anglesey was informed that arson on farms near Dundalk was apparently committed 'for no other reason than their having taken lands of which others were dispossessed either for misconduct or for nonpayment of rent.' He was determined not to give land to anyone who had been turned out: 'If the new tenant has not nerve to hold on in spite of threats, let the farm remain unrented. I would rather lose all rents than be dictated to by ruffians.' He knew some of the perpetrators but would never be able to secure testimony from anyone, 'so completely established is the reign of terror in these cases.' An agent on the Downshire estate tried in 1766 to determine whether there were competing claims to a farm by leaving it untenanted in order to discover whether it stayed waste.[198]

In the nineteenth century, amidst widespread poverty and land hunger on an estate, such complexities, aside from being inconvenient, could also be downright dangerous.[199] Devon commission witnesses testified that the only agrarian outrages in Ulster in recent memory had to do with the non-recognition of the right of renewal.[200] One landowner in Co. Armagh testified before the Devon commission that his agent had been murdered because he refused to give tenant right for his own land. In 1850 the managers of the Drapers' proportion explained to their employers the reasons for the murder of the agent of an estate in their neighbourhood. The Millers felt that he had been too quick to proceed at law against those who were behind in their rent, but added that it was 'very difficult to discriminate amongst a number of tenants who can pay and who cannot at particular periods.' They emphasized in a later letter the special difficulties surrounding the 'custom with tenants at will' where each joint tenant is responsible for only their share of the total, even though legally any one of them could be bound to pay the whole. The Millers were lucky to learn that excessive pressure on the wrong partners was clearly to be avoided.[201]

The enforcement of traditional property rights did not depend solely on the operation of secret societies or conspiratorial bands of arsonists, for quite often single tenants could enforce their own claims, even from a considerable distance. A man on the Fishmongers' estate who had been in jail for debt from 1828 to 1832 was one such tenant. He was liberated from jail on the promise that he would not molest the new occupier of his farm. But according to a deputy, 'he is so bad a fellow that, from the threats he holds out, no one has hitherto ventured to take the farm. . . . The farm is now merely grazed upon for the benefit of the company.'[202] Consider also the case of George Robb on the Gosford estate, whose aged father had allegedly left his farm to Robb's nephew in a will. Robb threw his nephew out and took possession of the farm in 1826 but had accrued arrears of over £60 by 1842. Robb refused to give the goodwill to anyone, so Gosford had him thrown in jail. By 1845 the arrears had mounted to £100 and his wife was unable to find anyone to take the farm other than the nephew. Clearly no one would come near this family dispute. This shows not so much the strength of tenant right as the ability of a single man to upset the normal patterns of estate management, and the legal weakness of the landlord to stop him.[203] In 1845 a Drapers' company tenant named Michael Hessan harrassed another tenant, John Moran, who was occupying the farm from which he had been ejected. Moran notified the Drapers' court of assistants that 'he has been subjected to a constant system of annoyance from the ejected tenant, which has had the effect of making him in arrear with his rent. . . .'[204] The agents explained that after Hessan was ejected, no one could be found to take the farm because it was situated so closely to Moran's. They eventually convinced Moran to take it, hoping that the two farms could be rationalized into one, and offered to abate the arrears which he had accumulated.[205] The practice of witholding the goodwill from tenants who replaced those who fell into financial difficulty and were forced off their farms long post-dated the elimination of the rundale system.[206] The concern for the integrity of the neighbourhood may have outlasted the rundale system itself, as the concern shown by many tenants to keep out 'bad neighbours' from vacated adjacent farms demonstrates.[207] Both landlord and tenant continued to share concerns about bringing in 'strangers' or 'outcasts from other estates' to a townland throughout the nineteenth century.[208]

Vaughan claims that local enforcement of property claims was not an important element of tenant right because only a 'formidable ruffian in the prime of life' could exact a high price for the goodwill of a farm. Such a measurement of the significance of local enforcement neglects the social basis of the tenant-right system. The physical strength of a pugnacious young tenant or the organized terror of a band of menfolk might not amount to much in the price of tenant right, but it often served to underpin the local fabric of goodwill and peaceable possession. The evidence shows that behind the occasional outburst lay the strength of the opinion of a large network of kin and community. Consider the case of a man on the Anglesey estate who forcibly took possession of another's mountain farm, set fire to his hay and pulled down his house. When the bailiff attempted to drive his cattle off, he 'was so dreadfully beaten by him and his friends as to endanger his life and, as I have been informed, to have been in great measure the cause of the poor man's death which took place soon after.' He was tried for this offence and imprisoned but 'still kept the possession, threatening the life and property of any person who interfered with them.' It was only after the agent had successfully 'ejected him and his *clan*' that the battle was won.[209] James Hamilton of the Abercorn estate discussed in a number of letters the case of Andrew Lowry, who 'is still in possession, and if he was out, it would be unsafe for a stranger to go there. . . . There is such a connection in that part of your lordship's estate, for they are all Lowrys or related to Lowrys, that unless the chain is somehow broke[n], there will be no living there for a stranger who will come into any of these farms.' Lowry was finally removed and later was convicted of cutting out the tongues of the incoming tenant's cattle and chopping down his trees. Quite often, the force of neighbourhood opinion prevailed, as in the case of Robert Glendenning of the Abercorn estate, 'who first made an agreement with Moses McCrea, but upon finding that some of the neighbours objected to McCrea's coming, afterwards agreed with John Kinkead, whom the neighbours liked better.' Matthew White, who rented a mill and an adjacent farm, was removed by James Hamilton after receiving a petition from 'John McCreiry, signed by Matthew Moody and many others, setting forth that Matthew White was a bad and dangerous neighbour.' Upon the sale of a farm in the townland of Momeen, James Huston was preferred over another purchaser because 'he was a man of substance and good character,' and because Hamilton had been informed that 'the people of Momeen, who would be his neighbours, would be very well pleased to have him fixed there.'[210] The strength of neighbourhood opinion was also revealed when agents carried out objectionable evictions or declined to renew leases. Examples abound in estate correspondence of the hostility of neighbours toward unwanted purchasers of farms and of the claim of neighbours to the right of renewal. A man on the Castleward estate who was denied possession of a farm by neighbours or undertenants responded by distraining their cattle:

> The tenants of Whitehill would not give possession to Terence Stockdale but threatened him with pitchforks. He put their cattle in Ballyculter pound, but they never came near them since, so they still remain in the pound. They went to Mr. Hill, who treated them as they deserved, and from him they went over the ferry to Dromerode and Tom Savage, who advised them to go straight to Dublin, but whether they be gone or not, Terence can't tell.[211]

James Hamilton lamented in 1795 that 'there are at present four waste farms, and although the former occupiers have removed and entirely resigned their claim, I cannot persuade or encourage the neighbouring tenants to lay aside their bigoted prejudice.'[212]

The boldness of individual behaviour should not obscure the basis of social power in the family and neighbourhood. As William Blacker remarked, 'anyone who knows the state of Ireland knows that it is not safe to emigrate even to an adjoining parish without paying for what is called goodwill of the person to whom he succeeds, which explains fully the reason why a sum of money nearly equal to the fee of the land is often given to get into possession of a farm under a regrettable landlord in a quiet neighbourhood, although the land may be subject to its full value in rent.'[213] For a very strict social code, enforceable by relatively rare instances of blackmail and outrage, to exist, it was not necessary to conjure up the image of a 'formidable ruffian in the prime of life' to sustain it. Tenant right, which operated without any of the usual aids needed for the transfer of property, courts, registration systems, lawyers and adjudicators, etc, was indeed 'a remarkable example of social cohesion,' because for a region where 'the average tenant was involved in only one transaction likely to lead to crime: the succession of his farm,' tenant-on-tenant crime was relatively low in Ulster.[214]

The preceding paragraphs discussed two different scenarios: one in which managers attempted to deal with rundale communities, and one in which they faced communities of family farms held in severalty, yet still tightly bound to community regulation of tenure. In both cases managers needed to somehow infiltrate and manipulate the relationships between neighbours and family members. Otherwise, the policy of attacking tenants individually would never succeed. The complicated social relationships between neighbours, though difficult for agents to accurately discern, were of crucial importance with respect to the goodwill which cemented a tenant's property rights in the community. The Millers recognized that they had little compass with regard to the expulsion of unwanted tenants in a closely-knit townland. Reflecting on the subject in 1846, they explained to the management committee in London that 'nothing in fact will induce one man to take another's land without giving him full value for it, unless the fear of being put out himself if he would not take it. It requires great caution in regulating farms in this country. In truth if such caution were not used this province like some of the other provinces, would become a by-word to the whole nation.' The squaring of townlands had allowed them to solve many of these problems. But regarding one troublesome case they wrote:

> If the court had been pleased to permit this as well as the other townlands to be squared Latimore's case would have been settled long ago – or if they will permit us to say to some one of the neighbouring tenants – he *must* take it or be *put out himself*, we will be able to attach it to another farm. But if we acted thus without your permission in all probability the tenant so coerced will forward a memorial to the court against us and we would have to enter into a long explanation to meet said memorial, or, if the court will consent to give up the arrear, then we shall be able to get a neighbour to take it, for he will in that case be able to give Latimore something for his tenant right, or goodwill as it is called.

They added that 'if we find however that we cannot prevail upon the neighbouring tenants to amalgamate these farms with their own we shall get us respectable tenants as we possibly can to take them. The tenants unfortunately are not in good circumstances adjoining these farms which makes it the more difficult to amalgamate them.'[215]

When attempting to infiltrate segregated rundale and small-farm townlands and place the best available tenant on vacated farms, estate managers risked trespassing on the sectarian sensitivities of the neighbours. Eighteenth-century managers, as was shown above, allowed and promoted the evolution of an ethnically segregated pattern of settlement. By the nineteenth century landlords were more concerned to let the operation of the land market eliminate small and inefficient farmers, regardless of their ethnic background. If this market could operate unhindered by ethnic segregation of townlands, then the latter was no longer relevant from a strictly financial point of view. According to Wright, 'the division of territory embodied in the notions of 'Protestant' and 'Catholic' farms was a restriction on free market mechanisms, but it would scarcely have been tolerated, let alone imposed, by landlords, if its economic impact on their rent-rolls had been significantly adverse. . . . It was a socially and politically possible strategy just because its economic impact was marginal.'[216] The tenant-right market may have operated to reinforce segregation. Evidence of sectarian exclusive dealing of tenant right was uncovered by the Devon commission, but Wright speculates that selling exclusively to those of your own religion was even more widely practised than Devon evidence indicates. Different townlands of many parishes in the west of the province were often occupied exclusively by members of one religion, and exclusive dealing helped to maintain the sectarian integrity of a townland.[217] There were, nevertheless, cases where the dictates of estate development began to conflict with the segregated status quo. An attempt by the Drapers' managers to break into a Catholic neighbourhood and place a Protestant tenant on a vacant farm in the 1820s reveals the nature of the problem. The minutes refer to tenants

> in Dunmurry and Moydamlaght of the Roman Catholic persuasion who had opposed the residence of a Mr. Hamilton amongst them on account of his being a Protestant, and who had by threats induced the said Mr. Hamilton to give up the farms of which he was about to become tenant. It is thereupon ordered that the clerk inform the company's agent that this court entirely approves of his conduct on this matter and to assure him of the entire support of this court in his resistance to the attempts of the inhabitants of the townlands in question to exclude Protestants from them.[218]

Henry Smith complained to a parish priest on the Drapers' estate in 1821 about

> the difficulty Mr. Rowley Miller experiences in placing a new tenant on a vacant farm in Dunmurry – his possession is opposed by the neighbours in the same townland and in Moydamlaght. This opposition must proceed

from a bigoted antipathy or from a spirit of lawless violence and a complete subversion of all right to property. . . . When they took possession of their estate, they found that by law and, it cannot be disguised also in some degree by prejudice, the Catholics were in a somewhat inferior condition to the Protestants. So far as was consistent with law and was in their power, they endeavoured to remove prejudices and to bring the Catholics and Protestants to the same level. Judge, then, what must be the feelings of those making such an endeavour to be met by an arrogant assumption of the inhabitants of any district that none but those of their own faith are worthy of being their neighbours or associates. . . . The company will never receive the dictation of any neighbourhood, [as] to whom or how they shall dispose of their property, and in the present instance they will vindicate their right to place upon their estates any man who is willing to become their tenant.[219]

The following day Smith told Rowley Miller that the court 'must commit an apparent inconsistency by instructing you that the vacant farm is on no account to be occupied by any person who is not decidedly a Protestant or Protestant Dissenter.'[220] It is not clear how this was resolved, and whether or not the company was successful in driving home their point that farms would be given to the most promising tenants, regardless of the views of the neighbours. But it is doubtful that Smith could have maintained this intemperate policy. Estate managers learned to rely on more tactful strategies.

THE IMPLOSION OF RUNDALE

Forceful interference in rundale communities was rare because stiff resistance in the neighbourhood often scared strangers away. When familial and communal ties within rundale communities were strained by the opening market for land, landlords and agents found a window of opportunity and a more subtle solution to the problem. By allowing promising partners in a rundale holding to step into a severalty agreement through the mechanism of a tenant-right purchase, agents promoted the individualization and rationalization of holdings from within a rundale community.[221] The internal tensions that threatened the rundale system were often the result of a collision between more aggressive, improving tenants and their less enterprising but jointly-bound partners. Estate managers often came to the defence of an improving tenant who wanted to escape from the collective responsibility of a joint lease. Many farms saw the implosion of joint tenancies into numerous severalty tenures at the expiration of the joint lease.[222] Though earlier in the century they found them to be convenient, eventually landlords wanted to break up joint tenancies. The dramatic change in attitudes toward the joint lease is reflected in the following comment by the Co. Armagh land agent William Greig: 'It is scarcely necessary to mention the trouble and mischief which generally results from granting joint leases, as the industrious have often to suffer for the indolence or poverty of those joined with them: it has often formed a great discouragement to improvement. No lease ought to be granted to more than one individual and the boundaries of the lands so leased ought to be distinctly defined as to lanes, streets, etc.'[223] Memorials and petitions from the threatened partners to their landlord document these collisions. John Gamble, a joint tenant with many others on the Barrett-Lennard estate, was residing in Antrim in 1715. He attempted to sell his portion to another impoverished tenant and refused to sell to the landlord except at an outrageous price. The joint tenants on the land declared that they would 'stand out' against any purchaser but the landlord.

> I believe he dare hardly sell it without giving it to your honour now, since the tenants that live on the eight tates . . . say they were all partners equally concerned with Gamble at the first taking from your honour. . . . They have always paid in their rent this nineteen years I have been here, and not to Gamble. . . . The tenants will stand out against Gamble or any that buys it from him except your honour.[224]

On the Conolly estate early in the eighteenth century a tenant named Boyle, infamous among the co-partners of a townland as an exacting farmer of tithes, purchased half the townland from an emigrating tenant. The partners petitioned Conolly as follows:

> That our neighbours have sold their part of Ballymore in order to go to the king's plantation in America, one half of it to John Boyle in Newtown Limavady, farmer of the tythe of the parish of Bally Kelly; that a great many parishoners of said parish have had severe and hard treatment by said Boyle, so that we, your petitioners, made offer of the same money that Boyle was to give for it, because we were afraid Boyle would put robbers or thieves among us; that [he] will oblige us, your lordship's tenants, to leave it, for he threatens us unless we deliver up the deed [so] that his agreement may be drawn on the back of it.

They expressed their fear of his 'racking' them with tithes. They tried and failed to separate themselves from him by a 'bond of performance of your lordship's rent for the half he had purchased' and 'for the payment of the falls of the lives of the deeds,' which he refused. Finally they asked him to go to Conolly and be received as a tenant, that is, to sever their partnership tenancy, but he also refused this.[225]

Occasionally, the threatened co-partners would win such battles. The largest holders in joint leases, once thought to be security for the entire group, were occasionally penalized for abusing their responsibilities by withholding their share of the rent, exploiting their poorer partners, or preventing the group from fairly redistributing shares.[226] More commonly, the landlord wanted to give the land, or some portion of it, to an ambitious and promising individual. A local linen merchant outbid the sitting jointly-bound occupiers of a town-land on the Anglesey estate after the letting had been provocatively advertised in the Newry papers in 1770. The agent then informed the smallholders that they would be ejected if they did not raise their bid. The residents petitioned, mustering a long list of justifications for their right of renewal: they claimed that their agricultural technique was sound, that their families had been in possession since the late Irish wars, and that they had built fences and manured 'as much as their abilities afforded' even though they never received a lease.[227] Eventually, the residents got new leases, both because while they were jointly bound, the rent was secure, and because Anglesey recognized their right. But, crucially, only the wealthiest among them were to be named in the leases: 'Perhaps your honour might think to give them leases; if so, one lease for each quarter will be safest, by taking in the three most [re]sponsible to each lease, and let them give articles to any others on the lands. It is doing nothing giving leases to poor people who have no stake for rent.'[228] Even though the threat from outside was warded off, the landlord took the opportunity to recognize the most promising of the sitting tenants.[229]

Such marginal tenurial victories by co-partners in competition with aggressive individuals were rare. It was more common for an aggressive individual within the community to use the tenant-right market to his advantage. The resistance by tenants on the McCartney estate to a redivision of their townland in 1774 was broken by a private offer from one among them. The agent had presented a new layout of farms which originally met with approval from the occupiers, but when it came time to settle on the new arrangement, they balked. The agent recounted that

> I told them they were acting wrongly for themselves by trifling and that they must take it as then layed out or determine to pay up their rent and leave the land, upon which I received a proposal privately from one of them at 12s. per acre for one of the new divisions which I think rather high. It appears to me that they were in combination and that the knot is now broke, and that the remaining part of the arable will set well.[230]

Another such tenant was Thomas Cunningham who in 1769 purchased the tenant right of half of a jointly-bound farm on the Abercorn estate, the other half of which was divided between two others. These two tenants 'were desirous that the farm should be made into thirds, and proposed joining with the purchaser and paying [rent] in proportion to make their parts a third instead of a quarter. But Cunningham would have all or none.' Eventually, he sold to another man willing to take only a third.[231] Fifteen years later, Cunningham was again in conflict with jointly-bound partners, this time claiming that he was suffering because of their arrears:

> At the time your lordship was pleased to order leases made out, some of them could not avail themselves of your lordship's goodness on account of their holding in common with others who did not merit such favour. Thomas Cunningham of Tillywhisker, who pays £10 10s. rent and is a punctual tenant, is one of those who has been barred of his lease. He has divided with his neighbours.[232]

Whether they were made amid tension and controversy or in a spirit of co-operative improvement, the redivisions made by the tenants themselves, as well as official divisions carried out by surveyors, caused a great confusion of property rights. Hamilton commented on the difficulties facing the rundale residents on the Abercorn estate in 1767:

> There are few divisions made by the tenants themselves that they abide by, though bound sometimes by oath. Sometimes they agree that one of themselves should divide and give the other a choice for some consideration in money; sometimes it is divided by indifferent persons and [the tenants] cast lots for the parts each is to have. . . . Divisions are the cause of most disputes, and [I] would therefore hope your lordship would give some orders concerning them.[233]

Tenant-right payments were a useful tool in settling these disputes in this dynamic system of landholding where a given estate might have rundale and severalty communities existing side by side, and often separated by ethnic and religious barriers. Such conflicts were often settled with 'some consideration in money.' After a redivision of an Abercorn estate townland, John McClintock observed:

> By the alterations McCrea has made, all the houses are on one division, and the other tenants insist on having their houses and gardens continued to them or getting a reasonable consideration for removing them, which I do not think unreasonable, as some had built houses immediately before the division and thought it might be insisted upon, as your lordship generally allowed a consideration to be paid by the tenant who continued in his houses to the one who removed.[234]

The tenants then chose 'two men to whom they referred the consideration for removing the houses.'[235] There were over 140 joint tenancies on the two northern estates of the Downshire family in Co. Down when Lord Downshire gave the following instructions to his agent in 1841:

> My tenants have for some time complained of the inconvenience arising from several persons holding farms in common, the head or good tenant among them being hampered by the poor or idle partner who is generally either unable or unwilling to keep his rent paid regularly. I therefore request Mr. Reilly to order a list to be sent me of the like with quantities, and to give the parties personally notice that they may arrange among themselves , so that this evil may be removed next November by the head purchasing the tenant right from his brother tenant, subject to Mr. Reilly's approval, after Mr. Henry Murray and Thomas Collins have examined each place.[236]

Although grand and forceful reorganizations of entire townlands were too confrontational and prohibitively expensive, a more tactful alliance with the insidious forces of the land market proved more effective in the long run. These forces manifested themselves in a variety of ways: as outsiders to a community sought to rent vacated land or land where a joint lease had recently expired, as prominent members of rundale communities desired independent leaseholds, and as the communities themselves moved toward market solutions to the manifold problems produced by the colonization and subdivision of land traditionally held in rundale.

Most of the evidence suggests that familial grids of inheritance stood in resistance to the unbending requirements of commercialized tenancies, but this was not always the case. It might also happen that familial relations were so poor that the tenants allowed a market solution to the problem of succession. The Drapers' company agents were drawn into an affair involving a father whose wife and son would not allow him to return to possession of a farm he had left in the care of the son in 1843. The agents insisted that he could sell the farm to any respectable man, but his family did everything that they could to prevent this from happening, threatening to take his life if he stepped near the farm. In such a case, the sale of the tenant right of the farm might serve to diffuse the family feud:

> If he attempts to go near his farm, they all attack him and in fact are putting the law at defiance and keeping possession by force. As magistrates, we will send three of his sons to jail if they do not give us sufficient security that they will keep the peace for two years toward their father. But as agents, we are of the opinion that no time ought to be lost in taking steps to remove them from Drumot farm. They are not only a disgrace to the estate but to the whole of the district, and it is the wish of the father, who is the company's tenant, that the farm should be sold and the money given to him. He would then, he says, give each of his sons a certain portion of the money to take them to America.[237]

The Drapers' company agents made a clear connection between the term 'goodwill' and the price that a farmer demanded for his removal from a community. This had nothing to do with the value of improvements or the difference between the Ricardan and the actual rent. It was a representation of the value of the membership of a farmer in a community, and the costs involved in extracting him from it. Later in the nineteenth century familial restrictions on the tenant-right market had become so weakened that even the endowment of a farm by a father to a son was exposed to the market, so that sons were required to pay the market tenant-right price in order to acquire their father's farms.[238]

AMALGAMATION OF FARMS AS IMPROVEMENT

The previous chapters discuss how the term improvement could be construed as something other than merely new buildings and fences. It referred also to the productive orientation of the tenant. That rundale tenants generally lacked such a productive orientation was widely recognized in the crisis decade of the 1840s. The Millers reflected in 1845:

> Lord Erne says in his speech to his Tenants 'It is quite impossible for him to force his Tenants to adopt any thing they do not wish.' His lordship is quite right. It is impossible to force a multitude to adopt any system they do not wish, and the most ignorant of the peasantry in this country consider that the reason the Gentlemen established farming societies and proposed an altered system of cultivation to the farming class, was, that they wished to improve the land in order hereafter to oppress them with heavy rents. This feeling was, that if they just went on in their old way, they would do well enough; and that they had a chance of getting their rent lowered, they were satisfied from year to year, if they could merely keep the potato crop for themselves and for their families and give up the remainder of their produce to the Landlord for the rent, they in fact had no desire to 'better themselves in the world' and hence the difficulty of improving their Condition, especially the tenantry in remote and backward districts, or those situated on the sides of mountains, where both climate and soil in general are bad.[239]

When in the nineteenth century the tenant-right issue came to revolve around compensation for improvements, landlords were concerned to restrict this connotation to tangible artifacts on the farms. In addition, they offered their own controversial connotation: the elimination of rundale was in itself an 'improvement,' in the sense that consolidated severalty farms were more economically stable, subject to greater control, and more easily coaxed toward an orientation to profit. The salient point is that landlords inevitably discovered that their various efforts to get their tenants to adopt modern techniques were futile where the confounding system of rundale operated.

This was particularly true of drainage.[240] 'Most of your farms are only half worked and in many cases between ditches and waste the third unoccupied,' claimed the earl of Antrim's agent in 1851. 'Had these men land for nothing it would be too dear.'[241] Referring to their conversations with visiting Devon commissioners about schemes for promoting drainage, the Millers wrote that the best policy 'is for the landlord to pay a portion of the outlay, say a half or a third, especially when the tenant holds at will. The thirteen townlands that were squared have been considerably improved by the new fences made thereon as it has drained them very much and the squaring of the farms will enable the occupiers a greater facility of making drains in the proper places.'[242] An unsigned report on the potential improvement of the earl of Antrim's estate highlighted the difficulties facing attempts at 'improvement' of landholding and husbandry:

> It would be easy to point to a system of husbandry calculated to improve the land and be beneficial both to the owner and the occupier, but I fear that were such a system laid down and inserted into the leases, no Irish tenant could be found to take the farms. And from the farms being in general small and the country people disliking strangers, I do not think it would be advisable to attempt the introduction of either English or Scotch farmers.

Furthermore, this reporter claimed, fences would be overgrown if put up and houses be allowed to deteriorate: 'I know not whether an Irish tenant would prefer his miserable hovel to any comfortable house.' Draining was much wanted but little understood on the estate, he remarked, and the taking of so many successive corn crops should be curtailed, 'but here again a difficulty occurs, for how can any of the Irish agents enforce a system the very reverse of which they practise themselves.'[243] The alleged productive deficiencies of rundale began to be more widely noticed in the 1830s and 1840s. Deputies reporting on the Skinners' proportion in 1836 sadly remarked that 'the estate is generally badly cultivated, and a great deal of it is still occupied in the mischievous and exploded way called rundale, which is a certain bar to good farming and solid improvement in cultivation.'[244] In his report on Lady Londonderry's Antrim estate in 1837, John Andrews listed what he felt to be the specific causes preventing improvement:

> Those specific causes are chiefly found in the old Irish system of allotment called rundale, under which land has been held promiscuously in mixed and scattered patches, effectually preventing enclosure and improvement, and in the inaccessible position of many tracts from the want of roads. The former has been steadily and judiciously obviated in every case where the expiration of leases has permitted it, and the latter has been removed as far as practicable without the command of adequate funds.[245]

As John Waring explained of a project to subsidize the drainage of some 4,000 perches of land on his estate in the 1840s: 'The agriculturalist and I have spent much time in endeavouring to get farms so divided as regarded fencing as to enable tenants to adopt a proper rotation of crops.' Waring also reported the planting of a large turnip crop.[246]

Ditching, draining, and new arable rotations were still important improvements before 1850. But with the post-famine increase in the relative viability of land-extensive production, 'improvement' came to mean destroying farms altogether. The Millers conjectured in 1848: 'Suppose the Company are about to grant leases and the estate is revalued. It follows that where two or more holdings have been joined together that the land(s) will be worth so much more per acre than when it has been held in one small piece.'[247] The marquis of Dufferin proposed in 1866 that a thirty-acre farm bordering two fifty-acre farms on his County Down estate be amalgamated whole to one of the two rather than divided between them, because the result of the latter option 'is to create side by side two farming centres, each of them smaller than we might ultimately wish as individual farms, but at the same time so large, and held by such good men, and so well furnished with buildings to make their amalgamation impossible.'[248] In a work published in 1870, Dufferin claimed that improvement on small farms was simply impossible. On small farms 'the deterioration of land, if justly estimated, would be found to outweigh, in most cases of eviction, the counter-claim of the tenant for compensation, it is improbable that many instances have occurred in which this condition has not been fulfilled.' The deterioration he referred to is not so much from the smallholders' agrarian practice as it is from the very fact of the existence of their farms. The opportunity cost in terms of the rent per acre obtainable on larger, consolidated farms outweighed the cost of compensating smallholders for the extermination of their farms.[249] In a letter to the Marquis of Downshire objecting to his opposition to tenant right and his support for coercion, William Sharman Crawford directly equated improvement with extermination, citing as evidence of this a Belfast newspaper report of over 250 men and women emigrating from Gweedore to Australia.[250] The landlord interpretation of the meaning of improvement had by 1870 been turned into the antithesis of their interpretation of it, c. 1700. Not only the rhetoric had changed; by 1870 managerial control over tenure had also dramatically increased, so that the deeds of a landlord like the marquis of Dufferin could match his words.

NOTES

1   The forms of settlement most commonly associated with rundale were known in
    lowland Scotland and England as the 'ferm toun,' in Ireland as 'baile,' and in the
    Scottish highlands as 'clachan.' The term was called variously 'runridge' in Mayo,
    'running-dale' in Galway, 'run and dale' and 'crossholding' in Donegal, and holding in
    'stock' in Fermanagh. Ian and Kathleen Whyte, The changing Scottish landscape
    1500–1600 (London, 1991), p. 4, 55–58; Desmond McCourt, 'The rundale system in
    Ireland: a study of its geographical distribution and social relations' (PhD. dissertation,
    Queen's University of Belfast, 1950), pp. 95, 301; J.H. Rutherford, 'The plantation of
    Lagan and its economy' in Donegal Annual (1959), p. 126; R. Buchanan, 'Field systems in
    Ireland' in Alan Baker and Robin Butler (eds.), Studies in field systems in the British isles
    (Cambridge, 1973), pp. 586–7. Smout distinguishes runrig, 'separate ownership of
    several scattered strips of arable, each one of which lay between those of different joint
    tenants to ensure a fair distribution of good and indifferent lands . . . ,' from rundale,
    'where some of the strips were consolidated into blocks which themselves lay
    intermingled with those of other joint tenants.' T.M. Smout, A history of the Scottish
    people 1560–1830 (Edinburgh, 1969), pp. 121–2. It is not clear on what evidence Smout
    bases his distinction, but if accurate it seems to fit with the pattern of plantation in
    Ireland which laid out farms in blocks rather than strips. Rutherford draws an analogy
    between the Irish rundale and the Scots runrig, and claims that the one existed
    beforehand and the other was imported by the Scots settlers. Rutherford, 'Plantation,'
    p. 126. Desmond McCabe defines rundale as 'the system of partible inheritance and
    dispersed land use, in open fields, under certain variable conditions.' Desmond McCabe,
    'Law, conflict, and social order: county Mayo 1820– 1845' (Ph.D. dissertation, University
    College Dublin, 1991), p. 20.
2   R.A. Dodgshon, Origin of the British field system (London, 1980), pp. 17–19; ibid.,
    pp. 30–2; McCourt, 'Rundale system,' pp. 85–7; D.N. McCloskey, 'English open fields
    as behaviour towards risk' in Peter Uselding (ed.), Research in economic history, vol. 1
    (Greenwich, Connecticut, 1976), pp. 124–70, cited in Dodgshon, Origin, pp. 22–4.
3   McCourt, 'Rundale system,' pp. 96–7. For descriptions of the similar system of runrig
    in Scotland, see Smout, History of the Scottish people, p. 122, and Ian D. and Kathleen
    Whyte, The changing Scottish landscape, 1500–1600 (London, 1991), p. 59.
4   Ibid., p. 4; McCourt, 'Rundale system,' p. 301.
5   Open-field cultivation and booleying were closely integrated: 'The days marking the
    departure of the herds and the first ploughing, and the return of the herds and the
    end of the harvest, grew to have a special significance.' Harold T. Masterson, 'Land
    use patterns and farming practice in County Fermanagh, 1609–1845' in Clogher record,
    vii, no. 1 (1969), p. 62; McCourt, 'Rundale system,' p. 236. Tenants in Donegal in 1682
    stored their valuables in a church during summer mountain grazing. A surveyor
    found minimal use of housing structures during the summer booleying of cattle.
    One building served many families. 'Survey by Thomas Knox of the estate of
    Termondmagrath, barony of Tirhugh, Co. Donegal, 1682,' N.L.I., Reports on private
    collections, viii, no. 220: Leslie papers in Possession of Mr. S. C. Ross. Where cattle
    could be pastured more proximately to the clachan, as in the Lagan area of east
    Donegal, there was no need for booleying. Rutherford, 'Plantation,' pp. 125–6.
6   Michel Foucault, Discipline and punish: the birth of the prison (New York, 1977) pp.
    220–1. Foucault focused on Bentham's panopticon, the prison he designed to control

its population through visual distinction and isolation. For the analysis of the panopticon, see pp. 195–228. Bentham had similar designs for control over land. See his 'Outline of a plan of a general registry of real property' (1831) in J. Bowring (ed.), *The works of Jeremy Bentham* (Edinburgh, 1843), p. 430, cited in J.H. Andrews, *Plantation acres: an historical study of the Irish surveyor and his maps* (Belfast, 1985), p. 140.

7 Bartolovich, 'Boundary disputes,' pp. 118–19. 'There is no overestimating the impact of maps; many viewers suddenly perceived their spacial existence in an entirely new way as they saw their houses from an aerial perspective. The maps were inviolable standards against which all customs and memories were judged. No longer did each villager carry with him a unique mental map of the land and community; once the surveyor's work was done one map alone ordered the landscape'. John Stigloe, 'Jack O'Lanterns to surveyors: the secularization of landscape boundaries' in *Environmental review*, i (1976), p. 22, cited in Bartolovich, 'Boundary disputes,' p. 203.

8 Bartolovich, 'Boundary disputes,' p. 87.

9 'Enclosure had a terrible but instructive visibility.' J. M. Neeson, 'The opponents of enclosure in eighteenth-century Northamptonshire' in *Past & present*, no. 105 (1984), quoted in Thompson, 'Custom, law, and common right,' p. 180.

10 D.B. Quinn, 'William Montgomery and the description of the Ards, 1683' in *Irish booklore*, ii, no.1 (1972), p. 37.

11 'A description of Onealand barony in the county of Armagh by William Brooke, Portadown,' 26 Oct. 1682, in *A natural history of Ireland, memories and notes relating thereto, made from communications to the Dublin Society* (2 vols), i, 222 (T.C.D., MS 883/1).

12 Young, *Tour*, ii, *passim*.

13 Robert Hutchinson to Henry Bayly, 24 Mar. 1778, P.R.O.N.I., Anglesey papers, D619/21/C/169. Survey of Bellaghan and Irish Grange, 13 Apr. 1778, ibid., D619/21/C/171.

14 John Robinson to Richard Waring, 19 Aug. 1804, P.R.O.N.I., McGildowney papers, D1375/3/4/24.

15 Waring to Robinson, 23 Aug. 1804, ibid., D1375/3/4/25. A year earlier, McGildowney and Waring exchanged speculations on whether a jury could be influenced to side with them against McDonnell. Edmund McGildowney to Richard Waring, 28 June 1803, ibid., D1375/3/3/22, and Waring to McGildowney [n.d.], ibid., D1375/3/3/25.

16 John Litton [?] to Earl of Lanesborough, 14 Feb. 1860, P.R.O.N.I., Earl of Lanesborough's papers, D1908/2/5.

17 McCabe, 'Law, conflict, and social order,' p. 395.

18 McCabe equates rundale with gavelkind inheritance, and notes that the latter was outlawed in 1605. However, the plantation legislation does not specifically refer to rundale. McCabe, 'Law, conflict, and property,' p. 395; Mary O'Dowd, 'Gaelic economy and society,' in Brady and Gillespie (eds.), *Natives and newcomers*, p. 141.

19 Andrews, *Plantation acres*, pp. 52–61, 83.

20 Hunter, 'Ulster plantation,' p. 429.

21 Ibid., p. 430. Hunter cites Marsh's Library, Dublin, Z4. 2. 6, pp. 537–8.

22 Ibid., pp. 430–1.

23 Henry Hatch to Henry Blundell, 29 June 1749, P.R.O.N.I., Downshire papers, D607/A/23; Henry Hatch to William Trumbell, 15 Mar. 1759, P.R.O.N.I., Downshire papers, film 17/1; Robert Hutchinson to Henry Bayly, 29 Apr. 1776, P.R.O.N.I., Anglesey papers, D619/21/C/134. In 1779 David McCool complained to Lord

Viscount Caledon of his Moville, Co. Donegal, estate that he had 'with some difficulty made out a new rent-roll, according to the present arrangement of the tenants,
and which indeed is every year in a fluctuating state, in consequence of purchasing,
selling, dying, transferring, bequeathing, etc., etc.' David McCool to Lord Viscount
Caledon, 8 Feb. 1799, P.R.O.N.I., Caledon papers, D2433/A/2/5/11. The obsolescence of maps caused a dependence on the opinions of old men for information
on the evolution of boundaries. Stanley Moncke to Thomas Conolly, 1 Dec. 1780,
T.C.D., Conolly papers, MS 3974–84/701.

24 Survey of the Manor of Clothworkers, 1840, Merchant Tailors' hall, N.L.I., film 1517.
For a similar statement from the Drapers' company estate, see the report by Nathanial
Stonard and W. Hamond, 27 Feb. 1817, minutes of the court of assistants, extracts
relating to Irish estates, Drapers' Hall, London, N.L.I., film 1529.

25 Ibid.

26 T.W. Freeman, 'Land and people, c. 1841' in Vaughan (ed.), *New history of Ireland*, v,
p. 243; R.V. Comerford, 'Ireland 1850–1870: post-famine and mid-Victorian' in
Vaughan (ed.), *New history of Ireland*, v, p. 374.

27 Giddens, *Contemporary critique*, p. 121.

28 Clay, *Economic expansion and social change*, i, p. 88.

29 Hunter, 'Ulster plantation,' p. 431.

30 'If no written leases existed, trouble could often ensue, and indeed there were frequent
disputes that would not have arisen earlier in the century when the pressure on
resources was lower. In at least one case brought before the Quaker meeting in Lurgan,
the root of the problem was that although there was an oral agreement between two
men over land boundaries, there was no corresponding written document.' Gillespie,
Settlement and survival, p. xxix.

31 Andrews, *Plantation acres*, pp. 117–18, 124–8.

32 [Thomas Dawson], *A dissertation on the enlargement of tillage, the erecting of public
granaries, and the regulating, employing and supporting the poor in this kingdom* (Dublin,
1751) and *The great importance and necessity of increasing tillage* (Dublin, 1754); Samuel
Pierson, *The present state of the tillage of Ireland considered . . .* (Dublin, 1725) and
Further considerations for the improvement of tillage in Ireland (Dublin, 1728); *Practical
agriculture epitomized and adapted to the tenantry of Ireland* (Dublin, 1771).

33 Andrews, *Plantation acres*, p. 205.

34 Works concerning the cultivation of the soil include: Edward Burroughs, *Essays on
practical husbandry and rural economy* (London, 1821) and *A view of the state of agriculture in Ireland* (Dublin, 1821); Henry Hoyte, *A treatise on agriculture addressed to the
noblemen and gentlemen of landed property in Ireland* (Dublin, 1828); William Blacker,
*Prize essay addressed to the agricultural committee of the RDS on the management of landed
property in Ireland* (Dublin, 1834) and *An essay on the improvements to be made in the
cultivation of small farm* (Dublin, 1834); Henry Lindsay, *Essay on the agriculture of the
county Armagh* (Armagh, 1836); Henry Crosley, *Hints to the landed proprietry and agriculturists of Great Britain and Ireland* (London, 1841); [William Hickey], *The farmer's
guide, compiled for the use of the small farmer and cotter tenantry of Ireland* (Dublin, 1841).

35 Evidence of farming societies survives from Clones, Draperstown, and on the
Annesley estate in County Down. J.R. Moore to Edward Mullen, 22 Sept. 1842,
P.R.O.N.I., Annesley papers, D1854/6/5; Rowley and J.R. Miller to Edward Lawford,
11 May 1845, P.R.O.N.I., Drapers' company papers, D3632/1/1. For reports on the
Clones Farming Society, see Nicholas Ellis to Thomas Barrett-Lennard, [?] Mar. 1839,

P.R.O.N.I., Barrett-Lennard papers, film 170/2; idem, 24 Sept. 1841, ibid., film 170/3; idem, n.d. [March, 1839], 24 Sept. 1841, 24 Sept. 1845, ibid., film 170/2. On other estates, see J.R. Moore to Edward Mullen, 22 September 1842, P.R.O.N.I., Annesley papers, D1854/6/5; Rowley and J.R. Miller to Edward Lawford, 11 May 1845, P.R.O.N.I., Drapers' company papers, D3632/1/1; Rowley Miller to W.H. Sawyer, 28 January 1875, ibid., D3632/1/4.

36 Smout, *History*, pp. 60, 72, 123.

37 Buchanan, 'Barony of Lecale,' p. 143.

38 Agent report, 1850, P.R.O.N.I., Earl of Antrim papers, D2977/6/5; J.B. Bankhead to Edmund McDonnell, 20 July 1851, P.R.O.N.I., Earl of Antrim papers, D2977/4/3.

39 A deputation to the Fishmonger's proportion appointed by the court of assistants in 1817 credited the Northwest of Ireland Agricultural Society with introducing the Scotch plough to the area and the straightening of furrows. Report of a deputation appointed by the court on the 12th of Apr. 1827, 1 Aug. 1827, Fishmongers' hall court minutes, N.L.I., film 1515.

40 [?] Webb to Andrew Nugent, 25 July 1817, P.R.O.N.I., Nugent papers, D552/A/7/6/14.

41 James Nugent to Andrew Nugent, 27 Nov. 1820, ibid., D552/A/7/6/61. In another letter he mentioned a particular tenant who could no longer make his rent out of 'a worn-out farm.' 'He had the benefit of it and made it what it is.' Idem, 12 Jan. 1821, ibid., D552/A/7/6/64. A survey of the Ballylam estate near Newtownards in 1833 reported the widespread exhaustion of the soil and argued for the necessity of evictions and the promotion of scientific farming. Survey of Ballylam estate by John Andrews, 2 October 1833, P.R.O.N.I., Londonderry papers, D654/N2/20

42 Nathanial Nesbitt to eighth earl of Abercorn, 26 Feb. 1753 and 19 Apr. 1757, P.R.O.N.I., T2541/IA1/2/154, T2541/IA1/4/67; Abercorn to Nesbitt, 4 Apr. 1757, P.R.O.N.I., D623/A/15/65; bills of cost from suits against tenants who broke subletting and successive ploughing covenants in the 1780s, N.L.I., Playdell papers, film 7648; Rev. George MacArtney to earl of MacArtney, 27 Apr. 1805, P.R.O.N.I., McCartney papers, D572/18/84; Robert Welsh to George Black, 2 Mar. 1792, ibid., D2225/7/52; Henry Prentice to [?] Hoffman, 15 Oct. 1857, P.R.O.N.I., Caledon papers, D2433/A/3/4.

43 Irish Society court minute books, 24 June 1842, N.L.I., film 1524.

44 Robert Welsh to George Black, 2 March 1792, P.R.O.N.I., McCartney papers, D2225/7/52.

45 Sir George Savile to James Murray, 28 May 1779, P.R.O.N.I., Murray of Broughton papers, D2860/17/4. See also the third report of Edward Oseland, 8 Nov. 1838, Merchant Tailors' Hall, Manor of Clothworkers' extracts from accounts, Box 131, N.L.I., film 1518.

46 See Chapter 5.

47 'The burning and carrying away of the surface is too much practised.' John Anderson, Moville, to 2nd Earl of Caledon, 18 Dec. 1815, P.R.O.N.I., Caledon papers D2433/A/2/15/1; Johnson and Fawcett to Dickens, 14 June 1832 and 27 June 1843, N.L.I., Playdell papers, film 7648; 'Notice to tenantry of Aughentaine prohibiting burning and stripping land,' 12 May 1842, P.R.O.N.I., Perceval-Maxwell papers, D3244/E/26/5; Dickson, 'Cork region,' p. 285–87.

48 Henry Prentice to Edward Evans, 11 January 1860, P.R.O.N.I., Caledon papers D2433/A/3/4.

49 Idem, 11 January 1864, ibid.

50 There were tillage and pasturing aspects of both rundale and severalty landholding. Enclosure was not exclusively associated with arable cultivation, just as rundale was more than a system of nomadic pastoralism. McCourt, 'Rundale system,' pp. 244–50; Young, *Tour*, i, 388; Johnston, 'Balfour rentals,' p. 101; Masterson, 'Land use patterns,' p. 65.

51 J.R. Wordie, 'The chronology of English enclosure, 1500–1914' in *Economic history review*, xxxvi, no. 4 (Nov. 1983), pp. 495, 502.

52 Robinson, *Plantation*, p. 180. A 1630 lessee was required to accompany the lessor or his assigns on horseback anywhere in the county of Tyrone. Lease of Castlestewart, County Tyrone, 1 Nov. 1630, P.R.O.N.I., Lenox-Conyngham papers, D1449/1/1.

53 Aalen, *Man and the landscape*, p. 163.

54 'A view of the archbishopric of Armagh by Thomas Ashe, 1703', P.R.O.N.I., T848/1.

55 Philip Robinson, 'The spread of hedged enclosure in Ulster' in *Ulster folklife*, xxiii, 1977, pp. 57–68. Robinson also relies on the excellent commentary in Dr. Thomas Molyneux's 'Journey to the North, August 7th, 1708' in R.M. Young (ed.), *Historical notices of old Belfast* (Belfast, 1896), p. 153. Molyneux had a sharp eye for enclosed vs. open landscape.

56 McCourt, 'Rundale system,' pp. 263–5.

57 Perceval-Maxwell argues that the Foyle valley resembles east Antrim rather than peripheral Ulster because of the ancient Scottish settlement in the Foyle. *Scottish migration*, p. 68.

58 Buchanan, 'Barony of Lecale,' pp. 98–100, 114, 140.

59 McCourt, 'Decline of rundale,' p. 130.

60 Kerr to Edmund McGildowney, 15 May 1814, P.R.O.N.I., McGildowney papers, D1375/4/10/9; James Fawcett to Lady Playdell, 9 June 1821, N.L.I., Playdell papers, film 7648; Fawcett to John Dickson, 25 Apr. and 9 July 1834, ibid.; Frederick Wrench to A.L. Barlee, 21 Jan. 1882, P.R.O.N.I., Brookeborough papers, D998/6/1. Robert Hutchinson to Henry Bayly, 24 June 1786, P.R.O.N.I., Anglesey papers, D619/21/D/14. Eight tenants petitioned in 1785 to hold their farms jointly. Tenant petition, 19 July 1785, ibid., D619/11/36; 'Observations for Mr. Park's assistance,' 18 July 1787, ibid., D619/14/C/4; Thomas Beer to [?] Rutherford, 20 Mar. 1845, ibid., D619/23/B/146; Robert Hutchinson to Henry Bayly, 21 May 1784, ibid., D619/21/D/15. E.E. Evans, 'Some survivals of the Irish open-field system' in *Irish geogr.*, xxiv, 1939, pp. 24–36; Desmond McCourt, 'Surviving Open Field in County Londonderry' in *Ulster folklife*, iv (1958), p. 26.

61 Report of a deputation to the Irish estate of the Clothworkers' company, 1849, Irish estate committee of management minutes, N.L.I., film 1517.

62 'Report of a deputation by the Court of Assistants of the Fishmongers' company the 18th of June 1832 to visit their estate in the County Londonderry, Ireland,' 25 Oct. 1832, Fishmongers' Hall court minutes, N.L.I., film 1515.

63 Currie argues that a combination of four different factors contributed to the disposition toward open-field farming and clustered settlement: (1) an inherited tradition in both Irish and planter families; (2) the need for co-operation in the colonization of land and the 'development of new landscapes;' (3) the plethora of mountain, bog, and natural meadow which lent itself to common use; and (4) the absence of any direct management of settlement practice by the property owners. Currie, 'Evolution,' p. 165.

64 Connolly, *Religion, law, and power*, p. 55.

65 McCabe, 'Law, conflict, and social order,' pp. 20, 28. See, for example, the hybrid phenomenon of 'proprietary runrig' in seventeenth-century Scotland. Ian D. Whyte,

Agriculture and society in seventeenth-century Scotland (Edinburgh, 1979), pp. 138–52. McCourt argues that partnerships and joint tenancy were coincident with rundale in Ireland, and Grey treated the terms rundale and outfield as interchangeable with respect to England. McCourt, 'Rundale system,' pp. 94–5; R.A. Dodgshon, Origin, p. 9.

66 Cormac Ó Gráda, 'Poverty, population, and agriculture,' in Vaughan (ed.), *New history of Ireland*, v, p. 126.

67 Whelan, 'Settlement and society,' pp. 54–56.

68 Buchanan, 'Barony of Lecale,' p. 157.

69 Ibid., p. 63; Philip Robinson, 'Irish settlement in Tyrone before the Ulster plantation' in *Ulster folklife*, xxii (1976), pp. 59–69; idem, *Plantation*, pp. 12, 94, 95. Robinson suggests that strategic concerns outweighed economic calculations of land quality, and that it was probable that 'there was an actual change in perceptions between the seventeenth and nineteenth centuries. In a rural economy less dependent on external communications and the need to produce a surplus for export, the isolation of areas with fertile soils in the west need not have been a disadvantage.' Ibid., pp. 14–15. See also Wright, *Two lands on one soil*, p. 172.

70 Macafee, 'Maghera region,' p. 83.

71 Ibid., pp. 83, 88. Given the defensive mobility of seventeenth-century native communities, we may question the adequacy of the concepts of 'core' and 'periphery,' since the embattled Irish apparently avoided the vulnerability of stable settlement in a 'core,' preferring a more mobile, although not exactly 'peripheral,' pattern of settlement. Macafee speculates: 'This idea is very tentative and it is obvious that more research is required into the distribution of the Irish. Where were the core areas of the Irish in pre-plantation times? Could it be that the Irish areas which are peripheral by present day standards were the core areas in an earlier environment?'

72 Johnston, 'Balfour rentals,' p. 95.

73 It is difficult to determine from estate evidence what type of communal system operated in a given townland. One indicator of communal production and fixed rundale was the joint lease. Smout describes similar circumstances in Scotland: 'To cultivate a farm by any method of joint tenancy inevitably made for communal work.' Smout, *History of the Scottish people*, p. 122.

74 Macafee, 'Maghera region,' p. 83.

75 E. A. Currie, 'Land tenures, enclosures and field patterns in Co. Derry in the eighteenth and nineteenth centuries' in *Irish geography*, (1983), p. 50.

76 Ibid., p. 84. Crawford writes: 'The evidence suggests that during the early years of the eighteenth century many of the colonists had to band together to acquire direct leases from the landlord and this led to their concentration in certain townlands.' W.H. Crawford, 'Economy and society in south Ulster in the eighteenth century' in *Clogher record*, viii, no. 3, 1975 p. 85. Joint leasing in Cork 'arose as much from its advantages to the lessor . . . as from its convenience to the lessees.' Dickson, 'Cork region,' pp. 269–70. See also Moody, *The Londonderry Plantation*, p. 133.

77 Cormac Ó Gráda, *Ireland: a new economic history 1780–1939* (Oxford, 1994), pp. 122–26.

78 [?] Armstrong to earl of Uxbridge, 3 letters of 1815, ibid., D619/23/A/81–83.

79 Currie, 'Evolution,' pp. 179, 210. McCourt associates the decline of rundale with improving landlords and concentrations of Protestant tenants. Native clachans survived in most of Derry because the London companies let to middlemen for the entire eighteenth century. McCourt, 'Rundale system,' p. 114.

80 William Mayne to Archibald Graham, 20 Mar. 1790, P.R.O.N.I., Barrett-Lennard papers, film 170/2.

81 Samuel McCrea to Thomas Conolly, 20 July 1760, T.C.D., Conolly papers, MS 3974–84/127.

82 McCrea to Conolly, 20 July 1760, ibid., MS 3974–84/127; Andrew Patton to James Murray, 2 Feb. 1770, P.R.O.N.I., Murray of Broughton papers, D2860/16/10.

83 Nick Dromgool to Edward Bayly, 5 Sept. 1738, P.R.O.N.I., Anglesey papers, D619/22/A/28.

84 John Bayly to Edward Bayly, 16 Sept. 1738, ibid., D619/21/A/46.

85 Earl of Uxbridge's directions to agents, n.d [c. 1770], ibid., D619/14/C/3.

86 Millers to Lawford, 14 June 1845, P.R.O.N.I., Drapers company papers, D3632/1/1.

87 MacAfee, 'Maghera region,' p. 84.

88 This is best revealed by surviving leasebooks. For two excellent examples, see Gillespie, *Settlement and survival*, and the 'Leasebook of the manor of Castledillon, Co. Armagh with very detailed observations by William Molyneux,' c. 1700, P.R.O.N.I., film 80/3.

89 Currie, 'Evolution,' p. 163; Macafee, 'Maghera region,' pp. 80–81.

90 On land outside plantation territory bogs might still have legal status as commons. Power, *Tipperary*, pp. 166–67, 170.

91 McCourt, 'Decline of rundale,' p. 124.

92 James Sinclair to eighth earl of Abercorn, 26 Mar. 1758, P.R.O.N.I., Abercorn papers, T2541/IA1/5/1.

93 Hamilton to Abercorn, 5 June 1764, ibid., T2541/IA1/6C/33.

94 Idem, 29 Dec. 1786 and 29 May 1787, ibid., T2541/IA2/4/2,40.

95 Currie, 'Evolution,' pp. 131, 138, 140. Kenneth H. Connell, 'The colonization of wasteland in Ireland, 1780–1845' in *Economic history review*, 2nd series, iii (1950), pp. 44–71.

96 Macafee, 'Maghera region,' p. 83.

97 Aalen, *Man and the landscape*, p. 140. David Ryan, in *The Irish practical farmers and gardeners* (Dublin, 1838, p. 80) wrote that potatoes 'are the greatest improvers of ground, so much so that they are the best preparatory crop for wheat.' Crawford, 'The political economy of linen,' pp. 140–143.

98 Buchanan, 'Barony of Lecale,' p. 146.

99 Hamilton to Abercorn, 21 Sept. 1785, P.R.O.N.I., Abercorn papers, T2541/IA1/15/25.

100 Report of the deputation appointed by the court of assistants of the Fishmongers' company, 22 Oct. 1846, Fishmongers' Hall court minutes, N.L.I., film 1515.

101 *Ordnance Survey Memoirs, County Londonderry*, quoted in Joel Mokyr, 'Irish history with the potato' in *I.E.S.H.*, viii, 1981, p. 11. There is early evidence of potato cultivation on the Murray of Broughton estate near Ballyshannon, Co. Donegal. James Hamilton to John Murray of Broughton, 11 July 1729, P.R.O.N.I., Murray of Broughton papers, D2860/12/22.

102 Dowling, 'Abercorn estate,' p. 29.

103 Joseph Calhoun to eighth earl of Abercorn, 11 Apr. 1745, P.R.O.N.I., Abercorn papers, T2541/IA1/1B/45.

104 Hamilton to Abercorn, 15 Apr. 1770, ibid., T2541/IA1/9/2; idem, 2 Sept. 1770, ibid., T2541/IA1/9/6; idem, 31 July 1778, ibid., T2541/IA2/2/4; idem, 27 July 1783, ibid., T2541/IA2/3/4.

105 James Hamilton, Jr., to ninth earl of Abercorn, 16 May 1800 and 18 May 1800, ibid., T2541/IA2/9/14, 20.

106 Idem, 11 June 1808, ibid., D623/A/99/27.

107 Idem, 22 Apr. 1783, 24 Apr. 1794, and 18 Apr. 1800, ibid., T2541/IA2/6/7, T2541/IA2/9/20, T2541/IA2/3/30.

108 William McDonnell to Sir Hugh Crofton, 8 Feb. 1822, N.L.I., MS 20,773.

109 Irish society court minute books, 20 Nov. 1845, N.L.I., film 1525, p. 73.

110 Report of the deputation appointed by the court of assistants of the Fishmongers' company, 22 Oct. 1846, Fishmongers' Hall court minutes, N.L.I., film 1515.

111 Report by John Lanktree, 1847, P.R.O.N.I., Earl of Antrim papers, D2977/6/4.

112 Ibid. The Drapers' company agent reported in 1845: 'The mountain districts where the soil is light have suffered less [from potato blight] than the lowlands where the soil is better, and better manured and cultivated.' Rowley and J.R. Miller to Edward Lawford, 7 Nov. 1845, P.R.O.N.I., Drapers' company papers, D3632/1/1.

113 Millers to Lawford, 31 May 1847, ibid. 'Every year since the squaring has been unfavourable for mountain crops [oats] upon which they depend for their rent and which are not cut until late in the season.' Millers to Lawford, 12 Feb. 1845, ibid.

114 See Greig's explanation of the demographic intensification over the previous sixty years from 1821. Greig, *General report*, p. 149.

115 Desmond McCourt, 'Infield and outfield in Ireland' in *Economic history review*, vii, no. 3 (April, 1955), p. 376. In his dissertation he argued that in Irish rundale 'collectivism and individualism are not evolutionary stages. The predominance of one over the other depends on technical and social conditions. They often thrive together in the same society.' McCourt, 'Rundale system,' p. 320.

116 Philip Robinson, 'Irish settlement in Tyrone before the Ulster plantation' in *Ulster folklife*, xxii (1976), p. 66.

117 For a discussion of the literature, see Dodgshon, *Origin*, p. 12.

118 By 'demographic context' we mean the conjunction of climatological and biological factors and technical forces of production governing the mortality rate, the social components of peasant agriculture bearing on the infertility rate, and the intrafeudal and intermonarchical warring that results in what cliometricians call 'excess mortality.'

119 Dodgshon, *Origin*, pp. 75–8.

120 William the Conqueror's devastation of Yorkshire provides his example. A.W.B. Simpson, *A history of land law*, 2nd ed. (Oxford, 1986), quoted in Thompson, 'Custom, law, and common right,' p. 127.

121 McCabe, 'Law, conflict, and social order,' p. 353. Subdivision was actually quite modest in Mayo between 1815 and 1845. Ibid., pp. 22–3.

122 Ibid., p. 127. McCabe also emphasizes that women bore the burden of the communal limits to subdivision operating in rundale communities, especially younger daughters and widows.

123 Ibid., pp. 22, 457–8.

124 Ibid., pp. 29–33, 35, 128–140.

125 The *locus classicus* is George Hill, *Facts from Gweedore*, reprint of fifth edition, with intro. by E.E. Evans (Belfast, 1971).

126 [?] Rutherford to [?] Beer, 17 Apr. and 13 Mar. 1841, P.R.O.N.I., Anglesey papers, D619/23/B/9,10; Rutherford to Beer, 16 Mar. 1842, ibid., D619/23/B/59.

127 Report of a deputation appointed by the court the 12th of Apr. 1827, 1 Aug. 1827, Fishmongers' Hall court minutes, Guildhall library, London, N.L.I., film 1515.

128 Rowley and J.R. Miller to Edward Lawford, 12 Feb. 1845, ibid., D3632/1/1.

129 See W.H. Crawford, 'Economy and society in eighteenth-century Ulster' (PhD. dissertation, Queen's University-Belfast, 1982), pp. 104–132.

130 [Brabazon] Noble to Thomas Barrett-Lennard, 18 Feb. 1760, P.R.O.N.I., Barrett-Lennard papers, film 170/2; Robert Hutchinson to Henry Bayly, 29 Aug. 1774, ibid., D619/21/C/100; letters of Edward McGildowney and Alexander Miller, 1839–40, P.R.O.N.I., McGildowney papers, D1375/3/79; 'Observations on the state of the tenantry in Leitrim,' 27 Dec. 1839, N.L.I., Leitrim papers, MS 3829; Rowley and J.R. Miller to Edward Lawford, 17 Aug. 1843, P.R.O.N.I., Drapers' company papers, D3632/3/4; memorial of the tenants of Brackaslievegallon division, 16 May 1844, ibid., D3632/1/1; memorial of James Kearney of Drumconready, 6 June 1844, minutes of the court of assistants, extracts relating to Irish estates, Drapers' Hall, London, N.L.I., film 1529.

131 [?] to [?], 15 Aug. 1843, N.L.I., Lane Fox papers, film 4063.

132 J.G.M. Harvey to G.V. Hunt, 21 Dec. 1876, P.R.O.N.I., Hart papers, D3077/G/15/30.

133 Rowley and J.R Miller to Edward Lawford, 1 October 1845, P.R.O.N.I., Drapers' company papers, D3632/1/1.

134 Edmund McGildowney to Robert McNaghton, 18 Jan. 1821, P.R.O.N.I., McGildowney papers, D1375/1/16; McGildowney to Lord Mark Kerr, 7 May 1821, ibid., D1375/1/16; agent memorandum, 18 May 1855, P.R.O.N.I., Brookeborough papers, D998/8/1. J.R. Moore to H. Wilson, 28 Feb. 1840, P.R.O.N.I., Annesley papers, D1845/6/1, p. 153. The supply of turf to urban centres was especially problematic. Edmund McGildowney to Richard Waring, 25 Aug. 1813, P.R.O.N.I., McGildowney papers, D1375/1/5.

135 William Maxwell to bishop Frederick Hervey-Bruce, 25 Aug. 1773, P.R.O.N.I., Hervey-Bruce papers, D2798/3/15.

136 J.G.M. Harvey to G.V. Hart, 15 July 1876, P.R.O.N.I., Hart papers, D3077/G/8,15/28.

137 Idem, 5 and 23 Apr. 1877, ibid., D3077/G/15/34.

138 George Joy, agent of the Mountcashel estate, allowed free turf and access to moss bawns. He threatened to take away these rights from a man who diverted the path of a watercourse. George Joy to Henry Raphael, 5 Apr. 1837, P.R.O.N.I., Mountcashel papers, T1289/19.

139 James Rooney to Nicholas Bayly, 30 Dec. 1742, P.R.O.N.I., Anglesey papers, D619/21/B/45; Stanley Monke to Thomas Conolly, 1 Dec. 1780, T.C.D., Conolly papers, MS 3974–84/701; Rev. John Wilson to William Ogilvie, various letters 1807–1808, P.R.O.N.I., Ogilvie papers, T1546/1; Edmund McGildowney to Lady Mark Kerr, 15 Oct. 1813, P.R.O.N.I., McGildowney papers, D1375/1/5; James Alexander to George Portis, 15 May 1772, P.R.O.N.I., Donegal papers, T1893; James Clulow to Rev. Kennedy, 26 May 1801, P.R.O.N.I., Perceval-Maxwell papers, D3244/B/4/12; James Fawcett to John Dickson, 5 Oct. 1833, N.L.I., Playdell papers, film 7648. Rev. Clotworthy Soden to bishop Frederick Hervey-Bruce, 18 June 1785, P.R.O.N.I., Hervey-Bruce papers, D2798/3/45; Irish Society court minute books, 10 Sept. 1805, N.L.I., film 1521.

140 [?] Armstrong to earl of Uxbridge, 6 May 1839, P.R.O.N.I., Anglesey papers, D619/23/A/301; idem, 30 June 1839, ibid., D619/23/A/310.

141 Idem, 26 Nov. 1839, ibid., D619/23/A/313; idem, 11 Apr. and 3 June 1840, ibid., D619/23/A/3/17,18; idem, 25 May 1840, ibid., D619/23/A/320, 321; S. Moore to Armstrong, 23 May 1840, ibid., D619/23/A/323.

142 John Anderson to earl of Caledon, 18 Dec. 1815, P.R.O.N.I., Caledon papers, D2433/A/2/15/1.

143 James Hamilton to eighth earl of Abercorn, 12 Dec. 1779, P.R.O.N.I., Abercorn papers, T2541/IA2/2/116.

144 James Hamilton, Jr., to ninth earl of Abercorn, 23 Nov. 1800, ibid., T2541/IA2/9/38.

145 Report of a statement made by the law and general agents, 3 Feb. 1817, Irish Society court minute books, N.L.I., film 1522.

146 George Joy to William Hutchinson, 11 June 1843, P.R.O.N.I., Mountcashel papers, T1289/19. The stated goal of the Brookeborough estate agent in 1883 was to get all turf rented to tenants at full price. Frederick Wrench to A.L. Barlee, 18 June 1883, P.R.O.N.I., Brookeborough papers, D998/6/2, p. 92.

147 'Report of a deputation by the Court of Assistants of the Fishmongers' company, the 18th of June 1832, to visit their estate in the County Londonderry, Ireland,' 25 Oct. 1832, Fishmongers' Hall court minutes, Guildhall Library, London, N.L.I., film 1514.

148 Rowley and J.R. Miller to Edward Lawford, 11 May 1844, P.R.O.N.I., Drapers' company papers, D3632/1/1.

149 Idem, 1 Mar. 1845, ibid.

150 James Hannah to James Agnew, 3 Sept. 1861, P.R.O.N.I., Earl of Antrim papers, D2977/4/3.

151 Archdeacon Trail to Robert McNaghton, 15 Apr. 1816, P.R.O.N.I., McGildowney papers, D1375/2/4/17.

152 Robert McNaghton to Edmund McGildowney, 16 Apr. 1816, ibid.

153 Petition of Redmond O'Hanlon of Ardaghy, 30 July 1785, P.R.O.N.I., Anglesey papers, D619/11/71

154 John Tasburgh to George Browne, 22 Mar. 1679, P.R.O.N.I., Kilmaine papers, T3134/1/1; lease of Cong to John Browne of Neale, n.d., ibid., T3134/3/10.

155 Johnston, 'Balfour rentals,' p. 94.

156 Gillespie, *Colonial Ulster*, p. 154.

157 Ibid., p. 125. For the use of the term 'peaceable possession' in Sligo in 1694, see Henry Crofton to Kean O'Hara, 14 Sept. 1694, P.R.O.N.I., O'Hara papers, T2812/4/120.

158 Edward Bayly to William Stannus, 26 Oct. 1716, P.R.O.N.I., Anglesey papers, D619/22/E/1.

159 Petitions, two identical, 14 Feb. 1778, P.R.O.N.I., Anglesey papers, D619/5/13,14.

160 James Rooney to Nicholas Bayly, 29 Jan. 1745, P.R.O.N.I., Anglesey papers, D619/21/B/66; Rooney to Bayly, 19 July 1742, ibid., D619/21/B/35; [?] to [?], n.d. [c. 1775?], P.R.O.N.I., McCartney papers, D572/18/48.

161 James Hamilton to eighth earl of Abercorn, 25 May 1781, P.R.O.N.I., Abercorn papers, T2541/IA1/13/98.

162 Idem, quoted in McCourt, 'Decline of rundale,' p. 124.

163 Petition, n.d., P.R.O.N.I., Anglesey papers, D619/11/21.

164 Petition of Henry Kearney and his partners, 29 July 1785, ibid., D619/11/69.

165 Petition of six tenants of Gortnamoyagh, n.d., ibid., D619/11/110.

166 [?] Armstrong to earl of Uxbridge, July 1836, ibid., D619/23/A/264.

167 Richard Waring to Edmund McGildowney, letters of 1802, P.R.O.N.I., McGildowney papers, D1375/3/2/1, 8, 10.

168 McGildowney to McNaghton, 13 Feb. 1819, ibid., D1375/2/7/2A; idem, 13 July 1819, ibid., D1375/2/7/17; idem, 18 Jan. 1821, ibid., D1375/1/16; McNaghton to McGildowney, 19 Jan. 1821, ibid., D1375/2/9/10.

169 McGildowney to McNaghton, 27 June 1820, ibid., D1375/1/15. The strategy was to sell Ballywillan bog, and therefore it was only to be set from year to year. McNaghton to McGildowney, 5 Apr. 1823, ibid., D1375/2/12/1.

170 McGildowney to McNaghton, 9 Apr. 1824, ibid., D1375/1/20.

171 Thomas Beere to Charles O'Hara, 21 June 1835, N.L.I., O'Hara papers, MS 20,321; [?] to M. Cooper, 5 May 1844, ibid., MS 20,321(13).

172 Award of Richard Jackson and Marcus McCausland, 3 Oct. 1775, P.R.O.N.I., Hervey-Bruce papers, D2798/3/25. This dispute was also referred to in Rowley Hedland to Bishop of Kilrea, 6 Oct. 1769, ibid., D2798/3/7.

173 R.C. Brush to earl of Belmore, 23 Dec. 1875, P.R.O.N.I., Belmore papers, D3007/V/131.

174 J.R. Moore to Mr. [?] Lees, 13 Jan. 1842, P.R.O.N.I., Annesley papers, D1854/6/2; Edmund McGildowney to James McNaghton, 8 Nov. 1814, P.R.O.N.I., McGildowney papers, D1375/1/6.

175 R.C. Brush to earl of Belmore, 25 Dec. 1875, P.R.O.N.I., Belmore papers, D3007/V/131.

176 Idem, 1 Jan. 1876, ibid., D3007/V/134.

177 Hunter, 'Ulster plantation,' pp. 423–4.

178 Brabazon Noble to Thomas Barrett-Lennard, 13 Nov. 1753, P.R.O.N.I., Barrett-Lennard papers, film 170/2. But in 1770 it was reported that plans for Nixon's bog had failed, the poor cottagers had not improved, claiming they had no security, and the grazing rights were left in dispute. Thomas Noble to Barrett-Lennard, 23 Jan. 1770, ibid.

179 John Todd to [Richard Barrett-Lennard], 11 Apr. 1755, ibid.

180 Memorial of tenants of Upper Drumcask near Swanlinbar, Co. Cavan, 24 July 1822, N.L.I., Letters to Sir Hugh Crofton relating to his Cavan and Monaghan estates, MSS 20,773.

181 John Alcock to Thomas Conolly, 5 Nov. 1800, T.C.D., Conolly papers, MS 3974–84/1368. It is interesting that Alcock *asked permission* to pay rent, so that his right to the cabin would remain clear, rather than accept at no rent the bog nearest to him: 'But give me leave sir to repeat my request of being charged a rent for the plain reason that as the nearest bog to me on your lands will allow me to make but four turns in a summer day's drawing, a more distant place even at no rent, though a kindness intended by you, would be hardly worth my acceptance. But when I am to pay rent, I may be permitted like any other tenant to negotiate for what will answer me.' Ibid.

182 Observations on Terrydremont, Limavady estate, c. 1770, P.R.O.N.I., Castletown papers, D2094/45.

183 These ambiguities of property rights often entered into the tensions between head tenants and undertenants, as in the case of George Leitch and Robert Harper of the Abercorn estate, who attempted to oust undertenants immediately after they had enclosed and ditched a great deal of land. James Hamilton to eighth earl of Abercorn, 13 Dec. 1770 and 2 Aug. 1771, P.R.O.N.I., Abercorn papers, T2541/IA1/9/87, T2541/IA1/9/133.

184 Henry Smith to Rowley Miller, 7 Apr. 1824, P.R.O.N.I., Drapers' company papers, D3632/3/2.

185 Lawford to Miller, 6 Dec. 1828, ibid.

186 Report of a deputation, 3 Dec. 1836, Irish Society court minute books, N.L.I., film 1523.

187 Masterson, 'Land use patterns,' pp. 61–2.

188 Agent report and valuation, n.d. [c. 1850], P.R.O.N.I., Earl of Antrim papers, D2977/6/5; 'Observations on the state of the tenantry in Leitrim,' 1838, N.L.I., Leitrim papers, MS 3238; [Thomas Beer] to Rutherford, n.d. [1841], P.R.O.N.I., Anglesey papers, D619/23/B/1.

189 The squaring project was described in a letter of 1845. Rowley and J.R Miller to Edward Lawford, 1 October 1845. They were apparently acting independently of the even more ambitious project of Sir George Hill in Gweedore, Co. Donegal.

190 Idem, 12 Feb. 1845, P.R.O.N.I., Drapers' company papers, D3632/1/1. Two years later, they recognized that there was much squaring still to be accomplished in the poorest townlands. Idem, 13 July 1847, ibid.

191 Richard Wilson to Lady Londonderry [cover letter to 'Report on Lady Londonderry's Antrim estate in two parts by James Douglas, agriculturalist,'] 26 Nov. 1856, P.R.O.N.I., Londonderry papers, D2977/6/10. Some years earlier John Lanktree, agent of the Earl of Antrim's estate, boasted that he had finally found a replacement for a tenant who was refusing to give his goodwill to anyone 'after much canvassing' in Newtownards. 'Report on Lady Londonderry's Antrim estate by John Lanktree,' 4 Sept. 1844, P.R.O.N.I., Earl of Antrim papers, D2977/6/3.

192 Henry Smith to James Smyth, 17 Dec. 1819, P.R.O.N.I., Drapers' company papers, D3632/3/1; minutes of the court of assistants, extracts relating to Irish estates, 16 Nov. 1843, Drapers' Hall, London, N.L.I., film 1529.

193 In 1851 the Millers warned that getting tenants from squared farms on to nearby estates was not sufficient 'as they will return and squat down as near as they can to where they formerly resided.' Rowley and J.R. Miller to Lawford, 26 Apr. 1851, P.R.O.N.I., Drapers' company papers, D3632/1/2; Millers to Lawford, 26 Jan. 1850, ibid.

194 Idem, 13 Dec. 1849, ibid.

195 James Hamilton to eighth earl of Abercorn, 31 Jan. 1780, P.R.O.N.I., Abercorn papers, T2541/IA1/13/6.

196 Memorandum of Thomas Addi of Donaghadee, c. 1730, P.R.O.N.I., Murray of Broughton papers, D2860/25/3/35.

197 Hamilton to Abercorn, 4 Sept. 1786, P.R.O.N.I., Abercorn papers, T2541/IA2/4/17.

198 [?] to earl of Uxbridge, 28 Jan. 1816, P.R.O.N.I., Anglesey papers, D619/23/A/93; Uxbridge to Armstrong, 13 Feb. 1816, ibid., D619/23/A/97; Uxbridge to Armstrong, 4 May 1817, ibid., D619/23/A/109; Rev. Edward Bailey to John Hatch, [?] Apr. 1766, P.R.O.N.I., Downshire papers, D607/A/265.

199 In Carlingford the practice of assassinating informers interfered with the agents' collection of information relevant to the management of the estate. Armstrong to Uxbridge, 26 March 1816, P.R.O.N.I., Anglesey papers, D619/23/A/99. The houses of farmers who had 'taken lands of which others were dispossessed either for mis-conduct or for non-payment of rent' were attacked. Others who had taken farms on the promise of paying the arrears outstanding from them, 'thereby assisting the person by whom the arrear had been incurred,' were attacked by a large mob. [?] to Anglesey, 28 Jan. 1816, ibid., D619/23/A/93. William Blacker's agriculturalist had twice narrowly escaped assassination. William Blacker to Kyle, 30 March 1846, P.R.O.N.I., Gosford papers, D1606/5/1.

200 Donnell, *Reports*, p. 91.

201 Millers to Lawford, 28 May, 11 June and 29 June 1850, P.R.O.N.I., Drapers' company papers, D3632/1/2.

202 'Report of the deputation appointed by the court of assistants of the Fishmongers' company on the 18th of June 1832 to visit their estate in the county Londonderry, Ireland,' 25 Oct. 1832, Fishmongers' Hall court minutes, N.L.I., film 1515. The agents of the Playdell estate in Leitrim advertised a farm for thirteen months without successfully filling the vacancy and had to return it to the former tenant and

forgive him his arrears of rent. William Johnston and Francis Fawcett to John Dickson, 27 January 1843, N.L.I., Playdell papers, film 7648.

203 Gourley, 'Gosford estate,' pp. 150–151.

204 Minutes of the court of assitants, extracts relating to Irish estates, 22 May 1845, Drapers' Hall, N.L.I., film 1529.

205 Rowley and J.R. Miller to Edward Lawford, 26 May 1845, P.R.O.N.I., Drapers' company papers, D3632/1/1.

206 For an interesting account, see Eull Dunlop (ed.), *Buick's Ahoghill, a filial account, 1901 of seceders in the Mid-Antrim village . . . from 1835 to 1980*, forward by Christopher Raphael and R.E.H. Uprichard (Maghera, 1987), pp. 95–97. See also R. C. Brush to earl of Belmore, 6 June 1881, P.R.O.N.I., Belmore papers, D3007/V/309; John H. Howe to marquis of Dufferin, 19 Feb. 1881, P.R.O.N.I., Dufferin papers, D1071A/K; James Crossle to Lady Verner, 2 Jan. 1882, P.R.O.N.I., Verner papers, D236/488/2, p. 341.

207 [?] Corbett to [Edward] Bayly, 26 Jan. 1734, P.R.O.N.I., Anglesey papers, D619/21/A/10; Michael Ward to Bernard Ward, 28 Oct. 1757, P.R.O.N.I., Castleward papers, D2092/1/8, p. 78; James MacCartney to Thomas Barrett-Lennard, 4 Feb. 1830, P.R.O.N.I., Barrett-Lennard papers, film 170/3.

208 Irish estate committee of management minutes, 29 Apr. 1847 and 1 Nov. 1849, Merchant Tailors' Hall, N.L.I., film 1517; J.R. Moore to Captain Despard, 29 May 1843, P.R.O.N.I., Annesley papers, D1854/6/5; Robert Perceval-Maxwell to James Murlands, 5 Dec. 1874, P.R.O.N.I., Perceval Maxwell papers, D1556/2/2; [?] to DL. Coddington, 30 June 1881, ibid., D856/B6/35.

209 Armstrong to Uxbridge, 26 September 1805, P.R.O.N.I., Anglesey papers, D619/23/A/15.

210 James Hamilton to eighth earl of Abercorn, 19 Jan. 1766, P.R.O.N.I., Abercorn papers, T2541/IA1/7/5; idem, 10 Feb. and 12 Apr. 1766, ibid., T2541/ IA1/7/57, 67; idem, 3 Oct. 1769, ibid., T2541/IA1/8/159; idem, 5 Sept. 1758, ibid., T2541/IA1/5/44; idem, 11 Sept. 1770, ibid., T2541/IA1/9/64.

211 Robert Ward to Justice Ward, 4 Nov. 1738, P.R.O.N.I., Castleward papers, D2092/1/5.

212 James Hamilton, Jr., to Abercorn, 25 May 1785, ibid., T2541/IA1/21/11. F.E. Foljambe wrote to his agent in 1799 to inquire into a dispute presented before him by a tenant who is 'still kept out of a part of his land by his neighbours.' F.E. Foljambe to James Speer, 24 July 1799, P.R.O.N.I., Foljambe papers, T3381/5/21.

213 Blacker, *Prize essay* p. 32.

214 Vaughan, *Landlords & tenants*, pp. 87, 161, 142.

215 Rowley and J.R. Miller to Edward Lawford, 16 May, 1846. 'The feeling in this country is *universal*, no man will enter into the farm of another without having his *goodwill* of it, that is he must satisfy the outgoing tenant with more or less money. . . .' Millers to Lawford, 23 June 1848, ibid.

216 Ibid., p. 87.

217 'It is a reasonable suspicion that the policy of each religion selling only to its own kind was yet another part of a growing fabric of accommodation between differentiated subsocieties.' Wright, *Two lands one soil*, pp. 86, 88, 99.

218 Minutes of the court of assitants, extracts relating to Irish estates, 6 Dec. 1821, Drapers' Hall, London, N.L.I., film 1529. Also in the minutes is a memorial of the Roman Catholics of the estate declaring that they are not Ribbonmen, with 509 signatures. The agent had two weeks previously recommended that those in this 'combination of Catholics' without leases should be put out. Henry Smith to Rowley Miller, 17 Nov. 1821, P.R.O.N.I., Drapers' company records, D3632/3/2.

219 Henry Smith to Rev. [?] Murphy, 11 Dec. 1821, P.R.O.N.I., Drapers' company papers, D3632/3/2.

220 Henry Smith to Rowley Miller, 12 Dec. 1821, ibid.

221 Robert Lowry enforced a rule on his estate in Westmeath that any tenant in common could force co-partners into a partition, with all sharing any litigation costs. Charles Gaussen [?] to Robert Lowry, 31 Mar. 1832, P.R.O.N.I., Lowry papers, D1132/1/4.

222 A tenant of Sir Hugh Crofton remarked on the high rent he was paying and noted that he has 'improved the farm and exhausted a great deal of money on it which now induces me to offer to become a tenant and take out a lease provided you make me the necessary abatement. It is the worst farm in Glynn, lying very high on the mountain and running in a narrow stripe to the road.' A. O'Brien, White Rock, Ballinamore, to Hugh Crofton, 22 July 1830, N.L.I., letters to Sir Hugh Crofton relating to his County Cavan and Monaghan estates, MS 20,773.

223 Greig, *General report*, p. 145.

224 Edmund Kaine to Dacre Barrett, 6 Oct. 1715, P.R.O.N.I., Barrett-Lennard papers, film 170/2.

225 Samuel Hynchman, *et. al.*, to Thomas Conolly, n.d. [c. 1720], P.R.O.N.I., Castletown papers, T2825/C/12/5; see also William Doherty to William McCausland, 18 May 1737, P.R.O.N.I., Pike-Fortescue papers, T2913/1/20.

226 R.C. Brush to earl of Belmore, 28 May 1863, P.R.O.N.I., Belmore papers, D3007/V/2; James Fawcett to Lady Playdell, 11 Dec. 1828, N.L.I., Playdell papers, film 7648; James Fawcett to John Dickson, 25 Apr. and 9 July 1834, ibid.

227 Robert Hutchinson to Henry Bayly, 11 Nov. 1770, P.R.O.N.I., Anglesey papers, D619/21/C/30; Hutchinson to Bayly, 11 Aug. 1770, ibid., D619/21/C/23; tenant petition, n.d., P.R.O.N.I., Anglesey papers, D619/11/38; tenant petition, 25 July 1785, ibid., D619/11/44.

228 Robert Hutchinson to Henry Bayly, 22 Nov. 1775, ibid., D619/21/C/128; Bayly to Hutchinson, 6 Feb. 1769, ibid., D619/21/C/5; Hutchinson to Bayly, 4 June 1783, ibid., D619/21/D/3. This problem affected another townland as well, and resisting tenants referred to the promise of the landlord's father 'that they should never be deprived of their holdings' or mentioned that 'they have been tenants in Sheeptown for sixty years.' Tenant petitions, 2 Jan. 1794, ibid., D619/11/81 and 16 Jan. [1790?], ibid., D619/11/109.

229 Open advertising might not necessarily mean that no right of renewal was recognised. The appearance of a market might hide actual practices of tenants refusing to bid each other up. Dickson, 'Cork region,' p. 303. In the 1770s large segments of land again came up for reletting in Munster. Bids were solicited in advertisements placed in such papers as the *Cork Evening Post, Finn's Leinster Journal* and the *Munster Journal*. This, according to Power, 'represented a departure from the customary practice of renewing the term and tenure of the sitting tenant. That these were not lands being let for the first time can be implied from the inclusion in the public notices declaring the landlords' intention of auctioning them, of the terms 'no preference given,' 'proposals in writing only,' and 'now in the possession of'.' Power, *Tipperary*, p. 135. Power does not provide any direct evidence of the customary practice of renewing sitting tenants. The result was the intimidation of bidders by the sitting tenants.

230 [?] to [?], 1 Oct. 1774, P.R.O.N.I., McCartney papers, D572/18/3.

231 James Hamilton to eighth earl of Abercorn, 17 Sept. 1769, P.R.O.N.I., Abercorn papers, T2541/IA1/8/155.
232 Idem, 18 Sept. 1785, ibid., T2541/IA1/15/24.
233 Idem, 19 Mar. 1767, ibid., T2541/IA1/7/63.
234 John McClintock to Abercorn, 26 June 1750, ibid., T2541/IA1/2/18.
235 Idem, 27 July 1750, ibid., T2541/IA1/2/19.
236 Maguire, *Downshire estates*, p. 133.
237 Edward Lawford to Rowley and J.R. Miller, 22 May 1843, P.R.O.N.I., Drapers' company papers, D3632/3/4; Millers to Lawford, 7 Nov. 1843, ibid., D3632/1/1; Millers to Lawford, 6 Feb. 1844, ibid.; minutes of the court of assistants, extracts relating to Irish estates, 22 Feb. 1844, Drapers' Hall, London, N.L.I., film 1529.
238 Frederick Wrench to Edward Bamford, 3 Mar. 1882, P.R.O.N.I., Brookeborough papers, D998/6/1, p. 854; Joseph Ferguson and John Williamson to D.L. Coddington, [?] Oct. 1879, A.S. Crawford to [?] Dixie, 15 Oct. 1879, P.R.O.N.I., Sharman Crawford papers, D.856/B6/38. See also agent valuation, n.d. [c. 1848], P.R.O.N.I., Earl of Antrim papers, D2977/6/5.
239 Millers to Lawford, 1 October 1845, P.R.O.N.I, Draper's company papers, D. 3632/1/1.
240 A report of 1831 stated that the smallness of farms also prevented effective drainage, unless closely regulated by the agent. Main drains would have to be built through numerous adjacent holdings. Report of Robert Stewart, 25 June 1831, N.L.I., Lane Fox papers, film 4064.
241 J.B. Bankhead to Edmund McDonnell, 5 Aug. 1851, P.R.O.N.I., Earl of Antrim papers, D2977/4/3. 'The agriculturalist and I have spent much time in endeavouring to get farms so divided as regards fencing as to enable tenants to adopt a proper rotation of crops.' Report of James McLanahan to John Waring, 28 March 1845, P.R.O.N.I., Perceval-Maxwell papers, D3244/E/26/17.
242 Millers to Lawford, 16 April 1844, P.R.O.N.I., Drapers' company papers, D3632/1/1A.
243 Anonymous letter on the possible improvement of the Antrim estate, c. 1812, N.L.I., MS 8125, 4.
244 Report of a deputation, 3 Dec. 1836, Irish Society court minute books, N.L.I., film 1523.
245 'Report on Lady Londonderry's estate in baronies of Glenarm and Kilconway by John Andrews,' 1837, P.R.O.N.I., Earl of Antrim papers, D2977/6/1.
246 Report of James McLanahan to John Waring, 28 Mar. 1845, P.R.O.N.I., Perceval-Maxwell papers, D3244/E/26/17.
247 Millers to Lawford, 25 May 1848, P.R.O.N.I., Drapers' company papers, D3632/1/1.
248 Marquis of Dufferin to Mortimer Thomson, 23 Feb. 1866, P.R.O.N.I., Dufferin papers, D1071A/K/Box 2.
249 Marquis of Dufferin and Ava, *Irish emigration and the tenure of land in Ireland* (Dublin, 1870), p. 196. He elaborated on this in Bessborough testimony, explaining that the reason that landlords do not invest in their estates is not so much that they lack the capital that the capital requirements are both unusually high and unremunerative on overcrowded estates where the farms are too small. *Bessborough comm. evidence*, question 1216. This also affected his view of a fair rent. Small farmers cannot survive because they could not pay a 'fair rent – such a rent as the occupants of adjoining farms of larger extent are able to pay with advantage to themselves.' Ibid., question 1483.
250 William Sharman Crawford to Marquis of Downshire, 1 Feb. 1859, P.R.O.N.I., Sharman Crawford papers, D856/D/140.

CHAPTER FIVE

The Advance of Estate Management

The inflation of property values, the growth of agricultural output, and the increasing density of the rural population in the half-century after 1780 deepened the complexity of the management of Irish estates. By the second third of the nineteenth century, the tenantry had become more socially differentiated, their tenurial histories more complex, economic opportunities more uncertain, the web of credit and debt between different strata of rural society more confusing and impenetrable, and the custom of tenant right more commercialized, than at any point in the history of rural Ulster before or since. The previous chapters revealed a number of the difficulties inherent in the management of eighteenth-century estates: problems dealing with untrustworthy agents and overmighty middlemen, the morass of multilayered tenancies (Chapter 2), the maintenance of a tenurial structure conducive to the development of viable rural commercial enterprises, the entanglements of credit and debt (Chapter 3), and the tenurial complications caused by the colonization, occupation, and cultivation of land in closely knit and demographically expanding farming communities (Chapter 4). The evidence from various northern estates in the eighteenth century rehearsed in these chapters shows a strong contrast between aggressively and effectively managed estates such as the Abercorn estate in County Tyrone or the Downshire estate in County Down and those on which competent and active management developed in the wake of dramatic economic change. As Crawford remarks, 'only when the transformation occurred did many landlords realize that they had lost effective control over their estates because there were too many tenants.'[1] As the previous three chapters make clear, there was much at stake in the effort to come to grips with tenant right. If estate managers could gain control of the tenant-right system operating on their estates, they could obtain a greater facility for managing the complicated tenurial and economic relationships of their tenantry, for promoting the productivity of their tenants and the profitability of their estates, for ridding their lands of impoverished and indebted residents, for rationalizing and visually reorganizing the layout of farms, and for replacing a communal, familial, and historical orientation to property rights with one based strictly on contracts. But in order to achieve these goals landlords had to embark on a concerted campaign to wrest control of the system from the tenants. The struggle took place over a wide range of times and places from the early seventeenth century to the Victorian period. This chapter suggests that by the famine decade of the nineteenth century a managerial revolution was largely complete.

THE INCREASING COMPLEXITIES OF ESTATE MANAGEMENT

The simple fact of demographic growth was itself a significant challenge to managers and should not be underemphasized. The problem was one of supervision. On the Abercorn estate after 1770 it was more common to find agents expressing concern for the size of the estate population, the nature of productive employment, and the size of specific groups of tenants: the poor, cottiers, widows, freeholders, and those available for military service.[2] In the last decades of the century Hamilton was more prone to refer to 'the poor,' the 'distressed,' or to 'the cottiers' when discussing the estate tenantry, rather than referring exclusively to specific individuals, as had been his earlier practice.[3] It was a difficult job, and not all agents were equal to the task. Ó Gráda judges that in tillage and protoindustrial zones throughout Ireland, 'a reluctance to negotiate leases and rent levels directly with hundreds of small tillage farmers made for a more passive landlordism.'[4] Because it was 'impossible to keep an eye on' so numerous a tenantry, an agent of the Downshire estate at Kilwarlin, Co. Down, in 1815, felt that covenants in the leases 'are almost considered generally as a mere dead letter.'[5] Perceptive landlords hired more and better qualified agents. The new breed were sometimes merchants or resident head tenants, but the most notable among them were attorneys. The scope of agent duties expanded beyond the traditional role of making leases and collecting rents to include accounting and collection of arrears, the distribution of plots of bog, and the management of large-scale relettings. Landlords ignored these developments to their own great financial peril. And those who did so were as likely as not to be liquidated by the crisis of the 1840s.[6]

The job of the land agent had as much to do with managing capital as with managing people. To properly control capital, agents had to control the vertical movement of assets from tenants to landlords in the form of rent, but also to manage the horizontal flow of capital between tenants through the tenant-right market. An example from the Anglesey estate in the 1730s shows how difficult this latter task could be. Captain Murray, a head tenant of a particularly valuable townland,[7] set the land to 'a numerous train of weak tenants – in number, they say, about fifty – and not ten of the whole tribe worth ten pounds apiece.'[8] In the following decade Murray was in such a poor financial condition that he mortgaged the lease, to the peril of both the landlord and the undertenants. The agent worriedly reported in 1743: 'As to Captain Murray's affair, I have no manner of hope of having his lease preserved, and I dread the consequence of it falling into the hands of a stranger; however, all that is in my power to serve him shall not be wanting, but the people's patience are worn out with promises and disappointments.'[9] A month later, the worst had happened: 'Captain Murray's lease is mortgaged; the money it is mortgaged for is about £100. The profit rent of it is above nine pounds a year, and if that lease was sold, as it soon must be unless redeemed, or if it was in the hands of a stranger,' it would mean a heavy loss to the estate because the land contained all the sea wrack. Apparently, there was a long-standing dispute between Murray and other tenants over the rights to the wrack. The undertenants pledged to pay no rent to the new owner of the lease and demanded the agent's support. Furthermore, it appeared that the rents not only of Murray but of his two mortgagees were intractably in arrears. Fearing an uproar from the undertenants, the agent recommended that the landlord find someone 'in trust to you' to buy out all three of them.[10]

By the latter third of the nineteenth century dealing with these local interconnections of indebtedness and the tenant-right system had become a routine aspect of estate management. The role of tenant right as collateral for loans increased dramatically in the nineteenth century with the increasing differentiation and complexity of the economic fabric of estates. Landlords had to be wary of tenants losing their farms to third parties after mortgaging them beyond their value, since mortgages or other debts, not the rent, might become the first lien on the tenant right of a farm.[11] Evidence from a number of estates suggests that the role tenant right played as collateral for loans from middlemen, neighbours, or banks interfered with estate management after the famine.[12] After two decades of haphazard management of tenant-right sales, Rowley and J.R. Miller of Draperstown began to systematize their approach to the problem in the 1850s. They reported with great exasperation in 1854:

> One thing is for certain: that we are very sick of regulating the private debts of persons who may sell their farms, and we are nearly to the resolution that when the sale of a farm takes place, we shall merely deduct the amount of the arrear due and hand the balance to the seller. It would save us a world of trouble and perplexity. The only thing against this would be that in many cases all creditors would be defrauded out of their demands, whether they were just or unjust. The court have every idea of the trouble we have in examining and sifting the claims of creditors. Where a farm is sold, a great portion of our time is taken up in such matters.[13]

By 1858 they seem to have resigned themselves to these difficulties, explaining that when a farm is sold, the amount is paid into the office, and we then deduct from said purchase money whatever arrear of rent may be due. We then have a meeting of the creditors, and after giving a fair allowance to the seller of the farm either to assist him to purchase a small place in another estate or to take him and family to America, we divide the remainder amongst his creditors according to the respective sums due to them. We have a vast deal of trouble in frequently ascertaining what may be fairly due, because many are apt to make out statements beyond the amount actually due, suspecting that they will only get a dividend in place of 20s. [in] the pound. By pursuing this plan, the purchaser is always safe as no subsequent claim or demand can come against his farm.[14]

The agent of the Verner estate in County Fermanagh resolved the difficulties of two brothers by interfering in the distribution of the proceeds of the tenant right of their farm. They were not only seriously in arrears in 1865, but also counted among their creditors a 'provincial' bank, a man from Aughnacloy, Co. Tyrone, and numerous other individuals, perhaps relatives in Australia.[15] Two other interesting examples survive from estate records in the 1860s and 1870s. Michael Murray on the Dufferin estate complained to his landlord in 1864 about one James Galway who

has contracted a debt with me to the amount of £18. The debt so con-tracted was for groceries advanced to him from time to time. I myself am a grocer in a small way and totally depending upon this business for the support of myself and a very large family. This debt I allowed to be con-tracted with the firm belief that if not otherwise paid, the tenant right of his farm would more than suffice to satisfy. This farm the said James Galway is willing to sell principally to pay me and the arrears which have been allowed to accumulate. Your agent, than whom there can be no better man, seems disposed to give it for a very small sum to a man called McJury, poor and anything but a solvent and a desirable tenant, his only recom-mendation being that he holds an adjoining farm. The sum of money, small as it is, he will have to borrow, and after paying the arrears, there will not be enough to satisfy my claim.

He recommended another neighbour who was willing and able to give 'as much for the tenant right as will pay off the arrears and satisfy my claim too.' Otherwise he asked for 'the use of the land for this crop, as he will be ejected in April, and by this means I might be enabled to pay myself. . . .'[16] The agent on the Caledon estate was also faced with a very complicated entanglement between debtors and creditors in 1872:

The facts are: Mr. Cadoo had on more than one occasion lent money to Davidson to pay his rent. In consideration of this Mr. Alexander [the agent] gave Mr. Cadoo a guarantee that should Davidson be compelled by circumstances to sell his place, the rent should first be settled out of the proceeds, and the residue, if any, handed to Mr. Cadoo towards paying his claim. This year Davidson was again in difficulties and he agreed to sell a portion of his farm to Mr. Cadoo. Mr. Alexander agreed to let Davidson sell upon the condition that the preference be given to the adjoining tenant, Cullen. Accordingly, Cullen became the purchaser slightly in excess of what Mr. Cadoo had agreed to give and Davidson had agreed to take. This bargain was completed, the money paid, and an agreement embodying the terms entered in a book in this office.

But unknown to Alexander, one Marshall 'was a creditor of Davidson's. On the 27th we heard that the sheriff had made a seizure under a decree, and that Davidson's interest of the whole concern, including the portion Cullen had already bought with Mr. Alexander's consent for £40. For the less valuable half Cullen had already paid Davidson £48 8s. 6d.'[17]

Debts to shopkeepers and neighbours complicated matters, but posed no serious threat to managers. The presence of overmighty creditors who took possession of their debtors farms in spite of the landlord had more alarming ramifications.[18] Creditors of heavily indebted sellers of tenant right were deliberately denied the privilege of buying them out on the Abercorn estate in the 1780s in order to put a stop to their aggrandizing ambitions.[19] The growing presence of banks began to overshadow these troublesome individuals in the nineteenth century. Regional banks began to play a large part in the network of credit and debt surrounding tenant-right exchanges, a situation which could create trouble for estate managers. In 1848 a cattle trader on the Drapers' company estate named John Mears, with debts totalling £800, only £50 of which was owed to the company, abandoned his wife and creditors and took ship to America. The bank held his lease, which served as collateral for occasional short-term loans which Mears required in his business. His wife consented to the sale of the farm for £400, but he returned and threw the purchaser's caretaker out of the house. The purchaser did not have the lease and thus legally could not proceed against him, and the company could not eject Mears because it had given possession to the caretaker. Legally, it was up to his creditors, and 'if a verdict should be given against Mears, he would take the benefit of the insolvent act and still hold possession.'[20] Early in the century landlords could restrict the mortgaging of leases by granting fewer of them,[21] but later, and especially after the 1870 land act, at-will or yearly tenancies were also commonly mortgaged. The earl of Belmore circulated a public notice dated 18 August 1864 which read in part:

> Whereas tenants often contract debts to their great disadvantage, on security of lands they hold by lease, or even at will, this is to give notice that the

proprietor of this estate will not sanction any such debts, and that he will utterly disregard the claims of any person or company who lends his tenants money on security of such lands . . . , [and such lenders] will do so entirely at their own risk.[22]

It is doubtful that a notice like this could effectively prevent mortgaging of assets. In one case on this estate during the 1870s there was concern that the Ulster Bank would sell the lands specified in a lease mortgage which it held and that the land act would leave the managers no remedy. The agent feared that

should the bank accommodation be withdrawn, it would seriously impede his [the lessee's] business. He has now a valuable interest on your lordship's estate and expends a great deal on tillage and improvements. Without a regular mortgage I believe the law is not quite clear as to power of ordinary creditors selling lands. It has been exercised and permitted to stand that landlords must pay in case of a refusal to acknowledge a sale. But I fancy the custom of the estate, where such a case arises, and the views of the particular barristers hearing the land case, have much to do in the matter.[23]

Only a manager who had gained the most firm control of tenant-right sales could argue that he held customary control of assets mortgaged by his tenants when the nature of the custom came to be determined by the courts set up by the land act of 1870.

Estate networks of credit and debt posed challenges, but the most serious form of debt, in the eyes of estate managers, was still that existing between the landlord and the tenant. The two available legal remedies against defaulting tenants were the distraint of goods or chattels for arrears of rent and ejectment for non-payment of rent, neither of which was satisfactory. The distraint of goods for the recovery of rent in the eighteenth century was a complicated and potentially expensive procedure, frought with uncertainties.[24] James Rooney, the Anglesey agent, approached the delicate task of distraining chattels for rent with considerable hesitancy in 1741. 'As to punishing the rest,' he wrote, 'you have no method but by distraining for last All Saint's rent immediately; though the custom is against us, yet the covenants of the lease empowers your doing so.'[25] Rooney's admission that custom was more powerful than the lease contract is further evidence of the weakness of estate management in the early eighteenth century discussed in Chapter 2. But even after they had established the legitimacy of the procedure landlords faced a number of obstacles. The first task was to actually gain possession of the goods placed under distraint. Abercorn's agent reported in 1793 'your lordship's bailiff in Donegal was most violently opposed and resisted while in the execution of his duty by five of your lordship's tenants, who not only rescued their cattle and treated him and his party very badly but declared they would have treated me worse. Early the next morning I set out with twenty men and before four o'clock had every hoof the men possessed safe in the pound.'[26] This was particularly challenging if the tenant lived on a remote farm or one bordering another estate. A landowner named Henry Wood brought to Andrew Nugent's attention his problems with two tenants, brothers-in-law named Sullivan and Mahon, the former a tenant of Wood's and the latter a tenant of Nugent's. He claimed that in 1831 Sullivan 'carried his corn and potatoes from his farm and drove off his stock by night, and carried the corn and potatoes to Mahon's farm' in order to defraud him of half a year's rent. For good measure Sullivan then collected a mob on that night round the house of the bailiff 'and prevented him from going out of his house to stop the proceedings.'[27] The Drapers' agents also failed to force a tenant to pay his arrears in 1845 because he kept his cattle on the border of the neighbouring Vintners' proportion.[28]

If an agent could successfully take possession of a tenant's cattle or crops, selling them created further problems. First there was the vexing problem of finding suitable buyers. 'I never took so much pains to get money in my life [as in] impounding cattle,' complained Edmund Kaine in 1721, 'and when I have done, am forced to let them out, for none will give me any money for them and I can do nothing with them myself.'[29] A century later, Andrew Newton, agent on the Lowry estate near Coagh, Co. Tyrone, had the same experience: 'I got the pound full and left it full. . . . The auction I am determined to go through with, but I dread the want of bidders. Should I buy for you, it would only saddle you with the keeping of cattle, for when the owners would make up the money, you could not refuse to give up the cattle to them.'[30] The Marquis of Dufferin's agent felt that though tenants would readily exchange cattle between themselves to resolve debts, 'they would seldom or ever buy at a distraint sale and the proprietor is often forced to have parties of his own to bid or allow the chattels to be sacrificed to characters who, for the sake of gain, are [resistant] to public odium.'[31] Even should the agent find buyers, distraint entailed the further risk of destroying the working capital of a farm, guaranteeing the accumulation of further arrears. As William Blacker told the Devon commission, 'it is a disgraceful thing to have the manor pound full of starving cattle; it is very injurious to the stock and is the most objectionable mode of recovering rent which can possibly be resorted to.'[32] Complaints that distraint had 'ruinous consequences to the owners' were common in the nineteenth century.[33] By the 1840s, the gathering in of arrears of rent had become 'perfectly impractical, since there is scarcely one of them who could pay a year's rent just now without disposing of their stock and chattels and leaving themselves without the means of support or payment of rent in the future.' Abatements were therefore necessary.[34]

Given the difficulty and inefficiency of distraint,[35] many agents resorted to ejectment, though the technicalities of the legal system also hampered this procedure. The power of the landlords to eject tenants from their farms was apparently quite weak at the beginning of the eighteenth century. Ejectments could only be served on lettings held under a written agreement which included a re-entry clause specifying the conditions of re-entry. In any proceeding the landlord had to document the legal title, the power of reversion, the lease, the property in question, and the amount owed. Given the bewildering complexity surrounding the registration of title before the reforms of the mid-nineteenth century, meeting such requirements could be not just tedious and expensive but impracticable altogether. This was particularly true in the case of tenants holding land without a lease, or holding a lease without the proper clauses, or holding leases over which the landlord did not hold a proper reversion.[36] The weakness of the law of ejectment can be seen in retrospect by observing the way in which it was amended during the eighteenth century. An act of 1712 (11 Anne, c. 2) was intended to overcome 'the many niceties that attend re-entries at common law' which tenants used to forestall distraint and ejectment. Another weakness of the law was that landlords could not proceed with ejectment until it was proved that sufficient distress could not be found on the premises. All the weaknesses of the distress procedure were therefore preliminary to ejectment. Amendments in 1717 (4 Geo. I, c. 5 and 8 Geo. I, c. 2), 1731 (5 Geo II), and 1752 (25 Geo. I, c. 13) attempted to further facilitate landlord legal re-entry to their leased property and circumvent the obstacles to the distraint procedure.[37] This body of law appears to have still left tenants with considerable defensive powers in the second half of the eighteenth century. If a tenant fell into arrears of at least half the yearly rent, the landlord then had to prove that the distrained goods were insufficient to compensate for the arrears, or that distressable goods had been fraudulently carried off or sold by the tenant. Only then did the clerk of the peace allow the landlord to post a 'notice to appear' at the next petty session or assize, requiring the tenant to defend himself against ejectment if he had not made up the arrears by that time. The whole process was costly and time-consuming. Fees paid to lawyers and to the court might amount to as much as the entire revenue raised from the distraint.[38] Even if a conviction was won, the tenant might be allowed until the next session of the court, in six months' time, to pay off the arrears, which could result in another expensive trial. The agent of the Anglesey estate was involved in a number of disputes over ejectments and the validity of leases in the years 1749–51. He expressed his frustration with 'badly brought' ejectments which 'failed on trial,' and concluded in 1751 that 'there is no doing business in the law but in the ordinary way, and the officers you see all play into one another's hands, so that the suitor by the rules of the court,

which must necessarily be pursued, may be a long time kept out of his right.'[39]
When the first in a wave of ejectments was carried out on the Abercorn estate
in 1769, Abercorn sought the aid of his Dublin lawyers because 'ejecting
tenants is so new a branch of business to me that it is necessary to [get] some
directions.'[40] The ejectment of tenants at will under this legal system was
obviously very cumbersome. Agents were occasionally awkwardly dependent
on their tenants for such directions. In 1819 the Millers complained:

> We shall get the particulars required by the court from the applicants them-
> selves, . . . but in many cases they cannot furnish what the courts require,
> namely the rent reserved and the arrear due by the applicant. Very many
> of the mountaineers have a very imperfect idea of these matters when they
> are in arrear. They can give the number and ages of their children but one
> of the other two we fear they cannot in many cases give. We shall however
> instruct them to the best of our power and explain to them what is meant
> by their reserved rent.[41]

Evidence of estate managers discovering the legal difficulties of ejecting
tenants, and learning the legal rules and technicalities of the process, is common in the eighteenth century,[42] and many others were still finding their
footing in the nineteenth century.[43]

All these technicalities offered ample opportunity for litigious tenants to
obstruct the proceedings. As Richey was to remark, 'to a man in possession,
a defendant in ejection, no system of law is so advantageous as one hope-
lessly entangled and incomprehensible.'[44] Landlords were understandably
suspicious of and hesitant to deal with tenants known to be sophisticated in
the ways of the courts. Such tenants might withhold their rents and use the
money to fight legal battles. In reference to a legal conflict with tenants in
1743, James Rooney attempted to get the court to 'grant an injunction to
quiet them upon paying one half year's rent into the exchequer immediately
before another half year becomes due, and by this they would be disarmed
of the sinews of war, the rents, and they would not think it worth their while
afterward to continue their suits.'[45] The widely adopted policy of keeping
rents low to promote peace and improvement backfired if it empowered
'litigious' tenants like the one McGildowney complained of in a letter to
Lord Mark Kerr in 1815:

> Had it not been for the good bargain of Ballytibbert which you were the
> means of his getting, he would neither be so ready or so able to fly to an
> attorney and go to law with your lordship as he has done, and you will
> please consider that my showing in this instance that you are determined
> to retain your rights may save the trouble and expense of deterring others
> from making similar attempts.[46]

The ejectment remedy was not only difficult and uncertain but forbiddingly costly. In 1788, Hamilton pointed out that 'the badness of the weather, the poverty of their cattle, and the backwardness of the labour prevented impounding as much as otherwise I would have done. Ejecting was certainly of great use, but the expense was grievous and it is attended besides with inconveniences.'[47] Of the forty ejectments served in 1790, only eighteen resulted in eviction. In the 1790s Hamilton's bailiffs needed the assistance of 'twenty to thirty men' to impound assets and enforce ejectments.[48] Referring to one townland with tenants in arrears, Edward Evans of the Foljambe estate near Dungannon, Co. Tyrone, observed: 'I have long threatened the others with ejectments, which I have declined to the last extremity, from the severe costs attending that mode, the only one that has effect.'[49] William Hudson reluctantly recommended that two men be served with ejectments in 1816, explaining that 'ejectment is an expensive proceeding and I am therefore cautious of going into it.'[50] Agents hoped that singling out one or two tenants might have a deterrent effect on the rest.[51] The hope that selective ejectment would terrorize the rest of the backward tenants was widespread,[52] but many agents soon realized that an established system of selective ejectment would eventually lose its deterrent effect.

Recent revisionist historiography emphasizes the infrequency of evictions, but it is clear that the capacity of agents to resort to ejectment and therefore their power to terrorize the tenantry at large dramatically increased in the nineteenth century.[53] They were greatly assisted by legislative changes. The infrastructure of the legal system through which tenants had to be pursued had been radically reformed by 1823. The dominant judicial institutions in the eighteenth century were the manor courts, most of which were established in the seventeenth century and often manned by a corrupt and autonomous magistracy.[54] A wide cleavage opened between the criminal statute law and the administration of justice in local rural communities in the eighteenth century, which discouraged both landlords and tenants from seeking redress through the judicial system.[55] The creation of the quarter session courts in 1796 and the petty session courts and the constabulary in 1823 marked a sea change in the local administration of justice, dramatically increasing its accessibility and effectiveness.[56] An act of 1816 (58 Geo III, c. 39) greatly facilitated the eviction procedures by allowing ejectment by civil bill in the quarter session courts. The procedure was much less costly but still technically exacting, with a high burden of proof. 'Before 1816 the expense of ejecting large numbers of tenants would have been very heavy, sufficient to deter most landlords from the attempt,' writes Maguire. It was not until the Civil Bills Courts, Ireland Act of 1851 that streamlined powers of ejectment were extended to all tenancies, written or implied, where arrears of rent had accumulated to at least the equivalent of one year's rent.[57] Between 1816 and 1851 'the civil bill procedure for recovery of rent could be used only against leaseholders, and not tenants at will or yearly tenants. It was necessary to serve notice to quit on the latter and then proceed against them, under the same statute, as overholding tenants, that is, tenants whose legal interest had been determined but were still in possession.'[58] The civil bill ejectment process now became a more effective threat to tenants. Quarter session civil bill ejectment only cost 5 or 6 shillings, so the risks involved in using it were greatly reduced.[59]

During this era of reform, land agents became much more confident in the exercise of ejectment. With costs reduced and effectiveness increased, only the adverse reactions of the tenants themselves would constrain them. And the tenants, having lost the legal upper hand, were forced to take their resistance out of doors. Of course, this was not an innovation. The agents of the Downshire estate in the 1750s expressed their frustration with tenant resistance to the process of distraint,[60] but they also recognized that the alternative of ejectment was not much better:

> The tenants in the north have hitherto paid very little. We were obliged to bring ejectments against some who refused to pay rent, upon which they grew so rebellious that they had like to have killed the sherriff who went to execute the process of the law. Wherefore we were of necessity of applying to the lord lieutenant and council to outlaw the offenders pursuant to an act of parliament in this kingdom. And we have accordingly got them proclaimed, which I hope will be such a terror to the rest that we shall for the future get the rent easy.[61]

Similar concerns were voiced by the agent on the Whyte estate nearly a century later. The agent worriedly urged Whyte to 'inquire and satisfy yourself as to the correctness of this report; at the same time do not let it get abroad that either he or I are *exterminators*. It is a dangerous and difficult task to make such changes in the landed property of the country as will meet the altered circumstances of the times, but it must be done as quietly and cautiously as possible.'[62] In two letters of February 1849 the Millers outlined the nuances of the ejectment policy they had developed over the course of nearly thirty years' experience. They stated that they would continue to serve ejectments, but that 'great caution ought to be used in the evicting of tenants. Great numbers should not in our judgement be put out at one time. We beg to mention to you that the sheriffs of each county have been directed to make a return of all ejectment decrees signed by them and on what estate the tenants lived.'[63] In 1850 the Millers commented, 'as to any tenant on the estate to give up his farm without having an ejectment decree over him, we might as well ask him, without any hope of success, to pay the national debt of England. They would nearly as soon give up their heart's blood as their bit of land.'[64] By 1878 William Stannus, the successor to the Millers, was able to boast:

> I am happy to say, however, that already a great number of cases have been satisfactorily arranged without incurring any law expenses on the part of the company. It does not follow that because a notice to quit is served, . . . it must be followed up at law – the terror of the law being in most cases sufficient to induce a refractory tenant ultimately to do what is required.[65]

MANAGEMENT OF THE TENANT-RIGHT SYSTEM

Some historians argue that the custom of tenant right was the manifestation of a special cultural or social bond between northern landlords and their tenants, a 'socio-cultural accomplishment' which produced a 'natural symbiosis' absent from the rest of Ireland.[66] Some even give landlords credit for cultivating this symbiosis, implying that those southern landlords who refused to allow tenant right to operate on their estates were behaving irrationally.[67] According to Vaughan, 'the inchoate nature of southern tenant right seems to have been largely due to a lack of co-operation between landlords and tenants, for much of the flexibility and certainty of Ulster tenant right came from the power of the estate office. . . . Indeed, without the agent's involvement, it is hard to see how the custom could have worked smoothly.'[68] This characterization of the relationship between social cohesion and powerful management may fit with the evidence of the economically buoyant mid-Victorian period, but it misses the subtleties of the relationship between the growth of the custom of tenant right and the development of managerial technique in the eighteenth and early nineteenth centuries. The custom of tenant right operated on some estates for over a century before it came to be properly understood and managed by the landowners. Moreover, this portrayal of the tenant-right system as a static, rational, socially cohesive system, masterfully controlled from above, rankles with the view that tenant right was, to quote Lord Palmerston's famous adage, 'landlord wrong.' Economists might justify its rationality and apologists for landlordism might highlight how enlightened managers used it to lubricate and soften social antagonisms, but contemporaries were always fully aware of the threat it posed to the property rights of landlords. Ulster managers did not devote so much attention to regulating tenant right simply because it made their jobs easier or simplified their lives. Just the opposite was true: agents and other commentators routinely expressed their disgust and frustration with the custom, and opinion to the contrary was rare and unpopular before the Devon commission testimonies were published. The regulation of tenant right was an unwelcome necessity accepted only because it proved to be a more flexible and adaptable method of management than the blunt, overly antagonistic, expensive, and ineffective alternatives of distraint of goods and the eviction of tenants. The impression one receives in reading through the business correspondence of Ulster estates is that as agents began to discover the technicalities, difficulties, and inadequacies of distraint and ejectment, they were simultaneously discovering something else: the practice of the custom of tenant right on their estates, while posing as a definite threat to their perceived property rights, held out for them the potential of more effective management. In the extant estate correspondence, a sense of outrage[69] at the effrontery and intransigence of the custom routinely, though gradually, gave way to more realistic assessments of its manageability.

The eighth earl of Abercorn was rather precocious in this respect. His correspondence in the 1770s and 1780s with James Hamilton reveals how they came to terms both with the disadvantages of the ejectment mechanism and their lack of control over tenant right. At times Abercorn was given to the expression of a naive confidence in his legal control of the land.[70] Two especially troublesome tenants in 1767 were cases in point: 'Matthew Glendenning . . . will not, I fear, pay up his arrears. I let him know, as I did the Cunninghams . . . and others that are far behind, that your lordship would allow them to dispose of their farms to discharge their rents, but they would not do it, though [the sale of] their leases would now clear them.' These two tenants would not sell until forced to do so by threats of ejectment: 'John Cunningham and Matthew Glendenning were the two that I thought first ought to be ejected. . . . Cunningham has, I know, been endeavouring to dispose of his farm and entreated that no proceedings be taken against him until the Lifford assizes [at] the end of this month, and that if he did not pay off, he would sell it to the highest bidder.' Other cases of conflicting claims and unauthorized sales began to mount in the following decades, and Abercorn became more concerned with the infringement of his legal rights and with the 'lawlessness' of the popular law: 'In every instance of this sort I feel myself the sufferer and am more and more convinced of the ignorance of the tenants of the principles of justice and common sense upon which the contract of a lease is founded.' Tenants who claimed the right of renewal of leases against Abercorn's will were forcefully admonished: 'Declarations, confirmed by oaths, that persons will be borne in pieces before they will leave houses which they have no right to, and which they solemnly covenanted that they would leave peaceably, are strong instances of barbarism; and the public is interested in having them rendered ineffectual.' Abercorn considered a refusal to sell a farm to be 'perverse' and 'unlawful.' In the 1770s he expressed the alarming opinion that over 400 farms should be sold and that the tenants 'ought to be made to feel that it will be themselves in the end who will suffer by their perverseness and unlawful proceedings, and all the tenants who are now going out will do well to consider that the more they discourage purchasers, the less their lands will sell for.' But his agent had all but acquiesced in the determination of tenants not to sell: 'Nothing but driving strictly or sending tenants to gaol will oblige them to sell, for though the tenant signed the advertisement for selling, I persuade myself that they express a concern for going out which prevents people from buying. . . . There are some who would lie in gaol so as to increase the arrear rather than give up.'[71]

The Hearts of Steel rebellion in County Antrim and other agrarian disturbances may have focused the minds of landlords on the strength of tenant conceptions of their property rights. Research into the activities of agrarian secret societies of the late eighteenth and early nineteenth centuries shows that questions of tenure and property rights were central, if not always predominant to the Hearts of Oak, Hearts of Steel, and Whiteboy agitations.[72] James Hamilton believed that tenant-right policy was the central issue in the rising of the Hearts of Steel: 'The first cause of those tumults [in Antrim, Down, and Derry] sprang from my Lord Donegall's taking fines and granting long leases to several purchasers and putting the occupying tenants into their hands to covenant for their holdings as they could. Many of them about Belfast gave up their lands, and upon it being stocked, the cattle were maimed and houses burned.'[73] Despite the other grievances of the Steelboys, what bore most heavily on Hamilton's mind was the way in which the outgoing tenants had allegedly been treated.

By the mid-1780s the administrators of the Abercorn estate had realized that the deterrent effect of spot ejectments had been minimal. A drastic change in policy was required if the massive arrears accumulated were to be reduced. Abercorn declared in 1787:

> I want an opportunity of entering fully with you on the subject of the vast arrear with which the estate is overwhelmed. You have for years been talking of the prospects of its diminution, but it never grows less and can no longer be endured. The system must be totally changed and decisive measures taken. What is called indulgence to the tenants is in the end cruelty. . . . I hope you will be able to inform me in your next letter that you have made a beginning and brought ejectment against the several principal defaulters. And I will not allow those who wait to be ejected the sale of the tenant right. I will take my chance on the arrears and let the lands by auction.[74]

Hamilton's response indicated his full agreement:

> The great arrears give me unspeakable concern . . . , and it must appear strange that there should be such difficulty when I myself see such instances

of farms for which there is no tenure selling at from eight to ten years' purchase; it is therefore evident that the system must be changed and decisive measures taken, and I am convinced that nothing in general can be so effectual as ejecting and, as your lordship observes, not allowing those who stand ejectment the benefit of a sale of tenant right.[75]

It was clear that unless they were willing to court an open rebellion, estate managers were not in a position in the late eighteenth century to accomplish large scale clearances of either tenants or arrears by the use of ejectment or forced tenant-right sales. By the early nineteenth century, best management practice was to accept the custom and attempt to manipulate it as much as possible. Both William Blacker and William Greig, two of the more articulate land agents in early nineteenth-century Ulster, clearly saw tenant right as a *substitute* for ejectment proceedings and argued that landlords should resign themselves to accepting it in order to manipulate it.[76] For Greig, tenant right has an overwhelming moral and social force, and its diminution could only be 'a work of time.' William Blacker also confessed to the Devon commission that 'I do not know how to get rid of it without incurring greater inconveniences. If you refuse to allow any tenant right you can scarcely ever get rid of a bad tenant, for the feeling of the country is so strong that no man will venture to take a farm without having the goodwill of the man who leaves it, and that man cannot leave it unless he has got something to carry away which will take him to America, or will obtain for it some other holding.'[77] John Andrews, agent to marquis of Londonderry, said that 'you would have a Tipperary in Down if [the curtailment of tenant right] was attempted to be carried out.'[78]

The salient realization was that if they could master the tenant-right system, agents could employ an ancient and widely recognized custom to accomplish controversial goals by more acceptable means. Landlords like Abercorn had come to grips with the question earlier, but it was not until the crisis decades of the 1830s and 1840s that many others had begun to wrest control of the tenant-right system from their tenants. By the mid-nineteenth century, the realization that the regulation of tenant right was a better mechanism for securing the rent than a policy of eviction had become more commonplace, especially among managers of the London companies' proportions.[79] Edmund McGildowney in Antrim felt that the expense of ejectment or other legal entanglements to the landlord was of the same order of magnitude as compensation for improvements, and was willing to buy out a tenant rather than serve an ejectment.[80]

This process of discovery, outrage, resignation, and manipulation is very clear on the estates of the London companies, where a virtually unmanaged tenantry had developed a strong tradition of tenant right in the eighteenth century. A surveyor of the Merchant Tailors' estate described how the custom of tenant right had become so strong by 1838:

> [Tenant right] no doubt originated from the tenant having built his house, enclosed and ditched the land, and made all the improvements on his farm without the least assistance from his landlords, and although the term of years originally granted may have been sufficient to repay him for all the outlay in capital and labour, still he never lost sight of the original expense and naturally looked to receive a compensation from his successor equal to the improved value of his farm, and as the landlord did not interfere so long as he received the rent (and the agent his fee for altering the tenant's name in his book), the custom has been handed down until it has established a right equal in effect to a law, for no one now can be found to take a farm unless the outgoing tenant is perfectly satisfied on leaving. Not a few cases have occurred recently, even in this peaceable part of Ireland, where parties have been ejected for non-payment of rent and other causes. Even when three or four years in arrears have not been demanded on the parties agreeing to quit, yet not having received a compensation for the tenant right for leaving, the incoming tenant's house and cornstacks have been set on fire. Under such circumstances I feel confident it would be impossible wholly to suppress the present system. Sales would be made privately, and no influence or power could counteract the secret combination to effect their determined purpose.[81]

He therefore recommended publicly accepting the custom and closely regulating its price. Edward Fletcher, deputy to the property of the Irish Society, recommended that leases should only be renewed to respectable tenants. As to the others,

> your agent must for the time being exert a combination of firmness and forbearance, of rigour and levity, to get such tenants ultimately off your rent-roll by tacitly sanctioning the buying out of the old tenant by a proper successor for a small consideration to indemnify the former for what is in Ireland termed 'the tenant right' – in other words, the paramount claim which by old custom every tenant in possession considers himself to have for a renewal in preference to any other person. Even taking cases after this method individually, your agent will have at times to encounter great difficulties, which, if presented in mass, would be found insuperable.

This method was apparently employed successfully by two generations of agents on the Fishmongers' estate, and had resulted in considerable consolidation:

> The tenantry are the most wealthy of any in the plantation, and these advantages have been accomplished without any complaints of hardship.

The very individuals who, when coerced to quit their farms, would raise a cry of oppression against their landlords are almost daily found disposing of them voluntarily if in embarrassed circumstances or if desirous of emigrating. . . . It is vain to refuse sanction altogether without the process of daily memorializing your honours and receiving a vote of court in reply being complied with. In some instances sellers would be half-way to America, and purchasers be installed in their place, before a reply would be received to an application, and the best bidder would be invariably accepted without reference to respectability or the interests of the lords of the soil.[82]

When the entire Drapers' company estate fell out of lease in May 1817, its owners naively assumed that tenants had no right to continue on lands held from the former leaseholder and that all rights of the tenants expired with their leases. The agent was instructed in 1818 to put up notices

to efface the erroneous impression, which seems to be entertained in many instances, that on the determination of leases the lessees have pretensions bordering on a right to continue [in] their holdings. The owners may have occasion or may choose to renew the possession or alter the disposition of the land, whereas the rights of the lessees arise entirely from, are regulated by, and expire with their leases. And the lessees on quitting can expect no compensation for anything which may have been done by them during their tenure without a special agreement for that purpose. Were it otherwise, all improvements even for the reciprocal convenience of the tenantry would be impractical.[83]

Outrage soon gave way to pragmatism on the Drapers' estate. Nearly every letter to Rowley Miller from tenants in 1823 concerned the sale of farms, and nearly every memorial from a tenant was a request to sell.[84] Inundated with exchanges of farms and aware of the lengths some tenants would go to defend the custom, the Millers soon recognized the necessity of regulating rather than attempting to abolish the tenant-right system. Their superiors in London, however, stubbornly refused to comprehend realities on the estate. In the 1840s the Millers had to emphasize repeatedly that they had no choice but to resign themselves to the existence of the custom, and that a sudden and massive removal of tenants from the estate was an impossibility. When presented with such a suggestion by one deputy, the Millers responded that

he has forgotten to point out how it is to be done. It would be a monstrous advantage *if it could be accomplished*, [but] there are only two ways of doing it, namely by turning adrift about 500 tenants composing about 3,000 individuals, or the company purchasing their own lands from the said 500 tenants at the rate of £10 or £12 per acre, *neither of which plans* are we prepared to recommend to the court of assistants. The first plan, of turning

> out so many individuals without *ample* remuneration, is totally out of the question, *it could not, and for humanity' sake ought not to be done, even if it could.* The second [plan] ... might have ... some feasibility ... if [the court] enabled us, where small farms were to be sold, to assist those tenants whose farms meared with them to purchase them by lending them either whole or part of the purchase money. . . .[85]

The following year they composed a lengthy disquisition on the subject for the benefit of the Londoners, attempting to drive home to them the serious nature of the question by relating the story of a Tyrone landowner named Brown, an acquaintance of theirs, who 'in order to improve his estate, turned out by ejectment many of his tenants and the consequence is that his life is in such jeopardy that he is obliged to keep policemen constantly in his house.' Another local landlord named Anderson behaved similarly, with the result that 'one of his houses has been burned to the ground and a Scotch steward he has, has been noticed that if he doesn't leave the country he will be shot. And it has been noticed to Mr. Anderson also that they will do all the injury they can both to him and his property.' Rather than behave like Brown and Anderson, the Millers argued that 'it is better for landlords to give way to the custom of a country than entirely to unhinge perhaps the frame of society.'[86] In letters over the next few years, they reiterated the anomalous nature of the custom, the impossibility of abolishing it, the risk of life or limb that would attend any attempt to do so, grasping for new metaphors with each attempt.[87] For their own part, they had settled on what they regarded to be the most effective policy in the prevailing circumstances:

> The general practice is, after an ejectment decree is obtained, to give the tenant time either to sell his interest in the farm or to make up the back-gone rent or a considerable part of it – the actual putting out of a tenant is the last resource unless he be a bad or a careless, slovenly man- when there is no hope of his doing well – when we are compelled to execute the decree, as we intend doing in 4 or 5 cases next week, we are obliged to *pull down all the houses*, if this were not done, the inmates thereof re-enter although such re-entry is a transportable felony.[88]

On numerous occasions in the 1840s, 1850s, and 1860s they made efforts to justify their policy by quantifying the reduction in the numbers of tenants on the estate, a task that was accomplished 'without any heart burning or unpleasant feeling because in no instance did a tenant ever have to leave the estate without receiving a fair and, may we add, ample remuneration for his holding.'[89]

The pre-famine period saw crucial developments in the relationship between landlords and their tenants. In the late eighteenth century an ineffective legal system and deeply entrenched custom handicapped management. A more streamlined and rationalized judicial system increased managerial power of tenants and tenures. With a more wieldy ejectment stick in their hands, agents were in a stronger position to pursuade insolvent tenants to sell their tenant right than they had been in the eighteenth century. The nature and extent of this strength will be considered in the final chapter. The evidence presented so far shows just how limited agents felt themselves to be in the aggressive use of the ejectment remedy and in obtruding on customary practices. None the less, by the famine decade, estate agents had moved past the stage of discovery, outrage, and resignation to the point where they began to secure ongoing managerial control of the tenant-right system. It was becoming clear that landlords threatened to gain the upper hand, and after the famine had thinned populations already considerably decimated by management policies promoting emigration, that clarity increased. It is also clear that this managerial revolution was politically contentious, and would dominate the discourse of Victorian rural politics in Ulster.

NOTES

1 Crawford, 'Landlord-tenant relations,' pp. 14, 17.
2 James Hamilton to eight earl of Abercorn, 14 Jan. 1770, P.R.O.N.I., Abercorn papers, T2541/1A/1/9/4; idem, 10 Aug. 1783, ibid., T2541/IA2/3/46; Robert Jamison to Abercorn, 21 July and 27 Aug. 1794, ibid., T2541/IA2/20/2, 29. Hamilton to Abercorn, 19 July 1778, ibid., T2541/IA2/2/4; idem, 18 May 1783, ibid., T2541/IA2/3/3; James Hamilton, Jr. to ninth earl of Abercorn, 26 Jan. 1790, ibid., T2541/IA1/17/1.
3 James Hamilton to eight earl of Abercorn, 1758, ibid., T2541/IA1/5/48; Hamilton found in 1767 that 'there are in some acres more than one tenant, and I thought that your lordship would not set less than an acre to anyone.' Idem, 15 Dec. 1767, ibid., T2541/IA1/7/1. During the economic downturn of 1783 Hamilton listed the number of cottiers, widows and herds on each division of the estate and commented that 'they may not all be poor; however, I am sure there are many hundreds of little tenants as poor as most of them.' Idem, 18 May 1783, ibid., T2541/IA2/3/32. See also James and Rowley Miller to Edward Lawford, 23 May 1848, P.R.O.N.I., Drapers' company papers, D3632/1/1.
4 Ó Gráda, *Ireland*, p. 33; Power, *Tipperary*, p. 164; Wakefield, *Account of Ireland*, i, p. 244. Dickson, 'Cork region,' p. 217. 'It was not until far into this century that Irish land agency became a well understood business and a profession for gentlemen.' Hugh de F. Montgomery, *Irish land and Irish rights* (London, 1881), p. 12.
5 Maguire, *Downshire estates*, pp. 115–116.
6 Donnelly, *Cork*, pp. 52–72.
7 Edward Bayly to [?], 15 Dec. 1733, P.R.O.N.I., Anglesey papers, D619/21/A/9.
8 Edward Rowland to Bayly, 23 Aug. 1734, ibid., D619/22/A/20.
9 James Rooney to Nicholas Bayly, 24 Sept. 1743, ibid., D619/21/B/57.
10 Idem, 15 Nov. 1743, ibid., D619/21/B/58.

11 R.C. Brush to earl of Belmore, 7 April 1866, P.R.O.N.I., Belmore papers, D3007/V/19; A.S. Crawford to [?] Dixie, 14 Feb. 1879, P.R.O.N.I., Sharman-Crawford papers, D856/B6/40.

12 The agent of the Dufferin estate realized in 1876 that it would be impossible to sell perpetuities, fine down rents, or induce tenants to purchase their holdings because the leases were so heavily mortgaged. J.L. Pattison to marquis of Dufferin, 20 Jan. 1876, P.R.O.N.I., Dufferin papers, D1071A/K/Box 2. In 1879 a man on the Crawford estate borrowed £700 at five percent on security of the tenant right to complete the purchase of a farm. Hugh Glass to D.L. Coddington, 15 Feb. 1879, P.R.O.N.I., Sharman Crawford papers, D856/B6/41. The holders of a mortgage on the Verner estate in County Fermanagh asserted their right to the farms of evicted mortgagees. James Crossle to Henry Harris, 13 Feb. 1882, P.R.O.N.I., Verner papers, D236/488/2, p. 432.

13 Millers to Lawford, 24 July 1854, P.R.O.N.I., Drapers' company papers, D3632/1/2.

14 Millers to W.H. Sawyer, 30 Dec. 1858, ibid.

15 James Crossle to R. Earnes, 3 April 1865, P.R.O.N.I., Verner papers, D236/488/1, p. 155.

16 Michael Murray to Dufferin, 8 Mar. 1864, P.R.O.N.I., Dufferin papers, D1071A/K/Box 1.

17 David Morris to J. Giran, 24 June 1872, P.R.O.N.I., Caledon papers, D2433/A/3/5. J.S. Crawford also had trouble with hidden creditors. James Lyons to J. S. Crawford, 27 Dec. 1862, P.R.O.N.I., Sharman Crawford papers, D856/B6/27.

18 James Johnston to D.L. Coddington, 19 Jan. 1881, P.R.O.N.I., Sharman Crawford papers, D856/B6/35.

19 Hamilton to Abercorn, 15 June 1784 and 18 June 1786, P.R.O.N.I., Abercorn papers, T2541/IA1/14/32, T2541/IA2/4/12.

20 Millers to Lawford, 7 Nov. 1848, P.R.O.N.I., Drapers' company papers, D3632/1/1. Lawford responded that Mears and Forsyth should settle the problem themselves without reference to the company. Lawford to Millers, 10 Nov. 1848, ibid., D3632/3/5.

21 Minutes of the court of assistants, extracts relating to Irish estates, 24 Jan. 1826, Drapers' Hall, London, N.L.I., film 1529.

22 R.C. Brush to earl of Belmore, 16 Feb. 1878, P.R.O.N.I., Belmore papers, D3007/V/196; idem, 13 Feb. 1880, ibid., D3007/V/262.

23 Idem, 14 Nov. 1874, ibid., D3007/V/94. In 1879 a tenant on the Belmore estate sued the Ulster Bank for illegal detention of his lease. John J. Benison to Belmore, 19 Apr. 1879, ibid., D3007/U/174.

24 A. G. Richey, *The Irish land laws* (London, 1880), p. 53.

25 James Rooney to Nicholas Bayly, 5 Dec. 1741, P.R.O.N.I., Anglesey papers, D619/21/B/29.

26 James Hamilton, Jr., to ninth earl of Abercorn, 13 Mar. 1793, P.R.O.N.I., Abercorn papers, T2541/IA1/19/21.

27 Henry Wood to Andrew Nugent, 3 June 1831, P.R.O.N.I., Nugent papers, D552/A/7/2/62.

28 Rowley and J.R. Miller to Edward Lawford, 26 May 1845, P.R.O.N.I., Drapers' company papers, D3632/1/1.

29 Edmund Kaine to Dacre Barrett, 15 Apr. 1721, P.R.O.N.I., Barrett-Lennard papers, film 170/2.

30 He closed this letter by remarking on the great scarcity of money and the fact that the best tenants were not paying rent. Andrew Newton to Robert William Lowry, 26 June 1814, P.R.O.N.I., Lowry papers, D1132/1/2.

31 Mortimer Thomson to marquis of Dufferin, 5 April 1866, P.R.O.N.I., Dufferin papers, D1071A/K/Box 3. 'To sell the cattle for another's debt is as every gentleman says one of the most unprecedented and tyrannical things ever done. . . .' Simon Kiernan to Robert Hamilton, n.d. [c.1815], P.R.O.N.I., Nugent papers, D552/A/7/4/15.

32 Gourley, 'Gosford estates,' pp. 270–1.

33 William Hudson to N.C. White, [?] July 1821, P.R.O.N.I., Whyte papers, D2918/3/4/36. Ant. Lock to Lady Ardglass, 15 Sept. 1688, P.R.O.N.I., Ardglass papers, D970/1/18; 'To distrain cattle would ruin our tenants and raise us no money.' William Gore to Claud Gilbert, 24 April, 1702, T.C.D., MUN/P/24/336. Similar commentary can be found in William Welman to Michael Ward, 22 April 1724, P.R.O.N.I., Castleward papers, D2092/1/1 p. 52, Francis Lascelles to Michael Ward, 5 November 1737, ibid., D2092/1/4; Brigadier Henry Conyngham to Lady Ann Murray, 2 October 1703, P.R.O.N.I., Murray of Broughton papers, D2860/5/16.

34 George Joy to Lord Mountcashel, 9 June 1842, P.R.O.N.I., Mountcashel papers, T1289/19. 'At this season I have no remedy as the people have nothing to distrain. . .' John Lanktree to Lord Londonderry, 16 Apr. 1844, P.R.O.N.I., Londonderry papers, D654/N2/27. See also McCabe, 'Law, conflict, and social order,' pp. 441–2.

35 By 1851 ejectment almost completely replaced distraint, because the 'spirit of combination and open active resistance' to the latter rendered it ineffectual. Ferguson and Vance, *Tenure and improvement*, p. 217. After the crop failure of 1872, H.R. Miller argued for a few ejectments because 'there are no goods to distrain. And besides, the distress causes an unpleasant clamour which is better to be avoided.' He urged leniency in light of the crop failure because 'the last batch of ejectments ordered acted as a warning, in consequence of which I believe that those who had any means at hand of paying have done so.' H.R. Miller to W.H. Sawyer, 1 May 1873, P.R.O.N.I., Drapers' company papers, D3632/1/4.

36 Donnelly, *Cork*, p. 71.

37 J.N. Finlay, *A treatise of the law of landlord and tenant in Ireland*, second edition (Dublin, 1835), pp. 411–46; A.N. Oulton, *Index to the statutes at present in force in or affecting Ireland, from the year 1310 to 1835 inclusive* (Dublin, 1836), pp. 180–2, 223–4, 335–8; Ferguson and Vance, *Tenure and improvement*, pp. 250–61; Hamilton to Abercorn, 27 Sept. 1787, P.R.O.N.I., Abercorn papers, T2541/IA2/4/p. 48.

38 Idem, 24 May 1772, 26 Dec. 1779, ibid., T2541/IA1/10/35, T2541/IA2/2/118.

39 James Rooney to Nicholas Bayly, 1 Apr. 1749, 13 Nov. 1750, 19 Feb. 1751, P.R.O.N.I., Anglesey papers, D619/21/B/81, 95, 98. And again in 1764 Bayly had to be informed that ejectment requires 'a description of premises, which is missing in this case, and precise proof of ownership.' [?] to Henry Bayly, 26 May 1764, ibid., D619/22/B/1. Two examples of lawsuits over the question of the validity of perpetuity leases on the Anglesey estate held by William Wallace: William Wallace to Nicholas Bayly, 18 January 1717, ibid., D619/22/A/5 and Rooney to Bayly, 10 August 1754 ibid., D619/21/B/115; petition with twenty signatures, 23 December 1753, ibid., D619/11/9, Rooney to Bayly, 10 Nov. 1741, ibid., D619/21/B/26; idem, 21 Nov, 1741, ibid., D619/21/B/27, and 5 Dec. 1741, ibid., D619/21/B/291.

40 Abercorn to Hamilton, 2 Nov. 1769, P.R.O.N.I., Abercorn papers, D623/A/20/105.

41 Millers to Lawford, 13 Dec. 1849, P.R.O.N.I., Drapers' company papers, D3632/1/2.

42 James Cottingham to [John Pomeroy], 22 Apr. 1780, P.R.O.N.I., Earl of Lanesborough's papers, D1908/2/1; Cottingham to Carroll, 29 Apr. 1780, ibid; Henry Hatch to [?]

Blundell, 24 Mar. 1753, P.R.O.N.I., Downshire papers, D607/A/23; James Rooney to Nicholas Bayly, 1 Apr. 1749, P.R.O.N.I., Anglesey papers, D619/21/B/81; [?] to Henry Bayly, 26 May 1764, ibid., D619/22/B/1.

43 David Gordon to John Savage, 25 Feb. 1796, P.R.O.N.I., Nugent papers, D552/A/4/2/68; Rev. John Wilson to William Ogilvie, 29 Aug. 1807, P.R.O.N.I., Ogilvie papers, T1546/1; James Craig to [?] Bailie, 24 Nov. 1810, P.R.O.N.I., Perceval-Maxwell papers, D3244/B/11/53; Edmund McGildowney to Lord Mark Kerr, 22 Apr. 1815, P.R.O.N.I., McGildowney papers, D1375/1/7; McGildowney to Kerr, 12 July 1815, ibid.; McGildowney to Michael Hughes, 1 Sept. 1816, ibid., D1375/1/8; McGildowney to Robert McNaghton, 3 Nov. 1825, ibid., D1375/1/21.

44 Richey, *Irish land laws*, p. 44.

45 James Rooney to Nicholas Bayly, 15 Nov. 1743, P.R.O.N.I., Anglesey papers, D619/21/B/58.

46 McGildowney to Kerr, 6 Feb. 1815, P.R.O.N.I., McGildowney papers, D1375/1/6.

47 James Hamilton to eighth earl of Abercorn, 24 Apr. 1788, P.R.O.N.I., Abercorn papers, T2541/IA1/16/16.

48 James Hamilton, Jr., to ninth earl of Abercorn, 11 July 1795, ibid., T2541/IA1/21/17.

49 Report of Edward Evans to F.E. Foljambe on rental of 1808, P.R.O.N.I., Foljambe papers, T3381/5/59; Evans to Foljambe, report on rental of 1811, 27 Dec. 1811, ibid., T3381/5/62.

50 William Hudson to N.C. White, 28 Dec. 1816, P.R.O.N.I., Whyte papers, D2918/3/3/129. Hudson served twenty ejectments in 1825, but only seven were executed. Hudson to White, 14 Apr. 1825, ibid., D2918/3/4/168.

51 Agents adopted the same policy with regard to distraint of goods. Edmund McGildowney to Archibald McElheran, 18 Apr. 1820, P.R.O.N.I., McGildowney papers, D1375/1/15; William Mayne to Thomas Barrett-Lennard, 4 Aug. 1805, P.R.O.N.I., Barrett-Lennard papers, D1232/1/12.

52 James Hamilton of the Abercorn estate hoped that the ejectment of one Thomas Cunningham in 1769 would have a deterrent effect on backward tenants throughout the estate. Hamilton to Abercorn, 7 May 1769, P.R.O.N.I., Abercorn papers, T2541/IA1/8/131. In 1770, Hamilton drew up a list of 'the five tenants who have been remarkably backward in rent payment' in each manor, and two or three of those five were served with eviction notices. Hamilton to Abercorn, 18 Nov. 1770, 23 May 1771, ibid., T2541/IA1/9/8,120. Hamilton believed that 'driving the rich would hurry those that are poorer almost as effectually as if they were driven themselves.' Hamilton to Abercorn, 8 June 1770, 2 June 1771, ibid., T2541/IA1/9/42, 122. In 1781 a similar policy was executed. Hamilton to Abercorn, 8 Apr. 1781, ibid., T2541/IA1/13/84. For similar policies on the Ogilvie estate, see Rev. John Wilson to William Ogilvie, 29 Aug. 1807, P.R.O.N.I., Ogilvie papers, T1546/1, and on the Crofton estate see Edward [Lowther] to Hugh Crofton, 15 Feb. 1822, N.L.I., MS 20,773.

53 Not all agents shared this view of the prohibitive expense of ejectment. See Brabazon Noble to Thomas Barrett-Lennard, 16 Nov. 1771, P.R.O.N.I., Barrett-Lennard papers, film 170/2; Thomas Gelston to Andrew Nugent, 1 Feb. 1827, P.R.O.N.I., Nugent papers, D552/A/6/5/12. Edmund McGildowney, became more aggressive in these years, particularly with tenants in arears whose leases had expired. Edmund McGildowney to Archibald Stewart, 26 Oct. 1814, P.R.O.N.I., McGildowney papers, D1375/1/6. In 1817 he informed one Mr. Dobbs of the 'ejectments to all the tenants of Caravanmurphy who are due one year's rent or upwards.' McGildowney to [?] Dobbs, 6 Jan. 1817 and 11 Nov. 1817, McGildowney to Robert McNaghton, 23 Nov.

1817, ibid., D1375/1/10–11. John Lanktree, agent to Lord Londonderry, wrote in the spring of 1844: 'tenants from year to year cannot be ejected without first serving notice to quit, of which I have issued above 500 just now, which will enable me to open a vigorous campaign after November.' John Lanktree to Lord Londonderry, 16 Apr. 1844, P.R.O.N.I., Londonderry papers, D654/N2/27.

54 W. H. Crawford and Brian Trainor (eds.), *Aspects of Irish social history, 1750–1800* (Belfast, 1969), pp. 129–131. 'The business of the manor courts,' writes Power, 'grew subsequent to an act of 1785, 25 Geo. III, c. 44 which confirmed and enlarged their powers in civil cases. Following its passage a number of manor courts were revived.' Courts leet had jurisdiction over boundary disputes, roads, markets, tolls, weights and measures, and courts baron over debts and small contracts. Power, *Tipperary*, pp. 163–4; Dickson, 'Cork region,' p. 240.

55 McCabe, 'Law, conflict, and social order,' p. 397. When they were needed to preserve the peace and the hegemony of landlords, as for example in the case of the trial of members of the Hearts of Steel in 1771, the assize courts proved less than adequate to the task. P.R.O.N.I., Donegall papers, T1893.

56 McCabe, 'Law, conflict, and social order,' pp. 451–2.

57 If a tenant refused immediately to give up possession, William Hudson suggested in 1824 that 'all that can be done is to serve him with a printed notice before the first of May desiring him to give it up on the first of November, and if he then refuses, an ejectment can be brought at the following sessions which come on in January. But no ejectment can be brought against a yearly tenant without giving him six months' notice. In this I am taking the worst view of the case.' William Hudson to N.C. White, 7 Apr. 1824, P.R.O.N.I., Whyte papers, D2918/3/4/111.

58 Maguire, *Downshire estates*, pp. 53, 60.

59 Ibid., pp. 56, 60.

60 Robert Isaac to Henry Hatch, 2 Jan. 1748, P.R.O.N.I., Downshire papers, D607/A/62; James Savage to Hatch, 12 June 1756, ibid., D607/A/148; Savage to Hatch, 16 Apr. 1764, ibid., D607/A/247.

61 Henry Hatch to William Trumbell, 24 Dec. 1757, ibid., film 17/1.

62 J.P. Kelly to John Whyte, 14 Mar. 1849, Whyte papers, D2918/3/7/166.

63 Millers to Lawford, 2 Feb. 1849, ibid., D3632/1/2. A similar statement is made in Millers to Lawford, 3 June 1850, P.R.O.N.I., Drapers' company papers, D3632/1/2. Still, they served thirty-six ejectments at the Magherafelt sessions of 1848, and they anticipated that 'the court [of assistants] will have a good opportunity now in many instances of enlarging the farms and diminishing the overgrown population of the mountain districts.' Millers to Lawford, 15 Jan. 1849, ibid. Fifteen additional tenants were ejected in the summer of 1852 for non-payment of rent. Millers to Lawford, 17 Jan. 1853, ibid.

64 Idem, 31 Dec. 1850, ibid.

65 William Stannus to W.P. Sawyer, 1 Feb. 1878, ibid., D3632/1/4.

66 Comerford, 'Ireland 1850–1870'; Vaughan, 'Ireland, c. 1870', in Vaughan (ed.), *New history of Ireland*, v, p. 749.

67 Guinnane and Miller, 'Bonds without bondsmen,' pp. 118–33; Wright, *Two lands on one soil*, pp. 81–2.

68 Vaughan, *Landlords & tenants*, p. 93.

69 The Anglesey agent wrote in 1845 that one of the tenants 'gave £100 for, I suppose, that abominable custom of 'goodwill' for the part allotted to him.' Beer to Rutherford, 25 Feb. 1845, P.R.O.N.I., Anglesey papers, D619/23/B/142.

70 Eighth earl of Abercorn to James Hamilton, 7 June 1758, P.R.O.N.I., Abercorn papers, D623/A/15/114; Abercorn to Hamilton, 11 Dec. 1773, ibid., D623/A/21/67; Abercorn to Hamilton, 7 Nov. 1779, ibid., D623/A/15/91.

71 Hamilton to Abercorn, 20 Dec. 1767, ibid., T2541/IA1/7/112; idem, 3 Mar. 1769, ibid., T2541/IA1/8/115; Abercorn to Hamilton, 31 Dec. 1775, ibid., D623/A/22/52; idem, 19 Dec. 1777, ibid., D623/A/23/1; idem, 7 Nov. 1779, ibid., D623/A/24/26; idem, 7 Nov. 1779, ibid., D623/A/24/26; Hamilton to Abercorn, 24 Dec. 1779, ibid., T2541/IA2/2/117. This last statement was made in the midst of a major effort to promote sales and clear the arrears which had been mounting since 1777.

72 See P.R.O.N.I., Donegall papers, T1893 and J.S. Donnelly, Jr., 'Hearts of Oak, Hearts of Steel' in *Studia Hibernica*, no. 21 (1981), pp 3–73.

73 Hamilton to Abercorn, 13 May 1772, P.R.O.N.I., T2541/IA1/10/18.

74 Abercorn to Hamilton, 15 Aug. 1787, ibid., D623/A/26/125.

75 Hamilton to Abercorn, 27 Sept. 1787, ibid., T2541/IA2/4, p. 48. Forty ejectment notices were served in 1790. James McFarland to Abercorn, 6 Nov. 1790, ibid., T2541/IA1/17/24.

76 William Blacker to J. McNulty, 23 Nov. 1833, P.R.O.N.I., Gosford papers, D1606/5/1, cited in Gourley, 'Gosfords estates,' p. 149. Greig, *General report*, pp. 27–8, 262, 271, 277.

77 *Devon comm. evidence*, cited in Gourley, 'Gosford estates,' p. 149.

78 J.P. Kennedy, *Digest of evidence taken before her majesty's commisioners of inquiry into the state of the law and practice in respect to the occupation of land in Ireland*, 2 pts. (Dublin, 1847), i, p. 296.

79 Millers to Lawford, 14 Apr. 1849, P.R.O.N.I., Drapers' company papers, D3632/1/2; third report of Edward Oseland, 8 Nov. 1838, Merchant Tailors' Hall, Manor of Clothworkers' extracts from accounts, Box 131, N.L.I., film 1518; P. O'Connor to J. P. Kelly, 7 Mar. 1849, P.R.O.N.I., Whyte papers, D2918/3/7/165.

80 Edmund McGildowney to Adam Hunter, 9 Apr. 1816, P.R.O.N.I., McGildowney papers, D1375/1/8.

81 Third report of Edward Oseland, 8 Nov. 1838, Merchant Tailors' Hall, Manor of Clothworkers' extracts from accounts, Box 131 (N.L.I., film 1518). The Clothworkers' company agent gave this acount of a tenant-right sale: 'Mr. Davock is fully entitled to sell his interest as is usually done on this estate – that is, by private bargain, the purchaser being required to sign a memorandum.' R.B. Touse [?] to C.J. Knox, 28 June 1859, P.R.O.N.I., Hervey Bruce papers, D1514/2/5/14).

82 Report of Edward Fletcher, agent of Irish Society, 6 Mar. 1840, Irish Society court minute books, N.L.I., film 1524.

83 Henry Smith to Rowley Miller, 6 Oct. 1818, Drapers' company papers, D3632/3/2. And exactly a year later, Smith endeavoured to impress this point on a tenant in Moneymore. Smith to R. Gibson, 30 Oct. 1819, ibid.

84 Various letters of 1821, ibid., D3632/3/2.

85 Rowley and J. R. Miller to Edward Lawford, 1 Oct 1845, ibid., D3632/1/1.

86 Idem, 16 May, 1846, ibid.

87 In 1846 they wrote: 'this Tenant Right or goodwill is an anomoly but we might almost as well endeavour to stop the course of the Thames as to stop it.' Ibid. And again two years later: 'The company might nearly as well endeavour to stem the ocean's tide as to stop the tenant-right question on their estate. It is kept by no proper bounds and that is all that can be done.' Idem, 25 May 1848, ibid. See also letters of 22 May 1847 and 23 June 1848, ibid.

88 Idem, 23 June, 1848, ibid.
89 Idem, 13 Nov. 1843, ibid. In 1864 Rowley Miller claimed that the population of the estate was 8,355, reduced by 2,500 since 1841, and was reported to be as high as 10,740 in 1818. 'The decrease on the estate up to 1861 of 2,500 has been owing almost entirely to the enlargement of farms upon the estate and to the wise regulation that a father cannot divide his farm with a son or sons. . . .' 220 farms had been amalgamated in this period. 'The tenants are all, thank God, invariably thankful and contented and acknowledge that they are much more comfortable than they formerly were.' Miller to W.H. Sawyer, 6 July 1864, ibid., D3632/1/3. This letter also includes figures for each division of the estate.

Part III

The End of Tenant Right

CHAPTER SIX

The End of Tenant Right

TENANT RIGHT AND POLITICAL ECONOMY

Chapter 2 traced the role that customary tenure played in signifying the legitimacy of the developing estate system in the eighteenth century. Throughout the period from 1790 to 1830, which saw an end to the moral economy in the 1790s, the 1798 rebellion and the Act of Union, and the struggle for Catholic emancipation, the legitimacy of that system was never seriously called into question. It could even be said to have become more secure as a growing body of enfranchised voters, yeoman, and others took opportunities to prove their loyalty to their landlord's interest. Even though historical claims for continuous tenure were frequently based on participation in political and military events, the custom of tenant right generally existed below the sphere of politics. Most of the evidence presented until now has been drawn from private and particular conversations between landlords, their agents, and their tenants. In the nineteenth century this began to change. From the 1830s, particular conversations formerly confined to estate correspondence began to be inexorably and irreversibly drawn into a public hegemonic battle over what has come to be called the 'land question.' There are both political and economic antecedents to this development. The Act of Union had already opened the question of the textual or representational tension between concepts of Irish and British unity, identity, and equality under the crown, and a reality that obstinately refused to conform to such concepts.[1] Meanwhile, the dramatic economic transformations throughout the British Isles in the early nineteenth century created paradoxes surrounding the Act of Union and the applicability of modern political economy to Ireland. These paradoxes surrounding Ireland's place within the first industrial nation would only deepen with the course of events and the hardening of ideological positions. The position of the small to middling farmer class, hit hardest by the post-Napoleonic deflation and industrial development, was the nub of the matter. Their place in contemporary society was threatened on a number of fronts. The threshold of economic viability in terms of farm size and productive output had begun to shift rapidly. The new aggressiveness in estate management identified in Chapter 5 was directed specifically at this population. In addition, its political position was weakened. The elimination of the political power of smallholders after the 1829 disenfranchisement of the forty-shilling freeholder, combined with the passage of the Poor Law in 1838, amended in 1843, which placed responsibility for the poor rates of those tenants paying under £4 rent on landlords, left this class politically exposed and powerless.[2] The Ulster smallholder, previously an important placeholder in the micro-society of the landed estate, was now disenfranchised, economically vulnerable, and subject to greater managerial control. The middling strata of farmers, suspicious of both the market and the growing power of estate management, developed a political defence of their status as farmers, tenants, and citizens. This defence would place the foundations of the land system in question and re-articulate the rules of private property in terms that would conserve their social power within a capitalist economy.

This was the milieu in which William Sharman Crawford, a landowner and member of parliament for County Down, introduced legislative initiatives that first politicized the land question. Crawford's 'persistent and indefatigable advocacy of tenant right'[3] in the 1830s and early 1840s forced the government to appoint the Devon commission to inquire into the occupation of land and agricultural practice in Ireland. The essential problems posed in these years were: how will the reality on Irish estates be made to conform to the text of the land law? Must that reality be drastically, even violently, altered to conform to the text? Or, alternatively, will the Irish legal text, written by legislation and judicial process to conform more closely to the English, be sufficient to rewrite that reality? From another angle, the question was: if indeed the law and Irish reality were irreconcilably separate, then what new law was appropriate to that reality? Serious consideration of this latter question leads on to a re-examination of the text of both the Union and the laws of political economy. The issues are eloquently captured in an exchange of letters between two political economists, Hutches Trower and David Ricardo, in 1822. Trower wrote to Ricardo:

> It appears to me that no permanent or substantial good can be done until all small farms and small tenancies are got rid of. These are the curse of Ireland. They are calculated to destroy the wholesome dependence of the lower upon the upper classes, which is one of the master links of society; and to encourage habits of idleness, which are the bane of all moral feeling. I am aware there would be difficulty in carrying this measure into execution, but the object is most important. The two deficiencies in Ireland are want of capital and want of industry. By destroying small tenancies you would obtain both.

Ricardo responded that Trower had identified the effect, not the cause. 'If Ireland had a good system of law – if property was secure – if an Englishman lending money to an Irishman could by some easy process oblige him to fulfil his contract and not be set at defiance by the chicanery of sheriff's agents in Ireland, capital would flow into Ireland.'[4] For Trower the law is useless until Irish reality is changed. For Ricardo, reality flows from texts: the text of the law and the text of the market. This distinction corresponds to two different approaches to the land question in the first half of the nineteenth century. For those who felt as Trower did, Irish reality must be made to conform to English law, and this conformity required mass emigration and the education and re-indoctrination of those who remained. For Trower, proper political economy would function only if the ignorant Irish peasant could be either eliminated or culturally adapted to it. Henry Gould's pamphlet of 1847 argued that the small farmer class must 'be abolished, and become labourers at money wages, to the more opulent, in order that a more productive mode of cultivation may be pursued.'[5] Edward Burroughs, William Blacker, and William Hickey, in tracts published between 1821 and 1841, emphasized the need for education of tenants toward cleanliness, efficiency, and new crop rotations. Borroughs highlighted the following problems: supine and unpatriotic land-lords, lack of capital and skill, the ignorance and indolence of the tenantry, uncertain implementation of agricultural law by landlords, unfair tithes, and the shortage of circulating medium.[6] Richard Griffith attacked what he saw as a lazy and conservative Irish peasantry. Better transport and more bog recla-mation could ameliorate Irish problems, but he also urged the adoption of a liberal system of religious and moral education for the poor.[7] Re-indoctrination was also the implicit solution in J. E. Bicheno's *Ireland and its political economy*, which complained of Irish Catholics' 'moral antipathy to economic rationality, their perceived opposition to individualism, and their refusal to see land as merely a commodity and regarding the landlord-tenant relation as of a "social nature," and not just as a contract between buyers and sellers.'[8] The reports of the commissioners inquiring into the 'condition of the poorer classes in Ireland' in 1838 were also concerned primarily with social and economic, not legal, reforms. They recommended a program of social engi-neering on a massive and expensive scale: to bring wasteland into cultivation, drain and improve existing farms, provide agricultural instruction to raise the standard of farming and loans to construct or extend the economic infra-structure generally, and offer large scale assistance for emigration.[9]

As opposed to manipulating society to conform to the text, Ricardan utili-tarianism had it that it was only necessary to change the text – the text of the legal system and the text of the market – and reality would naturally adjust itself to the ideal. The proper solution to the failure of political economy, according to the Ricardan line of reasoning, was more and better political economy. Under the laws of proper political economy, both landlords and tenants were 'free' to negotiate however they might. An undated letter fragment from the Anglesey estate, apparently from the agent to a tenant sometime in the mid-eighteenth century, shows the situation of those economically weak tenants who were subjected to the 'freedom' of the market: 'I have some reason to believe the rent which you are to pay for the lands you hold of me not to be so secure as I would wish. I am content you should continue tenant still, provided you can get me such security for the rent as I shall approve of. If not, I shall take myself to be at liberty to look out for another tenant . . . , and you have the same liberty also.'[10] Landlords and their apologists were fond of pointing out that land was no different than any other commodity and landlords and tenants no different than any other traders of commodities. The marquis of Dufferin made an analogy between landed property and a merchant ship; the tenant was the seaman, and the landlord the shipowner.[11] The landlord Robert Perceval-Maxwell advised a tenant in 1863 that 'the purchase of the interest in your lease must stand by itself, totally irrespective of any other transaction, just as if the sale was made to a Belfast merchant or any other person.'[12] Lord Palmerston, perhaps the most powerful mouthpiece for the views of Irish landlordism in his day, railed against fixity of tenure as 'communistic and totally at variance with the social organisation to which the country has attached so much value, and on which the interests of the country depends. I say let the owners and the tenants settle their own affairs – give each full liberty to do so.'[13]

Ricardan views naturally had academic proponents as well. William Neilson Hancock, the sometime Professor of Political Economy in Trinity College and brother of John Hancock, a northern land agent, argued that the poor state of Irish agriculture was due to the state of the land law. The solution lay not in the reform of individual practices, nor in the voluntaristic infusion of various types of capital investment, nor again in forced clearances of estates, but in removing legal and institutional impediments to free trade in land and the application of capital to land. Legal violations of the maxims of political economy such as fixity of tenure were the cause of, not the solution to, Ireland's ills. Free trade in land was for Robert Longfield paramount, and would eventually eliminate problems such as ethnic differences in productivity, poor crop rotations, etc.[14] Jonathan Pim argued that Irish economic backwardness was attributable neither to creed nor to Celtic origin. 'Irishmen succeed in America,' he noted, 'why not at home?' His answer pointed to the sorry history of bad laws and investment-depressing agitation, and to the correctives of free trade in land and the rationalization of tenures.[15]

The Ricardan tendency was much in evidence in Westminster. There is a certain Ricardan direction to legislative reform in the pre-famine decades, of which the increasing power of ejectment discussed in Chapter 5 was a part. The stream of Irish land legislation in the period 1800–1840 was designed, in Oliver MacDonagh's synopsis, 'to secure the landlord's position, as absolute owner, by cheapening and facilitating ejectments, evictions, and the consolidation of holdings. They were moreover accompanied by statutory attempts to render these courses of action safer by coercion methods, militia laws, suspension of *habeas corpus* and other methods for stamping out peasant counteraction.'[16] The successive encumbered estates acts are another example of this trend. By facilitating the replacement of bankrupt capitalists, these laws aspired to change personnel in the hope that the game of political economy might be better played.[17] Ricardan legislation was no more or less callous than Trower's proposed social revolution, for the problem and the solution were formulated in terms of abstract structures,[18] not concrete historical agents. Ricardo's technique, Marx complained, was to 'begin with pauperizing the inhabitants of the country, and when there is no more profit to be ground out of them, when they have grown a burden to the revenue, drive them away, and sum up your Net Revenue! The number and welfare of productive individuals is irrelevant, the only concern is 'that grammatical entity, "the national wealth".'[19] Whether by Trower's forced annihilation or Ricardo's equally efficacious legislative reform, the end was to be the same. As *The Times* put it on 16 April 1858, 'England has submitted to the change necessitated by the consolidation of farms and the migration of small freeholders and copyholders into towns, and so must Ireland'.[20]

The problem facing both conservative reformers and Ricardan utilitarians was the inescapable and seemingly unbridgeable gap between social reality and legal text. *Laissez-faire* could only work, as a *Times* editorial singled out for abuse by Marx had it, 'under proper conditions of society.' These conditions would obtain, Marx was not the last to point out, only with 'the interference of the soldier, of the policeman, and of the hangman.'[21] James A. Lawson, Whately Professor of Political Economy at Trinity College during the 1840s, pointed out that the science of political economy itself was born out of this difference between the ideal and the real. Political economy owed its existence to 'the misfortunes and calamities caused by offending against the laws of nature.'[22] If political economy, as natural law, could only become immanent artificially, then the policy of *laissez-faire*, paradoxically, had to be interventionist, not a passive and minimalist application of natural law.[23] This paradox put *laissez-faire* ideologues in a rather unfortunate rhetorical situation. Consider for example the speech of the marquis of Londonderry to the House of Lords in 1850 at the height of the tenant-right agitation in the vicinity of his County Down estate. He complained of the incitements by Presbyterian ministers to tenants to break their private contracts with landlords. He hesitated to propose that the county be proclaimed, 'but really something must be done to put a stop to such outrages. . . . Because, my lords, I must maintain, the laws of property are the laws of the land and, if it came to be discussed, I should like to know if the relation between landlord and tenant is not after all merely commercial, standing upon the same footing as a merchant with his customer – the public has no business with them. Each value their own bargains with their eyes open.'[24] The paradox of this plea is clear: if the relationship is purely commercial and 'the public has no business with it,' then surely the marquis has no business begging the House of Lords to do something on his behalf. If on the other hand the issue is public, then the agitation by enfranchised tenants for reform of the law is no less legitimate than the marquis' pleas for protection.

These intractable paradoxes created the political space for the articulation of a legislative reformism that recognized Irish singularity. Conceptually, this position is a radical version of Ricardanism where the law is altered to conform to an unalterable reality. For the likes of Trower this was an impossibility because under the Union, Irish laws which 'infringed the rights of property' might set a dangerous precedent for England.[25] Such fears help to explain the shrillness of the Victorian reaction to the idea of an 'Irish political economy'[26] which set out a 'sacral' alternative to the economistic chain of signifiers of English political economy: 'property, rent, productivity, upkeep, improvement, impoverishment, ownership, tenant right, landlord right, buying and selling, state purchase, redistribution, and so forth.'[27] Proponents of a peculiarly Irish political economy such as Mitchell, Davitt, Lalor, and Gavan Duffy formulated an alternative discourse around the terms 'soil' and 'earth.' These symbols were anterior to land and property, representing a state that preceded the plantations and the conquests, ontologically and metaphysically more fundamental than land as a 'politico-legal entity.'[28] As such they were held to be more powerful symbolically by way of their natural materiality. There was sympathy for these conceptions even from within the ranks of the political economists. 'There must be something wrong in a theory,' wrote political economist Samuel Laing, 'which is so universally condemned by the secret instinct of good sense and right feeling of the public mind, when the very first step is taken by an individual landlord in Ireland to bring the theory into practice on his estate.'[29] A number of political economists, most prominently J. S. Mill, defended a more radical form of utilitarianism by which the land law should be altered in order to preserve and cultivate essential aspects of Irish reality, especially the small-farm community.[30] Defence of the four-to six-acre farm as a viable economic unit occupied a number of authors in the early nineteenth century.[31] Following Mill, William Sharmon Crawford offered economic defences of the small farm in an effort to justify land law reform on economic rather than ethical or political principles. Sharman Crawford argued that small farms were productive in Ireland because of poor soils, falling prices which benefited the subsistence farmer, and capital shortage. A small-farm society, he argued, could supply industrial labour complete with a subsistence safety-net to mitigate the exploitation inflicted by urban industrialists. If the six-acre farm failed, it was because of oppressive rents, insecure tenure, lack of information, but not for reasons of productivity.[32] Sharman Crawford dismissed race, religion, population density, or the want of manufactures as causes of Irish poverty in order to highlight the predominant role of property relations. Authorities such as Mill, LeQuesne, Thornton, and Laing all agreed, he argued, that when smallholdings were held under secure tenures, prosperity followed.[33]

The year 1835 marks the entry of this more radical reformism into Irish politics. Two important events occurred in that year: Sharmon Crawford introduced an Irish land bill in parliament, and the first public meeting urging the legislative recognition of the custom of tenant right took place in Comber, County Down. Tenant right from this date forward became a nation-wide question, though not yet a question of nationhood. The question of how the economic surplus of the economy was to be socially distributed would heretofore be a question of the rights of property, despite O'Connell's efforts in the 1830s to articulate it in terms of the rights of the Anglican church.[34] During the crisis of the 1840s, the total value of tenant right in Ulster came to be viewed in terms of the macroeconomic capital stock of the province. When newspapers began to speak of the £20–30 million (*Banner of Ulster*, 24 June 1845) or £60 million (*Belfast Vindicator*, 22 March 1845) value of tenant right,[35] it had taken on a new political significance and symbolic value in a public sphere that would be radically restructured by the famine and the Representation of the People Act of 1851.[36] In these decades the question of the applicability of political economy to Ireland took the form of a debate over the meaning and significance of tenant right.

The ideological problems surrounding the definition of tenant right in historical writing discussed in Chapter 1 were first seriously broached in these decades. The appointment of the Devon commission made a national issue of tenant right, marked the definitive end of an age of innocence with regard to the meaning of the custom, and began a process of defining and finally eliminating tenant right. Gone were the days when the custom was left unexamined as long as the rent was tolerably well paid. A new divisiveness centered around the effort to make the meaning of tenant right 'uni-accentual' ensued. Looking back from the year 1875 on the history of landlord and tenant before this politicization of the question, Robert Donnell wrote: 'Happy, says the sage, was the man who never knew he had a stomach. To be envied were the

Ulster tenants when dispossession being unknown, and improvements uncon-fiscated, while enjoying in reality the protection of the usage of the province, they were unconscious that they possessed what the jurists called tenant right. The right was not spoken of till the wrong had been wrought.'[37] 'Landlords,' suggests Vaughan, 'put up with tenant right only as long as its implications remained obscure.'[38] The more closely they examined tenant right, as the marquis of Dufferin quipped to the Bessborough commission, 'the more clearly right and wrong declare themselves.'[39] It was, in Bakhtin and Thompson's terms, a classic hegemonic battle over the uni-accentual nature of the sign.

It is clear from both estate correspondence[40] and Devon commission testi-mony that agents, priests, and Presbyterian ministers were stuck in the middle of this battle. Some witnesses were clearly struggling to explain the ambiguous nature of the custom to the landlordist Devon committee. John Hancock, Lord Lurgan's agent, considered tenant right to be 'the claim of the tenant and his heirs to continue in undisturbed possession of his farm so long as the rent is paid, and in case of a change in occupancy it is the sum of money which the new occupier must pay to the old for the peaceable enjoyment of the holding.'[41] The Rev. John Brown, a Presbyterian minister from County Londonderry, testified:

> I wish to define what I mean by tenant right. It is the interest a tenant should have in the capital he has expended in money and labour, in build-ing houses and making improvements . . . ; [but] it is practically carried much further and understood by the people to carry to their property; they think they have a claim on it. The general impression in our country is that every man who owns land or houses has a certain interest in them, the value of which is regulated by the interest of the country. Upon that principle it is they that unfortunately wish, and it is the wish of human nature, to have a claim upon the soil, and that is what causes the people to offer far more than what the land is worth.[42]

The Devon inquiry and the report of the commissioners raised expectations and provoked strong responses. One Leitrim land agent observed 'that there is a strong feeling in the minds of the lower orders here that any tenants evicted in the last forty years are to be put into possession again by the land commissioners.'[43] More generally, and more realistically, tenants perceived that 'land legislation would effectively outlaw the custom by ignoring it.'[44] The agent of the Merchant Tailors' proportion reported in 1843 that tenants had become more aggressive since 1840. They 'used to ask indulgence as a favour, now they demand it as a right, and often speak with careless indifference about what a landlord *can do* in the enforcement of his demands.'[45] The Millers of Draperstown offered a typically insightful, though in retrospect perhaps overly alarmist, commentary on the situation in a letter of 1848:

The land commission with Lord Devon at its head has we conceive done much mischief in bringing this point so prominently before the public because it has unsettled the minds of men, not only in the other provinces, but in this. The tenantry everywhere talk of matters connected with land now in a manner they never thought of before and what may be the upshot time can only unravel, but one thing *we are convinced* of is that if the *Government* or the *Landlords* will not make a rallying point for the loyal men of Ireland and that soon the country may be lost before they are aware of it. There is a spirit abroad which would at once overwhelm the Government if it were not that the dissatified portion of the Protestant community are afraid to join the Romans lest they themselves should be cut off after a bit by the latter. Feeling strongly as we do on this subject we hope the court will excuse us speaking strongly. We believe, *humanly speaking*, that if a rallying point be not made, and we are inclined to think that Orangeism and muskets combined are the only sure one just now, an outbreak may take place which may cost a vast loss of life and property. . . . If we lived in other times there would be no difficulty in keeping separate our acts as agents of the company from our public acts but at present there might be, *although there ought not to be* more or less difficulty in doing so.[46]

In this context, attempts at even-handed definitions of the custom gave way to strident polemic. Landlords and their ideological defenders attempted to delimit and determine the meaning of tenant right within the acceptable boundaries of the 'rights of property.' This meant, in effect, restricting the meaning of tenant right to its tangible, financial aspects. The Devon report, for example, recommended only a compensation for improvements bill, sidestepping the thornier issues of inheritance and free sale. The strategy proposed was to ignore these latter aspects of the custom, neither to legalize nor to ban them. Legalizing the custom, according to the report, would be an unthinkable abrogation of the 'just rights of property,' but on the other hand social turmoil 'would result from any hasty or general disallowance of it.'[47] William Neilson Hancock used his brother John's evidence to the Devon commission concerning the management of Lord Lurgan's property to conclude that 'the tenant right of Ulster, when considered economically, is only a recognition, by long established custom, of the right of the tenant to the fair profit of the capital vested by him, by purchase or expenditure, in the permanent improvements of the land, or to the inherited profit arising from such improvements, when made by some of his ancestors.'[48] According to Robert Dudley Baxter, tenant right has nothing to do with the length of tenure, which is agreed upon independently or implied as yearly.[49] On the other hand, the radical end of the tenant-right movement[50] put forward its own more capacious but no less monolithic definition of tenant right, which amounted to a community-based valuation of improvements and a perpetual tenure at a fixed rent. William Connor, a landowner from Maryborough, who is often described as 'the earliest and most indefatigable apostle of land reform,'[51] claimed in an 1840 tract that the tenant 'by virtue of his cultivation of the soil, possessed a right to its undisturbed occupation which the landlord should not be entitled to challenge as long as he received his rent.' Connor's advocacy of a 'valuation and perpetuity' at a meeting of the Tenant League in 1847 went far beyond the avowed purpose of the league, namely, 'extending the tenant right of Ulster to Tipperary.'[52] The 'valuation and perpetuity' solution was clearly beyond the permissible range of opinions on the land question at this stage.[53] He was successfully prosecuted for sedition for articulating this view in an inflammatory speech at a tenant-right meeting in Mountmellick and sentenced to six months imprisonment in 1843.[54]

Crawford's legislative effort was clearly informed by the idea of fixity of tenure and fair rents. But as a landlord and parliamentary representative his radicalism had strict limits. Crawford argued in an 1837 pamphlet that God is the only absolute owner of the soil, and that a fair and honest living from the soil is everyone's natural right.[55] He attempted to articulate a position somewhere between bourgois free traders and radical peasant proprietors with a rhetoric of 'joint interest' in the soil. But he had great difficulty reconciling his liberal views of the land question with the pressures he faced discharging family debts with the revenue of his County Down estate. He wrote in the 1850s:

> What I should want is a power of offering some terms of tenure which would enable me honourably to raise the rents to a fair, improved value, and if I could give a perpetuity interest I could raise the rent still higher. I could take fines which would enable me to pay off the debts. It is undoubtedly a losing scheme in my opinion to refuse largely increased rental on the denial of a *legal* interest whilst that interest practically exists by a *custom* which cannot be honestly or honorably denied by the landlord.

Other members of his family, and in particular John, who managed the estate, were uncomfortable with the position William had put them in. When parliament failed to legislate on the subject, William had felt obliged to give the tenants a private contract which would guarantee 'that security to which they have a right.' His brother was hurt by what he mistakenly regarded as William's 'doubts on his future conduct on the improvements question.'[56] Whatever the impact of his private scruples, the ideological composition of the House of Commons and the clearly stated opposition to fixity of tenure by Peel's government forced Crawford to focus on those reforms that he felt had some chance of a hearing in parliament. His bills restricted themselves to establishing guarantees for compensation for improvements[57] which required no previous registration of improvements or restriction on the type of improvements, and no limitation on the length of tenure beyond which improvements might be considered exhausted. They also provided that the amount of compensation be determined by local arbitration, without preset limits.

Notwithstanding the wild rhetoric of Connor in the 1840s, tenant-right activists were also generally careful to emphasize individualist commercial ambitions of Ulster farmers, trimming their rhetoric for parliamentary ears. A petition submitted to parliament from Comber in 1835 opened by recognizing that Irish circumstances 'are such as to offer every facility and prospect of success to the pursuits of commercial enterprise,' but went on to complain of the circumstances that 'dog improvement in agriculture' and 'fetter that commercial energy which can only be brought into useful action by the prosperity of the husbandman.'[58] Their rhetoric focused on compensation for improvements. Connor's rhetoric about perpetual tenures was conspicuous by its absence: 'Petitioners maintain that landlords have a right to a fair rent for their land, but they also maintain that tenants are equally entitled to a remuneration for such improvements as are calculated to increase the value of property.'[59]

It appears then that in the 1830s and 1840s landlords were largely successful in reducing the controversy over tenant right to the tangible and acceptable issue of compensation. Edward Driver, deputy to the Clothworkers' company, explained the custom in these terms in 1840:

> I consider it very probable this right originated in some manner . . . from the tenant having originally enclosed the land and brought it into cultivation, erected a house and other necessary buildings, made subdivisions, fences, and other improvements principally at his own expense, but it cannot be denied that on the company's estates these operations must be mostly of such ancient date, probably far exceeding a century, that it may be presumed long leases were at those times granted to such adventurers, and which have very long since expired, and the parties may have continued in the occupation a series of years, probably in many cases equal to the original leases.[60]

Driver concluded that the present tenants could not possibly have any unexhausted improvements, as the company's estate has been out of lease for seventy years. Having discussed the origins of tenant right with a number of agents and gentlemen, he claimed that he had 'found scarcely any two agreeing on the origin of it, its practical treatment hitherto, or upon a remedial provision for alleviating the bad effects or extirpation of the system altogether.'[61] The marquis of Dufferin's agent also saw the importance of articulating the problem in terms of tangible rather than intangible factors. He wrote to Dufferin in 1854:

Inasmuch as it is necessary in all cases of outgoing tenants to allow them certain sums as compensation for something not easily definable it will be a matter of some importance to have said sums recognized as having been given for some tangible objects instead of for an imaginary thing under the name of 'tenant right.' I would thereupon suggest that as to farm buildings it would be better not to limit compensation as to tenure for in nine instances out of ten the claim as to farm buildings could have lapsed and that in the event of a sum still being looked for and very likely conceded it would only in my opinion be perpetuitary Tenant Right.[62]

Dufferin responded that 'in time the tenant's interest in all improvements must lapse. The only question is the duration of the term necessary to exhaust his interest. This is a matter of exact calculation. You say that an interest which has no relationship to improvements is transferred under the Tenant-right Custom – this is quite true and under no circumstances could you make so indefinite, so intangible a value the subject of legislation.'[63]

This rhetoric of compensation did reflect the concerns of tenants whose tenant-right values had been eroded by the post-Napoleonic deflation and had plummeted severely in the famine decade, but it is difficult to see how the purely material aspect of compensation for improvements could have motivated this mass movement. By many accounts the departure of a tenant from a farm with unexhausted improvements was a rare occurrence, limited to cases where recently improved land had unexpectedly changed hands. The Devon commissioners concluded from their inquiry that 'the tenant right is seldom sold by improving tenants . . . ; even if the price of tenant right be at all affected by the improvements made on the farm, a fact doubted by some witnesses, it is not so influenced in proportion to the value of the improvements.'[64] In fact, most discussions of compensation for improvements that surfaced in estate correspondence involved unexpected terminations of tenancies. On the Abercorn estate Hamilton noticed that the subject arose either because of a surveyor's rearrangement of a holding or upon the death of a tenant,[65] and there are many examples of this from the records of various Ulster estates.[66] It is also questionable how the tenant-right system affected farm investment. Witnesses before the Devon commission argued almost in the same breath that the custom of tenant right promoted and retarded capital investment in agriculture.[67] Few modern economic historians are willing to defend the so called 'land tenure hypothesis' which blames low investment on uncertain tenures.[68] Parties on both sides of the question placed compensation for improvements high on the political agenda for ideological rather than material reasons, to the great frustration of radicals. The bishop of Kerry, for example, wrote to Isaac Butt in May of 1867 that 'it riles me to see men who assume the leadership in a question like this shouting for compensation for improvements while they leave both tenure and rent in the arbitrary powers of the landlord.'[69]

Crawford's bills to guarantee compensation for improvements were nevertheless ritually howled at by the landlordists in parliament. Yet between 1845 and 1848, the government introduced three bills to compete with Crawford, signalling a shift in landlord position from one of posturing about sacred contracts to a more pragmatic attempt to address the problem of compensation for improvements on their own terms. The first of these bills required that any new improvement be registered and agreed to by the landlord, and spelled out strict time limits after which tenants could no longer claim compensation for improvements – 31 years for houses, 14 for drainage – and strict limits on the amount of compensation to be given. The earl of Lincoln's bill of 1846 was much the same. The earl of Sommerville's bill of 1848, the third government-sponsored bill, provided a mechanism for public notice of planned improvements, set a limit on compensation for improvements of no more than the equivalent of three years' rent, further limited such compensation only to holdings valued over £10 p.a., and banned any retroactive claims for compensation for improvements before the bill would take effect. The bill was amended to include the appointment of an 'Inspector of Improvements' responsible for arbitrating disputes over the value of improvements. None of these bills was destined to make it through the House of Commons, castigated by radicals as 'milk and water delusions' and by landlordists as legislative robbery.[70] The tenant-right movement, which had showed some promise in the late 1840s of becoming a national political force, collapsed under the weight of its own internal conflicts over strategy in relation to the governments of the day.[71] With the collapse of that movement in the economically resurgent 1850s, 'milk and water' solutions were replaced by more straightforward *laissez-faire* proposals in the Ricardan mold.

COMPENSATION FOR IMPROVEMENTS AND CALDWELL'S ACT OF 1860

In 1850, Joseph Napier, a leading sponsor of land bills over the next decade, asked two barristers to prepare a report on the land law in Ireland. The result was Ferguson and Vance's *The tenure and improvement of land in Ireland, considered with reference to the relation of landlord and tenant in Ireland and tenant right* (1851), a work which became an important reference in the next two decades and the intellectual foundation of Deasy's and Caldwell's acts of 1860 – the enshrinement of capitalist property relations in Irish land law.[72] In step with the divisiveness of the previous decade, Ferguson and Vance articulated the land question in terms of an unambiguous dichotomy between feudalism and capitalism. Landlord and tenant relations could be founded on only one of two bases: feudal law or Roman civil law. The former implied 'mutual support and dependence, correlative rights and duties,' while the latter took the form of 'conventional contract between two independent parties, founded on considerations of mutual convenience and self-interest, and regulated by terms and conditions to be faithfully and literally complied with.'[73] Clearly, tenant right had to land on one side or the other of this dichotomy. Ferguson and Vance associated the ideas of the tenant-right movement with both feudalism and revolution, those of 'all good men' with contract.[74] The fact that tenant right was a custom that developed among a tenantry that saw itself neither as feudal nor revolutionary but progressive and modernizing, the very foundation of the Ulster economy, was inadmissible to Ferguson and Vance. In their conclusion they wrote:

> The tenant right in respect to mere occupancy, formed not upon prescriptive enjoyment or indulgence, but on inherent right, with its revolutionary doctrines of fixity of tenure and valuation of rents, we have noticed for the information of those who may be ignorant of the Tenant League agitation in Ireland, rather to warn them of the embarrassments in which the general subject is involved, than to confute or reason upon such wild and dangerous projects. The consequences of this agitation are such as to lead every lover of peace and order to remove from the mouths of such orators every possible pretext for their agitation, and every semblance of injustice, by placing the question on a fair and liberal footing.[75]

Ferguson and Vance split the meaning of tenant right into two unequal halves: (1) tenant right of occupancy, with its hereditary and historical claims to the soil – this was to be demonised and suppressed – and (2) tenant right of compensation for improvements, which was given a much more sympathetic treatment. They disengenuously pretended confusion by calling tenant right 'a phantom that melts away under every attempt to define it, and that, chameleon-like, appeared to assume a different aspect every time it presents itself,'[76] and they repeated the recommendation of the Devon commission that parliament should ignore it rather than either outlaw it or legalize it. The strategy, which was to be embodied in government bills over the next decade, was to suppress the controversial meaning of tenant right, and hope that generous compensation for improvements would appeal to the tenantry and soften the rhetoric of the agrarian radicals. It is clear that they were aware of competing interpretations and that they were hoping that the defenders of such interpretations, like tenant right itself, would melt away like so many phantoms.[77]

Caldwell's act of 1860 required that tenants publicly register their proposed improvements and accept a specified and fixed twenty-five-year annuity as compensation. The act was an unqualified failure, according to testimony before parliamentary committees. Neither landlord nor tenant saw much use in it. On the side of the landlord, the marquis of Dufferin argued that given the size of farms prevailing in Ulster, their primary objective was the tearing down of improvements and consolidation of farms, not more improvements. Tenants, on the other hand found the terms of the annuity incomprehensible, objectionable, or both.[78] Privately, Dufferin recognized the inadequacy of Caldwell's act as a guide to the management of his own estate by increasing the limit of a tenant's claim for an agricultural improvement from twenty-five to forty-one years. 'Make them agree and sign to the 7.5 percent as the rate of tenant's compensation as well as the rate for the purchase of the annuity,' he wrote to his agent in 1866. 'If they object to the forty-one year limit, tell them that by rights their lease ought to be the limit, and every year beyond the twenty-five for which that is value is an act of grace on my part.'[79] Two of his tenants, however, refused to accept anything but a system of arbitrated valuation of the improvements. David Anderson and James Dickson complained to Dufferin about his restrictions on the value of tenant right in 1865:

> We respectfully submit that we do not consider the terms of arbitration which we have received from [the agent] Mr. Thomson altogether equitable. We are willing to be bound by them so far as the buildings on both the leased and unleased land are concerned. But with regard to the unexhausted improvements on the farm, we take the liberty of saying that suitable fences in good keeping made more than twenty-one years ago are not only as good but better now than when constructed, that places converted into arable land where once there were only rocks and marshes are as valuable now as the year after the rocks were removed or the marshes filled up. The same view holds in some measure with respect to draining – if properly done, its efficiency or value is not exhausted in twice fourteen years. We respectfully admit to your lordship that it is fair and equitable to leave [it] to the arbitration to determine what is the present value of these improvements, be it much or little.[80]

The effort to redirect the question of tenant right toward the more 'tangible' issue of compensation for improvements touched on intractable social and conceptual difficulties surrounding landlord-tenant relations. The difficulties of crediting the landlord and the tenant in correct proportions for the change in the value of the land occurring during a tenure were inherently problematic. Marx argued that the relative value of a farm, which he called the 'differential rent,' depended on two interrelated quantities: the natural fertility of the farm (DR1) and the capital invested in the farm (DR2). The relationship between DR1 and DR2 is twofold: first, each sets a limit on the other, capital invested sets a limit on fertility, fertility on the returns to capital; second, according to David Harvey's analysis of the problem, their interaction makes it 'impossible for either landowner or capitalist to separate the two forms of rent, to distinguish what is due to the flow of capital and what is due to the 'permanent' effects of natural differences in fertility. The true basis of the appropriation of rent is rendered opaque.'[81] When a certain quantity and form of capital investment (and with it, a particular orientation of production) becomes generalized, the 'natural' differences between farms are no longer the same. For example, Ulster arable land that was once considered unproductive becomes more desirable once the infrastructure of the linen industry is built up, and the reverse is true when it disintegrates. DR2 thus silently graduates into DR1, improvements are naturalized. 'The complex interactions of DR1, owing plainly to the landlord, and DR2, at least partially due to capital, make it impossible to distinguish who should get what,' according to Harvey's gloss. 'There is no way to ensure that the appropriators of rent take their due and only their due. . . . The landlord is perpetually caught between the evident foolishness of taking too little and the penalties that accrue from taking too much.'[82] This opacity complicates a number of issues associated with tenant right – the rent level, the length of tenure, responsibility for investment, and compensation – and plagued managers of Ulster estates over the entire period considered in this book. There was no easy solution to the problem of compensation for improvements, so that, 'like the contract over the working day, so central to the relation of capital to labour, it is ultimately regulated by the state, either by legislation or by legal precedent.'[83]

The issue was especially confused in Ireland because of Irish landlords' historical inability or unwillingness to invest in their land. The fundamental distinction between English and Irish agrarian capitalism was that in England the landlord took responsibility for major capital investments in the land, whereas in Ireland the tenant shouldered these responsibilities. According to Brady, the law implied that

> when a tenancy ended the principle *quicquid plantatur solo, solo cedit* [translated by Justice Shee as 'tenants' improvements are landlords' perquisites'] applied, and the landlord was legally entitled to resume possession not only of the land but also of any appurtenances that became attached to it during the tenancy. In England, however, improvements such as buildings and fencing were customarily made by the landlord, but in Ireland by the tenants, so the plight of an outgoing tenant in Ireland was exacerbated by the law.[84]

How could Irish landlords be given credit for the increase in value of agricultural property? As Ó Gráda has acerbicly suggested, 'the old orthodoxy was crude and sometimes silly, yet it sought to make the point that landlords did precious little to justify their annual income. Perhaps there was little they could do; in any case, had *phytophthora infestans* destroyed landlords instead of potatoes in 1845, agricultural output would have only been marginally affected. In this Marxian sense the tenantry as a group were indeed being exploited.'[85] If this stereotypical distinction were accurate, the issue of compensation for improvements would have been tricky enough. Matters were made worse by landlords who, in fits of optimism and enlightenment, violated the truism that they were not inclined to invest in their estates.[86] Some of the London companies, after close to two centuries of total neglect of their estates, suddenly became 'progressive' in the early nineteenth century after long leases to middlemen expired. The head agent of the Drapers' company, for example, claimed that the company had invested 'very nearly the whole of our profits of our estate for the first three years of our possession' on the construction of flax-mills, school-houses, and churches.[87] At the same time that they were subsidizing emigration, the managers of the Drapers' company were also subsidizing the construction of houses. The head agent warned a prospective leaseholder in 1821 against claiming interest in buildings erected with subsidies from the estate.[88] The general policy adopted in 1835 was to offer four-percent loans for building houses.[89] Other London companies also subsidized housing, although not so extensively as the Drapers' company. In 1852 the Merchant Tailors' company called a halt to its subsidization of improvements until the rent question was settled.[90] The managers of the Perceval-Maxwell estate gave away slates for houses in 1845 to all but the smallest tenants.[91] John Lanktree posted a notice on the Londonderry estate in County Antrim in 1845 that read: 'The marchioness of Londonderry, who by her late generous distribution has shown so great a concern for the personal comfort of the tenantry, has given orders to assist all those who desire to improve [their holdings with slate roofs and pig houses].'[92] Landlords also invested in drainage projects and the reorganization of farm boundaries.[93]

These landlords were rightly suspicious of the trouble that might lay ahead of them. Edward Lawford of the Drapers' company speculated on the risks of assisting tenants with the construction of buildings in 1829, emphasizing that the correct allocation of rights became very difficult with time:

> The policy of this kind of assistance is doubted by some of our friends and seems to me to admit of question, for if the tenant afterward sells his holding, he would in fact sell the company's property and put the company's money into his own pocket. It is true that we might refuse to allow him to sell, or we might put him under some terms as to his selling which should obviate this objection, but in order to do this, the fact of an advance to him must always be borne in mind, which would not be very likely, and besides, after some lapse of time it would be very difficult to impose terms which should be perfectly fair to all parties.[94]

The Fishmongers' company offered interest-free subsidization of farm buildings, hoping that there would be no confusion as to tenant right of these improvements,[95] a problem that was also recognized in this 1852 report from a deputation to the Fishmongers' proportion:

> The particular circumstances of every holding must be taken into consideration: whether, for instance, the improved value, if any, was the result of the tenant's own outlay and exertion or wholly or in part brought about by the assistance of the company; how long such improved value had been enjoyed by the tenant, and if long enough to have afforded a reasonable compensation for his outlay. On all these points the only guide for us was the knowledge and experience of the agent. These points would occur principally or only in the case of mountain farms brought gradually into cultivation.[96]

Faced with obstacles such as these it is no wonder that some landlords abandoned investment policies altogether. As one agent put it to his landlord: 'I most certainly would not recommend you to lay out money and in these days of Tenant Right why should the landlord lay out money?'[97]

Traditionally, landlords looked to avoid the difficulties of such calculations by granting to tenants a tenure of adequate length to allow for the full enjoyment of improvements. But this only displaced the question: what was the appropriate length of tenure to guarantee that improvements would be fully enjoyed by the tenant? Across two centuries, there was little consensus on this issue. One thing was clear. Unless the right of renewal was absolutely guaranteed, at-will tenures were seen to be deficient. The agent on the Downshire estate complained in 1757 of the condition of the at-will tenants: 'No tenant will raise marl without a lease, and without marl the yearly rent will not be got.'[98] The Anglesey agent reported in 1783 that tenants were clamouring for leases and seemed distressed because 'under uncertain tenures they are unwilling to make the necessary and useful repairs many of the habitations require.'[99] One such tenant was Owen Reilly. In a petition of 1785 he claimed that his forbears had been resident for time out of memory on a farm that was originally 'barren and uncultivated, which cost him a great deal of labour and money to improve it and bring it into culture.' He claimed that he had limed and manured extensively and was 'afraid to be at any more expense, his lease being uncertain and a great many gaping for it and ready to supplant him when the lease expires.' He requested 'encouragement to go on with improvement of the land, and that you will suffer none other to enjoy the benefit of his labour.'[100] Echoing a growing consensus, the Merchant Tailors' committee passed a resolution in 1841 stating that 'the holding of land from year to year deprives the occupier of one of the strongest incentives to industry and improvement, and therefore they believe . . . that the tenantry should obtain leases of their holdings for a fixed term at fair and moderate rents.'[101]

If leases were necessary, how long should they be? The term of twenty-one years was widely regarded by those familiar with the management of English estates as sufficient to guarantee the full benefit from improvements. The 21-year lease became increasingly popular after 1790.[102] The Anglesey estate agent penned the following argument in 1811:

> Since the prospect of a certain tenure has been held out, twenty-one years and one life, a general spirit of improvement is manifested throughout the estate. But to promote that to any extent and to induce them to pay an increase of rent cheerfully, a term not shorter than one life and twenty-one years is indispensable. The responsibility of extending this encouragement to such persons only as are able and likely to improve I will take upon myself.[103]

Thomas Beer maintained in 1847 that a twenty-one-year lease was fair and just, because a good tenant would get a renewal and would have been compensated for improvements, and the landlord would be given the opportunity to replace a bad one.[104] He saw no reason for a lease longer than twenty-one years, 'as such a term is considered with us in England to be quite sufficient to remunerate a farmer for his outlay of capital by a rotation of crops or any improvement he may make upon his farm – including even draining.'[105] But there was equally widespread doubt as to whether even twenty-one years provided sufficient security. William Ogilvie, a landowner in County Down, admitted that twenty-one years were not sufficient without a further guarantee of a right of renewal. He offered his tenants twenty-one years and their own lives, and sixty-one years were to be given to those who would build town houses. Tenants were given the right to renew, but Oglivie reserved his right to readjust the rent according to his perception of the changing levels prevailing in the area. This, he hoped, would satisfy both owner and occupier: 'The tenant will be encouraged to improve from the certainty of his tenure, and the landlord will share the advantage of his improvements. This term I mean to introduce generally as the leases fall in.[106] Some believed that thirty-one years or more were necessary. John Lanktree, an advisor to the earl of Antrim, recommended that thirty-one-year leases be given to some improving tenants in Antrim because 'a shorter lease than this would not be satisfactory to tenants who have spent much and have much to spend in building and agricultural improvements, and who look to enjoy for their own lives the labour they have performed.'[107] One tenant under the management of Edmund McGildowney agreed to lay out a considerable sum of money on his farm in 1821 only if the landlord granted him a lease of thirty-one years and three lives. 'No doubt,' McGildowney concluded, 'a lease for twenty-one years and one life is not sufficient inducement to lay out much money in building.'[108]

Whatever the length, many regarded the lease as useless for conserving investments unless it had an indeterminate expiry date. Tenants nearing the end of their term might disinvest in the holding by letting improvements deteriorate, thus ensuring that the improvements had been exhausted. This was known to happen on the Abercorn estate as early as 1749,[109] and was found to be quite common in the time of the Devon commission.[110] Henry Hatch, who managed the property of Henry Blundell before the Downshire family purchased the estate, believed that lives were preferable to years in leases because with years tenants 'let improvements go to ruin and rack the land by plowing in the last few years, whereas the uncertainty of lives prevents this.'[111] One anonymous reporter on an Antrim estate observed that 'the present mode of letting leases for years and lives [leaves] the tenant, after the expiration of the years, in such an uncertainty that he will never attempt any improvement, and of course the land gets into the utmost state of exhaustion.'[112]

Finally, there were others who believed that only tenures tantamount to perpetuity would suffice. A new middleman on the Trinity College estate in County Armagh, looking back on the tenurial history of his land, judged that his holding was in such great condition because the undertenants had been given perpetuities. The previous middleman, a Mr. King, 'finding these lands totally unimproved and not seeing any prospect of their becoming otherwise if he did not give longer terms than twenty-one years, determined as an encouragement to his tenants to improve to give them leases with a [toties quoties] covenant upon paying proportionably of fine and raise in rent.' The present middleman, a Mr. Barry, emphasized how important these long renewable leases had been to the development of the townland. He claimed that the college had repeatedly assured him that it would not increase the rent because the value of the lands had been improved, and that the occupiers knew this:

> [Barry] often told the tenants of this promise, who, relying upon it and considering themselves as having perpetuities of their lands and thinking that they should have the full benefit of their improvements, did apply themselves to them with great expense and industry, having erected many buildings for carrying on the linen manufacture and manured a great part of their lands with lime, which they were obliged to purchase at a distance of seven or eight miles, there not being any limestone upon their lands. . . . It is observable that no bleaching mills could ever have been built on those lands if longer leases had not been given them than for twenty-one years, and that land improvements were consequential to the erecting of such buildings.[113]

The agent to the Derby estate in County Louth would have agreed with this assessment. He claimed in 1773 that the former leases were so short that 'the lower class of tenants would have hurt the lands by endeavouring to make the most of them. This, I hope, will not appear to be the case now, as continuing the former tenants in most of the farms has given them expectations of further terms being granted and of course induced them to treat the farms in a husbandlike manner.'[114]

In short, confusion reigned over the issue. Uncertainty dampened investment, but perpetuity bred absenteeism. Smart rents drained capital supplies, but beneficial rents rewarded indolence. The Ulster Custom promoted improvements; no, it sapped the incomer of his vital working capital. The evidence could be read in support of Trower's prognosis and against Ricardo's rebuttal concerning Irish ills and solutions. The problem lay in the structure of the society, not the form of its institutions. As a Cork landlord opined in 1724: 'the spirit of improvement is more in the man than the length of his lease. . . . I know no encouragement that will prevail on men who love not improvement.'[115] But the problem was not that tenants 'loved not' their improvements, it was that they loved them too much, so that no tenurial agreement was sufficient to settle the question of compensation. As two of Dufferin's tenants argued,[116] only arbitration, the basis of Crawford's bills, would suffice; or as thousands of others would later insist, only the tenant right of 'free sale' was sufficient. John Martin of Killinchy, County Down, explained in 1856:

> In my neighbourhood the price of the outgoing tenant's interest was always determined by the increased value which the holding received from the care, labour, and expenditure he had given it. And that was very simply and easily ascertained by the bidding of the competitors for the farm in the market. It was not the *outlay* by any means which fixed the market price, it was the improved value produced by the outlay and generally the management of the tenant. . . . When the outgoing tenant looks to the landlord and not to the new tenant for the price of his interest, and where the price is to be settled not by competition for the farm but under some rule, . . . the increased letting value should be the measure of compensation. The Ulster tenant-right custom, according to which the only question to be settled was how much a *bona fide* purchaser would give a tenant for his interest, was very simple and saved all the trouble of calculations to the landlord.[117]

From the tenants' view of the matter, all the nice calculations concerning the value of unexhausted improvements and the length of tenure were irrelevant to tenant right. When a tenant chooses to leave a farm, only the present value of the farm is of concern. The problem comes back to the inscrutability of the value of the past labour invested in the farm, and the perpetual discursive battle that inscrutability caused within agrarian capitalist societies. The issue of compensation, as Martin of Killinchy recognized, folded into the equally contentious issue of fair rent.

DEASY'S ACT AND THE HISTORICIST TURN

In 1860 a majority of members of parliament in Westminster were convinced that a law consolidating Irish land law on English principles would effect a definite solution to the land question. In a society where contracts had clearly proven to be inadequate, the solution was more contracts. Deasy's act endeavoured to follow Ferguson and Vance's suggestion to abolish the customary property rights of the Irish peasantry and finally eliminate ancient feudal relationships. Section 3 of the law provided exactly this by insisting that 'the relation of landlord and tenant shall be deemed to be founded on the express or implied contract of the parties, and not upon tenure or service, and a reversion shall not be necessary to such relation, which shall be deemed to subsist in all cases in which there shall be an agreement by one party to hold land from or under another in consideration of any rent.'[118] While section 3 banished feudalism, sections 41 and 42 reinaugurated capitalism by spelling out what the modern lease implied: (a) 'that the landlord has a good title to make a lease,' (b) that 'the tenant will have quiet and peaceable enjoyment without interruption,' and (c) that the tenant must obey any lease covenants, pay the rent, and, most crucially, give up quiet possession at termination. Such agreements, as befitting legislation based on the ideology of freedom of contract, were to be recognized as 'equality of treatment for landlord and tenant.'[119]

In modern historiography, Deasy's act lies hidden in the shadows of the more momentous legislation of 1870, 1881, and 1887. Its importance, conceptually as well as historically, is not often recognized.[120] With the passage of Deasy, the battle between Irish reality and English political economy came to a head, and the implications of the conversation between Trower, Ricardo, and Mill were realized. Deasy's act was the ultimate embodiment of Ricardan philosophy in that it attempted to rewrite a set of laws that were thought to have been corrupted by outmoded feudal and Hibernian holdovers in the expectation that real change would naturally follow. After Deasy, Ricardans could no longer argue that the law was in need of further reform, a situation which raised the stakes in the debate against those who argued for the embodiment of custom in the land law. The ultra-Ricardan position, for which the marquis of Dufferin was a prominent exponent, now placed the sovereignty of the market over any proposed legislation that might backtrack from the perfection of Deasy. For example, Dufferin argued that the market, not the landlord, was responsible for the mass emigration of tenants in the nineteenth century. If legislation effectively removed the landlord, the market would still remain.[121] Dufferin viewed radical proposals in terms of their market effects, and argued forcefully that lofty rhetoric about ancient rights, compensation for improvements, and fair rents, was a cover for a movement to usurp rather than eliminate the market power of the landlord. He attacked Mill's suggestion that landlords be forced to sell their land to tenants at a price fixed by parliament. This would bankrupt landlords, especially recent purchasers in the landed estates court, and ignore the plight of labourers without any property rights. But more importantly, it would be ineffective. Changing the old landlords for a new landlord – the government – would not prevent the basic problems of subdivision, rack-renting and impoverishment.[122] As for the idea of a 'fair rent,' he wrote:

> It is amusing to observe that the same persons who are anxious to mitigate the effects of competition by imposing on the owner of land a rent fixed by Act of Parliament, always contend that the person in whose favour this beneficial interest is to be created should have the right to dispose of it to the highest bidder: that is to say, though I am to be precluded from receiving the market value of my land, my tenant is to be allowed to do so, by extracting a fine from whoever may be induced to make the most extravagant offer for his goodwill.[123]

Conservative spokesmen for Irish landlords were not the only commentators to realistically assess the sovereignty of the capitalist market. In one of his few writings on the subject of the Irish land question, Marx performed a similar yet opposing manoeuvre, cleverly turning the contemporary 'bourgeois' critiques of the absolute rights of the British landed monopoly – those of Ricardo, Newman, and Spenser – against those who would divorce the issue of property rights from the discussion of the question of tenant right.[124] In an article for the New York *Daily Tribune* of 22 March 1853, Marx noted that the growth of productive power in agriculture was pressing on the agricultural population of Ireland, that 'landlordism, concentration of farms, application of machinery to the soil, and introduction of modern agriculture on a great scale' required mass emigration from the countryside. He quoted *The Economist* to the effect that 'the departure of the redundant part of Ireland and the Highlands of Scotland is an indispensable preliminary to every kind of improvement.'[125] But he was careful to distinguish his position from both the triumphalism of the Ricardans on the one hand and the romanticism of celebrants of outmoded agriculture on the other:

> Now I share neither in the opinion of Ricardo, who regards 'Net Revenue' as the Moloch to whom the entire populations must be sacrificed, without

even so much as a complaint, nor in the opinion of Sismondi, who in his hypochondriacal philanthropy, would forcibly retain the superannuatated methods of agriculture and proscribe science from industry, as Plato expelled the poets from his Republic. Society is undergoing a silent revolution, which must be submitted to, and which takes no more notice of the human existences it breaks down than an earthquake regards the houses it subverts. The classes and the races, too weak to master the new conditions of life, must give way. But can there be anything more peurile, more short-sighted, than the views of those Economists who believe in all earnest that this woeful transitory state means nothing but adapting society to the acquisitive propensities of capitalists, both landlords and money lords?[126]

Marx would not be caught between colonial capitalism and an outmoded nativism.[127] He emphasized the progressive aspect of colonialism to unsettle armchair radicals who condemned it without doing anything to promote real technical progress and emancipation, and who idealized pre-capitalist societies as romantic utopias.[128] Aware that colonial economic progress would not wash away a corrupt and anti-democratic form of resistance whose dominant ideology was a 'nostalgic nativism,' both Marx and Engels viewed the 'non-reforming nationalisms' of 1848[129] with deep scepticism, a scepticism they extended to the Irish Fenians as well.[130]

Both Dufferin and Marx offered hard-nosed prognoses for a prolonged and painful adjustment, the former in the name of the sacrosanct property rights of landlords, the latter in the name of a socialism that would finally abolish and overcome the pain and contradictions inherent to that system of private property. Neither of these positions would get far in Ireland. Within the ideological gamut spelled out here, Marx could be viewed as a radical Trowerian. He would have agreed with Trower that the problem and its solution were essentially social in nature, even as he opposed what he considered to be Ricardo's callous structural legalism. In fact, he took the opportunity to chide the *Times* for its Trowerian position, noted above, when it claimed that the institutions of private property could only function under the 'proper conditions of society.'[131] Unlike Trower, who looked for a social revolution to achieve conformity with the law, Marx struggled for a revolution that would destroy the law and replace it with a new, though never clearly specified, set of arrangements. Judging such a revolution politically premature, Marx and Marxists left Ireland to its own devices.[132] Dufferin, however, was also whistling in a typhoon. His economics were sound, but his political position was rapidly becoming an anachronism. Dufferin had missed the vital political point underneath the apparent duplicity of tenant-right advocates on the issue of 'fair rent.' He was right to complain that fair rents and fixed tenures would merely allow sitting tenants to exploit those below them and those

who came after them. Politically, however, the result would be a demo-
craticization and strengthening of the social power of the private property
system. As Wright commented, 'perhaps a few million secure landholders
would have been as greedy as a few thousand landlords had been. But at least
the selfishness would have spread its advantages and disadvantages more
evenly, and the arrogance of monopolistic power would have been broken.'[133]
Metropolitan capitalists had already begun to see that the landlord monopoly
of rural property would have to be sacrificed in order to preserve private
property itself. This position, as Marx had pointed out in 1853, was already
justified conceptually by Ricardo and others. As one handbook of statecraft
published in Germany rendered it:

> The peasantry forms the physically soundest and strongest part of the
> population, from which the cities, in particular, have constantly to be
> recruited. It forms the core of the army. . . . Politically its settled character
> and attachment to the soil make it the foundation of a prospering rural
> community. . . . The peasantry has at all times been the most conservative
> element of the state. . . . Its appreciation of property, its love of the native
> soil makes it into the natural enemy of urban revolutionary ideas and a
> firm bulwark against social democratic efforts. It has therefore been rightly
> described as the firmest pillar of every sane state, and with the rapid
> growth of large cities, its significance as such increases.[134]

This type of thinking marks the transition from *laissez-faire* capitalism to a
self-consciously administered capitalism which recognized that whole regions
and entire classes might lay permanently outside the ambit of proper metropolitan capitalism, a historicist retheorization of the development of private
property which attended to the 'imperious conditions of time and place.'[135]
The new thinking allowed for the consideration of policies of a far more
radical nature because it was assumed that they would not be applicable to
England. The inflammatory ideas that had landed William Connor in jail in
the early 1840s had begun to enter the mainstream two decades later. As a
result, both high landlordism and socialism would be marginalized.

The emergent radicalism was not that of Marx but of his counterparts in
the Trower/Ricardo ideological spectrum – the Radical Ricardans who followed
in William Sharman Crawford's footsteps. The radicalism of Connor, Sharman
Crawford, and J. S. Mill differed fundamentally from Marx's in that it espoused
a reformed system which preserved the private property system and the
legitimacy of the state which founded it. Where Marx attacked the legitimacy of the bourgeois state and sought its overthrow, the radical Ricardans
made the sovereignty and legitimacy of the state the centrepiece of its reform
plan. The historicist turn against the *laissez-faire* conceptions of property was
underpinned by Mill's politico-theoretical justification of state intervention

into property relationships. The state, according to this thinking, was the natural representative and collective owner of the divinely bestowed land of the nation. Dufferin rendered Mill's position with these words: 'Because land is a thing which no man made, which exists in limited quantity, which was the original inheritance of all mankind, which, whoever appropriates, keeps others out of possession, it is competent for parliament to deal with private estates in land in whatever manner may prove most conducive to the well-being of the community.'[136] James McKnight, the tenant-right propagandist and sometime editor of the *Londonderry Standard*, was one of the first Victorians to to put forward the idea that the customary nature of Irish land law was the direct result of the state's rightful intervention into Irish property relations in the reign of James I. The Victorian state, in other words, still held the power to administer economic relationships in a precapitalist manner. Land was still something other than a tradeable parcel like capital and labour. The profits and other privileges of ownership granted to landholders during the plantation were subordinate to the 'inherent trusteeship' over landed property held by the state. The escheatment of lands under the plantation explicitly subordinated private profit to imperial trust. 'So far as Ulster is concerned,' McKnight wrote, 'the idea of *absolute private ownership*, on the part of the Landlords, is the most arrant assumption.'[137] Empirically, McKnight made some questionable extrapolations. He imagined that the article of plantation requiring that tenures be such as to provide 'certain estate' in fact meant fixity of tenure. In other words, fixed and certain tenures, the language of the seventeenth century, was equated with 'fixity of tenure' in the language of the nineteenth century.[138] This interpretation of the plantation served both to undermine *laissez-faire* arguments about landlord rights and legitimize the role of the contemporary state, thus navigating between Dufferin and Marx.

McKnight's argument became very popular in the 1860s and 1870s, and was articulated in different formulations by Peter Maclagan, Isaac Butt, Robert Donnell, and William Henderson.[139] The key to the argument was to establish the legal fiction that, to quote E.P. Thompson again, 'customary usages must have been founded on some original grant, from persons unknown, lost in the mists of antiquity. The law pretended that, somewhere in the year dot, the commons were granted by benevolent Saxon or Norman landowners, so that uses were less of right than by grace.' The legal fiction was purely ideological. As Thompson wrote, 'it guarded against the danger that use rights might be seen as inherent in the users, in which case the successors of the Levellers or Diggers might arise and plead their original title.'[140] These grants, in the words of James I, quoted by Isaac Butt, were given not merely to benefit the grantees but to 'do service to the crown and commonwealth,' their primary function being the 'advancement of the public service.' Butt marshalled the evidence of Pynnar's seventeenth-century surveys of escheated counties to claim that the right of occupancy 'originated in the evasion by the grantees of Ulster property of the conditions imposed on them to place an estated tenantry on their lands.' In order to keep tenants, they had to be given fixity, i.e., perpetuities. Butt's justification emphasized that the historical peculiarities of private property in Ireland resulted from the failures of the plantation.[141] Seen in this light, contemporary proposals to give security of tenure to farmers, far from being revolutionary or communistic, were consistent with the spirit of the original patents granted by the Stuart monarchy.

Propagandists for *laissez-faire* doctrine met this argument with historical and political-theoretical rebuttals. Dufferin felt that the origin of tenant right had 'nothing to do with James' settlement.' The leases of that era, he rightly argued, were in Gourley's words 'terminable leaseholds on which perfect freedom of contract was intended to supervene.'[142] Tenant right, according to Dufferin, was merely the result of competition for land since the late eighteenth century.

> Tenant right, i.e. the custom under which one tenant is supposed to sell his *goodwill* to another, at an enormous price, is evidently the creature of competition; but in those days, the occupation of land in Ireland was not an attractive adventure, and, until the last increase of population brought a pressure upon the soil, such competition did not exist, and as a consequence, '*tenant right*' as I have often heard my old aunt, Lady Dufferin, say, was not heard of.[143]

Dufferin's argument was that historically-based claims to property rights cut both ways, and that the evidence showed his historical attachment to the land was better than his tenants: 'By the Clandeboye maps of A.D. 1630 we can ascertain the names of the then occupants of the farms in a large portion of county Down, and from the information we there obtain, it is evident that the present class of landlords are, for the most part, the true representatives of the then tenants; and that the present tenants are either the product of subsequent immigration, or the descendants of persons brought over as subtenants, labourers, or military dependants, by the former tenants, ancestors of the present landlords.'[144] But Frederick Seebohm chided Dufferin for forgetting that his conception of the absolute ownership of the land by landlords is in fact a historical result, and still subject to the restrictions of many manorial customs in England that were not allowed to grow in Ireland. Faced with the rising power of the English trading classes, Seebohm argued, these landlords cling to their old feudal maxims, but not when faced with the complaints of their Irish tenantry.[145]

By the middle of the 1860s all the options available within the Ricardo-Trower discourse seem to have been exhausted, and the line of thinking which originated with William Sharman Crawford and the tenant-right movement of the 1830s gained ground. The famine and mass emigration had effected a massive change in Irish reality along the lines that Trower envisaged in the 1820s, yet that reality still did not conform to the legal model. On the other hand, the 1860 centrepieces of Ricardan legislation were also failing. In Richey's influential view of the matter, the choice was either to force the new contract law down the throats of the Irish and transform social conditions to suit the new legal framework 'or to introduce legislation of an admittedly retrograde character, for the purpose of palliating patent evils and allaying not ill-founded discontent.'[146] For economists like Mill and Cairnes, difference was once again ascendant. They had come to the realization that 'all attempts to assimilate the Irish land system to the English' would merely 'aggravate the Irish sense of grievance and end in failure.'[147] Sir Robert Peel could declare in 1863 that 'the act of 1860 had effected a final settlement of the agitated question, and they did not feel included to re-open it,'[148] but in fact almost immediately after Deasy's act the ideological trend was away from the tenets of section 3. The historian must take care not to cast a hegemonic shift such as occurred in the 1860s with the appearance of inevitability, but it is nevertheless true that, as Black commented, there was in the years 1867–70 'a noticeable tendency for the development of informed public opinion, both in England and in Ireland, to outpace the growth of policy. Whilst successive ministries fumbled before an unsympathetic House with measures for limited compensation, an increasing body of opinion in Ireland was massing behind the idea that fixity of tenure was the minimum acceptable solution of the land problem.'[149] The Fenian uprisings of the 1860s, though not directly motivated by the land question, nevertheless are relevant to the abandonment of *laissez-faire* for legislative measures geared toward liquidating smallholders at landlord expense and strengthening the social and tenurial position of large farmers.[150]

Alarmed by Fenianism, British political élites appear to have lost their stomach for Trowerian strong-arm *laissez-faire* policies. Abandoned by Marx, and Marxism, Ireland would follow a path over the next decade of adjustment to the requirements of the capitalist market, stumbling backwards and unintentionally toward that end, sedated by romantic ideologies and palliative legislation, pummelled when deemed necessary by coercion bills and the suspension of *habeus corpus*. Gladstone espoused the evolutionist and historicist conception of the Irish land question in his speech introducing the Land Bill of 1870: '[In Ireland], where old Irish ideas were never supplanted except by the rude hand of violence – by laws written on the statute book, but never entering into the heart of the Irish people – the people have not generally embraced the idea of the occupation of land by contract; and the old Irish notion that some interest in the soil adheres to the tenant, even though his contract has expired, is everywhere rooted in the popular mind.'[151] Irish social and political reality had run past the grasp of *laissez-faire* nostrums. The new discourse, historicism, based on the questionable presuppositions of evolutionary determinism, the idealization of a communal customary past, and the ascription of such an ideal past to the present situation in Ireland, was no more adequate to the reality of the Irish land question. However, it served its dual purpose of offering an alternative to all but the most die-hard *laissez-faire* ideologues as well as providing Irish élites, for the time being, with a coherent representation of their difference from the English norm.[152]

THE LAND ACT OF 1870 AND THE END OF TENANT RIGHT

In order to legislate on the question of tenant right, it was necessary to deal with the difference between a static, generalized definition of the custom and the variegated production of its meaning at the level of the estates themselves. Gladstone famously described his experience of this conundrum in a letter to the earl of Clarendon in September 1869: 'I have puzzled and puzzled over it and cannot for the life of me see how it is to be legalized without being essentially changed. It is like trying in Algebra to solve a problem of two unknown quantities with only one equation.'[153] One could read the hand-wringing over the meaning of tenant right – its alleged chameleon-like quality, its seeming likeness to an unsolveable equation – as only an excuse for the inability or unwillingness of legislators and commentators to define the custom in a way that recognized its most enduring historical aspiration: to represent a claim for continuous possession. Any definition with this capacity gainsayed both the letter of Deasy's act and the intentions of capitalist estate management. Still, Gladstone did have a point. His algebraic equation was an apt metaphor for the definition of the Ulster custom of tenant right because it implied that the custom could only derive meaning from the relationship between two incalculable social forces operating both in the public sphere and on individual estates. To adhere to Gladstone's analogy, the two unkown quantities were: (1) the strength of the custom of tenant right both as a practical matter of the particular usages on Ulster estates and as a symbolic means to 'pacify' Ireland politically; (2) the strength and resilience of land-lordism, both in terms of the private control landlords had secured over the operation of the custom and the collective role they might continue to play in the political governance of Ireland. A static definition, no matter how capacious, was a political and conceptual impossibility: too generous a definition threatened both the gains many landlords had made over the previous decades and their traditional capacity as a paternal and stabilizing presence within Irish politics and society; too limited a definition, on the other hand, risked the political alienation of the northern tenantry and the upsetting of that paternal stability. The 1870 act in effect recognized that customary tenure, based on history rather than contract, could never be committed to legal script. It is testimony to Gladstone's political genius that he managed to secure passage into law a bill that legalized the Ulster custom while refusing to define it, allowing liberals to adopt the rhetoric of the 'final solution' to the land question while permitting the battle between landlords and tenants over the meaning and regulation of tenant right to continue on their estates. The 1870 act opened to public view the clash between landlord usage of the custom to defend their property rights and the profits they gained therefrom, and tenant defence of ancient rights against these modern usages and the vicious operation of the market.

It was clear to Gladstone that fixity of tenure would alienate landlords, but at the same time mere compensation for improvements had proved unworkable as a legislative program. The goal, as he saw the matter in the late 1860s, was to figure out how to symbolically offer more. The answer he hit upon was to legalize tenant right where it existed without defining it and establish mechanisms for landlord provision of compensation for improvements and 'disturbance.' The intention of the act was to allow for the continued liquidation of the unwanted portion of the tenantry by using the mechanism of the Ulster custom – and where it did not exist, compensation for improvements and disturbance – to make the landlords pay for the social adjustments that the *Times*, Dufferin, and Marx had all recognized as inevitable.[154] The act distinguished between two types of tenancies, those that were either covered by pre-existing custom or subject to the new mechanisms for compensation of improvement and disturbance, and those that were explicitly excluded from such mechanisms either in the legislation itself or in new contracts. The intention of the act was to provide a mechanism for the peaceful elimination of the former and the expansion of the latter. Tenants in the former category who appeared before the courts were essentially sacrificing the right of renewal for a cash reward. The act did not reverse the requirement to give up peaceable possession of a farm at the end of a tenancy, upheld since Deasy at least; instead it allowed for compensation for the disturbance of having lost this right. The report of the Bessborough commission described the tenant's Hobson's choice: 'In order to raise a question before the court, he is forced to begin by a surrender of the only thing for which he cares. The plaintiff in a land claim, if he fails to prove his case, is turned out without the compensation that he claimed; but if he proves it, he is turned out all the same. . . . In a word, once the tenant comes into court all the law can give him is compensation in money.'[155]

Ulster tenants were put in a precarious position because the definition of their tenant right was left in the hands of the courts. Suspicions of the act were voiced almost immediately at tenant-right meetings in Belfast and Portadown in March of 1870. Tenants noticed that the act did nothing to protect the right of renewal, in particular it failed to address the right of renewal of the holders of expired leases, a right explicitly abrogated by Deasy. Tenants also recognized that the act's failure to define the custom left them completely vulnerable to the legitimation of landlord 'usages' that the tenants regarded as merely come-lately infringements on ancient practices. Finally, and most seriously, the act said nothing about fair rents, leaving tenants open to the very real danger that their tenant right could be effectively destroyed either by rent increases or, as happened in the 1840s, by plummeting prices and volumes of their produce. There were some apparent advantages to the act for Ulster tenants. Those who freely parted with their farms were at least able to make claims for compensation based on local custom rather than under the rules spelled elsewehere in the text of the act.[156] Ulster tenants who had the protection of the custom were therefore potentially immune from the 'Hobson's choice' facing tenants who had to give up their their tenures as a precondition of their appearance in the land court. They could not, in other words, be 'capriciously' evicted – in order to consolidate two farms into one, for example – if they paid a fair rent. What was the nature of this protection? It clearly hinged on conceptions of fair rent, an issue taken up below. This mechanism proved useful to a significant number of northern tenants in the early years of the act. Though the *Coleraine Chronicle* alleged in 1874 that 'the Ulster Custom is being gradually dropped in the land courts, owing to the difficulty of proving it,' the amount of compensation decreed under the tenant-right section of the act never fell below 50% of the Ulster total in these years.[157] The tenant-right advocate W.D. Henderson drew this balanced conclusion on the operation of the act in its first four years: 'Whilst upon some points, and especially the legalization of leasehold tenant right, we have been defeated, upon other points – such, for example, as the incidence of estate usages – we have got more than we have hoped for, although certainly not more than we were entitled to. . . .' Henderson was none the less careful to emphasize the persistent and ominous weaknesses of the legislation: tenant right had now been reduced to a claim to compensation, not continued occupation, and the act gave 'no security whatever against capricious eviction,' and no right to renew a lease.[158]

The main difficulties presented by the 1870 act in these years were the implicit contradiction between Deasy's act and the tenant-right section of the 1870 act with respect to leaseholders, the effect on perceptions of the 'usages' of tenant right under aggressive management, and the rapid turnover in land ownership since the installation of the encumbered estates court. These difficulties manifested themselves in two notorious court decisions. The first was judge Barry's decision in *McKeown vs. Beauclerc* which found that at the expiry of a lease a tenant had no claim under the custom, a decision that, as Wright noticed, 'was in direct conflict with pre-1870 realities and did much to actually weaken the custom.'[159] Of equal notoriety was an appeal decision by Justice Christian which ruled that the first section of the land act could not protect tenants on a newly purchased estate.[160]

The right of renewal of a lease was the most contentious issue. Explicitly ruled out by section 3 of Deasy's act, tenant right on leasehold farms was also especially difficult to prove because farms on which leases had expired were only rarely sold, leaving little in the way of tangible evidence concerning the operation of this usage.[161] Tenant-right advocates were understandably adamant about the existence of this right, notwithstanding Deasy or the bounds of a lease. Legislating that tenants must give up quiet possession at the termination of their contracts merely shifted the question. After the tenant formally gives up the quiet possession, what happens next? In the legislative dream world, the farm is placed in a competitive market and the best bidder gets it. But in reality, that market was saturated by a customary practice that controlled the succession of the farm. Donnell argued that under English judge-made law in 1831, a custom which may contradict the terms of a tenancy 'applies only at the *expiration* of the tenancy.' So too, according to Donnell, did the custom of tenant right apply to tenants who held leases which specifically outlawed tenant right of renewal after the lease expired.[162] The 1870 act was designed to dovetail with Deasy's promotion of the lease contract by exluding leases of thirty-one years or longer in length from the jurisdiction of the act and permitting landlords to contract themselves out of the act in leases set to tenants paying £50 or more yearly rent. Far from promoting leases, however, the outlawing of leasehold tenant right soured the attitudes of tenants for leases, especially if they were living on estates where the tenant right of at-will tenants were recognized. The Bessborough inquiry revealed that yearly tenants regarded the long lease as 'not a lengthening of the yearly tenancy, but a shortening of the continuous traditional tenancy.'[163] The Drapers' agents noted that 'those holding from year to year with the tenant right attached to their holdings by the land act of 1870 are quite as independent and enjoy equal privileges with those holding under lease.' Indeed a few weeks later one tenant who had a thirty-one year lease and who had 'bought up a large number of smallholdings from time to time' told the agent that he would tear up his lease 'if I would hand him back his lease money, so little did he estimate the value to be attached thereto [because] it imposed restrictions that tenants from year to year did not lie under. It is unfortunate,' he continued 'that while one portion of the tenantry are extolling the liberality of the Drapers' company that the remaining portion and by far the most influential should be dissatisfied or even entertain the idea that their circumstances have not been as favourable as their poorer neighbours.' Unlike the relatively contented and docile tenants at will, these thirty-one-year leaseholders were 'saturated with all Parnell's pernicious doctrines' and were 'holding aloof, paying no rent.'[164] The marquis of Dufferin's agent advised him 'to offer to cancel your leases in the case of any tenant who thinks he would be better off without one' because, anticipating that Dufferin might wish to sell the estate, he felt that 'your lordship's position, and the saleable value of the estate, will be quite as good, if not stronger, in relying upon the custom of the estate as it will be under leases.'[165]

The status of all usages, not just the application of the custom to lease-holders, was further complicated by the vicissitudes of the market for landownership. The managerial characteristics of an individual landlord were often critical to tenant perceptions of the nature and value of tenant right, and even the appearance of a new heir or heiress could be quite traumatic. A landlord or agent with favourable qualities enhanced the value of a holding and was reflected in the price of tenant right.[166] James Hamilton attempted to explain the effect of landlord behaviour on tenant-right payments in a letter of 1778: 'The price farmers sell at would prove their bargains to be good, yet I cannot help thinking there is more in it that makes them so very tenacious. I cannot express it. The phrase is purchasing your lordship, the getting into your lordship's estate. It has always been considered as a sure inheritance and protection.'[167] In the post-famine period tenants could rely less and less on the sure inheritance and protection of an old planter family. Closer manipulation of the tenant-right system and occasionally capricious if not extractive increases of rent contributed to the tenant unease, but the more important factor was the uncertainty caused by the activity of the landed estates courts.[168] Nearly a quarter of all land in Ulster changed hands in the period 1849–1879, and many landlords who did not sell out must have seriously considered their options.[169] Although the purchasers were probably on average no better or worse than the sellers, their reputation among tenant-right activists was poor. They were considered to be mere speculators who treated their new assets as purely commercial instruments, and who were, in the words of the Bessborough report, 'ignorant of the traditions of the soil.' There was no provision for the compensation of tenants for improvements upon the sale of an encumbered estate and the Bessborough commission noted that estates were often advertised as being ripe for rent increases at the expiration of leases.[170] Robert Longfield testified before the Maguire commission in 1865 that purchasers in landed estates courts had been extinguishing tenant right by having a condition of their purchase that the custom be no longer recognized on the estate.[171]

The experience of tenants of two of the London companies exemplifies the jeopardy into which the change of landlords might place tenants. The Clothworkers' proportion was purchased by Sir Hervey Bruce over the heads of the resident middlemen, who incidently made strong claims to their right to purchase based on the improvements they had made as tenants.[172] True to the stereotype of a new purchaser, he promptly increased the rent by 40%, served 130 notices to quit on those who objected to the measure, and attempted to restrict tenant-right sales to five years' purchase.[173] The Skinners' company took the management of their proportion into their own hands in 1872, the last of the London companies to do so. Until then it was in the hands of the Ogilby family, the principal of whom, according to minutes of 1857, 'seldom resides on it and seems to consider the estate in the light of a property that he is interested in making the most of while the lease lasts. He has now two surviving lives and twenty-five years in concurrent terms at £1,500 a year.'[174] The entire estate was held at will by the occupiers. When the Ogilby lease expired in 1872 the Skinners' management committee had no intention of recognizing any custom of tenant right. They seemed not to have an understanding of tenant right on the estate, proving that even after forty years of public and private disputation and the passage of Gladstone's act, landlords were capable of sustaining a complete ignorance of the custom.[175] They were told that the agent for Ogilby 'admitted the Ulster custom in a limited form,' only on permission of the landlord and only rarely by auction. Preference was always given to neighbours or others on the estate, 'at a price fixed between themselves or by arbitration if the parties could not agree.'[176] But three years later, after complaining about the exorbitant payments of tenant right for houses in Dungiven, the Skinners' managers surmised that

> as no allusion was made in the lease to tenant right it is conceived that no such right existed when the lease was granted as against the lessors the Skinners' company. The estate was let to Mr. Ogilby without it being claimed or recognized and it is conceived that as he took the estate unfettered by such a right he could have no power to create it or suffer it to grow into existence as against his lessors the Skinners' company, who it is conceived are entitled to have their estate delivered up to them perfectly free and unfettered by any claim whatsoever according to the condition contained in the lease.

The managers wished to find some proof that tenant right did not exist on the estate before the Ogilby lease began in 1802, but they were informed that if the usage of the custom could be established under Ogilby then the company would not be able to disallow tenant right.[177]

How was the existence of the custom on a given estate to be determined? How would the courts judge whether, in the words of Carter's seventeenth-century thesis on custom, tenant right 'groweth to perfection' and 'obtaineth the force of law?'[178] Matthew Dutton's tract on Irish land law published in Dublin in 1726 defined custom as follows:

> Of every custom there are two essential parts, time and usage, time out of mind, and continual and peaceable usage without lawful interruption. It is said by Coke, both to customs and prescriptions, these two things are incident and inseparable, viz. possession or usage, and time. Possession must have three qualities, it must be long, continual, and peaceable. My lord Coke tells us, in respect to the variety of customs in most manors, it is not possible to set down any certainty, only this incident inseparable, every custom must have, viz. that it be consonant with reason. For how long-soever it hath continued, if it be against reason, it is of no force in law.[179]

Under the 1870 act, the burden of proof of the custom lay with the tenants, and the standard of proof of the existence of a restrictive usage was nothing near to Dutton and Coke's standard of reasonableness, i.e. that it be shown to exist beyond 'past memory of man' or 'time out of mind.'[180] Even so, the success of one tenant was a victory for every tenant on the estate.[181] The stakes were therefore very high in individual cases before the county chairmen. As one agent wrote, 'the Land Act only legalized the various tenant-right 'usages' as it found them, yet that where one exception to a restricted tenant right was proved to have taken place on an estate where a restricted tenant right as a general rule had been allowed, the unrestricted right became applicable to all those holdings in respect of which no particular custom could be proved to exist.'[182] A crucial amendment to the land bill changed the word 'usage' to 'usages,' in the clause of the first section legalizing tenant right where it existed. This oriented the land courts toward the particular practices of an estate, not the general usage of a district, county, or province.[183] As James McKnight complained to Gladstone, 'the change of the word 'usage' to 'usages,' it appears to me, will inevitably legalize all the estate orders that have anywhere been made in violation of the custom.'[184] The general, bird's-eye view of the the situation was confusing and rapidly evolving: some estate offices had in recent decades been struggling gradually to come to grips with the various challenges of estate management, including regulating the tenant-right system, others had maintained a stable pattern established by managers many decades previously. Still others, because of the changes wrought by sale and inheritance, had seen abrupt reversals in managerial style. Against this variegated backdrop, an out-of-doors agitation began pressing for the universalization of the most radical possibilities of the custom. Opinions on what constituted the essence of tenant right varied greatly. Devon commission testimony could be used by later partisans either to play up the vagaries of the custom and its variety of local usages or to aggregate them together in order to define its essential characteristics, and witnesses before the Bessborough commission claimed that it was the controversy stirred up by the Devon commission that spurred landlords to develop estate rules infracting on tenant right that were unknown in the 1830s and earlier. Vaughan argues that 'most, but not all, of the definitions that included security of tenure and fair rents came from the later part of the period, apparently stimulated by debates on the land act of 1870.' He cites the testimony of a Monaghan man in 1852 who felt that the 'old' tenant right of Ulster was of a much more limited nature than the inflated version put forward by the Tenant League.[185] But William Morris, who toured the country in 1869 felt that the strength of the tenant-right custom was in decline as a result of more careful regulation.[186] Alert landlords certainly became aware in the 1840s of the implications of the precedents they set by regulating tenant right. The Millers of Draperstown explained to Edward Lawford what was at stake in 1846:

> Their tenant right had not been interfered with either by their landlords or their agents, except to check it so as to prevent an improper person being introduced on to the estate. In the address put in by the deputation signed by the four gentlemen there are *seven matters* they touch upon. The first is tenant right – this paper seems, we think, *to emanate from themselves* and they are solicitous to have some security from the Company – that tenant right shall not be interfered with. We suppose they mean that *they* should regulate it and not your *agents*, and that every man should sell his holding to whom he pleases to the highest and best bidder. If this should be ever conceded in about ten years all the bad characters from every estate in the province who has money would become tenants on this property.[187]

Lawford complained in 1848 that 'I have my misgivings whether what we are doing in arranging with the tenants for the sale of their holdings may not at some future period be construed into such recognition of the right as may lead to the prejudice of the Company.'[188] That same year John Hancock, the Lurgan land agent, warned that the law allowed landowners to settle their estates with anti-tenant-right policies and that tenant right must be put on a legal basis because it now depends on varying estate management regimes.[189]

Without going so far as to second guess or pass judgement on the behaviour of the land courts, it is possible to set out the range of usages of the custom that developed on a small sample of Ulster estates. The intention here is to show the range of possibilities over the entire period, not to establish the exact state and provenance of a particular usage c. 1870 on each estate. Estate managers manipulated the system in five ways: by banning the sale of certain types of tenancies, by taxing the sale of tenant right, by regulating the price of tenant-right sales, by exercising a veto over purchasers, and by direct investment in the tenant-right market. The least frequent of the five was an outright ban on the sale of certain types of property and tenures. Estate managers often restricted tenant right according to the type of tenure. The managers of both the Drapers' company and the Clothworkers' company attempted to allow the disposal of leases but not of at-will tenures, and also applied different rules for leases of different lengths.[190] Landlord concern to control the tenure of urban tenements and town parks from the tenant-right market resulted in a ruling under the 1870 act which excluded them from the custom. But usage could still prove against this judgement. A report on the tenant right of town parks on the Drapers' estate in 1878 considered whether the tenant right applied to the parks around Moneymore and Draperstown. The reporter considered that 'there has been such buying and selling of these parks as would warrant a judge in holding that tenant right did attach to them. . . . The company would, if they ejected any of the holders, have to pay them tenant right.' The report concluded that it would be difficult to trans- form the town parks to fit the description in the 1870 act and thereby extin- guish tenant right thereof.[191] Mills, kilns, bleach greens, and other assets critical to local estate economies might also fall under restriction.[192]

A second form of regulation was a tax on the sale of tenant right in the form of a covenant in leases penalizing their sale. Abercorn at first charged one year's rent but later reduced the fine to a half-year. This policy had been in limited operation early in the eighteenth century but only slowly became accepted by the tenantry. John McClintock complained in 1736 that 'the tenants have not paid any penalties forfeited by disposing of their leases, nor do I believe they will if I don't impound and apprize [*sic*] their cattle; those who purchased the tenant right of Castledowney park refuse positively and say they would rather give it up entirely.'[193] But by 1773 it appears that James Hamilton had everything under control.[194] Other estates taxed sales only retroactively if they were discovered to have taken place without the agent's foreknowledge and permission. The leases of 1777 on Lord Kerr's Antrim estate prohibited alienation 'without special liscence [sic] and consent' of the landlord.[195]

A third form of restriction on sales was a crude regulation of the price by preventing the holding from being publicly 'canted' or auctioned, an event that might bring the price of a farm to a level price with which estate man- agers were uncomfortable. Abercorn wished to avoid large payments which might burden the estate, particularly if the seller was leaving the property. A salient example was described by James Hamilton, Jr., in 1801:

> I have done all I could to discourage the sale of Mrs. Pue's farm and will attend the auction on the sixth of August, which has been advertised in

both Derry and Strabane newspapers. I can hardly suppose anyone will be hardy enough to purchase without having had your lordship's permission. I had given notice to Mrs. Pue that your lordship would not consent to the sale of her farm. I hear that £1,200 has been offered for it. It is thought to be the best farm in your lordship's estate.[196]

These auctions were not easily regulated by estate agents. In 1770 a farm on the Nugent estate was canted, but the agent suspected that it was a sham and that both the buyer and the price to be paid had been previously arranged: 'They bid each other up to keep up the form of a cant . . . , [but] it was plain from the purchase money being pounds, shillings, and pence that the purchase was on some agreement made privately.'[197] The Millers of Draperstown explained their technique of infiltrating an auction to a tenant who had advertised his farm for sale in 1844: they would place a friend at the sale to outbid everyone 'and then privately approach the highest acceptable bidder underneath him and offer him the farm at that price.'[198] Of course, the best solution was to avoid auctions altogether by prohibiting them and appointing an independent arbiter to fix the price. The marquis of Dufferin told his agent in 1847 to 'attempt no change [of tenants] except on terms as shall secure to the tenants a little more than may be considered by an independent person an equivalent for what he surrenders. Should he attach to his occupation a far greater value than it really possesses, it would be best to humour him a little and affect a compromise.'[199] Arbitration, not auctions, also set the price of farms on the Brookeborough and Belmore estates.[200]

Agents might also peg tenant-right prices by employing mathematical formulae that incorporated various quantities: the number of 'years' purchase,' a specific rate per acre, a ratio of the Griffith's valuation, the price the seller had paid for the tenant right when he entered the farm, etc. The Mercers' company allowed five years' purchase, that is, a tenant-right price could be no higher than five times the yearly rent,[201] while the Clothworkers' company fixed tenant right at three years' purchase, although five years was allowed in a special case in 1866. In doing this, they were following the rules established on the neighbouring McCausland estate.[202] Dufferin warned his agent in 1869 against letting competition drive the price of a lease beyond a set limit.[203] One correspondent of Dufferin's recommended eighteen years' purchase on Griffith's valuation as the general fair rate of purchase.[204] The owner of Islandmagee, Co. Antrim, limited the sum to be given as tenant right to £12 an Irish acre, and on the Shirley estate in County Monaghan a limit of £10 per acre was set.[205]

A fourth way of regulating tenant-right sales, and by far the most important, involved a veto over the incoming tenant.[206] This was closely related to regulation of the price since the landlord's choice of incomer might not have offered the best price to the seller. Sellers often insisted on their right to the best sale which the market would yield, referred to as the 'outside price,' complaining that regulated or arbitrated prices were unfair to them. A Drapers' tenant was given liberty to sell his farm in 1825 to a neighbour 'if he will give what *you* [Miller, the agent] *consider a fair price* for the lease. If no tenant would give a fair price, he may alienate to any stranger whom you may approve of as tenant, but if he can get a fair price from one of our own people, he must not be permitted to alienate to a stranger because he can get more.'[207] One Mr. Wade, who wanted to sell his Drapers' company farm in 1824, objected to the limitation on the range of buyers, arguing that 'it would not sell so well if he was restricted as to purchasers.' He was told 'that the agreements for the lease [state] . . . that any liscence [*sic*] to alienate would be so limited, and therefore if one of four tenants who can occupy with his present holding will give him a price approaching the actual value, you may intimate [that] the company [give] consent to the alienation.' If not, then the agent was instructed to find a good stranger.[208] In 1843, Henry Crosset presented his case personally before the Drapers' court, claiming that 'he would have got £120 for his interest in [his farm] from an unexceptional tenant, and that he was ordered to give it up to Smith Davidson for £55.'[209] Another Drapers' company tenant complained in 1862 of Hugh Elkin, his neighbour, who paid £200 for his farm; but the seller insisted that 'it was worth £300,' which 'he would have got for it if we had permitted him to sell to a person not residing upon this estate.'[210] Two years later, the Millers told Elkin that if he was unhappy with his neighbours and his rent, he should sell to a neighbour and Miller would 'procure you a purchaser who will not only give you a fair but an outside price for it.'[211] The agent of a property in Ardmalin, Co. Donegal, found the auctioning of farms, or any form of competition or bidding between potential purchases, objectionable. He wrote in 1878:

> The highest bidder may be from another estate altogether, and where it is known that the landlord will insist upon an adjoining tenant or tenants getting a preference and that they have a natural desire to enlarge or square their holdings, persons who may dislike them, or who may be in collusion with the seller, will bid the land up beyond its fair value so as either to force the parties who should get the land into giving too much, or else to drive the landlord into taking someone who should not get it.[212]

The veto power over purchasers was particularly crucial to the process of amalgamating farms. Chapters 3 and 4 concluded by noting that the regulation of tenant-right sales was directed mainly at eliminating the tenure of the occupiers of farms whose size and layout was a legacy of the evolution of the rundale system and the linen rural trades. Giving the right of renewal or the right of first refusal to the tenants of farms adjoining the seller allowed managers to positively reinforce the customary claims of stronger farmers while attacking those of their weaker neighbours, directly playing the one off the other.[213] This required that the agent infiltrate community and family control over inheritance. Only by requiring that the buyers of farms be unrelated to the seller, and ensuring that they pull down the houses and re-draw boundaries on the farm, could the sale of the farm coincide with management objectives. The result of such policies was that many sons were prevented from inheriting portions of farms from fathers or widows.[214] In the 1750s Abercorn attempted to insert a covenant that bound leaseholders against passing the tenant right on to their families, a move discouraged by his agent: 'The clause against bequething [sic] to their families their interest will, I'm afraid, frighten them and make them think that they have no interest in anything.'[215] A century later, no tenant on the Drapers' estate who paid under £5 in rent was allowed to leave holdings to their children or to sell to anyone but the adjacent farmer. The agents would attempt to secure an 'outside value' for the purchaser,[216] and all except one home would be pulled down: 'Where farms are thus consolidated, it should be upon condition that the farm buildings are brought into one spot so as practically to prevent the farm being occupied by more than one person.'[217] In 1823 the Drapers' agents prevented a man from dividing his farm among his children, forcing him to sell the holding and divide the money instead. Furthermore, they directed that if the adjoining tenant purchased the farm, that tenant could hold the right of renewal, but if a stranger purchased it, his interest in the farm would expire with the lease. These directives were accompanied by the following lecture on property rights from the head agent:

> Your reasoning for the division of the farm you hold under the Drapers' company has no foundation in fact to support it. It seems to assume that the land is in fact your property. In this you are mistaken. It is only the quick stock upon it which you have a right to look to as the provision for your family. Whenever you want to divide your property amongst them, you have only to sell your lease and turn your stock into money and each child may have a share of all you are worth.[218]

William Blacker, agent for the Gosford estate, insisted that the freedom of the outgoing tenant to choose his successor 'was not a right, but an indulgence,' though on the Downshire estate passing the farm on within the family was allowed.[219] The Drapers also appeared to have softened their policy over the years. The Millers spelled out their strategy in 1849: 'When a tenant wishes to sell his farm, if it be a small one, we use every exertion to induce his neighbour to purchase. Sometimes they are willing enough to do so and often either unwilling or unable to purchase; if the latter, we permit the tenant's son to purchase, and if we fail in this we open it up to a stranger.'[220]

These concerns for resolving debts and amalgamating farms peacefully within the context of the demands of the neighbours and kin were important, but the overriding goal of the exercise of the veto on purchasers was to secure tenants who were wealthy and Protestant.[221] In the eyes of managers, it was much more important that 'one tenant not be changed for a worse,' that 'a man of good substance and character' be found, whether or not neighbours and kin agreed with the choice.[222] An agent in Bangor, Co. Down, reported in 1745: 'James Blackwood has purchased Thomas Cowden's tenant right of the house adjoining his, and I would wish that what he proposes would be agreeable to my lord and you, as it is exchanging a very good for a very bad tenant.'[223] Agents usually revelled in their descriptions of successfully attracting a capitalist to their estates. For example, after giving much detail of their past investment activity, the Drapers' agents described two wealthy tenants who were interested in purchasing the tenant right of a farm as 'highly respectable and industrious persons and, we are bound to say to the court, they are deserving of any complements the court may be pleased to grant them. . . . These Andersons have come out of a neighbouring estate. Be assured [that] it is such men, especially in Ireland, that *landlords ought by every means in their power* [to] induce to settle on their property.'[224] Robert Farrell, who planned to erect a factory of an unspecified nature, told the agent of the Whyte estate in 1859 that he would take thirty acres presently occupied by some tenants and deal with the tenants himself. The pleasure with which the agent read this proposal can easily be imagined:

> This would do away with the necessity of your dealing with the tenants at all and would leave the payment of their tenant right to me, as I would take the land out of their hands. In this case I can arrange to pay Mr. White £1,000 or £1,500 for a ninety-nine-year lease, as [a] thirty-one-year lease would scarcely be sufficient to extend my works and put up machinery on.[225]

David Wilson, a tenant on the Speer estate near Fivemiletown, described his improvements and asked permission in 1866 to dispose of his farm: 'we therefore hope you will not object to our getting the liberty sought, and we will endeavour to satisfy you with a good Protestant tenant in our places.'[226]

Instead of or in addition to regulating tenant-right sales, many landlords plunged directly into the tenant-right market by purchasing their own tenancies, hoping to extinguish the custom by doing so. One County Down resident felt that 'a landlord purchasing openly his own property would be considered so injurious to the Right of Property that it is never done,'[227] but in fact the practice was well known in his neighbourhood.[228] Why would landlords buy their own property? Some calculated that it was worthwhile to purchase in order to be free to advance the rent.[229] Others secured their veto power over the incoming tenant simply by buying all farms that were to be sold and vacated.[230] Still others purchased tenant right to amalgamate farms, supervise improvements, or redraw boundaries.[231] Landlord purchases of tenant right were also motivated by efforts to preserve woods, desmesnes, or town parks.[232] Such exchanges between a landlord and his tenants are the clearest reminder of the landlord's inability to eliminate the system in any other way than by participation in it. This policy of buying back their own property, signifying as it did the artificiality of confiscation and ownership, appears as a premonition of the eventual sale of property rights under the land acts.

THE EXISTENCE OF TENANT RIGHT AFTER THE 1870 ACT

The question which Gladstone so skilfully evaded by leaving it in the hands of the courts was not made less difficult by narrowing its scope to the level of the estate. If, as must have been the case on the majority of estates, the custom existed in some form before it was discovered, regulated, and restricted by progressive managers, then the questions were: how far had that custom been changed? Were those changes to be regarded as legitimate? That is, could they be considered customary according to the widely known legal standard of custom? The difficulties judging the nature of the custom were manifold. Consider the following hypothetical scenario. Over a period of years (how many?) a certain number of tenant-right exchanges (how many? how exemplary were they?) occurred on an estate. The estate office regulated a number of these on an *ad hoc* basis, others they accepted explicitly or implicitly in retrospect. The estate office developed its rules into a consistent policy (over how long a period?). Exchanges continued to occur, some governed by the rules (when did this establish the legitimacy of the rules?). By 1870 there could exist an enormous chasm between landlord and tenants in relation to perceptions of the status of these regulatory usages. The proper answer to each of these questions must consider not only empirical evidence of usages, but also judgements about their age, the appropriate length of time necessary to confer legitimacy, and other conceptions about what legitimates custom. The problem, in the last instance, was how to determine the 'existence' of something which had since Deasy's act, if not for centuries, been technically beyond the law.

Landlords who had within the previous few decades embarked on restrictive regulative policies might simply deny the existence of the custom, asserting that any sale of a farm was merely an act of kindness or indulgence, not the recognition of a right. Agent-landlord correspondence often gives the impression of careful enforcement of estate rules, but without any corroborating evidence the suspicion must remain that old practices had not been entirely eliminated and that new office rules such as controlling the price and vetoing purchasers were circumvented by the tenants. Landlord and agent claims about the nature and extent of the custom cannot be taken at face value. For example, a County Down agent asserted in 1856 that 'as I have never acknowledged Tenant Right further than an equitable act of favour and kindness from a good landlord to a tenant, I have therefore given no attention to the rules that guide it . . . '[233] The following day, however, another correspondent from the district wrote a long letter explaining in detail how the tenant-right system operated to guarantee compensation for improvements in the locality.[234] Robert Perceval-Maxwell warned a tenant in 1870 that 'the custom of selling farms to which you alluded in conversation with me does not exist upon this estate. The better way for you to do [sic] is to give me a written statement of any claims you may wish to prefer against me and I shall take them with consideration and let you know the result, having seen the crops at present on the ground.'[235] Two years later one of his tenants made an itemized claim on his landlord which included £183 for the value of buildings, improvements and manure, £110 for 'disturbance' and £40 for 'tenant right.' Perceval-Maxwell told his solicitor, 'I could not admit his claim of disturbance or tenant right as that custom did not prevail on my estate. But I offered him the sum of £150 for all compensation to which I acknowledged him entitled under the fourth section of the land act. . . .' The tenant accepted this arrangement and Perceval-Maxwell made him sign a statement that 'he will not directly or indirectly receive any further sum from the incoming tenant under any pretext or denomination whatever.'[236] The incoming tenant was required to sign a similar statement before taking possession. This evidence clearly poses two questions: why, if tenant right was not customary on the estate, had the landlord to go to such lengths to ensure that it not be practised; and secondly, how did these two tenants settle the issue of 'goodwill' between them?

The records of the Colebrooke, Co. Fermangh, estate of Lord Brookeborough give another example of how this battle over the existence of the custom might be played out. William Morris, reporting on his tour from Galway to Enniskillen in 1870, claimed that Fermanagh was a tenant-right county and drew a clear distinction between landlord and tenant relations in that county with those further south, due primarily to 'the famous custom, which, so to speak, is the visible expression of this harmony between the landed classes.' In Fermanagh, he observed, tenant right sold on average for three to six years' purchase.[237] But the agent of the Brookeborough estate claimed ten years later that 'tenant right generally did not exist in Fermanagh, so that it would be very hard to prove that there were bigger prices on adjoining estates.'[238] The Brookeborough estate had been aggressively managed from at least the 1850s, especially with respect to the exchange of farms. The agent asserted in 1876 'that the estate is more absolutely under the landlord's control than any other estate with which I am acquainted in Ireland.'[239] In 1866 one tenant who had purchased a plot without permission and now wanted to be 'accepted as tenant' for an additional farm was told that he would have to give up the purchased plot without compensation. Another tenant who had purchased a lease without permission was warned that the landlord 'would not recognize the sale and that he had bought at his peril as Sir Victor would put any rights he had in force and would not renew with him as tenant at the fall of the lease.'[240] But even here where the custom had apparently been regulated out of existence, the landlord occasionally allowed it to exist unofficially. An agent diary of 1871 refers to the case of the ejectment of Thomas Noble Jr. in the county land courts. Noble's claim for compensation was refused by the chairman. 'Ulster Tenant Right [was] proved not to exist on the Colebrooke estate. Not wishing to ruin Noble I agreed with Mr. J. Rea, Belfast, . . . to give Noble £70.' The chairman 'approved though he stated I was not bound to give one shilling.'[241] For the agent and the county chairman, this may only have been an act of indulgence; for Mr. Noble, it may have been a vindication of his beleaguered but ancient right.

A landlord might be able to satisfy himself, and the court, of the restricted nature of a tenant-right usage on his estate even though his agent was unwilling or unable to enforce those restrictions. The marquis of Dufferin, for example, could not trust his agent to stamp out the operation of tenant right on his own estate and had to constantly monitor him on this issue. In the 1860s he forced purchasers of farms to sign statements like the following: 'So as not to interfere with the landlord's opportunity of putting the land into proper shape for the advantage of the cultivator, I was clearly to understand that it was the tenant's beneficial interest in the land and that alone I had purchased and should consequently be required on termination thereof to surrender possession of same.'[242] Dufferin's agent, more out of pragmatism than sympathy, was much less strict in his dealings with tenants, much to the consternation of his employer. After one sale took place Dufferin complained:

> In the advertisement of the sale which I have seen, he describes the farm as his 'property' and he sells not only his existing lease but a twenty-one year lease at the back of it. . . . Immediately on hearing this, I sent for him for the purpose of quashing the whole proceeding, but he at once met me by stating that he had received your sanction for everything he had done before you went to London.[243]

Thomson replied almost immediately:

I explained to Mr. Knox [the seller] and the purchaser tha
bought was simply Mr. Knox's beneficial interest in his
expiration thereof no matter what amount he gave for it h
claim whatever against your lordship on account ther
would simply occupy Mr. Knox's shoes and be entitle
twenty-one years not at the present rent but at the current rent of the day
and at the end thereof all claim would cease.[244]

Thomson was in an unenviable position. Like any competent land agent, he knew that effective management required an intimacy with the affairs of the tenants and a tactful recognition of their conceptions of their 'property.' Unfortunately, he was employed by one of the most strident and vocal opponents of tenant right in the nineteenth century. Dufferin complained that Thomson 'will spend hours relating disputes between a couple of litigious tenants, or the members of a family that have quarrelled, though the matters in dispute are no affairs of mine, and yet he cannot find one hour in each week in which to write a reply to my most pressing communications.' Dufferin did not trust Thomson, but he could not bring himself to let go a man who gave the best years of his life to the estate. Another agent named Henry Pattison was brought in to work along side Thomson when Dufferin's public career brought him to Quebec.[245] Pattison made repeated written requests to Thomson in the early 1870s for information about tenants who were compensated or leases that had changed hands,[246] and reported in 1874 that Thomson 'is very ready to explain any points to me regarding both his papers and dealings with his tenants, and I am doing my best to master the ins and outs of tenant right.'[247]

Over the next couple of years it became apparent that the most important managerial duties, namely rent collection, serving ejectments at assizes, and arranging for the sale of farms, were to remain in Thomson's hands.[248] Thomson was also to prove his irreplaceability in the land courts. In 1877 a dispute with a tenant named Lowry over the existence of the Ulster Custom on the Dufferin estate came to a head and was reported in the regional press.[249] Thomson called Lowry 'an old and very stupid man' who allegedly purchased tenant right from his mother around 1830. He was trying to sell the fifteen-acre farm for £250. Thomson traced his family's presence on the estate back to his father's lease in the 1790s. Lowry's lawyer, who was connected to the Tenant Right League, was attempting 'to prove that we had a custom notwithstanding the custom of the lease and that we were bound by this custom.' Thomson's defence was 'to show that although we did adopt a certain restricted practice, it was a matter of favour the granting of permission and not a right that could be demanded, and fortunately the barrister took this view of the case.'[250] Once again, the 'existence' of the custom depended on the crucial difference between 'favour' and 'right.' An experienced agent like Thomson, who spent his whole career navigating the porous border between favour and right, was in a position to tip the balance of the scales of justice toward his employer's side in a highly publicized case. In 1878 Thomson decided to go to Canada to look for a farm for himself, the prospect of which left Pattison with 'a great deal of out-of-door work in the next three months, as I cannot find that he has kept up any history of the several farms, and I think to avoid risks after legislation.' Pattison remarked that 'I hardly know how we should have got on without Mr. Thomson in regard to much that has to be done for the landed estates court.'[251]

The 1870 act only exacerbated the ambiguities surrounding the question of the existence of tenant right that had been an inherent part of its history for over a century. It has already been noted that the custom could not legally exist under the orders and conditions of the plantation. Deasy's act of 1860 was merely a recodification of this longstanding fact. On the face of it, the provision of the 1870 act legalizing tenant right where it existed was an absurdity. The act did, however, provide a legal mechanism for bringing the custom's existence and the ways in which landlords had come to grips with it out of the shadows of the private sphere of the estates themselves. Whether the decisions of the courts legalizing landlord restrictions on the custom settled the problem of its existence is another question. Long accustomed to asserting their amorphous rights against evolving management practices, tenants in the 1870s continued to hold on to a conception of tenant right with more universal connotations than those allowed by judicially-proved usages. Tacit acceptance of decisions restricting free sale and the right of renewal in the generally economically buoyant, post-famine decades kept these tensions in precarious balance. By the end of the decade, that balance had disappeared. As the Bishop of Clogher informed a Fermanagh landlord in 1881:

> We are looking out with intense anxiety for the ministerial proposals on the Irish land question. Some change is absolutely necessary. There is scarce a shred of Tenant Right, properly so-called, now surviving in the counties of Monaghan and Fermanagh. Gladstone's land act of 1870 has been the annihilation of tenant right amongst us, of course *indirectly*. After the passing of that Act landlords set themselves at once to suppress tenant right and they have succeeded in this to perfection. Except on your estate and one or two others, the confiscation of tenant's rights and improvements is now complete.[252]

The advantages of hindsight on the nature of tenant right in Victorian Ulster are strictly limited. The intention here is not to solve Gladstone's equation by filling in the missing explanatory variables with the evidence of estate records. The question is unsolvable by that means, even if the records of all the estates in Ulster had existed and survived. The question faced by Gladstone was not to be anwered by an empirical accounting of the operation of the Ulster Custom, because it addressed more abstract and fundamental questions about the threefold relationship between (1) the general rules governing the political economy of land (the question of the proper form of property, the governance of the distribution of rights to property, and the fair valuation of the product of labour and the soil), (2) the particular relationships between landlords and tenants which simultaneously embody and infract those general rules, and (3) the history of the evolution of these fractious relationships into a master narrative referred to as the 'Ulster custom' or the 'land question.' The question, at its root, is one of the mutual constitution of property, citizens, and the state in Ireland and Britain.

THE QUESTION OF FAIR RENT

The custom was conceptually protean, a bundle of 'usages' tightly faggotted together into a social fabric. The most crucial seam in this fabric, the linchpin of the custom, was a fair rent. What good, after all, was fixity of tenure at an unfair rent? Who would buy a farm that had neither an affordable rent nor a recognized property right? The three F's were always intertwined, even if tenant right was not articulated as the trinity of fair rent, free sale, and fixity of tenure until the 1870s. Victorian experts like Hancock, Seebohm, and Henderson all agreed that a fair rent was an essential component of the custom.[253] Donnell argued that a system of fixing rents by competition 'could not co-exist with a tenant right, an essential condition of which is a fairly valued rent. The rent may be raised so as to encroach upon or even to extinguish it.'[254] The managers of the Drapers' company estate used this fact to put pressure on those who refused to sell their farms and leave the estate. Tenants were to be informed that 'no renewal of lease shall be made to them and . . . they [will] be put under a small advance of rent as a warning to them that the longer they defer complying with the reasonable wishes of their landlords, the less valuable their tenant right, as it is termed, will become.'[255]

Ulster tenants at will, or those whose leases had expired, could argue that they held a right of continuous possession as long as they paid their rents. But what would happen if they could not pay? What would happen if the surrounding economic circumstances drove up real rents to the point where the tenant right of their farms became worthless, as had happened in the late 1840s? Nothing galvanized the political agitation for legal recognition of the fair rent component of tenant right more than a narrowing of the difference between nominal rents and the nominal value of farm output. The crisis periods of 1846–48 and 1879–82 are two cases in point. Economic recoveries in the 1850s and late 1860s brought tenant-right values back into line, a welcome change for both landlords and the stronger tenants, aiding and abetting the process of consolidation of farms and removal of smallholders.[256] The failure of the 1870 act to address the relationship between fair rent and tenant right was a time bomb that ticked almost inaudibly through the buoyant early 1870s, only to explode in the deep depression at the end of the decade. Historians have expended a great deal of effort on establishing an accurate quantitative picture of the material determinants of the relative economic positions of landlords and tenants during this period. The goal of this literature has been to explain the material – though, given the heroic nature of many of the assumptions, highly abstract – determinants of the land war.[257] This is an important line of study, since greater objective certainty concerning the distribution of income between landlords and tenants will remain a cornerstone of any full understanding of the *dénouement* of the land question. But the cornerstone is not the house; it may help explain *when* the tenantry finally revolted against the landlord system, but it does not explain *why* that revolt occurred.[258] It was a crisis neither of material welfare nor of empirical politics, but of *the political* itself.[259] The governance of Ulster since the plantation had rested on the landed estate system where an oligopoly of landlords held all legal rural property and the mass of society, both native and newcomer, rented that land. The legitimacy of this system of governance was based on the accumulated and innumerable agreements between landlords and tenants, cemented with each half-yearly payment of rent. The system was based on a fabric of co-operation between landlord and tenant which gave legitimacy to rent payments.

The legitimacy of the estate system rested on the method by which rents were set. This methodological question could not, and still cannot, be placed on a sound conceptual or logical foundation. Intellectually, one may construct a system which determines an equilibrium rent, but this is no guide to its social determination, except in a society in which the hegemony of the 'free contract' was absolute. The value of land, as capital, can be regarded in such a system as simply the annuity payable to its owner based on its physical fertility and the opportunity costs of investments of labour and capital into it. Even in its own terms, this calculation is complicated by the constantly changing nature of the alternative uses – the opportunity costs – of agricultural land and labour, the most important of which in the Irish context were the development of the textile proto-industries and the widening of the international labour market.[260] Capital, land, labour, and the commodities produced by their combination can only be measured as an exchange value determined by the social abstractions of the wage rate and the rate of interest. The classical economic measurement of the value of land fails to open the question of its intrinsic value because it stops short of raising questions about the historical production of the social mechanisms by which the wage and the interest rate are determined. The inscrutability of the value of land is the result of social contradictions over the distribution of the surplus of labour (whether consumed or conserved as capital), not intellectual failure or the unknowability of the thing in itself. Rent was a mechanism through which the power relations between landlords and tenants flowed. Its quantity was the result not only of differential fertility and capital investment but the class conflict between owners and differential strata of occupiers over the surplus of production. The payment and receipt of rent therefore effectively reproduced the classes engaged in the system (farmers as farmers, labourers as labourers, landlords as landlords, etc.). The setting of the rent level was therefore a social and political calculation as much as it was an economic one. How should rents be determined? This is not a question that was historically and conceptually settled before the 1870s only to be upset by external material and political crises. Rather it is a question that is conceptually impossible to answer, and has been historically answered only as a result of social compromises. These compromises often lasted for centuries, but they did not constitute definitive answers. New compromises may result in a revolution in the form the question takes, as when the 'land war' between landlords and tenants mutated into the the 'ranch war' between tenants, but the question persisted, and persists to this day. Owner occupancy may be a very powerful politico-symbolic solution to the problem, but it is just a displacement of the tension between private landed property and capital.[261]

What was a fair rent? The question has never received a proper answer, and opinions vary to extremes. Ferguson and Vance, following Adam Smith, invoked a tradition whereby a third of product of the land went to landlord, the tenant, and to other expenses (taxes, capital, labour).[262] On the other hand, the radical Presbyterian Rev. David Bell moved the following resolution at a Tenant Right meeting in 1848: 'That no proprietor of land is justly entitled to a larger sum in the form of rent than the produce of the land would be worth in its natural state.'[263] Landlords across the centuries recognized that in practice the rent of a particular farm depended completely on that opaque factor – the labour of the farmer. The Anglesey agent appreciated in 1770 that the valuation of a property 'depended on the fancy of a tenant,' and in particular certain lands were 'worth a great deal more to an improving tenant.'[264] Edmund McGildowney judged as useless any attempt to put a value on a farm until its occupant had laboured it for a few years. In 1817 he informed a tenant who had requested a lease at a modest rent:

As I am very sure neither you nor his lordship wishes for anything but what would be fair and right on both sides, and as neither of you can at present or until after a few years' trial do more than guess at the value, I shall recommend to his lordship to accept of your offer and grant you a lease for a few years, at the end of which you will both be able to know what will be the fair and equitable terms to grant a long lease at.[265]

N.C. White was informed by his agent in 1816 that 'you know the object we have in not immediately granting leases was the hope of being able to ascertain the probable value of land.'[266] William Blacker felt that tenants should be charged rent commensurate with the amount of skill and capital they possessed.[267] A report to the Fishmongers' company argued that 'great dissatisfaction would have been occasioned by a comparison in cases where the rent of an improving tenant had been raised [along] with those on holdings which, not having been improved, were necessarily either lowered or allowed to remain at the existing rent, though such absence of improvement might be the result of want of due industry and enterprise.'[268]

The level of rent was an important but unpredictable device for discovering the productive capacity of a farmer. Some landlords forced the rent as high as they could in order to find the maximum that could be produced.[269] Most, however, calculated that 'fair' rents would have a beneficial effect on long-term surplus extraction. The rent level had an unpredictable influence on two related decisions on the part of the tenant: whether to divide up and sublet the farm, and whether to invest in improvements. Some thought that 'beneficial' rents, like long leases, induced tenants to cultivate and improve rather than sublet a property. The agent of the Perceval-Maxwell estate noted in 1823 that no increase in rent was to be sought from good tenants, as a higher rent forced them to sublet.[270] Rack-renting was also undesirable because it might indirectly threaten the tenants on the ground. On the Foljambe estate in 1788 the agent gave this account of a head tenant whose only resource for meeting his financial obligations seems to have been his ability to persecute his undertenants:

George Armstrong, who has set almost all his holding to undertenants, is now suing them for the rent and recovering it by law so that they are prevented paying it to me, which was the only prospect I had of securing a very considerable arrear due on that holding, as Armstrong has very little property or distress on the land. He also talks of suing me for having sold a small quantity of cattle off his holding last year. . . . The truth is his holding is not worth the arrear due upon it, which makes him unwilling to sell. He therefore wishes to hold the land and pay no rent if possible.[271]

An easy rent was also seen as the best way to promote improvement. Rather than hazard investments themselves, landlords hoped that by allowing their tenants to accumulate capital they would develop the farms. Early in the plantation the simplest way to affect the economy was to indulge tenants with 'beneficial' leases. A survey of land in County Donegal by Thomas Knox in 1682 urged that 'a landlord ought to give good encouragement to people to farm his land and not look for the value at first setting but let them have their farms easy for some time.'[272] Arthur Brownlow included houseboot and turf in his mid-seventeenth-century leases, but these perquisites were eliminated from leases later in the century. He also adjusted the rent 'so that it was lower in the early years of the lease.'[273] Nicholas Ellis gave an example of the policy which had been in operation on the Barrett-Lennard estate for some decades in 1830:

> William Smith's immediate tenant was a General Murray, who had purchased the interest of William Nixon. The lease had been made in the year 1744. . . . The style in which it is kept would do credit to an English farmer. . . . I always encouraged his improvements by an assurance to him that when the land came out of lease, I would make a special effort to you on the subject, and he might rely upon it that he should not be charged for anything he did to better the condition of the house and farm. . . . My idea is that he should be charged just such a rent as the land would bring now as if it had been under the usual cause of treatment.[274]

On the Anglesey estate rents were also occasionally set below the 'lettable value.' After the turn of the century Lord Uxbridge, the owner of the Anglesey estate, was concerned to balance increases of rent with a 'fair and equitable interest' to the tenants.[275] The risk of giving a beneficial lease was that the tenant might relet the land at a profit rather than improve the farm himself. Seeing the accumulation of large profit rents in the hands of middlemen in the eighteenth century, some landlords responded by rack-renting them when the first opportunity arose. Sir George Savile, a Tyrone landowner, remarked that 'if farms are let for anything less than the highest rent, it is not an easy matter to prevent second bargains.'[276] William Greig proposed to strike a balance between the beneficial and the rack-rent, arguing that 'any sum beyond what will have the effect of exciting tenants to exertion, may be oppressive and have an opposite tendency.' He proposed setting the rent just high enough to 'prove a spur to industry than any bar to improvement.' This he called a 'smart rent.'[277]

Conceptions about cultivating improvement and inhibiting subletting were not the only guides to setting the rent. The rent level also had to be socially acceptable. The goal was to maintain an active, improving, and above all *contented* tenantry, what one agent referred to as 'the English plan.' The

English plan had an ancient lineage. Since the dawn of post-feudal pater-nalism in the English countryside, landlords and their apologists had concerned themselves with 'the moral obligations which were to govern landlord-tenant relations.'[278] The records of the Barrett-Lennard estate in Monaghan provide an interesting view of the process of setting the rent. William Mayne felt that the long-term interests of the landlord were best served by allowing the tenants a certain degree of comfort. In 1808 he explained to Barrett:

> A sharp agent certainly, with the approbation of the landlord, might charge more. However, I never let land for any of my employers at the highest rate. I let it at what I think the tenant can pay without oppression. And of course, the landlord receives a fair honest rent, the tenant is content, does not run into arrear, has no cause for any change in the government, land-lord, or agent, and an appearance of English comfort runs through the estates.[279]

He reiterated the point again in 1809, noting that there were many landlords in south Ulster charging much higher rents than he did, 'yet by so doing, that link between landlord and tenant was broken, the tenantry had no interest in the country.' In 1814 he described the appropriate strategy: 'The present idea is that land will lower in yearly value, yet increase in purchase, that is, we shall be more on the English plan, content with less interest in landed pro-perty than hitherto and tenants to become more respectable.'[280]

Mayne formed his attitude based on his observation of the troublesome effects of the more exploitive policies of other landlords around Clones, Co. Monaghan. 'You don't hear of murders, burnings, or tenantry failing about Clones, which to the disgrace of many parts of Ireland, is the case, and all proceeding from oppression,' he remarked, in defence of indulgent rents. 'Give the poor Irish only English indulgence,' he advised, 'and they will be content.' The disruption of the Clones market by a mob in 1816 resulted in the jailing of forty men, most of whom were from outside the Barrett estate. The incident prompted Mayne to comment on the advantages of a moderate rent and to criticize those 'high-flying landlords and clergymen who advance their rents and tithes to an exorbitant rate.' And in the following year he appealed again to Barrett-Lennard's lenity: 'Within the last four years I have been spurred on to lay rather a heavier rent on your lands than I wished. . . . I did believe you wished I should take example from Dean Roper and others who had properties in the neighbourhood of Clones.'[281] The Anglesey agent expressed a similar point in 1821: 'The apparent happiness of a tenantry, numerous, unfortunately, almost beyond calculation may be attributed to your lordship's liberality in the first instance in sanctioning a proportionate reduction of rents to those whose means of paying it arose entirely from the produce of agriculture.'[282] If an agent like Mayne was cognizant of developments further afield than his own district, he would have found much more evidence in support of his strategy. Much of late eighteenth and early nineteenth century agrarian outrage in Munster was directed at inhibiting landlords from allowing an open competitive market to set new rents on farms with expired leases. According to one magistrate in 1809, 'it is well known that farmers who are nearly or out of lease are principally the cause of all the disturbances and outrages, which are done to deter others from bidding for their farms and their landlords from raising their rents.'[283] This kind of activity was intermittent and short-lived, but it 'doubtless modified the open letting of farms in the last fifteen years of the century; whether they really affected rent levels significantly is doubtful, but the desire for peace on an estate and the fear of disturbance probably somewhat enlarged the chances of renewal for sitting tenants.'[284] Over the next twenty years, these constraints persisted, if not tightened. Ellis remarked in 1845 that 'the setting of land is now a peculiarly delicate thing. I must not go too high and bring 'Molly Maguire' upon me and I must not show a fear of her by going to law.'[285]

If rents on well-managed estates were not set at the 'lettable value' or by open competition between tenants, the question, then, was how to set the rent level so that it would be 'fair and judicious.' As one agent put it, 'I am satisfied that it is impossible to judge accurately of the value of land in Ireland, for practically speaking, that depends very much on the will of the landlord.'[286] This was, of course, a managerial as well as conceptual problem. It was the boast of an efficient agent such as Richard Purcell that he could 'give a shrewd guess to the ability of every tenant on the estate, and I will surely oblige such to pay who are able to do so without suffering their stock to be sold.'[287] But a corrupt agent could have the opposite effect. In County Down in the early eighteenth century, Henry Blundell's difficulties with two agents, Gwynn and Meredyth, prevented an accurate valuation of the estate. In 1720 Blundell criticized Gwynn for misleading Meredyth about the value of the properties and being 'too much in the interest of the tenants.' Blundell recognized that Gwynn knew 'the value of every acre around Dundrum, and if you were as much in my interest as you pretend, you would have given me your assistance in letting them to the best advantage.'[288] With larger populations later in the century, the uncertainty and expense of the task dissuaded most agents from setting rents without expert assistance. One popular procedure for fixing rents was to hire professional surveyors to value the farms. Their opinions were often controversial, however, and their calculations often needed to be revised with the aid of other individuals and devices. Rowley Miller felt that he could not trust the work of the surveyor of the Drapers' company estate in 1854: 'We did not think it right to follow him throughout, for we knew what he could not know: the improvement of farms by [the] hard work and industry of the owners thereof within the last few years. We do not consider it judicious to value an estate too frequently because the industrious man, if the valuator be a stranger, will be taxed for his improvements whilst the indolent and careless too frequently escape, and the result of frequent valuations stops improvements on an estate altogether.'[289] The valuer's science often amounted to nothing more than a sense of what bargains might be struck. Valuers often merely abided by the rent level that appeared to be customary in the vicinity of their estates. A revealing example of this is the Downshire estates, where rents were set by professional valuation from at least 1800 on properties in County Down and King's County. The valuers took a consistently different view of the southern estate than they did of the Down estate. The estate's agent told the Devon commission that he kept the rent below one-fourth the value of the produce, which he thought was a valuation 'that will let the tenant live.' Nevertheless, he set the rents higher on the southern estate because of the general level of rents of other estates in the neighbourhood. This was his best guide to just how well the tenants might live in the midlands.[290]

The entry of these issues into the public sphere did nothing to solve the problem. William Sharman Crawford, for example, declared his intention in 1835 to implement on his own estate the rules of his tenant right bill should it fail in parliament. He had no idea, though, what the terminology in the bill regarding fair rents would mean in practice.[291] The 1870 act prompted all concerned to recognize the intimate link between fair rents and tenant right.[292] The problem was that tenant right could now be attacked under the act in two ways, by increasing rents and by lowering the awards given in the courts below the market level.[293] The Bessborough commission report concluded that 'no principles for the calculation of a fair rent, as distinguished from a full commercial rent, have ever been so generally received as to become part of the custom.'[294] Northern tenants, fearing that landlords would respond to the bill by rack-renting,[295] drafted a resolution at a meeting in Portadown urging that all rents should be set by third-party arbitration. The primary purpose of the arbiters was to preserve the value of tenant right. Rent increases became a leading grievance by the late 1870s even thought the general rent level was not overly exploitive.[296] Some evidence of the growing tension surfaces in the Drapers' company papers. A new valuation of 1875 raised rents by as much as 17% in one townland on the estate.[297] The agent Walter Stannus wrote in December of 1875 that 'only 91 out of the entire estate have agreed to the terms offered, and these principally from the smaller class of leaseholders.'[298] A stand-off ensued between Stannus and the more prominent tenants. A meeting in Draperstown of the Tenant

League noticed in the *Belfast News Letter* was chaired by a tenant named Dickson. Stannus recommended the following strategy: 'As Mr. Dickson has put himself so prominently forward and is doing so much to disturb the minds of the tenants, I would suggest to the committee the propriety of 'taking the bull by the horns' and demanding possession from Dickson. If he was made an example of it would have a very good effect and would induce a number of others to assent to the new valuation.'[299] The estate won ejectment cases in Magherafelt against Dickson and many others. 'In each of the cases,' according to Stannus, 'the chairman gave costs against the tenants so that we have every hope that further legal proceedings will be unnecessary and that the tenants will forthwith comply with the company's terms.'[300]

The earl of Belmore, operating in a more politically sensitive context of a by-election in 1873, was not able to be as aggressive as Stannus. He wanted his estate revalued and set on new terms in 1876, but his agent R.C. Brush worried that 'professional valuators do more harm than good. There were three separate ones employed by Lord Powerscourt on his estate [near Benburb, Co. Tyrone] and I don't believe the valuation of any one was adopted, although it cost his lordship eight or nine hundred pounds for valuing 9,000 acres, and all is not yet settled after four years of confusion.'[301] Nevertheless a valuation of 34 townlands was conducted the following year which, if implemented, would have increased the rent by six per cent. Brush advised against implementing the increase, citing the rebellion of the Powerscourt tenantry, the excitement kept alive by the land bills of Butt, Crawford, and Smyth, and the possibility of provoking 'knots of individuals' and giving a 'handle' to demagogues.[302]

What was the relationship between tenant right and the rent level? The tenant-right payment, like any commodity exchange, gave retroactive confirmation of exchange value. But the meaning of this information still had to be interpreted. Agents who were just coming to grips with the custom thought high tenant-right prices meant that rents could be increased.[303] Henry Smith advised tenants in 1821 that 'no licence to alienate will ever be granted but on a full and candid disclosure of the consideration to be received by the vendor. This is not from any jealousy that the tenants have had their leases on too good a terms, but as a guide to ascertain in future lettings what is the real current value of the land.'[304] Over twenty years later Edward Lawford was equally adamant on this matter:

> It would be no answer to the court for the tenant to state that he had given a large sum for his lease, for that would only be considered as evidence that the rent at which the premises were let was under their value. And that is the way the court look upon the subject when they see a tenant at will selling a holding upon which he has not expended a shilling of his own in

the way of improvement for four or five years' purchase, and it leads the court to believe that the whole of the estate is greatly underlet.[305]

In 1842 George Joyce, the agent to Lord Mountcashel, referred to a tenant who had requested a rent reduction and speculated that 'if he were to offer his farm for sale tomorrow, I make not the least doubt he would get £100 at once, and unless he is wanting to do so in order to get as high a price as possible for it, is wishing to have his rent reduced as much as possible so that a purchaser may pay more for it. I cannot imagine what other object he has in view of the line of conduct he has adopted.'[306] But landlords (and historians) were mistaken if they believed that high tenant-right prices implied that rents lost to tenants (who were then presumed to have the ability to capitalize on their good fortune[307]) could be recouped by rent increases. Fair rents, once capitalized, mortgaged, or otherwise collateralized, began to circulate through the rural economy. Because a tenant-right sum was not a static lump, hidden under tenant mattresses, landlords were incapable of retrieving it from a particular tenant. Increasing the rent of a tenant who had just paid a high price for a farm could easily ruin him and his family. Fair rents, anomalous as this may have seemed to many, became competitive rents once expectations about tenant-right prices were generalized.[308] The Millers struggled to communicate this point to the Drapers' management committee in 1848:

> The value of tenant right, no matter how much the out-going tenant may get for his holding, does not one way or the other weigh with the landlord or evaluator as to the *acreable value* of the land. This is an anomoly and difficult to explain but nevertheless it is the fact. . . . It is no criterion whatever as to the estate being set too low because the owner of a farm may get a considerable sum for his tenant right. There have been instances of landlords taking up this point, who raised their rents and injured their tenants and ultimately themselves for doing so.[309]

The anomalous nature of fair rents folds back into to the anomalous nature of the estate system itself, its artifice and its contingency. In rare instances in the estate records, these links appear within the experience of a single tenant and her family. The following example from the records of the Irish Society clearly shows the way in which the custom of tenant right mediated between the functioning of the economy and the social foundation of that economy, between competition and privilege. The case concerns William and Samuel Moore, who held land in County Londonderry under a lease dating from the middle of the eighteenth century. William renewed while Samuel continued in his position under the old lease. Eventually, Samuel died, the old lease expired, and his widow and brother requested a new lease. According to a report on the case:

The Society were pleased to consider the widow as having the tenant right, but a strife and competition [arose] between the family of Samuel and his widow. They raised and bid up the premises against her to a rent of £50 a year, at which rent the Society was pleased in the month of December of 1812 to order a lease to be made to Mrs. Moore, a widow, at the said rent of £50 a year.

Having outbid her competitors, Patience Moore later petitioned for a rent reduction and got a new rent of £38. Noting that she had just accepted a lease of twenty-one acres for thirty-one years and one life at an increased rent of £40 17s., increased from £9 3s. to £50,[310] one deputy to the Irish Society proportion felt it necessary to add a detailed comment on the important difference between the holding of land based on competition and the holding of land based on custom. Despite the awkward prose, this comment demonstrates the author's awareness of the distinction between the basis of tenant right on historicity and the basis of tenant right on production:

Seeing that an opinion of tenant right or the preferable claims of tenants in possession appears to prevail among tenants of the Society, and to have been hitherto invariably prevailed between landlord and tenant from the time of the charter, under which both have prospered, and as your committee conceived the liberality of the Society must always have had in view the circumstances of their being in for all intents and purposes absentee landlords, they cannot help calling to their minds the very strong presumptive evidence of a corresponding return from their tenants, who in the late rebellion in Ireland appear to have resisted in its contagion, although tempted, by its approach to the very confines of Londonderry and Coleraine. Your committee cannot conclude this report without alluding to the circulation of opinions that some other mode of letting [than] by means of competition ought to be resorted to. Upon this point your committee feel themselves deeply impressed.[311]

Here is an instance where an Ulster land agent clearly recognized an extra-economic basis for 'tenant right' or the 'preferable claims of tenants in possession' and spelled out two of these extra-economic characteristics considered in detail in previous chapters: the long history of their occupation under the conditions of absentee ownership and their allegiance to the political arrangement established by the plantation in times of violent upheaval. By appealing to the 'liberality' of the Irish Society, the reporters also declared allegiance to a fundamental feature of liberalism: that certain realms of society should be preserved from the rule of the market. There is a close association between the custom of tenant right and the category of factors we have named the 'extra-economic,' with these factors taking the form of rent policies that inhibited competition, were attuned to fairness and liberality, or followed an 'English plan.' But the extra-economic reward given to tenants – that their families and kin be given a tenant right which preserved them from competition – was already dissolved within the economy. Any deterioration in the value of that reward, in the form of rent increases or price deflation, could destroy the meaning of tenant right.

THE END OF TENANT RIGHT

Once the *laissez-faire* project embodied in Deasy had reached its ideological *cul de sac* and it became widely recognized that some form of palliative legislation was inevitable, those responsible for that legislation stepped into a no man's land. If Irish land law was to be based on principles other than those spelled out in Deasy, then what would they be? If the conceptual basis of land reform was a new system more attuned to the balance of agrarian class power in the countryside, then how was this balance to be measured? In the run-up to the 1870 act, questions like these raised anxieties on all sides about the pace of change and the nature of the battle to come. 'The landlords know that a land bill is inevitable,' wrote the *Northern Whig* in April of 1870, 'it is folly, therefore, for tenants to talk of remaining as they are. They cannot remain as they are. Their position must either be made better by immediate legislation, or be infinitely worse than in Ulster, at least, it ever was before. The days of kind, indulgent landlords, with 'moral' but no legal obligations to their tenants, are over.'[312] William Morris also recognized the inherent instability of the situation in which the custom was 'repudiated by law and upheld only by strong yet not invincible custom.'[313] The honeymoon granted to the 1870 act, if there was one, was short lived. After the recommendations of the landlordist Chelmsford commission had manifested themselves in obnoxious rulings on the existence of leasehold and town park tenant right,[314] a series of outdoor meetings took place, including one of national scope in Dublin in 1873. Over the next two years tenant righters began to recognize the urgency of a situation in which the foundations of the land law had become unstable. As Samuel Smyth proclaimed at a tenant meeting in Moira, Co. Down, in 1874: 'We have shifted our moorings and we cannot remain where we are. It is quite evident [that] the guardianship of feudalism will afford us no further shelter, and the protective wing of British law has not yet taken us in.'[315]

This movement against the 1870 act represents an epochal shift in the long history of tenant right, and the culmination of the developments both in the public sphere of politics and in the private sphere of the estates themselves over the previous half-century. Throughout the course of its history, the custom of tenant right was defended as a particularity – particular to the history of a family, its relationship to the landlord and to the land settlement at large – against the universality of both the regime of private property and the capitalized land market, and the political regime of colonial Ulster and the union. In this characteristic, the Ulster custom resembled many of the customary tenures that had preceded it in early modern England and Scotland. These forms of tenure came into existence at 'the interface between law and agrarian practice' only after the law of private property began to take on a universal appearance. Customary tenures were, throughout history, viewed as local, *lex loci*, from the Archimedean position of the common, universal law.[316] Isaac Gilpin, a contemporary authority on the sixteenth-century tenures wrote that 'customs, especially in the Northern Parts of this nation, are so various and differing in themselves that a man might almost say that there are as many several customs as manors or Lordships in a county.'[317] To recall the arguments of Chapter 1, tenant right, the last of a long heritage of customary tenures, was contentious and open to attack because it attempted to represent the labour of the plantation, which was and is objectively unrepresentable. This unrepresentable phenomenon residing at the interface of law and agrarian practice balanced the defence of traditional attachments to the soil against the incredulous assertions of capitalist private property. In the history of all customary tenures there is a moment when the ambiguous tension between custom and the legal text reaches a crisis.[318] As Maitland characterized it, the broad trend of land law may have been 'neither from communalism to individualism, nor yet from individualism to communalism, but from the vague to the definite.'[319] In the case of customary tenures, definitiveness was quickly followed by obsolescence. The first written definitions of customary tenures, the first legal efforts to specify them, are a result of circumstances under which the definitions come into question and are the subject of controversy, circumstances under which capitalists are seeking their elimination. Before this time customary tenures were well understood even if they were not legally specified. When a custom had an *immediate* meaning in a stable context, there was no *process* of definition.[320] In the case of early modern customary tenures like Scottish kindly tenure or border tenant right in the north of England, a combination of commercialization and legal inquisition gradually eroded their status. The growing market for customary tenancies diluted the inheritance claims formerly attached to them. At the same time, the efforts of landlords and judges to define them more accurately gradually reduced them to the modern lease contract. This process in relation to border tenant right has been described by Mildred Campbell as follows:

> That the full and exact nature of tenant right had never been clearly defined seems evident from the records of certain cases that came into the Elizabethan courts. . . . The inability of witnesses on either side to clarify the matter [of whether tenant right more closely resembled inheritable freehold

than at-will tenancy] and their confusion, arising apparently from their own uncertainty rather than from a desire for evasion, makes one suspect that the tenure had never been specifically defined in their own minds. Anciently, this would have mattered little. But now that the land was coveted by both the landlord and the tenant, it was of moment to both.[321]

Landlords in Scotland and England won the battle over definition, replacing customary tenures with modern contracts. Irish landlords were clearly threatening to do the same in the nineteenth century, but they failed in the end. Tenant right would not be dissected by the legal Occam's razor established by the 1870 act, largely because of the ability of the agitation in response to the 1870 act in the early 1870s to recodify the meaning of tenant right in terms of the 'three Fs' fair rent, fixity of tenure, and free sale.[322] The emphasis was now on the universal essence of the custom, not its singular and local characteristics. Under the 1870 act, argued Robert Donnell, the term 'usages' could only mean the ancient essences of the custom, not the numerous restrictions pressed upon it by various agents in the nineteenth century. Donnell argued that estate regulations of tenant right were 'high-handed violations thereof, wrought at a time when the custom had no legal protection.'[323] In parliament, this movement was represented by James Sharman Crawford, now occupying the seat once held by his father. With support of some Ulster conservatives and the editors of the *Belfast Newsletter*, who feared mass defection of Ulster tenants to the Land League, Sharman Crawford introduced bills in the late 1870s designed to amend the 1870 act so that 'the Ulster custom should be presumed to exist unless the landlord was able to prove to the contrary.'[324] With the coining of the three Fs and Crawford's effort to legislate a universally applicable definition of tenant right, the longstanding relationship between particular a custom and universal law in Ulster was reversed. Landlords, after half a century or more of developing techniques to maximize their control over their tenants, under the 1870 legislation defended these *particular* set of practices against the accusation by tenant-right propagandists of a generalized, universal, historically actual, and legally imprescriptable custom. 'Basically what the Ulster tenant associations were seeking,' writes Francis Thompson, 'was not the legalization of the custom as it actually operated at this time but the uniform enforcement of the custom in its integrity throughout the whole province.'[325] The only way to ensure against high-handed violations was to make the essence of the custom universal.

The test of the validity of this gesture, according to Matthew Dutton, was reason. The Ulster custom of tenant right was reasonable, but paradoxical as well. This book has argued that the customary claims of Ulster tenants had their basis in the inauguration and maintenance across many decades of those relationships between tenants and landlords that cemented a new land system in place, transformed the economy, and reorganized the landscape according to a new model. The result was, after many painful transitions, a highly commercialized and productive rural economy. The paradox lay in the fact that customary tenure has usually been one of the first casualties of this multifaceted transformation. Lowland Scotland, for example, saw a transformation in its rural economy c. 1700–1820 that was very similar in its timing and nature to that which occurred across the water in Ulster.[326] However, customary tenures had been extinguished long before this era, and the commercial contract ruled landlord-tenant relations. Scotland never needed its own version of Deasy's act. Why? Only a more detailed comparison of the social and political power and legitimacy of the respective landed classes could deliver a complete answer. The Scottish landed élite were cohesive, their power concentrated, and their cultural and ethnic connections with their tenantry relatively strong. They held the project of agrarian capitalism safely in their own hands, met with little significant resistance in the countryside, and were able to capitalize on the strength of the towns in and around their estates in a period of urbanization and industrialization unparalleled in western European history.[327] The Scottish countryside was not lacking in class tensions over the adjustment to capitalist landlordism, but the tensions were localized and never materialized in the political realm. Ulster landlords, by contrast, were a much less cohesive and powerful force, not least because of their diverse background and rapid rate of turnover. Their social connection to their tenantry, the key to the establishment of a culture of legitimacy and deference, was also weaker than in Scotland. Landlord and tenant relationships were plagued by, on the one hand, mistrust and anxiety (Orangeism), and on the other, resentment and alienation (Ribbonism). The agrarian capitalist project was prosecuted with less authority and faced greater resistance. When it succeeded, Ulster landlords were not in a position to capitalize on it.

In Scotland and England, the countryside had by the nineteenth century long entered the modern world alongside the town. The representation of the Irish countryside after the Act of Union, by contrast, vacillated between two dystopian tropes: Ireland the sacred ancient culture oppressed by its colonizers, and Ireland the barbaric political economy unfit for the modern world. In both cases, according to Seamus Deane, Ireland was viewed romantically 'either as a representation of a sacral community oppressed by a secular, modernizing colonial state, or as a representation of an irretrieveably uncivilized community not fitted for survival in the modern world.'[328] Ulster landlords and tenants sat uneasily within this bi-polar representation. The novels of Maria Edgeworth exemplify their predicament. In Tom

Dunne's reading, Edgeworth was preoccupied with the fate of a paternalist colonialism struggling to incorporate Ireland within a liberal United Kingdom. The deep irony and pessimism of *Castle Rackrent*, according to Dunne, reflects the objective situation of the Edgeworth family: liberal and progressive landlords sandwiched between shrill High Orangeism on the one hand and a recalcitrant and outmoded peasantry on the other.[329] On the one hand, according to Edgeworth's rubric, the countryside was populated by a violent and inscrutable tenantry governed by a 'Ribbon Code' that 'resents all interference by the landlord in the use of the land: to throw farms together is an offence; to prevent subletting is an offence; to prevent the admission of lodgers is an offence. In fact, every act of ownership is an offence.'[330] On the other hand, and in direct opposition, stood a belligerent alliance of Orangemen and landlords. In between Ribbonism and Orangeism, still following Dunne's mapping of the situation of Edgeworth's fiction, there was a Liberalism which thrived in Ulster only in special demographic and political circumstances.[331] In the context of the land question, Liberalism involved an alliance between ethnically, politically, and economically secure strong farmers and their landlords which tacitly excluded rural residents with more meagre capital endowments. In stark contrast to both the belligerence of the Orange-landlord alliance and the discord of the Ribbon-landlord antagonism, the Liberal alliance displayed some potential for settling Irish property relationships on a new hegemonic footing. Gladstone, and the historicists who influenced his thinking, believed in the possibilities of that middle ground upon which a reintegration and reconciliation of the two classes could be legislated, returning landlords to that idealized position 'marked by residence, by personal familiarity and by sympathy with the people among whom they live, by long, traditional connection handed down from generation to generation and marked by a constant discharge of duty. . . .'[332]

For those who accepted that the survival of this liberal class alliance required a different form of political economy, based on different customs and institutions, the crucial question, inextricably binding the land question to the national question, was whether this articulation of Liberalism was elastic enough to hold together in one parliament under one crown communities governed by separate economic rules and legal texts. Wright observed that precisely this issue distinguished the northern Protestant from the Catholic reaction to the land act of 1870. For the northern champions of Gladstone, the 1870 act was evidence of the efficacy of 'a wider Liberal alliance within the British constitutionalism; for many southerners Gladstone's was yet another unsympathetic response to the moral and physical force of Fenianism.' Northern Protestant tenants were satisfied with the 1881 act as a final measure because they were satisfied with the nature of their citizenship, the state, and the role of a limited landlordism in that polity.[333] The northern view of tenant right was bound up with the existence of landlordism, however weakened, and the opposition to the nationalism of Davitt and Parnell was embodied most forcefully in a landlord-tenant alliance in the Orange Order. For the mass of Catholic tenants, however, the legalization of the 'three Fs' in 1881 was only a correction of the failings of the 1870 act, and was widely regarded as a minimum transitional measure on the way to peasant proprietorship. Northern Catholic tenants were long accustomed to defending their tenant-right claims in the same terms as their Protestant neighbours,[334] but their claims to the soil were now more deeply rooted in an alternative, and, in the circumstances of the land war, antithetical myth of origin.[335] The northern struggle for tenant right focused on the degradation of an established custom rooted in the historicality of tenures dating from the century of the plantation. In the middle of the nineteenth century, this rhetoric served to briefly unite tenants north and south behind a program of reformed landlordism. The political failure of that movement, the shock of the famine, and the development of a more utopian rhetoric concerning ancient rights to Irish soil left the mass of Catholics disenchanted with the colonial myth of origin and the legislation directed toward it. By the late 1860s, Butt's efforts to justify land reform by reference to plantation statutes was falling on deaf ears. In parts of south Ulster, tenants had already surrendered in the battle over usages. Speeches at tenant-right meetings in Monaghan, Cavan and even in Magherafelt in 1869 emphasized that tenant right was a myth. A resolution at a Scotstown, Co. Monaghan, meeting read that security of tenure was 'nothing more than wishing that the people should be allowed to live on the soil which God had made for their use.'[336] From this perspective, Gladstone's effort to rehabilitate a landlordism based on the various plantations of the sixteenth and seventeenth centuries was doomed. The land war of 1879–1881 ended the era of the limnality or in-betweenness of tenant right, and destroyed the middle ground between landlords and tenants upon which a liberal class alliance might be based.

By legalizing free sale, fair rent, and fixity of tenure, the land act of 1881 made tenant right the universal law of the land. Tenant right had for centuries existed outside the text of the colonial estate system, as defined by the orders and conditions of plantation and later by Deasy's act. It supplemented that textual reality.[337] Irish private property in the form of the landed estate system was held to be the genetic form and the most natural condition of capitalist relations of production in the countryside. The private property system posed as an already complete whole, outside of which tenant right marked the historical and contingent development of that system. If this capitalist posture was real, to follow the logic of the supplement, the supplement would be nothing: everything is presumably already included within the whole. If the supplement is something rather than nothing, it must expose the *defect* of the whole, for any whole that is able to accommodate the addition of a supplement testifies thereby to the lack of something *within* itself. The supplement outside stands for the missing part inside the whole. It is because the whole does not succeed in *being everything* that a supplement from without must be added, in order to compensate its defective totality.[338]

Landlords and political economists regarded the custom of tenant right with curious distrust. To them it was merely a derivative and debilitating property relationship. The land question of the nineteenth century was an index of the degree to which the agrarian capitalism they espoused was disturbed and corrupted by the anomalies of the plantation. But far from proving private property to be the foundation or origin of this discourse, and tenant right as merely a parasitic growth, this dangerous supplement called tenant right threatened to usurp private property by exposing the illusory character of its foundational myth. Tenant right was a supplement entering into the heart of the discourse on Irish property, defining its very nature and condition. This discourse was subject to a wrenching from within, which prevented it from carrying through the logic of its own professed intention. The Protestant-identified, individualist, capitalist community in the north-east, whose socio-cultural profile *was* compatible with the presuppositions of political economy, whose own history in Ireland was one of alliance with agrarian capitalism, brought to the arena of nineteenth-century discourse and politics a customary practice which threatened the *laissez-faire* hegemony and scuttled Deasy's act. The danger of this supplement was finally realized in the land acts of 1870 and 1881.

The time between the passage of the 1870 act and the introduction of effective legal mechanisms for land purchase was a volatile and provocative period, both conceptually and historically. An agitation was set in train whereby custom, from time immemorial *lex loci*, threatened to establish itself *lex universalis*. But the 'wrenching from within' never amounted to a complete undoing of the private property system, only a reconfiguration or mutation of the landlord system into a system of peasant proprietorship and, eventually, into a new and divided nation of proprietors. Tenant right, by the end of the century, had become a worn out ideological sign, withdrawn from the pressures of the social struggle. The custom of tenant right had exposed important questions about the nature of capital and private property that have been since rendered opaque, questions surrounding the legitimacy of property, the determination of the value of labour and rent, and the social context of private contracts. The demise of customary tenures is the result of the hegemony of private property, which buries these questions or co-opts the potential questioners. If history has closed the question of tenant right, the intention of this book has been to reopen it by attending to the extra-economic supports of the economy, the social allegiances which maintain those supports, and the social customs like tenant right which mediate between the two. This strategy makes no pretence at originality. It is only a gesture in solidarity with the spirit of the work of Edward Thompson, who envisioned the following context for the study of pre-capitalist customs in one of his last published statememts:

> As capitalism, or 'the market' made over human nature and human need, so political economy and its revolutionary antagonist came to suppose that this economic man was for all time. We stand at the end of a century when this must now be called in doubt. We shall not ever return to pre-capitalist human nature, yet a reminder of its alternate needs, expectations, and codes may renew our sense of our nature's range of possibilities. Could it even prepare us for a time when both capitalist and state-communist needs and expectations may decompose, and human nature may be made over into a new form? This is, perhaps, to whistle into a typhoon. It is to reinvoke the discovery, in new forms, of a new kind of 'customary consciousness,' in which once again successive generations stand in apprentice relation to each other, in which material satisfactions remain stable, if more equally distributed and only cultural satisfactions enlarge, and in which expectations level out into a customary steady state. I do not think that this is likely to happen. But I hope that the studies in this book may illuminate how custom is formed and how complex is its operation.[339]

NOTES

1 Terry Eagleton, *Heathcliff and the great hunger* (London, 1995), pp. 124–44.

2 Donnelly, *Cork*, pp. 112, 236.

3 Francis Thompson, 'Land and politics in Ulster, 1868–86' (Ph.D. dissertation, Queen's University of Belfast, 1982), pp. 103–105.

4 Both letters are quoted in R.D.C. Black, *Economic thought and the Irish question, 1817–1870* (Cambridge, 1960), pp. 18–19.

5 Henry Gould, *Thoughts on a judicious disposition of land in Ireland, calculated to promote the best interest of landlord and tenant . . .* (Dublin, 1847).

6 Burroughs, *Essays on practical husbandry* and *A view of the state of agriculture in Ireland*; similar arguments are made in Horatio Townshend, *A view of the agricultural state of Ireland in 1815* (Cork, 1816), and William McCombie, *The Irish land question practically considered* (Aberdeen, 1869). The 'lazy indolence of the Irish tenant' was emphasized in Francis Wyse, *The Irish Tenant league: the immoral tendency and entire impracticability of the measures considered, in a letter addressed to John O'Connell, M.P.* (Dublin, 1850). For Dean, the problem was the excessive power of priests and the consequent need for

liberal education. G.A. Dean, *A treatise on the land tenure of Ireland, and the influences which retard its progress* (London, 1869).

7 Richard Griffith, *Practical domestic politics, being a comparative and prospective sketch of the agriculture and population of Great Britain and Ireland* . . . (London, 1819).

8 Cited in T.A. Boylan and T.P. Foley, *Political economy and colonial Ireland: the propagation and ideological function of economic discourse in the nineteenth century* (London, 1992), p. 147.

9 Oliver MacDonagh, 'The economy and society, 1830–1845' in Vaughan (ed.), *New history of Ireland*, v, p. 226.

10 Nicholas Bayly to a tenant, n.d. [c. 1734], P.R.O.N.I., Anglesey papers, D619/6/2.

11 Dufferin *Irish emigration*, pp. 183–5.

12 Robert Perceval-Maxwell to Rev. Isaac Mack, 29 April 1863, P.R.O.N.I., Perceval-Maxwell papers, D1556/2/2, p. 250.

13 Black, *Economic thought*, p. 49. See also *Examination of the landlords' and tenants' case, illustrated by the revaluation of the earl Romney's farms* . . . (London, 1851).

14 William Neilson Hancock, *On the economic causes of the present state of agriculture in Ireland*, 4 pts. (Dublin, 1849), i. Hancock's *laissez-faire* dogma was qualified by a patriarchal and paternal moral code to be enforced by the church on capitalists and family members. The church was to serve as a countervailing force against bourgeois economics. Boylan and Foley, *Political economy and Ireland*, pp. 144–5. Robert Longfield, *Report on the legislative measures requisite to facilitate the adoption of commercial contracts respecting the occupation of land in Ireland* (Dublin, 1851).

15 Jonathan Pim, *Conditions and prospects of Ireland and the evils arising from the present distribution of landed property* (Dublin, 1848).

16 Oliver MacDonagh, *States of mind: a study of the Anglo-Irish conflict 1780–1980* (London, 1983), pp. 35–36.

17 Black, *Economic thought*, p. 39.

18 Polanyi described the Ricardan position as follows: 'Hobbes' grotesque vision of the State – a human Leviathan whose vast body was made up of an infinite number of human bodies – was dwarfed by the Ricardan construct of the labour market: a flow of human lives the supply of which was regulated by the amount of food put at their disposal.' Karl Polanyi, *The great transformation: the political and economic origins of our time* (Boston, 1944), p. 164.

19 Karl Marx and Frederick Engels, *Ireland and the Irish question*, edited by R. Dixon (New York, 1972), pp. 54–58.

20 Ibid., p. 45.

21 Marx, 'Indian question – Irish tenant right,' in Marx and Engels, *Ireland and the Irish question*, p. 61.

22 Quoted in Boylan and Foley, *Political economy and Ireland*, p. 3.

23 W. N. Hancock's *Impediments to prosperity in Ireland* (London, 1850) argued that *laissez-faire* was an active policy in Ireland, not passive as in England. 'In Ireland,' according to Black's gloss, 'progress was hampered by outmoded legislation and advocated the removal of unnecessary restrictions.' Black *The statistical and social inquiry society of Ireland, centenary volume 1847–1947* (Dublin, 1947), pp. 59–60.

24 *Hansard's parliamentary debates*, 3rd ser., civ, pp. 224–5.

25 Black, *Economic thought*, p. 37, citing a letter from Charles Wood to the fourth earl of Clarendon, 26 October 1847.

26 William Neilson Hancock argued the Irish political economy was 'about as reasonable as proposing to have Irish mechanics, Irish mathematics, or Irish astronomy.' Hancock,

'On the economic views of Bishop Berkeley and Mr Butt. . . .' in *Transactions of the Dublin statistical society*, i (1847–9) cited in Boylan and Foley, *Political economy and colonial Ireland*, p. 9.

27 Seamus Deane, 'The production of cultural space in Irish writing' in *boundary 2: an international journal of literature and culture*, xxi, no. 3 (fall, 1994), p. 125.

28 Ibid., p. 130. For Davis, these symbols were legitimized by the existence of 'the communal land system of ancient Europe, and particularly 'Celtic' Ireland.' This discourse was highly ambivalent, attractive to romantic conservatives like Burke and to proto-socialists like Davis.

29 Black, *Economic thought*, pp. 22–3.

30 See E.D. Steele, 'J.S. Mill and the Irish question: the principles of political economy 1848–1865' in *The historical journal* xii, no. 2 (1970), pp. 216–236; idem, 'J.S. Mill and the Irish question: reform, and the integrity of the empire, 1865–1870' in ibid., xii, no. 3 (1970), pp. 425–427.

31 Henry Hoyte, for example, claimed that half of a six–acre farm could support two cows, the other half could feed a family with the proper tillage rotation. Hoyte, *Treatise on agriculture*. See also Mathew Carey, *Vindication of small farmers, the peasantry and labourers of Ireland* . . . (Philadelphia, 1836), [William Hickey], *The farmer's guide, compiled for the use of the small farmer and cotter tenantry of Ireland* (Dublin, HMSO, 1841), and Henry Crosley, *Hints to the landed proprietry and agriculturists of Great Britain and Ireland* (London, 1841). One series of treatises published under the name 'Eight Seven' argued for the creation of a smallholding class of five-acre farmers who would cultivate flax to supply the textile industry, and food for subsistence. Eight Seven, *A simple and effectual mode of providing for the labouring classes; and, at the same time promoting the landed interest* (Dublin, 1825); *Prosperity of the labourer the foundation of universal prosperity* (Dublin, 1827); *Practicability of a legislative measure for harmonizing the conflicting interests of agriculture* . . . (Dublin, 1830); *An antidote to revolution or a practical comment on the creation of privilege* . . . (Dublin, 1830).

32 William Sharman Crawford, *A defence of the small farmers of Ireland* (Dublin, 1839). Crawford employed the 1841 census to provide evidence that small farms and impoverishment were unrelated in Ulster. This case was put to the Devon commission. J.P. Kennedy (ed.), *Devon comm. digest*, i, p. 402 quoted in Kennedy, 'Struggle for tenant right,' p. 13. For a later defence of 'la petite culture,' see Thomas E.C. Leslie, *Land systems and industrial economy of Ireland, England, and continental countries* (London, 1870).

33 William Sharman Crawford, *Depopulation not necessary. An appeal to the British members of the Imperial parliament* (Dublin, 1850).

34 Frank Wright, *Two lands on one soil*, p. 138.

35 Kennedy, 'Struggle for tenant right,' p. 10. A poster with the legend 'Robbery! Robbery! Robbery!' circulating in 1848 asked whether the 'Men of Ulster' would submit to be 'actually and unmistakably robbed, of millions of capital which you have had always available in the recognised Ulster tenant right?' Ibid., p. 160. McKnight's discussion of tenant right also refers to the 'reduction in value of nature property' in *Banner of Ulster*, 12 October and 13 November 1849.

36 For the importance of the changing structure of the electorate see T.K. Hoppen, *Elections, politics, and society in Ireland, 1832–1885* (Oxford, 1984), chapter 1. The expanding electorate of 1851 and 1867, according to Comerford amounted to 'a major new reality in Irish life, the rising social importance of the middling and large tenant farmers as a class.' R.V. Comerford, 'Churchmen, tenants, and independent opposition' in Vaughan (ed.), *New history of Ireland*, v, pp. 382, 399, 400.

37 Donnell, *Reports*, p. 19. As Rev. Blakely asked in 1851, 'has it become necessary that an act should be passed containing some forty of fifty sections, for the guidance and government of two parties whose interest it is to cultivate the most friendly discourse?' F. Blakely, *Letters on the relation between landlord and tenant*, (Belfast, 1851). Welch lamented the loss of natural and familial relations between landlord and tenant. James Welch, *Tenant-right: its nature and requirements; together with a plan for a legislative act for the readjustment of the relationship between landlord and tenant, for the promotion of agriculture* (London, 1848), as did Ferguson and Vance, *Tenure and improvement*, p. 2.

38 Vaughan, *Landlords & tenants*, p. 73.

39 *Bessborough commission evidence*, questions 1231–1232.

40 Attentive agents had of course long been aware of these ambiguities, that tenant right had both a strict financial meaning and a broad connotation with respect to property rights. James Hamilton use both the phrase 'given up the quiet possession' and the more financial 'sells his interest' or 'disposes of his farm' when referring to tenants who left their farms to others. James Hamilton to ninth earl of Abercorn, 12 Dec. 1766, and 27 Jan. 1771, 17 Apr. 1785, 25 Jan. 1792, P.R.O.N.I., Abercorn papers, T2541/IA2/5/5, T2541/IA1/15/11, T2541/IA1/7/50, and T2541/IA1/9/99; Hamilton to Abercorn, 8 Feb. 1765 and 17 Sept. 1769; James Sinclair to Abercorn, 2 Feb. 1767, ibid., T2541/IA1/6C/110, T2541/IA1/8/155, and T2541/IA1/7/56.

41 *Devon comm. evidence*, pt. i, xix, p. 483. Similarly, the agent of the Grocers' estate in 1870 defined tenant right as 'a payment by the incoming tenant nominally for improvements effected by the outgoing tenant, but really for the quiet and peaceable possession of the premises.' Olive Robinson, 'The London companies and tenant right in nineteenth-century Ireland' in *Agricultural history review*, xviii (1970), p. 59.

42 *Devon comm. evidence*, pt. i, xix, p. 633.

43 Joseph Kell to George Lane Fox, 9 April 1844, N.L.I., Lane Fox papers, film 4063.

44 Comerford, 'Churchmen, tenants, and independent opposition,' p. 399.

45 Letter placed before the committee from Mr. Knox, agent, 28 Nov. 1843, Merchant Tailors' Hall, Irish estate committee of management minutes, N.L.I., film 1517. This agent gave the following reason for the increasing boldness of the tenants: 'Although they are almost all against O'Connell and his political movement, they take advantage of the present agitation to press their claims saying, as one of the tenants told me the other day, they had held the country in former times for the Protestant landlords and they had a claim upon them for liberal treatment.' The Millers also commented that 'since the land commission went its rounds' no tenants would accept shorter than a twenty-one-year lease. Millers to Lawford, 14 June 1845, P.R.O.N.I., Drapers' company papers, D3632/1/1.

46 Millers to Lawford, 25 May 1848, ibid.

47 *Devon comm. report*, p. 15 quoted by Brady, 'Legal developments,' p. 456 and Kennedy, 'Struggle for tenant right,' p. 84.

48 Hancock, *Tenant right considered economically*, pp. 33–34, 43. Dobbs attacked Hancock's theory, marshalling Devon evidence showing that tenant right was much more than compensation for improvements and carried much further to include the sale of 'goodwill.' Conway E. Dobbs, *Some observations on the tenant right of Ulster* (Dublin, 1849), pp. 6–7.

49 Robert Dudley Baxter, *The Irish tenant-right question examined by a comparison of the law and practice of Ireland; with suggestions on the basis of legislation, and the consequences which would follow the adoption of fixity of tenure or the Ulster tenant right* (London, 1869).

50 See Kennedy, 'Struggle for tenant right,' *passim*.

51 John E. Pomfret, *Struggle for land in Ireland, 1800–1923* (Princeton, New Jersey, 1930), p. 60; Kennedy, 'Struggle for tenant right,' p. 71; Philip Bull, *Land, politics & nationalism: a study of the Irish land question* (Dublin, 1996), pp. 28–34. In 1825 James Pike had already published a tract criticizing absenteeism, high rents, and uncertainty of tenure and arguing that tenants should possess a 'secure and permanent tenure' through purchase at government-valued prices by a joint stock company which in turn sells to tenants. [James M. Pike], *Statement of some causes of the disturbances in Ireland, and of the miserable state of the peasantry . . .* (Dublin, 1825).

52 *The Nation*, 25 September 1847; *Londonderry Standard*, 24 Sept. and 1 Oct. 1847, cited in Kennedy, 'Struggle for tenant right,' p. 136.

53 Black, *Economic thought*, pp. 24–5. Connor's argument was that only a government valuation and a perpetuity could prevent rack-renting, because of the peculiar nature of land, the only non-increasing resource. William Connor, *The prosecuted speech; delivered at Montmellick in proposing a petition to parliament in favour of a valuation and perpetuity on his farm to the tenant* (Dublin, 1842), and *A letter to the tenantry of Ireland, containing an exposition of the rack rent system; and pointing out a valuation and perpetuity as its only effectual remedy* (Dublin, 1850). Connor's views were too radical for both O'Connell's Repeal Association and the Tenant League. In the Nation of 8 and 15 April 1843, O'Connell rejected Connor's plan for transferring 'the monopoly of land from the landlord to the tenant' as too radical.

54 R.V. Comerford, 'Churchmen, tenants, and independent opposition,' p. 399. Bull, *Land, politics, and nationalism*, pp. 28–9.

55 William Sharman Crawford, *Observations showing the necessity of an amendment in the laws of landlord and tenant . . .* (Belfast, 1837). See also Vincent Scully, *The Irish land question with practical plans for an improved land tenure and a new land system* (Dublin, 1851); H.D. Hutton, 'The Land Question issued as a sociological problem . . .' *JSSIS*, iii (1861–3) p. 225, Boylan and Foley, *Political economy and Ireland*, pp. 147–8.

56 W. S. Crawford, memoranda, n.d. [c.1857–8], P.R.O.N.I., Sharman Crawford papers, D856/D/126, 131, 133.

57 Kennedy, 'Struggle for tenant right,' pp. 27–8.

58 *Northern Whig*, 19 November 1835, cited in Kennedy, 'Struggle for tenant right,' p. 49.

59 Ibid., pp. 48–51.

60 Survey of the Manor of Clothworkers, 1840, Merchant Tailors' Hall, N.L.I., film 1517.

61 Ibid.

62 Mortimer Thomson to marquis of Dufferin, 18 Feb. 1854, P.R.O.N.I., Dufferin papers, D1071A/K Box 1.

63 Dufferin to Thomson, 20 Feb. 1854, ibid.

64 *Devon comm. digest*, i, p. 291.

65 James Hamilton to eighth earl of Abercorn, 7 July 1769, P.R.O.N.I., Abercorn papers, T2541/IA1/8/131.

66 Richard Gwynn to [?] Blundell, 22 June 1747, P.R.O.N.I., Downshire papers, D607/A/37; petition of Bernard Rice, 1843, P.R.O.N.I., Anglesey papers, D619/11/112; petition of William Allen to provost and senior fellows, Aug. 1810, T.C.D., MUN/P/24/397.

67 *Devon comm. evidence*, pt. i, xxii, pp. 403–20; J.C. Brady, 'Legal developments,' p. 455. One common attack on the irrationality of the system of tenant right was that it also reduced tenant investment in farms. Sellers of tenant right were alleged to have stripped everything they could from the farm and sold at the highest possible price;

buyers offered far more than they could manage to pay without borrowing heavily. James Walker, *Remarks addressed to landlord and tenant farmers of Ireland* (Belfast, 1860). Lord Londonderry called this theory 'absurd' in a letter to William Sharman Crawford in 1847: 'Surely the proprietor or agent can examine and ascertain all the qualities and characteristics of the new tenant (as we do all of our servants). We may occasionally be deceived but the chances are much the other way.' Lord Londonderry to William Sharman Crawford, 14 Feb. 1847, P.R.O.N.I., Sharman Crawford papers, D856/D/88.

68 Joel Mokyr, *Why Ireland starved*, pp. 81–7, 99–103; Ó Gráda, *Ireland before and after the famine: explorations in economic history, 1800–1925* (Manchester, 1988), pp. 32–35, 128; idem, 'Poverty, population, and agriculture,' p. 129.

69 Black, *Economic thought*, p. 53.

70 Kennedy, 'Struggle for tenant right,' pp. 75, 93–120, 168. 'None of the measures introduced between 1852 and 1867 went as far as Sharman Crawford's tenant-right bill of 1852. . . . Of the ministerial bills – and these were the only bills ever likely to be passed – only one, that of the Tory Irish attorney-general Joseph Napier in 1852, recognized the principle of retrospective improvements.' F. Thompson, 'Land and politics in Ulster,' p. 163.

71 See James S. Donnelly, Jr., 'A famine in politics' in Vaughan (ed.), *New history of Ireland*, v, p. 364; J.H. Whyte, *The tenant league and Irish politics in the eighteen-fifties* (Dundalk, 1972); Comerford, 'Churchmen, tenants, and independent opposition;' and Bull, *Land, politics, and nationalism*, pp. 43–4.

72 Alan Dowling, 'The genesis of Deasy's act' in *Northern Ireland legal quarterly*, xl, no. 1 (spring, 1989), pp. 53–61.

73 Ferguson and Vance, *Tenure and improvement*, p. 1.

74 Napier, who had clearly digested this, spoke in parliament of the warnings made by Sir John Davies and Edmund Spenser in the seventeenth century of the paramount importance of the application of English land tenure in Ireland, when introducing his bill to consolidate the law of landlord and tenant in 1852. Napier associated feudalism with the at-will tenancy. *House of Commons debates*, 3rd series, 22 Nov. 1852, columns 309–10. See Dowling, 'Genesis of Deasy's act,,' p. 53.

75 Ferguson and Vance, *Tenure and improvement*, pp. 436–8.

76 Ibid., p. 301, quoted with approval in Vaughan, *Landlords & tenants*, p. 67.

77 These recommendations were taken up and embodied in Napier's collection of four bills of the 1850s, the precursors to Caldwell's act and Deasy's act of 1860. Dowling, 'Genesis of Deasy's act.' In a pamphlet of 1853 Napier opposed compensation for 'spurious' improvements and claims by evicted tenants, arguing that the goal of legislation should be to assist in identifying *bona fide* improvements and arrive at an exact compensation for unexhausted proper improvements by solvent tenants. Joseph Napier, *The landlord and tenant bills* (Dublin 1853), pp. 54–57.

78 *Maguire commission evidence*, passim; *Bessborough commission evidence*, question 1216.

79 Marquis of Dufferin to Mortimer Thomson, 13 Jan. 1866, P.R.O.N.I., Dufferin papers, D1071A/K/Box 2.

80 David Anderson and James Dickson to Dufferin, 21 Dec. 1865, ibid., D1071A/ K/Box 1.

81 David Harvey, *The limits to capital* (Oxford, 1982), p. 357.

82 Ibid., p. 362–4.

83 Ibid.

84 Brady, 'Legal developments, p. 455; Shee's translation is cited by Donnell, *Reports*, p. 103.

85 Ó Gráda, 'Poverty, population, and agriculture,' p. 129.

86 See Vaughan *Landlords & tenants*, pp. 120 ff.

87 Henry Smith to Rowley Miller, 19 March 1822, P.R.O.N.I., Drapers' company papers, D3632/3/2

88 Henry Smith to 'Messrs. Gressum and sons,' 5 Mar. 1821, P.R.O.N.I., Drapers' company papers, D3632/3/1.

89 Edward Lawford to Rowley and J.R. Miller, 1 Dec. 1834, 30 Dec. 1835, 10 Aug. 1838, P.R.O.N.I., Drapers' company papers, D3632/3/4; Millers to Lawford, 4 May 1844, 9 Mar. 1846, ibid., D3632/1/1; report of a deputation, minutes of the court of assistants, extracts relating to Irish estates, 6 Feb. 1840, Drapers' Hall, London, N.L.I., film 1529; Millers to W.H. Sawyer, 25 Mar. 1861, P.R.O.N.I., Drapers' company papers, D3632/1/3. Millers to Lawford, 14 June 1845, 26 May 1846, ibid., D3632/1/1. The Drapers' company adopted a general policy whereby the principal of loans to tenants did not have to be repaid, although there were a number of exceptions. During the period 1856–1862 twelve loans were made to tenants, five for £100, two for £150, one for £500, and the rest for under £50. Miller to Sawyer, 3 Jan. 1865, ibid., D3632/1/3.

90 Irish estate committee of management minutes, 1 Apr. 1852, N.L.I., Merchant Tailors' Hall records, film 1517; [?] to Edmund Stronge, 15 May 1863, P.R.O.N.I., Clothworkers' company papers, D1514/2/5/15; Irish Society court minute books, 15 Aug. 1845, N.L.I., film 1525.

91 [?] Lanahan to John W. Maxwell, 15 Aug. 1845, P.R.O.N.I., Perceval-Maxwell papers, D3244/E/26/22.

92 Report on Lady Londonderry's Antrim estate by John Lanktree, 1845, P.R.O.N.I., Earl of Antrim papers, D2977/6/4.

93 The Abercorns financed the construction of a canal, along with other projects. Dowling, 'Abercorn estate,' pp. 116–64. The Millers wrote in 1845 that it was the general trend of landlords to underwrite drainage. Millers to Lawford, 8 Apr. 1845, P.R.O.N.I., Drapers' company papers, D3632/1/1. The Drapers' company put an end to their assistance to drainage projects in 1856, arguing that tenants who had recently paid large sums for tenant right could afford to drain themselves. Millers to Sawyer, 7 Feb. 1859, ibid., D3632/1/3. The Earl of Belmore gave allowances for building drains which made the land safe for cattle. R.C. Brush to earl of Belmore, 4 Apr. 1866, P.R.O.N.I., Belmore papers, D3007/V/18.

94 Edward Lawford to Rowley Miller, 7 Mar. 1829, P.R.O.N.I., Drapers' company papers, D3632/3/3.

95 Fishmongers' Hall court minutes, 14 Nov. 1850, N.L.I., film 1515.

96 'Report of the deputation appointed by the court on the 8th of July 1852 to visit the company's estate in Ireland,' Court minutes relating to Irish estates, 30 Sept. 1852, Fishmongers' Hall records, Guildhall Library, London, N.L.I., film 1514.

97 J.B. Bankhead to Edmund McDonnell, 5 Aug. 1851, P.R.O.N.I., Earl of Antrim papers, D2977/4/3.

98 James Savage to Henry Hatch, 5 Dec. 1757, P.R.O.N.I., Downshire papers, D607/A/171.

99 Robert Hutchinson to Thomas Hanson, 4 June 1783, P.R.O.N.I., Anglesey papers, D619/21/D/3.

100 Petition of Owen Reilly of Corbett, 25 July 1785, ibid., D619/11/45.

101 Letter of S.W. Greer in support of memorial from tenants, 29 July 1841, Merchant Tailors' hall, Irish estate committee of management minutes, N.L.I., film 1517.

102 Dickson, 'Cork region,' pp. 272–77.

103 [?] Armstrong to earl of Uxbridge, 22 Mar. 1811, P.R.O.N.I., Anglesey papers, D619/23/A/60.

104 Thomas Beer to Rutherford, 5 Jan. 1847, ibid., D619/23/B/206.

105 Idem, 25 Feb. 1845, ibid., D619/23/B/142.

106 William Ogilvie to Rev. John Wilson, 1, 21, and 26 July 1807, P.R.O.N.I., Ogilvie papers, T1546/1.

107 Report by John Lanktree, 1848, P.R.O.N.I., Earl of Antrim papers, D2977/6/4.

108 Edmund McGildowney to Lord Mark Kerr, 10 Mar. 1821, P.R.O.N.I., McGildowney papers, D1375/1/16.

109 Nathanial Nesbitt to eighth earl of Abercorn, 24 Feb. 1749, P.R.O.N.I., T2541/IA1/1D/44.

110 Mokyr, *Why Ireland starved*, p. 102.

111 Henry Hatch to Henry Blundell, 1 Aug. 1754, P.R.O.N.I., Downshire papers, D607/A/23.

112 Anonymous letter on the possible improvement of the Antrim estate, n.d. [c. 1812], N.L.I., MS 8125(4).

113 Case of Berry Barry submitted to provost and senior fellows, n.d. [but after 1775], T.C.D., MUN/P/24/383.

114 Arthur Mcguire to lord [?] Stanley, 25 Oct. 1773, P.R.O.N.I., Derby papers, film 368/1.

115 Dickson, 'Cork region,' p. 184.

116 See above, note 80.

117 John Martin to George Mahon, 22 April 1856, N.L.I., George C. Mahon papers, MS 22,191.

118 Brady, 'Legal developments,' p. 459. As Brady describes it, the previous custom held that leases, which were originally held to be personal contracts, distinct from claims to land such as copyhold or freehold, 'came to be regarded as estates in land, and by a process of analogy the concept of tenure, by which all land was held in return for services, was applied to them, the tenant holding in return for a service, which was the payment of rent.' Ibid., p. 458.

119 Ibid., p. 463. Brady comments that the 'concepts of mutual agreement and free choice were scarcely the common currency of rural life in mid-nineteenth century Ireland.'

120 See Alan Dowling, 'The landlord and tenant law amendment act (Ireland) 1860' (Ph.D. dissertation, Queen's University of Belfast, 1985).

121 Dufferin, *Irish emigration*, pp. 115–128.

122 Idem, *Mr. Mill's plan for the pacification of Ireland examined* (London, 1868). Given his views on the necessity of emigration and the supremacy of markets, one may question the sincerity of Dufferin's sympathy with the plight of labourers. On his own property he made sure that labourers residing on the skirts of farms were absolutely barred from the exercise of tenant right. Dufferin remarked in 1884: 'I am quite willing to have the cottage you mention pulled down and one put in repair for a labourer, provided he is changed from time to time [so] that he may not acquire any tenant right.' Marquis of Dufferin to John H. Howe, 18 Mar. 1884, P.R.O.N.I., Dufferin papers, D.1071A/K Box 2. Vaughan also uses the plight of landless workers to complain about tenant aspirations. Vaughan, *Landlords & tenants*, p. 10.

123 Idem, *Irish emigration*, p. 121. Montifort Longfield argued in similar terms against any arrangement to establish fixity of tenure through government-valued purchase.

The market would still operate to the same end, and any such system would merely give a windfall to those presently in possession at the expense of the present owners and future occupiers. Longfield, *Tenure of land in Ireland*.

124 Marx, 'The Indian question – and Irish tenant right,' pp. 59–65.

125 Idem, 'Forced Emigration . . .' in ibid., pp. 54–58.

126 Ibid., p. 57.

127 This refers to his controversial statement of the 'double mission' the bourgeoisie was to perform in India, for which Marx has been accused of celebrating triumphant capitalism and denigrating colonial resistance. Ahmad argues that Marx consciously disassociated himself both from the Orientalist position ('I share not the opinion of those who believe in a golden age of Hindustan') and the colonial-modernist position ('the misery inflicted by the British on Hindustan is of an essentially different and infinitely more intensive kind than all Hindustan had to suffer before') in his first article on India in 1853. Ahmad argues that Marx's position is essentially tragic, rather than romantic or ironic. In passages such as these Marx deploys 'an enraged language of tragedy – a sense of colossal disruption and irretrievable loss, a moral dilemma wherein neither the old nor the new can be wholly affirmed, the recognition that the sufferer was at once decent and flawed, the recognition also that the history of victories and losses is really a history of material productions, and the glimmer of a hope, in the end, that something good might come of this merciless history.' Aijiz Ahmad, *In theory: nations, classes, literature* (London, 1992) pp. 227–8, 235.

128 Marx and Engels, *Selected correspondence*, p. 79.

129 Erica Benner, *Really existing nationalisms: a post-communist view of Marx and Engels* (Oxford, 1995), p. 179. His later correspondence with Russian agrarian radicals further reveals that Marx was not an historical determinist on the subject of the development of agrarian societies in the face of capitalism. It was in this context that Marx famously denied being a Marxist. Concerning the specificity of the Russian scene, and by implication, the Irish and Indian as well, he wrote: 'By studying each of these developments separately, and then comparing them, one may easily discover the key to this phenomenon. But success will never come with the master-key of a general historico-philosophical theory, whose supreme virtue consists in being supra-historical.' Marx, 'A letter to the editorial board of Otechestvennye Zapiski,' in Teodor Shanin, *Late Marx and the Russian road*, p. 136

130 Engels wrote to Marx in 1867: ' . . . as to the Fenians, you are quite right. The beastliness of the English must not make us forget that the leaders of this sect are mostly asses and partly exploiters and we cannot in any way make ourselves responsible for the stupidities which occur in every conspiracy.' Engels to Marx, 29 November 1867, in Marx and Engels, *Ireland and the Irish question*, pp. 145–6.

131 'Has, perhaps, the *Times* been converted into a social revolutionist? Does it want a *social* revolution, reorganizing the "conditions of society," and the "arrangements" emanating from them, instead of "parliamentary enactments"?' Marx, 'The Indian question – Irish tenant right' p. 61.

132 Marx viewed Ireland in terms of a model of capital accumulation in the British economy, emphasizing its role as supplier of food and raw materials and consumer of finished goods, not in terms of a model of colonial exploitation. Hazelkorn argues that Marx's view of Ireland was clouded by his miscalculation of the historical and revolutionary importance of the English working class, from which followed a preoccupation with the effect of the Irish working class in England on class relations

there. According to Hazelkorn, Marx 'never envisaged the [anti-landlord national struggle] leading the way to socialism but only to the development of capitalist agriculture. A socialist revolution in Ireland was another day's work.' Ellen Hazelkorn, 'Reconsidering Marx and Engels on Ireland,' in *Soathair*, ix (1983), p. 86.

133 Wright, *Two lands on one soil*, p. 175.

134 Quoted by Eric Hobsbawm, *The age of capital, 1848–1875* (London, 1975), p. 182.

135 T.E. Cliff Leslie, quoted in Boylan and Foley, *Political economy and Ireland*, p. 9.

136 Dufferin, *Mr. Mill's plan*.

137 James McKnight, *The Ulster tenant's claim of right; or landownership a state of trust; the Ulster Tenant-Right an original grant from the British crown, and the necessity of extending its general principle to other provinces of Ireland* (Dublin, 1848), pp. 15–16. McKnight's paper is Greer's source on the origins of tenant right. Samuel M'Curdy Greer, *The law of landlord and tenant. Amount of compensation for tenant's improvements. To the tenant farmers of Great Britain and Ireland* (Coleraine, 1850). James Fintan Lalor, inspired by William Connor's pamphlets, made similar arguments. Bull, *Land, politics, and nationalism*, pp. 29–30.

138 McKnight, *The Ulster tenant's claim of right*, p. 25.

139 Isaac Butt, *Land tenure in Ireland: a plea for the Celtic race*, p. 49; Butt, *Irish people and Irish land* (Dublin, 1867), pp. 232; H.F. Hore, 'Archaeology of Irish tenant right' in *Ulster journal of archaeology*, vi (1858); Donnell, *Reports*, p. 51; W.D. Henderson, *Ulster Tenant Right, an historical and economic sketch* (Belfast, 1875), pp. 11–12; Peter Maclagan, *Land culture and land tenure in Ireland. The result of observations during a recent tour . . .* (Dublin, 1869); W.F. Bailey, 'The Ulster tenant-right custom: its origins, characteristics, and position under the land acts' in *JSSIS*, x, (Sept., 1895), p. 12; R.B. O'Brien, *Parliamentary history of the Irish land question from to 1869; and the origin and results of the Ulster custom* (London, 1880), pp. 151–167.

140 Thompson, 'Custom, law, and common right,' pp. 160–1.

141 Butt, *Irish people and Irish land*, pp. 33–51, 221–3.

142 Gourley, 'Gosford estates,' p. 146. See Henry Hutton (ed.), *Lord Dufferin's speeches and addresses* (London, 1882).

143 Dufferin to Charles William Hamilton, 14 Feb. [1866], Hamwood papers, Hamwood House, Co. Meath, A/26/3. The origin of tenant right on an estate in Monaghan was said to have issued from the first leases given to the actual occupiers of land in the 1760s. 'The Ulster custom,' generally traceable from the plantation of Ulster, has, according to this account, 'never optained in the barony of Farney. In that barony, at least, the phrase 'tenant right' can scarcely be traced beyond the present century, and must be limited to the purchase of the interest of the tenant during the existence of the lease or tenancy at will under which he holds . . . ' [W.S. Trench], *On 'Tenant-Right,' or 'goodwill' within the barony of Farney, Co. of Monaghan, Ireland* (London, 1874), p. 18.

144 Dufferin to Charles William Hamilton, 14 Feb. [1866], Hamwood papers, Hamwood House, Co. Meath, A/26/3. See also Dufferin, *Irish emigration*, pp. 182–3.

145 Frederic Seebohm, [*The Land Question. In three parts*] (Dublin, 1869), pp. 234–40.

146 Richey, *Irish land laws*, p. 61.

147 Black, *Economic thought*, p. 54, 64.

148 Armstrong, *Economic history of agriculture*, p. 36.

149 Black, *Economic thought*, p. 51. Clive Dewey, 'Celtic agrarian legislation and the Celtic revival: historicist implications of Gladstone's Irish and Scottish land acts, 1870–1886,' *Past & present*, no. 64 (August, 1974), pp. 30–70.

150 The felt need to respond to the threat of the spread of Fenianism with land reform is clear in the speeches and writings of Isaac Butt and J.S. Mill. R.V. Comerford, 'Gladstone's first Irish enterprise' in Vaughan (ed.), *New history of Ireland*, v, p. 450; E.D. Steele, 'J.S. Mill and the Irish question: reform, and the integrity of the empire, 1865–1870' in *The historical journal*, xii, no. 3 (1970), pp. 425–427.

151 Dewey, 'Celtic agrarian legislation,' p. 59.

152 Ibid., pp. 30–70.

153 Vaughan, 'Ireland, c. 1870,' p. 749.

154 For the details of the passage of the act, see ibid., pp. 746–758; Vaughan, *Landlords & tenants*, pp. 93–102; Armstrong, *Economic history of agriculture*, pp. 32–54.

155 Brady, 'Legal developments,' p. 466.

156 Vaughan, 'Ireland, c. 1870,' p. 752.

157 *Coleraine Chronicle*, 31 Oct. 1874; F. Thompson, 'Land and politics,' p. 226.

158 Henderson, *Ulster Tenant Right*, pp. 18–20.

159 Wright, *Two lands on one soil*, p. 436; Donnell railed against those who agreed with Barry's decision. 'So far from the claim being novel or unwarrranted, [leasehold tenant right] was put plainly and expressly in every form which Sharman Crawford's Tenant-right Bill assumed from 1835 to 1858; and it came directly before parliament in an amendment [excluding the custom from leaseholds] on the Land Bill of 1870.' Donnell, *Reports*, pp. 60–61, 242.

160 F. Thompson, 'Land and politics,' p. 218.

161 Ibid., pp. 217–23.

162 Donnell, *Reports*, pp. 126–7.

163 Brady, 'Legal developments,' p. 466 quoting *Bessborough commission report*, p. 21.

164 Walter Stannus to W.H. Sawyer, 8 Nov. and 6 Dec. 1879, 3 and 10 Jan. 1880, P.R.O.N.I., Drapers' company papers, D3632/1/4.

165 Henry Pattison to marquis of Dufferin, 20 Jan 1876, P.R.O.N.I., Dufferin papers, D1071A/K, Box 2.

166 A Londonderry magistrate testified before the Devon commission that although 'the value of the tenant right is affected by tenure, it is as much affected by the character of the landlord.' *Devon commission evidence*, pt. i, xix, 665–9. Similarly, Henry Prentice, agent of the earl of Caledon's estate in Tyrone, declared that 'the amount of the sale of tenant right is dependent very much on the landlord under whom the farm may be held. If he is a good landlord and a man of character in the country, the price will be higher. If he is an inferior landlord, the price will be comparatively low.' Ibid., p. 837.

167 James Hamilton to eighth earl of Abercorn, 18 Oct. 1778, P.R.O.N.I., Abercorn papers, T2541/IA2/2/52.

168 F. Thompson, 'Land and politics,' pp. 103–105.

169 Both Crawford and Dufferin contemplated selling their estates or offering their tenants perpetuities. A correspondent to Dufferin recommended that he consider selling to tenants under the landed estates act rather than proceeding under part ii of the 1870 act. S.J. Lynch to Dufferin, 16 April 1872, P.R.O.N.I., Dufferin papers, D1071A/K Box 3. He later considered giving perpetuities or fining down the rents, but in the end decided that getting the consent of mortgagers 'would raise such difficulties that the plan could not be carried out.' Henry Pattison to Dufferin, 9 Dec. 1875 and 12 Jan. 1876, ibid., box 2.

170 Brady, 'Legal developments,' pp. 456–7. Newer landlords 'tended to be more commercial and to appear more grasping simply because they generally could not afford

to be as benevolent or altruistic as the bigger landowners.' F. Thompson, 'Land and politics,' p. 149.

171 *Maguire committee evidence*, questions 135–6, 620, 638, 652, 697. 'I have heard of more than one clear instance in which purchasers in the landed estates court have directly invaded the Tenant Right that existed for ages upon the lands.' Morris, *Letters on the land question of Ireland*, p. 258.

172 See Chapter 2, p. 67.

173 F. Thompson, 'Land and politics,' pp. 138–39.

174 Skinners' company Irish committee minutes, 7 July 1857, Skinners' Hall, London, N.L.I., film 1520.

175 The Skinners' company told their agent that the company 'are taking the opinion of council on the subject of tenant right' and that he should not recognize any sales until further notice. 'Letter from Mr. Clarke dated 23 August,' Skinners' hall extracts from court minute books relating to Irish estates, 17 Dec. 1872, N.L.I., film 1520. The following spring the minutes record that a number of tenants were allowed to sell, although 'no claim of tenant right' was to be allowed for houses in Dungiven. Ibid., 14 Jan. and 24 Apr. 1873.

176 Michael King to Skinners' company, [n.d.] c. 1870, P.R.O.N.I., D1550/10.

177 Court minutes of 13 February 1873, N.L.I., Skinners' Hall court minute books relating to Irish estates, film 1520.

178 Thompson, 'Custom, law, and common right,' p. 97, quoting Carter, *Lex customaria* (1696).

179 Matthew Dutton, *The law of landlord and tenants in Ireland* . . . (Dublin, 1726).

180 Thompson, 'Custom, law, and common right,' p. 97.

181 For example, in *McCausland vs. McCausland* the landlord proved that his rule that only two years' purchase be given for tenant right was a prevailing usage. F. Thompson, 'Land and politics,' p. 225.

182 J.G.M. Harvey to G.V. Hart, 21 Feb. 1878, P.R.O.N.I., Hart papers, D3077/G/15/39.

183 F. Thompson, 'Land and Politics,' pp. 224–6. The County Down court decision *Kenan vs. Lord de Ros* judged that 'whatever practice prevailed for any reasonable time previous to the passing of the act, and not imposed in contemplation of the act, was the tenant right legalized upon that estate, no matter what the tenant right might be in the district round about.' Armstrong, *Economic history of agriculture*, p. 44, n. 289.

184 James McKnight to Gladstone, 2 April 1870, Gladstone MS 44426, f. 68, quoted in F. Thompson, 'Land and politics,' p. 191, n. 24.

185 Vaughan, *Landlords & tenants*, p. 69.

186 O'Connor Morris, *Letters on the land question of Ireland*, pp. 256–8.

187 Rowley and J. R. Miller to Edward Lawford, 30 Nov, 1846, P.R.O.N.I., D3632/2/2.

188 Idem, 25 May, 1848, ibid.

189 John Hancock, *Observations on tenant right legislation; being an answer to a deputation of Lord Lurgan's tenantry* (Dublin, 1848).

190 Henry Smith to J.R. Miller, 26 Mar. 1822, P.R.O.N.I., Drapers' company papers, D3632/3/2. R.B. Touse to C.J. Knox, 22 Feb. 1859, P.R.O.N.I., Hervey Bruce papers, letterbook relating to Clothworkers' company estate, D1514/2/5/14.

191 'Mr. Glover's report on town parks,' 30 Dec. 1878, P.R.O.N.I., Drapers' company papers, D3632/1/4.

192 Henry Smith to Rowley Miller, 21 Dec. 1823, ibid., D3632/3/2.

193 John McClintock to Viscount Paisley, 8 Jan. 1736, P.R.O.N.I., Abercorn papers, T2541/IA1/1A/21.

194 James Hamilton to eighth earl of Abercorn, 25 Apr. 1773, ibid., T2541/IA1/10/85.

195 Unsorted box of leases, etc., P.R.O.N.I., McGildowney papers, D1375/9/1; Robert McNaughton to Edmund McGildowney, 13 Feb. 1819, ibid., D1375/2/7/6.

196 James Hamilton, Jr., to ninth earl of Abercorn, 26 July 1801, P.R.O.N.I., Abercorn papers, T2541/IA2/10/22.

197 David Buttle to John Savage, 2 Oct. 1770, P.R.O.N.I., Nugent papers, D552/A/4/2/8.

198 Rowley and J.R. Miller to Robert Bryan, 6 Aug. 1844, P.R.O.N.I., Drapers' company papers, D3632/1/1. 'Generally tenants get ten years purchase for their farms, but in order to prevent men from intruding themselves into the estate, we never permit a farm to be sold *by auction*. We must know who the new intended comer is before we allow the transfer of a farm. . . .' Millers to Edward Lawford, 30 Nov, 1846, ibid.

199 Marquis of Dufferin to John Howe, n.d. [1847], P.R.O.N.I., Dufferin papers, D1071A/K/Box 1.

200 Frederick Wrench to Edward McSuaran, 10 Feb. 1879, P.R.O.N.I., Brookeborough papers, D998/6/1, p. 441; Wrench to Luke P. Knight, 14 July 1879, ibid., p. 492. Mathew Saukey appointed two men in 1856 to arbitrate the price of a sale of a small farm and dwelling houses. Memorandum of Mathew Saukey, 20 Feb. 1856, ibid., D998/8/2. After the land act this had become an established rule. The agent told Miss Jane Alexander in 1878 that she could 'dispose of the interest in your lease by arbitration according to the rules of the estate and *in no other way*. On hearing from you as to whom you select to act as your arbitrator, Sir Victor will decide on the future tenant for the holding.' Frederick Wrench to Miss Jane Alexander, 15 Oct. 1878, ibid., D998/6/1, p. 405. Brush, agent of the Belmore estate in County Tyrone, prohibited auctions and insisted on local purchasers. R.C. Brush to Earl of Belmore, 7 Oct. 1873, P.R.O.N.I., Belmore papers, D3007/V/69; idem, 8 Aug. 1874, ibid., D3007/V/88; idem, 25 Dec. 1875, ibid., D3007/V/131.

201 Survey of Manor of Clothworkers by Edward Driver, 1840, Merchant Tailors' Hall, N.L.I., film 1517.

202 R.B. Touse to Edmund Stronge, 17 Mar. 1866, P.R.O.N.I., Clothworkers' company papers, D1514/2/5/15, p. 219.

203 Marquis of Dufferin to Mortimer Thomson, 22 Mar. 1869, P.R.O.N.I., Dufferin papers, D1071A/K/Box 3. Pattison wrote to Dufferin in 1879: 'One of the grounds on which assent is refused is the rule of the estate that no assent is given to any sale where the price exceeds the valuation of the improvements plus the value of the unexpired term in the lease.' J.L. Pattison to Dufferin, 9 Jan. 1879, ibid., D1071A/K/Box 5.

204 Mr. Le Fanu to Dufferin, 31 Mar. 1872, ibid.

205 Robert Perceval-Maxwell to James Murlands, 5 Dec. 1874, P.R.O.N.I., Perceval-Maxwell papers, D1556/2/2; [W.S. Trench], *On 'Tenant-Right,' or 'goodwill' within the barony of Farney*, p. 17.

206 In 1858 the Clothworkers' estate allowed a memorialist to sell by auction provided the agent could veto the purchaser. R.B. Touse [?] to C.J. Knox, 6 Aug. 1858, P.R.O.N.I., Hervey Bruce papers, D1514/2/5/14. The restrictions James Crawford set on the potential purchasers of the farm of one Sam Neil of Ballybrick, Co. Down, in 1864 were typical. He would consider (a) those who are solvent; (b) those willing to pay a higher rent in case of an increase; and (c) a person already a tenant or willing to become a tenant on the property. Sam Neil to James S. Crawford;

memorandum of James S. Crawford, [?] July 1864, P.R.O.N.I., Sharman Crawford papers, D856/B6/29, 30.

207 Henry Smith to Rowley Miller, 1 July 1825, P.R.O.N.I., Drapers' company papers, D3632/3/2.

208 Idem, 5 Aug. 1824, ibid.

209 Edward Lawford to Rowley Miller, 22 May 1843, ibid, D3632/3/4. In the next letter he was ordered to be removed from the estate.

210 J.R. Miller to W.H. Sawyer, 9 Dec. 1862, P.R.O.N.I., Drapers' company papers, D3632/1/3.

211 Millers to Hugh Elkin, 18 Jan. 1864, ibid., D3632/1/3.

212 J.G.M. Harvey to G.V. Hart 21 Feb. 1878, P.R.O.N.I., Hart papers, D3077/G/15/39.

213 ' . . . One child only ought to be kept at home with a view to succeeding to [the largest farms]. In the smaller ones it would be desirable if all could be sent out so that as the holders die off they may be added together.' Rowley Miller to Henry Smith, 11 June 1822, P.R.O.N.I., Drapers' company papers, D3632/3/2. Another County Londonderry agent wrote that the only remedy for smallholders who were behind in their rent payments was 'the throwing of two farms into one and giving it to the most industrious tenant of the two.' H. Gamble to [?] Babington, 10 Dec. 1855, P.R.O.N.I., Hervey-Bruce papers, D1514/2/5/18/24.

214 Widows were particularly vulnerable previous to the maturity of sons or daughters. Robert Hutchinson to Henry Bayly, 6 June 1778, P.R.O.N.I., Anglesey papers, D619/21/C/174; Rowley and J.R. Miller to Edward Lawford, 7 Feb. 1844, P.R.O.N.I., Drapers' company papers, D3632/1/1.

215 Nathanial Nesbitt to eighth earl of Abercorn, 19 Apr. 1757, P.R.O.N.I., Abercorn papers, T2541/IA1/4/67.

216 Rowley and J.R. Miller to W.H. Sawyer, 11 Sept. 1857, P.R.O.N.I., Drapers' company papers, D3632/1/2.

217 Henry Smith to Rowley Miller, 18 Sept. 1821, ibid., D3632/3/2. When it was discovered that the rules against subdivision were violated, the right of renewal was usually revoked. In 1844 the Millers explained how many families evaded the proscription against dividing among sons. One instance was revealed at death of the father. Another was uncovered when an agent detected two smokestacks on the farm. Millers to Lawford, 6 Aug. 1844, ibid., D3632/1/1; Millers to W.H. Sawyer, 28 Oct. 1863, ibid, D3632/1/3; minutes of the court of assitants, extracts relating to Irish estates, 17 July 1856, Drapers' Hall, London, N.L.I., film 1530. The agent on the Hart estate also discovered 'the second fire' on a farm in 1875, and the tenants were to be put out for subdividing. J.G.M. Harvey to G.V. Hunt, 21 Dec. 1876, P.R.O.N.I., Hart papers, D3077/G/15/30.

218 Henry Smith to William Smith, 14 Mar. 1823, P.R.O.N.I., Drapers' company papers, D3632/3/2.

219 William Blacker to R.B. Weany, P.P., 4 March 1840, P.R.O.N.I., Gosford papers, D1606/5/1 p. 217, cited in Gourley, 'Gosford estates,' p. 149; Maguire, *Downshire estates*, pp. 113–115; R.B. Touse to C.J. Knox, 22 Feb. 1859, P.R.O.N.I., Hervey-Bruce papers, D1514/2/5/14.

220 Rowley and J.R. Miller to Edward Lawford, 14 Apr. 1849, P.R.O.N.I., Drapers' company papers, D3632/1/2; Walter Stannus to W.H. Sawyer, 6 Mar. 1878, ibid., D3632/1/4.

221 See above, pp. 93–99.

222 Hamilton to Abercorn, 17 Sept. 1769, 11 Sept. 1770, 3 Apr. 1773, P.R.O.N.I., Abercorn papers, T2541/IA1/8/155, T2541/IA1/9/64, T2541/IA1/10/85.

223 Charles Brett to Judge Ward, 27 Feb., 1745, P.R.O.N.I., Castleward papers, D2092/1/6, p. 88; George Brett to Justice Ward, n.d. [c. Dec. 1747], ibid., D2092/1/7, p. 52.

224 Rowley and J.R. Miller to Edward Lawford, 25 Mar. 1850, P.R.O.N.I., Drapers' company papers, D3632/1/2.

225 Robert Farrell to J.P. Kelly, 14 July 1859, P.R.O.N.I., Whyte papers, D2918/3/8/60.

226 David Wilson to Mrs Jane Graham, 15 Feb. 1866, P.R.O.N.I., Stuart papers, D847/27/4.

227 James Bailie to George Mahon, 28 April 1856, N.L.I., George C. Mahon papers, MS 22,213.

228 'When the landlord himself desired to obtain occupation of a farm, which sometimes happened, there was a general understanding in the neighbourhood that he was entitled to the farm at a somewhat lower price than the new tenant, provided the old tenant was disposing of his interest of his own accord. But when the landlord dispossessed the tenant for his, the landlord's convenience, it was expected that he should pay fully as much as the highest bona fide bidder among new tenants.' John Martin to George Mahon, 22 April 1856, ibid., MS 22,191.

229 Ann Babington to John Murray, 23 Mar. 1791, P.R.O.N.I., Murray of Broughton papers, D2860; John Litton [?] to earl of Lanesborough, 14 Feb. 1860, P.R.O.N.I., Earl of Lanesborough's papers. D1908/2/5. The Merchant Tailors' company purchased a tenant's 'beneficial interest' in 1849. Irish estate committee of management minutes, 27 Dec. 1849, Merchant Tailors' Hall, N.L.I., film 1517.

230 Address to tenants, c. 1845, P.R.O.N.I., Perceval-Maxwell papers, D3244/E/29/40; John Burnett to J. Pinkerton, P.R.O.N.I., Earl of Antrim papers, D2977/4/3.

231 R.C. Brush to earl of Belmore, 24 Feb. 1876, P.R.O.N.I., Belmore papers, D3007/V/139; [?] to [?], 4 Mar. 1803, P.R.O.N.I., McCartney papers, D572/18/62; William Hudson to J. White, 20 Sept. 1808, P.R.O.N.I., Whyte papers, D2918/3/2/29; Hudson to White, 20 Nov. 1808, ibid., D2918/3/2/35; J.R. Moore to [?] Lees, 13 Jan. 1842, P.R.O.N.I., Annesley papers, D1854/6/2. [?] to [?], 4 Mar. 1803, P.R.O.N.I., McCartney papers, D572/18/62; William Hudson to J. White, 20 Sept. 1808, P.R.O.N.I., Whyte papers, D2918/3/2/29. Hudson to White, 20 Nov. 1808, ibid., D2918/3/2/35; Henry Prentice to Rev. Dr. Montgomery, 4 July 1864, P.R.O.N.I., Caledon papers, D2433/A/3/4; 'Reply to petition of Robert Campbell' by Henry Prentice, 11 June 1864, ibid., D2433/A/3/4.

232 The Drapers' company bought the tenant right of six acres in order to remove the best wood on the estate from public access in 1876. H.R. Miller to W.H. Sawyer, 11 Nov. 1876, P.R.O.N.I., Drapers' company papers, D3632/1/4. In 1876 the agents tried to put an end to town-park tenant right by buying up land at £5 an acre, spending a total of £120. Miller to Sawyer, 5 January 1876 and 3 March 1876, ibid. The Anglesey agent purchased a farm on the estate on behalf of the bailiff which ended up as part of the estate desmesne. Thomas Beer to [?] Rutherford, 28 June 1843, P.R.O.N.I., Anglesey papers, D619/23/B/105.

233 James Bailie to George Mahon, 21 April 1856, N.L.I., George C. Mahon papers, MS 22,213. He recommended consulting with James Crawford, estate agent and son of William Sharman Crawford, and reading 14 & 15 Vic., Chap. 23, Sec. 3.

234 John Martin to George Mahon, 22 April 1856, ibid.

235 Robert Perceval-Maxwell to Robert Robinson, 22 July 1870, P.R.O.N.I., Perceval-Maxwell papers, D1556/2/2, p. 372.

236 Perceval-Maxwell to James Murland, 6 Jan. 1872, ibid. In another letter Maxwell claimed that the rule on the estate was to allow the tenant compensation for improvements but not to allow a sale. Robert Perceval-Maxwell to Chas. C. Russell, Belfast, 3 Feb. 1872, ibid.

237 O'Connor Morris, *Letters on the land question of Ireland*, p. 250.

238 Frederick Wrench to A.L. Barlee, 9 Feb 1884, P.R.O.N.I., Brookeborough papers, D998/6/1/95, D998/6/2, p. 216.

239 Frederick Wrench to F.J. White, 28 Dec. 1876, ibid., D998/6/1/95.

240 Agent memoranda book, 27 March and 26 Dec. 1866, ibid. D998/8/12. See also 17 May and 2 July 1872, ibid., D998/8/18, and letters of Frederick Wrench to various tenants in 1877–78, ibid., D998/6/1 pp. 104, 112, 134, 181, 228, 245, 249, 329, 400, 403, and 405. 'Jim Beatty undertenant to Maguire, told me his landlord was going to sell the lease and I replied that anyone who bought it could only by the interest for the residual of the lease and that he must be accepted by the landlord and by the rules of this estate if he expected to have any claim.' Agent memoranda book, 4 July 1873, ibid, D998/8/19. See also Frederick Wrench to Anderson Fowles, 8 August 1877, ibid., D998/6/1, p. 231.

241 Diary of Mathew Saukey, 30 April 1871, ibid, D998/8/17.

242 Memorandum, 19 Jan. 1866, P.R.O.N.I., Dufferin papers, D1071A/K Box 2. The farm in question here was reclaimed from exhausted bog forty years previously and was very awkwardly shaped.

243 Marquis of Dufferin to Mortimer Thomson, 26 August 1869, P.R.O.N.I., Dufferin papers, D1071A/K, box 1.

244 Thomson to Dufferin, 28 August 1869, ibid.

245 Dufferin to Henry Pattison, 16 July 1874, ibid.

246 Pattison to Thomson, 1 July 1870, Pattison to Dufferin 9 April 1874, Dufferin to Pattison, 8 May 1874, Dufferin to Pattison, 30 April 1874, ibid.

247 Pattison to Dufferin, 18 June 1874, ibid.

248 Ibid., 25 March 1875, 30 March 1876, 11 May 1876, ibid, box 2.

249 *Northern Whig*, 11 April 1877; *Belfast Morning News*, 18 Feb. 1881.

250 Thomson to Dufferin, 12 April 1877, P.R.O.N.I., Dufferin papers, D1071A/K, Box 3. For an account of another case which Dufferin lost, see W.F. Bailey, *The Ulster Custom [the Ulster tenant right custom, the Dufferin estate] decision by W.F. Bailey legal land commissioner delivered at Dublin on Saturday, 30 April, 1888.*

251 Pattison to Dufferin, 31 Jan. and 11 April 1878, ibid., box 4.

252 James Donnelly [Bishop of Clogher] to Hugh de Fellenberg Montgomery, 5 Dec. 1881, P.R.O.N.I., Montgomery papers, D627/327b.

253 Hancock, *The tenant right of Ulster considered economically*, pp. 8–9. The rents charged in areas where the Ulster custom applies are not competition rents but 'customary rents.' The rents are variable, not fixed, but still customary in the sense that it is not competition determines them but some other conception of fair value. Seebohm, *The Land Question*, p. 637. According to Henderson, tenant right in the eighteenth century meant that at the expiration of leases the new rent was set to the farmer in possession by fair valuation, not competition. Henderson, *Ulster Tenant Right, an historical and economic sketch.*

254 Donnell, *Reports*, p. 80. He used Devon testimony to allege that there was no competition for land in Ulster, that tenant right required that all land be valued fairly by experts who consciously conceded a tenant-right value to the tenant. Ibid., pp. 80–87.

255 Report of Edward Fletcher, agent of Irish Society, 6 Mar. 1840, Irish Society court minute books, N.L.I., film 1524.

256 Wright, *Two lands on one soil*, p. 384. Deflated tenant-right values represented a managerial crisis for agents as well. The effectiveness of the tenant-right system as a managment tool depended on the buoyancy of the tenant-right market. The Millers observed that 'it was consolation to landlords and agents when they were obliged to put out tenants that they had something to fall back upon, namely 'tenant right.' Tenant right however being here so deteriorated, those poor tenants that we intend to put out next week have little hope before them but the workhouse with their families and the feeling in this country is universal respecting the workhouses, that nothing but starvation will induce any one to become an inmate therein.' Millers to Lawford, 23 June 1848, P.R.O.N.I., D3632/1/1. The Millers noted with some concern in 1849 that 'tenant right is fast going to the winds; it is entirely gone in houses everywhere, there are lots of houses to let in every town and village.' Millers to Edward Lawford, 1 May, 1849, ibid.

257 In place of a very lengthy account of this literature, see the discussion and bibliography in Michael Turner, *After the famine: Irish agriculture 1850–1914* (Cambridge, 1996). For an example of the problems concerning assumptions, see Turner's discussion of the implications of choosing the proper year to begin and end periods and subperiods of analysis. Ibid., pp. 199–200, 208–9, 215.

258 If Turner's recent conclusion that the distribution of income between landlords, tenants, and labourers was largely *stable* in the period 1850–1880 survives the scrutiny it will surely receive, then the debate over whether the situation of the 1870s and 1880s was a 'crisis of poverty and tyranny' or a 'crisis of prosperity,' to quote Vaughan's characterization, is no longer relevant.

259 '*The political* is the manner in which, explicitly or implicitly, a society defines or represents itself to itself and to others as a social unity.' Dick Howard, *From Marx to Kant* (New York, 1993), p. 88. Emphasis added.

260 Wright, *Two lands on one soil*, pp. 29, 84–87, 98–9. Greig recognized this when he argued that in England the sight of improved farms and efficient agricultural practice could safely be regarded as proof of a fair rent, but in Ireland the linen economy, which diverted the tenant's attention away from the land and caused excessive competition and land hunger, confounded judgments about the true value of land. 'To fix a fair and equitable rent on lands in this country is a most difficult matter. In countries where the tenants are substantial and skilful, lands will more easily find their true level as to what they can yield in rent, but in a country where the great body of the tenants are only in part dependent on agriculture, manufacture furnishing a part and are possessed of means and industry almost as various in degree as their numbers and situations, it is a most difficult task.' Greig, *General report*, p. 123.

261 Harvey, *The limits to capital*, p. 365.

262 Ferguson and Vance, *Tenure and improvement*, pp. 67–8.

263 *Northern Whig*, 13 January 1848, cited in Kennedy, 'Struggle for tenant right,' p. 153.

264 Robert Hutchinson to Henry Bayly, 2 Dec. 1770, P.R.O.N.I., Anglesey papers, D619/21/C/42.

265 Edmund McGildowney to [?] Turnley, 21 June 1817, P.R.O.N.I., McGildowney papers, D1375/1/10.

266 William Hudson to N.C. White, 18 Dec. 1816, P.R.O.N.I., Whyte papers, D2918/3/3/128.

267 Blacker, *Prize essay*, chapter 1.

268 'Report of the deputation appointed by the court on the 8th of July 1852 to visit the company's estate in Ireland,' Court minutes relating to Irish estates, 30 Sept. 1852, Fishmongers' Hall records, N.L.I., film 1514.

269 George Rye, a small Cork landowner and author of *Considerations on agriculture* (1730) believed that low rents discouraged investment in land. Dickson, 'Cork region,' p. 142.

270 J.B. Johnson to John Waring Maxwell, 22 June 1832, P.R.O.N.I., Perceval-Maxwell papers, D3244/E/8/9B.

271 James Speer to F.E. Foljambe, 15 Mar. 1788, P.R.O.N.I., Foljambe papers, T3381/5/10. The managers of the Irish Society ordered in 1822 that agents should secure the rents from middlemen by levying distraints on their undertenants, and that the undertenants were to be subject to ejectments if necessary to recover the rent. Minutes of the Irish Society, 7 Dec. 1822, N.L.I., film 1522. On the Downhire estate, however, the agent was less sure of his ability to be so aggressive toward the undertenants. He complained that while it was true there were goods to be distrained on the premises, these could only be taken 'at the expense of breaking the poor undertenants who owe but little, and wasting the lands.' James Gwynn to Henry Hatch, 3 Jan. 1746, P.R.O.N.I., Downshire papers, D607/A/27.

272 'Survey of the estate of Termondmagrath in the barony of Tirhugh, Co. Donegal' by Thomas Knox, 1682, N.L.I., *Reports on private collections*, vii, no. 220: Leslie papers, in possession of Mr. S.C. Ross.

273 Gillespie, *Settlement and survival*, p. li.

274 Nicholas Ellis to Thomas Barrett-Lennard, 30 Jan. 1830, P.R.O.N.I., Barrett-Lennard papers, film 170/3.

275 [?] Armstrong to earl of Uxbridge, 20 Apr. 1804, P.R.O.N.I., Anglesey papers, D619/23/A/3.

276 Sir George Savile to James Murray, 28 May 1779, P.R.O.N.I., Murray of Broughton papers, D2860/17/4.

277 Greig, *General report*, pp. 122, 138–39.

278 The theme with which Stone opens his chapter on leasing policy is morality, not economics. He quotes from various landlords' advice to their heirs, such as the 1st Lord Montagu: 'Be moderate in taking fines and sparing in raising of rents that [the tenants] may have cause both to pray and praise God for you.' Stone, *The crisis of the aristocracy*, p. 304.

279 William Mayne to Thomas Barrett-Lennard, 7 May 1808, P.R.O.N.I., Barrett-Lennard papers, D1232/1/74.

280 Idem, 12 June 1809, ibid., D1232/1/98; idem, 12 June 1814, ibid., D1232/1/199.

281 Idem, n.d. [c. May 1810], ibid., D1232/1/113; idem, 11 June 1816, ibid., film 170/2; idem, 20 Apr. 1817, ibid.

282 [?] Armstrong to earl of Uxbridge, 18 Dec. 1821, P.R.O.N.I., Anglesey papers, D619/23/A/138.

283 Power, *Tipperary*, pp. 190–1.

284 Dickson, 'Cork region,' p. 312.

285 Nicholas Ellis to Thomas Barrett-Lennard, 5 Sept. 1845, P.R.O.N.I., Barrett-Lennard papers, Mic.170/3.

286 [?] Armstrong to earl of Uxbridge, 28 June 1843, P.R.O.N.I., Anglesey papers, D619/23/B/105. 287 Dickson, 'Cork region,' pp. 223–4.

288 Henry Blundell to James Gwynn, 3 Jan. 1720, P.R.O.N.I., Downshire papers, D607/A/12.

289 Rowley Miller to Edward Lawford, 14 Feb. 1855, P.R.O.N.I., Drapers' company papers, D3632/1/2.

290 Maguire, *Downshire estates*, pp. 42–45.

291 William Sharmon Crawford to John S. Crawford, 31 July 1835, P.R.O.N.I., Sharman Crawford papers, D856/D/36.

292 Donnell, *Reports*, p. 86.

293 The courts did occasionally rule on the issue of fair rent. Vaughan notes the case of *Carraher vs. Bond*, where a tenant was given an award based on a tenant-right value of £12 an acre even though the estate office had calculated the rent based on a tenant-right value of £8 an acre. Vaughan, *Landlords & tenants*, pp. 97–98. But many observers claimed that the county chairmen were generally allowing nowhere near the market value of tenant right in their awards, thus ratifying as a 'usage' office rules restricting tenant-right prices. F. Thompson, 'Land and politics,' p. 227.

294 *Bessborough commission report*, p. 3.

295 *Belfast Newsletter*, 19 March 1870.

296 F. Thompson, 'Land and politics,' p. 232.

297 Stannus to W.H. Sawyer, May 1875, P.R.O.N.I., Drapers' company papers, D3632/1/4.

298 Ibid., 29 Dec. 1875, ibid.

299 Idem, 10 March 1876, ibid.; This reletting drew the unwelcome attention of the *Derry Sentinel*. Idem, 3 March 1876, ibid. One tenant, 'a leading man among the tenant-right party [who] was mainly instrumental in getting up the memorial,' refused to accept the new valuation. Idem, 1 Jan. 1876, ibid.

300 Idem, 10 and 19 April, 6 and 24 July 1876, ibid.

301 R.C. Brush to earl of Belmore, 19 Dec. 1876, P.R.O.N.I., Belmore papers, D3007/V/152.

302 Idem, 29 June 1877, ibid., D3007/V/156.

303 See Chapter 1, p. 6.

304 Henry Smith to Rowley Miller, 18 Sept. 1821, P.R.O.N.I., Drapers' company papers, D3632/3/2.

305 Edward Lawford to J.R. Miller, 17 Mar. 1848, P.R.O.N.I., Drapers' company papers, D3632/3/5. After remarking on the high prices of some recent tenant-right sales, the court of assistants recorded the following comment in the minutes of their meeting of 6 August 1855: 'These tenants, among other things, allege this as a reason why their rents ought not to have been increased, a reason which the committee apprehend has a contrary tendency inasmuch as it shows that the rents paid by the former tenants must have been considerably below the value of the lands held by them, or such large sums would not have been given for the interest thereon.' Minutes of the court of assistants, extracts relating to Irish estates, Drapers' Hall, London, 6 Aug. 1855, N.L.I., film 1530. The managers of the Clothworkers' proportion held similar opinions. Report of a deputation to the Irish estate of the Clothworkers' company, 1849, N.L.I., film 1517; R.B. Touse [?] to C.J. Knox, 22 Feb. 1859, P.R.O.N.I., Hervey-Bruce papers, D1514/2/5/14.

306 George Joy to Lord Mountcashel, 18 Jan. 1842, P.R.O.N.I., letterbook of George Joy, T1289/19.

307 Vaughan, *Landords & tenants*, p. 74. On the other hand, tenants were in no position to capitalize on their good fortune by selling tenant right unless they left rural society altogether, since otherwise they would be forced to sink the money into another highly-priced farm.

308 Greig argued that tenant right was acceptable, and represents a fair rent, in the case of leaseholders, even where those leases expressly forbid it. Greig, *General report*, p. 169.

309 Rowley and J.R. Miller to Edward Lawford, 25 May 1848, P.R.O.N.I., Drapers' company papers, D3632/1/1. The Millers had already attempted to describe the anomalous nature of tenant-right payments for land 'let at a fair value' in a letter of 1 October 1845. The following year they tried again to explain the anomaly to an uncomprehending court of management in London, concluding that 'it is difficult to explain this, but it is nevertheless the fact.' Millers to Lawford, 1 May, 1849, ibid.

310 Report on the memorial of Patience Moore, 15 Dec. 1812, N.L.I., film 1521. There is no mention of accidental competition or any other bidders for this farm, but the agent did ask whether Moore should get the farm.

311 Report as to the extent of the Society's lands and probable means of improvement, 8 Feb. 1813, ibid. A military officer recommended in 1797 that all landlords give their old tenants 10% reductions in rent as a mark of respect for their loyalty. Brigadier-General Knox to Thomas Pelham, 19 April 1797, P.R.O.N.I., T755/4/2.

312 *Northern Whig*, 18 April 1870, quoted in F. Thompson, 'Land and politics,' p. 193.

313 William O'Connor Morris, *Letters on the land question of Ireland* (London, 1870), p. 267–8.

314 Urban holdings in Strabane were usually let by the eighth earl of Abercorn 'with the condition that [the tenant is] not to be understood to have any tenant right to it.' John Hamilton to Abercorn, 18 Nov. 1770, P.R.O.N.I., Abercorn papers, T2541/IA1/9/80. Sir Victor Brooke denied 'any saleable interest in town parks' on his estate in County Fermanagh. Frederick Wrench to Joseph Alexander, 26 Apr. 1881, P.R.O.N.I., Brookeborough papers, D998/6/1. See also John Howe to marquis of Dufferin, 6 Nov. 1880, P.R.O.N.I., Dufferin papers, D1071A/K, box 1.

315 *Northern Whig*, 11 July 1874, quoted in F. Thompson, 'Land and politics,' p. 233.

316 Thompson, 'Custom, law, and common right,' p. 97.

317 Ann Bagot, 'Mr. Gilpin and manorial customs' in *Trans. Cumberland and Westmoreland Ant. Soc*, lxii, (1963) pp. 67–8; Tawney, *Agrarian problem*, pp. 286, 293; Campbell, *English yeomen*, p. 145; Batho, 'Noblemen, gentlemen, and yeomen,' p. 293.

318 A similar moment was reached with respect to kindly tenure in mid-sixteenth-century Scotland and border tenant right in early seventeenth-century northern England. See the literature cited in chapter 1, note 40.

319 Dodgshon, *Origin*, p. 53. According to Hoyle, 'manorial custom was rarely committed to paper except when its existence or details were subject to doubt.' R.W. Hoyle, 'Lords, tenants, and tenant right,' p. 40.

320 Clay suggests that the erosion of customary tenures in England was in fact a process of definition: 'Even where tenures had been undeniably customary there had been innumerable disputes between manorial lords and their tenants about what exactly local custom prescribed, and in particular how much the tenants could be made to pay for their tenancies. . . . By the middle of the seventeenth century, however, these controversies were dying down, in part because . . . common law had clarified many formerly contentious issues. . . .' Clay, 'Landlords and estate management,' pp. 198–99.

321 Campbell, *English yeomen*, pp. 148–9. For Scottish kindly tenure, see Dodgshon, *Land and society*, pp. 60–1

322 'It would appear that the term the 'the three F's' was first used by Rev. N.M. Brown at a tenant right meeting in Ballymoney in February 1873.' Armstrong, *Economic history of agriculture*, p. 55, n. 348. Donnell defined the essence of tenant right by the

following trivium: 'There are three things essential to the existence of a tenant right interest: 1. The fairly valued rent. 2. The continuousness of the interest beyond the legal determination of the tenancy. 3. The right of realizing the value of the interest before removal.' Donnell, *Reports*, p. 111.

323 F. Thompson, 'Land and politics,' p. 85. In particular, office restriction of price could not be a usage. Robert Donnell, *Reports*, pp. 136–140.

324 'The *Newsletter* had evidently reached the conclusion that some concession would have to be made to the tenant farmers of the north lest they should be tempted to flock to the standard of the Land League.' Armstrong, *Economic history of agriculture*, pp. 59–60. Armstrong cites Locker Lampson, *Considerations on the state of Ireland*.

325 *Belfast Newsletter*, 5 March 1870, cited in F. Thompson, 'Land and politics,' pp. 188–190; Armstrong, *Economic history of agriculture*, p. 33. 'The contemporary justification for the introduction of plural usages was that the practice of the custom was not uniform; but this view ignored that behind all the variations, variations which were imposed by the landlords, there lay an ineluctable custom the essential attributes of which were clearly understood and stated by tenant farmers and which were moreover recognised on several large estates.' Ibid., p. 44.

326 See T.M. Devine, *The transformation of rural Scotland: social change and the agrarian economy, 1660–1815* (Edinburgh, 1994), especially chapters 2–4.

327 Ibid., especially pp. 35, 60–64, 73.

328 Deane, 'Production of cultural space,' p. 122.

329 Tom Dunne, *Maria Edgeworth and the colonial mind* (Cork, 1984), pp. 6–8.

330 Maclagan, *Land culture and land tenure in Ireland*, p. 46. On the activities of Ribbonmen in Westmeath in the 1820s, see the correspondence of Andrew Nugent, P.R.O.N.I., Nugent papers, D552/A/7/6–7; in north Antrim see the letters of Edward McGildowney, P.R.O.N.I., McGildowney papers D1375/1/16, 17, 21; in Leitrim in the 1840s see correspondence of George Lane-Fox, N.L.I., Lane-Fox papers, film 4063; in Louth in the 1840s and 1850s see correspondence of Thomas Rutherford and Thomas Beer, P.R.O.N.I., Anglesey papers, D619/23/B. On the Molly Maguires in Leitrim in the 1840s, see the correspondence of William Johnston, John Dickson, and James Fawcett, N.L.I., Playdell papers, film 7648; Molly Maguires were discussed in the House of Commons, see *Hansard* lxxxiii, pp. 1537–8, lxxxiv, pp. 1174, 1360. On the Tommy Downshires in Co. Down see Kennedy, 'Struggle for tenant right,' pp. 26–39.

331 Wright's work is valuable for suggesting how to delineate the rather fluid boundary between popular Orange landlordism and more radical tenant-righters. He traces how the alliance between strong-farmer tenant-righters and Whig landlords was disturbed at mid-century by a more broadly based Presbyterian agitation for low rents which had its advocate in James McKnight, editor of the *Londonderry Standard*. Wright associated Liberal strength with large-farm areas serviced by agriculturally dependent towns (like Ballymoney) where Catholic threats to landholding were perceived as minimal. It was large-scale Protestant tenant farmers, insulated from Catholic populations, who formed organizations like the Route Tenant Defence Association, an active and aggressive body in the 1870s. Wright, *Two lands on one soil*, pp. 96, 171–2, 395–7, 404, 437, 453–8.

332 Gladstone speaking in parliament, quoted in Dewey, 'Celtic agrarian legislation,' p. 60; Bull, *Land, politics, and nationalism*, pp. 50–51.

333 Wright, *Two lands on one soil*, pp. 437–8. *Ulster Weekly News*, 24 Jan 1874. Wright carefully distinguishes between a position advocating 'the stripping of [landlord's] monopolistic privileges and prerogatives' from 'their outright expropriation.' Ibid., p. 204.

334 See chapter 2, pp. 93–99.

335 David Miller, *Queen's Rebels*, pp 76–8; Wright, *Two lands on one soil*, p. 172.

336 Wright, *Two lands on one soil*, p. 388; *Northern Star*, 4 November 1869; *Weekly Northern Whig*, 6 and 27 November 1869.

337 Jacques Derrida performed a provocative and useful reading of the term 'supplement,' defined in the *Oxford English dictionary* as 'a thing added to remedy deficiencies,' when he analyzed 'that dangerous supplement' that writing is to speech in the work of Jean Jacques Rousseau. Jacques Derrida, *Of Grammatology*, trans. Gayatri Chakroavorty Spivak (Baltimore, 1974), pp. 141–64. This paragraph owes much to Christopher Norris' concise gloss in his *Deconstruction: theory and practice* (London, 1982), pp. 33–4.

338 Vincent Descombes, *Modern French philosophy*, trans. by L. Scott-Fox and J.M. Harding (Cambridge, 1980), p. 148.

339 Thompson, *Customs in common*, p. 15.

Bibliography

I. SOURCES

A. MANUSCRIPTS

1. *Public Records Office of Northern Ireland*

a. Family estate papers

Abercorn papers:

> Transcripts of letters from various agents of the Abercorn estate around Strabane, Co. Tyrone, 1736–1801. T2541/1A1/1–21, T2541/1A2/1–10, T2541/1B1/1–4.
>
> Letters of agents James Hamilton, Sr. and James Hamilton, Jr. to the ninth earl of Abercorn, 1802–10. D623/A/94–100.
>
> Letters from the eighth and ninth earls of Abercorn to various agents of the Abercorn estate, 1744–88. D623/A/12–26.
>
> Letters from Captain J. Humphries, agent of the Abercorn estate, to the first duke of Abercorn, 1849–58. D623/A/269.
>
> Report on the management of the Abercorn estate by Henry Harrison. D623/A/271/4.
>
> Leases, lease books, and one book of tenant right payments. D623/B/10–14.
>
> Rent account books arranged by manor, 1794. D623/C/4.
>
> Color map of the Abercorn estate. D623/D/1/22.

Anglesey papers: Attornments, proposals, and petitions of tenants near Omeath, Co. Louth, to their landlord, 1735–1851. D619/5, 6, 11; Letters from various agents, 1716–1804. D619/21–23.

Annesley papers: Legal notebooks of Richard Annesley, law student, 1750–64. D1854/4/2, 4, 6, 7; Letter books of J.R. Moore, trustee of the Annesley estate in Castlewellan, Co. Down, 1836–80. D1854/6/1–8.

Antrim papers: Reports of the agent of the marchioness of Londonderry's estate around Carnlough, Co. Antrim, 1837–62. D2977/6/1–14.

Ardglass papers: Letters from agents of the estate of the countess of Ardglass, Ardglass, Co. Down, 1682–92. D970/1.

Barrett-Lennard papers: Letters from various agents of the Barrett-Lennard estate around Clones, Co. Monaghan, 1684–1850. Film 170; Letter book of William Mayne, agent of the Barrett-Lennard estate, 1806–1815. D1232/1.

Belmore papers:

> Correspondence of the earl of Belmore primarily with other landlords. D3007/O/1.
>
> Letters from agents in Ballyconnell, County Cavan to the earl of Belmore, 1875–85. D3007/U/1–350.
>
> Letters from agents in the Moy, County Tyrone to the earl of Belmore, 1863–85. D3007/V/1–499.

Brookeborough papers:

> Out-letterbooks of Frederick Wrench, agent of the Brookeborough estate in Colebrook, Co. Fermangh, 1876–88. D998/6/1–2.
>
> Memoranda books of the agents of the Brookeborogh estate, 1855–76. D998/8/1–22.
>
> Notes on a court case concerning a bog dispute, 1884. D998/25/1.

Caledon Papers:

> Letters from various agents of the Caledon estates near Castle Derg, Co. Tyrone, and Moville, Co. Donegal, 1790–1880. D2433/A/2
>
> Letterbooks of agents of the Caledon estates, 1790–1886. D2433/A/3.
>
> Cash books of agents of the Caledon estates. D2433/A/11/2–6.
>
> Writ banning tenant right sales on the Caledon estate, c. 1867. D2433/A/12/4.
>
> Leases of lands in Castle derg, Co. Tyrone, 1780. D847/5.

Castle Stewart papers: Correspondence referring to lands near Eary, Co. Tyrone, 1653–7. D.1618/15/2.

Castleward papers: Letter books of Justice Ward, Bangor, Co. Down, 1723–64. D.2092/1/1–8.

Castletown papers: Introduction by A.P.W. Malcomson. T2825/Introduction; Leases, letters from tenants, and agent correspondence, 1720–94. T2825/C/10, 12, 15, 20, 25–29.

Clanbrassil papers: Rental, family letter book, and memoranda book referring to lands on the Ards peninsula, Co. Down, 1632–1715. T761/1, 3, 7; Rentroll, 1670. T2253.

Clifford papers: Letterbooks of the agents of land purchased by John Mulholland near Downpatrick, Co. Down, 1879–83. D1167/12A/1–2.

Donegall papers: Estate correspondence concerning the Hearts of Steel outrages, Co. Antrim, 1771–5. T1893.

Downshire papers: County Down estate correspondence, 1707–1801. D607/A/1–637; Letters from estate agent Henry Hatch concerning lands owned by the Blundell family, 1753–86. Film 17/1.

Dufferin papers: Correspondence between Lord Dufferin and various agents of his estate in Co. Down, 1870–84. D1071A/K.

Edmonstone papers: Letters concerning disputes between tenants near Red Hall, Co. Antrim, 1769–1780. D233/1–15.

Ellis papers: Letters and petitions concerning tenants on the See of Derry Diocesan lands, seventeenth century. D683.

Foljambe papers: Estate documents referring to the Manor of Cecil, Newtown Savile (formerly Tamlaght), Co. Tyrone. T3381.

Guthrie Castle papers: Correspondence of the estate of the bishop of Raphoe in County Londonderry, 1637–63. T1547.

Hart papers: Correspondence and other papers concerning the Hart estate in Kilderry, near Muff, Co. Donegal, 1820–1880. D3077/G, H.

Hervey-Bruce papers: Papers of Bishop Frederick Hervey-Bruce referring to the estates of the Bruce family of Coleraine and of the Clothworkers company in Downhill, Dunboe, Magilligan, and Ballyscullion, Co. Londonderry, 1790–1802. D1514/2 and D2798.

Kirk-Vesey papers: Letters concerning the Kirk estate, Carrickfergus, Co. Antrim, 1718–1735. T2524.

Lanesborough papers: Letters from the agents of the Earl of Lanesborough concerning land in counties Fermanagh and Cavan, 1780, 1860–4. D1908/2/1, 5.

Lenox-Conyngham papers: Letters concerning tenants near Derry city, 1630–1717. D.1449/1.

Londonderry papers: Letter and order books of agents to the Londonderry estate near Newtownards, Co. Down, 1834–70. D654/N1, N2, N5; Correspondence of Lord Londonderry, 1790, 1807 (Cleland papers). D714/6/13.

Lowry papers: Correspondence concerning the Lowry estate near Pomeroy, Co. Tyrone, 1812–32. D1132/1/1–7.

Macartney papers: Agent correspondence, 1770–1810. D572/18 and D2225/7/4–80.

McGildowney papers: Correspondence of Edmund McGildowney, landowner and agent, Ballynaglogh and Ballycastle, Co. Antrim, 1808–34. D1375/1–4.

Montgomery papers: Correspondence of Hugh de F. Montgomery, landowner near Fivemiletown, Co. Tyrone, 1873–1882. D627/248–344, 428.

Mountcashel papers: Letter book of George Joy, land agent to Lord Mountcashel, Galgorm Castle, Co. Antrim, 1835–48. T1289/19.

Murray of Broughton papers: Correspondence, accounts and a survey of the Murray estate near Donegal town, 1680–1799. D2860.

Nugent papers: Correspondence relating to the Nugent estates near Portaferry House, Barony of Ards, Co. Down, 1721–1851. D552/A/2–9; Rental of the Nugent estate in Co. Down recording the sale of tenant right, 1722. D552/B/3/2/93.

O'Hara papers: Correspondence referring to the estate in county Sligo. T2812/1–8;

Survey of the economic development of county Sligo in the eighteenth century by Charles O'Hara. T2812/19.

O'Neill papers: Letters concerning the O'Neill estate near Dunmore, Co. Antrim, 1702–1707. D1470/3.

Ogilvie papers: Letter book of William Ogilvie, landowner near Ardglass, Co. Down, 1807–10. T1546/1.

Perceval-Maxwell papers: Letters mostly to John Waring Maxwell, referring to estates near Bangor and Lecale, Co. Down, 1802–1876. D3244/B, C, E; Letterbooks of Robert Perceval-Maxwell, Groomsport, Bangor, Co. Down, 1859–84. D1556/2/1–4.

Pike Fortescue papers: Letter concerning tenants near Dungannon, 1737. T2913/1/20.

Rossmore papers: Letters concerning land near Rathmore, Co. Monaghan, 1687–1713. T2929/1–2.

Sharman Crawford papers: Letters of Arthur, James, and William Sharman-Crawford concerning their estate in Co. Down, 1836–65. D856/A6, B6, C6, D.

Stuart papers: Letters referring to tenants near Omagh, Fivemiletown, and on the Stuart Estate, Drumasple, Co. Tyrone, 1715, 1866, 1870. D847/27/1, 4, 7.

Verner papers: Letterbooks of agents to the Verner estates in counties Armagh, Tyrone, and Monaghan, 1850–90. D236/488/1–5.

Waring papers: Letters of William Waring concerning land near Waringstown, Co. Down, 1656–1689. D695.

Whyte papers: Letters from various legal and land agents to John J. and Nicholas C. Whyte, landowners near Loughbrickland, Co. Down, 1773–1889. D2918/3/1–11; Legal documents concerning the estate. D2918/5.

b. Papers relating to the estates of the City of London and its livery companies

Irish Society papers:

> Irish Society correspondence, 1873. D1960.

> Survey of Irish Society's estate in county Londonderry, [n.d. c.1872]. D573/6.

> Court minutes, letterbooks, and account books of the Irish Society, 1617–1871. Film 9A.

Drapers' company papers:

> Letterbooks of correspondence from agents of the Drapers' company estate near Moneymore and Draperstown, Co. Londonderry, to members of the committee of management of the Drapers' company, Drapers' Hall, London, 1843–88. D3632/1/1–5; film 495/1–4.

> Letterbooks of correspondence from members of the committee of management to agents, 1817–83. D3632/3/1–8; film 495/8–11.

> Letterbook of correspondence from the solicitor to the Drapers' company, Magherafelt, Co. Londonderry, 1881–6. D3632/4/1; film 495/13.

> Bundles of letters concerning tenant right. D3632/K/6/1/4, 6; D3632/K/6/2/11.

> Registry of the tenants in the Drapers' estate who have sold their farms and the names of those who have bought from them and the sums paid, 1828–1870. D3632/K/6/1/1.

> Registry of sales of tenant right on the estate of the Drapers' company, 1872–81. D3632/K/6/1/3.

Papers relating to other London Companies:

> Accounts extracted from 'Orders of Courts, 1683–1700'; agent correspondence, 1840–73; proceedings of the joint board of the Irish Society, 1854–65. Film 146/9.

> Accounts, agents reports, and correspondence of various London companies, 1822–76. Film 9b.

Articles of agreement of a lease on the Haberdashers' estate, 8 April, 1616. T2208/1.

Rentroll of the Vintners' company proportion of lands, 10 Oct. 1718. D2094/21.

Report of a deputation appointed by a special general court of the Ironmongers' company held 14 May 1841. D382.

Report to the Skinners' company on the regulation of tenant right, by Michael King, c. 1870. D1550/10.

Volume of maps of Skinners' company estate by William Sampson and Charles McQuaid, 1830–70. D1550/27.

c. Other manuscript material

Lease assignment of a graveyard, 1693. T1062/45/124.

Letter of Alex Brennan, 1 April, 1852. T2140.

Letterbook of Andrew Spotswood, agent of estates in County Londonderry, 1861–71. D.1062/1.

Letterbooks of George Moore, 1780s. D2309/4/3,4.

Leasebook of the manor of Castledillon, Co. Armagh, with very detailed observations by William Molyneux, c. 1696. Film 80/3.

View of the lands of archbishop of Armagh, 1703. T848

2. National Library of Ireland

a. Manuscripts

'Journal of a tour of parts of England, Wales, and Ireland, 3 June to 12 Aug. 1773' by Reverend J. Burrows, MS 23,561.

Hans Stevenson papers: Correspondence between William Hamilton and Hans Stevenson, 1694–1710 referring to land in Co. Down. MS 1702.

Fingall papers: Letters referring to lands in counties Meath and Cavan, c. 1725. MS 8025.

Crofton papers: Letters to Sir Henry Crofton relating to Cavan and Monaghan estates, 1809–30. MS 20,773; Surveys of Crofton estate, 1719–1794. MS 20,798.

Dawson papers.

Survey of the Dawson estate in County Monaghan, 1719. MS 3180.

Notes on the Dawson estate in County Monaghan, 1768–89. MS 1647.

Survey of the Dawson estate, now the property of Lord Cremone, 1841–2. MS 1698 (also P.R.O.N.I. D266).

Journal of a tour to Dawson's Grove by Rev. J. Burrows, June to August, 1773. MS 23,561.

O'Hara papers: Letters from agents in Coloomey, Co. Sligo. MSS 20,321, 20,353–54.

Vernon papers: Letters concerning estates in Cavan and Monaghan, 1848–80. MSS 18.948, 18,949, 18,953.

Surveys of the estate of the marquess of Antrim in Glenarm, Larne, and Coleraine, Co. Antrim, 1811–13. MS 8125.

'Observations on the state of the tenantry in Leitrim,' 1838. MS 3829.

Dr. Michael Quaine papers relating to the Royal School, Armagh and Royal School, Cavan estates, 1830–50. Mss 17,920 (1,2), 17,912(6).

Letterbook of the Murray Stewart estate in County Donegal, 1875–79. MS 4273.

Memoranda of Captain Joseph Erskine concerning the Hearts of Steel, 10 April 1772. MS 8179.

Letters to Edward Brice concerning his estate at Ballywilliam, Co. Down, c. 1800. MS 13,537.

b. Microfilm in possession of the National Library

Conolly papers: Letters of Robert McCausland, Limavady, to William Conolly, 1718–29, and other estate material. Film 6950–6951.

Drapers' Hall records: Minutes of the court of assistants of the Drapers' company concerning their Irish estate, 1805–1828. Film 1529–30

Fishmongers' Hall records: Extracts of court minutes relating to Irish estates, 1822–50. Film 1514–6.

Irish Society court minute books, 1797–1871. Film 1521–1528

Lane-Fox papers: Letters on the management of Waterford and Leitrim estates, 1830–50.

Merchant Tailors' Hall records: Court minutes and reports of the Clothworkers' company. Film 1517–1519.

Playdell papers: Letters concerning the Playdell estates in Drumlane and Doobally, Co. Cavan. Film 7648–7650.

Shirley papers: Copies of ordnance survey reports on the productive economy of several parishes in County Londonderry, 1834–8. Film 4646.

Skinners' Hall records: Extracts from Court minutes relating to Irish estates, 1800–1868. Film 1520.

Southwell papers: Letters concerning Southwell estate near Downpatrick, Co. Down. Film 521.

3. Trinity College, Dublin

Records of Trinity College estates in Ulster, 1610–1860. MUN/P/24.

Conolly papers: Letters concerning estates of William Conolly in Counties Londonderry and Donegal, 1709–1850. MSS 3944; 3974–84.

'A view of the hearth money in the several provinces and counties of Ireland as let to farm in the following years' in *A natural history of Ireland*, T.C.D., MS 883/1.

B. PRINTED MATERIAL

1. Historical Manuscripts Commission Reports

Hastings MSS (Hist. MSS. Comm. Rep. Hastings MSS, Vol III, 1934, pp.152–3): Letter of Elizabeth, Countess of Moirs, to Earl of Huntington, 4 Feb. 1771.

Hastings MSS (Hist. MSS. Comm. Rep. Hasting MSS, Vol IV, 1947 pp 86–8): Draft of a letter of Bishop Bramhall to the Lord Deputy Wandesford concerning farming conditions in Ulster. April 16, 1640.

Cowper MSS (Hist. MSS. Comm. Rep. 12, App. 1, p.416): Memorial by Sir Thomas Phillips to the King on the Ulster Plantation. 9 Nov. 1630.

2. *National Library of Ireland,* Reports on Private Collections

No. 6. Report on the Fingall papers (from 1557) in N.L.I. relating to the Plunkett family and to lands in Meath and Cavan.

No. 9. Report on the Madden papers, property of J.W.R. Madden of Clones.

No. 113. Report on the Rossmore papers concerning the property of Lord Rossmore in County Monaghan.

No. 142. Report on the Shirley papers, property of Lieut. Col. E.C. Shirley, Lough Fea, Carickmacross, Co. Monaghan.

No. 220. Report on the Leslie papers (from 1664) preserved at the estate office, Glaslough, Monaghan, relating to the Leslie family and to lands in counties Monaghan, Cavan, and Donegal.

3. *Parliamentary Papers*

Report from her majesty's commissioners of inquiry into the state of the law and practice in respect to the occupation of land in Ireland [605], HC 1845, xix, 1.

—— *Minutes of evidence,* pt. i [606], ibid, 57.

—— *Minutes of evidence,* pt. ii [616], HC 1845, xx, 1.

—— *Minutes of evidence,* pt. iii [616], HC 1845, xxi, 1.

Report from the select committee on the tenure and improvement of land (Ireland) Act; together with the proceedings of the committee, minutes of evidence, appendix, and index, HC 1865 (402), xi, 341.

Two reports for the Irish government on the history of the landlord and tenant question in Ireland, with suggestions for legislation. First report made in 1859; second, in 1866, by W. Neilson Hancock [4202], HC 1868–9, xxvi, 1.

Report from the select committee of the house of lords on the landlord and tenant (Ireland) act, 1870; together with the proceedings of the committee, minutes of evidence, and index, HC 1872 (403), xi, 1.

Report of her majesty's commission of inquiry into the working of the landlord and tenant (Ireland) act, 1870, and the acts amending the same [c 2779], HC 1881, xviii, 1.

—— *Minutes of evidence,* pt. i [c 2779–i], HC 1881, xviii, 73.

—— *Minutes of evidence,* pt. ii [c 2779–ii], HC 1881, xix, 1.

—— *Index to minutes of evidence and appendices* [C 2779–iii], HC 1881, xix, 825.

4. *Contemporary Published Works*

Bailey, W.F. 'The Ulster tenant right custom; its origins, characteristics and position under the land acts,' *Journal of the statistical and social inquiry society of Ireland,* x (1893–4), pp. 12–22.

Baxter, Robert. *The Irish tenant right question examined by a comparison of the law and practice of England with the law and practice of Ireland.* London, 1869.

Bicheno, James. *Ireland and its economy.* London, 1830.

Blacker, William. *Prize essay addressed to the agricultural committee of the Royal Dublin Society on the management of landed property in Ireland.* Dublin, 1834.

—— *An essay on the improvements to be made in the cultivation of small farm.* Dublin, 1834.

Blakely, F. *Letters on the relation between landlord and tenant.* Belfast, 1851.

Burroughs, Edward. *Essays on practical husbandry and rural economy.* London, 1821.

—— *A view of the state of agriculture in Ireland.* Dublin, 1821.

Butt, Isaac. *Land tenure in Ireland; a plea for the Celtic race.* Dublin, 1866.

—— *The Irish people and Irish land.* Dublin, 1867.

Calendar of state papers relating to Ireland, 1509–1670. 24 vols. London, 1861–1912.

Carey, Mathew. *Vindication of small farmers, the peasantry and labourers of Ireland . . . .* Philadelphia, 1836.

Cliff Leslie, T.E. *Land systems and industrial economy of Ireland, England, and continental countries.* London, 1870.

Connor, William. *The prosecuted speech; delivered at Montmellick in proposing a petition to parliament in favour of a valuation and perpetuity on his farm to the tenant.* Dublin, 1842.

—— *A letter to the tenantry of Ireland, containing an exposition of the rack rent system; and pointing out a valuation and perpetuity as its only effectual remedy.* Dublin, 1850.

Crawford, William Sharman. *Observations showing the necessity of an amendment in the laws of landlord and tenant. . . .* Belfast, 1837.

—— *A defense of the small farmers of Ireland.* Dublin, 1839.

—— *Depopulation not necessary. An appeal to the British members of the imperial parliament against the extermination of the Irish people.* London, 1849.

Crosley, Henry. *Hints to the landed proprietry and agriculturists of Great Britain and Ireland.* London, 1841.

Davies, Sir John. *A discovery of the true causes of why Ireland was never entirely subdued until His Majesties happie raigne.* London, 1612.

[Dawson, Thomas]. *A dissertation on the enlargement of tillage, the erecting of public granaries, and the regulating, employing and supporting the poor in this kingdom.* Dublin, 1751.

—— *The great importance and necessity of increasing tillage.* Dublin, 1754.

Dean, G.A. *A treatise on the land tenure of Ireland, and the influences which retard its progress.* London, 1869.

Dobbs, Conway E. *Some observations on the tenant right of Ulster.* Dublin, 1849.

Donnell, Robert. *Reports of one hundred and ninety cases in the Irish land courts; with preliminary tenant right chapters.* Dublin, 1876.

Doyle, Martin. *An address to the landlords of Ireland, on subjects connected with the melioration of the lower classes.* Dublin, 1831.

Dubourdieu, John. *Statistical survey of county Antrim.* Dublin, 1812.

Dufferin and Ava, first marquis of. *Irish emigration and the tenure of land in Ireland.* London, 1867.

—— *Mr. Mill's plan for the pacification of Ireland examined.* London, 1868.

Dutton, Matthew. *The law of landlord and tenants in Ireland* . . . Dublin, 1726.

[Eight Seven]. *A simple and effectual mode of providing for the labouring classes; and, at the same time promoting the landed interest.* Dublin, 1825.

—— *Prosperity of the labourer the foundation of universal prosperity.* Dublin, 1827.

—— *Practicability of a legislative measure for harmonizing the conflicting interests of agriculture.* . . Dublin, 1830.

—— *An antidote to revolution or a practical comment on the creation of privilege* . . . Dublin, 1830.

Examination of the landlords' and tenants' case, illustrated by the revaluation of the earl Romney's farms. . . . London, 1851.

Ferguson, William Dyer, and Vance, Andrew. *The tenure and improvement of land in Ireland, considered with reference to the relation of landlord and tenant and tenant right.* Dublin, 1851.

Furlong, Joseph Smith. *A treatise of the law of landlord and tenant as administered in Ireland.* Dublin, 1845.

Gould, Henry. *Thoughts on a judicious disposition of land in Ireland, calculated to promote the best interest of landlord and tenant.* . . . Dublin, 1847.

Greer, Samuel M'Curdy. *The law of landlord and tenant. Amount of compensation for tenant's improvements. To the tenant farmers of Great Britain and Ireland.* Coleraine, 1850.

Greig, William. *General report on the Gosford estates in Armagh, 1821.* Edited with an introduction by F.M.L. Thompson and D. Tierney. Belfast, 1976.

Griffith, Richard. *Practical domestic politics, being a comparative and prospective sketch of the agriculture and population of Great Britain and Ireland.* . . . London, 1819.

Hancock, John. *Observations on tenant right legislation; being an answer to a deputation of Lord Lurgan's tenantry.* Dublin, 1848.

Hancock, William Neilson. *The tenant right of Ulster, considered economically.* . . . Dublin, 1845.

—— *Report on the landlord and tenant question in Ireland, from 1860 to 1866; with an appendix, containing a report on the question from 1835.* Dublin, 1866.

—— *Report on the state of Ireland in 1874.* Dublin, 1874.

—— *Impediments to prosperity in Ireland.* Dublin, 1880.

Henderson, W.D. *The Irish land bill.* Belfast, 1870.

—— *Ulster Tenant Right, an historical and economic sketch.* Belfast, 1875.

[Hickey, William]. *The farmers guide, compiled for the use of the small farmer and cotter tenantry of Ireland.* Dublin, HMSO, 1841.

Hill, Rev George. *An historical account of the plantation of Ulster at the commencement of the seventeenth century, 1608–1620.* Belfast, 1877.

—— *An historical account of the MacDonnells of Antrim.* Belfast, 1873.

Hill, George. *Facts from Gweedore.* Facsimile reprint of fifth edition (1887) with an introduction by E. Estyn Evans. Belfast, 1971.

Hore, H.F. 'The archaeology of tenant right' in *Ulster journal of archaeology,* vi (1858), pp. 109–25.

Hoyte, Henry. *A treatise on agriculture addressed to the noblemen and gentlemen of landed property in Ireland.* Dublin, 1828.

Hutton, H.D. 'The Land Question issued as a sociological problem . . .' *Journal of the social and statistical inquiry society of Ireland,* iii (1861–3).

The Irish land question and the twelve companies in the county Londonderry. Belfast, 1869.

Kennedy, J.P. *Digest of evidence taken before her majesty's commissioners of inquiry into the state of the law and practice in respect to the occupation of land in Ireland,* 2 pts. Dublin, 1847.

Lawes, Sir John Bennet. *Exhaustion of the soil in relation to landlord's covenants and the valuation of unexhausted improvements.* London, 1870.

Lindsay, Henry. *Essay on the agriculture of the county Armagh.* Armagh, 1836.

Longfield, Montifort. *Systems of land tenure in various countries: series of essays published under the sanction of the Cobden club.* London, 1870.

McCombie, William. *The Irish land question practically considered.* Aberdeen, 1869.

McEvoy, J. *A statistical survey of County Tyrone.* Dublin, 1802.

MacLagan, Peter. *Land tenure and land culture in Ireland.* London and Edinburgh, 1869.

—— *Land culture and land tenure in Ireland. The result of observations during a recent tour. . . .* Dublin, 1869.

McKnight, James. *The Ulster tenant's claim of right; or landownership a state of trust; the Ulster Tenant-Right an original grant from the British crown, and the necessity of extending its general principle to other provinces of Ireland.* Dublin, 1848.

Montgomery, Hugh de F. *Irish land and Irish rights.* London, 1881.

A natural history of Ireland, memories and notes relating thereto, made from communications to the Dublin society. 2 vols. 1683.

O'Brien, R.B. *Parliamentary history of the Irish land question from to 1869; and the origin and results of the Ulster custom.* London, 1880.

O'Connor Morris, William. *Letters on the land question of Ireland.* London, 1870.

Ordnance survey, memoir of city and northwest liberties of Londonderry, parish of Templemore. Dublin, 1831.

Oulton, A.N. *Index to the statutes at present in force in or affecting Ireland, from the year 1310 to 1835 inclusive.* Dublin, 1836.

Pierson, Samuel. *The present state of the tillage of Ireland considered.* Dublin, 1725.

[Pike, James]. *Statement of some causes of the disturbances in Ireland, and of the miserable state of the peasantry . . .* Dublin, 1825.

Pim, Jonathan. *Conditions and prospects of Ireland and the evils arising from the present distribution of landed property.* Dublin, 1848.

—— *The land question in Ireland: suggestions for its solution by the application of mercantile principles to dealings with land.* Dublin, 1867.

Practical agriculture epitomized and adapted to the tenantry of Ireland. Dublin, 1771.

Richey, Alexander G. *The Irish land laws.* London, 1880.

Ross, David. 'The tenant right of Ulster, what it is, and how far it should be legalized and extended to the other provinces of Ireland,' *JSSI,* iii, no. 24 (July, 1863), pp. 390–404.

Russell, Robert. *Ulster tenant right for Ireland; or notes upon notes taken during a visit to Ireland in 1868*. London and Edinburgh, 1870.

Scully, Vincent. *The Irish land question with practical plans for an improved land tenure and a new land system*. Dublin, 1851.

Seebohm, Frederick. [*The Land Question. In three parts*]. Dublin, 1869.

Suttie, Sir George Grant. *On land tenure and the cultivation of the soil*. Edinburgh and London, 1876.

[Trench, W.S.], *On 'Tenant-Right', or 'goodwill' within the barony of Farney, Co. of Monaghan, Ireland*. London, 1874.

Townshend, Horatio. *A view of the agricultural state of Ireland in 1815*. Cork, 1816.

Wakefield, Edward. *An account of Ireland, statistical and political*. 2 vols. London, 1812.

Wyse, Francis. *The Irish Tenant league: the immoral tendancy and entire impracticability of the measures considered, in a letter addressed to John O'Connell, M.P.* Dublin, 1850.

Young, Arthur. *A tour in Ireland, with general observations on the present state of that kingdom made in the years 1776, 1777 and 1778*. Constantia Maxwell (ed). Cambridge, 1925.

II. LATER WORKS

A. PUBLISHED WORKS

1. General

Ahamad, Aijiz. *In theory: nations, classes, literature*. London, 1992.

Appelby, Andrew. 'Agrarian capitalism or seigneurial reaction? The northwest of England, 1500–1700' in *American historical review*, lxxx (1975), pp. 574–94 .

Arthur, C.J. *Dialectics of labour: Marx and his relation to Hegel* Oxford, 1986.

Asch, Ronald G. (ed.). *Three nations – a common history? England, Scotland, Ireland, and British history c. 1600–1920*. Bochum, Germany, 1993.

Aston, T.H. and Philpin, C.H.E. (eds). *The Brenner debate: Agrarian class structure and economic development in preindustrial Europe*. London, 1985.

Baker, A.R.H. and Butlin, R.A. (eds). *Studies of field systems of the British Isles*. Cambridge, 1973.

Bakhtin, Mikhail. *The diologic imagination*. Trans. Caryl Emerson and Michael Holquist. Austin, Texas, 1981.

Balibar, Etienne. 'The basic concepts of historical materialism' in Louis Althusser and Etienne Balibar, *Reading capital* (London, 1970), pp. 209–16.

Bagot, Ann. 'Mr. Gilpin and manorial customs' in *Transactions of the Cumberland and Westmoreland antiquarian society*, lxii, (1963) pp. 67–8.

Batho, Gordon. 'Nobleman, gentlemen, and yeomen' in Joan Thirsk (ed.), *Agrarian history of England and Wales*, vol. iv, *1500–1680*. Cambridge, 1967, pp. 276–305.

Benner, Erica. *Really existing nationalisms: a post-communist view of Marx and Engels*. Oxford, 1995.

Blum, Jerome. 'English parliamentary enclosure' in *Journal of modern history*, liii (1981), pp. 477–504.

Bouch, C.M.L. and Jones, G.P. *The lake counties 1500–1830: a social and economic history.* Manchester, 1961.

Bourdieu, Pierre. *Outline of a theory of practice.* Trans. by Richard Nice. Cambridege, 1977.

Bowden, Peter. 'Agricultural prices, farm profits, and rents' Joan Thirsk (ed.), *Agrarian history of England and Wales,* vol. iv, *1500–1680.* Cambridge, 1967, pp. 593–695.

Brenner, Robert. 'The origins of capitalist development: a critique of neo-Smithian Marxism' in *new left review,* no. 109 (1977), pp. 25–92.

—— 'Economic backwardness in Eastern Europe in light of developments in the west: in Daniel Chirot (ed.), *The origins of backwardness in eastern Europe: economics and politics from the middle ages until the early twentieth century* (Berkeley, 1989), pp. 15–52.

—— 'Bourgeois revolution and transition to capitalism' in A.L. Beier, David Cannadine, and James M. Rosenheim (eds.), *The first modern society: essays in English history in honour of Lawrence Stone* (Cambridge, 1989), pp. 271–304.

—— *Merchants and revolution: commercial change, political conflict, and London's overseas traders, 1550–1653.* Cambridge, 1993.

Britnell, Richard. *The commercialization of English society, 1000–1500.* Cambridge, 1993.

Britnell, Richard and Campbell, Bruce M.S. *A commercializing economy: England 1086 to c. 1300.* Manchester, 1995.

Buchanan, R.H., et. al. (eds). *Man and his habitat: essays presented to Emyr Estyn Evans.* London, 1971.

Campbell, Mildred. *The English yeomen under Elizabeth and the early Stuarts.* New York, 1968.

Carr, David. *Time, narrative, and history.* Bloomington, Indiana, 1986.

Clay, Christopher. 'Lifeleasehold in the western counties of England, 1650–1750' in *Agricultural history review,* xxix, pt. ii (1981) pp. 83–96.

—— *Economic expansion and social change: England 1500-1700.* 2 vols. Cambridge, 1984.

—— 'Landlords and estate management in England' in Joan Thirsk (ed.) *The agrarian history of England and Wales,* v, pt. ii; *1640–1750: agrarian change* (Cambridge, 1985), pp. 214–24.

Cohen, G.A. *Karl Marx's theory of history: a defence.* Oxford, 1978.

de Vries, Jan, *The economy of Europe in an age of crisis, 1600–1750.* Cambridge, 1976.

Deane, Seamus. 'The production of cultural space in Irish writing' in *boundary 2: an international journal of literature and culture,* xxi, no. 3 (Fall, 1994), pp. 117–144.

Derrida, Jacques. *Of Grammatology.* Trans. Gayatri Chakravorty Spivak. Baltimore, 1974.

—— 'White mythology' in Jacques Derrida, *Margins of Philosophy.* Trans. with additional notes by Alan Bass (Chicago, 1982), pp. 217–18.

Descombes, Vincent. *Modern French philosophy.* Trans. L. Scott-Fox and J.M. Harding. Cambridge, 1980.

Devine, T.M. 'Social responses to agrarian 'improvement': the highland and lowland clearances in Scotland' in R.A. Houston and I.D. Whyte, (eds), *Scottish society 1500–1800.* London, 1989.

—— *The transformation of rural Scotland: social change and the agrarian economy, 1660–1815.* Edinburgh, 1994.

Dickenson, W. Croft. *Scotland from the earliest times to 1603.* Third edition, Archibald A.M. Duncan (ed.). Oxford, 1977.

Dobb, Maurice. *Studies in the development of capitalism.* London, 1946.

Dodgshon, R.A. *Land and society in early modern Scotland.* Oxford, 1981.

Foucault, Michel. *The order of things: an archaeology of the human sciences.* New York, 1970.

—— *Discipline and punish: the birth of the prison.* New York, 1977.

Giddens, Anthony. *Central problems in social theory: action, structure, and contradiction in social analysis.* Berkeley and Los Angeles, 1979.

—— *A contemporary critique of historical materialism, volume i.: Power, property, and the state.* Berkeley and Los Angeles, 1981.

Glennie, Paul. 'In search of agrarian capitalism: manorial land markets and the acquisition of land in the Lea valley c. 1450–1560' in *Continuity and change,* no. 1 (1988), pp. 11–40.

Godelier, Maurice. *The mental and the material: thought, economy, and society.* London, 1986.

Goody, J.J., Thirsk, Joan, and Thompson, E.P. (eds.). *Family and inheritance.* Cambridge, 1976.

Gottlieb, Roger. 'Feudalism and historical materialism: a critique and synthesis' in *Science and society,* xlv, no. 1 (Spring, 1984), pp. 1–37.

Grant, I.F. *The social and economic development of Scotland before 1603.* London, 1930.

Gunst, Peter. 'Agrarian systems of central and eastern Europe' in Daniel Chirot (ed.), *The origins of backwardness in eastern Europe: economic and politics from the middle ages to the early twentieth century.* Berkeley, 1989.

Harte, N.B. 'The rise of protection and the English linen trade 1690–1790' in J.B. Harte and K.G. Ponting, (eds.), *Textile history and economic history.* Manchester, 1973.

Harvey, David. *The limits to capital.* Oxford, 1982.

Harvey, P.D.A. (ed.), *The peasant land market in medieval England.* Oxford, 1984.

Hilton, Rodney (ed.). *The transition from feudalism to capitalism.* London, 1978.

Hobsbawm, Eric. *The age of capital, 1848–1875.* London, 1975.

Houston, R.A., and Whyte Ian D. (eds.). *Scottish society, 1500–1800.* London, 1989.

Hoyle, R.W. 'Lords, tenants, and tenant right in the sixteenth century: four studies' in *Northern history,* xx (1984), pp. 38–63.

—— 'An ancient and laudable custom: the definition and development of tenant right in northwestern England in the sixteenth century' in *Past & present,* no. 116 (1986), pp. 24–55.

—— 'The land-family bond in England: comment' in *Past and present* no. 156 (Feb., 1995), pp. 151–74.

Howard, Dick. *From Marx to Kant.* New York, 1993

Kerridge, E. *Agrarian problems in the sixteenth century and after.* London, 1969.

Lachman, Richard. *From manor to market: structural change in England, 1536–1640.* Madison, Wisconsin, 1987.

MacFarlane, Alan. *The origins of individualism: the family, property, and social transition.* Oxford, 1978.

—— *The culture of capitalism.* Oxford, 1987.

Marcuse, Herbert. *Hegel's ontology and the theory of historicity*, trans. and intro. by Seyla Benhabib, London, 1987.

Marx, Karl. *Pre-capitalist economic formations.* Edited with an introduction by Eric J. Hobsbawm, trans. Jack Cohen. New York, 1965.

—— *Capital: a critique of political economy.* Volume 1. Intro. by Ernest Mandel, trans. by Ben Fowlkes. New York, 1977.

—— *Capital: a critique of political economy.* Volume 3. *The process of production as a whole.* Edited by Frederick Engels. New York, 1967.

Marx, Karl and Engels, Frederick. *The German ideology: part one with selections from parts two and three and supplementary texts.* Edited with an introduction by C.J. Arthur. New York, 1970.

Mudimbe, V.Y. *The invention of Africa: gnosis, philosophy, and the order of knowledge.* Indiana, 1988.

Munshi, Surendra. 'Social formation and the problem of change' in *Science and society*, lv, no. 2 (Summer 1991).

Neeson, Janet M. *Commoners: common right, enclosure, and social change in England, 1700–1820.* Cambridge, 1993.

Nicholson, J. and Burn, R. *The history and antiquities of the countries of Westmoreland and Cumberland. 1777*, reprinted. Yorkshire, 1976.

Norris, Christopher. *Deconstruction: theory and practice.* London, 1982.

Pippin, Robert. 'Marcuse on Hegel and historicity' in *Philosophical forum*, xxv, no. 3 (Spring, 1985), pp. 183–4.

Pirenne, Henri. *The economic and social history of medieval Europe.* New York, 1937.

Polanyi, Karl. *The great transformation: the political and economic origins of our time.* Boston, 1944.

Quilligan, Maureen. *The language of allegory: defining the genre.* Ithaca, 1979.

Roth, Michael. *Knowing and history: appropriations of Hegel in twentieth century France.* Ithaca, 1988.

Sanderson, Margaret. *Scottish rural society in the sixteenth century.* Edinburgh, 1982.

Scott, J.C. *The moral economy of the peasant: rebellion and subsistence in Southeast Asia.* New Haven, 1976.

Searle, C.E. 'Custom, class conflict, agrarian capitalism: the Cumbrian customary economy in the eighteenth century' in *Past and present*, no. 110 (1986), pp. 106–133.

Shanin, Teodor. *Late Marx and the Russian road: Marx and 'the peripheries of capitalism'.* London, 1993.

Smith, Richard (ed.). *Land, kinship, and lifecycle.* Cambridge, 1984.

Smith, Tony. *The logic of Marx's Capital: replies to Hegelian criticisms.* Albany, New York, 1990.

Smout, T.M. *A history of the Scottish people, 1560–1830*. Edinburgh, 1969.

Sreenivasan, Govind. 'The land-family bond at Earls Colne, Essex, 1550–1650' in *Past and present*, no. 131 (May, 1991).

—— 'The land-family bond in England: reply' in *Past and present* no. 156 (Feb., 1995), pp. 174–188.

Stone, Lawrence. *The crisis of the aristocracy, 1558–1641*. Oxford, 1964.

Tawney, R.H. *The agrarian problem in the sixteenth century*. London, 1912.

Thirsk, Joan, (ed.). *The agrarian history of England and Wales. Volume iv: 1500–1640*. Cambridge, 1967.

—— *The agrarian history of England and Wales. Volume v: 1640–1750*. 2 vols. Cambridge, 1985.

Thompson, E.P. *Whigs and hunters: the origins of the Black Act*. New York, 1975.

—— 'The grid of inheritance: a comment,' in J. Goody, J. Thirsk, and E.P. Thompson (eds.), *Family and inheritance* (Cambridge, 1976), pp. 328–60.

—— 'Eighteenth-century English society: class struggle without class?' in *Social history*, x, no. 2 (1978), pp. 133–165.

—— 'Custom, law, and common right' in *Customs in common: studies in traditional popular culture* (New York, 1991), pp. 97–184.

Tupling, G.H. *The economic history of Rossendale*. Chetham, 1927.

Volosinov, V.N. *Marxism and the philosophy of language*. Trans. by Ladislave Matejka and I.R. Titunik. London, 1986.

Wallerstein, Immanuel. *The modern world system, ii: mercantilism and the consolidation of the European world-economy, 1600–1750*. London, 1980.

Watts, S.J. 'Tenant-right in early seventeenth-century Northumberland' in *Northern history*, vi (1971), pp. 64–87.

Whyte, Ian D. *Agriculture and society in seventeenth-century Scotland*. Edinburgh, 1979.

—— 'Written leases and their impact on Scottish agriculture in the seventeenth century' in *Agricultural history review*, xxvii, pt. i (1979), pp. 1–9.

Whyte, Ian D. and Whyte, Kathleen. *The changing Scottish landscape, 1500–1600*. London, 1991.

Williams, Penry. 'The northern borderland under the early Stuarts,' in H.E. Bell and R.L. Ollard (eds.). *Historical essays, 1600–1750, presented to David Ogg* (New York, 1963), pp. 1–17.

Wordie, J.R. 'The chronology of English enclosure, 1500–1914' in *Economic history review*, xxxvi, no. 4 (Nov., 1983), pp. 483–505.

2. Works Concerning Ireland

Aalen, F.H.A. *Man and the landscape of Ireland*. London, 1978.

Anderson, James. 'The decay and breakup of the rundale system in the Baroney of Tirhugh' in *Donegal annual*, vi, no. 1 (1964), pp. 1–42.

Andrews, J.H. *A paper landscape: the ordnance survey in nineteenth-century Ireland*. Oxford, 1975.

Armstrong, D.L. *An economic history of agriculture in Northern Ireland, 1850–1900*. Oxford, 1989.

Bartlett, Thomas J. *The fall and rise of the Irish nation: the Catholic question 1690–1830.* Dublin, 1992.

Bartlett, Thomas J. and Hayton, W.D. (eds). *Penal era and golden age: essays in Irish history, 1690–1800.* 2nd edition, Belfast, 1977.

Beckett, J.C. and Moody, T.W. (eds). *Ulster since 1800: a political and economic survey.* London, 1954.

Bell, Jonathan and Mervyn Watson. *Irish farming: implements and techniques, 1750–1900.* Edinburgh, 1986.

Black, R.D.C. *The Statistical and social inquiry society of Ireland, centenary volume 1847–1947.* Dublin, 1947.

—— *Economic thought and the Irish question 1817–70.* Cambridge, 1960.

—— *A catalogue of pamphlets on Irish economic subjects 1750–1900 in Irish libraries.* Belfast, 1969.

Bottigheimer, K. *English money and Irish land: the 'adventurers' in the Cromwellian settlement of Ireland.* Oxford, 1971.

Boyd, H.A. 'Dean William Henry's topographical descriptions of the coast of county Antrim and North Down, c. 1740,' in *Glynns*, ii (1974).

Boylan, T.A. and Foley, T.P. *Political economy and colonial Ireland: the propogation and ideological function of economic discourse in the nineteenth century.* London, 1992.

Brady, Ciaran and Gillespie, Raymond G. (eds). *Natives and newcomers: The making of Irish colonial society 1534–1641.* Dublin, 1986.

Brady, J.C. 'Legal developments, 1801–79' in W.E. Vaughan (ed.), *A new history of Ireland, v: Ireland under the union, 1, 1801–1870* (Oxford, 1989), pp. 451–81.

Buchanan, R.H. 'Common fields and enclosures: an eighteenth-century example from Lecale, County Down' in *Ulster folklife*, xv (1970), pp. 99–118.

—— 'Historical geography of Ireland pre 1700' in *Irish geography*, xvii, suppl (1984), pp. 129–166.

Bull, Philip. *Land, politics, and nationalism: a study of the Irish land question.* Dublin, 1996.

Butlin, R.A. 'Land and people, c. 1600' in T.W. Moody, F.X. Martin, and F.J. Byrne (eds.) *A new history of Ireland, iii: early modern Ireland 1534–1691* (Oxford, 1976), pp. 142–67.

Canny, Nicholas. 'Hugh O'Neill, Earl of Tyrone, and the changing face of gaelic Ulster' in *Studia Hibernica*, x (1970), pp. 7–35.

—— 'Migration and opportunity: Britain, Ireland, and the new world' in *I.E.S.H.*, xii (1985), pp. 7–32.

—— 'A reply,' in *I.E.S.H.*, xiii (1986).

Canny, Nicholas, et. al. (eds). *The westward enterprise: English activities in Ireland, the Atlantic, and America 1480–1650.* Liverpool, 1978.

Clarke. Aidan. 'The Irish economy, 1600–1660' in T.W. Moody, F.X. Martin, and F.J. Byrne (eds.) *A new history of Ireland, iii: early modern Ireland 1534–1691* (Oxford, 1976), pp. 142–67.

Comerford, R.V. 'Ireland 1850–1870: post-famine and mid-Victorian' in W.E. Vaughan (ed.), *A new history of Ireland, v: Ireland under the union, 1, 1801–1870* (Oxford, 1989), pp. 372–95.

—— 'Churchmen, tenants, and independent opposition, 1850–56' in W.E. Vaughan (ed.), *A new history of Ireland, v: Ireland under the union, 1, 1801–1870* (Oxford, 1989), pp. 396–414.

—— 'Gladstone's first Irish enterprise, 1864–70' in W.E. Vaughan (ed.), *A new history of Ireland, v: Ireland under the union, 1, 1801–1870* (Oxford, 1989), pp. 396–414.

Connell, K.H. 'The colonization of waste land in Ireland, 1780–1845' in *Economic history review,* second series, iii (1950), pp. 44–71.

—— *The population of Ireland, 1750–1845.* Oxford, 1950.

Connolly, Sean. *Religion, law, and power: the making of Protestant Ireland 1660–1760.* Oxford, 1992.

Cox, J.M. 'Local economics in the Clogher valley' in *Clogher record,* vii, no. 2 (1970), pp. 236–250.

Crawford, W.H. 'The rise of the linen industry' in L.M. Cullen, (ed.), *The formation of the Irish economy* Cork, 1969).

—— 'The origins of the linen industry in north Armagh and the Lagan valley' in *Ulster folklife,* xvii (1971), pp. 42–51.

—— 'Ulster landowners and the linen industry' in T.J. Ward and R.G. Wilson, (eds.), *Land and industry: the landed estate and the industrial revolution* (New York, 1971), pp. 117–144.

—— *Domestic industry in Ireland: the experience of the linen industry.* Dublin, 1972.

—— 'Landlord-tenant relations in Ulster, 1609–1820' in *I.E.S.H.,* ii (1975), pp. 5–21.

—— 'The case of John McNeelans of Shanoney, 1773' in *Ulster folklife,* xxiii (1977), pp. 92–96.

—— 'The Murray of Broughton estate, 1730' in *Donegal annual,* xii (1977)..

—— 'Change in Ulster in the late eighteenth century' in Thomas Bartlett and David Heyton (eds.), *Penal era and golden age: essays in Irish history, 1690–1800* (Belfast, 1979), pp. 186–203.

—— 'The Ulster Irish in the eighteenth century' in *Ulster folklife,* xxviii (1982), pp. 24–32.

—— 'Ulster as a mirror of the two societies' in David Dickson and T.M. Devine, (ed.), *Ireland and Scotland, 1600–1850: parallels and contrasts in economic and social development* (Edinburgh, 1983), pp. 43–62.

—— 'The political economy of linen' in Ciaran Brady, Mary O'Dowd, and Brian Walker, (eds.) *Ulster: an illustrated history* (London, 1989), pp. 134–58.

—— 'The significance of landed estates in Ulster 1600–1820' in *I.E.S.H.,* xvii (1990), pp. 44–61.

Crawford, W.H., and David Trainor (eds). *Aspects of Irish social history.* Belfast, 1969.

Crotty, Raymond. *Irish agricultural production: its volume and structure.* Cork, 1966.

Cullen, L.M. 'Problems in the interpretation of eighteenth-century Irish economic history' in *Transactions of the Royal Historical Society,* 5th ser., xvii (1967), pp. 1–22.

—— *Anglo-Irish trade, 1660–1800.* Manchester, 1968.

—— *An economic history of Ireland since 1660.* London, 1972.

—— *The emergence of modern Ireland.* London, 1981.

Cullen, L.M. and Furet, F. (eds). *Franco-Irish symposium on social and economic history.* Dublin, 1977.

Cullen, L.M. and Smout, T.C. (eds). *Comparative aspects of Scottish and Irish social and economic history.* Edinburgh, 1976.

Cunningham, J.B. 'William Conolly's Ballyshannon estate, 1718–26' in *Donegal annual*, xxiii (1981), pp. 27–44.

Currie, E.A. 'Fining down the rents: management of the Conolly estates in Ireland, 1734–1800' in *Derriana*, ii (1979), pp. 25–38.

—— 'Land tenure, enclosure, and field patterns in county Londonderry in the eighteenth and nineteenth centuries' in *Irish geography*, ix (1976), pp. 50–62.

—— 'Landscape development in south Derry in the eighteenth century' in *Studia Hibernica*, no. 19 (1979), pp. 87–101.

Curl, James Stevens. *The Londonderry plantation 1609–1914: the history, architecture, and planning of the estates of the City of London and its livery companies in Ulster.* Chichester, 1986.

Denman, D.R. *Tenant right valuation in history and practice.* Cambridge, 1942.

Devine, T.M. and Dickson, David (eds). *Ireland and Scotland, 1600–1850: parallels and contrasts in economic and social development.* Edinburgh, 1983.

Dickson, David. *New foundations: Ireland 1660–1800.* Dublin, 1986.

Dewey, Clive. 'Celtic agrarian legislation and celtic revival: historicist implications of Gladstone's Irish and Scottish land acts, 1870–1886' in *Past & present*, no. 64 (Aug., 1974), pp. 30–70.

Dickson, R.J. *Ulster emigration to colonial America, 1718–75.* London, 1966.

Donnelly, James S., Jr. *The land and the people of nineteenth-century Cork: the rural economy and the land question.* Boston, 1975.

—— 'Landlords and tenants,' in W.E. Vaughan (ed.), *A new history of Ireland, v: Ireland under the union, 1, 1801–1870* (Oxford, 1989), pp. 332–49.

—— 'A famine in politics' in W. E. Vaughan (ed.), *A new history of Ireland, v: Ireland under the union, 1, 1801–1870* (Oxford, 1989), pp. 357–71.

Dowling, Alan. 'The genesis of Deasy's act' in *Northern Ireland legal quarterly*, xl, no. 1 (Spring, 1989), pp. 53–61.

Duffy, P.J. 'The territorial organization of Gaelic landownership and its transformation in County Monaghan 1591–1640' in *Ir. Geogr.*, xiv (1980), pp. 1–26.

—— 'The evolution of estate properties in south Ulster 1600–1900' in William J. Smyth and Kevin Whelan (eds), *Common ground: essays on the historical geography of Ireland presented to T. Jones Hughes* (Cork, 1988), pp. 84–109.

Dunlop, Eull, (ed.). *Buick's Ahoghill: A filial account (1901) of seceders in the mid-Antrim village. . . .* Maghera, 1987.

Dunne, Tom. *Maria Edgeworth and the colonial mind.* Cork, 1984.

Ellis, Stephen G. *Tudor Ireland: crown, community, and the conflict of cultures 1470–1603.* Essex, 1985.

Evans, E.E. 'Some Survivals of the Irish openfield system' in *Geography*, xxiv (1939), pp. 24–36.

Freeman, T.W. 'Land and people, c. 1841' in in W.E. Vaughan (ed.), *A new history of Ireland, v: Ireland under the union, 1, 1801–1870* (Oxford, 1989), pp. 242–71.

Foster, Roy F. *Modern Ireland: 1600–1972*. New York, 1988.

Gill, Conrad. *The rise of the Irish linen industry*. Oxford, 1925.

Gillespie, Raymond G. *Colonial Ulster: the settlement of east Ulster 1600–1641*. Cork, 1985.

—— (ed). *Settlement and survival on an Ulster estate: the Brownlow leasebook 1667–1711*. Belfast, 1988.

—— 'The small towns of Ulster' in *Ulster folklife*, xxxvi (1990), pp. 23–31.

—— *The transformation of the Irish economy, 1550–1700*. Studies in Irish economic and social history, 6. Dundalk, 1991.

Guinnane, Timothy, and Miller, Ronald I. 'Bonds without bondsmen: tenant right in nineteenth-century Ireland' in *Journal of economic history*, lxi, no. 1 (March, 1996), pp. 113–142.

Hayes-McCoy, G.A. 'Gaelic society in Ireland in the late sixteenth century' in *Historical studies*, iv (1963), pp. 45–61.

Hazelkorn, Ellen. 'Reconsidering Marx and Engels on Ireland' in *Saothair*, ix (1983), pp. 79–88.

Hill, J. Michael. 'The origins of the Scottish plantations in Ulster to 1625: a reinterpretation' in *Journal of British studies*, xxxii (Jan., 1993) pp. 24–43.

Hogan, Patrick. 'The migration of Ulster Catholics to Connaught, 1795–6' in *Seanchas Ardmacha*, ix, no. 2 (1979).

Hoppen, Theodore. *Elections, politics, and society in Ireland, 1832–1885*. Oxford, 1984.

—— *Ireland since 1800: conflict and conformity*. London and New York, 1989.

Hunter, R.J. 'Towns in the Ulster plantation' in *Studia Hibernica*, xi (1971), pp. 40–79.

James, Francis Godwin. *Ireland in the empire 1688–1770: a history of Ireland from the Williamite wars to the eve of the American revolution*. Harvard, 1973.

Johnson, J.H. 'The distribution of emigration in the decade before the great famine' in *Irish geography*, xxi (1988), pp. 78–87.

Johnston, John. 'Settlement on a plantation estate: the Balfour rentals of 1632 and 1636' in *Clogher record*, xii, no. 1 (1985), p. 92–109.

Kennedy, Liam. 'The rural economy, 1820–1914' in Kennedy, Liam and P. Ollerenshaw (eds). *An economic history of Ulster 1820–1940*. Manchester, 1985.

—— 'Farm succession in modern Ireland: elements of a theory of inheritance' in *Economic history review*, xliv, no. 3 (1991), pp. 477–99.

Kirkham, Graham. 'Economic diversification in a marginal economy: A case study' in Peter Roebuck, (ed.), *Plantation to partition*, pp. 64–81.

Lucas, A.T. *Cattle in ancient Ireland*. Kilkenny, 1989.

Lyons, F.S.L. and Hawkins, R.A.J. (eds.) *Ireland under the union: varieties of tension*. Oxford, 1980.

Macafee, William. 'The colonization of the Maghera region of south Derry' in *Ulster Folklife*, xxiii (1977), pp. 70–91.

MacCarthy-Morrogh, M. *The Munster plantation: English migration to southern Ireland 1583–1641*. Oxford, 1986.

McCourt, Desmond. 'The rundale system in Donegal: its distribution and decline' in *Donegal annual*, iii, no. 1 (1954), pp. 47–60.

—— 'Infield and outfield in Ireland' in *Economic history review*, vii, no. 3 (2nd series, 1954), pp. 369–76.

—— 'Surviving open field in county Derry' in *Ulster Folklife*, iv (1958), pp. 24–28.

—— 'Traditions of rundale in and around the Sperrin mountains' in *Ulster journal of archaeology*, xvi (1963), pp. 67–84.

—— 'The use of oral tradition in Irish historical geography' in *Irish geography*, iv (1972), pp. 394–410.

MacDonagh, Oliver. *States of mind: a study of Anglo-Irish conflict 1780–1980*. London, 1983.

——'The economy and society, 1830–1845' in W.E. Vaughan (ed.), *A new history of Ireland, v: Ireland under the union, 1. 1801–1870* (Oxford, 1989), pp. 218–41.

Maguire, W.A. *The Downshire estates in Ireland, 1801–45: the managemant of Irish landed estates in the early nineteenth century*. Oxford, 1972.

—— (ed). *Letters of a great Irish landlord: a selection from the estate correspondence of the third Marquess of Downshire, 1809–45*. Belfast, 1974.

Malcomson, A.P.W. 'Absenteeism in eighteenth-century Ireland' in *IESH*, i (1974), pp. 15–35.

—— 'The politics of "natural right": The Abercorn family and Strabane borough, 1692–1800' in G.A. Hayes (ed), *Historical Studies*, x (1976), pp. 43–87.

—— *John Foster: the politics of the Anglo-Irish ascendency*. Oxford, 1978.

Marx, Karl and Engels, Frederick. *Ireland and the Irish question*. R. Dixon (ed). New York, 1972.

Masterson, Harold T. 'Land use patterns and farming practice in county Fermanagh 1609–1845' in *Clogher record*, vii, no. 1 (1969), pp. 56–88.

Miller, Kerby A. *Emigrants and exiles: Ireland and the Irish exodus to North America*. Oxford and New York, 1985.

Mitcheson, Rosalind and Peter Roebuck (eds). *Economy and society in Scotland and Ireland 1500–1939*. Edinburgh, 1988.

Mokyr, Joel. 'Uncertainty in prefamine agriculture' in T.M. Devine and David Dickson (eds), *Ireland and Scotland, 1600–1850*. Edinburgh, 1983, pp. 89–101.

—— 'Irish history with the potato' in *I.E.S.H.*, viii (1981), pp. 3–29.

—— *Why Ireland starved: a quantitative and analytical history of the Irish economy, 1800–50*. Boston, 1983.

Moody, T.W. *The Londonderry plantation, 1609–1641: the City of London and the plantation in Ulster*. Belfast, 1939.

—— 'The treatment of the native population under the plantation of Ulster' in *Irish historical studies*, i, no. 1 (1939), pp. 59–63.

Nicholls, Kenneth W. *Land, law, and society in sixteenth century Ireland*. Dublin, 1976.

O'Dowd, Mary. 'Land and inheritance in early modern Sligo' in *I.E.S.H.*, x (1983), pp. 5–18.

—— 'Gaelic economy and society,' in Ciaran Brady and Raymond G. Gillespie (eds). *Natives and newcomers: The making of Irish colonial society 1534–1641* (Dublin, 1986), pp. 120–147.

O'Flanagan, Patrick, Ferguson, Paul and Whelan, Kevin (eds). *Rural Ireland: modernization and change 1600–1900*. Cork, 1987.

Ó Gráda Cormac. *Ireland before and after the famine: explorations in economic history, 1800–1925*. Manchester, 1988.

—— 'Irish agricultural history: recent research' in *Agricultural history review*, xxxviii, pt ii (1989), pp. 165–173.

—— 'Poverty, population, and agriculture' in W.E. Vaughan (ed.), *A new history of Ireland, v: Ireland under the union, 1, 1801–1870* (Oxford, 1989), pp. 108-36.

—— *Ireland: a new economic history, 1780–1939*. Oxford, 1994.

O'Mearain, Lorcan. 'The Bath estate 1700–1777' in *Clogher record*, vi, no. 2 (1967), pp. 333–360.

—— 'The Bath estate 1777–1800' in *Clogher record*, vi, no. 3 (1968), pp. 555–573.

O'Neill, Kevin. *Family and farm in pre-famine Ireland: the parish of Killashandra*. Madison, Wisconsin, 1984.

O'Tuathaigh, Gearoid. *Ireland before the famine, 1798–1848*. Dublin, 1972.

Ohlmeyer Jane, (ed.). *Ireland from independence to occupation, 1641–1660*. London, 1995.

Pawlisch, Hans S. *Sir John Davies and the conquest of Ireland: a study in legal imperialism*. Cambridge, 1985.

Perceval-Maxwell, Michael. *The Scottish migration to Ulster in the reign of James I*. London, 1973.

—— *The outbreak of the Irish rebellion of 1641*. Dublin, 1994.

Power, Thomas. *Land, politics, and society in eighteenth-century Tipperary*. Oxford, 1993.

Pomphret, John E. *The struggle for land in Ireland 1800–1923*. Princeton, 1930.

Quinn, D.B. 'William Montgomery and the decription of the Ards, 1683' in *Irish booklore*, ii (1972), pp. 29–45.

Robinson, Olive. 'The London companies and tenant right in nineteenth-century Ireland' in *Agricultural history review*, xviii (1970), pp. 54–63.

Robinson, Philip. 'Irish settlement in Tyrone before the Ulster plantation' in *Ulster folklife*, xxii (1976), pp. 59–69.

—— 'The spread of hedged enclosure in Ulster' in *Ulster folklife*, xxiii (1977), pp. 57–69.

—— 'British settlement of county Tyrone, 1610–66' in *I.E.S.H.*, v (1978), pp. 5–26.

—— 'Urbanization in northwest Ulster, 1609–70' in *Irish geography*, xv (1982), pp. 35–50.

—— *The plantation of Ulster: British settlement in an Irish landscape, 1600–1670*. Dublin and New York, 1984.

Roebuck, Peter. 'The making of an Ulster great estate: the Chichesters, 1599–1648' in *Proceedings of the Royal Irish Academy*, lxxix, sect C, no. 1 (1979), pp. 1–25.

—— (ed). *Plantation to partition: essays in Ulster history in honour of J.L. McCracken*. Belfast, 1981.

Rutherford, J.H. 'The plantation of the Lagan and its economy 1600–1900' in *Donegal annual* (1959), pp. 122–140.

Simms, J.G. 'Donegal in the Ulster plantation' in *Irish geography*, iv (1972), pp. 386–93.

Smyth, William J. and Kevin Whelan (eds). *Common ground: essays on the historical geography of Ireland presented to T. Jones Hughes.* Cork, 1988.

Solow, Barbara L. *The land question and the Irish economy, 1870–1903.* Cambridge, 1971.

Steele, E.D. 'J.S. Mill and the Irish question: the principles of political economy 1848–1865' in *The historical journal* xii, no. 2 (1970), pp. 216–236.

—— 'J.S. Mill and the Irish question: reform, and the integrity of the empire, 1865–1870' in *The historical journal* xii, no. 3 (1970), pp. 425–427.

—— *Irish land and British politics: tenant right and nationality 1865–70.* Cambridge, 1974.

Stock, Leo Francis (ed.), *Proceedings and debates of the British parliaments respecting North America,* 5 vols. Washington, 1924–1941.

Truxes, Thomas M. *Irish-American trade, 1660–1783.* Cambridge, 1988.

Turner, Michael. *After the famine: Irish agriculture 1850–1914.* Cambridge, 1996.

Vaughan, W.E. *Landlords and tenants in Ireland 1848–1904.* Studies in Irish economic and social history, no. 2. Dundalk, 1984.

—— 'Ireland, c. 1870' in W.E. Vaughan (ed.), *A new history of Ireland, v: Ireland under the union, 1, 1801–1870* (Oxford, 1989), pp. 726–801.

—— *Landlords & tenants in mid-victorian Ireland, 1848–1904.* Oxford, 1994.

Whelan, Kevin. 'Settlement and society in eighteenth-century Ireland' in Gerald Dawe and John Wilson Foster (eds.) *The poet's place: Ulster literature and society* (Belfast, 1991), pp. 45–62.

Whyte, J.H. *The Tenant League and Irish politics in the 1850s.* Dundalk, 1963.

Wright, Frank. *Northern Ireland: a comparative analysis.* Dublin, 1987.

—— *Two lands on one soil: Ulster politics before home rule.* Dublin, 1996.

B. UNPUBLISHED THESES AND DISSERTATIONS

Bartolovich, Crystal Lynn. 'Boundary disputes: surveying, agrarian capital and English renaissance texts.' PhD. Dissertation, Emory University, 1993.

Buchanan, R.H. 'The Barony of Lecale, County Down.' PhD. dissertation. Queen's University of Belfast, 1958.

Crawford, W.H. 'Economy and society in eighteenth-century Ulster.' PhD. dissertation. Queen's University of Belfast, 1983.

Currie, Edward A. 'The evolution of cultural landscapes in the northwest and southeast regions of County Derry in the eighteenth and nineteenth centuries with particular reference to the Rae and Moyola valleys.' PhD. dissertation. Queen's University of Belfast, 1981.

Dickson, David. 'An economic history of the Cork region in the eighteenth century.' PhD. dissertation. Trinity College Dublin, 1977.

Dowling, Alan. 'The landlord and tenant law amendment act (Ireland) 1860.' PhD. dissertation, Queen's University of Belfast, 1985.

Dowling, Martin W. 'The Abercorn estate: economy and society in northwest Ulster, 1745–1800.' M.A. thesis. University of Wisconsin-Madison, 1986.

Gourley, Robert. 'The social and economic history of the Gosford estates, 1610–1876.' M.S.Sc. thesis. Queen's University of Belfast, 1974.

Hunter, R.J. 'The Ulster plantation in the counties Armagh and Cavan 1608–41.' M.Litt. thesis. Trinity College Dublin, 1969.

Johnston, John I.D. 'The Clogher valley as a social and economic region in the eighteenth and nineteenth centuries.' M.Litt. thesis. Trinity College Dublin, 1974.

Johnston, J.D. 'The plantation of County Fermanagh 1610–41: an archaeological and historical survey.' M.A. thesis. Queen's University of Belfast, 1976.

Kennedy, Brian. 'The struggle for tenant right in Ulster 1829–1850.' M.A. thesis. Queen's University of Belfast, 1943.

Kirkpatrick, Robert W. 'Landed estates in mid-Ulster and the Irish land war, 1879–85.' PhD. dissertation. Trinity College Dublin, 1977.

McCabe, Desmond. 'Law, conflict, and social order: county Mayo 1820–1845.' PhD. Dissertation. University College Dublin, 1991.

MacCarthy, Robert B. 'The estates of Trinity College Dublin in the nineteenth century.' PhD. dissertation. Trinity College Dublin, 1982.

McCourt, Desmond. 'The rundale system in Ireland: a study of its geographical distribution and social relations.' PhD. dissertation. Queen's University of Belfast, 1950.

Robinson, Olive. 'The economic significance of the London companies as landlords during the period 1800–1870.' PhD. dissertation. Queen's University of Belfast, 1957.

Thompson, Francis. 'Land and politics in Ulster, 1868–86.' PhD. dissertation. Queen's University of Belfast, 1982.

Vaughan, William E. 'A study of landlord and tenant relations between the famine and the land war, 1850–78.' PhD. dissertation. Trinity College Dublin, 1974.

Index

Abercorn estate (Tyrone and Donegal) 3,
6, 24, 64, 71, 86, 95, 98, 123, 127, 136,
143–4, 147–8, 150–1, 154, 189, 191,
193, 201, 204, 212, 214–5, 220–1,
241–2, 245, 249, 254, 280, 288
Abercorn, eighth earl of 3, 6, 71–6, 91,
123, 130, 136, 142, 145, 148, 150, 212,
249, 253–5, 301, 305, 308
ninth earl of 91–2, 142, 201, 246, 305–6
Absenteeism 124, 289, 325
Acheson estate (Co. Cavan) 182
Acts of Parliament
Act of Union (1801) 269, 329
Caldwell's Act (1860) 281–2
Catholic Relief Act (1793) 90
Civil Bills Courts (Ireland) 250
Deasy's Act (1860) 281, 290, 296–300,
310, 314, 326, 329, 331–2
Land Act (1870) 296, 298–300, 302–5,
310, 314, 316, 322, 326, 328, 330–2
Land Act (1881) 332
Linen Bounty Act (1745) 140
Navigation Acts 140
Octennial Act (1768) 89–90
Poor Law (1838) 270
Representation of the People Act
(1851) 275
Addi, Thomas 212
Agents 3–4, 6, 30, 56, 59–60, 63, 72–3,
76–8, 80, 85, 92, 94, 97–8, 119, 125,
134, 136, 146, 152–3, 156, 158, 161,
178–9, 181–4, 189–90, 192–4, 197–201,
204, 207, 210, 212–5, 217–22, 241–3,
246–7, 249, 251–2, 255–7, 259, 269,
272, 285–6, 304, 306, 308, 310–14,
317–8, 320–3
Agrarian capitalism 7–14, 16–19, 27–8, 32,
118, 120, 329, 331–2
Agrarian violence 151, 200, 214–7, 246–7,
251, 254, 256, 258, 273–4, 320–1, 323
Alcock, John 209
Alexander, Leslie 67, 86

America 77, 86, 127–132, 139–40, 143–4,
212, 219, 222, 245, 255, 257, 272
American Indians 29
Anderson family 309
David 283
Andrews, John 224, 255
Anglesey estate (Co. Louth) 59, 64, 77–80,
84, 87–8, 133–4, 141, 145, 149, 155,
179, 181, 189–90, 198, 204–5, 212,
214, 219, 242, 246, 248, 272, 286–7,
317, 319–20
marquis of (see also Uxbridge, earl of)
78–80, 84–5, 87, 220
Anne, Queen 248
Annesley estate (Co. Down) 153
Antrim 23, 54, 60, 82, 85, 92, 95, 123, 128,
147, 155, 179, 204, 224, 249, 254–5,
285, 287–8, 305–6
town 219
earl of 194, 202, 224, 287
glens 185, 194, 205
Ardglass (Co. Down) 155
Ardmalin (Co. Donegal) 307
Ards peninsula (Co. Down) 145, 178, 183,
185
Ardstraw (Co. Tyrone) 91
Argyllshire (Scotland) 120
Armagh 48, 50, 52, 54, 60, 65, 76, 80, 93,
95, 123, 127, 129–30, 134, 141, 148,
153, 178, 180, 184–5, 207, 213, 219,
288
archbishop of 180, 185
Armstrong, George 318
John 30
William 80–1
Arrears of rent (see Debts)
Ashe, Thomas 185
Aughnacloy (Co. Tyrone) 131, 244
Australia 225, 244

Babington, Andrew 70
Backfence (Co. Tyrone) 137

Backlands (Co. Donegal) 199
Bagenal, Nicholas 30
Baily, John 205
Bakhtin, Mikhail 276
Balfour estate (Co. Fermanagh) 50, 76, 96–7, 188, 203
Ballinamore (Co. Cavan) 192
Ballycastle (Co. Antrim) 155
Ballyclare (Co. Antrim) 147
Ballyculter (Co. Down) 215
Ballykelly (Co. Londonderry) 219
Ballymacrea (Co. Antrim) 85
Ballymagorry (Co. Tyrone) 72
Ballymore (Co. Londonderry) 219
Ballynascreen (Co. Londonderry) 95
Ballyshannon (Co. Donegal) 55, 147, 208
Ballytibbert (Co. Antrim) 249
Ballywillan (Co. Antrim) 205
Banagh barony (Co. Donegal) 71
Banbridge (Co. Down) 24
Bangor (Co. Down) 59, 309
Banks 244–6
Bann river 23, 65, 99, 135, 153
Bantry, earl of 80
Baronscourt (Co. Fermanagh) 86
Barrett, Dacre 56, 59, 76, 130–1, 141–2
Barrett-Lennard estate (Co. Monaghan) 30, 58–9, 64, 76–7, 81, 92, 97, 99, 125, 128, 134–6, 142–3, 145, 155, 207–8, 219, 319–20
   Thomas 92, 133, 320
Barry, Judge 300
Bartlett, Thomas 90, 96
Bath estate (Co. Monaghan) 94
Batho, Gordon 12
Baxter, R.D. 277
Bayly, Edward 134
   Nicholas 31, 204
Bealalt (Co. Donegal) 189
Beer, Thomas 287
Belfast 55, 92, 146, 206, 225, 254, 272, 299, 312
Belgium 140
Bell, David 317
Bellaghy (Co. Londonderry) 66, 192
Belleghan (Co. Louth) 87
Belmore estate (Co. Tyrone) 91, 306
   earl of 91, 206–7, 245–6, 323
Belturbet (Co. Cavan) 179
Benagh (Co. Louth) 79–80
Benburb (Co. Tyrone) 323

Beresford family 91, 129
Bessborough Commission 276, 298, 300–1, 304, 322
Bicheno, J.E. 271
Black, R.D.C. 296
Blacker, George 51
   William 91, 182, 215, 247, 255, 271, 308, 318
Blackwood, James 24, 309
Bligh, Thomas 125
Blundell estate (Co. Down) (see also Downshire estate) 63–4
   Henry 136, 288, 321
Bodley, Josias 180
Bogs 190–202, 205–9, 242, 271
Booleying 177
Boylagh barony (Co. Donegal) 71
Boyle, John 219
Boys, Abraham 212
Brackaslievegallion (Co. Londonderry) 95
Brady, Ciaran 20
   J.C. 284
Brenner, Robert 8, 12, 19–20
Brogan, Augustine 99
Brooke, William 178
Brookeborough estate (Co. Fermangh) 306, 311–12
   Lord Victor 311–12
Broughton, James Murray of 124, 126, 183
Brown, John 24
   Rev. John 276
   Patrick 69
   Roger 68–9
   Thomas 68–9
   William (Jnr) 68
   William 68
Brownlow estate (Co. Armagh) 53, 127, 182
   Arthur 49, 51, 141, 319
Bruce, Frederick Hervey, bishop of Derry 67, 81, 85, 199–200, 302
Brush, R.C. 206–7, 323
Buchanan, R.H. 187, 192
Burroughs, Edward 271
Burrows, J. 149
Butt, Isaac 280, 294–5, 323, 331

Cairnes, J.E. 296
Caledon estate (Co. Antrim) 244
   earl of 155, 202
Calvert, Thomas 24

Campbell, Mildred 22, 327
Canny, Nicholas 15–16, 19, 121
Capital (see Money)
Capitalism 7–12, 14, 16–17, 19–20, 27–8,
  32, 83, 98–9, 118, 120, 135, 137–9,
  160, 177, 181, 197, 270, 273, 282, 290,
  292–3, 327, 329, 331–3
Captain Rock 205
Carey, Henry 90
  Tristram 73, 149
Carland, William 212
Carlingford (Co. Louth) 65, 200, 204
Carrickfergus (Co. Antrm) 128, 144
Carroll, James 61
Carrow (Co. Monaghan) 30
Carter, S. 303
Castle Stewart (Co. Tyrone) 53, 94
Castledillon (Co. Armagh) 24, 94, 134
Castledowney (Co. Donegal) 305
Castlefin (Co. Donegal) 189
Castletown estate (Co. Fermanagh) 54
Castleward estate (Co. Down) 55, 59, 215
Cavan 50, 54, 56, 76, 86–7, 99, 121, 157,
  179, 182, 185, 192, 208, 331
Charles II, King 96
Chelmsford Commission 326
Chichester, Arthur 48, 71, 203
Christian, Justice 300
Churton, Robert 12
Clachans 185
Clandeboye maps 295
Clarendon, earl of 297
Clarke, Aidan 50, 121–2
  John 78
  Mrs John 78
  Michael 125
Clay, Christopher 13, 123
Clements, John 206–7
Clerkill (Co. Down) 153
Clogher (Co. Tyrone) 76
  bishop of 314
Clones (Co. Monaghan) 30, 56, 58–9, 64,
  76, 97, 99, 125, 128, 135–6, 142, 145,
  189, 320
Clothworkers' company 23, 56, 67, 81–2,
  90, 154, 181, 185–6, 279, 302, 305–6
Coagh (Co. Tyrone) 247
Cochran, Bob 151
Coke, Edward 119, 303
Colebrook (Co. Fermanagh, see also
  Brookeborough) 311–12

Coleraine (Co. Londondery) 25, 65, 88,
  90, 325
Collins, Thomas 222
Comber (Co. Down) 275, 279
Combination 212
Cong (Co. Mayo) 203
Connacht (see also Connaught) 122
Connaught 155, 178
Connolly, Sean 20, 186
Connor, William 278–9, 293
Conolly estate (Co. Londonderry) 147,
  209, 219
  Thomas (Jnr) 66, 87, 90, 153, 189, 208–9
  Thomas (Snr) 55, 130, 219
  William 90
Conway estate (Co. Antrim) 24
Conyngham, Capt. 125
  William 85
Cookstown (Co. Tyrone) 141
Cork 57–8, 80, 98, 125, 133, 141, 289
  Earl of 135
Cottiers (see also Undertenants) 73, 119,
  148–9, 151–2, 154, 157–9, 181, 207, 241
Cowden, Thomas 24, 309
Cox, Richard 141
Crawford, J.S. 278, 328
  W.H. 17, 26, 48, 53, 141, 241
  W.S. 225, 270, 274–5, 278, 281, 289, 293,
    296, 322–3, 328
Crofton, Hugh 193, 208
Cromwell, Oliver 51, 96
Crosset, Henry 307
Cullen, L.M. 26, 123, 140
Culmore (Co. Londonderry) 29
Cunningham, John 253
  Thomas 220–1
Currie, E.A. 66, 189, 191
Customary tenures 7–11, 13, 16, 21–3, 25,
  27–8, 31, 68, 99–100, 120, 269, 298,
  327–9, 332

Dartrey estate (Co. Monaghan) 149
Davidson, Smith 307
Davies, John 15, 119
Davitt, Michael 274, 331
Dawson's Grove (Co. Monaghan) 149
Dawson, Thomas 133
de Vries, Jan 138
Deane, Seamus 329
Debts 49, 56, 89, 91, 126–8, 130–2, 143,
  149–50, 152, 157, 198, 207, 213–4,

216, 221, 242–50, 252–6, 259, 273, 278, 309, 318
Derby estate (Co. Louth) 289
Derry city 24–5, 68, 71, 88, 136, 142, 144, 147, 188, 201, 306
Derry, bishop of 24, 55, 124
Derrygoon (Co. Tyrone) 150
Devon Commission 22, 71, 98, 210–11, 213, 217, 224, 247, 252, 255, 270, 275–7, 280, 282, 288, 303–4, 322
Diamond, battle of the (Co. Armagh) 129
  Hugh 24
  Murtagh 24
Dickson, David 125
  James 283
Distraint 56, 64, 80, 145, 215, 246–8, 250, 253
Doherty, Charles 86
Donaghkeady (Co. Tyrone) 67
Donegal 52, 54–5, 59–61, 64, 71, 76, 90, 95, 118, 124, 127, 133, 146, 189, 199, 201, 208–9, 212, 246, 253, 307, 319
Donegall, Lord 130, 254
Donnell, Robert 91, 275, 294, 300, 315, 328
Doobally estate (Co. Leitrim) 93
Dormollen, Cornelius 87
Down 24, 26, 51, 54, 59–60, 63, 89, 123, 129, 136, 141–2, 145, 153, 155, 178, 180, 183, 187, 192, 204, 221, 225, 241–2, 254–5, 270, 273, 275, 278, 287, 289, 295, 309, 311, 321–2, 326
Downshire estate (Co. Down) 55, 60, 64, 145–6, 181, 213, 241–2, 251, 286, 288, 308, 321
  family 221, 288
  2nd marquis of 64
  3rd marquess of 91
  4th marquis of 221–2, 225
Drainage 224–5
Draper, Robert 134
Drapers' company 75, 82, 88, 90, 93–5, 131–2, 153, 156–9, 189–90, 198, 202, 211–14, 217, 222, 225, 245, 247, 257, 285, 300–1, 304–5, 307–9, 315, 321–2, 324
Draperstown (Co. Londonderry) 131, 160, 199, 211, 243, 276, 304–6, 322
Driver, Edward 82, 181, 279
Drogheda (Co. Louth) 58
  earl of (see also Moore) 97
Dromerode (Co. Down) 215

Dromnavaddy (Co. Down) 24
Drumot (Co. Londonderry) 222
Dublin 60, 119, 123, 137, 139–40, 142, 145, 188, 215, 249, 303, 326
Dublin Society 182
Dufferin estate 157, 244, 313
  Lady 295
  marquis of 25, 89, 225, 247, 272, 276, 279–80, 283, 289–92, 294–5, 298, 301, 306, 312–3
Duffy, Gavan 274
  P.J. 76
Dundalk (Co. Louth) 79, 83, 180, 212
Dundrum (Co. Down) 64, 321
Dungannon (Co. Tyrone) 141, 146, 250
Dungiven (Co. Londonderry) 302
Dunlop, Jack 202
Dunmurry (Co. Londonderry) 217
Dunne, Thomas 329–30
Dutton, Matthew 303, 328
Dysart (Co. Londonderry) 183

Edenderry (Co. Offaly) 136
Edgeworth, Maria 329–30
Ejectment 68, 70, 89, 135–6, 213–4, 220, 246–56, 258–9, 273, 276, 299, 312–3, 323
Elizabeth I, Queen 15, 18–19, 327
Elkin, Hugh 307
Ellis, Nicholas 136, 156, 319, 321
Enclosures 181–2, 184–5, 192, 197, 204, 209, 224–5, 285
Encumbered estates 86, 300–1
Engels, Frederick 292
England 8, 10, 12–21, 49, 57, 81, 86, 95, 97, 117, 120, 123, 126, 137–40, 182, 184–6, 188, 195, 252, 273–4, 284, 286–7, 293, 295–7, 300, 320, 327–9
  border tenant right 22–3, 327
  Cambridgeshire 12
  Essex 56
  Lancashire 140
  Leicestershire 12
  Manchester 139, 147
  Wiltshire 12
Enniskillen (Co. Fermanagh) 311
Erne river 185
Erne, Lord 223
Estate managers (see Agents)
Estates, division of 12, 75, 152–4, 156, 179, 220

Europe 12
Evans, Edward 250
Eviction (see Ejectment)
Ewing, John 68

Farming techniques 182–4, 225
Farney (Co. Monaghan) 94
Farnham, Lord 129
Farrell, Robert 309
Fenians 292, 296, 330
Ferguson, W.D. 5, 57, 281–2, 290, 317
Fermanagh 50, 53–4, 56, 60, 92, 95–6,
     121, 185, 188, 244, 311, 314
Feudalism 8–10, 22, 50, 62, 138, 282, 290,
     295
Fews (Co. Armagh) 65
Fines 12, 19, 48, 55, 59, 66–7, 153, 200, 305
Fingal (Co. Dublin) 97
Fingal, earl of 86–7, 126
Finglas (Co. Dublin) 61
Firrbreage (Co. Armagh) 180
Fishe estate (Co. Armagh) 48
Fisher, James 77
Fishmongers' company 66, 86, 90–1, 95–6,
     186, 194, 198, 201, 213, 256, 286, 318
Fivemiletown (Co. Tyrone) 309
Fletcher, Edward 256
Foljambe estate (Co. Tyrone) 131, 250,
     318
     F.E. 92
Foster, Roy 56
Foucault, Michel 177
Four Mile Water river (Co. Antrim) 180
Foyle river 64, 71, 76, 136, 142, 185
France 12, 140
Freedoms (Co. Donegal) 200
Freeholds 12, 15–16, 19, 50, 62–3, 90, 120,
     125, 127, 137, 161, 242, 273, 327

Galbraith, James 206
Galt, Robert 155
Galway 311
Galway, James 244
Gamble, John 219
Garvagh (Co. Lomdonderry) 70, 73
Gavelkind 15
George I, King 248
George II, King 248, 250
Germany 139–40, 293
Giddens, Anthony 10, 181
Gillespie, R.G. 14, 19–21, 23, 27, 137, 204

Gilpin, Isaac 327
Gladstone, W.E. 7, 296–8, 302–3, 310,
     314–5, 330–1
Glassbole (Co. Donegal) 62
Glendenning, Matthew 253
     Robert 215
Goldsmiths' company 56, 68, 86
Goodwill 1, 3, 214–6, 222, 295, 311
Gore, William 55
Gosford estate (Co. Armagh) 95, 153, 82,
     213, 308
Gould, Henry 271
Gourley, Robert 295
Great Britain 138, 140, 315
Greenore (Co. Donegal) 133
Greig, William 219, 255, 319
Griffith, Richard 181, 271, 306
Grocers' company 86, 90, 159
Grumbley, John 69
Guthrie, Francis 52
Gweedore (Co. Donegal) 225
Gwynn, Hugh 63
     James 321

Hamburg 140
Hamilton, James [I] 48, 60–1
     James (Jnr) 90–2, 129, 149, 151, 154–5,
          193, 201, 305
     James (Snr) 3–4, 72–5, 90, 127, 143–4,
          147–8, 150–1, 153–4, 192–3, 212,
          214–5, 221, 242, 250, 253–5, 280,
          301, 305
     Joseph 61
Hancock, John 272, 276–7, 304
     W.N. 272, 277, 315
Hanlon, James 79
     John 79–80
Harper, Robert 73, 149
Harrison, Thomas 80
Hart estate (Co. Donegal) 199–200
Harvests 124, 143–5
Harvey, David 284
Hatch, Henry 60, 288
Hazlett family 88
     Robert 88
Head tenants 25, 47, 49, 52, 56–7, 59–60,
     62, 67–8, 70, 74, 76–9, 82, 90, 125,
     147–9, 151, 157, 160, 190, 222, 242,
     316, 318
Hearts of Oak 254
Hearts of Steel 254

Henderson, W.D. 294, 299, 315
Henry, William 146, 152
Hertford estate (Co. Antrim) 130
Hessan, Michael 214
Hickey, William 271
Hill, George 70–1, 73
Hillsborough (Co. Down) 141
Hillsborough estate (Co. Down) 130
  Lord 141
Hobsbawm, Eric 138
Holdings, abandonment (see Leases,
  alienation)
  amalgamation of 12, 131, 214, 216,
    223, 225, 258, 299, 307, 309
  division of 72, 186, 196, 198, 206, 210,
    291, 318
  size of 12, 152–4, 158, 283
  value of 124–5, 154
Holland 138, 140
House of Commons (Ireland) 122, 139,
  161
House of Commons (UK) 140, 278, 281,
  296
House of Lords 139, 273–4
Hudson, William 250
Hughes, Jones 187
Hunter, Adam 205
  R.J. 48–9, 61, 180, 207
Huston, James 215
Hutchinson, James 147
  Robert 78–80

Improvements 6, 12–13, 29, 52–3, 55, 57,
  61–9, 71, 78, 81, 86, 88, 118–21, 129,
  132–7, 142, 159, 182, 184–5, 189,
  191–2, 199, 202–3, 207, 209, 218,
  223–5, 255–8, 271, 276–86, 288–9,
  291, 298, 302, 309, 319, 322, 324
Inishowen (Co. Donegal) 71, 199, 201
Ireland, colonization of 17–21, 49, 95–6,
  98–9, 120, 127, 133, 139
Irish Society 25, 55, 65, 67–71, 78, 82, 88,
  179, 201, 256, 324–5
Islandmagee (Co. Antrim) 306
Isle of Man 51

Jackson, George 67
  Richard 67, 90
  William 56
James I, King 22–3, 25, 48, 51, 65, 203, 294

James II, King 51, 57, 96
Johnston, John 76
Joy, George 201
Joyce, George 324

Kaine, Edmund 76, 125, 128, 130, 142, 247
Kennedy, David 92
  John 67
Kerr, James 149
  Mark 82, 85, 205, 249, 305
Kerry 134
  bishop of 280
Killinchy (Co. Down) 289–90
Killybegs (Co. Donegal) 127
Kilmacrenan (Co. Donegal) 71
Kilmore, bishop of 25, 47
Kilwarlin (Co. Down) 242
King's County (see Offaly)
King, William 53, 97
Kingsborough, Lord 80
Kinkead, John 215
Knox, General John 92, 98
  Thomas 319

Labourers 158–9, 271
Lagan (Co. Donegal) 71
Lagan river 185
Lagan valley 55, 123
Laing, Samuel 274–5
Lalor, Fintan 274
Land League 328
Land Question 269–71, 273–82, 290–1,
  293–4, 296
Land War 331
Landed Estates Court 291, 298–301,
  303–4, 310, 312–4, 322–3
Landlords 1, 6, 9–13, 20–3, 25–9, 52, 54–5,
  57–61, 66–7, 70, 73–4, 78–9, 81–4,
  86–92, 96–8, 100, 118–9, 124–7, 134,
  141, 143–4, 146, 148, 152, 161, 176,
  178–83, 189, 191, 194, 197, 200–1,
  203–7, 209–12, 218–21, 223–5, 241–3,
  246–50, 252–6, 258, 269, 272–4, 276–7,
  279, 280–5, 287, 290–1, 293, 295–8,
  302, 304–12, 316–9, 324–7, 329, 332
Lane Fox estate (Co. Leitrim) 199
Lanesborough, Earl of 179
Lanktree, John 285, 287
Lawford, Edward 210, 285, 304, 323
Lawson, J.A. 273

Leases 5, 13, 30, 48, 57, 61, 71, 91–2, 94,
  125, 135, 141, 148, 189, 201, 205, 225,
  245, 248, 254, 272, 286–90, 299–301,
  307, 309, 312–13, 317–8
  alienation of 48–9, 52, 57–9, 72–3, 117,
    124–8, 203, 210, 307, 323
  litigation 125
  renewal of 5, 16, 24–6, 29, 31, 50, 52,
    55, 58, 68, 70–2, 74, 77–8, 82–3,
    85–9, 98–9, 126, 133, 149, 206, 208,
    213, 215, 220, 224, 253, 256–7,
    287–8, 299–300, 307–8, 312, 314–5,
    324–5
Lecale (Co. Down) 123, 155, 187, 192
Lecky, A.H. 88
Leinster 60, 178
Leitch, George 73–4, 148
Leitrim (Co. Tyrone) 56
Leitrim 87, 93, 199, 276
Lennox, William 52
Leslie, James 52
  Patrick 52
Lewis, Samuel 181
Liberalism 330
Lifford (Co. Donegal) 75, 253
Limavady (Co. Londonderry) 30, 130, 219
Lincoln, earl of 281
Linen industry 137–57
Lisburn (Co. Antrim) 55, 141, 146
Listimore (Co. Tyrone) 73–4, 149
Litigation (see also Leases, Tenant Right)
  12, 85, 149, 200, 205–6, 213–4, 216,
  245–53, 259, 298–300
Livestock 13–14, 118, 120, 123, 147, 149,
  156, 196, 247, 318
Locke, John 28–9
London 60, 132, 140
  City of 63, 65, 140
  companies 23, 25, 50, 54, 62–8, 70, 82,
    86, 88, 91, 132, 159, 185, 194, 216,
    255, 257–8, 285, 302
Londonderry county 23, 25, 29, 53–4, 56,
  64–71, 73, 85, 87, 90, 92, 95, 123, 143,
  147, 154, 180, 188–9, 191, 206,
  209–10, 243, 254, 276, 302, 324–5
  marchioness of 211, 224, 285
  marquis of 91, 255, 273, 285
Longfield, Robert 272, 301
Longford 155
Lough Foyle 95
Lough Neagh 185

Loughbrickland (Co. Down) 99, 153
Loughinsholin barony (Co. Londonderry)
  65
Louth 26, 30–1, 64, 77, 88, 179, 185, 204, 289
Lowry estate (Co. Tyrone) 247
  family 214
  Andrew 214–15
Lurgan (Co. Armagh) 49, 141–2, 304
  Lord (see also Brownlow) 276–7

Macafee, William 23, 65, 188–92
McCabe, Desmond 196
McCadanes, Daniel 69
McCartney estate 183, 220
McCausland estate 306
  Robert 130
McClellan, Robert 23, 93
McClintock, John 221, 305
McCourt, Desmond 185, 195
McCrea, Moses 215
  Samuel 189
McCreiry, John 215
MacDonagh, Oliver 273
McDonnell, Randal 179
McElhargy, John 85
McEvoy, J. 147, 152
McFarland, George 206
  Patrick 87
McGildowney, Edmund 82, 85, 202, 205,
  249, 255, 287–8, 317
McGuire, James 78
  Peter 78
McKelver, James 206–7
McKeown v Beauclerc 300
McKinley, John 68–9
McKnight, James 294, 303
Maclagan, Peter 294
McMahon family 49
McMechan, Jane 24
McReevy, Robert (Jnr) 69
  Robert (Snr) 69
Magee, William 69
Magennis family 51
Maghera (Co. Londonderry) 23, 56, 156,
  188, 192
Magherafelt (Co. Londonderry) 323, 331
Maguire Commission 301
Maguire family 204
  W.A. 4–5, 152, 250
Mahary, Frances (nee Brown) 68
  Matthew 68–9

Maitland, F.W. 327
Major, Alexander 69
  Henry 147–8
  Thomas 69
Marshal, John 24
Martin, John [I] 29
  John [II] 289–90
Martin, Solomon 29–30
Marx, Karl 9–10, 17, 273, 283, 285, 291–4,
  296, 298
Massereene, Lord 66–7
Masterson, H.T. 210
Matthews, Patrick 78
Maxwell, James 25
  Robert 25, 47, 50, 52
  William 199–200
Mayne, Charles 77
  William 77, 99, 136, 145, 189, 320–1
Mayo 129–30, 197, 203
Mears, John 245
Mellifont, Treaty of 15
Mercers' company 91, 159, 192, 306
Merchant Tailors' company 88, 91, 156,
  158, 256, 276, 285–6
Middlemen 59–63, 71–3, 75–7, 80–2, 90,
  119, 152, 189, 191, 209, 241, 243, 302
Mill, J.S. 274–5, 290–1, 293–4, 296
Miller, H.R. 131–2, 157, 160, 194, 199,
  202, 211, 213, 216, 223–5, 249, 251–2,
  257–8, 276, 304, 306–8, 324
  J.R. 131–2, 156–7, 160, 194, 199, 202,
    211, 213, 216, 223–5, 243–4, 249,
    251–2, 257–8, 276, 304, 306–8, 324
  Kerby 127
  Rowley 157, 210, 217–8, 243–4, 257,
    307, 321
Mitchell, John 274
Moira (Co. Down) 326
Molesworth, Robert 97
Molly Maguire 321
Molyneux estate (Co. Armagh) 24
Momeen (Co. Donegal) 215
Monaghan 30, 49, 54, 56, 64, 82, 97, 125,
  128, 142, 149, 180, 185, 189, 304, 306,
  314, 320, 331
  town 76
Money 6, 9–10, 118, 137–8, 143, 145–6,
  152–3, 158, 177, 206, 242, 270–1, 275,
  280, 283–4, 287, 289, 294, 316–7, 319,
  332

Moneymore (Co. Londonderry) 95, 156,
  305
Montgomery, Hugh 48
Moody, Matthew 215
  T.W. 15, 18, 65
Moore, Henry 97
  J.R. 153
  Patience 29, 324–5
  Samuel 29, 324–5
  William 324
Moran, John 214
Morris, William 304, 311, 326
Mortgages (see Debts)
Mount Sedborough estate (Co.
  Fermanagh) 76
Mountcashel, Lord 324
Mountmellick (Co. Laois) 278
Moydamlaght (Co. Londonderry) 217
Moyola river 65
Mudimbe, V.Y. 17–18, 27
Mullattee (Co. Louth) 30–1
Munster 60, 135, 141, 178, 321
  Plantation 117, 121
Murlough family 146
Murnaghan, Brian 87
Murray, Capt. 242–3
  General 319
  Henry 222
  John 127
  Michael 244

Napier, Joseph 281
Nesbitt, Nathanial 145
Netherlands (see Holland)
New England 128, 130
New York 291
Newcastle (Co. Down) 153
Newry (Co. Down) 84, 94, 141–2, 146,
  180, 220
Newton, Andrew 247
Newtown Limavady (see Limavady)
Newtownstewart (Co. Tyrone) 76
Nicholls, K.W. 120
Nine Years' war 15
Nixon, William 319
Noble, Thomas (Jnr) 312
  Thomas (Snr) 58, 76, 136, 142, 145, 155
Nugent estate (Co. Down) 125, 145, 183,
  306
  Andrew 247
  James 183

O'Connell, Daniel 275
O'Connor, P. 153
O'Dolan, Andrew 93
    Philip 93
Ó Gráda, Cormac 187, 242, 284
O'Haggan, James 85
    John 85
O'Hara estate (Co. Sligo) 59, 129, 205
    Charles 81
    Keane 59
O'Neill family 21, 50, 65, 122
    Hugh (earl of Tyrone) 15–16, 66, 90
    Matthew 15
    Phelim 21
    Shane 15
O'Neille, Martha 53
Offaly 136, 322
Ogilby family 302
Ogilvie, William 155, 287
Omagh (Co. Tyrone) 71, 76
Omeath (Co. Louth) 88, 94, 141, 146,
    185, 198
Orange Order 93, 99, 277, 329–31
Oseland, Edward 91

Pale, the 76, 122
Palmerston, Lord 252, 272
Parnell, C.S. 301, 331
Partible inheritance 176
Pastoralism 14, 117–9, 122–4, 127, 132,
    134–5
Pattison, Henry 313–4
Pawlisch, H.S. 120
Payne, John 61–2
Peaceable possession 1, 62, 70–1, 73, 83,
    202–4, 206–7, 214, 290, 298, 300
Peel, Robert 278, 296
Pemberton, Thomas 92
Perceval-Maxwell estate 285, 318
    Robert 272, 311
Perceval-Maxwell, Michael 19, 120–1
Perceval/Egmont estate 134
Peyton, Rose 129
Pim, Jonathan 272
Plato 292
Playdell estate (Co. Leitim) 87, 93
Plunkett, James 87
    Oliver 94
Polanyi, Karl 20
Political agronomy 90–1
Political economy 271–5, 329, 332–3

Portadown 299, 322
Power, Thomas 57
Powerscourt, Lord 323
Price, John 49
Production 31–2, 117–161
Property relations 9, 25
Proudfoot, Lindsey 195
Provisions 150–2
Purcell, Richard 321
Pynnar, William 295

Quebec 313
Quinn, James 192

Rack-rent 6, 59, 62, 73, 77, 81, 128, 130,
    184, 291, 318–9
Raphoe (Co. Donegal) 52, 127
    bishop of 52
Rathmore estate (Co. Monaghan) 56
Raven, Thomas 180
Rawdon, William 55
Rea, J. 312
Reilly, Owen 286
Rents 1, 6, 49–50, 52–6, 62–3, 66, 71, 76,
    78–81, 85, 88, 93, 96, 98, 121, 124,
    128, 130–1, 141, 143, 145–6, 148–50,
    154–5, 157–8, 188–9, 194–7, 201,
    208–9, 212, 220, 222, 225, 242, 245–6,
    249–51, 253, 256, 272, 275, 278–9,
    282, 284–5, 288–90, 299, 301, 304,
    309, 313, 315–26, 331–2
    abatement of 55, 81, 87, 126, 155, 247
    waste (see Leases, Alienation)
Ribbonism 329–30
Ricardo, David 6, 158, 223, 270–4, 281,
    289–91, 293, 295–6
Richardson family 81
    Robert 24
Richey, A.G. 249, 296
Robb, George 213
Robinson, Philip 18, 135, 185, 188, 195
Roebuck, Peter 48, 191
Rogers, John 199–200
Rooney, James 134, 246, 249
Roper, Dean 320
Rosnagallagh (Co. Londonderry) 68–70
Ross, Robert 149
Rossmore, earl of 55–6, 97, 126
Rowley, Hercules 67
    Hugh 24
    J.R. 75
    William 90, 189

Ruish, Francis 52
Rundale 74, 176–82, 184–92, 195–200, 203,
    206, 209–11, 214–5, 217–18, 221–4, 307

Said, Edward 32
Salaman, Redcliffe 192
Salters' company 56–7, 192
Sampson, G.V. 198
Sanderson, Margaret 22
Sartre, J.P. 21
Savage family 60, 178
    Joseph 24
    Thomas 215
Savile, George 183–4, 319
Scotland 12, 21–2, 49, 52, 71, 75, 81, 86,
    93, 95, 97, 120, 123–4, 137–8, 126,
    147, 182, 185, 188, 195, 291, 327–9
    kindly tenures 22, 327
    Wars of independence 12
Scotstown (Co. Monaghan) 331
Seebohm, Frederick 295, 315
Segregation 19, 93, 95–8, 189, 191, 217–18
Seven Years' War 89
Shelbourne, Lady 126
Shirley estate (Co. Monaghan) 81, 306
Silthorp, Stephen 58
Simpson, A.W. 196
Sinclair, John 22
Singons, Col. 56
Skinners' company 90, 224, 302
Slieve Gullion (Co. Armagh) 65
Sligo 59, 81, 147, 205
Slutmulrony (Co. Fermanagh) 61
Smallholders 150, 155, 157, 159–60, 179,
    184, 190, 194, 198, 220, 225, 270, 275,
    296, 300, 316
Smith, Adam 8, 317
    Dowltagh 204
    Henry 82, 210–11, 217–8, 323
    Samuel 72
    William 319
Smout, T.M. 182
Smyly, John 149
Smyth, Samuel 326
    W.J. 95
Solow, Barbara 5, 7
Somerville, earl of 281
Speer estate (Co. Tyrone) 309
    James 131
Spenser, Edmund 27, 119, 291

Sperrin mountains (Co. Londonderry) 65,
    185
Spotswood, Andrew 147
    John 66, 153
Stannus, Walter 252, 322–3
    William 204
Steelboys 90
Stewart, Ezekiel 128–9
    Robert 53
Stockdale, Terence 215
Storey, Leo 179
    William 97
Strabane (Co. Tyrone) 3, 24, 68, 71, 76,
    90, 136–7, 142, 145, 149, 306
Strettle, Amos 66
Stroud, Major 24
Subletting 13, 58, 60
Sunderland, earl of 140
Swanlinbar (Co. Cavan) 208

Talbot, Richard 96
Tanistry 13, 15, 120
Tasburgh, John 203
Temple, John 51
    Thomas 51
    William 51
Tenant League 304, 313, 323
Tenant right, elections 89–92
    emigration 127–32, 152, 212, 219,
        257
    end of 326–33
    improvements 5, 26, 30, 52, 58, 311
    justification for 7, 31, 118
    legislation 270, 273, 278, 281, 290, 298,
        302–4, 314
    litigation 84–5, 126
    management of 131–2, 252–9, 269–70,
        304–314
    meaning of 5, 25–32, 276–7, 297,
        302–4
    origin of 1, 11, 16, 21–5, 57, 279
    sale of 127, 130–2, 253, 254–5, 259,
        302, 305–11, 313, 323–4
    value of 275, 301, 316, 322, 324
Tenures, at will 94, 126, 190, 224, 245,
    286, 300, 302, 305, 315, 328
    attornment 85
    fixity of 50, 55, 73, 82, 94, 186, 272,
        278, 282, 286–9, 292, 294–6, 298,
        325, 328, 331

Tenures *(contd.)*
  hereditary 23, 99
  in common 207
  joint 176, 179, 189–90, 196, 198, 210,
      218–22
  perpetual 66, 190, 202, 288–9,
      295
Terrydremont (Co. Londonderry) 209
Thompson, E.P. 9, 11, 16, 28–9, 276, 294,
      333
  Francis 328
Thomson, Mortimer 312–4
'Three Fs' 315, 328–9, 331
Tillywhisker (Co. Louth) 221
Tipperary 57, 80, 119, 255, 278
Toaghy (Co. Armagh) 25
Todd, John 142, 208
Tonagh (Co. Tyrone) 73
Trail, Archdeacon 202
Trimble, John 64
  Joshua 64
Trinity College Dublin 25, 47, 49–55,
      59–61, 80–1, 133, 207, 272–3, 288
Trower, Hutches 270–1, 273–4, 289–90,
      292–3, 295–6
Truxes, T.M. 140
Tuam, archbishop of 203
Tyrconnell, earl of (see also Talbot) 96
Tyrone 22, 24, 54, 71–5, 91, 129, 147, 183,
      185, 195, 241, 244, 247, 250, 258, 309,
      319, 323
  earl of 15–16, 66, 90

Ulster Custom 1–2, 4, 6, 289, 298–9,
      302–3, 310, 312–5, 327–8
Ulster, Plantation 12, 16–23, 27, 47–51,
      54, 62, 63, 65, 76, 83–4, 93–8, 117–22,
      126–7, 135, 138, 177, 180, 185, 188,
      190, 195, 209, 256, 294
Undertenants 49–50, 58–60, 63–4, 66–82,
      84, 119, 125, 149, 158–9, 206–10, 215,
      243
United Irishmen 92–3
United Kingdom 157, 330
Uxbridge, 1st earl of 31, 78–80, 84, 94,
      141, 319–20

Valuations 321–3
Vance, Andrew 5, 57, 281–2, 290, 317
Vaughan, W.E. 4–5, 7, 214, 252, 276, 304
Verner estate (Co. Fermanagh) 244
Vesey, Agondish 147
Vincent, Thomas 133
Vintners' company 66, 128, 189, 247
Virginia (Co. Cavan) 86–7, 99
Volosinov, V.N. 2, 11

Wakefield, Edward 90, 123
War of the Roses 12
Ward, Charles 59
Waring estate (Co. Down) 55
  John 225
  Richard 179, 205
  William 51, 55, 57, 61, 141
Waringstown (Co. Down) 51
Warner family 80
Warrenpoint (Co. Down) 141
Watson, Robert 69
Wentworth, Thomas 180
West Indies 130, 139
Westminster 272, 290
Weston, William 14
Westport (Co. Mayo) 129
Whelan, Kevin 187
Whistler, Gabriel 56–7
White, George 200
  Matthew 215
  N.C. 318
Whiteboys 254
Whitehill (Co. Down) 215
Whitestown (Co. Louth) 78
Whyte estate (Co. Down) 153, 251, 309
  John 251
William III, King 51, 53, 56, 96–7
Willoughby, Hugh 30
Wilson, David 309
  John 155
  Richard 211
Wood, Henry 247
Wright, Frank 99, 129, 141, 156, 217, 293,
      300, 330

Young, Arthur 80, 147, 151, 178